Assisting Emigration to Upper Canada

THE PETWORTH PROJECT, 1832–1837

The 1830s were years of social and political change in Britain. Rural unrest in 1830-31 spurred politicians and landlords to reexamine the roles government and individuals should play in fighting poverty. *Assisting Emigration to Upper Canada* demonstrates the effect of new attitudes and new rules of relief for the English poor on poor English immigrants arriving in Upper Canada.

Using a rich collection of contemporary sources, this study focuses on one group of English immigrants sent to Upper Canada from Sussex and other southern counties with the aid of parishes and landlords. In Part One Wendy Cameron follows the work of the Petworth Emigration Committee over six years and traces how the immigrants were received in each of these years. In Part Two, Mary McDougall Maude presents a complete list of emigrants on Petworth ships from 1832 to 1837, including details of their background, family reconstructions, and additional information drawn from Canadian sources.

WENDY CAMERON is a partner in Wordforce and a visiting scholar at the Northrop Frye Centre, Victoria University at the University of Toronto.

MARY McDOUGALL MAUDE is a partner in Wordforce and Shipton, McDougall Maude Associates, a coordinator of the Publishing Program at Ryerson Polytechnic University, and a visiting scholar at the Northrop Frye Centre, Victoria University at the University of Toronto.

ASSISTING EMIGRATION
TO *Upper Canada*

THE PETWORTH PROJECT
1832–1837

Wendy Cameron
and
Mary McDougall Maude

McGill–Queen's University Press
Montreal & Kingston • London • Ithaca

Legal deposit third quarter 2000
Bibliothèque national du Québec

Printed in Canada on acid-free paper

Publication of this book has been made possible by a grant from the Jackman Foundation.

McGill-Queen's University Press acknowledges the financial support of the Government of Canada through the Book Publishing Industry Development Program (BPIDP) for its activities. It also acknowledges the support of the Canada Council for the Arts for its publishing program.

Canadian Cataloguing in Publication Data

Main entry under title:
Cameron, Wendy
Assisting emigration to Upper Canada : the Petworth project, 1832–1837

Includes bibliographical references and index.
ISBN 0-7735-2034-1

1. Ontario—Emigration and immigration—History—19th century. 2. England—Emigration and immigration—History —19th century. 3. Petworth Emigration Committee. 4. Great Britain—Emigration and immigration—Government policy—History—19th century. 5. Immigrants—Ontario—Registers. I.Maude, Mary McD. II. Title.

FC3071.9.14C34 2000   325'.342'09713   C00-900269-3
F1058.C34 2000

CONTENTS

Tables, Figures, Maps

MAPS

FOREWORD

It is with great pleasure and anticipation that I write a Foreword for this book and for its companion volume, *English Immigrant Voices: Labourers Letters from Upper Canada in the 1830s*, edited by Wendy Cameron, Sheila Haines, and Mary McDougall Maude. These books have been dear to my heart for many years. The question that you, the reader, may ask is, why have we written such a detailed work on what has been a relatively obscure – at least until now – event in our history? My answers constitute the essence of this Foreword.

First, there was the personal desire to know more about the origins of my own Jackman ancestors and why they came to Canada. Like far too many Canadian families, after over a century and a half in our adopted homeland we had only the vaguest recollections of our origins. We knew only that our Jackman ancestors had come from Goring in Sussex, England, sometime in the middle of the nineteenth century, but we knew nothing of where they first settled in what is now the Province of Ontario. Either as a direct result of these volumes or as a result of private research conducted over many years in parallel with them, many of these details are now known. In this regard, I am particularly grateful to Ellen Megannety.

Like us, our grandparents and great-grandparents were products of their time – and my forebears wanted to leave the countryside for the rapidly growing cities of their new homeland. Memories of their rural roots on both sides of the Atlantic soon began to fade, and it took family historians such as my brother Hal and myself many years to uncover these traces. We offer the thanks of all our family to Brenda Dougall Merriman and Leigh Lawson who have written our family genealogy with such attention to detail.

However, this quest for one's own family roots, while of great interest on a personal level, began to pale in comparison with the much bigger story that could be told. Members of our family did not come to the new world entirely on their own initiative or using their own resources – they came as part of a larger immigration plan which we have called "the Petworth Project, 1832-1837." This story has to be told not only for its own sake but also as the story of an English-based emigration scheme. Here in Ontario, attention to the stories of Celtic immigrants from Great Britain to Upper Canada – the Scots and the Irish and even the Welsh – has tended to obscure the fact that large numbers also came from England itself. This comparative neglect of the English among the thousands of immigrants arriving in Canada persists into our more recent history and needs to be redressed.

The English did not just appear in Canada: they too have their stories of why and how they came. The fact that most of us speak English in Ontario should not obscure that some of us have in addition a more particularly English heritage. The distinct contributions of the English pioneers in Canada needs study as a component of the whole. Thus, we hope these volumes will be a worthy addition and complement to Canada's overall immigration history.

As recorded in this history and in the personal letters printed in *English Immigrant Voices*, our ancestors sent by the Petworth Emigration Committee were fortunate, comparatively speaking, in the conditions of their passage and of their settlement in Upper Canada. These volumes were possible because people in charge in England and Canada thought record-keeping important and because the participants were able to send letters home. We remember and thank those who left us these records of our past. May we never take our English heritage for granted!

Finally, the Petworth emigration scheme did not just happen by itself. There were outstanding personalities who ensured that it came about. Even though their names may no longer be well-known in today's condensed histories of the period concerned, yet to me they remain as unsung heroes. First, there is Lord Egremont himself, whose political foresight and financial generosity made the entire scheme possible. Then there is the Reverend Thomas Sockett, whose determination and organizational skill ensured that the plan went forward. Finally, there is Sir John Colborne (later Lord Seaton), who arranged for the safe settlement of the newly arrived immigrants in Upper Canada. To these and all those who assisted them, our most heartfelt gratitude.

We spent many years researching and writing this history, and I have much enjoyed sharing in the process with our author-editors, Wendy Cameron, Sheila Haines, and Mary McDougall Maude, and meeting other people seeking out their own ancestors who were part of this scheme. I have had the pleasure of visiting nearly every locale in Sussex and Surrey from whence our immigrants came and many of their destinations in Ontario. In this latter regard, there is still much research to be done. May those of us of Petworth-scheme ancestry continue to share our experiences and to deepen our knowledge of what was done for us so many years ago. May these pages help us never to forget!

Reverend Edward John Rowell Jackman,
sponsor and patron of these volumes,
and a proud descendant of Petworth pioneers

Toronto, Ontario
March 2000

PREFACE

In each of the years from 1832 to 1837, emigrants from Sussex and neighbouring counties in southeast England were sent off to Upper Canada (Ontario) on ships chartered by the Petworth Emigration Committee. Recognized by contemporaries for their humanitarian intent and effective organization, the Petworth emigrations stand out in a field where much of the record is sorry and unhappy. They – along with a few other schemes – demonstrate that a properly conducted assisted emigration could open the door to a better life for the individuals involved. They also serve as examples of the parish-aided emigration that for a brief period, from 1830 to 1837, flowed to Upper Canada from the southern counties of England.

Part One of this book discusses the history of the Petworth emigrations in the context of the politics surrounding poor law reform and assisted emigration. These subjects had a direct influence on private schemes of emigration because decisions about whether emigrants would be assisted, and about who among the applicants would get assistance, were made by politicians in London and by local leaders who acted as sponsors in the sending communities. Part One also traces the selection of the Petworth emigrants, follows them in their travels from England to Upper Canada, and looks at their patterns of settlement within the province. Although very different, these two lines of inquiry inform each other. On the one hand, we can see that policy makers and sponsors shaped the course of assisted emigration and, on the other, we can see in the Petworth emigrations how policies and plans informed the reality of assisting emigration to 1830s Upper Canada.

Part Two consists of a list drawn from our files on individual Petworth emigrants. The research behind this list was an exercise in both family and social history. As we searched to identify emigrants on both sides of the Atlantic Ocean, we recorded our information within a number of fields in order to present it in a way that would be useful to other researchers as well as ourselves. By presenting the background and family composition of Petworth emigrants, and by tracing those we can to their place of first settlement in Upper Canada, we hope to encourage further investigation of the English farm labourers and artisans who came to this country in considerable numbers in the 1830s.

In England, parish-aided emigration and the poor laws were inextricably connected, since the parish paid for part or all of emigration assistance under both the old poor law and the new post-1834 poor law. Initiatives to deal with unemployment and unrest in rural England lay behind parish-aided emigration to Upper Canada in the 1830s, and this helps to explain its peaks and valleys.

The 1837 rebellions in the Canadas caused a hiatus in immigration from Britain. From that time onward, the Petworth Emigration Committee sent relatively few emigrants and without any of the supervision of the earlier period. Parish-aided immigration overall did not regain the same importance in Upper Canada.

In investigating the impact of 1830s poor law reforms on the Petworth emigrations, we discovered that changing attitudes and policies towards assisted emigration paralleled the evolving thinking on the poor laws. The study of these emigrations helps to explain how the British government moved away from the paternalistic Colonial Office experiments of the 1810s and 1820s, whereby it helped smaller numbers of emigrants become frontier farmers, and towards the laissez-faire approach that opened the ports of British North America to large numbers of very poor immigrants in the 1840s. The Petworth immigrants arrived in a transition period, and in their reception the rules governing assistance can be seen to tighten.

For British historians such as Sydney and Beatrice Webb or Michael Rose and Anne Digby, who have studied the civil responsibilities of English parishes and the long history of the English poor laws, or for those such as J.R. Poynter who have examined the origins of poor law reform, assisted emigration is just a brief subsection of the nineteenth-century story. If the point of view is reversed, the rich history of rural England becomes the background to parish-assisted emigration and to government policies affecting both assistance and the reception accorded new immigrants in Upper Canada. Although these policies had their genesis in England and in the circumstances of the English poor, they were applied to all arriving immigrants.

In the 1830s, immigrants arriving in Upper Canada from all parts of the British Isles were directly affected by new thinking on poor relief in England because in these years the Colonial Office still instructed the lieutenant-governor of Upper Canada concerning his spending on poor immigrants. The philosophy and policies behind the new poor law are associated with followers of Jeremy Bentham, who sought to introduce the principles of centralization and inspection to government. Alan Greer and other Canadian historians have held that the reforming principles of Bentham's disciples were brought to bear in the administration of the Canadas only with the arrival of Governor Charles Edward Poulett Thomson (later Lord Sydenham) and the union of Upper and Lower Canada in 1840. Significant changes in instructions from the Colonial Office concerning arriving immigrants, however, preceded both legislative amendment of the poor law in England and the beginnings of administrative reform in the colony.

Historians of English poor law reform study – as Anthony Brundage noted in the preface to *The Making of the New Poor Law* – "the exercise or attempted exercise of power – the power of cabinet ministers, M.P.s, reformers, officials, magistrates, and landowners." A case study of the evolution of policies towards assisted emigration from England and assisted immigration to Canada as revealed in the Petworth emigrations takes us into similar realms, the world of the politicians and wealthy sponsors, whose decisions affected the course of events described in this book.

Records kept about the poor, however, are equally useful to social historians who investigate their lives. The records of the Petworth emigrations are similarly helpful in this respect. So far, investigations of the migration patterns of poor and assisted immigrants to Upper Canada have concentrated on the Scots, who were important early migrants to Upper Canada, and on the Irish, who formed the great majority of all immigrants in the first half of the nineteenth century; examples are Marianne McLean's *People of Glengarry*, Bruce Elliott's *Irish Migrants in the Canadas*, and Catharine Ann Wilson's *A New Lease on Life*. The English immigrants have drawn less attention, perhaps because English working people such as those sent by the Petworth committee are notorious for having vanished quickly into the population of Upper Canada. Assistance, however, gives the historian a handle. Parish-aided emigration is emerging from the shadows, as historians (Bruce Elliott in Canada and Gary Howells in England, for example) have begun to look at emigration records such as those created by the Poor Law Commission appointed in 1834.

The extensive documentation of the Petworth emigrations makes it possible to assemble a case study that draws on many different sources. The Petworth committee methodically selected groups of emigrants from the class of agricultural labourers and rural craftsmen under very similar circumstances in each of six years. The records thus created – and preserved to a degree unusual in parish-aided migration – span the period of transition from the old to the new poor law, when new policies towards the able-bodied poor were being set in England and applied to immigrants arriving in Canada. These sources have allowed us to study the Petworth Emigration Committee and its relations with sponsors and government during this period. They have also allowed us to identify the emigrants and follow the fortunes of a number of them from the time they left Portsmouth until they established themselves in readiness for their first winter in Upper Canada.

One obstacle that hampers parish-emigration research has been the paucity of detailed listings of the participants. Because ships' passenger lists for Canadian destinations have not survived for this period, historians must find alternative sources. Those that are available for Petworth emigrants are discussed in the introduction to Part Two. We began our attempt to identify the Petworth emigrants by combing the records preserved in the estate office at Petworth, now the Petworth House Archives. On the basis of these records, we have been able to identify about 1,600 of the 1,818 emigrants recorded as having been sent on the Petworth committee ships between 1832 and 1837. The two main problems we encountered in tracing these emigrants were, first, in making the link between an individual or family and the fact of emigration on a Petworth ship, and, second, in filling in information on family members, who very often appear only as numbers associated with a head of family. Our compilation does not replace the missing ships' lists, and because we resorted to a broad range of sources in pulling it together, we are more positive in identifying some emigrants than others. The list presented in Part Two does not include all the Petworth emigrants, and it may include some emigrants from these communities who arrived in Canada on a different ship. These reservations aside, we believe that our list is a fair representation of the kind of people sent by the Petworth Emigration

Committee and accurate enough to serve as a sample of parish-assisted immigrants to Canada.

Our project on the Petworth emigrations expanded to include a second book, for as we collected material for this history, one of the sources grew in importance. From the beginning of the project, letters written by Petworth immigrants in Upper Canada to correspondents in England proved invaluable in our attempt to uncover the history of the scheme and to reconstruct Petworth families and kin groups. These letters have been gathered in *English Immigrant Voices: Labourers' Letters from Upper Canada in the 1830s.* Along with the letters, we have offered brief snapshots of the writers' lives before and after they sailed, as gleaned from other research. The letters are appealing documents in themselves, with interesting stories to tell, and are also a remarkable source for a class of people who left few written records, and they raise many questions concerning the emigrant experience.

Our two books can be read independently, and some people will be interested only in one or the other. The reader willing to take on both accounts will find a rounded picture of the same emigrant experience seen from both above and below. The narrative facts of the emigrations are the same, but the perspectives are different. The one book focuses on the people responsible for sending and receiving assisted emigrants, the other on the newly arrived labouring immigrants. The resulting differences in perception are in themselves remarkable and a study for the social historian.

A micro-study such as this one also brings out differences in language usage between England and Canada and between the past and present. We have tried to explain terms that may be unfamiliar or archaic in one place or the other, particularly with respect to geography, and have included maps that we hope will clarify the principal administrative units with which the project is concerned. In both the text and maps, we have used the 1830s boundaries for counties and parishes in England and for districts and townships in Upper Canada. We have, however, taken the liberty of writing East Sussex and West Sussex even though Sussex was not formally divided into two counties until 1888. In Upper Canada, many villages and towns were named, or renamed, during the 1830s, and for these we have used modern names after the first mention to avoid confusion. Toronto, which was known as York until 1834, generally appears as Toronto (except in quotations and discussion specific to pre-1834), and the town plot of Blandford Township is given its later name of Woodstock.

THE INDIVIDUAL RESPONSIBLE for this project is the Reverend Edward Jackman. A keen student of history, he has long felt that, among emigrants from the British Isles, the English have been neglected by historians. After archivist Alison McCann of the West Sussex Record Office drew his attention to an article by Wendy Cameron on the Petworth emigrations (which in 1836 included his ancestor William Jackman and family), he began to consider the possibility of exploring the emigrations further. This volume is the result and it is the product of a collaborative effort. The project was devised and coordinated by Wendy Cameron and Mary McDougall Maude in consultation with Father Jackman. Part One was written by Wendy Cameron with some editorial advice from Mary McDougall Maude, who also collaborated on the figures and tables. The latter designed the fields for the project files used in Part Two and coordinated the presentation of the data. Sheila Haines and Leigh Lawson were responsible for genealogical research in England and for the intricate and demanding work of family reconstruction. They also collected a large portion of the English research materials used in Part One. Brenda Dougall Merriman took over responsibility for genealogy in Canada and the daunting task of linking immigrants in Upper Canada with the passengers who boarded Petworth ships at Portsmouth. She prepared the tables detailing occupation of lots in Adelaide and Woodstock. Gwen Peroni did much of our computer work and helped in making our files for individuals an effective research tool. Susan Rowlands of the Geography Laboratory of the University of Sussex prepared the English maps, and Byron Moldofsky of the Cartography Office of the University of Toronto those for Canada. For thanks and acknowledgments please turn to page 345.

Part One

THE PETWORTH EMIGRATIONS FROM SUSSEX TO UPPER CANADA, 1832–1837

Wendy Cameron

George O'Brien Wyndham, third Earl of Egremont (1751–1837), painted at the time of the Petworth emigrations

Thomas Phillips, *The Third Earl of Egremont*
Courtesy of the National Trust Photographic Library

Egremont greeting royalty at Petworth. The main figures in the centre of the picture are (from left to right) the King of Prussia, the Duchess of Oldenburg, the Emperor of Russia, and the Earl of Egremont. The six children of Elizabeth Illive are in the group behind Egremont.

Thomas Phillips, *The Allied Sovereigns at Petworth, 24th June 1814*
Courtesy of the National Trust Photographic Library

Egremont's entourage in 1814 included people later involved in the story of the Petworth emigrations. Lord Egremont [1]; his sons Colonels Henry [2] and George [5] Wyndham; his son-in-law Sir Charles Burrell [3]; and the Reverend Thomas Sockett [4].

Thomas Phillips, *The Allied Sovereigns at Petworth, 24th June 1814* (detail)

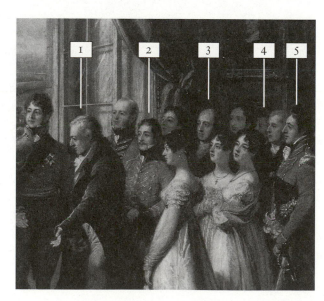

The Reverend Thomas Sockett; rector of Petworth and organizer of the Petworth emigrations
Thomas Phillips, *The Reverend Thomas Sockett*
Courtesy of The Lord Egremont; photograph, Courtauld Institute of Art

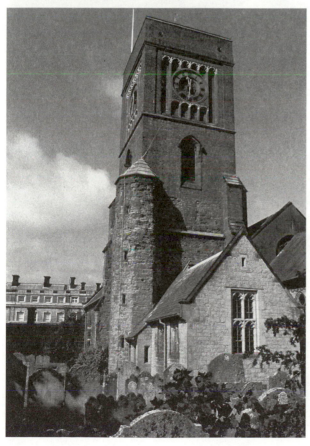

St Mary the Virgin, Sockett's church at Petworth, with Petworth House in the Background
Photograph: Patrick Burrows

A celebration at Petworth House showing the facade facing the park. Egremont is on horseback.
William Frederick Witherington, *Fête in Petworth Park* (detail), 1835

Goodwood House, the estate of the Duke of Richmond
From J.D. Parry, *Historical and Descriptive Account of the Coast of Sussex* (1833), facing p. 407
Courtesy of Sussex Archaeological Society

Charles Lennox, fifth Duke of Richmond (1771-1860)
From Baxter, *Library of Agriculture*, vol. 1, frontispiece (4th ed., Lewes, 1846)
Courtesy of the Sussex Archaeological Society

Barkford House, Kirdford, the Home of Richard Hasler, one of Sockett's Sussex Sponsors.
Photograph: Patrick Burrows

The cottage at the crossroads. The young Petworth emigrant Robert Chalwin
lived with his large family in one half of the original cottage.
Photograph: Patrick Burrows

INTRODUCTION

Eighteen hundred men, women, and children travelled from Portsmouth, England, to Upper Canada under the auspices of the Petworth Emigration Committee in the years 1832–37. The men were primarily agricultural labourers, although there were rural artisans among them. Some of the men and women were single, but most emigrated in families and many of the parents were middle-aged with several children. These emigrants came from the southeast of England, mostly from parishes around Petworth in West Sussex but also from East Sussex and neighbouring counties. Many had received assistance from their parishes from time to time in the past. They were poor and many of them emigrated because they had financial assistance from great landowners such as Petworth's George O'Brien Wyndham, the third Earl of Egremont, from lesser parish notables, and from the parishes themselves.

The Petworth emigrations were initiated under Egremont's patronage by Thomas Sockett, rector of Petworth, personal chaplain to Egremont, and founder and chairman of the three-man Petworth Emigration Committee. Sockett was the committee's prime mover and made the important decisions. The other two members, local businessmen Thomas Chrippes and William Knight, confined their attention to practical matters. The Petworth emigrants sailed from Portsmouth on ships chartered by the committee, and when they reached Montreal in Lower Canada, the committee's superintendent conducted them to York (renamed Toronto in 1834) (see map 1). Many Petworth immigrants received help from the government of Upper Canada in travelling beyond Toronto, and a number of the families had additional help in getting settled. They settled in south-central and western Ontario – in the urban areas of Toronto and Hamilton and their vicinities; in communities along the Grand River valley in the Gore District; in the London District, particularly in a settlement created by the government in 1832 in the Township of Adelaide and later in the area of Woodstock; and, in fewer numbers, in the Western District.[1]

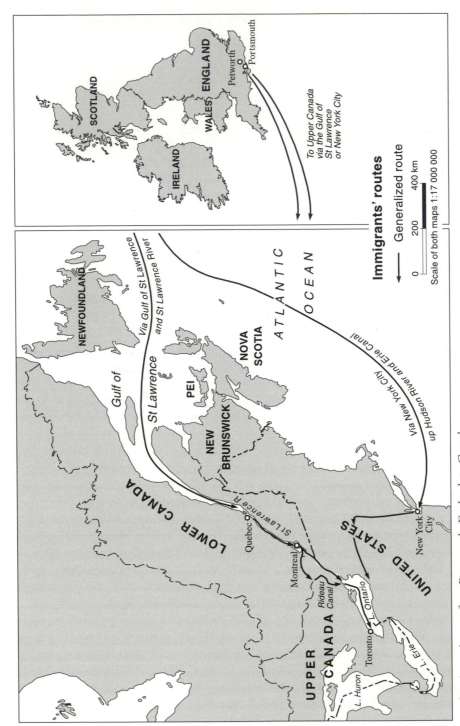

1 *Immigrants' routes from Portsmouth, England, to Canada*

In all, close to one hundred parishes sent emigrants on at least one of the Petworth ships. Parishes were the smallest unit of civil government in early nineteenth-century England. When Sockett devised his plan of emigration, each parish was responsible for its own social services, and poor relief was financed by a "poor rate" – a tax raised by local authorities on the assessed value of buildings and property. Different forms of administration and a variety of other local factors meant that paupers in one parish might receive either more or less aid than those of a neighbouring parish. Even if people moved about, however, if they applied for assistance in any other parish they could be sent back to their parish of legal "settlement," a settlement being a right to parish aid normally acquired by birth or, for women, by marriage. If a parish decided to assist emigration, the emigrants it sent were chosen from among people with a settlement in that parish.[2]

Parishes varied in size and population. Sussex parishes were not particularly large (map 2). The 6,000-acre parish of Petworth, which included the great house and the town of that name, held about 3,000 people in 1831. Sockett's other West Sussex parish, Duncton, was 1,300 acres in size with only 272 inhabitants listed on the 1831 census. In addition to Petworth and Duncton, Egremont owned all the land in Tillington, Northchapel, and Egdean, and had substantial holdings in several other West Sussex parishes. The parishes where the earl owned all or much of the land made up the heartland of the Petworth emigrations.

As lord lieutenant of Sussex, Egremont had certain responsibilities for the whole county, most of them having to do with the militia. With respect to the emigrations, his most significant role was as the dominant landlord and magistrate in an area in the northwest quadrant of West Sussex. His patronage was important to everyone, from lesser magistrates to tradesmen and farmers (many of whom were his tenants), and he did not have to stir from Petworth House to make his wishes known. In their history of southeast England, Peter Brandon and Brian Short borrow the words of a nineteenth-century authority on rural society in England, Richard Jefferies, in describing a sphere of influence like Egremont's as "a little kingdom," an agricultural area dominated by an alliance of landowners and tenant farmers with a market town as capital.[3] The core area under Egremont's control was surrounded by satellite parishes whose leading citizens also deferred to him, adopting his policies on parish issues even if he did not own land in their parishes.

Petworth, the market town and administrative centre for this "kingdom," is about forty miles southwest of London in a district of downland farms and rolling hills. To the north, this district carried into the arc of the clay hills and forests of the High Weald, and to the south, it merged into the chalk hills of the South Downs (see map 3). Egremont's Petworth House dominated the town literally as well as figuratively. Unlike most great houses, it backed on the town, which was built right up to the walls of the house and of the park made famous by the design of Capability Brown. An 1820s traveller estimated that the house with its walled garden, stables, and outbuildings occupied an area almost as large as the town centre.[4] The town-side entrance to Petworth House was right beside Sockett's church, and his rectory was only a short walk away.

2 *West Sussex parish boundaries in the 1830s*

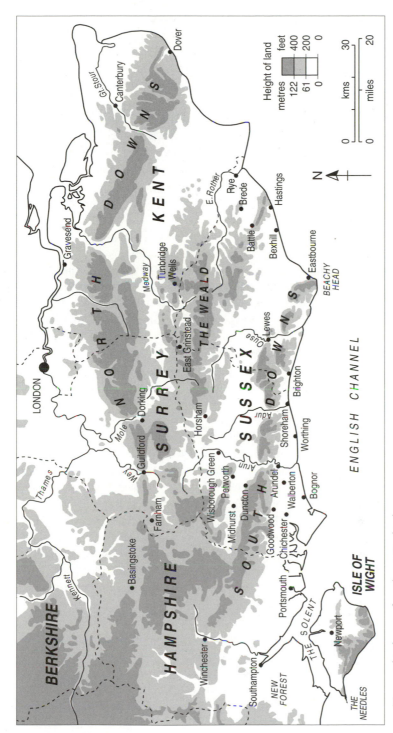

3   Topographical map of southeast England

The second great landlord important to the Petworth emigrations was Charles Gordon Lennox, the fifth Duke of Richmond. Richmond's Goodwood House was located south of the hills that cut Petworth off from the coastal plain. It had a setting more characteristic of great houses, being placed well back in its park, and to this day it is surrounded by farmland. During a long political career, Richmond served both Tory and Whig prime ministers, always, as he said, with the goal of advancing the "Agricultural Interest."[5] He entered the House of Lords in 1819 and first made a name for himself as an advocate of measures to protect British agricultural products. During the 1840s he returned to this subject with a vigorous campaign in favour of the corn laws. From the end of 1830 until he resigned in the summer of 1834, Richmond was a minister in the Whig administration of Charles Grey, the second Earl Grey.[6] This was a period when Richmond focused his attention on poverty and unrest among agricultural labourers, believing these to be the most important issues facing rural England; and in 1832 Sockett's first emigrants travelled under Egremont's patronage with the benefit of Richmond's political goodwill.

Egremont maintained and visited houses in London and Brighton, but he had retired to the country and made his life at Petworth more completely and at an earlier age than was usual for one of his rank. Inheriting Petworth House and its estates as a child in 1763, Egremont had been fortunate to live during years of "unprecedented prosperity" for the great landowners of England,[7] and he had added to his fortune by inheritance in Ireland and by purchase in England.[8] His tenure is described as the "golden age" of Petworth House: he made the house a showplace for British artists and its grounds the site of the latest experiments in agriculture.[9] His hospitality to rich and poor at Petworth was legendary, but by 1832 he was old – eightyone years of age. Court diarist Charles Greville, a frequent visitor in the 1830s, described him as an eccentric, distanced from the household that revolved around him by his habit of keeping constantly on the move so that talk with him could be had only in snatches.[10] Egremont was set in his ways and not much influenced by the ideas of his peers in a House of Lords he no longer attended. Richmond was a generation younger, an affable and popular member of court circles, as well as an active politician. He worked closely with Egremont in county matters, but in London he was exposed to the social issues of utilitarian reformers and absorbed new ideas about government. As a member of the cabinet from 1830 to 1834, he took part in setting new policies for the nation, policies that held no interest for Egremont.[11]

Sockett had joined Egremont's household at an early age. Through the interest of a poet friend of the earl, he came to Petworth House in 1797 as tutor to Egremont's eldest acknowledged son, George Wyndham, who had been sick and unhappy at boarding school. Just three years earlier, when he was nineteen and employed by John Holroyd, the first Earl of Sheffield at Sheffield Place in East Sussex, Sockett had taken his meals with the servants. Sheffield's daughter dismissed him as a "wry necked" young secretary "intended for Country use," possibly describing a manner that failed to amuse rather than a physical disability not evident in portraits or photographs.[12] In his new position at Petworth, Sockett thrived in the community of

interesting people – the French émigré noblemen who gave way over time to natural scientists and artists – and he stayed to tutor the three boys among the five children of Egremont and Elizabeth Illive who survived infancy.[13] (Illive's origins are
not certain, though she may have been the daughter of a schoolmaster. In any case,
she did not match Egremont in rank, and their long relationship did not survive their
private marriage in 1801.) When his children no longer required a tutor, Egremont
kept Sockett on by sponsoring his education as a clergyman.

Egremont's regard for Sockett's abilities was evident when he picked his sons' young
tutor to be the next rector of the Church of St Mary the Virgin at Petworth. Having made his choice, he held to it even in the face of obstacles that might have con-
founded someone less used to having his own way. Sockett travelled to Surrey for
baptism in the Church of England, but the Bishop of Chichester refused to waive
the requirement of a degree before ordination. Undeterred, Egremont sent Sockett,
his own son Charles (Sockett's pupil at the time), and a servant off to Oxford, paying "every expense in the most delicate and liberal manner." Admiringly, Sockett confided to his diary, "he *is* a Patron."[14] Egremont then supported Sockett in parishes
where he owned the right of appointment until the Petworth post became vacant
in 1816, nine years after he had first raised the subject on one of the rare evenings
when he and Sockett dined alone at Petworth House.[15] In return, Sockett gave years
of efficient and tactful service as the well-respected rector of St Mary's. He controlled
the vestry in the parish of Petworth to suit Egremont's wishes, and he was also one
of the people who distributed Egremont's personal charitable giving in West Sussex.

Egremont's wealth allowed him to promote in surrounding parishes the policies
he favoured and to employ people like Sockett. He encouraged the Petworth emigrations by assuming the financial risk of chartering ships and certain other over-
head expenses. In addition, he paid the full passage for all emigrants sent to Toronto
from parishes where he owned all the land and a part passage for emigrants sent from
many others. This gift of a passage was conditional. Egremont helped only those emigrants whose parish contributed a portion of their expenses (a few emigrants provided this contribution themselves). At the least, the parishes paid to outfit their
emigrants and transport them to Portsmouth, these being judged responsibilities
already in the parish sphere.

Once Egremont agreed to the emigration scheme, he delegated full authority to
Sockett. Sockett had no written instructions, and we have been unable to determine
whether he drew money through the Petworth estate accounts, even though he and
his committee members kept financial records down to the last stamp. Emigration
may have been one of the charities paid out of Egremont's private income. Whatever his source of funds, Sockett had no precise upper limit on his spending. Egremont had mentioned an appropriate sum for the first ship before turning the scheme
over to him, certain that Sockett would manage the money wisely and conduct the
affair with due regard for his patron's peace of mind and reputation.

Sockett's parish of Petworth served the Petworth emigrations as a kind of flagship,
setting the tone for the manner in which the other parishes under Egremont's influ-

ence conducted assisted emigration. Yet knowing what Egremont would think was the "right" thing to do in a particular situation could not always have been easy. Sockett walked a fine line in deciding how much money he should spend on promoting emigration and sending emigrants to Upper Canada. Looking back from 1838 at the Petworth emigrations, he expressed but one regret, that he had not pursued his contacts outside Sussex more aggressively and publicized his method of proceeding more widely.[16]

Egremont's hold on his area of deference remained firm through the six years of the Petworth emigrations, a period in which English local government changed significantly. The movement for a reform of the poor law gained strength as a result of the Swing disturbances of 1830–31, serious unrest among agricultural labourers in counties of the south and southeast. These were the counties examined and considered by the Royal Commission on the Poor Laws, which prepared the way for the introduction of the new poor law.[17] To the extent that legislators also considered assisted emigration in this decade, policies were designed for the same region that would address the particular problems of agricultural districts like those represented in the Petworth emigrations. The Petworth emigrations offer a concrete example of the interaction between poor law reform and assisted emigration and of the impact of new thinking about poverty and poor relief on a scheme devised under the old rules.

The Poor Law Amendment Act, passed by Parliament in 1834, was intended both to redesign local government in England and to bring the poor law into line with new ideas about the proper management of the poor. This act replaced the local authority of the autonomous parish vestry with the central authority of a three-man poor law commission in London.[18] The importance of the parish as a unit of local government was greatly diminished, although parishes did continue to pay for a number of services to their own paupers, including assisted emigration.[19] The Amendment Act provided for parishes to be grouped together into poor law unions. (The minority of parishes that had united in different kinds of unions under earlier legislation were given a choice in 1834 of remaining as they were or disbanding and forming a new union.) The local boards of guardians in charge of newly created poor law unions answered to the Poor Law Commission. The guardians were expected to enforce rules laid down by the commissioners, and an assistant commissioner paid them regular visits to check on their proceedings.[20]

The new poor law challenged the culture of providers and dependents represented by the pre-1834 poor law.[21] The poor law commissioners believed that if they could replace the old system with a free market in labour, new jobs would be created and wages would rise as the poor rates fell.[22] They attributed many of the social ills of their time to the overuse of parish aid and to the practices by which it was diverted to supplement labourers' wages. They labelled the diversion of parish funds to the support of the able-bodied the "allowance system," and they blamed this system for causing the whole of the labouring population in affected counties to take on many of the undesirable characteristics of paupers. The purpose of the commissioners' notorious "workhouse test" was to isolate able-bodied paupers in the workhouse and thus make a clear distinction between them and labourers working independently of parish support. Where the test was fully applied, the able-bodied were denied relief unless they and dependent family members agreed to enter a workhouse – a degree of destitution rare among Petworth emigrants.[23]

The newly appointed poor law commissioners took office with considerable public support because the shortcomings of the old system had been so apparent in many parts of the country. Sockett himself was among those who thought many parishes overdue for administrative reform in 1834, but he was not prepared for the form that change would take under the poor law commissioners. Over the next three years, he discovered how relentlessly the commissioners intended to apply their rules, and he became one of a growing number of their middle-class opponents.

When they first sent assistant commissioners into the rural districts, the poor law commissioners sought to win the cooperation of large landowners like Egremont. Egremont could have single-handedly converted the area in his sphere of influence to the new poor law – as Richmond did in making a model union of Westhamptnett. (Those who have studied the role of the landed aristocracy in the introduction of the new poor law have missed a lovely example in these adjoining unions.)[24] The two assistant poor law commissioners successively responsible for West Sussex during 1835 and 1836 needed Egremont's help in dissolving the Sutton Gilbert Union (formed by authority of Gilbert's Act of 1784) to the east of Petworth so that they could create new unions with logical boundaries.[25] They also tried to get him to use his influence to smooth their paths in setting up these unions (see map 4).[26] Egremont's intransigence was a serious setback, but so long as they had any hope of winning Egremont over to support the new poor law, they had no desire to cross him on the matter of his pet emigration project and Sockett's scheme was safe.

By 1837, it was obvious to everyone that Egremont would not be won over and that his silent opposition had set the tone for his district and stiffened the resistance of "this troublesome, headstrong board [of guardians] at Petworth."[27] Sockett must have had Egremont's consent to appear as a key witness before a parliamentary select committee on the administration of the poor law called at the insistence of John Walter, the proprietor of *The Times* and the principal parliamentary opponent of the poor law commissioners.[28] Walter chose Petworth as the first union to be investigated and Sockett as the first of a number of witnesses whose combined testimony would cause even the large majority of the committee members in favour of the act to lean slightly in the direction of more discretion in granting relief.[29] In a rueful tribute to Egremont's power, Assistant Poor Law Commissioner William Hawley wrote from Sussex to Edwin Chadwick, the commissioners' secretary, of the "utter improbability" of finding a suitable person in the Petworth Union to defend the Poor Law Commission. All for miles around were under the influence of "that autocrat" at Petworth House.[30] Such an admission of his failure with Egremont, however, left Hawley bitter. He carried a grudge against Sockett that appears to have affected his dealings with parishes hoping to send some of their poor with the 1837 Petworth emigration.

The Petworth emigrations were brought to an end when Egremont died in November 1837, before Sockett's tussle with the commissioners was fully played out.

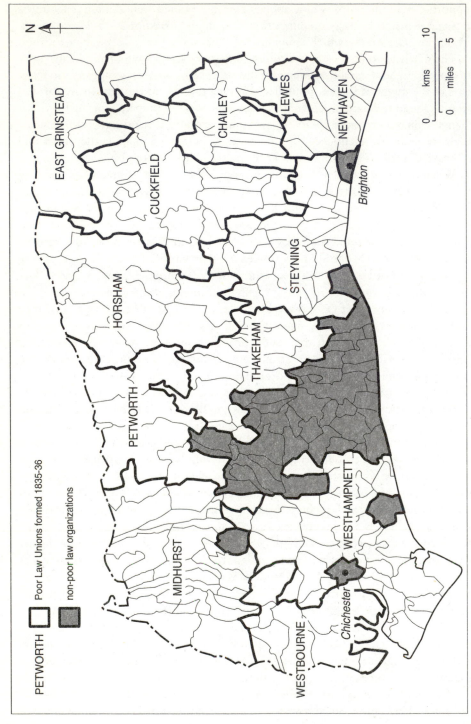

N

PETWORTH ☐ Poor Law Unions formed 1835-36

▨ non-poor law organizations

EAST GRINSTEAD

CUCKFIELD

CHAILEY

LEWES

NEWHAVEN

Brighton

HORSHAM

STEYNING

PETWORTH

THAKEHAM

MIDHURST

WESTHAMPNETT

WESTBOURNE

Chichester

kms   0   10

miles   0   5

4   West Sussex Poor Law Unions formed 1835–1836

The chances of their revival were weakened when news of rebellions in the Canadas at the end of the same year all but cut off emigration from England in 1838. Egremont's son, George Wyndham, who inherited Petworth, was a very different person from his father. Although he gave Sockett a hearing and sent numbers of emigrants to Upper Canada from his estates in Ireland, he decided against continuing his father's emigration scheme. He also declined to take up a project Sockett had been promoting since 1834, to buy land in Upper Canada as a "Sussex" settlement.

Wyndham had grown up with the stigma of his illegitimate birth, uncertain that even Petworth would be his. Egremont's will made him the largest landowner in Sussex, with substantial holdings in Yorkshire and Ireland, but both his wealth and his standing were less than his father's. The entailed title went to Egremont's nephew, who also inherited Egremont's lands in Somerset and the west of England. In addition, Egremont left his Cumberland estates with their valuable mines and substantial sums of money to his younger children.[31] Although still very wealthy, Wyndham downsized the staff at Petworth and did nothing on the same expansive scale as Egremont.

Upper Canada (now Ontario), the destination of the Petworth emigrants and the province favoured by British emigrants to the Canadas in this period, was one of a number of settlement colonies administered through the Colonial Office. During the years from 1791 to 1840 in Upper Canada, immigration fuelled the rapid growth of a population already favoured with a high rate of natural increase. A population estimated at 14,000 in 1791 multiplied to 83,000 in 1817. Reaching 166,000 in 1826, the number would increase to 374,000 in 1836.[32] By mid-century, in 1851, a census recorded 952,000 people in the province then known as Canada West, and most of the available farm land had been taken up. (See Appendix B for complete figures on emigration from Britain in the period 1821–51.)

Seen from Britain in 1832, Upper Canada appeared vast and ripe for development. The colony was divided into large districts that were being subdivided into townships; these latter, the smallest unit of local government, were many times the size of any Sussex parish. The population was still spread mainly along the principal waterways. As the eye travelled westward over the map, there were large areas not yet surveyed into townships. An intensive publicity campaign by the Canada Company, a land company based in London, contributed to the impression at this time that these lands only waited for people to arrive from Britain to become productive.

Petworth emigrants sent to Upper Canada between 1832 and 1837 were part of a wave of emigrants from the British Isles who came to North America during the three decades following the Napoleonic Wars. As the century wore on, successive waves of migration grew in size. Most British immigrants settled in the United States, although in the early period many came first to the British North American colonies to take advantage of cheaper fares. Between 1815 and 1865, more than one million people left Britain for British North America. Irish immigrants predominated during the first half of the nineteenth century. English immigration in the period before the 1840s has been overshadowed by the far greater numbers who arrived in Canada from England towards the end of the nineteenth century and in the early twentieth.[33]

Within this broad picture, the Petworth immigrations belonged to a mini-wave, a brief "mania" for emigration from England to Upper Canada. This particular migration was largest in 1831 and 1832, a time when the people of Upper Canada were moving quickly to open new areas and bring them into cultivation. It weakened in the face of recession and political discontent in the colony in mid-decade, and died away with rebellion and unrest in the Canadas in 1837 and 1838. Although English immigration to Canada is traditionally more from the north, the immigration of the 1830s is characterized by a movement from southern counties.[34] Parish-aided emigrants came mainly from the south and from East Anglia. They were a significant component of the arrivals with an English background and helped to give the group its south-of-England character.

Parish-aided immigrants arriving in Upper Canada in 1831 and 1832 stepped into an established tradition of assistance. Looking at European emigration to North America between 1815 and 1930, Dudley Baines offers the educated guess that perhaps 10 per cent of emigrants were officially assisted by institutions, such as governments, land companies, or railways.[35] In Upper Canada, the aid that immigrants received to help them settle in the province was given both separately from and in conjunction with assistance in crossing the Atlantic, and it has to be included in the calculation. The numbers that can be recaptured are estimates based on the records of formal aid from government.

By the time of the Constitution Act of 1791, which divided the old Province of Quebec into Upper and Lower Canada, assisted settlements had strong roots in the province. The settlements created to provide a home in British territory for loyalists who came north after the American Revolution had set the precedent of free land grants from the government, in these cases given as a reward for military service and a compensation for losses. Bruce Wilson estimates that in 1785 in the area of Upper Canada there were 7,500 loyalist settlers (Scottish and Scots-Irish, with aboriginal people, blacks, Irish, German, English, and native-born American colonists). They had been assisted to establish themselves in the hinterland of the present towns of Prescott, Brockville, and Picton in the east and in a smaller community at the western end of the province near Niagara.[36]

In the early nineteenth century, the most influential government initiatives in assisted emigration were made by the Colonial Office during the long tenure of the Tories and Colonial Secretary Lord Bathurst. Under different terms, several parties of immigrants were located in Upper Canada between 1815 and 1825. The majority were Irish or Scots and they were settled in different parts of the province, for the most part east of Toronto.[37] Lillian Gates estimates that by 1822 there were 10,763 persons settled with assistance in the Bathurst District (this number includes people already in the province, a number of them former soldiers who had served in British regiments during the War of 1812–14).[38] In a count of immigrants given assisted passage from Britain as part of aid overseen by the Colonial Office in the period 1815–25, H.J.M. Johnston arrives at a total of 6,700 or more. Making inge-nious use of sketchy records and weighing them to account for natural increase and leakage to the United States, he reckons that this category of state-aided immigrants accounts for about one-sixth to one-fifth of the immigrant arrivals in these years.[39]

Parish-aided immigrants to Upper Canada are more difficult to count because they were sent by many different parishes and no single authority was responsible for them. In these years, parish-aided immigrants were by definition English and Welsh. Ireland had no poor laws before 1838, and since the Scottish poor laws of this era did not permit aid of this kind to the able-bodied, there was no corresponding movement there.[40] Until 1834, the best totals for parish immigration to the Canadas were kept in the Emigrant Office at Quebec. The figures were compiled and sent to the Colonial Office by Alexander Carlisle Buchanan, who had been appointed as agent in 1828. Buchanan worked with a nephew of the same name as his. Before ill-health forced his uncle to resign and he replaced him as agent in 1838, the younger Buchanan took over an increasing amount of the work of the office and filled in during his uncle's periods of sick leave, which included the winters of 1835, 1836, and 1837. From 1831 to 1834, Buchanan relied on letters from sponsors, on infor-mation he picked up about arriving ships, and on the immigrants who came to his office and told him that they had been assisted. Using these informal sources, he recorded a total of 12,677 immigrant arrivals assisted by parishes and landlords. In the next three years, from 1835 to 1837, the Quebec Emigrant Office recorded another 7,239 immigrants in this category. Thus the Buchanans' total for assisted immigration between 1831 and 1837 was 19,333.[41]

After 1834, the Quebec Emigrant Office relied in part on poor law commissioners to supply numbers. From 1834, the commissioners listed assisted emigrants in their annual reports, but their partial responsibility was reflected in partial records. Their count was restricted to emigrants from those parishes that had applied to them to approve a loan. Using these figures as the best available after 1835, Bruce Elliott reports that the commissioners recorded the departure of about 10,000 emigrants to British North America between 1835 and 1847, two-thirds having left in 1835–37 and one-quarter in 1842–45.[42]

In an assisted settlement in late eighteenth- or early nineteenth-century Ontario, new immigrants from Britain were assigned lots of land on terms of deferred pay-ment and given more or less generous help with food, shelter, and medical care, help which had overtones of the old poor law. If the immigrants could not find work on their own, the government hired them as road builders – the traditional occupation of the pauper employed by an English parish. The main spokesperson for assisted emigration that would include additional aid in the colony was Robert John Wilmot Horton, colonial under-secretary from 1821 to 1828. Horton is best remembered as a champion of emigration from Ireland, but he was also an advocate of parish-assisted emigration.[43]

Horton's influence still predominated the field of colonization theory when Sock-ett designed his scheme, and his Tory paternalism was a comfortable fit with that of

Egremont and Sockett. His influence was also strong in Upper Canada in 1832, where another like-minded Tory paternalist, Sir John Colborne, had been lieutenant-governor since 1828. In England, however, Horton's idea that assisted settlements should be an integral part of assisted emigration no longer resonated in the Colonial Office. After Horton had left office as under-secretary, the policies of past administrations to freely alienate crown lands to serve any convenient purpose had come under criticism. One of these policies had been to assign land free or on easy credit terms to indigent immigrants (such as those sent by Horton in the 1820s).

The thrust of Colonial Office policy since 1830 had been to impose a simplified sales system in all colonies and to maximize revenues from colonial lands remaining in the possession of the crown. The colonial theorist who found most favour in the 1830s was Edward Gibbon Wakefield. Wakefield's ideal colony included immigrants who would work for others until they had saved to pay a "sufficient" price for crown lands. Even if Colonial Office officials had wanted to apply Wakefield's full model to Upper Canada, they would have been prevented by the ease with which immigrants who were dissatisfied in the Canadas moved across the open border to the United States. Wakefield's endorsement of higher prices for wild lands, however, lent respectability to a decision made in 1831 to raise the prices.[44]

Viscount Howick (later the third Earl Grey), the under-secretary who set out to imprint the values of the 1830s on the Colonial Office, had added weight as the eldest son of the prime minister and is seen as having dominated a weak colonial secretary.[45] Having put his mark on a new policy of land sales, Howick was instrumental in leading his father's government to a decision against making government a prominent player in parish-aided emigration to British North America. He also turned his attention to the reception given poor immigrants in Upper Canada and the high cost of assisting the able-bodied among them.

The Colonial Office set policy in Upper Canada by sending instructions to the lieutenant-governor, thus bringing issues of the old versus the new poor law to the colony. In 1832 and thereafter, Lieutenant-Governor Sir John Colborne's instructions were to reduce and, as much as possible, to phase out aid to the able-bodied among arriving immigrants. These instructions in fact anticipated changes in the poor law at home, as Upper Canada had no poor law and there was no need to wait for new legislation. Petworth immigrants were affected along with everyone else, although they received extra attention from local authorities who were aware of Egremont's sponsorship and were impressed by his rank and influence.

Colborne, like Egremont in Petworth, resisted the new rules of assistance, being a paternalist of the old school who had an agenda of his own. He did not have the same kind of control over Upper Canada as Egremont did over his area of Sussex, and he was in a more direct chain of command leading to the Colonial Office; but he did have the self-confidence of someone who had enjoyed a long and distinguished career. Most of his life had been spent in command in the army, and he was used to facing situations not foreseen in his orders and acting on his own initiative.[46] His instincts towards the poor were in line with the old poor law, and his resistance to new ways of dealing with poverty was reflected in the help given Petworth immigrants in his colony.

Apart from having a different vision of the needs of the poor, Colborne had ambitious plans for his province that accommodated assisted settlement. He sent survey parties out along the waterways to foster improvements in transportation and harbours, and he made a start on improving arterial roads. The settlers he wanted for these newly opening townships were British. He saw the high proportion of American-born settlers in western Upper Canada as both a military liability in the event of hostilities with the United States and a threat to British customs and institutions. His answer was to encourage communities in which a mix of British immigrants included people of the officer class who would act as magistrates and employers and poor immigrants who would supply labour and services. To this end, he was tireless in interviewing, entertaining, and wooing new immigrants who arrived with capital, and he used every opportunity to direct the destination of assisted settlers.

Many Petworth emigrants received help in travelling within Upper Canada. In addition, two groups in particular benefited from Colborne's settlement policies. In 1832, a number of Petworth emigrants were sent to become part of a government-supervised settlement in Adelaide Township in the London District, where poor settlers were given land on special terms and assistance in getting established. A second plan, in place from 1834 to 1837, was directed to some of the families sent by the Petworth committee and other parish sponsors, giving them temporary possession of a five-acre lot and a log house in close proximity to communities where rapid expansion ensured employment. Under this plan, Petworth emigrants went to Woodstock and Brantford.

Colborne's successor as lieutenant-governor was Sir Francis Bond Head, who replaced him early in 1836. Head arrived in Upper Canada fresh from his success as an assistant poor law commissioner, in which capacity he had quickly and efficiently introduced the new poor law to much of Kent.[47] He is known in Canada primarily for his eccentric and divisive political presence. His personal intervention in an election in the summer of 1836 achieved the short-term effect of sweeping those who supported his conservative views to victory, but at the price of polarizing opinion and embittering the opposition, and he is thought to have precipitated the brief rebellion led by William Lyon Mackenzie in December 1837 by sending the regular troops in his jurisdiction out of the province to Lower Canada. Investigation of Head's impact on the social services of the colony has only begun, but the influence of his connection with the poor law commission is obvious.[48]

The continuation of Colborne's five-acre-lot plan under Head probably owed as much to institutional memory and its small scale as to any thought the new lieutenant-governor gave to its merits. Head encouraged the sending of parish emigrants, but under his direction this program and all those for their reception were starved of money. His intention was to force the communities that he believed were benefiting from immigration to look after immigration's casualties. Under Colborne, all agents in the Crown Lands Department (the government department responsible

for lands still in the possession of the crown) had given more or less of their attention to poor immigrants and had helped find jobs or a location for many who were
capable of work. Head made a beginning on separating the duties of emigration
agents from those of crown lands agents and restricting the activities of emigration
agents to the main points of entry.

Under Head, the emigration agents, now reduced in number and on very strict
budgets, had to report to Anthony Hawke, the chief immigration agent in Toronto,
before giving the most minor amounts of relief. Hawke's instructions to these agents
were as stringent as any issued by the Poor Law Commission in London. These
instructions signalled not only a change in the kind and amount of help given to
able-bodied immigrants but also changing attitudes and intentions more widely based
than the personal opinions of two lieutenant-governors. Colborne saw in parish-
aided immigrants a pool of settlers whom he wanted to encourage to take over empty
lands. Head saw the parish poor as immigrants in the same light as the parish paupers he had dealt with in his brief career as an assistant poor law commissioner in
England, as people who needed to be pressured to find work and support themselves. The Petworth emigrations straddled the six years when changes in attitudes
and policies towards poverty initiated in England were crossing the Atlantic and influencing the policies governing the reception of poor immigrants in Upper Canada.

Chapter I

"emigration ... the best if not the only remedy": from "swing" to parish-assisted emigration

Emigration ... begins to go very prosperously in the neighbourhood, and I am convinced that it is the best if not the only remedy for the evils of a superabundant population in a district like this.

Egremont to Richmond, 22 March 1832[1]

Nothing will prevent a continued stream of emigration flowing toward U.C. but the impossibility of parishes raising the necessary funds, & ... they cannot ... unless some legislative enactment be provided.

Sockett to Richmond, 22 October 1833[2]

The British government seriously considered legislation supporting parish-aided emigration early in 1831, and the possibility of a nationally organized scheme came up again in 1834. Thomas Sockett was not involved in lobbying for assisted emigration in 1831, and his role in 1834 was a minor one. Nonetheless, he believed that the long-term future of parish-aided emigration and of his own scheme at Petworth depended on the government passing favourable legislation. He thought that the Poor Law Amendment Act of 1834 was the legislation he needed, but the impetus it gave to the Petworth emigrations proved temporary. The support that sustained Sockett's emigrations came from the Earl of Egremont. Egremont hoped for more from assisted emigration than a quiet winter, although he was not unaware of this effect. He backed Sockett's emigration scheme as a humanitarian way of encouraging workers who could not earn a living to move away from his district permanently. After his patron's death in November 1837, Sockett was unable to charter another ship for emigrants from Sussex.

In government circles, assisted emigration was seen mainly as a pacification measure motivated by concerns about renewed unrest in rural parishes on the scale seen during the Swing disturbances of 1830–31. With each year that passed without major disturbances in the countryside, government support for the measure weakened, and the lobby for government-sponsored assisted emigration to British North America lost out to a stronger lobby demanding poor law reform.

Many parishes embraced assisted emigration for a year or two following the Swing disturbances, and others turned to it with the introduction of the new poor law a few years later. Assisted emigration had the beauty of obtaining an immediate result by removing a number of people whose poverty and unemployment constituted a threat. Sending emigrants was expensive, however, and long-term benefits to the individual ratepayer were questionable. Over time, those who believed in the lasting

effects of poor law reform were more persuasive and carried the day. They were successful in part because they incorporated assisted emigration into their own argument. They presented it as a temporary measure that could help the government to
impose effective social control and create the conditions needed to bring in sweeping reforms. Thus the Duke of Richmond was as comfortable supporting Sockett's
project as Egremont; he simply offered a more qualified support.

Sockett, Egremont, and Richmond were practical men who dealt with the poor
in terms of their own personal experience – as a clergyman in Sockett's case and as
a magistrate and landowner in Egremont's and Richmond's. In West Sussex they
encountered ample evidence to convince them of a Malthusian "surplus" in the large
numbers of labourers unemployed every winter. By March 1830, Richmond was convinced that something needed to be done, and he raised the matter in the House
of Lords. He presented evidence of the poverty among labourers in both rural and
urban communities and unsuccessfully called upon Wellington's Tory government
to launch an inquiry into the state of the working classes.[3]

England in the early nineteenth century was undergoing rapid change. The years
following the final defeat of Napoleon in 1815 saw a remarkable increase in population. The census for 1831 tabulated close to 5 million more people in England and
Wales than had been recorded in 1801, an increase from about 8.9 to 13.9 million.
Figures for Sussex show an increase in population from 159,000 to 273,000.[4] The
postwar period was one of uncertainty for many. Returning soldiers had difficulty
finding civilian jobs. In manufacturing districts, some workers were displaced as a
result of technological advances and others because of shifts in patterns of trade and
in consumer demand in a country now at peace. The number of agricultural labourers, the largest single occupation group recorded in the 1831 census, increased
markedly while opportunities for work in agriculture and related trades stagnated.[5]

Although the recession in agriculture was not felt equally in all years or in all
parts of the country, large numbers of wage labourers in arable areas of southeast-
ern counties suffered unremitting poverty. The source of their misery had changed
from the high prices and scarcity of the years when England was at war with France
to the insecurity and seasonal unemployment of the postwar recession, but many
families and individuals continued to rely on the parish to supplement inadequate
wages.[6]

THE SWING DISTURBANCES

By the autumn of 1830, the situation was far more serious than anything Richmond
had predicted at the beginning of the year. People in England had seen revolution
breaking out once again on the Continent. The turmoil in France and Belgium had
potential social as well as political implications for Britain. By the end of the harvest season, rural labourers in one community after another in southern England were
burning ricks and barns, destroying the threshing machines that were taking their
winter work, and joining forces to demand higher wages and more job security. These

scattered disturbances came to be collectively known by the name of the mythical Captain Swing – the signature used on some of the anonymous threatening letters sent to landowners and farmers. In all, there were risings in over twenty counties in 1830–31: across the southeast to the west country, in the home counties and the midlands, in East Anglia, and even in a few communities in the regions slightly affected to the north and west of Lincoln.[7]

The common threads in the Swing disturbances were the demands for higher wages, better working conditions, and full employment. In many rural parishes, for weeks or sometimes months, employers intimidated by fear of incendiary fires or mob action paid more than before, but they took back these concessions as soon as they felt safe in doing so. Historians have interpreted the outbursts of 1830–31 as forms of protest that threatened property, not life, perpetrated by people whose objectives were bound by local limits.[8] Among contemporaries, fear of full-scale revolution in England – fear of the chaos of France and republicanism – meant harsh action against those involved and a more calculated look at measures to alleviate rural distress, and these included emigration.

Charles Grey's Whig government was elected at the height of the Swing disturbances in November 1830. As one part of its platform, Grey's government promised more rigorous suppression of unrest and measures to prevent future disturbances. This attitude was stiffened by aristocratic landowners such as Richmond who were horrified by the failure of many rural magistrates to stand up to the Swing protesters.

Even as Grey's cabinet was being formed, Richmond's responsibilities in Sussex drew him back to Goodwood to deal with a situation too serious to leave to his younger brothers. Disturbances, which in the summer had appeared to be mainly localized in Kent, had suddenly begun to spread westward rapidly and unpredictably. As Egremont wrote to Home Secretary Sir Robert Peel in early November, rural labourers were susceptible to contagion in even the "quietest and best disposed districts."[9] Soldiers, members of Peel's new London police, or the coast guard could bring any one situation under control; the difficult question facing the government was how to deploy limited forces without risking being caught seriously out of position by the next outbreaks.

Magistrates carried a heavy responsibility for law and order in rural England in 1830. The methods of both rural mobs and their rulers had roots in the traditions of a society where very few controlled the many. If Egremont was too old to ride out as Richmond did at the head of a hastily assembled force of tenants and retainers to disperse a mob with a speech,[10] he was a past master at getting his way by using a judicious blend of theatre, behind-the-scenes intervention, and timely reminders of the force that backed his suggestions.[11] Egremont called on Peel to send soldiers to Petworth so that he would have the "terror of the name" at his disposal, but he did not use them and soon sent them away.[12] Although the radical town of Horsham, northeast of Petworth on the London road, caused him and his son-in-law Sir Charles Burrell prolonged concern,[13] the disturbances Egremont confronted in his district were not serious enough to cause him to question methods of social control that had served him well in the past and seemed to him to be a sufficient response in 1830.

Lesser magistrates in Egremont's area of influence had not all fared so comfortably. Aristocrats like Egremont assumed local leadership and relied on their own very considerable resources, but they also knew that a request from them for soldiers would be quickly honoured. In many isolated areas, lesser magistrates and employers found ways to rationalize their own capitulation to their labourers' demands: a "temporary concession" on wages, "as long as the Demands are not very unreasonable," was "an Evil, & a great Evil," but it was a lesser evil than the fires that would result from refusing the workers' demands.[14] This was the kind of thinking that led the government to find the magistracy wanting and to seek more reliable instruments for controlling the poor.

Richmond himself was as confident as Egremont and personally popular, but he saw a more menacing side to the disturbances in parishes centred around towns such as Worthing, Arundel, and Chichester. He described the snowball effect of a tumultuous crowd, how it became "more drunk and more daring" as it rolled across the flat coastal plain. Workers who on their own would have done nothing were intimidated and gathered up into the mob. During the night, parties broke off to extort money from isolated houses.[15] In this district, Richmond moved quickly to counter the destruction of machines, arson, and cases of intimidation and extortion by making examples of those whose guilt seemed clear.[16] Before leaving Chichester to return to London, he drew on military experience gained in the French wars to organize a paramilitary force of civilian constables "after the manner of a military occupation by a hostile army."[17]

In the autumn of 1830, Egremont, Richmond, and others among the great landlords of Sussex took a two-pronged approach to dealing with the disturbances, an approach that reflected their two different roles. As magistrates, they were responsible for public order, and they responded with firm measures to make an example of labourers who took the law into their own hands. As landowners, they were "country gentlemen," in normal circumstances bystanders in the wage negotiations between farmers and labourers.[18]

Both Egremont and Richmond were on record as thinking that farmers ought to pay their workers more than they had in recent years, but they could only imagine redress as coming from above.[19] In the situation in which they found themselves in 1830, aristocratic landlords often tried to save appearances by encouraging employers to make concessions before they received threats. Disturbances appeared to hop and skip across the county in part because of their interventions.[20] In many Sussex parishes, noble landlords smoothed the way so that no incidents occurred of a magnitude to be noticed by historians.

Aristocratic magistrates presided in person over public meetings of tenants as well as magistrates' meetings, which in addition to raising constables and watchmen passed euphemistic resolutions on aiding the suffering poor.[21] As a practical incentive to farmers to raise wages, Egremont and other landlords reduced their rents. This lead was sometimes followed with a similar reduction in tithes by the clergy and other tithe holders in the area they influenced.[22] Specifically, they wanted farmers to maintain the higher rates of pay into the winter months and to keep their casual workers on as regular employees of a single master. At the height of the disturbances, anxious farmers looked to them for leadership and did as they suggested.

Egremont mediated negotiations between respectful delegations of farmers and labourers.[23] His agent encouraged farmers to dismantle threshing machines in anticipation of trouble.[24] Just before a fair day in late 1830, when riots were widely expected, Sockett guided the Petworth vestry to a typical conclusion. The first order of business dealt with raising a liberal subscription for guarding the town. The second would see the vestry set a new scale in raising the parish wage "to such a sum that it is thought there can now be no legitimate ground for complaint."[25] The new rate paid by the parish – usually somewhat below that paid by farmers and hence a sort of unofficial minimum wage – was twelve shillings a week (see Table 1.1). Egremont signalled his approval by adopting the "scale of wages adopted by the Petworth

Table 1.1
Petworth Wage Scale, 1830

Daily wage scale negotiated by Petworth special vestry, 17 November 1830	
Man and wife and 2 children[a]	2s.
Man and wife and 1 child	1s. 8d.
Man and wife	1s. 6d.
Single man over 18 years of age	1s.
Youths aged 15 to 18	8d.

SOURCE: WSRO, PHA 8558, Petworth parish vestry, 17 November 1830.
[a] The wage scale stops at two children because in Petworth a child allowance
was paid to families with three or more young children.

Farmers" for his own workmen (those he employed directly as opposed to those who worked for his tenants) "under the several Departments [of his estates] and in other parishes as well as Petworth."[26]

Just as Egremont had criticized farmers who had ignored his opinion in the past and kept wages too low, so he castigated those who panicked during the disturbances and conceded more than was "right" or was expected by labourers in better-managed parishes like Petworth.[27] What was "right" constrained the earl as well as the farmers. In practice, Egremont continued – after 1830 as before – to treat his labourers rather better than the community norm, but he always respected the expectations of local farmers that he would not pay wages and benefits too far out of line with theirs. Egremont, for all his wealth and benevolence, saw no anomaly in criticizing farmers for paying their labourers too little while he himself employed some who depended on additional support from the parish.[28]

Once the Swing crisis passed, farmers paid their labourers as little as or less than before.[29] In parts of East Sussex, militant labourers had been in a strong enough bargaining position to ask for fourteen shillings a week year-round, and wages in some districts were still at this level in 1832.[30] In the west, as early as December 1830, labourers who had been promised farm employment petitioned Richmond because they were back working in the parish gravel pits and at a rate of pay lower than promised.[31] By February 1831, Sussex newspapers carried accounts of farmers acting together on wage reductions.[32] Over the next few months, these same newspapers reported arson and other incidents in which workers had risen up against employers who brought in itinerant labourers to help with their harvest.

Such reminders of the labourers' dissatisfaction kept Richmond and his landowning associates in cabinet searching for legislation that would prevent the rural poor from ever again being in a position to pose a similar threat to the existing social order.[33] The landowners had to bide their time, however, as the national spotlight had shifted from rural to urban disturbances, and from rural protest and social reform issues to the Reform Bill agitation of 1831 and 1832 and electoral politics.[34] In the interval, Richmond in particular never let the government forget the importance of agricultural labourers and their needs. He thought that the "labouring poor" deserved concrete evidence that government was working to better their condition.[35] The means he proposed were measures already available under the old poor law, measures that should be applied as a "palliative for present evils until a more permanent amelioration could be decided upon."[36] Witnesses before a select committee of the House of Lords, of which Richmond was a member, offered evidence that helped confirm him in this opinion. They testified that in the spring of 1831 only gentlemen farmers still willingly kept on extra labourers; the majority of farmers used savings from reductions in rents and tithes to pay down old debts or absorbed them into general farm revenues.[37]

Richmond failed in a spirited attempt to have the Lords' committee issue a report endorsing assisted emigration, and he turned in disgust from its timid deliberations and looked for other ways to help poor labourers. As an emigration bill relating to parish emigration was in the process of being put forward from the Colonial Office, Richmond himself sponsored legislation intended to encourage the employment of surplus workers through the use of a parish labour rate. When a parish had a labour rate, ratepayers either hired extra labourers according to an agreed formula or paid a penalty in cash. As with assisted emigration, parish officers in normal circumstances had difficulty persuading everyone to agree to the extra charge. This bill made it easier for parishes to override minority opposition, and it was adopted as a temporary measure to last for one year. Proposals for an extension beyond 1832 ran into stiff opposition in Parliament from interest groups who suffered financially from its imposition, and it was not extended into a second year when it came up for renewal.[38]

Although a labour rate might seem to have nothing to do with emigration, in the case of the Petworth emigrations there was a fortuitous connection through Sockett. Bishops in the House of Lords had strongly opposed the labour rate as particularly injurious to members of the clergy (they paid rates on their tithes but had little occasion to employ many labourers), and the bill ran against Sockett's self-interest as the second largest ratepayer in Petworth after Egremont.[39] Egremont, however, supported the bill, and his son-in-law Burrell championed it in the House of Commons. Sockett thus obligingly headed petitions in its favour.[40] Whether he was already preparing to approach Egremont with his emigration scheme or whether he devised it as an alternative to a labour rate, Sockett applied evidence collected for these petitions to his proposal for assisted emigration.

Using evidence from his own parish, Sockett demonstrated the impact of recent disturbances, though he tactfully omitted any direct reference to them. In the year 1830–31, expenditure on the relief of the able-bodied poor in the parish of Petworth had tripled or quadrupled over that of the previous two decades.[41] During the midwinter months of December 1830 and January 1831, the parish employed more than 100 men and supported some 330 people if their wives and dependent children were counted in.[42] In Sockett's view, these people would benefit most if they were sent to the colonies, a move which would also ensure that neither they nor their children would be a future drain on the parish poor rate. The savings to ratepayers that Sockett predicted in parishes sending emigrants probably reflected the inflated costs of using parish funds to employ "redundant" workers in the aftermath of Swing.

In later years, Sockett said that he had approached Egremont in 1831 on the subject of assisted emigration, offering Malthusian warnings that the poor, having once reduced the middle classes to their own level, would finally consume even the wealth of the landowners.[43] This argument for assisted emigration appealed more to middle-class ratepayers like Sockett than to a man of Egremont's wealth. Nevertheless, Egremont liked Sockett's plan of assisted emigration, probably because it did not ask too much of him and did not require disturbing innovations. He had for years launched large, labour-intensive projects at times of high unemployment,[44] and Sockett proposed to run his emigrations on a similar pattern.

Although Egremont's recommendation of assisted emigration to Richmond also had Malthusian overtones, he looked at surplus population from the different perspective of a hereditary landowner. He wrote that he had seen the labouring population of his district increasing over many years. Over the same period of time, the number of acres under cultivation had remained constant – the cultivated acreage had not increased "by one acre in a century." Assisted emigration, he argued, would restore a better balance between land and labour at home. It would be "happy" in its outcome because of the improved prospects of those who emigrated.[45] During his remaining years, Egremont saw no reason to change this opinion and he therefore continued to back Sockett's annual emigrations.

With Egremont convinced, Sockett was ready to start his scheme. In the early spring of 1832, he was too busy to think much of the big picture, and he began his lobbying for a government plan of assisted emigration only after he had finished the task of organizing his second emigration from Petworth. He had no way at that time of knowing that the most important decisions affecting parish emigration had already been made.

The likelihood that Grey's government would fully support parish-aided emigration was greatest in December 1830 and January 1831. At the height of the crisis of the Swing disturbances, assisted emigration was attractive to the government, since it offered government the same quick results it offered sponsors in individual parishes. In *Society and Pauperism*, J.R. Poynter describes the reform of the poor law as the end process of a long and tortuous debate that had roots in the eighteenth century and had resurfaced in the strong case for abolition of the poor law made in the period 1817–20. While Poynter sees the Swing disturbances as precipitating action, he argues that the reforms to the poor law adopted in 1834 took time to emerge and more time to win acceptance. In 1831, with no other resolution in sight, parish-assisted emigration appeared to be a solution ready for implementation.

PARISH-ASSISTED EMIGRATION AND GOVERNMENT

The subject of assisted emigration had been discussed at great length in select committees chaired by the colonial under-secretary, Robert John Horton, in 1826 and 1827.[46] After the failure of his plans for Ireland, Horton had braved the hostility of colleagues thoroughly bored by the subject and kept parish emigration before Parliament in the form of a bill enabling parishes to mortgage their poor rates in order to assist emigration.[47] Although Horton liked to think of himself as a lone campaigner, Colonial Secretary Sir James Murray had in fact appointed John Richards in April 1830 as a one-man commission to British North America to investigate possible sites for large settlements of pauper immigrants. In the late autumn of 1830, Richards was back in England and busy preparing a final report based on material he had been sending to R.W. Hay in the Colonial Office.[48] For a brief period, serious consideration was given to dusting off Horton's scheme and making it over as a Whig measure.

The new colonial secretary was a former Tory, Frederick Robinson, Viscount Goderich (Earl Ripon in 1833). Strongly influenced – some say dominated – by his under-secretary, Viscount Howick, the son of the prime minister and the future third Earl Grey,[49] Goderich appears to have left the matter of assisted emigration almost entirely to Howick. In December 1830, in the immediate wake of Swing, Goderich wrote a private letter in support of removing 50,000 "industrious individuals" from the southern counties,[50] but by the beginning of March 1831, when he sent off a non-committal response to a paper on the subject sent to him by his friend Richmond, he seems to have returned to his more settled attitude of distrust of large schemes.[51]

The first document to test the waters of public opinion on the subject of assisted-emigration legislation was a pamphlet circulated in January 1831 entitled *Remarks on Emigration*, written by political economist Nassau Senior. The pamphlet included a draft bill drawn up with the silent assistance of James Stephen, the permanent counsel to the Colonial Office.[52] Senior was a former professor of political economy at Oxford and an important adviser to Grey's government. He modelled his plan on Horton's, with the administrative difference of putting parish emigration under a central commission rather than under the Colonial Office, but he presented it with a flamboyance that had none of Horton's laboured logic. Senior met the issue of the cost of a national scheme of assisted emigration on high ground by claiming that the benefits to society justified the expense.[53] Recognizing fear of the mob as the most compelling reason to pay for assisted emigration, he used it shamelessly: "the peasantry will rise again – confident from having been successful; and furious, from having been deceived." Assisted emigration was "the sole immediate remedy" to prevent this outcome in the perhaps one-third of English parishes where there was a surplus population of labourers.[54] Although Senior's reputation as an adviser to government rests on his work on poor law reform, this work had barely begun. In this pamphlet, poor law reform appears only in a vague list of measures to prevent a future population explosion after emigration had done its work.

Horton happily endorsed Senior's draft bill as maintaining the spirit or "principle" of the emigrations to Upper Canada he had organized under the superintendence of Peter Robinson in 1823 and 1825. Just as the bill was about to be presented to Parliament, he learned that Howick had introduced a thoroughly upsetting change. Howick's bill "completely abandoned" Horton's emphasis on locating parish immigrants on the land and replaced it with an emphasis on wage labour.[55] On 22 February 1831, two days after receiving Horton's blistering memo, Howick introduced a bill "to facilitate voluntary Emigration to His Majesty's possessions Abroad"[56] – modestly claiming no more credit for himself than the merit of adopting Horton's ideas.

The publicity surrounding Howick's emigration bill attracted attention in many parishes where sponsors and parish officials had not seriously considered assisting emigration before the outbreak of the Swing disturbances. The bill did not specify any government responsibilities for assisted emigrants once they reached the new jurisdiction of the colonies and assigned none to sponsors. Although many were willing to send a small amount of landing money, sponsors and parishes took up assisted emigration on the assumption that they would be free of the emigrants once they reached the other shore. Horton had modified his own scheme to limit private sponsors' contributions in this way, but he had assumed that government would take over in the colonies. He rightly identified Howick's intention to rely on the private sector to receive emigrants in British North America as well as to send them from Britain as having huge implications for the colonies. As he knew from his years in the Colonial Office, these colonies had a seasonal workforce and a limited capacity to absorb poor newcomers. In speaking to the bill, Howick dealt with the commissioners' role in the colony by wishing away difficulties. He glossed over problems of long distance and primitive transport, and he waved aside the cost of establishing immigrant settlements on crown lands as an eventuality unlikely to be necessary. In his hands, the question of wage labour versus assisted settlement became one of the moral advantages of self-help with no doubt as to the answer. On the basis of this assumption, he ventured the opinion that "there were strong reasons to believe that "once begun, and conducted on a systematic principle, its [assisted emigration's] expense would be trifling."[57]

Despite his initial role in introducing the emigration bill, Howick was apparently responsible for allowing a revised version to die on the order paper at the end of the session. If he had ever really believed that assisted emigration might be simple or cheap, he soon heard enough to convince him otherwise. He explained his reasoning in December 1831 in responding to George Poulett Scrope, who had sent him a draft of an emigration bill radically simplified to make it easier for parishes to borrow. Howick did not want the legislation because of the many "embarrassing questions" that would be raised by government involvement. He also thought it unnecessary for the government to encourage a process that was going "almost as fast as we can desire."[58]

Howick had rejected assistance to parish-aided emigration to North America at a time when Richmond still hesitated, and it took Howick the better part of a year to bring Richmond to his way of thinking. By April 1831, Richmond was ready to agree with Howick that the emigration bill could not pass in its present form, but he was still anxious to take at least a small step towards removing "the excess of labourers" before another winter again brought hardship and unemployment.[59] Howick seems to have suggested the idea of a commission. Richmond spoke to Goderich, and in July Goderich appointed a five-man commission to be chaired by Richmond with Howick as one of its members. The government allowed the Emigration Bill to drop but left the way open for the subject to be taken up again in the new session in 1831–32.

Goderich's instructions to Richmond's commissioners stated explicitly that they did not have the financial powers envisaged for the commission described in Howick's emigration bill. Their task was to collect information and make recommendations.[60] Because they had not convened until the season of emigration to British North America was largely over, the commissioners were too late to consider encouraging further emigration in that direction during 1831. Probably at Howick's instigation, they turned this apparent disadvantage around by starting their deliberations with the Australian colonies of New South Wales and Van Diemen's Land.

Howick's papers reveal that he had a stronger interest in assisting emigration to Australia than to North America. These distant colonies were not attracting the labouring immigrants they needed. Even as a measure of relief for England, assisted emigration to the Southern Hemisphere had the great advantage of taking agricultural labourers at the best time of year. Emigrants left for North America in spring, when employment was picking up and their own ability to contribute to the expense was at its lowest. If they went to Australia, they could leave in the autumn, at the beginning of the season when their presence was a threat and when they still had the extra money earned during the harvest.[61]

While there was undoubtedly exaggeration in claims crediting the Emigration Commission with beginning the assisted emigration to Australia of persons "accustomed to earn their Subsistence by Manual Labour, such as Agriculturalists, Artisans, or Mechanics,"[62] the commissioners did preside over the first steps towards active government involvement in the movement of free emigrants to Australia in place of convict labourers. They helped to persuade shipowners to offer a cheap passage aimed at working people, and they had a part in convincing the government to make a modest trial of a bounty system, payments made to assist the emigration of the people most needed in the colony. They also helped to make known the all-important willingness of receiving colonies in the Southern Hemisphere to devote a portion of their land revenues to assisting emigration from Britain.

These beginnings in assisted emigration to Australian colonies were limited in scope and in numbers sent, but the commissioners' report identified sources of funding and showed the way. Policies initiated during the 1830s, and strengthened during the following decade, resulted in Australasia replacing North America as the principal destination for assisted emigrants from southern England. By the time this redirected assisted emigration was flowing strongly, changes in the poor law made working people like those sent to Upper Canada by the Petworth committee ineligible for parish aid. Under the new regime, English paupers were likely to be unable or unwilling to perform the hard work expected of new immigrants or else so miserably poor that they had no alternative to the workhouse. Thus, the financial assistance that colonial governments offered emigrants to Australia (and later New Zealand) came with conditions that increasingly discouraged those identified as paupers.[63]

The commissioners' policy recommendations for North America emerged more slowly. Richmond had focused his own research on unemployment in his county of Sussex in the winter of 1831–32. The results confirmed his conviction that "the distress – more particularly in the south-eastern districts of the country, arose from a superabundance of population."[64] In January 1832, Richmond still expected and wanted legislation on assisted emigration in time for spring departures.[65] Howick countered by reminding Richmond of the realities of English politics. The colonial secretary was heavily occupied with impending legislation to end slavery in British colonies, and a host of other issues awaited legislation. The response from outside Parliament to the proposed bill on assisted emigration had been much more lively than from within. Parishes and individuals had sent unprecedented numbers of emigrants in 1831 and seemed set to do so again, but they would only act if they were not distracted by hopes of legislation offering easier funding. Why not wait, Howick suggested, to see what happened in the 1832 season and, if necessary, reintroduce the bill in the session of 1833.[66]

Richmond chaired a committee charged with gathering evidence on the condition of slaves in Jamaica, and his prominence ensured him a certain involvement in the politics of the Reform Bill of 1832. Until this bill was passed in March 1832, its central goals – to abolish rotten boroughs, increase representation in cities and counties, and allow a limited widening of the franchise – dominated parliamentary debate.[67] Richmond was nonetheless as concerned as ever about persistent reports of rural protests.[68] He let Howick persuade him to give up the bill on assisted emigration, but he gave way only because he believed he was on the track of a better solution. He had been demanding a full investigation into the state of the poor since 1829, and now it was about to happen.

An abiding concern of the upper levels of Grey's government was that during the Swing disturbances agricultural labourers had discovered the power of numbers. They feared that the Swing disturbances had had "a permanently bad effect upon the character of the agricultural population."[69] This concern lay behind Richmond's belief that neither assisted emigration nor other measures of the old poor law could provide a complete answer to this challenge. Assisted emigration touched only the people directly involved; he wanted a measure that would be felt and recognized by all labourers.

Although Richmond is not usually named among the people who suggested it, a cabinet document proposing the Royal Commission on the Poor Laws bears his name.[70] This document made explicit the mandate of the commission to concentrate its investigations in the counties most involved in the rural uprisings of 1830.[71] In the document, Richmond accepted the opinion of reformers such as Senior who claimed that under the old poor law labourers had been corrupted by bad administration. He also accepted their argument that reforms could restore to the proper balance of some unspecified and happier time in the past the relations between the three parts of society represented by employers, labourers, and paupers.[72] Once he accepted that reform of the poor law was the legislation he had hoped for, legislation that would positively effect the whole of the labouring population, Richmond was prepared to accept Howick's advice on the subject of assisted emigration.

Howick's papers contain an early draft of the final report that the emigration commissioners submitted to Lord Goderich on 15 March 1832. Although must of this draft was used, it was significantly longer than the final version. The deleted passages explained Howick's position and pertained to important policy recommendations accepted before the final report was submitted. The draft report sets out Howick's candid arguments in favour of government staying at arm's length from parish-aided emigration. In 1831, Howick noted, 8,000 immigrants had arrived at Quebec within one week, 2,000 of them within in a single day. With so many people leaving all parts of England at the same time, a public authority could not oversee their selection and sending with the necessary efficiency. Parishes would take advantage of government participation to rid themselves of the idle and profligate, and colonists would be loud in complaints, of which the Colonial Office already had a sample.[73] Howick carried the day and the final report of the Emigration Commission was predicated on the decision to wind up the commission and transfer its few remaining duties to the Colonial Office.

The emigration commissioners stated categorically that emigration to British North America should be left to the workings of the laissez-faire marketplace. In the view it offers of labouring immigrants, their report submitted in March 1832 foreshadows the better-known report of the Royal Commission on the Poor Laws presented two years later in 1834.[74] Anticipating the sentiments of the restructured poor law, the commissioners swept away difficulties posed by the cost to government of assistance to the able-bodied poor by denying that such help was necessary or beneficial. Government officers in home and colonial ports should do their best to ensure that emigrants were not misinformed or defrauded, but emigrants in the final analysis would have to rely on their own good sense and prudence, or on that of those who acted for them.

Richmond's commissioners took the position that government had no direct part to play in assisting emigration to North America. Their report dismissed Horton's planned settlements as a technique of the past: "however beneficial to the parties actually removed, the measure was far too costly to be persevered in to an useful extent." Immigrants arriving in the North American colonies, they wrote, must not expect aid – not grants of land, not provisions, not tools. Sponsors were advised that it was impolitic for government "to undertake the entire charge of large bodies of people, and thus destroy in them the habit of reliance upon their own personal exertions." As well as being impolitic, government interference on behalf of able-bodied immigrants was not needed in colonies "where there exists a great and constant demand for labour." Advice to new immigrants to work at the trade they had followed at home flowed from this line of thought. With the assumption that all could find work, it seemed that forcing newcomers to save to buy land did them the favour of ensuring that they first learned the ways of the country. In the body of the report, the commissioners admitted that a few emigrants to Upper Canada in 1831 had needed government assistance. They trusted that such people would in future find employment on public works financed by an expanding colonial economy. The theme of "those who desire to work cannot fail to do well for themselves" became a refrain that gained added respectability from repetition in official sources.[75]

The commissioners noted their initiatives with regard to Australia for Goderich's consideration, pointing out that a portion of the land revenues could be used to bring people to these colonies. With regard to North America, they left assisted emigration to parishes and private sponsors. They did not recommend that parishes be given new powers to help them raise money. Following Howick's recommendation to Richmond, the commissioners did not raise the possibility of future government involvement, preferring to wait to see what parishes would do on their own.

In one area, the commissioners spearheaded a new government initiative. According to instructions they had been given, they prepared *Information Respecting the British Colonies*, a series of pamphlets for the various colonies which the Colonial Office would update and reissue over many years. Alexander Carlisle Buchanan, the emigration agent at Quebec since 1828, also published the first of his information pamphlets for emigrants at the end of 1832. Richmond used his position as postmaster general to support a heroic effort in the Colonial Office to send information on emigration to the Canadas to parish authorities throughout England and Wales. Much of Kent and Sussex was covered before the logistics of mass mailing defeated the project.[76] Sockett received the pamphlet on the Canadas within days of publication, but it was too late to make a great difference around Petworth in 1832.

The practical contribution of Richmond's commission to the Petworth emigrations was undoubtedly its high profile, in part because of the attention Richmond's name attracted locally and in the county press. Perhaps by design, the report itself seems to have received little publicity. As late as October 1832, Sockett was unaware that Goderich had disbanded the commission after receiving its report the previous March.[77]

The parish emigration of 1832 was indeed as large as that of 1831, and it may have been larger, as the cholera epidemic got in the way of counting. Using very informal sources such as the letters of sponsoring gentry, Buchanan at Quebec counted in each of these years roughly 5,000 immigrants who had come out "under Parochial aid, or by assistance of their Landlords." In common with all immigration to the Canadas, these numbers fell substantially in 1833 and 1834. In 1833, Sockett entered the public debate over government assistance, urging that government facilitate parish borrowing for purposes of sending emigrants. As Richmond was arguably the strongest supporter of assisted emigration in the cabinet, Sockett was in a good position to lobby with some small effect.

Sockett was well respected in his district, and his voice could only have strengthened Richmond's conviction that government must deal with the short-term glut of labourers as well as the long-term goals of poor law reform. Sockett wrote to Richmond on the subject of declining support for his scheme in 1833.[78] In 1834, he wrote again, informing Richmond that seven parishes in his area had been ready to send emigrants if they could have found the money. There were far too many men working for the parish and too many young "beer shop boys" in the jail at Petworth. Sockett had the candidates for assisted emigration; now he sought legislation to aid parishes in raising money. Sponsors he had relied upon were unwilling to make further advances until parishes paid back unsecured loans from 1832 and 1833.[79]

Like many of his contemporaries with a point to make, Sockett resorted to publication. His *Letter to a Member of Parliament* was sent to most members of both houses.[80] In it, Sockett advocated legislation that would allow parishes to borrow money for assisted emigration on easier terms, enabling them to spread repayment over several years. Although his specific suggestions for raising money had too much of the old poor law about them to find favour, he had identified the one issue in parish emigration that government was now willing to address.

Interest in assisted emigration was revived among politicians because of fears that labourers would rise in defence of the traditional forms of assistance that were to be abolished that year under the Poor Law Amendment Act. Richmond was said to be the strongest advocate of assisted emigration in the cabinet committee reviewing the draft Poor Law Amendment Act. This committee was advised by Nassau Senior, whose enthusiasm for assisted emigration had spilled over from his pamphlet into the report of the Royal Commission on the Poor Laws submitted in 1834. Senior apparently still favoured separate legislation covering assisted emigration, although there seems to have been little chance that he would be heard.[81] There was no separate legislation and the final text of the act covered emigration in two clauses. These clauses dealt only with the issue of parishes raising funds and seemed tuned to Richmond's wish that assisted emigration be available to parishes as a means of cushioning the impact of stricter rules of poor relief.

Although these measures fell far short of the Emigration Bill of 1831, Sockett was satisfied that they were all he needed to continue with his private scheme. He believed that the act enabled parishes to raise their share of the expense of sending emigrants and that he would be left to manage all other aspects of his emigration. He was of this opinion because he had not yet felt the power of the poor law commissioners to interfere in local matters. Clauses 62 and 63 of the act set out the terms under which a parish might obtain loans for purposes of assisting emigration by mortgaging its poor rates for up to five years, but executive authority under the act rested with the poor law commissioners in this as in other matters. The commissioners controlled the application process for loans and had the power to approve or reject applications before they went to the Exchequer Bill Loan Commission.[82]

Independent information collected by American consuls, although sketchy, supports the second report of the poor law commissioners, which shows that the largest emigration resulting from the act left East Anglia in 1836 and was bound mainly for Quebec. Only a few emigrants were approved for United States destinations (the poor law commissioners made exceptions for those joining family members).[83] East Anglia had already proved fertile ground for emigration at the beginning of the decade,[84] but in 1836 parish emigration in this district received an impetus not given elsewhere or at other times. The assistant poor law commissioner for East Anglia, James Kay (later Kay-Shuttleworth, prominent in educational reform), took an unusual stand in favour of assisted emigration. Kay had just started forming poor law unions in Norfolk and Suffolk at the beginning of 1836, and he was able to convince his superiors that, if he did not offer the option of assisted emigration, landowners and potential guardians would refuse to accept the commissioners' workhouse test. Despite misgivings in London, Kay was given permission to proceed for one year.[85] The following year, there was no special emigration initiative and the commissioners directed that parish aid in that district too be denied to the able-bodied unless they entered the workhouse.

By 1836 the Colonial Office had turned its back on assisted parish emigration to North America. Under the Amendment Act, the Poor Law Commission still had to play a part, but it did so with increasing disapproval and resistance. These attitudes were more evident in the Blything Union of Suffolk in East Anglia than in Petworth, where Egremont's dislike of the new poor law complicated relations with the commissioners. The Earl of Stradbroke, the dominant nobleman in the Blything Union, was a prominent supporter of the new poor law; yet he had great difficulty extracting even a negative answer to his request to the Colonial Office that it give his district special consideration by chartering a ship to carry assisted emigrants to Upper Canada.[86] Within Stradbroke's new union, the rector of Wrentham had his loan application mistakenly rejected by bureaucrats in the Poor Law Commission who did not know or care about the size of his parish or his local standing. He wrote to London with growing fury as he attempted to straighten out this misunderstanding only to find that the supply of forms he needed was exhausted.[87] Despite all these annoyances, his emigrants did get off.

The Poor Law Commission complied with clauses 62 and 63 of the Amendment Act in authorizing loans for assisted emigration, but it required parishes to go through a complex and protracted process, and Edwin Chadwick, its hard-pressed secretary, gave perfunctory attention to this aspect of his job. At first, Chadwick probably found consolation for the extra paperwork in Bentham's dictum that assisted emigration was the least objectionable use of poor relief for the able-bodied. Within a year or two, the commission started to see a connection between parishes with an interest in assisted emigration and parishes where local authorities were resisting instructions to enforce new rules of relief to the full.

Animosity between Sockett and Assistant Commissioner Hawley first burst into the open over the issue of assisted emigration. The exchange was set off by Hawley, who compounded the annoyance of an inaccurate report on the emigration with a description of Petworth emigrants as "vicious characters who, steeped in vice and habitual pauperism, have preferred the uncertain advantages of expatriation to honest industry at home."[88] Sockett countered in a letter to John Walter, a member of Parliament and the proprietor of *The Times*. Sockett's letter, published in the London *Standard*, began with a defence of the character of his emigrants and then broadened into a general condemnation of the commissioners' approach to emigration.[89]

The main thrust of Sockett's attack was against the commissioners' indifference to the fate of the people sent as emigrants. Using his own area, Sockett had no trouble finding examples of careless record keeping and deficient numbers in the statistics published in the commissioners' second annual report. He believed that new sponsors would turn to the commissioners' report for guidance, and that neither the text nor the lengthy list of parishes for which loans were approved revealed the full cost of assisted emigration. Sockett thus feared that sponsors would be misled into entrusting their people to an underpriced and unsafe carrier. He was critical of the cynicism exemplified by Hawley in West Sussex, and he judged the commissioners irresponsible in putting their names to misinformation.

Sockett applied simple arithmetic to the commissioners' summary of their loans, pointing out that the parish of Pulborough had apparently sent one emigrant to New York for the astronomical amount of £200. In a rare attempt at a joke, Sockett also pointed to the "cheap ones" from Swanington – "possibly they swam over." He then returned to his more serious objection to figures that might appear plausible. The entry for Petworth listed only the money raised by the parish, not Egremont's contribution. For the parish of Tillington, next door to Petworth, the commissioners listed fewer than half the emigrants sent in the two seasons covered by their report – twenty-four of fifty-one – and recorded expenses of £140. Sockett's figure for the parish was £212, and Egremont had contributed another £376. In Petworth and Tillington, additional funding had come from a landlord, but parishes without an Egremont or an emigration society could also find extra funds. The commissioners, for instance, had not mentioned in their report that a number of parishes financed assisted emigration out of the proceeds from the sale of poor-houses, cottages, or other property that was no longer needed after the formation of the new poor law unions.

Sockett's concern was less with correcting the record with respect to the numbers of emigrants sent from parishes such as Tillington than with making it known that these parishes had spent far more than the poor law commissioners had implied. Our research on the surviving records of the Poor Law Commission, however, confirms his scepticism about the numbers, turning up only about half the numbers of emigrants we know to have sailed on Petworth ships between 1835 and 1837. This may be an anomaly; Bruce Elliott and Gary Howells, for example, believe that Norfolk records are much more complete. To the extent that this difference reflects the different attitudes of Hawley in Sussex and Kay in East Anglia, there may be other parts of the country as badly served in the commissioners' records as the parishes sending emigrants on Petworth ships.

FEAR OF UNREST at home was an uncertain foundation for a program of assisted emigration. The economic hardships that caused social disturbances also prompted people to emigrate. Once the ice was broken with a successful first venture, someone like Sockett could count on emigrants coming forward. The problem lay with sponsors. When a local crisis such as a disturbance was the principal reason for sending emigrants, the interest of most sponsors would evaporate once life returned to normal. Petworth was an exception because, although the disturbances were a trigger to starting up a program of assistance, Egremont continued his support for other, largely humanitarian, reasons. Sockett believed that some form of steady support from government would encourage other sponsors to provide more regular backing, but he had little time to put this opinion to the test.

As under-secretary for the colonies, Howick saw widespread distrust of parish-assisted emigration in British North America, and he interpreted this distrust as one more strong reason for government not to get involved. He succeeded in persuading the members of Richmond's Emigration Commission to take his advice. The framers of the Poor Law Amendment Act and the cabinet committee that approved the final draft had no one to make the strong case for the Colonial Office point of view, which Howick had presented to the Emigration Commission. They gave their main attention to the English counties disrupted by the Swing disturbances without considering opinion in the colonies. The report of the Royal Commission on the Poor Laws and the Poor Law Amendment Act of 1834 encouraged parishes to assist emigration without taking into account its impact in the receiving colonies. Colonial administrators were left to manage the reception and integration of parish immigrants as best they could. The response of one such administrator, Lieutenant-Governor Sir John Colborne, and the reception he accorded the Petworth emigrants will be the subject of later chapters.

CHAPTER 2

"DECENT ACCOMMODATION": SETTING A STANDARD FOR THE PETWORTH EMIGRATIONS

My only fear is – lest it [economy] may be carried *too far*, so as to materially interfere with the comforts, and even endanger the lives of the emigrants ... It will be understood that, by the term[s] I have used, I mean nothing *luxurious*, only such *decent* accommodation as is absolutely necessary to persons of heretofore *decent* habits.

Sockett to Charles Barclay, Dorking, 8 March 1833,
copy sent to Richmond[1]

Sockett devised his own standards of safety and comfort for his ships. These were based on the community standards of his parish rather than on legislated standards set by government, and he defended them vigorously under both the old poor law and the new. As he was well aware, the issue was cost. He believed that sponsors and parishes should pay what was necessary to maintain a "decent" standard, even if they could get emigrants to leave for less. From 1832 to 1837, Sockett charged more than the going rate for a passage from Portsmouth to Quebec. He was convinced that brokers competing to cut prices to the lowest level must send emigrants "too much in the Irish style," overcrowded in ill-fitted, rotting ships. He used the extra funds to satisfy himself that conditions on board ship were safe and healthy and to send his emigrants under a superintendent who was in charge of all aspects of management that were not the direct responsibility of the shipmaster. Sockett was rewarded with a low mortality rate at sea and praise for his ships by the inspecting officers at the Grosse Île Quarantine Station on the St Lawrence River, the first stopping point for emigrants to Quebec. As he did in his parish, Sockett achieved his standard on ships chartered by the Petworth Emigration Committee by careful management of an existing system rather than by innovation.

Petworth emigrants were part of a mass movement of poor emigrants carried as return cargo on timber ships bound for British North America. The cheap fares induced poor emigrants to keep using the timber ships bound for Quebec and Saint John, New Brunswick, even though these vessels were less comfortable and often slower than the passenger ships bound for United States ports. The spread in price was partly the result of government measures. The British government encouraged the timber trade by allowing British ships with a British destination to carry a higher number of passengers in relation to their tonnage than those going to U.S. ports, while

American states penalized ships' captains if their passengers became dependent on state institutions.[2]

By 1832, Irish emigrants to North America had become synonymous in the minds of people such as Sockett with the poorest passengers travelling under the worst conditions. This had not always been the case. In the early years of the century, emigrants from Ireland had been mainly aspiring farmers. By 1832, however, Sockett had good reason to assume that ships carrying Irish emigrants represented the lowest possible standard.[3] By supplying their own food, Irish emigrants could find fares of thirty to fifty shillings for a passage to Quebec. Such low fares bought high risks.[4]

The worst excesses of the trade in human cargo from Britain to British North America were well known by the time Sockett launched his scheme. Once on board an unseaworthy, overloaded, or undersupplied ship and at sea, emigrants had to tough out the journey as best they could. Some lives were lost to shipwrecks and a few cases of starvation grabbed headlines, but the great tragedy of the emigrant trade was contagious disease – ship-fever (typhus and typhoid), smallpox, cholera, and childhood diseases such as measles. These diseases were brought on board with the emigrants; they spread among undernourished people in the crowded and unsanitary conditions in the holds of many emigrant ships; and they took a further toll in the quarantine stations, hospitals, rooming houses, and tent cities where emigrants congregated on arrival.[5] Sockett not only recoiled from the idea of such conditions for his own people, but he feared that his scheme might be tarnished, and perhaps destroyed, if disasters occurred and word got round that a ship carrying Sussex emigrants had been lost or suffered an epidemic.[6]

The Petworth emigrations began at a time when government was widely expected to come to the assistance of parish-aided emigration. Egremont's sponsorship and wealth allowed Sockett to put his own standards in place in a private scheme while he waited to see what the politicians would do. Nassau Senior warned that government must do something if emigrants assisted by English parishes were not to find themselves as badly off as the poor Irish. He demanded the supervision of an emigration commission because he had no faith in parish officers. They would "as a matter of course" select the lowest tender. Private contractors would profit at "an immense expense of individual suffering" and recreate the tragic conditions of an earlier season in 1827 following the temporary repeal of the Passengers' Act.[7]

The Passengers' Act as reintroduced in 1828 set minimum standards for emigrant ships in matters such as the space allocated to each individual and supplies of food and water. These standards were stiffened to some degree by amendment in 1835. The decision made in 1832 against government supervision left parish emigrants with no protection other than this act, and the government had ample evidence that it was frequently evaded. In their report, Richmond's emigration commissioners put the best face possible on the situation by placing agreements relating to the Atlantic passage firmly in the private sector. The final responsibility for passengers' well-being, they wrote, rested with the emigrants themselves or (a reminder to parishes) with

Table 2.1
Ships chartered by the Petworth Emigration Committee, 1832–1837

Year	Ship	Nos. of Emigrants	Superintendent and Surgeon	Registered Tonnage	Ship's Master	Port of Departure	Date of Departure	Port of Arrival	Date of Arrival
1832	Eveline	} } } 603	Stephen Goatcher (Surgeon Mr Curry)	A1, 301 tons		Portsmouth (Spithead)	11 April	Quebec Montreal York	28 May 31 May 8 June
	Lord Melville		William Penfold (Surgeon Mr Lascelles)	A1, 425 tons	Captain Royal	Portsmouth (Spithead)	11 April	Quebec Montreal York	28 May 8 June 19–22 June
	England (brig)	164	J.C. Hale	A1, 320 tons	Captain Lewis	Portsmouth (Spithead)	8 May	Quebec York	15 June 1 July
1833	England	200	J.C. Hale	A1, 320 tons	Captain Lewis	Portsmouth (Spithead)	25 April	Quebec Montreal York	17 June 20 June 1 July
1834	British Tar (brig)	135	J.M. Brydone	A1, 383 tons	Robert Crawford	Portsmouth (Spithead)	17 April	Quebec Montreal Kingston Toronto	1 June 4 June 13 June 14 June
1835	Burrell (barque)	252	J.M. Brydone	A1, 402 tons	J. Metcalf	Portsmouth (Spithead)	23 April	Quebec Montreal Toronto	9 June 18 June 25 June
1836	Heber	264	J.M. Brydone	A1, 441 tons	Captain Rue	Portsmouth (Spithead)	28 April	Quebec Montreal	5 June 9 June
1837	Diana	198	J.M. Brydone	A1, 321 tons	Edward Lane	Portsmouth (Spithead)	27 April	Quebec Montreal	15 June 20 June

SOURCES: Compiled from WSRO, Goodwood MS 1473, 1474; PHA 137, PHA 140. Numbers of emigrants are those given in Sockett's table found at PRO, MH 12/13060; CO 384/41, 352; and WSRO, PHA 140, "Abstract...1837." Dates of arrival are derived from letters and contemporary newspapers.

those who sent them. The problem with the commissioners' statement was that it failed to take into account the great gap between emigrants who were poor, often unsophisticated, and ignorant about the conditions that they agreed to, and the people who preyed on them in ports and misled and cheated them on the passage.

Distressing cases multiplied, and news of them spread with the great increase in emigration from Britain at the beginning of the 1830s. Government gave a partial answer by creating a new service. Responsibility for the emigrants in the most-used ports was taken out of the hands of customs officers and given to emigration agents who reported to the Colonial Office. The first of these agents, Lieutenant Lowe, was appointed to Liverpool in 1833; seven other appointments followed in 1834. These officers, chosen from among naval officers on half-pay, acted as advisers to and advocates for emigrants, and they tried to bring offenders to justice in the most serious cases of fraud, negligence, or illegal overcrowding.[8] In less-used ports, such as Portsmouth, customs officers continued to handle duties connected with emigrants. When the mayor of Portsmouth received a circular asking if an agent was needed at his port, he declined, explaining that most of the emigrants from Portsmouth to Quebec and Montreal were sent by the Petworth committee.[9]

In 1832, Sockett set the price of a full adult passage on a Petworth ship at £10. This rate included food, supervision, medical care, and additional travel from Quebec to Toronto. Children up to the age of thirteen travelled for half fare and infants under one year of age had a free passage. Sockett probably chose Portsmouth as his port of departure because it had good connections by road with parishes sending emigrants on Petworth ships. He was also comfortable with a port where light emigrant traffic made it easy to keep his people together and where, if he did need official help, he had a certain influence through Richmond.

EMIGRATION UNDER THE PETWORTH COMMITTEE

Table 2.1 details information about the ships and their dates of departure and arrival. With the regularity that was Sockett's trademark, all the ships chartered by the Petworth Emigration Committee sailed in the month of April. In April 1832, the *Lord Melville* and the *Eveline*, the first two Petworth charters, were superintended by William Penfold and Stephen Goatcher. A third ship, the *England*, was commissioned by people based in the parish of Wisborough Green. Although the *England* was not chartered by the Petworth Emigration Committee, Sockett always included its emigrants in his numbers. His committee helped with the arrangements for the Wisborough Green ship and probably referred passengers who were too late in applying for its own vessels. The *England* sailed on 8 May with Captain J.C. Hale as its superintendent. In 1833, the Petworth committee hired Hale and chartered the *England* for a second voyage. From 1834 to 1837, the Petworth superintendent was James Marr Brydone. The *British Tar* sailed in 1834, followed by the *Burrell*, the *Heber,* and the *Diana* in the following years. With the exception of the *Diana*, all these ships were obtained from Carter and Bonus, a London company of established reputation which was one of the largest carriers of emigrants to North America in the 1830s and 1840s.

When Sockett launched his scheme, he was confident about the standards of conduct towards the poor he had established in his parish over the twenty years he had been in charge of the Petworth vestry, but he was a neophyte in the transatlantic emigrant trade. His first two years were a learning experience, and he made significant changes in 1833 and 1834 before arriving at arrangements that fully satisfied him. In 1832, he knew that Egremont would wish to send his emigrants at better than the minimum standards set out in the Passengers' Act, but he had only a general idea of what this would entail or of how to achieve it. He took no chances. On the point of printing an announcement that his committee would charter from the local Portsmouth firm of Garratt and Gibbon, Sockett drew back and decided in favour of Carter and Bonus, the most widely recognized firm in the field. He was equally cautious in insisting on ships certified A1 by Lloyds of London as proof that they were seaworthy.

In 1832, Sockett lacked the confidence of experience needed to personally direct the whole scheme, and his committee employed a broker, James Waddell of London, to handle certain aspects of it. Waddell acted as a liaison with the shipowner. He also advertised the ships himself, offering a passage to either Quebec or Montreal as well as Toronto and to people not sailing under the Petworth superintendent. At three pounds ten shillings without provisions, Waddell matched the prices to Quebec of Garratt and Gibbon, his principal rival. His rate with provisions was higher than Garratt and Gibbon's, perhaps because he used the Petworth stores.[10] Another London broker who approached Sockett was Edward Charles Mitchell, who was acting for the Dorking Emigration Society in Surrey. Mitchell was looking for a convenient ship leaving at the same time, and he negotiated a group rate on the Petworth ship bound for Quebec (three pounds seven shillings and six pence per adult passage) for a large number of Dorking emigrants. Mitchell supplied provisions for the Dorking Society, and the society hired its own superintendent and paid the expenses of its emigrants between Quebec and Montreal.[11]

One reason that the first Petworth emigrations came together as smoothly as they did was that the people most involved acted according to their established roles in the community. Egremont provided both seed money to start the scheme and an overarching sponsorship that helped Sockett keep it going. In the small world of parish politics, the descriptions "benevolent" and "munificent" used of him probably referred as much to his willingness to extend his patronage beyond his sphere of personal interest as to the amount of his expenditure.

As patron of the Petworth emigrations, Egremont incurred the considerable financial risk inherent in chartering a ship, absorbed organizational costs, and covered unexpected expenses. In addition, he was the largest single sponsor of the immigrants on the Petworth ships and he gave passage money outright rather than requiring repayment from the parish. Each year from 1832 to 1837, he paid for emigrants from five parishes around Petworth where he owned all the land – Petworth, Tillington, Northchapel, Egdean, and Duncton. By 1836 he had sent over 200 people from these five parishes. According to the degree of his ownership or interest, he also paid a proportion of the cost of the transatlantic passage for emigrants in thirteen other parishes.[12] The understanding that evolved between Egremont and Sockett was that the Petworth Emigration Committee would recoup the basic costs of passage for emigrants who were not counted among Egremont's own people.

The files of the Colonial Office contain a number of examples of officials chartering ships only to have signed-up emigrants melt away, either because their courage failed, the prospects for local employment improved, or they heard bad reports from the proposed destination. Sockett tried to minimize the risks of losing people by requiring a two-pound deposit before he would reserve a passage, but he worried about even a few empty spaces.[13]

Sockett provided the leadership for the Petworth project. He determined where and how the emigrants would travel, and he corresponded in his own name, or the name of the committee, with sponsors, the Canada Company, and government departments. Leadership in parish emigration was often supplied by magistrates who as a class had a reputation for short-lived enthusiasms in parish matters.[14] As a result of their lack of commitment, assisted emigration as a community effort lasted in most parishes perhaps for a single season, rarely more than two in a row. Sockett was not a magistrate – in Sussex the clergy were prohibited from sitting on the bench – but aside from the judicial function, he fulfilled the role. With his unusual commitment to emigration, he kept his scheme going for six consecutive years, filling his ships by drawing together emigrants from a different configuration of parishes in each year.

Although Sockett associated the names of the other committee members, Knight and Chrippes, with his own in the committee's many business transactions, executive direction rested with him. Administering a scheme like this one, he advised, required a team designed for quick and confidential action. There were decisions requiring "a good deal of delicate management, and a discretionary power vested somewhere, to act at the *last moment.*" There were also matters "not to be talked about" – perhaps taking people at a lower price was one.[15] Another issue, mentioned discreetly by Sockett and openly by others, concerned the choice of a destination distant enough to make return difficult. In a section of his report subsequently published in the sessional papers, Charles Hope Maclean, an assistant to the Royal Commission of 1832, explained that Petworth sponsors had sent their emigrants all the way through to Toronto to "remove as much as possible both inducement, and facility, to return, before a fair trial had been made of the country."[16]

Knight and Chrippes represented the farmers, shopkeepers, and others at that social and economic level who kept parishes running on a day-to-day basis. Sockett chose them to provide the business experience he needed to outfit emigrants and charter and provision a ship. Both these men were entrepreneurs with the variety of talents necessary to earn a living in the small town of Petworth. William Knight was a corn chandler, a dealer in grain. He had in addition an agency for the Sun Insurance Company, and although he was not strictly qualified as an accountant, he served in this capacity for the Petworth and Sutton Gilbert Unions. His brother-in-law, Thomas Chrippes, kept a shop as a cabinetmaker and upholsterer. By 1839, Chrippes was listed in Pigot and Co.'s directory as a carpenter and builder and also worked as an auctioneer and surveyor (evaluator). He served as the committee's book-keeper, recording receipts and making a careful record of disbursements. When Egre-mont died, Chrippes was employed as an appraiser to make inventories of Petworth House and of Egremont's London and Brighton houses.[17]

Sockett's father had been a printer and stationer in London before his business failed, and Sockett worked closely with Petworth printer John Phillips in publiciz-ing his plan. Phillips published books and pamphlets for Sockett as well as immi-grant letters on single sheets and in small pamphlets, which were sold for two pence or distributed free of charge. In 1832, before he had his own promotional material, Sockett was helped by the general upsurge of interest in emigration to Upper Canada and in particular by the Canada Company's publicity for Upper Canada and the Huron Tract. The company's speaker, William Cattermole, lectured in Guildford in Surrey, just within the area served by the Petworth committee during a sixteen-month tour that also took him to Suffolk, Norfolk, Essex, and Kent.[18] Not long after-wards, emigrants from Guildford and nearby Dorking embarked on a Petworth ship. Sockett did much of his own research on Upper Canada in books written to a greater or lesser degree in the interest of the Canada Company, and these books were promi-nent on the list of recommended reading that accompanied his major publications.[19]

Beyond the publicity generated by Phillips's publications, Sockett made sure that his emigration was prominently featured in the county press. He was helped again in 1832 by the upsurge of interest in emigration to Canada that was sweeping the south, but through his own efforts he managed to sustain considerable interest in his scheme after this interest died down. The level of detail in reports on the Pet-worth emigration in the *Sussex Advertiser* in 1832 suggests that the information was supplied by the committee. After 1834, when a number of emigrants from East Sus-sex sailed on the *British Tar*, the *Brighton Herald* also carried detailed articles date-lined Littlehampton, where Sockett leased a beach house.[20] As soon as he received them, Sockett sent some of the first letters to arrive from Petworth emigrants in Upper Canada to the *Portsmouth Herald*. In later years, newspapers carried letters that seem to have come from Sockett and others that the editors found through their own contacts.

In addition to a broad publicity campaign aimed at both sponsors and emigrants, Sockett advertised his ships in places where likely emigrants congregated. Early in the season, the committee's messengers travelled three or four days at a time, pin-ning up broadsheet advertisements in public places in villages and along the main roads where toll gates offered a stopping point and a convenient wall. Inns and pubs helped to spread news of the ships. Peter Scovell, the innkeeper at The King's Head at Haslemere, Surrey, passed on correspondence from emigrants whom he may have assisted before they left. Writing from Upper Canada, Ann Mann assumed that the owner of the Onslow Arms would display a copy of her letter to "let everyone see that I lives in Adelaide."[21] A second broadsheet printed and circulated at the end of

March, or in early April at the latest, updated the information on the impending sailing. If the ship was not full, this was the time to encourage last-minute passengers; if plans changed, this was the best way to communicate a delayed sailing date.

The first sign that an immigrant ship would fill was when sponsors and parishes began paying deposits and purchasing outfits. Members of the public could obtain information or make deposits at Phillips's office in Petworth or in Portsmouth, where Sockett had a temporary headquarters at 20 Penny Street. The committee also finalized their lists of needed clothing and "necessaries" for the voyage and, in what became a local make-work project, encouraged the officers of other parishes to examine samples in Chrippes's shop and buy at Petworth (see Tables 2.2 and 2.3).[22] Parish officers in the parishes whose emigrants received a free passage from Egremont con-

Table 2.2
List of Necessaries for Emigrants to Upper Canada, 1832

Families should take their	*Single men must have*
Bedding.	A Bed or Mattress.
Blankets.	Metal Plate or wooden Trencher.
Sheets. &c.	Some kind of Metal Cup or Mug.
Pewter Plates or wooden Trenchers.	Knife. Fork and Spoon.
Knives and Forks and Spoons.	
Metal Cups and Mugs.	
Tea Kettles and Saucepans.	
Working Tools of all descriptions.	All, or any of which, may be procured at
(A large tin Can or watering Pot would be useful.)	Portsmouth, if the Parties arrive there unprovided.

Various other portable articles in domestic use (especially of metal) according as families may be provided.

SOURCE: *Emigration: Letters* (1833), v.

tributed five pounds per adult and three pounds five shillings for children and infants to cover the outfit (clothing, bedding, and utensils needed on the voyage), internal travel, and landing money.[23] Other parishes might supply an outfit of lesser value, but there was a consensus among sponsors that the parish must contribute something, that a subscription for emigration raised among the better off should go towards "those expenses which do not come under the head of parish relief."[24]

When in 1832 Sockett set five pounds per adult as the contribution of parishes receiving free passages from Egremont, he intended that the emigrants would be outfitted in a manner befitting Egremont's rank. If parishes followed his recommendations, they provided clothing well beyond the usual expectations of parish charity.[25] The first year's experience showed that heavy baggage added to the cost and difficulty of travel within the Canadas, where even by water the allowance for free carriage was much less than at sea. Emigrants were also supplying their acquaintances back home with first-hand advice tuned to the availability of different goods in different parts of the province. In later years, Sockett chose to trust the emigrants more than he had initially. He still asked for a five-pound contribution from parishes where

Table 2.3
Outfit Recommended to Parishes for Labourers, 1832

Cost at Petworth	£	s.	d.
A Fur Cap	0	1	8
A warm Great Coat	0	11	9
A fluching[a] Jacket	0	8	9
Ditto Trowsers	0	5	4
A Duck Frock[b]	0	2	10
Ditto Trowsers	0	2	11
A Canvas Frock	0	2	11
Two pair Trowsers	0	5	10
Two Jersey Frocks 2s. 2d.	0	4	4
Four Shirts 2s.6d.	0	10	0
Four pair Stockings	0	4	0
Three pair Shoes	1	8	0
A Bible and a Prayer Book.			
TOTAL	4	7	6
Deduct for Articles of Clothing each Person may be supposed to possess	1	17	6
The Average cost will be about	2	10	0

Women in the same proportion, especially a warm cloak.
(The Average cost of Clothing for Women in addition to what they in general possess is about 37s.)

SOURCE: WSRO, Goodwood MS 648, f. 61.
[a] *flushing*, A rough, thick woollen cloth.
[b] A smock made of strong linen or cotton, lighter than canvas.

his influence prevailed, but he recommended that emigrants bring as much as they could of their own store of clothing, cooking utensils, and tools, and that parish authorities transfer all the money remaining in the allocation made for an individual or a family to Toronto in their names.

The Petworth Emigration Committee's one surviving minute book covers the hectic months beginning in January 1832 when emigration must have consumed Sockett's time and that of his associates.[26] Sockett's committee had to deal simultaneously with major issues and small details and to refer to the Colonial Office and the Canada Company for information on unfamiliar subjects. The first entry in the minute book concerned the passage to North America; the second, a fur hat suitable for Upper Canada and the question of whether to purchase in London or find a pattern for local manufacture. Chartering a ship was difficult and worrying. Sockett opened negotiations with shipowners in January, writing very tentatively, still quite unsure of his numbers.

In February, the committee's negotiations with the broker James Waddell revolved around the Petworth emigrants' occupying part of a ship. If the committee guaranteed 150 passages, Waddell would bring a ship from London to Portsmouth and take on the risk of filling it to capacity himself. By the beginning of March, the committee had engaged its own ship, and by 21 March, it had spoken for two. As

Waddell juggled ships, trying for the perfect match at the right time, the Privy Council unexpectedly entered the equation.

In 1831, cholera had spread from Asia, across Europe, and to Great Britain. On 26 and 28 March 1832, the office of the Privy Council issued an order reinstating health provisions that had been dropped from the Passengers' Act of 1828 in the interest of a cheaper passage. All ships bound for North America with more than fifty people on board were required to carry a qualified surgeon and a medicine chest equipped to the standard adopted on a ship of war.[27]

Sockett had already been promised a surgeon for one of his ships; now in competitiion with too many others, he scrambled to find one for the other, the *Lord Melville*. A young man known to Chrippes declined, Sockett's contact also failed, and the surgeon finally found by the firm Carter and Bonus was arrested and removed from the *Lord Melville* by the police. Robert Carter and Sockett joined others in complaining to T.F. Elliot at the Colonial Office of difficulties in finding doctors and the unnecessary expense of such an elaborate list of medicines. The rules were soon relaxed, and the *Lord Melville* was one of the ships given permission to carry a less-qualified surgeon. By the end of April, the Privy Council had rescinded the order concerning the medicine chest for all ships on which there was no sign of sickness three days after the passengers had embarked. Once this was established, the ship could sail without the chest. Sockett, however, would continue to send a well-equipped medicine chest on all his ships.[28]

The *Lord Melville* secure, Waddell asked to make a final replacement and bring in the *Eveline*. Each time Waddell substituted one ship for another, the committee checked that the new vessel was certified A1 with Lloyds.[29] All surviving contracts entered into by the Petworth committee showed the same attention to detail. The terms were similar from year to year, spelling out costs and holdbacks; the responsibilities of the shipowners and the committee if either should cause delay; the facilities to be provided for emigrants by the ship – water, casks, buckets, and tubs; upper limits on the profits allowed if emigrants ran short of provisions and purchased from the captain; and the arrangements on arrival – where the emigrants were to be landed, who would pay the head tax, and who would pay the steamboat that towed the ship from Quebec to Montreal. In addition, the committee's contracts specified that the captain would allow no one on board without the consent of the committee; that he would not sell liquor or any other article to emigrants without the consent of the superintendent on penalty of £50; that he would not bring any emigrant from his ship back to England on penalty of £10; and that he would return the committee's medicine chest free of charge.[30]

Even as he negotiated with Waddell, Sockett corresponded with a widening circle of sponsors, trying to finalize numbers and collect deposits. In February, he canvassed parishes where Egremont was landlord – parishes immediately around Petworth and between Petworth and Arundel – asking in his covering letter for a list of poor persons of good character wishing to emigrate to Upper Canada. On 1 March 1832, he published his *Information to Persons desirous of emigrating this Neighbourhood to*

Upper Canada, which included practical advice on preparations. He wanted his emigrants to be "decently clad" for the journey (he was perhaps concerned about the appearance in Portsmouth of hordes of emigrants who had all been advised by others to wear their oldest clothes on the ship), but he warned that they must be prepared to send the bulk of their luggage to the hold. The recommended container was a cask no larger than a hogshead or sixty gallons. "All packages should be marked with the Owners name, in large letters" – a precaution that did not prevent some going astray in Upper Canada. In addition, emigrants should have "a small Tin Case" to carry important personal records – certificates of marriage and baptism or the discharge papers of a former soldier – and references as to character and past employment.[31]

By early March 1832, Waddell was advertising his two ships in the *Brighton Gazette*. The list of recipients of a second version of Sockett's *Information*, issued on 19 March, showed how quickly interest in the scheme had spread beyond the neighbourhood of Petworth.[32] Waddell gave out copies at the Sutton Workhouse, and the committee also referred him to various Brighton addresses and the offices of another Brighton paper, the *Guardian*.[33] To the north of Petworth, Magistrate William Henry Yaldwyn, whose Blackdown House was in the parish of Lurgashall, booked fifty-one passages for emigrants from his home parish (where Egremont owned one-fifth of the land but paid two-fifths of the cost) and half as many again for emigrants from three neighbouring parishes. He and John Knight Greetham, the rector of Kirdford, personally conducted large contingents of emigrants to Portsmouth. Sockett sent literature as far as Guildford over the county border with Surrey. In addition to the seventy-five sent by the Dorking Society, another fifty-five emigrants came from Surrey, most of them from parishes in the Dorking area. Hearing somehow of the scheme, Charles Beldam, a landowning magistrate and church warden from the Royston area of Cambridgeshire, opened negotiations. He was too late for the committee's first ship, but Sockett held space for his people on the second after a spirited correspondence convinced Beldam that the committee would not go below nine pounds ten shillings per passage for twenty-four men, women, and children.[34]

The third ship sent in 1832, the *England*, sailed partly as a result of recruiting by James Knight, a former shopkeeper and maltster from Wisborough Green who had gone to Ohio. Knight had become an agent for the Courtauld family, and he sent several letters home to Sussex newspapers to promote his settlement at Nelsonville in Athens County, Ohio. Sockett printed 400 copies of one of Knight's letters for circulation, and John Napper in Wisborough Green offered local sponsorship. The seventy people sent by Wisborough Green formed the nucleus that led to the engagement of the *England*. In addition to this group, the *England* carried forty-five emigrants from Sussex parishes to the south of Wisborough Green – Arundel, Binstead, and Bersted; twenty-four from Hampshire, mostly from Portsmouth; and twenty-five from Kent.[35]

In the final days before the ships sailed, the committee members received the last of the money to be transferred to Toronto for distribution to individual emigrants. Sockett had investigated Colonial Office arrangements for sending money through to Alexander Carlisle Buchanan, its agent at Quebec, and had decided to improve on them.[36] He had arranged through the Canada Company for his committee to receive the money in Petworth or Portsmouth and to transfer it as a lump sum to Toronto in the name of its superintendent. On arrival, the superintendent drew out this money and distributed it to individuals and heads of families. Emigrants who had money of their own, or gifts from family or sponsors, were free to use this service as well; it was safe, economical, and intended as one more incentive to keep them with their superintendent until they reached the committee's preferred destination.[37]

Sockett, Chrippes, and Knight travelled to Portsmouth to oversee the final arrangements for each ship. Before the emigrants arrived, they had business to conduct with suppliers for the ship and with port officials whose goodwill Sockett sought to secure by using Richmond's influence.[38] The emigrants' departures from their home parishes were timed so that they could board their ship the same day. Emigrants gathered at collection points, and large parties were accompanied to Portsmouth by a sponsor or someone else.[39] With carters to feed as well as emigrants, the Petworth committee ordered cold suppers for 170 at one inn en route. A reporter for the *Portsmouth Herald* in 1832 estimated that there were 500 emigrants in a single convoy that paraded through town, announced by bugles and with flags flying from their wagons. In May, emigrants for the *England* arrived in sixty-two wagons.[40] In later years, sponsors continued to make an occasion of emigration. The emigrants who left Brighton in East Sussex in 1834 were sent off with a roast beef dinner, a speech from the popular vicar of St Nicholas, and gifts of Bibles, prayer books, and tea.

The Brighton party in 1834 left for Portsmouth at five in the morning in two caravans with two wagons for their luggage. They stopped for a hot dinner at Havant and reached Portsmouth Point twelve hours after leaving Brighton. Although they had travelled on good roads across the coastal plain, parents must have been exhausted that evening as they settled tired children into their berths. Despite all this, the party responded to the novelty of the trip and the excitement of being the centre of unaccustomed attention. Visitors the next day reported them in high spirits.[41] Second thoughts were a private matter. In 1835, reports were the same: "they were all in high spirits, and we could not discover a countenance of regret among the whole party."[42]

The rumours in 1832 that emigrants were fleeing the ships to enlist as soldiers in preference to sailing for the Canadas perhaps arose because those who arrived late in the day could not be ferried to the ship after nightfall and had to stay in the town. The committee's denials of such rumours were published by the same newspaper that reported only two confirmed cases: one faint-hearted family from Sullington and two brothers who had slipped away to return to their home parish and "Sir Charles's pheasants." The committee may in fact have booked more passages than the ship could hold, overcompensating for last-minute defections and non-arrivals, as another newspaper report told of people being sent home to await a later ship – probably the *England*.[43]

The last days of preparation in 1832 had their share of disasters. A careful count on 30 March revealed that the committee was six passages short of the optimum number for the two vessels. As the committee members filled the ships with last-minute emigrants and purchased outfits for them in Portsmouth, the sailing of the *Lord Melville* was suddenly put in doubt. Approaching Portsmouth Harbour, the captain fell sick and died. The vessel and all aboard were clamped under quarantine. A few days later, with the crew still healthy, the *Lord Melville* and the *Eveline* were ready to board.[44]

Even this short delay beyond the announced date of Thursday, 5 April, meant that another flurry of messengers was dispatched to the relevant parishes by the committee, which was anxious to avoid the costs of holding emigrants in Portsmouth. Approximately 170 emigrants arrived in town on Saturday, 7 April, but most of the convoys of carts were directed to arrive Monday and Tuesday, Tuesday being the latest time possible for emigrants to board the two ships. Finally, all passages were paid up, the last visits were made to the ships, and the emigrants set sail. Sockett sent a sermon for the first Sunday with the superintendents and returned to Petworth to fret until he heard of their safe arrival at Quebec City.

The emigrants of 1832 must have settled down on the ships amid considerable confusion. In later years, the committee assigned berths before the emigrants boarded the ship. Families and people from the same community were kept together as much as possible. Single men and boys over fourteen years of age were allowed to join their families in the day, but they were sent to their own compartment in the fore steerage at night. The *England* in 1833 had a vacant berth which could be used as a hospital.[45] On the *British Tar* in 1834, a partition divided the family quarters in half, each half reached by its own hatchway. The partition allowed room for a cistern with a water closet for each section.[46] Beginning in 1833, Petworth ships also offered a few second-class or intermediate cabins. Lydia Hilton wrote to her father, urging him to book one of these cabins if he came out. For an extra two pounds he would have a place to himself at night instead of having to bed down with the young men.

There is no single description of a Petworth ship, but numerous references give some idea of the living quarters. In addition to being the only space available for cooking, exercising, and hanging laundry, the deck accommodated toilet facilities and a variety of animals. Sockett sent hogs, cattle, and Southdown sheep to his son George, who settled near Guelph in 1833, and to George's neighbours.[47] Other animals were destined for the table of privileged cabin passengers. The ship provided steerage passengers with two cooking hearths and fuel so that they could cook for themselves. Brydone organized the cooking on the *British Tar*; we do not know how sharing was arranged before he took over as superintendent. Cooking on deck had its hazards. In 1834, John Barton fled from his assignment as cook after the rolling of the ship overturned copper pots full of boiling beef. Hannah Tilly still limped several weeks after she scalded her foot.

In rough weather, the men might climb to the deck to escape the "sickness and closeness of the 'tween decks," though they faced a drenching; women and children remained below.[48] Writing of the transatlantic passage, William Cobbett singled out the need to walk across the deck to a toilet as the ultimate humiliation for a woman of "decent habits" compelled by circumstances to travel in the steerage; he claimed that he had seen women make themselves ill rather than do so. Sockett supplied the two water closets between decks on his ships out of concern that women might choose to stay below and make "the steerage a scene too filthy to think of."[49] In fact, in bad weather they had little choice.

Captain Hale's *Instructions to Persons intending to Emigrate*, which Sockett reprinted more than once and kept in circulation in the Petworth area into the 1840s, was written on the assumption that his readers knew that they would be going down between decks to travel in tiers of double bunks six feet square lining both sides of a central passage.[50] Each passage on the *Lord Melville* bought a sleeping space of nine superficial feet, so that a single berth might serve two adults and four young children.[51] On later ships, the allocation of sleeping space was increased to twelve superficial feet. By this calculation, three adults shared a six-by-six-foot berth. The committee also reserved the right to direct the placing of the head and feet of all the berths in order to ensure that none were set up against the bulkheads, where they would block the centre aisle. The crew slept forward of the young men in their own quarters with no access to the emigrants.

Hale's *Instructions* were full of hints on how to make the best use of the little space available. Emigrants should bring a box to hold cutlery, as well as a gimlet, hooks, nails, and leather straps. Children must be trained to replace their possessions in the berth or to hang them up immediately, or they would be sure to be lost to the rolling of the ship. For water, he suggested a two- or three-gallon tin bottle of the type used to store oil in shops. With a handle for pouring, these bottles rested on a flat side, and the best ones had a hinged top rather than a cork. An old piece of carpeting made a handy wrapping for anything stored beside the berth or it could be laid under the bedding. Hale recommended taking lots of blankets and suggested that emigrants stuff their mattresses with chaff or straw rather than with feathers. Feathers would be difficult to maintain on board ship and cheap to replace once they reached Canada. Only vigorous cleaning would keep the berth clear of lice.[52] The upper berths, which Hale recommended, had a clearance on the *British Tar* of only two and a half feet under the uncovered beams supporting the deck above. On the 1834 crossing, Tabitha Ditton's daughter was born in one of these berths in a four-hour delivery attended by Brydone and a woman who acted as nurse. Both mother and baby did well, and less than three weeks later Tabitha was one of those dancing on the deck to celebrate their arrival in the Gulf of St Lawrence.[53]

Although the port of departure was Portsmouth, sailing was marked from Spithead outside the harbour. In 1832, after his ship was towed by steamboat from the harbour, James Rapson guessed that 275 of the 300 passengers on the *Lord Melville* fell sick at Spithead as the ship rocked throughout the night and into the next day, waiting for favourable sailing conditions. In 1833, the *England* took four or five days to work her way out to the open water of the Atlantic. She had barely cleared the Needles into the Channel before numbers of emigrants were acutely sick. Hale, who had seen it all before, characterized seasickness as a "most terrible bore." He tried to distract his charges with something special – grog and tobacco for men, brandy, hot coffee, and soft food for women, and a treat of gingerbread for children. A surprising number of emigrants wrote that bacon was the best food for the seasick. Brydone thought coffee the most "grateful beverage" for the nine on the *British Tar* who suffered severely, but he, like emigrant Ann Thomas, believed that the most certain remedy was to lie quietly in a berth.

In the context of what we know of emigrants sent under the Petworth committee, the references they make in their letters to the sea voyage tell as much about themselves as about the passage. For Ann Thomas, "the worst part of it is getting over."[54] John Ayling, who described a sudden snow flurry and throwing snowballs on the deck till his clothes were soaked, dismissed the fears of those at home with the boast that "I should not care no more of coming over the water than I should of going over the sheep wash."[55] Thomas was the pregnant mother of four young children whose baby was born towards the end of her voyage. Ayling was a single nineteen-year-old man enjoying a break in a life of hard toil. Although Charlotte Willard lived in fear that some member of her large family would fall overboard, she admitted that her children felt at home on board ship. Emigrants less anxious than Charlotte wrote excitedly of seeing porpoises and small whales and distant icebergs "as big as the whole of the buildings on your farm."[56] More than one shipboard romance resulted in a marriage in Upper Canada. Good sailors without too many family responsibilities could enjoy themselves. Even those who merely endured the crossing might form or cement lasting friendships. In surviving records, the Petworth emigrants with the most serious complaints of hardship during travel wrote of the inland portion of their journey rather than the Atlantic crossing.

ADJUSTING SHIPBOARD ARRANGEMENTS AND CONDITIONS

Sockett was provoked into a written defence of the standard his ships set in 1832 by Charles Barclay, the owner of the Bury Hill estate in Surrey. Barclay, perhaps because of his travels to the United States, led the Dorking Emigration Society which had sent over seventy emigrants with the Petworth committee. Barclay's *Letters from the Dorking Emigrants* appeared at the same time as Sockett's *Emigration: Letters from Sussex Emigrants, … 1832* and covered similar ground.

THE FINANCIAL ACCOUNTS of the Dorking Society published in *Letters from the Dorking Emigrants* revealed that the assistance given an adult emigrant in Dorking had been in total about two-thirds the amount spent on a similar person sent by Egremont and one of his parishes (see Table 2.4); yet Barclay suggested that on the strength of this experience the amount could be further reduced "without diminishing the comforts of the emigrants."[57] Although he included letters from four of Sockett's Sussex emigrants, Barclay did not mention the Petworth committee or its part in chartering the ship on which the Dorking emigrants had sailed. His authority for the lower rate was Mitchell, his London broker, whom he recommended enthusiastically. Sockett responded in a strongly worded letter. He thought Mitchell could not send emigrants safely at the rate he offered in 1833, and he gave a number of

Table 2.4
Dorking Emigrant Society Expenses, 1832

	£	s.	d.
Society expenses			
Printing, stationery, postage, rent of a room at the infant school for meetings	7	0	10
Emigrant expenses[a]			
Clothing and tools	104	18	0
Proportion of utensils, etc., at 5s. 11½d. each	18	9	5
Conveyance to Portsmouth and related expenses, at £1.13.2 each	101	11	3
Passage money, Portsmouth to Montreal, at £3.7.6 each	209	5	0
Provisions, Portsmouth to Montreal, at £2.1.4 each	128	3	6
Steam tug, Quebec to Montreal, at 3s. 4½d. each	10	9	8
Passage and provisions, Montreal to York (Toronto), at £12s. 6d. each	69	15	0
Pocket money, for Mr Christopher Able, the superintendent	5	0	0
for 45 adults and 18 [*sic*] children	54	18	4
for the Willard family	8	0	0
Commission paid to Edward Charles Mitchell[b]	25	4	1
TOTAL EXPENSES REPORTED	742	15	1

SOURCE: Reported by John Niblett, treasurer (Barclay, *Letters from the Dorking Emigrants,* [12–13]).

[a] The society calculated the expenses "for adults and children taken together as equivalent to 62 adult travelers." The society paid all the expenses of 45 adults and 15 children. Rather than litigate the disputed settlement of the Willard family of 11 (8 adult passages) with Dorking, the parishes of Shere and Albury agreed to pay £60.0.0 to the society on the Willards' account. Three men paid the society £25.15.0 for fitting them out and sending them with the Dorking party.

[b] The commission was paid on £504.0.11, expenses for provisions, passage, and pocket money.

specific examples of the ways the emigrants would suffer.[58] Not surprisingly, there was no resolution, and no more emigrants from Dorking sailed in Petworth ships.

As Barclay demonstrated, the erosion of standards of emigrants' comfort and safety was the result of more than a simple decision to consider only the lowest rate. From Sockett's point of view, Barclay endorsed a bid that was too low because he had not taken the trouble to do the kind of independent research that Sockett thought necessary. In 1833, after a good experience with Mitchell in 1832, the Dorking Society was willing to trust that he knew what he was doing and could safely lower his rate. Sockett believed that Mitchell had gone too far in a very competitive market.

Sockett's first two emigrations revealed a learning process. The main object of the changes he made was to take more control into his own hands. After 1832, he eliminated the use of a broker (possibly a reason he never again considered sending more than one ship), and he took steps to find a different kind of person as superintendent, someone familiar with the sea and better able to take charge. He also worked towards a single steerage passage in which all emigrants travelled under the Petworth superintendent.

Advertisements for Petworth ships show Sockett offering additional incentives to bring in people who would travel under the committee as well as on its ship. In 1833, the same ten-pound fare charged a year earlier paid for additional space on board ship and included the head tax of five shillings per passage paid at Quebec. Parishes where Egremont owned some property received the same proportional contribution from him as before, although their rate was now eight pounds, and all other parishes within five miles of Petworth could send emigrants for nine pounds. Sockett promised special consideration for young women going to join family or friends irrespective of their parish.[59] In 1836, Sockett retained the incentives, but he specified that all passengers must opt for rations supplied by the committee and issued under the direction of its superintendent.[60]

In the first year, Sockett misjudged the demands of the superintendent's job. His committtee appointed men who at home might have served as parish officers. William Penfold on the *Lord Melville* was from Thakeham, east of Petworth, but an emigrant letter describes him as "of Easebourne work-house" at Midhurst.[61] He left England with many concerns of his own. William Tyler, Egremont's agent, had pursued him for a sizeable debt just as the *Lord Melville* was about to sail, and Chrippes fussed about security for the considerable sums which of necessity were advanced for Penfold's use as the emigrants travelled inland.[62] Penfold had brought along his pregnant wife, who gave birth during the voyage. When a whole tier of berths along one side of the *Lord Melville* collapsed during a storm, Penfold must have been distracted in dealing with the resulting "confusion" among the emigrants, all of whom were fortunate in escaping any serious injury.[63] The committee never again sent a man with a family as superintendent.

Stephen Goatcher, the superintendent on the *Eveline*, and Christopher Able, sent by the Dorking Society on the *Lord Melville*, were farmers who had taken on the job as a means of going to see for themselves what prospects North America offered. Goatcher, a Pulborough farmer and churchwarden, had left his wife behind to look after the farm. Two of the letters Goatcher wrote to his wife (printed by Sockett) revealed his delight in his place at the captain's table, his wonder at being received in person by the lieutenant-governor of Upper Canada, but also his carping about the size of his party and the trouble involved in looking after so many.[64]

Able, for his part, was in the unenviable position of having less material assistance than the Petworth superintendent to give his charges, and he seems to have had little control over them. Emigrants from Dorking saw their rations reduced to a diet of bread and salt beef for the last weeks of the voyage. They may not have understood that their sponsors had paid less than those whose emigrants were victualled by the Petworth committee; they certainly noted with scorn that Able continued to eat in relative luxury as he gave out their limited fare. Charlotte Willard's complaints reflected his shortcomings as a superintendent. Her voyage had been disturbed by the daily quarrelling and fighting of a "very uncomfortable set." Her new blankets had been taken and replaced with one old one, and the family had lost various items of clothing. Although Charlotte thought she knew where to look for her possessions, she felt powerless to get them back.

Resolved to find a professional superintendent in 1833, Sockett's committee turned to Carter and Bonus for advice. They received a strong recommendation for J.C. Hale, who at the height of the 1832 cholera epidemic had successfully conducted

the Wisborough Green party from the *England* south to Ohio. This recommendation, his past experience as master of his own merchant ship, and his acquaintance
with the Canadas all counted in Hale's favour, and Sockett was pleased with the good
sense of his *Instructions*. When the Petworth committee sent the *England* as its own
ship in 1833, it appointed Hale as superintendent.[65]

Despite his promising references, Hale's reputed bad conduct in 1833 caused Sockett more grief than any other single incident in the course of the Petworth Emigrations. The problem seems to have been that Hale drank and drank heavily on the
1833 voyage. This activity left him open to accusations that he was stealing from the
committee's stores and using his position to profit at the expense of the emigrants
in his charge. Egremont's name appeared in a newspaper story incorporating these
accusations, a story that spread from Canadian papers to the Brighton paper read
by Egremont. Egremont was "much vexed" and Sockett correspondingly distressed.[66]

Sockett had an immediate public-relations problem and the future problem of
having to put matters to right for the following year. In the interest of damage control, he went public, publishing, and sending to Sussex and Upper Canadian newspapers, copies of the letter of reference Hale had brought to the committee and of
every mention of Hale in letters received to date from the emigrants of 1833.[67] The
Colonial Office had turned down Sockett's request to have Lieutenant-Governor
Colborne investigate, and he had to make do with a self-justifying letter from
Anthony Hawke, the agent in charge in Upper Canada.[68] On the question of Hale's
behaviour towards them during the voyage, as on most questions of importance, emigrants who bothered to raise the topic at all split unhelpfully in their opinions. Comments ranged from the highly favourable – "Capt. Hale did every thing in his power
to make us comfortable" – to the libellous – Hale was "not fit to drive a pig to market."[69] The *Montreal Gazette*, however, had found a cabin passenger prepared to speak
out, but to remain unnamed, against Hale's treatment of the people in his care.

Sockett was satisfied that Hale had not been thieving, but he could only hope
that the accusations of "habitual drunkenness" were overblown. In fact, Hale stood
partly condemned by his own reports of the Atlantic crossing. Hale represented his
emigrants, both men and women, as wheedling for drink on every possible occasion, even before they left the English Channel. He seemed to have responded freely,
perhaps taking a share for himself?[70] Yet, as Sockett confided to Richmond, the committee was at a loss as to where to turn for someone more qualified than Hale, who
at the least had successfully conducted two emigrations totalling over 400 people.[71]
The answer to Sockett's dilemma came in a friend's misfortune.

James Marr Brydone was a veteran of the battle of Trafalgar, one of many army
and navy officers whose connection with Upper Canada in the 1830s began when
he lost his job. In his case, Brydone also lost the house that went with his job and
he was put on half pay with a young family to support. He had been employed most
recently at the naval yard at Deptford, in charge of the medicine chests put on navy
ships (the very complete medicine chest sent on Petworth ships probably reflected
his advice), but he had many years' experience of the sea.[72]

Sockett's own hard experience in building a career in the shadow of wealthy patrons is evident in his private letters to Brydone. He readily agreed that Brydone had been "darkly dealt with" when he lost his position, but he urged that Brydone remain quiet and live to fight another day, warning frankly that "*all bigwigs hang together*."[73] After unsuccessfully sending out Richmond to see if he would find Brydone some employment at Portsmouth, Sockett applied to him again to make sure that Brydone had nothing to lose by being out of the country. He then persuaded his friend to take charge of the *British Tar*.[74]

Brydone was "from education; habits; and situation; of quite a different class from those who have heretofore gone out as superintendents of our parties."[75] He was the "magistrate" whom Sockett needed to impose order on the ship and negotiate on equal terms with authorities in Upper Canada. The fact that he was also a qualified surgeon lifted another worry from Sockett's shoulders. Brydone's account of the 1834 emigration, published under the title *Narrative of a Voyage*, served as a blueprint for the Petworth emigrations of 1835, 1836, and 1837, which Brydone also supervised.[76] Once he was confident that his standard was met, Sockett was satisfied and kept less-detailed written records about the voyages of the remaining ships.

One of Sockett's concerns with the Passengers' acts of 1828 and 1835 was the crowding they allowed. He demanded ships that were "lofty between decks; and capable of being well ventilated." Although the *Lord Melville*, which measured seven feet between decks, and the *Diana*, at six feet six inches, seemed none too high for two levels of bunks, the acts required only five feet six inches.[77] Despite requiring extra height and sending only two-thirds of the maximum numbers allowed by the Passengers' Act of 1828, Sockett believed that his emigrants had been overcrowded in 1832. The acts of 1828 and 1835 set number limits according to the tonnage of the ship. Beginning in 1833, Sockett used a different method, calculating his upper limit according to a superficial measurement of the space actually available for the emigrants' use. Years later, Robert Carter commended him for having applied this new formula long before it came into general use or was adopted by government.[78]

Emigrants did not complain publicly about crowding. Many of them did complain about the food, and some, such as Charlotte Willard, about the conduct of fellow passengers. Others complained about the superintendents – Hale, but also Brydone in one case in 1837. Complaints from emigrant ships were difficult to deal with, partly because of the problem of finding credible witnesses but also because of their sameness, which suggested that they could be endemic. Those who dealt regularly with emigrants had to sort out problems that could be solved from those that arose naturally from the situation – the "inevitable annoyances of a cold and tedious passage," the stress of travelling in close quarters with alarming shipmates.[79]

When they addressed shipboard conditions in 1833 and 1834, Sockett and the members of his committee relied on Hale's practical knowledge and Brydone's naval experience. In 1832, the Petworth committee sent one gallon of water per day for each passenger over fourteen years of age (those younger were allotted a half-gallon) and rations for sixty-three days, taking nine weeks as the outside length of the crossing. As required by law, the ship carried additional emergency rations. (Over six years, the Petworth ships took from five and a half to seven weeks from Spithead to Quebec City and arrived at Montreal with rations to spare.) The superintendent and the few cabin-class passengers ate "fresh meat and fowls" and drank porter with the captain. From the steerage, emigrants wrote that they found it almost impossible to eat the highly salted Irish beef that was the usual fare of sailors.

For the *England* in 1833, the committee sent aboard beef salted to their own specifications at Portsmouth and bacon and pork that was either home cured at Petworth or of the best quality from Ireland. Nevertheless, Hale reported that there had been problems, beginning at Portsmouth when bacon and potatoes were taken on board in the rain. Ship's mates, he informed the committee, were notoriously careless with supplies that did not belong to the ship. Both items deteriorated further in a damp hold, and by the end of the voyage, the list of supplies seriously affected by moisture had lengthened to include bread and oatmeal. All but a few fish on top of a cask of English cod had rotted and the coffee was musty. The bacon, although "unquestionably the best sea-meat for Country People," had lost in volume to constant scraping and cleansing (which may help to explain emigrants' complaints about short weight in their rations), and the bacon from Petworth had been shipped too green. The meat Hale had found easiest to manage and most useful was "fresh" pork, which had a higher proportion of lean and came cut in regular-sized pieces of four pounds each, but the children in particular ate little meat. Hale recommended replacing some of it with more tea, sugar, butter, and lard in order to bring the rations another step closer to the food available to labourers at home.[80]

In 1834, the committee wrote a new clause into the contract for the *British Tar*, requiring that a small storeroom for the Petworth provisions be built against one of the partitions between decks. Brydone reported that the provisions travelled well and gave satisfaction. In 1836, the *Heber*, the Petworth ship with the largest number of passengers, carried about 4,000 pounds of pork and bacon cured at Petworth and a "great quantity" of corned beef prepared at Portsmouth a few days before sailing.[81] There was a complaint of moldy bread again in 1837;[82] perhaps some deterioration was accepted by experienced sailors like Brydone.

Changes instituted by Brydone addressed the way life on board ship could be organized to ensure order, cleanliness, and the greatest possible efficiency in distributing and cooking food. He believed that those who complained about insufficient food let their own supplies, which they were issued a week at a time, go bad by storing them improperly through carelessness or because they lacked space. It was a question of wastage. In 1834, he refined the "scale of victualling," giving daily rather than weekly quantities and appointing a steward to ensure fair distribution. Under this regime, he actually reduced the total issue of some items, and emigrants on the *British Tar* had three meatless days out of seven (see Table 2.5). With the *British Tar*, Sockett arrived at the standard of provisioning he wanted. The list of provisions loaded on the *Burrell* in 1835 is given in Table 2.6. Two years later, the basic menu on the *Diana* was very similar to what had been established on the *British Tar*, with the minor

Table 2.5
Scale for the Issuing of Provisions, *British Tar,* 1834

Daily	Bread, ½ pound; water, ½ gallon
Sunday	Beef, 1 pound; potatoes, 1¾ pound; rum and water, ½ pint
Monday	Flour, ½ pound; raisins, ¼ pound; cheese, ½ pound; butter, ¼ pound
Tuesday	Pork, 1 pound; potatoes, 1¾ pound; brandy and water, ½ pint
Wednesday	Flour, ½ pound; raisins, ¼ pound; cheese, ½ pound; butter, ¼ pound
Thursday	Beef, 1 pound; potatoes, 1¾ pound; rum and water, ½ pint
Friday	Flour, ½ pound; raisins, ¼ pound; cheese, ½ pound; butter, ¼ pound
Saturday	Pork, 1 pound; potatoes, 1¼ pound; brandy and water, ½ pint
Weekly	Tea, 2 oz., or coffee, 4 oz.; sugar, 1¼ pound
When required	Vinegar, mustard, and soap
	Preserved meat, and porter, for the use of the sick

SOURCE: Brydone, *Narrative,* 5.

Table 2.6
Provisions Taken on Board the *Burrell,* 1835

Goods	Amount	Weight
Flour	10 barrels	
Biscuits	40 bags	
Soft bread		300 lbs
TOTAL FLOUR AND BREAD		7,580 lbs
Potatoes		11,900 lbs
Beef		1,976 lbs
Petworth pork and bacon		1,500 lbs
Mess pork	18 casks	
TOTAL MEAT		7,076 lbs
Cheese		22 cwt
Sugar		19 cwt
Coffee		167 lbs
Tea		117 lbs
Butter and raisins		±½ ton each
Peas	12 bushels	
Rice		56 lbs
Also vinegar, tobacco, soap, molasses, jams, bottled fruit, pickles		
Brandy	54 gals.	
Rum	60 gals.	
Porter	3 hhds	
Port and sherry	9 dozen	
Large supply poultry and vegetables		

SOURCE: *Brighton Herald,* 2 May 1835.

addition of peas for soup on the two days when the emigrants received pork.[83]

A superintendent had a fine line to tread in keeping order, and in day-to-day matters his success perhaps depended as much on the mix of emigrants as on his own leadership skills. Hale put up with the antics of "turbulent characters" until the *England*

Table 2.7
Rules and Regulations on the *British Tar,* 1834

Spithead, 17th April, 1834

Rules and Regulations of J.M. Brydone to be Observed by the Emigrants on Board the British Tar

1st	The bread and water will be issued daily, between six and seven in the morning.
2nd	The beef or pork, on Sundays, Tuesdays, and Saturdays, at ten in the forenoon; and on these days, brandy, or rum and water, at two in the afternoon.
3rd	The flour, raisins, cheese, and butter, on Mondays, Wednesdays, and Fridays, at ten in the forenoon.
4th	The tea, or coffee, and sugar, on Saturdays, at four in the afternoon.
5th	One man to be selected from each mess, to draw the provisions and water. Four of the young men, in daily rotation, to assist the cook in getting up the provisions, coals, and water, fill the water cisterns, and keep the upper deck clean and dry.
6th	John Gamblin [Gamblen], William Green, and William Martin to attend the issuing of the provisions and water, in daily rotation, to see that the messes occasion no delay, and that justice is done to all.
7th	The heads of the messes in the fore steerage; T. Perring [Perrin], H. Snelling, C. Voice, and W. Warren, in the middle steerage; J. Bassam, G. Coleman, Thos Ditton, and W. West, in the after steerage; to see that the berths and deck of the ship be properly cleaned every morning, before nine, the deck swept up after every meal, and the water cistern kept constantly supplied with water, by the young men in rotation; who are also requested to give some assistance to the families, if required by the superintendent to do so.
8th	John Gamblin, William Green, and William Martin to visit the berths daily, and when clean, report to the superintendent prior to his inspection, in the forenoon.
9th	All the parties before named, to prevent smoking between decks, swearing, or improper conduct of any sort: and all are requested to refrain from such acts as may tend to disturb the peace, comfort and harmony of the whole.
10th	No person to remove, or take a light from the lamps, or move the lamps from their position, unless directed by the superintendent, or master of the ship, to do so; and all complaints, or causes of complaint, to be submitted to the superintendent, who will immediately enquire into them, and as far as in his power cause them to be removed.

SOURCES: WSRO, PHA 138; and Brydone, *Narrative,* 4–5.

was in the Gulf of St Lawrence; once there, he issued a belated set of regulations and threatened to note names for prosecution on arrival. Although he reported that his "Reform Bill" was taken in good part, he was accused by some immigrants of intimidation.

In 1834, emigrants on the *British Tar* were greeted with a list of ten "rules and regulations" outlining how they were to conduct themselves on board ship (see Table 2.7). Families and individuals were divided into messes, and heads of messes received the rations for their group and were assigned specific supervisory duties in the emigrants' living areas. Single young men were given jobs to ensure that they kept themselves busy, the ship clean, and the routine of life predictable and regular. Brydone drew on his experience in the navy and as a doctor/superintendent of a convict ship to Australia in 1819 for these regulations.[84] In this, as in many other measures, the Petworth committee anticipated the government-appointed Colonial Land and Emigration Commission, which in the 1840s also used the regulations on convict ships as a guide in drawing up those for assisted emigrants.

Brydone relied on the willing cooperation of the emigrants, assigning them various tasks, but he did have one treat to offer those who performed special duties. He doled out extra liquor rations to his steward, his two cooks, and their assistants, and (a dig at Hale) made the point in his report that everyone did their share without asking for spirits. A final bottle of rum went each week to the crew in the interest of good relations. His success on the *British Tar* – where the only cases of "improper conduct" were the minor effects of "the thoughtlessness of youth" – was repeated over the next two years. His recorded difficulties came on the *Diana* in 1837.

In 1837, an anonymous letter published in the *Brighton Patriot* struck out against the *Diana*'s passengers, some of them "sent by the parishes" and "the greatest blackguards on earth"; against "old S," who charged more than a London or a Liverpool passage and did not deliver the expected benefits; and particularly against Brydone, "this villain of a superintendent" who gave short rations and treated the writer like a convict, denying him porter during illness.[85] Sockett's quick and firm response in the same newspaper closed the case on the anonymous accusations, and they were not repeated in any other source. The one charge that lingered because it couldn't be answered was that Brydone was fined two pounds and costs for brutally kicking "a poor friendless boy" (the author claimed he'd been drunk).[86] There were emigrants who found Brydone high-handed and perhaps in this case he had been too harsh or had lost his temper, or perhaps Sockett was justified in ignoring a charge he considered undeserving of an answer.

The routine report of Edward Lane, the master of the *Diana*, reduced the criticisms to familiar problems: dissatisfaction with the rations and irritation with misbehaving young men (people who kept the ship "in a state of mutiny all the way over" in the anonymous letter). Lane wrote appreciatively of Brydone's work, praising his impartiality in issuing rations and stating that Brydone had "gained the respect of the elder and more sensible part of the passengers."[87]

If nothing else, Brydone's difficulties in 1837 highlighted his successes in the three previous years. Preserving order and decency on an emigrant ship was no easy task.

When the new poor law was first introduced, Sockett hailed the emigration clauses that secured loans and made it easier for parishes to raise money. He believed that with access to this financing, parishes in his area would send more emigrants and that he could be sure of filling his ships. So far as his own plan was concerned, he expected it to continue as before with this one change. He had no intention of making any compromises in his standards to attract additional sponsorship.

Sockett charged different rates for a passage depending on the circumstances of the emigrant, but in 1835 his norm was probably about one pound higher than the eight pounds and ten shillings parish officers paid if they booked their emigrants a passage with Carter and Bonus from London to Toronto through James Denham Pinnock, an agent appointed to work with the poor law commissioners.[88] Sockett did not comment on this rate, but he took strong issue with cut-rate brokers operating in Sussex. In a printed notice to parish officers, he wrote that his ships represented more than a ten-pound value because Egremont had generously provided funding beyond the total raised in passage money. Although he acknowledged that they could send their emigrants to North America for substantially less, he warned that they risked failure by doing so. An apparent saving might prove no saving at all if the individuals and families "got rid of" on the cheap returned destitute and dependent on their parish. Sockett urged that they contrast this picture with "the cheering accounts sent back by those who emigrated under the management of this Committee."[89]

THE ROLE OF SPONSORS

After 1834 as before, Sockett succeeded best in rural parishes where he had a prominent sponsor willing to pay for a somewhat higher standard than the norm and to trust him to achieve it. For sponsors of means, Sockett offered convenience as well as quality. Richard Hasler of Kirdford, a magistrate married to Egremont's niece, echoed Egremont in his answer to the "Rural Questions" of the 1832 Royal Commission on the Poor Laws: "In my opinion, Emigration, if carried out judiciously, and to considerable extent, is the best, if not the only means of relieving both parishes and the Poor; and I mean both the Poor who emigrate and the Poor who remain at home."[90] Other prominent sponsors of Petworth emigrants who lived in Egremont's shadow were Sir Charles Burrell, Egremont's son-in-law; William Henry Yaldwyn from Lodsworth, and Richard Prime of Walberton. Sockett cited Prime, "who always paid the full price," as an example of a gentleman glad to pay someone else to see to the details who was "loud in expressing his satisfaction" with the committee's work.[91]

SOCKETT STARTED HIS SCHEME with the hopeful expectation that aristocratic landowners would duplicate his plan. He had half hoped in 1832 that Richmond might assume Egremont's role in assisting emigration from the Chichester area "south of the hills" that separated Petworth from Goodwood.[92] Although Richmond did sponsor emigrants in 1832 and brought a member of the Baring family, and probably the Dorking Society, into the scheme, he did not act on Sockett's hints. Another potential patron in West Sussex, Bernard Howard, the twelfth Duke of Norfolk and the leading Roman Catholic in the Sussex aristocracy, pointedly ignored the Petworth emigrations. After talking to Sockett, the mayor of Arundel wrote regretfully to Richmond in 1832: "If our noble Duke was to follow the example of the Petworth noble Earl, we might not be in difficulties; but it is otherwise."[93] Few emigrants were sent on Petworth ships from the district that deferred to Norfolk.

Two noble landlords of Richmond's acquaintance whose interest in chartering a ship can be traced to the Petworth emigrations both sent emigrants, but they each fell far short of a shipload. Their endeavours lacked the crucial elements of the Petworth scheme: Sockett's commitment and Egremont's willingness to pay more that his share. Lord Suffield, one of these noblemen, wrote to Richmond from Norfolk that he had not lacked for willing candidates; he blamed his failure to fill a ship on having begun the enterprise too late in the season and on difficulties in raising money in parishes where he owned the land.[94]

Table 2.8
Lewes Emigration Committee, East Sussex, 1833

West, George John, fifth Earl De la Warr [Delaware], Cambridge and Sussex landowner
Cope, Charles Cecil, third Earl of Liverpool, Buxted Park, Buxted
Pelham, Henry Thomas, third Earl of Chichester, Stanmer House, Stanmer
Hall, Henry, fourth Viscount Gage, Firle Place, near Lewes
Cavendish, Charles Compton (later first Baron Chesham), MP for the Eastern Division of Sussex,
    Compton Place, Eastbourne
Shiffner, Sir George, Bart, Coombe Place, Hamsey, near Lewes
Shelley, John Villiers, Esq., Maresfield Park, Maresfield
Curteis, Herbert Barrett, Esq., MP for the Eastern Division of Sussex, Windmill Hill, Peasmarsh
Partington, Thomas, Esq., Offham, near Lewes
D'Oyley, Thomas, Sergeant at Law, East Sussex
Courthope, George, Esq., "Whiligh," Ticehurst
Cripps, John Marten, Esq., "Stantons," East Chiltington
Gew, R., Esq.
Richardson, Thomas, Esq. (Camoys Court from 1835), Barcombe

SOURCE: *Hampshire Telegraph*, 25 November 1833; and project files.

The noble patron whose role in assisted emigration most closely duplicated Egremont's part in Sockett's scheme was the Earl of Chichester of East Sussex. In the autumn of 1833, Chichester sent to Sockett for information to help him set up an emigration committee similar to Sockett's.[95] The sponsors Chichester drew to his Lewes Emigration Committee were of similar social standing to those from West Sussex who were attracted to the Petworth scheme by Egremont's name (see Table 2.8). In Brighton, Chichester's participation overcame the doubts that had caused plans for assisted emigration to fail in 1832. The crucial difference between Egremont and Chichester was that Chichester was unwilling to take on the risk of chartering a ship. He ignored Sockett's warnings about "the Loss of Time and other Inconveniences that would result from a numerous Executive" and proceeded by committee.[96]

The Lewes Emigration Committee planned for 300 emigrants. They proposed to hire a superintendent and charter a ship to sail in April 1834 from Newhaven to Montreal and, if demand warranted, on to Toronto. But with no Egremont to back the charter, the Lewes committee had to ask the landowners to commit before the end of December to half the estimated cost of a passage and to a promise of security for the share to be contributed by parishes where the sponsor owned land.[97] Sockett could have told the Lewes meeting that neither sponsors nor potential emigrants would be easy to pin down so far in advance. The Lewes committee's 1834 venture became one of many examples of plans for assisted emigration that had to be scaled down as participants vacillated and time ran out. The committee was unable to fill a ship, and the Petworth ship provided Chichester with a means of making good a promise to those who had booked a passage from Lewes or Brighton.

In addition to large landowners whose holdings were often in more than one parish, Petworth sponsors included men, and a few women, who gave assistance to one or just a few emigrants from their own parish. The people they helped might have represented a particular burden on the poor rates, but the letters of thanks or greetings to individual sponsors or former employers from some emigrants suggested a more direct connection. Quite often, these messages came from women who had been servants before leaving England.

The sponsors also included smaller landowners like John Biddulph of Burton Park or Levi Bushby of Goring, or farmers like Charles Farhall of Clarksland, Billingshurst, who was attacked by Charles Chitty for encouraging the emigration of "other people's good workers." Or they might be people who owned property in a village. Susan Loud, the fourth-highest ratepayer in the village of Angmering, made a loan of £200 to her parish to send emigrants in 1832. In larger communities, Charles Chaplen, who lent £100 to send thirteen people from the parish of Cocking in 1836, sold linen retail at Midhurst, and Henry Hurly of Lewes, another contributor to the scheme, was a banker. As might be expected given the role of the clergy in many parishes, several members of the clergy appear as Petworth sponsors: the Reverend Charles Neal of Stoke, the Reverend William Peckham Woodward at West Grinstead, and Thomas Pannel, rector of Burton with Coates.

Henry Wagner, the vicar of St Nicholas, Brighton, typified urban sponsors and those who worked within the framework of a committee. In Brighton in 1834, a Mr King of the Provident and District Society distributed information and received applications. The decidedly urban members of the Brighton Emigration Committee included James Cordy, a wine and spirit merchant and the head of the committee; Lewis Hyam, a silversmith, jeweller, and pawnbroker; and James Collins, a coal merchant and shipowner, who accompanied the 1834 emigrants to Portsmouth.[98] In yet another configuration typical of parishes that were the sites of small towns, the people attending the special vestry meeting on assisted emigration in Dorking had a mixture of rural and urban occupations (see Table 2.9).

Authorities on the Isle of Wight represented the only large institution sending any number of Petworth emigrants. Under an incorporation act, a single House of Industry at Newport had served the island since the eighteenth century. The *Hampshire Telegraph* reported in 1834 that the thirty paupers sent from the House on the *British Tar* were selected from among the healthiest and most industrious and were fitted out for emigration with care and attention.[99] In 1837, the governor of the House justified his use of discretionary authority to exceed the original vote for assisted emigration with a reference to the "standard of comfort intended by the Guardians of the Poor."[100] The accounts prepared by the governor showed that he had accepted Sockett's recommendations on the passage and the outfit (see Table 2.10 and compare with the Dorking accounts in Table 2.4). The only sign of pennypinching of which Sockett would not have approved was the sum of £44 12s. sent to Toronto for distribution as landing money for seventy-eight people. If this was indeed the total, the Isle of Wight emigrants of 1837 received less than their counterparts sent by the Dorking Society in 1832.

Sockett's standards became an issue for a second time in 1837. This time, his opponent was more formidable than Charles Barclay had been in 1833. The poor law

Table 2.9
Dorking Special Vestry, 1832

Members of Special Vestry, Dorking, 10 February 1832, which passed unanimously a resolution to assist excess labourers to emigrate

Reverend George Feacham, vicar of St Martin's, Dorking, and chair of meeting
John Philps, churchwarden and tailor
William Combes, churchwarden
Richard Wit Philps, overseer
Samuel Bothwell, overseer
William Crawford Esq., Pippbrook estate, Surrey, MP for City of London, 1833–41
Charles Barclay, Esq., MP, member of banking and brewing family, owner of Bury Hill
Samuel Jackson, Esq.
Alfred Dawson, minister, Congregational Church, Dorking
James White, estate agent, auctioneer, and surveyor
John Niblett, undertaker and bookseller
William Alloway, butcher
Joseph Sawyer, grocer
James Tewsley, farmer
William Deene, ironmonger and furniture dealer
James Wells, corn dealer
John Beckett, painter, decorator, plumber, and artist
John Adie Carter
Philip Cooke, ale taster
Robert White, plumber and painter
Thomas Rose, grocer and cheesemonger
George King, butcher
George Duidney (Dewdney), saddler or miller
Richard Fielder, linen draper and salesman
Charles Cosens
William Miller, cabinetmaker and auctioneer
Henry Miller
William Curtis, cabinetmaker
Robert Marsh, linen draper

SOURCE: SRO (GMR), PSH/DOM 9 (3); Dorking Museum files.
NOTE: A vestry minute on 31 October 1832 records "Cash paid on account of Emigration Expenses" £226.9.3.

commissioners were seeking to extend the uniformity they sought in parish assistance to the assistance in emigrating offered under the loans they approved. At least with regard to Petworth ships, this measure was an obvious attempt to assert authority. Writing to the commissioners in 1837, Sockett defended his standards as vigorously as ever and criticized them sharply for theirs. He returned to the themes of his attack on Mitchell and Barclay in 1833. Ten shillings for an outfit was not enough to supply bedding and clothing; in the between decks of a ship, a clearance of five feet under the beams was not sufficient space for English men and women – he was angry enough to suggest that even convicts were sent at a higher standard.[101]

The surviving records of the Poor Law Commission contain at least one example of the commissioners successfully diverting emigrants originally intented for the

Table 2.10
Isle of Wight House of Industry Emigration Expenses, 1837

	£	s.	d.
64 passages (78 persons) Portsmouth to Toronto, £10 per passage less 5 per cent discount	608	0	0
Clothing, shoes, and bedding average £5 per head	390	9	0

Incidentals
   including redeeming clothing and shoes from pawn, supplies
   purchased from Petworth Emigration Committee, wagons
	23	19	3

Letters of credit sent on to the commissioners of the Canada Company at Toronto landing money	44	12	0
Expenses not found or not explained	20	7	8
FINAL ACCOUNT	1086	17	11
Average cost per head for 37 men, 13 women, 17 boys, and 11 girls	13	16	8

SOURCE: Reported by T. Pike, governor (Isle of Wight Record Office, z/HO/ BI, f. 89; z/HO/44, ff. 133-4).

Diana. In a letter that would have pleased Sockett immensely, C. Strong, a guardian of the Cuckfield Union writing for the parish of Balcombe east of Hosham, informed the poor law commissioners that the parish intended using Egremont's ship "which all Sussex Emigrants prefer well knowing the comfort and decency attaching to it." He expected some of the Balcombe people to refuse to go on any other.[102] In a second letter, Strong questioned the commissioners' calculation of four dollars, or seventeen shillings and four pence, for inland travel from Montreal to Upper Canada as "too close" and raised the concern that it might "prejudice the cause." Petworth emigrants, he added, might choose any Upper Canadian port on Lake Ontario and take advantage of Brydone's presence to get a recommendation to a government agent in Upper Canada.[103]

Strong's Cuckfield Union was also at odds with the poor law commissioners in 1837. The conjunction of Cuckfield and Petworth, two trying unions, may have reinforced the commissioners' determination to turn down Balcombe's request for a loan. The grounds they cited were that the parish proposed to raise more money than was necessary or reasonable, and they pressed Strong to accept a rate much lower than that advertised by emigration agent Pinnock in 1835. Strong accepted the commissioners' broker and presumably sent his people at a rate of five pounds for a passage to Montreal, provisions included.[104]

The fate of the Balcombe emigrants on the *Auxilier*, one of two ships on which the poor law commissioners sent emigrants from London in 1837, bore out all Sockett's concerns about the risks of a cheap passage. Sixty-four emigrants from this ship were hospitalized at Grosse Île, and four young children from Balcombe were among the ten or twelve passengers who died of smallpox. Although he described the English paupers on this ship as "generally well provided" (because they had landing money), the Quebec agent Buchanan arranged to send them free of charge from Quebec up to Montreal, where adults each received their twenty shillings sterling according to the commissioners' instructions.[105]

SOCKETT EQUATED THE SUCCESS of his scheme with his emigrants' success in Canada, as well as with the numbers he sent. He needed to offer a certain level of comfort and decency to attract the kind of people he believed best able to relocate to advantage. In lowering the rate of passage, the commissioners not only put the safety of the emigrants at risk but lowered the bar for purposes of selection. Sockett was anxious to make sure that "respectable" people of "decent" habits would be comfortable on his ships and would recommend them to like-minded emigrants of subsequent years.

In bringing his emigrations to the standard he wanted, Sockett worked independently of government. He argued for assisted emigration in terms popularized by Horton in the 1820s, but he showed no particular knowledge of Peter Robinson's proceedings in 1823 and 1825. Because Horton had directed those emigrations from the Colonial Office, the Navy Board had chartered Horton's ships and arranged for rations and medicines to be put on board. An ex-navy surgeon superintendent had been in charge of the emigrants on each ship.[106] Sockett never sought guidance from the past experience with chartered ships in the Colonial Office, and it was 1834 before he reached a comparable level of administrative control. On the other hand, his independence opened the way for some forward-looking practices. His insistance on ships certified A1 by Lloyds, his methods after 1832 of calculating and allocating space, and Brydone's regulations for passengers were all measures that the Colonial Land and Emigration Commission adopted during the 1840s. It speaks well for Sockett that he worked in advance of government regulation in identifying these measures and implementing them in an emigration scheme.

The fact that Sockett was able to discover the keys to a better standard for the Atlantic passage independently of cumulative Colonial Office experience is an indication that the knowledge of how to make shipboard life safer and less unpleasant was available to sponsors who cared to seek it out. Although fraud and deception were problems for inexperienced sponsors as well as for naive emigrants, Sockett was justified in thinking that a sponsor looking for the cheapest passage was one of the worst hazards faced by assisted emigrants. He also proved over six years that there were sponsors and parishes willing to consider more than the cheapest possible price. He found people in each of these years who were quite content to pay rates above the minimum to give their emigrants a safe passage and a better chance at success.

*The Home of the Rick
Burner* from *Punch*, 1844
*As this date indicates, the
problems associated with the
Swing disturbances continued
in rural England.*

*Emigrants travelling to the
port of departure*
The Emigrants' Farewell *from
Illustrated London News,
13 April 1844 (detail)*

Ploughing, harrowing, stacking hay, the work of an English farm
From Jeffreys Taylor, *The Farm* (1832)

Reaping and threshing
From Jeffreys Taylor, *The Farm* (1832)

EMIGRANTS sent out to UPPER CANADA by the PETWORTH EMIGRATION COMMITTEE.

Places from which they came	1832 Adults M	F	Under 14 M	F	TOTAL	1833 Adults M	F	Under 14 M	F	TOTAL	1834 Adults M	F	Under 14 M	F	TOTAL	1835 Adults M	F	Under 14 M	F	TOTAL	1836 Adults M	F	Under 14 M	F	TOTAL	Total Number in the 5 Years from each Place
Petworth	25	9	8	7	49	11	5	5	3	24	4				4	5	4	4	1	14	9	3	2	2	16	107
Tillington	4	6	2	4	16	1	2			3					—					—	10	15	14	11	50	69
Northchapel	6	5	6	8	25					—	1				1					—	1	1	1	2	5	30
Egdean					—					—	1				1					—	1	1	3		5	9
Duncton					—	2				2					—	2				2	1				1	9
Lavington					—					—					—					—	1				1	1
Graffham					—					—					—					—	1	1	2	2	6	6
Sutton	5	2	3	3	13	1		1		2					—					—					—	15 E
Bignor	4	2	7	8	16					—					—					—					—	16
Coates	2	3	2	2	9					—					—					—					—	9 E
Fittleworth	2		1		3	2	1			3	3		1		4			1		2					6	18 E
Barlavington	1				1					—					—	1	1			2	3	2	1		6	11 E
Bury			1		1					—					—					—					—	1
West Grinstead					—					—	2				2	2	2	5	2	11					—	13 E
Shipley	4	1	1	2	8	1	1	4		6					—	9	7	4	7	27					—	41
Billingshurst					—					—	4	2	3	1	10					—	8	4	5	2	19	29 E
Wisborough Green	3				3					—					—	6				6	6	5	8	3	22	31 E
Kirdford	18	12	13	15	58	7	3	1	3	14					—					—					—	72 E
Lurgashall	21	14	22	18	75	2	1		1	4					—					—					—	75 E
Lodsworth	1	2	3	3	9					—					—	3	1			4					—	17
Linchmere & Frensham	2	1			3					—					—	1	1	2	4	8					—	11
Farnhurst and Steep	5	3	4	6	18	6	4	6	7	23					—					—					—	41
Ambersham					—	6				1					—					—					—	1
Easebourne					—					—					—					—	2	1	2	2	7	7
Cocking					—					—					—					—	4	1	3	2	10	10
Bepton					—					—					—	2	2	4	5	13					—	13
Pulborough	2	2	5	1	10					—	1	1	2	1	5					—					—	15 E
Greetham					—			1		1					—					—					—	1
Sullington	2	2	3	5	12					—					—	1	1	4	2	8					—	20 E
Storrington					—					—					—	1				1					—	1 E
Chiltington					—					—					—	1		1		2					—	2
Thakeham	2	2	2	1	7					—					—					—					—	7
Wiston & Washington					—					—	4				4	2	1			3					—	7
Rackham					—					—					—	2	1	5		8					—	8
Burpham					—					—					—	1	3	2	4	10	1	2	1	4	8	18
Clapham					—					—					—					—					—	1
Findon					—					—					—					—	11	9	11	7	38	38
Goring					—					—					—	7	2	2	5	16	12	6	5	4	27	43
Heene					—					—					—	2	2	2	4	10					—	10
Tarring					—					—					—					—					2	2
Angmering	3	1			4					—					—					—					—	4
Arundel					—					—					—					—	1				1	1
Climping					—					—					—	2	6	3	6	17					—	17
Yapton					—					—					—	6	4	1	1	12					—	12
‡ Felpham and Merston	4	4	6	6	20	3	2	2	1	8					—	20	7	8	9	44					—	72 E
Walberton	13	4	3	1	21	1				1					—	6	2	2	1	11	11		1		12	45
Oving					—	1	1			2					—					—					—	2
Boxgrove					—	1	1			2					—					—	1				1	3
Chichester					—	5	1	2	1	9					—					—					—	10
Pagham	1	1	1		4					—					—					—					—	4
Stoughton	1	1	2	1	5					—					—					—					—	5
Seaford					—					—					—	1				1					—	1
Brighton & Lewes, &c.					—					—	26	12	11	8	57					—	3				3	60
Mrs. Jones and Family		1	7		8					—					—					—					—	8
Stoke (Guildford)	8	5	2	6	21					—					—					—					—	22
Haslemere	3	2	2	2	9	3	3	6	1	13					—					—					—	22
Chiddingfold	8	4			12	3			1	4					—					—					—	16
Hascomb and Witley	3	1			4					—					—					—	3	3		1	7	14
Dunsfold and Ockley	4				4	7				7					—					—					—	14
Alfold					—					—					—					—					—	4
Southampton					—					—	1	1	1		3					—					—	3
Isle of Wight					—	16	1	1		18	34	3		6	43					—					—	61
Portsmouth					—					—					—	1				1					—	1
Buriton					—					—					—					—	1				1	1
Itchingstoke and Northington	8	1	1		10					—					—					—					—	10
Ivington	3	1	1		5					—					—					—					—	5
Bath					—					—					—	3	3	2	3	11					—	11
Warminster					—					—					—					—	1				1	1
Hindon, East Knowle & Cricklade (Wilts)					—	25	8	11	7	51					—					—					—	51
Kempsford (Gloucestershire)					—					—					—	1		1		2	2				2	4
London	2	1	1		6					—	1	1			2	1			1	2	1			2	3	13
Ongar (Essex)					—					—					—	2				2					—	4
Attleboro (Norfolk)					—					—					—	1			1	2	2				2	4
Royston (Camb.)	6	5	8	5	24					—					—					—					—	24
Scotland					—					—					—	1				1					—	1
Single Passages, (i. e.) Persons from various Places	11				11					—					—					—					—	11
*Dorking & Neighbourhood	36	20	24	22	102					—					—					—					—	102
§Wisborough Green & some Parishes in Hants					—					—					—					—					—	164
TOTAL					769					200					135					252					264	1620

* These went in the same ship with those sent by the Committee, under the charge of the same medical man, but of a separate superintendent, who attended them up the country.

Emigrants sent … by the Petworth Emigration Committee, 1836

PRO, MH 12/13060, f.123817, reproduced as Table 3.1, page 85

Between decks on an emigrant ship

Emigrant Vessel – Between Decks, from *Illustrated London News*, 10 May 1851

The Anchorage at Quebec City, 1832

Sketch by Henry Byan Martin

NA, C115003

St Lawrence Durham boat
Sketch by Henry Byan Martin
NA, C115051

Locks and Dams at Davis' Mill on the Rideau Canal. The steamboat preceded the barges out of lock and will take them in tow once more.
Thomas Burrows, *Lock, Dam etc. at Davis' Mill*, 1840
AO, C100050

CHAPTER 3

"PAUPERISM [IS] ALMOST UNIVERSAL": WHO WERE THE PETWORTH EMIGRANTS?

The ordinary prejudices against paupers can hardly apply to those of these two counties [Sussex and Hampshire]. Pauperism, being there almost universal among the labouring classes through the mistaken kindness of making up wages out of the poor rates, is not, as in more fortunate counties, a proof either of idleness or of dishonesty.

Montreal Herald, in an article on emigration and the Earl of Egremont, copied by the *Brighton Gazette*, 9 July 1835

Petworth emigrants left their homes in England because they were in economic difficulties and feared that their situation might get worse rather than better in the future. They typically emigrated either as part of a family that depended on the wages of a single wage-earner trapped in a low-wage occupation, or as single men who had difficulty finding a permanent job. Agricultural workers in arable districts of southeast England lost purchasing power in the late eighteenth century during the wars with France when a scarcity of foodstuffs caused rising prices. During the period of adjustment to a peacetime economy in the early nineteenth century, the central issue was not so much prices as the rapid increase in population and the resulting competition among labourers for too few jobs. The three bad harvests that led up to the Swing disturbances in West Sussex threw many people out of work, and the threshing machines so bitterly attacked during the disturbances pointed the way to a future in which reduced numbers of men would be employed in farming. When times improved at the end of the 1830s, there was more employment but the numbers of labourers wanting work kept wages low in West Sussex.[1]

Although food riots in 1795–96 and at the turn of the century occurred in the towns of Sussex rather than in the Sussex countryside, the effects of grain shortages were felt everywhere.[2] Farmers and magistrates chose to make use of the poor laws to support their labourers rather than raise wages to keep step with the rising price of flour and face the problem of sustaining or lowering these wages when prices corrected. In variations of a practice labelled the "Speenhamland system," eligible paupers received help in kind or in money when the price of flour or bread rose above a specified limit.[3] In the postwar years, farmers hit by reductions in their own incomes paid no more for labour than a necessary minimum.

An incomplete but extensive survey of Sussex parishes compiled for the Duke of Richmond in 1831–32 identified 3,283 able-bodied male labourers out of work that winter.[4] This survey suggests that parishes with significant winter unemployment could be found in all parts of Sussex from the fertile coastal plain to the High Weald along the border with Surrey and Kent. By the 1830s the Speenhamland system had largely lapsed, but farmers continued to use the parish poor rates to supplement their labourers' wages in parishes where they controlled how the rates would be used. In comparison with other counties, spending on relief in Sussex was high, with the corollary that Sussex agricultural labourers were not quite so badly off as some.[5] Even a full-time labourer was judged unable to support more than two – or three – young children on his wages, and the principal form of poor relief to the able-bodied in this era was a child allowance given after the birth of the third or – in some parishes – the fourth child.[6]

Sockett provided some evidence of the amount of aid given families under the old poor law and hence of the impact in his parish of the poor law commissioners' campaign against outdoor relief (that is, aid to people living in their homes rather than in a workhouse). He insisted that the members of the Petworth vestry (which he controlled until the parish was taken into the Petworth Poor Law Union) had judged all applicants for relief on their individual merits. He left the impression, however, that a large family with a total income from all sources under fifteen shillings a week would be considered eligible for help.[7] The poor law commissioners first had the guardians of the Petworth Union replace a child allowance in money with an allowance of flour and then, in June of 1836, ordered West Sussex poor law unions to stop all kinds of outdoor relief to able-bodied paupers. At the time the Petworth guardians stopped the child allowances of money and flour, the weekly wage of agricultural labourers in Sussex hovered around ten shillings.[8]

In unions like Petworth, guardians forced to stop the child allowance and other benefits took exception and proved inventive in finding new ways to provide some relief. Guardians of the poor and even long-time parish officials were touched by the plight of the children: "I was hurt in my feelings to see the pitiful cries of the poor; it would hurt any man to see a parcel of young children, and have no more to give, it would touch the heart of a flint-stone; I could not bear it."[9] Edward Butt, the relieving officer for the district of Petworth and Kirdford in the Petworth Union who made this statement, reported that in the winter of 1836–37 his district had sixty-six labouring families with five or more children. All told, these families had 366 children aged twelve or under, a reminder – in comparison with the England of today – of the relative youth of the population of the 1830s, when close to two out of every five persons were under fifteen.[10] The first strategy adopted in Petworth, and in a number of other unions, was to take one, two, or even three children from large families into the workhouse.

Sockett tried other strategies on his own. He persuaded Egremont (and, on his own telling, only Egremont) to join him in paying a premium on wages when flour rose above a certain price, an interesting step back into the days before the child allowance but one that did not resonate with employers younger than his patron.[11] In another move that was perhaps also limited to Sockett's district of West Sussex, he sent some exceptionally large families to Upper Canada on the *Diana* in the spring of 1837. Of eleven families from Sussex, ten travelled with from six to thirteen children. The only family from Sussex on this ship with a lesser number was the family headed by Sarah Hopkins, a woman who travelled alone with three children under fourteen.

K.D.M. Snell argues that agricultural wages in the south fell significantly between 1833 and 1837 and were lower in 1850 than in 1833. In the southeast, "the area where the New Poor Law was applied most rapidly and fully," fifteen of sixteen counties fell within his "hardest-hit category."[12] Most historians who study the later nineteenth century cast doubts on there having been any firm trend of improvements in farm workers' wages and living conditions relative to the rest of the English population. Those who do see improvements suggest that they were a gradual consequence of the new balance in supply and demand for farm labour, resulting from large-scale migration to the cities and, to some extent, from emigration.[13]

A PROFILE OF PETWORTH EMIGRANTS

In the context of a period when the economic outlook for rural workers was generally bleak, the records of the Petworth emigrations provide various keys as to which rural workers were most likely to be among the crowd of emigrants who disembarked from Petworth ships at Montreal. Sockett wanted his scheme to be better known, and on several occasions he provided information on his emigrants to newspapers, government departments, and parliamentary committees. The profile of the emigrants in this chapter rests on these accounts and on our own information on individuals and families (see Part Two). The selection of emigrants for assistance under the Petworth scheme was always an individual decision made by a sponsor or parish, but some determining factors such as occupation, family circumstance, and age can be picked out as common components of the decision.

Occupation, particularly male occupation, was probably the most important factor in the selection of parish emigrants. R.W. Hay, writing from the Colonial Office in 1831, explained that "pauper, as used in emigration schemes, means a redundant labourer, who may be either a good or bad character – the redundancy being determined by the demand for labour as compared to the supply, and not by the individual character of the labourers soliciting employment."[14] The Petworth emigrations were launched as an answer to this kind of redundancy, and they were misused if sponsors managed to include anyone certain to become dependent on public aid in Upper Canada.

In his role as the rector of Petworth, Sockett explained the needs of the poor to the rich and powerful by citing examples of the way they lived and the daily hardships they faced. He took care also to explain to the 1837 Select Committee on the Poor Law Amendment Act how he gathered his information, because in those difficult times even the clergy were suspected of inciting discontent. Sockett described how he entered cottages where he was well known, how he engaged in small talk and then listened to the labourers and their wives as they told of their troubles large and small. From these conversations and his own local knowledge, he was able to decide on which issues were most important for the whole district and sometimes – as in the case of assisted emigration – he could come up with solutions.

Sockett spoke on behalf of the poor as a sympathetic observer moved to act by seeing labouring people in deeper poverty than their community should tolerate. He did not supply a definition of that poverty, but Adam Smith's description of basic necessities as "whatever the customs of the country renders it indecent for creditable people, even of the lowest order, to be without" seems to cover Sockett's intention and may even lie behind his own definition of the standards for Petworth ships.[15] As the reformers of his time were inclined to shift the blame for unemployment onto the poor, Sockett occasionally went beyond describing living and working conditions to defend the character of people he knew both as individuals and as a collective identity, "the poor." Although he did not cite them in this regard, the letters from Petworth emigrants in Canada that he had received and published are good evidence for his case.

Figure 3.1 gives the occupations we know of for the heads of households listed in our family reconstructions in Part Two. We could not identify the occupations of almost 46 per cent of heads of households, but of the number whose occupations were identified, almost 70 per cent were involved in some form of agricultural labour. Another 20 per cent were craftsmen – blacksmiths, bricklayers, carpenters, sawyers, tailors, shoemakers, and so on. The other 10 percent had varied ways of earning a living. Contemporary records help to establish who among the people in these occupations were most likely to emigrate, and supply examples from a particular year and sometimes from a particular place or area within the region sending Petworth emigrants.

In 1851, James Caird presented a map of English agriculture divided into four main regions. According to his broad characterizations, the southeast suffered from the double disadvantage of both the low rents (and, by implication, low profits) associated with corn (cereal crops) in the eastern part of the country and the low wages associated with the south.[16] If there was a typical labourer on a Petworth ship, he came from an arable farm such as Caird thought typical of his region. On this farm, he was likely to have derived his wages from cultivating and harvesting a commercial crop of some kind.

On nineteenth-century English farms like those around Petworth that were large enough for a division of labour, historians have found a clear distinction between the people who worked with animals and those who did not.[17] Petworth emigrants were likely to come from the latter group. Few people involved in animal husbandry or the care of horses are identified among Petworth emigrants, although there was no lack of such people in the Petworth area. The Petworth and Goodwood estates were noted for their sheep and cattle, to say nothing of their racing stables and foxhounds. Sockett himself employed a number of carters. But the pay scale of shepherds, carters, and even gatekeepers on Egremont's estates differed from that of other labourers. Workers who cared for animals had a year-round task that involved extra

Figure 3.1
Occupations of Identified Petworth Emigrants, 1832–1837

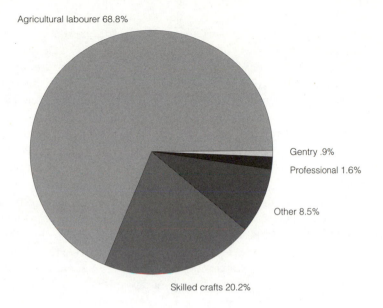

Agricultural labourer 68.8%

Gentry .9%

Professional 1.6%

Other 8.5%

Skilled crafts 20.2%

SOURCE: Project files, list of emigrants

NOTE: Only heads of households are included in this chart. The occupation of almost 46 per cent of identified Petworth heads of households is unknown. Many of the heads of households emigrating, both those for whom we have found occupations and those for whom we have not, were receiving parish relief. *Agricultural labour* includes those designated agricultural labourer, farm labourer, farming man, and labourer. *Skilled crafts* includes a baker, several blacksmiths, bricklayers, carpenters, a cooper, two fellmongers, sawyers, a number of shoemakers, tailors, weavers, a wheelwright, among others. *Other* includes a bailiff, five farmers and one yeoman, a gardener, miller, postman, several soldiers or sailors, and servants. The *professional* category includes several naval officers, a schoolteacher, and a surgeon, most of them cabin passengers.

hours and therefore extra pay. Gatekeepers had the cottage that went with the job. Regular house servants at Petworth were sure of their weekly wage and perquisites. Neither farm workers who looked after animals nor the servants in Petworth House were barred from the Petworth ships of 1832–37, but there is little evidence of their presence. They were not the ones burdening the rates, and they were not prime candidates for assisted emigration.

The term "agricultural labourer" as applied to the majority of Petworth emigrants was elastic as to which outdoor workers it included. In predominantly farming country, a man who spent part or much of the year at work in the forest could be classed as an agricultural labourer. In the wooded parish of Chiddingfold in Surrey, the principal employment from May until the harvest was cutting timber. After a break for the harvest, these labourers went from forest to coppice for winter work.[18] In other districts, summer field workers moved to the coppice during the winter. In coppices, broad-leafed trees were cut back and the shoots that grew around the trunk harvested according to a rotation that depended on the variety of tree and the intended use.[19] Although this work kept a number of men in Sockett's district busy over the winter, they were at the mercy of the weather. A heavy snowfall in a year like 1836–37 drove them out of the woodlots to join those looking to the parish for temporary aid.

Apart from the agricultural workers, the other occupation groupings of Petworth emigrants of significant size were those of rural artisans. Men with a trade had a certain status, enough standing to be distinguished from agricultural labourers on lists of Petworth emigrants or lists of people out of work in Petworth. However, they felt threatened. An 1834 resolution of the Midhurst vestry offered evidence that men in the building trades could not be certain of maintaining a higher standard of living than field workers. According to the vestry, bricklayers and carpenters earned good wages in the summer, and for this reason, the vestry's members had decided not to give them any more relief in the off-season than would bring their total income up to the annual wage of an agricultural labourer. If workers in the building trades could not make ends meet on this amount, they would have to enter the workhouse.[20] For those who considered themselves craftsmen and a cut above labourers, the declining status implied by this decision must have been added incentive to emigrate.

On the list of men "employed" by the parish of Petworth (and therefore out of regular work) in the years 1830–31, farming men were the most numerous. How these men came to be out of work is suggested by a few surviving pay lists prepared by Egremont's tenant farmers in the parish of Tillington.[21] These lists demonstrate both the low wages paid in a labour-intensive farming industry and the sharp seasonal fluctuations in the size of the workforce. The records of payments are most complete for 1830 and 1831 on the 150-acre Dean Farm.[22] The payments entered for Dean Farm were mainly for day work with some for task work (payday was traditionally Saturday). If these books represent a complete account, no one had a full year's work from his employer. Although Henry Miles was the only certain Petworth emigrant among employees of Dean Farm, the surname of several other emigrants match surnames on the farm.[23] Henry Miles and his brother John were the two men most constantly employed in 1831: thirty-seven weeks for Henry and thirty-eight for John.

The Dean Farm paybook records encapsulate the experience of many agricultural labourers in 1830s Sussex where they had to contend both with the seasonal fluctuations of employment in a labour-intensive farming industry and with low wages. The farmer made payments to fifty-six and fifty-seven different workers in each of 1830 and 1831. Most were men, but a few women worked at small tasks such as sewing sacks and did field work. The majority of both men and women were hired for short periods of from a few days to two months, and a few names are recorded only once or twice. The men most regularly employed in the work of the farm received ten shillings for a six-day week. Some male workers received both more and less than this amount, and during harvest men received three shillings a day. At all times of the year, women were paid six to eight pence a day with a maximum of four shillings and six pence a week.[24]

Apart from the ever-present agricultural labourers, other "redundant" workers dependent on the parish of Petworth in midwinter 1830–31 were people from the building trades and shoemakers. Bricklayers were listed with their assistants (two bricklayers' labourers for every bricklayer). Shoemakers were out of work as a secondary effect of seasonal unemployment. The trade was easy to enter, shoemakers were many, and if they depended on poor clients they might join their customers in maintaining the parish roads in seasons when these people had no money to buy. When they reached Upper Canada, Petworth emigrants evidenced two kinds of shoemaker: those like John White for whom it was their living, and others like William Goldring who was a shoemaker among a variety of other occupations. Emigrant lists do not reveal such distinctions or distinguish a person fully experienced in a trade from one hoping to parlay a handy skill into employment in the colony. People who had more than one occupation were common in rural England, however, and many Petworth immigrants proved ready to work at either a trade or farming in Upper Canada as opportunity offered.[25]

Petworth emigrants in 1832 were "agricultural labourers" (by far the largest proportion), blacksmiths, carpenters, wheelwrights, shipwrights, tailors, shoemakers etc.[26] In 1833, after first setting aside the "greater part" who were agricultural labourers, Sockett published another sampling of the proportional representation of certain trades for (male) emigrants aged fourteen and over on the ships that sailed in 1832 and 1833. From the building trades, there were thirteen bricklayers and three brickmakers, seven carpenters, and nine sawyers. Apart from eight shoemakers and six gardeners, there were only one or two individuals to represent each of the other occupations listed.[27] In addition to people with skills obviously useful in a new country, Sockett included on this list a landscape painter, a printer, and a wool-stapler (the person who sorted and graded wool).

A newspaper account of the Dorking emigrants sent from Surrey in 1832 characterized them as ranging in background from the small copyholder (a system of land tenure derived from manorial days) and the shopkeeper down to the labourer and the pauper.[28] Mention of the small copyholder introduces a different kind of rural experience than was to be had working for Egremont or his tenant farmers on the outskirts of Petworth. In his detailed study of Lodsworth, a thin strip parish in Sussex stretching northward from Petworth into the Weald, Michael Reed explored the lives of people who lived in this region of hills and heavy clay. Reed found that small family farms were still common in this part of the world, years after consolidation had become the norm for much of English agriculture.

Pressures on these farms help to explain the considerable emigration from this area of England in the 1830s. Many families in Lodsworth maintained a way of life based on small parcels of land owned or rented by the farmer. These farmers might not hire at all if they had children of an age to help, or they might hire one man, perhaps a relative. Another class of smallholder Reed identified in Lodsworth farmed for subsistence as a secondary interest to a trade or other occupation – perhaps the small shop of the newspaper article. In this community, people with little ready cash bartered goods and labour among themselves and proved themselves very resourceful in their use of credit.[29] James Rapson, a Petworth emigrant of 1832 from Lodsworth, settled at first near Guelph and then in Waterloo Township, surrounded on both occasions by relatives or friends who supported one another by dividing their attention between farming and working in other ways off their own property as opportunity allowed. Such skills were never touted by middle-class writers who recommended the Canadas to the industrious labouring man, but their presence helps to explain why some British labourers adapted more readily than others to conditions in rural Upper Canada.

A Sussex newspaper of 1834 described the Petworth emigrants of that year as the sons of farmers, mechanics, and agricultural labourers, a description that brings us back to the agricultural roots of the Petworth emigrations.[30] Sockett believed that the announcement that Brydone would superintend the *British Tar* had tipped the scale for several respectable families who had been wavering in their desire to emigrate.[31] In 1835 another newspaper identified a number of occupations apart from the main one of agricultural labourer among emigrants on the *Burrell*. Among ninety-three males over fourteen years of age, there were three bricklayers, three shoemakers, and one each of farmer, blacksmith, wheelwright, gardener, watchmaker, and butcher.[32] A final listing for the *Diana* in 1837 distinguished married men from single. With the exception of a farmer with nine children and a farrier with seven, the married men were agricultural labourers and all had a good reference. The occupations of single men were more varied and included a sailor and a "working jeweller" as well as agricultural labourers and shoemakers.[33]

Sockett did not often deal in large numbers, but he did make one attempt to tabulate his committee's results in 1836, charting the numbers of men, women, and children sent from different parishes.[34] Sockett's original table covering parishes that sent emigrants between 1832 and 1836 is both reproduced in Table 3.1 and included in our illustrations.[35] True to the orientation of his scheme, Sockett worked with the parish as his primary unit of organization in selecting and sending emigrants. For each parish named, he listed the number of emigrants sent in any particular year under the four headings of males and females above and below the age of fourteen. A fifth column gave the total number sent by that parish. He undoubtedly chose fourteen as the age to define the end of childhood because children under that age paid a half passage. Sockett himself also included infants under the age of one in his totals. As they travelled free of charge, we cannot be sure that they were always included in other counts of Petworth emigrants.

Sockett prepared his table to set the record straight at the office of the poor law commissioners, and he also sent a copy to the Colonial Office. He had particular points to make. He emphasized the importance of Egremont's contributions to the scheme by marking parishes in which Egremont had contributed all or part of the emigrants' passage. Although not a complete listing of every parish participating in his scheme, his chart was extensive enough to demonstrate that the Petworth committee had drawn together emigrants from a large number of parishes covering a wide geographic area that extended into several counties. Only the parish of Petworth had sent emi-

Table 3.1
Emigrants Sent Out to Upper Canada by the Petworth Emigration Committee, 1832–1836, Prepared by Thomas Sockett

Places From Which They Came	1832 Adults M	1832 Adults F	1832 Under 14 M	1832 Under 14 F	1832 Total	1833 Adults M	1833 Adults F	1833 Under 14 M	1833 Under 14 F	1833 Total	1834 Adults M	1834 Adults F	1834 Under 14 M	1834 Under 14 F	1834 Total	1835 Adults M	1835 Adults F	1835 Under 14 M	1835 Under 14 F	1835 Total	1836 Adults M	1836 Adults F	1836 Under 14 M	1836 Under 14 F	1836 Total
Petworth, West Sussex	25	9	8	7	49	11	5	5	3	24	4	:	:	:	4	5	4	4	1	14	9	3	2	2	16
Tillington, West Sussex	4	6	2	4	16	1	2	:	:	3	:	:	:	:	-	-	-	-	-	-	10	15	14	11	50
Northchapel, West Sussex	6	5	6	8	25	:	:	:	:	-	:	:	:	:	-	-	-	-	-	-	1	1	1	2	5
Egdean, West Sussex	:	:	:	:	-	:	:	:	:	-	1	:	:	:	1	-	-	-	-	-	-	-	-	-	-
Duncton, West Sussex	:	:	:	:	-	2	:	:	:	2	:	:	:	:	-	2	-	-	-	2	1	1	3	-	5
Lavington, West Sussex	:	:	:	:	-	:	:	:	:	-	:	:	:	:	-	-	-	-	-	-	1	-	-	-	1
Graffham, West Sussex	:	:	:	:	-	:	:	:	:	-	:	:	:	:	-	-	-	-	-	-	1	1	2	2	6
Sutton, West Sussex	5	2	3	3	13	1	1	:	:	2	:	:	:	:	-	-	-	-	-	-	-	-	-	-	-
Bignor, West Sussex	4	2	7	3	16	:	:	:	:	-	:	:	:	:	-	-	-	-	-	-	-	-	-	-	-
Coates, West Sussex	2	3	2	2	9	:	:	:	:	-	:	:	:	:	-	-	-	-	-	-	-	-	-	-	-
Fittleworth, West Sussex	2	:	1	:	3	2	1	:	:	3	3	:	1	:	4	-	-	1	1	2	1	1	3	1	6
Barlavington, West Sussex	:	:	:	:	-	1	:	:	:	1	:	:	:	:	-	1	1	-	-	2	3	2	2	1	8
Bury, West Sussex	:	:	1	:	1	:	:	:	:	-	:	:	:	:	-	-	-	-	-	-	-	-	-	-	-
West Grinstead, West Sussex	:	:	:	:	-	:	:	:	:	-	2	:	:	:	2	2	2	5	2	11	-	-	-	-	-
Shipley, West Sussex	4	1	1	2	8	1	1	4	:	6	:	:	:	:	-	9	7	4	7	27	-	-	-	-	-
Billingshurst, West Sussex	:	:	:	:	-	:	:	:	:	-	4	2	3	1	10	-	-	-	-	-	8	4	5	2	19
Wisborough Green, West Sussex	3	:	:	:	3	:	:	:	:	-	:	:	:	:	-	-	-	-	-	-	-	-	-	-	-
Kirdford, West Sussex	18	12	13	15	58	7	3	1	3	14	:	:	:	:	-	6	-	-	-	6	6	5	8	3	22
Lurgashall, West Sussex	21	14	22	18	75	:	:	:	:	-	:	:	:	:	-	-	-	-	-	-	-	-	-	-	-
Lodsworth, West Sussex	1	2	3	3	9	2	1	1	:	4	:	:	:	:	-	3	1	-	-	4	-	-	-	-	-
Linchmere & Frensham, West Sussex	2	1	:	:	3	:	:	:	:	-	:	:	:	:	-	-	-	-	-	-	-	-	-	-	-
Farnhurst & Steep, West Sussex	5	3	4	6	18	6	4	6	7	23	:	:	:	:	-	1	1	2	4	8	-	-	-	-	-
Ambersham, West Sussex	:	:	:	:	-	1	:	:	:	1	:	:	:	:	-	-	-	-	-	-	-	-	-	-	-
Easebourne, West Sussex	:	:	:	:	-	:	:	:	:	-	:	:	:	:	-	-	-	-	-	-	2	1	2	2	7
Cocking, West Sussex	:	:	:	:	-	:	:	:	:	-	:	:	:	:	-	-	-	-	-	-	4	1	3	2	10

Table 3.1 (continued)

Places From Which They Came	1832 Adults M	1832 Adults F	1832 Under 14 M	1832 Under 14 F	1832 Total	1833 Adults M	1833 Adults F	1833 Under 14 M	1833 Under 14 F	1833 Total	1834 Adults M	1834 Adults F	1834 Under 14 M	1834 Under 14 F	1834 Total	1835 Adults M	1835 Adults F	1835 Under 14 M	1835 Under 14 F	1835 Total	1836 Adults M	1836 Adults F	1836 Under 14 M	1836 Under 14 F	1836 Total
Bepton, West Sussex	:	:	:	:	—	:	:	:	:	—	:	:	:	:	—	2	2	4	5	13	:	:	:	:	—
Pulborough, West Sussex	2	2	5	1	10	:	:	:	:	—	1	1	2	1	5	—	—	—	—	—	:	:	:	:	—
Greetham, West Sussex	:	:	:	:	—	:	:	1	:	1	:	:	:	:	—	—	—	—	—	—	:	:	:	:	—
Sullington, West Sussex	2	2	3	5	12	:	:	:	:	—	:	:	:	:	—	1	1	4	2	8	:	:	:	:	—
Storrington, West Sussex	:	:	:	:	—	:	:	:	:	—	:	:	:	:	—	1	—	—	—	1	:	:	:	:	—
Chiltington, West Sussex	:	:	:	:	—	:	:	:	:	—	:	:	:	:	—	1	1	—	—	2	:	:	:	:	—
Thakeham, West Sussex	2	2	2	1	7	:	:	:	:	—	:	:	:	:	—	1	1	—	—	2	:	:	:	:	—
Wiston & Washington, West Sussex	:	:	:	:	—	:	:	:	:	—	4	:	:	:	4	2	1	—	3	8	:	:	:	:	—
Rackham, West Sussex	:	:	:	:	—	:	:	:	:	—	:	:	:	:	—	2	1	5	2	8	:	:	:	:	8
Burpham, West Sussex	:	:	:	:	—	:	:	:	:	—	:	:	:	:	—	1	3	2	4	10	1	2	1	4	8
Clapham, West Sussex	:	:	:	:	—	:	:	:	:	—	:	:	:	:	—	1	—	—	—	1	1	—	—	:	1
Findon, West Sussex	:	:	:	:	—	:	:	:	:	—	:	:	:	:	—	—	—	—	—	—	11	9	11	7	38
Goring, West Sussex	:	:	:	:	—	:	:	:	:	—	:	:	:	:	—	7	2	2	5	16	12	6	5	4	27
Heene, West Sussex	:	:	:	:	—	:	:	:	:	—	:	:	:	:	—	2	2	2	4	10	:	:	:	:	—
Tarring, West Sussex	:	:	:	:	—	:	:	:	:	—	:	:	:	:	—	—	1	—	—	—	1	1	:	:	2
Angmering, West Sussex	3	1	:	:	4	:	:	:	:	—	:	:	:	:	—	—	—	—	—	—	:	:	:	:	—
Arundel, West Sussex	:	:	:	:	—	:	:	:	:	—	:	:	:	:	—	1	—	—	—	1	1	—	—	:	1
Climping, West Sussex	:	:	:	:	—	:	:	:	:	—	:	:	:	:	—	2	6	3	6	17	:	:	:	:	—
Yapton, West Sussex	:	:	:	:	—	:	:	:	:	—	:	:	:	:	—	6	4	1	1	12	:	:	:	:	—
Felpham & Merston, West Sussex	4	4	6	6	20	3	2	2	1	8	:	:	:	:	—	20	7	8	9	44	:	:	:	:	—
Walberton, West Sussex	13	4	3	1	21	1	:	:	:	1	:	:	:	:	—	6	2	2	1	11	11	1	:	:	12
Oving, West Sussex	:	:	:	:	—	1	1	:	:	2	:	:	:	:	—	—	—	—	—	—	:	:	:	:	—
Boxgrove, West Sussex	:	:	:	:	—	1	1	1	:	3	:	:	:	:	—	—	—	—	—	—	:	:	:	:	—
Chichester, West Sussex	:	:	:	:	—	5	1	2	1	9	:	:	:	:	—	—	—	—	—	—	1	—	—	:	1
Pagham, West Sussex	1	1	1	1	4	:	:	:	:	—	:	:	:	:	—	—	—	—	—	—	:	:	:	:	1
Stoughton, West Sussex	1	1	2	1	5	:	:	:	:	—	:	:	:	:	—	—	—	—	—	—	:	:	:	:	—
Seaford, East Sussex	:	:	:	:	—	:	:	:	:	—	:	:	:	:	—	1	—	—	—	1	:	:	:	:	—

This page reproduces a wide tabular statement (rotated on the page) listing places of origin against a repeating set of count columns (the pattern of four counts followed by a total is consistent throughout, e.g. *Men / Women / Boys / Girls / Total*). The clearly legible parish list and figures are set out below.

Brighton and Lewes, &c., East Sussex	26	12	11	8	57		3
Mrs. Jones and Family	:	1	7	:	8		—
Stoke (*Guildford*), Surrey	8	5	2	6	21		—
Haslemere, Surrey	3	2	2	2	9		—
Chiddingfold, Surrey	8	4	:	:	12		—
Hascomb & Witley, Surrey	3	1	:	:	4		—
Dunsfold & Ockley, Surrey	—	7	:	:	7		7
Alfold, Surrey	4	:	:	:	4		—
Southampton, Surrey	:	:	:	:	—		—
Isle of Wight, Hampshire	16	1	1	:	16		—
Portsmouth, Hampshire	:	:	:	:	—		1
Buriton, Hampshire	:	:	:	:	—		—
Itchingstoke & Northington, Hampshire	:	:	:	:	—		—
Ivington, Hereford	8	1	1	:	10		—
Bath, Somerset	3	1	1	:	5		—
Warminster, Wiltshire	:	:	:	:	—		1
Hindon, East Knowle & Cricklade, Wiltshire	25	8	11	7	51		—
Kempsford, Gloustershire	:	:	:	:	—		2
London	2	1	1	2	6		3
Ongar, Essex	:	:	:	:	—		—
Attleboro', Norfolk	:	:	:	:	—		2
Royston, Cambridgeshire	6	5	8	5	24		1
Scotland	:	:	:	:	—		—
Single Passages (i.e., persons from various places)	11	:	:	:	11		—
Dorking, Surrey, & neighbourhood*	36	20	24	22	102		—
Wisborough Green & some parishes in Hants	:	:	:	:	164		—
TOTAL					769	200	264

Grand-total figures shown along the foot of the several columns: 769, 200, 135, 200, 252, 264.

NOTE: Original spelling of parish names has been retained. County names have been added; see illustration of original.

*These went in the same ship with those sent by the committee, under the charge of the same medical man, but of a separate superintendent, who attended them.

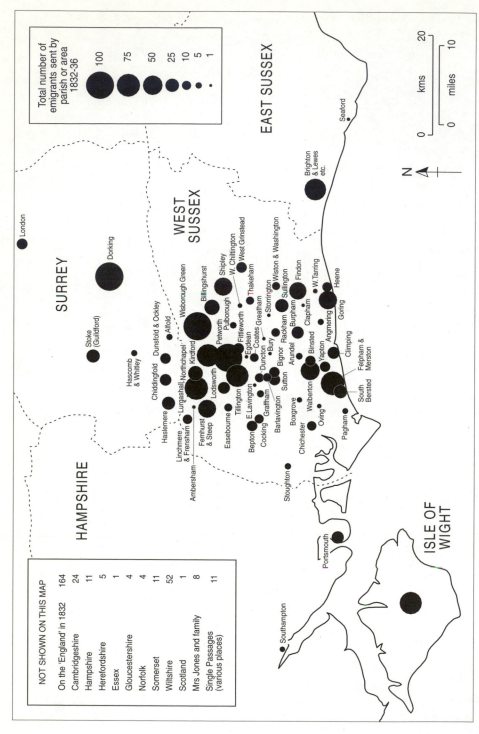

NOT SHOWN ON THIS MAP

On the 'England' in 1832	164
Cambridgeshire	24
Hampshire	11
Herefordshire	5
Essex	1
Gloucestershire	4
Norfolk	4
Somerset	11
Wiltshire	52
Scotland	1
Mrs Jones and family	8
Single Passages (various places)	11

Total number of emigrants sent by parish or area 1832-36

100
75
50
25
10
5
1

SURREY

HAMPSHIRE

WEST SUSSEX

EAST SUSSEX

ISLE OF WIGHT

London

Dorking

Stoke (Guildford)

Hascomb & Whitley

Dunsfold & Ockley

Altold

Wisborough Green

Chiddingfold

Haslemere

Linchmere & Frensham

Ambersham

Fernhurst & Steep

Lurgashall Northchapel

Kirdford

Lodsworth

Petworth

Pulborough

Fittleworth

Easebourne

Tillington

Bepton

Cocking

E.Lavington

Graffham

Barlavington

Duncton

Sutton

Bignor

Bury

Coates Greatham

Egdean

Shipley

W. Chiltington

West Grinstead

Billingshurst

Thakeham

Storrington

Wiston & Washington

Sullington

Findon

W.Tarring

Heene

Goring

Angmering

Climping

Felpham & Merston

South Bersted

Yapton

Binsted

Walberton

Clapham

Burpham

Rackham

Arundel

Boxgrove

Oving

Chichester

Stoughton

Pagham

Portsmouth

Southampton

Brighton & Lewes etc.

Seaford

N

kms

0   20

miles

0   10

5 *Number of emigrants sent by the Petworth Emigration Committee, 1832–1836, as recorded by Thomas Sockett*

grants every year, but an impressive number had sent emigrants more than once. Sockett's total of over 1,600 emigrants was also an impressive figure.

As his purpose was to convey a broad picture of the accomplishments of his committee, Sockett satisfied himself with a degree of accuracy that served this end. In general, it is safe to assume that his information was most accurate in parishes where the committee was most involved and that his accuracy decreased with the distance of the sending parish from his headquarters in Petworth. When it came to noting the participation of parishes in distant Wiltshire, Sockett did not even check the spelling of Chicklade and East Knoyle, which he entered incorrectly.

Table 3.2
Places Sending Emigrants in 1832, Recorded by Sockett in 1833

Place	Males	Females	Total
Sussex			
Arundel	2	2	2
Binsted	10	6	16
Bersted	14	11	25
Wisboro' Green	35	35	70
Hants			
Odiham	7		7
Portsmouth	10	7	17
Kent	12	13	25
TOTAL	90	74	164

SOURCE: *Emigration: Letters* (1833), xii.
NOTE: Although these places are omitted from Sockett's 1836 chart (see Table 3.1), the number of emigrants may be accounted for by the 164 he added for passengers on the *England* in 1832.

Despite its orderly appearance, Sockett's table cannot be reconciled totally with figures and detail he himself published in 1833.[36] Table 3.2 records parishes, and the numbers from those parishes, identified by Sockett in 1833 but not mentioned separately on his 1836 chart. Only a few parishes, and a few emigrants, are affected because Sockett handled parishes sending fewer than five people differently in his two sources. A larger number of parishes were omitted in 1836 because he sometimes grouped people from several parishes under a single name. Emigrants on the *England* in 1832 are from "Wisborough Green and some Parishes in Hants [parishes in Hants that he could have listed from his own publication]." Other 1832 emigrants from a number of Surrey parishes outside Dorking are subsumed under "Dorking and neighbourhood." Emigrants sent from East Sussex by the Brighton and Lewes emigration committees in 1834 are brought together under the names of those two places, and Sockett did the same for the Isle of Wight, where different parishes contributed to emigration even if they sent people already lodged in the union workhouse at Newport. Finally, at the end of his chart, Sockett grouped eleven single passages unhelpfully as "from various places." In Part Two, we have been able to sup-

Table 3.3
Total Number of Emigrants Arriving at Port of Quebec and Montreal, 1832-1837, Compared with Petworth Emigrants, Number and Percentage

| | Quebec and Montreal arrivals | | | | | | |
| | Males 14 & over | | Females 14 & over | | Children under 14 | | Total |
	No.	%	No.	%	No.	%	
1832	n.a.		n.a.		n.a.		51,746
1833	9,204	43	6,444	30	5,918	27	21,566
1834	13,565	44	9,685	31	7,681	25	30,935
1835	5,597	45	3,866	31	3,064	24	12,527
1836	14,447	52	7,833	28	5,448	20	27,728
1837	11,740	54	6,079	28	4,082	19	21,901

| | Petworth emigrants | | | | | | |
| | Males 14 & over | | Females 14 & over | | Children under 14 | | Total |
	No.	%	No.	%	No.	%	
1832	231	39	117	20	246	41	594
							164*
1833	98	49	37	18	67	33	202
1834	81	60	20	15	34	25	135
1835	93	37	53	21	106	42	252
1836	99	38	57	22	108	41	264
1837	62	33	28	15	96	52	191

SOURCE: Figures for Quebec arrivals in 1833 are from the report of emigration agent A.C. Buchanan in PRO, CO 384/35, f.123v, and those from 1832 and 1834 on are published in Appendix No. 1 to Report on Emigration in the Sessional Papers. Buchanan's figures can vary. Petworth figures for 1832 to 1836 are from PRO, CO 384/41, f. 362; those for 1837 are from WSRO, PHA 140.
* The only breakdown for the 164 people who travelled in the England in 1832 is found in Emigration: Letters (1833), which gives 90 males and 74 females. The sex of 5 children over 14 travelling in 1837 could not be determined; these children are not included in the figures under males and females but are included in the total.

ply some of the parish names omitted by these shortcuts, though most emigrants from the Isle of Wight appear under that designation.

Sockett's count of children throws some light on family composition and can be compared with similar statistics kept by Buchanan, the emigration agent at Quebec, of all men, women, and children recorded arriving in Quebec and Montreal (see Table 3.3). The comparison shows a higher percentage of travellers under age fourteen with the Petworth committee in every year but 1834. The lower percentage of females over fourteen years of age recorded by Sockett is not by any means definitive, but it points towards larger families.

In another set of figures, this time drawn from 1831 ships' lists of British emigrants arriving without assistance at United States ports, Charlotte Erickson remarks that,

Figure 3.2
Number of Identified Male and Female Emigrants, 1832–1837, by Age Cohorts, Numbers

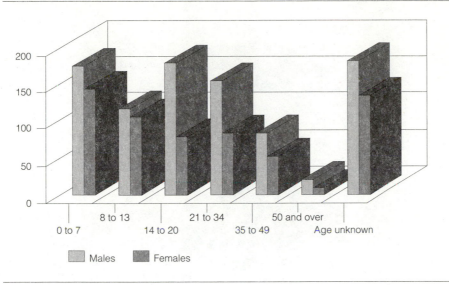

SOURCE: Project files, list of emigrants.

NOTE: Just under 1,500 emigrants have been identified and listed in Part Two. We know the ages of all but 20 per cent of the males and 22 per cent of the females.

as we found for Petworth emigrants, this class of English emigrants also travelled with more children than their Irish contempories. In her sample, a very high 77 per cent of English and Welsh emigrants travelled with other members of their family, and more of them travelled as part of a nuclear family than did emigrants from Ireland.[37]

Other contemporary sources record the additional information that many Petworth emigrants who left as children were so young as to be totally dependent. As well as the influence of Egremont's name, the presence of an unusual number of young children may help to explain why emigration agents in Upper Canada singled out large families among Petworth emigrants and were anxious to see them settled and housed with all possible despatch. In 1832, when the *Portsmouth Herald* distinguished two age groups among the children, 173 adults on the *Lord Melville* travelled with 91 children under seven and 45 between the ages of seven and fourteen. On the *Eveline*, there were 166 adults, 60 children under seven, and 24 between seven and fourteen.[38] Although Sockett's chart did not include figures for 1837, a separate source shows that a very high proportion of the children on the *Diana* were eligible for a half passage and thus were under fourteen.[39] Parishes had an obvious interest in sending off children, who might grow up to be as poor as their parents, for half the price of sending an adult.[40]

An analysis of our reconstructed families leads to similar conclusions about the passengers on Petworth ships. Figure 3.2 is an analysis by age cohorts of some 1,500

Figure 3.3
Family Composition of Identified Petworth Emigrants, 1832–1837

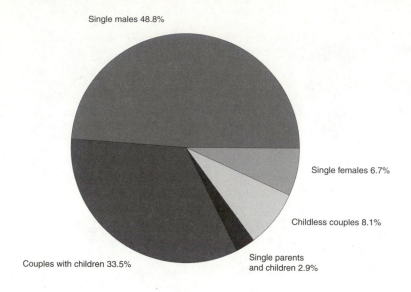

Single males 48.8%

Single females 6.7%

Childless couples 8.1%

Single parents
and children 2.9%

Couples with children 33.5%

SOURCE: Project files, list of emigrants.

NOTE: Just under 1,500 emigrants have been identified and listed in Part Two; of these, 203 family units (composed of parent or parents and children) emigrated in the years 1832–37. The average size of these families was 6. Two hundred and seventy single males emigrated and 37 single females. Forty-five childless couples emigrated.

emigrants whom we have identified and listed in Part Two. Bearing in mind that boys between fourteen and twenty were counted as adults, we note that even so the Petworth emigrants travelled with a lot of young men. Figure 3.3 shows the family composition. Two hundred and seventy single males emigrated and as a proportion they almost equal the other household groups. The next largest segment is composed of couples with children and single parents with children, together making up about 36 per cent. There were 203 of these family units and the average size of the families was six. We found just 37 single females (6.7 per cent). The fact that only 45 childless couples (8.1 per cent of the family units) emigrated reflects not only that children followed marriage quickly, if they did not precede it, but also that it was older couples with a number of children who were encouraged to emigrate. As can be seen on Figure 3.1, we found many children under seven.

If Petworth "heads of families" were married men, most travelled in families with children. The one clear impression that emerged from an attempt to equate family size with age was that the average family size grew steadily for heads of households between the ages of thirty and fifty. Our information on age is limited, perhaps too limited to say more. We have ages for 133 of the heads of families who travelled with children, but they are scattered unevenly through the six years of the emigrations and through different age groups within these years. Of thirty heads of households who were in their thirties or forties when they left England in 1832, nine were between thirty and thirty-four. This group emigrated with an average number of 2.2 children. The four who were between forty-five and forty-nine had nearly three times as many children with them, an average number of 6.3.

Although many of the "families" in the Petworth emigrations were in fact nuclear families (parents travelling with their children), others are better described as "household" groupings.[41] In a number of the sources we gathered to create the list in Part Two, the only surname name given, and often the only Christian name, is that of the head of the "family." Much of our work of family reconstruction has been devoted to identifying the other people in the group.

In listing the accompanying "family" or "household" members in Part Two, we chose to preserve the groupings as we found them on the assumption that their logic had meaning to the people concerned. The logic of shipboard families seems to be that of the records kept for parish relief. This "family" did not include children left behind or (usually married) adult children travelling in another unit, and it often enough included people who were not children of the family head. In this respect it probably reflected the "household" of a pauper applying for relief – the "family" included both his dependents and the people who might be expected to contribute to the household in which they lived.

The shipboard family was defined loosely in order to place as many emigrants as possible under a responsible head, and a number of people on Petworth ships travelled in extended family groups. As already noted, "heads of families" were almost always men. According to Sockett, just fourteen of the women on the Petworth ships of 1832 and 1833 travelled on their own without some connection to an emigrating family, and only one family was headed by a widow. Nephews, nieces, and sisters-in-law were included. Second marriages were common. Half-sisters and -brothers came along. Fathers might list their daughters' illegitimate children with their own. Occasionally, a person who was no relation was included in a family for purposes of travel.

Within the shipboard "family" units, the nuclear family had a cohesion over time not extended to everyone in the group. A test came when someone fell ill on the journey between Quebec and the emigrants' Upper Canadian destination. If either the marriage partner or young children fell ill, this nuclear family dropped out of the travelling party and stayed together. Adult brothers and sisters left their siblings' families behind and travelled on. They might leave a young person to assist, but the second family pressed on. If the person to fall ill was a temporary addition to the household for purposes of emigration, he or she might be left behind alone in the care of a third party.

In addition to being households or domestic units of considerable flexibility, Petworth families had many interconnections through both male and female relatives. Where we can, we have indicated examples in Part Two. Sockett considered Brydone a relative as well as a friend because Sockett's first wife was a half-sister of Brydone's wife. Similarly tenuous relationships among his emigrants are almost impossible to discover unless they are revealed in correspondence, but they do emerge often enough to indicate many layers of connection between the people who sailed on these ships.

At the same time as we stress interconnection, we need to insert a warning about the small name pool in Sussex and the number of surnames on Petworth ships that were common in Sussex and sometimes also in Upper Canada. We have Phillipses and Coopers who were father and son or brothers and Phillipses and Coopers who are no apparent relation.

Participants in the Petworth emigrations largely fall into the same age groups as the men who earlier took part in the Swing disturbances. Among those sent to trial for Swing disturbances, Hobsbawm and Rudé picked out "young men" and "men of early-middle years."[42] The men on Petworth ships were for the most part workers who had guarded their "character" in a tight labour market with outward deference or, as Sockett insisted, had worked with good humour and good will to make the best of difficult lives. No individual on a Petworth ship could have participated in the Swing disturbances so openly as to be named and prosecuted, but men at these same two stages in their lives were well represented.

The single young men among those convicted for riots, strikes, and other acts of open defiance, and perhaps sent to the penal colonies in Australia, had their counterparts on Petworth ships. The readiness of young men who were unemployed and single to leave for Canada is no surprise, nor is the willingness of sponsors to send them from areas such as Dorking in 1832 or the Isle of Wight in 1833 and 1837, where unemployment was an issue of public order.

The court trials for Swing offences of middle-aged fathers with large families is more of a surprise. And 1830–31 was not their only moment of desperate defiance. In his analysis of the participants in William Courtenay's abortive uprising in Bosenden Wood in Kent in 1838, Barry Reay finds middle-aged men in their thirties and forties over-represented in comparison with men of this age in the total populations of their parishes. He believes that these men, and the wives who encouraged their actions, were victims of a poverty cycle associated with numerous children. Most of the men in his study group were employed in 1838, and more than half of them had received parish aid in the 1820s and the 1830s.[43]

As farm labourers or as rural craftsmen, workers found themselves worst off (and most dependent on the poor rate) as young people just getting established or as parents with several young children. As these children grew up, they in turn experienced difficulty in entering the workforce. Sockett was typical of his time and place in believing that discriminatory employment and relief policies pushed single labourers into early and improvident marriages. These traditions died hard. By 1838, Sockett might write that "a job of work is worth whatever it is worth, no matter who performs it,"[44] but many farmers held to old ways. They hired single men last, paid them less than the married men, and laid them off first. Our project files show many young men who had help from the parish the winter before they set sail.

Single farm labourers, often young boys, no longer lived as a matter of course in the farmer's house until they married. With the exception of the Weald, where farms were small and the custom of farm servants living-in was more often continued, single men in the south and east were usually hired on a temporary basis as casual labourers.[45] In a report of 1842, the poor law commissioners dealt briskly with the nostalgia of people bemoaning the trend away from live-in farm servants and the supervision implied by that status:"whatever real ground there may be to regret the change, it appears to be one generally preferred by both parties, and there appears to be no reason to expect that the ancient system will be revived."[46]

THOMAS SOCKETT AND RURAL POVERTY

From a humanitarian point of view, the poverty that most concerned Sockett was that of the middle-aged heads of families, poverty that of course was also that of women and children. When Sockett tried to draw Parliament's attention to the plight of labouring families, he took his place in a well-established tradition. In 1796 David Davies, another rural clergyman, had published the *Case of the Labourers in Husbandry*, which drew on his personal experience in his small parish in Berkshire to demonstrate that a hard-working and frugal labouring family could not support more than two children on the maximum wages of a single breadwinner. Davies made the connection with the sermon tradition explicit, using "the labourer is worthy of his hire" (Luke 10:7) as the text of his sermon to legislators.[47] A generation later, Sockett, who spoke in this regard of his parochial duties as a clergyman, brought a similar message to the Select Committee on the Poor Law Amendment Act of 1837.

In March 1837, Sockett travelled to London with several members of the Petworth vestry to protest the impact of sudden changes in poor relief on families with young children. *The Times* had criticized the Royal Commission on the Poor Laws for not questioning poor men directly.[48] At the hearings of the Select Committee on the Poor Law Amendment Act, Sockett was asked to bring to the committee a "steady intelligent working man" from Petworth, a long-time resident "whose evidence if given here would be satisfactory to the working community in the neighbourhood."[49] Sockett came back with four such men. As all four of them had large families of from six to ten children, they represented what was probably the lowest standard of living among potential Petworth emigrants. Contemporaries recognized their poverty by such marks as the absence of a pig kept by all cottagers able to afford one. But Sockett's four witnesses described working conditions common to the district, and other families who embarked on Petworth ships would have recognized their struggles to feed, warm, and clothe their children.[50] The evidence given by Sockett's witnesses is summarized in Table 3.4. Three of them were from Kirdford and one was from Petworth. All were asked similar questions about their family members and their work, income, assistance, and hours of work.

James Slements, age forty-seven, lived about a mile outside Petworth and was the one who belonged to that parish. He worked for Egremont and described himself as a common labourer who did all kinds of work. Slements mentioned spending pennies a week on soap, candles, sugar, tea, and butter. He begged gruel from a gentle-

Table 3.4
Summary of Evidence on Work and Wages Given before Select Committee on the
Poor Law Amendment Act, 1837

	Witness	
	James Slements	*Henry Sopp*
	age 37 6 children, 5 at home	age 47 7 children, 4 at home
Parish	Petworth	Kirdford
Employer	Earl of Egremont	parish, surveyor of roads previously Mr Eade, farmer previously, a soldier
Occupation	common labourer (all kinds of work) constant: full time; "wet or dry"	pauper, roads and quarry
Wages (weekly)	10s. standing, extra 1s. 6d. tied to price of corn	parish: 9s. roads parish: 10s. quarry Eade: 10s. (no beer)
Assistance (old poor law)	money, then 2 gals flour weekly; about 1 soverign towards annual rent	3 gals flour weekly; relief money for rent from birth of 3rd child until 4 years before

Additional income
  Harvest
  Task work
	about £3
	barking (not every year)[a], not allowed haying
	or other task work when he is needed
		about £3
		None while a parish pauper

Hours of work	12 – 1 hr for dinner, 2 half hr breaks	10 – 7–5, 1 hr for dinner
	Edward Pullen	*George Ayling*
	age 43 10 children, 6 at home	age 45 8 children, 6 at home
Parish	Kirdford	Kirdford
Employer	Earl of Egremont	farmer
Occupation	labourer (in the copse & cutting wood); day work	farm labourer; probably day work
Wages (weekly)	10s. standing, extra 1s. 6d.	10s. (no beer); tied to price of corn
Assistance (old poor law)	4s. to 5s. a week (1s. 4d. a week for over 2 children; elsewhere 20d.)	3 gals flour (worth 3s.) Formerly got flour for 5 children

Additional income
  Harvest
  Task work
	about £3
	barking
	hay making
	reaping
	mowing
		about £3
		hedging
		threshing
		barking
		mowing

Hours of work	not given	10 – some overtime

SOURCE: BPP 1837 (131), XVII, pt 1, First Report of the Select Committee on the Poor Law Amendment Act.
[a] *barking:* removing bark from felled trees or from the poles cut out of coppiced woods

man when his family had influenza. Edward Pullen, age forty-three, also worked for Egremont, but at day work, without the certainty of a permanent place. Except during the harvest, Pullen worked for most of the year in coppices and woodlands. Pullen believed that he could have worked "a great deal better" with more to eat. George Ayling, forty-five, who lived about a mile out in the country and worked as a farmer's labourer, agreed with a leading question suggesting that the same would be true of "pretty nearly all the labourers in your part of the country." When he went to London as a witness, Henry Sopp, a forty-seven-year-old ex-soldier, had been working for the parish of Kirdford for eight weeks, after having been laid off by a Kirdford farmer. After two of his children were taken into the workhouse, the rest of the family had had to survive on the meagre parish pay of nine shillings and six pence a week. Sopp said that they lived on bread while on the parish pay list. A friend had given them six pence to buy candles and milk for their baby.[51]

The committee explored with Sockett's witnesses the possibility of earnings beyond their regular wage. During harvest, the men estimated that they earned about an extra three pounds over their regular wage. At other times of the year, task work, which as the name implied was paid by the piece rather than by the day or week, paid less well in 1837 than it had within the memories of these men. As a condition of his regular work, Slements was not given task work and was forbidden to take on extra work except at harvest, when extra hours were rewarded. Other piecework might not be as profitable as it seemed, as labourers were expected to provide and maintain their own tools even if they were uncertain of being hired again another year.

All four men were in debt, and three of the four were behind on the rent. Whether they lived in a single or double cottage, or in a tenement shared with five other families, all four families lived in four small rooms, two up, two down, but they were anxious to stay where they had a garden and could grow potatoes and cabbage sufficient for perhaps four to five months of the year.[52] Talking of the past, Sockett's four labouring witnesses described a traditional pattern of annual outlay. They had paid the rent and bought items such as clothing and fuel after the harvest or whenever extra earnings offered an opportunity. In 1837, they still purchased shoes once a year, but their families wore clothes bought before the changes in the poor law. A year later, Sockett heard reports of labouring families taking down the checked curtains from bed or window to make clothing for their children.[53] One farmer witness described labourers' clothing as "bad" and spoke of "a miserable little pinched-up piece of fire" as further evidence of privation and distress."[54]

Edward Butt, the relieving officer for Petwork and Kirdford, left the impression that it was the women who came to him to collect the child allowance. Presumably they were the ones able to get away in the daytime. Historian Robert Allen claims that, as English agriculture evolved towards larger farms, the most dramatic savings in labour were made by reducing the use of women and children. He writes that women employed on farms almost always had a male relative at work on that farm, and he suspects that boys and girls who grew up on farms were much more likely to be working there than the children of landless labourers.[55] Another historian, Hugh

Cunningham, in summarizing the answers to the rural questions circulated in 1832 by the Royal Commission on the Poor Laws, concluded that there was little work available for children up to the age of fourteen – this despite a universal belief in the agricultural districts that work was the proper occupation for children.[56]

Witnesses from the Petworth Union, Sockett himself, William Stapley from the Sutton Union, and Sockett's four labourers all confirmed the lack of paid work for women and children.[57] Such opportunities as existed were very poorly paid: Sockett thought a woman would be fortunate to take in washing, and Ayling's wife earned less than six pence a week making straw hats. In an area of limited grassland, women competed with boys for stone-picking work and boys, described by Stapley as little twopenny boys whom he mixed in with older six- and eight-penny boys, were to be had in numbers for the asking. Most married women could only make a direct contribution to the family income by gleaning with their children in the wheat fields during the harvest.[58]

The select committee heard of equally bleak prospects for child workers. Young boys who had traditionally earned pennies in the fields scaring crows away from the grain had been displaced by older boys.[59] Boys might be taken into service as young as twelve, as opposed to fourteen for girls, but at this age, they worked for board and depended on their parents for clothes. A girl of eleven was taken into service only as an act of charity; the presence at home of a girl fourteen or more had to be explained by her mother's need for help around the time of a birth. Although boys of sixteen were not mentioned in this evidence, many parishes had begun to list boys of this age on the parish pay lists.

If Sockett had found a way, the single men on Petworth ships would have been more evenly matched by single women. Labourers' daughters were expected to find work in service until they married, and Sockett's concern was that there was an over-supply of such young women in the Petworth area. If they could find work, girls employed as house servants on a farm rarely earned anything beyond their board until they were eighteen or nineteen, and the top wage in this position was five pounds per annum.[60] Reports from Upper Canada promised that girls would find work without difficulty. In 1832, Sockett offered a protected environment on Petworth ships so as to encourage "respectable unmarried Females, who may wish to join any Relations or Friends already settled in Upper Canada."[61] In 1834, he wrote to Richmond suggesting a bounty on female emigration to Canada on a similar plan to the Australian, and in 1835 he proposed to Hay at the Colonial Office that the cost might be shared between the government and Egremont.[62] After both approaches failed, he arranged through Egremont in 1835 to offer reduced fares to "a few single women, not belonging to families now emigrating, but who may wish to go to friends already settled in Canada."[63] If they took advantage of the offer, the presence of such women may be hidden because they travelled as part of an unrelated family (Frances Upton's mother brought his son's fiancée with her in 1835), but they cannot have been many.

A supervised emigration also offered a possibility of providing for orphaned and indigent children by apprenticing them in the colonies.[64] Petworth emigrants wrote home about farm apprentices being given substantial gifts in kind if they stayed to the ages of eighteen or nineteen. Petworth emigrant William Upton deeply regretted the fee his family paid superintendent William Penfold to take his brother Clifford to Upper Canada as his apprentice, having come to believe he could have found a carpenter at Toronto willing to pay Clifford a total of $300 by the end of his seven years. Henry Heasman was twenty when he apprenticed himself to a Woodstock blacksmith for four years in an agreement that provided him with his board and keep and a progressive annual payment as he gained experience.

Sockett apparently knew that such positive accounts only told one side of the story. He was quite definite when Robert Gouger contacted Brydone in 1835 about taking children for his Children's Friend Society. Sockett wrote to Brydone: "We are better without them at *any price*. If you are to make an answer, it may be, that we could not take them *under price* if we *had* room, but that we *have not*."[65]

As with labourers, apprentices came from different backgrounds and varied greatly in skill and potential. Sockett may have had bad reports of the group of perhaps sixteen unaccompanied boys sent from the Isle of Wight on the *England* in 1833. We have not been able to discover the fate of these boys, but their beginnings were not promising. There was a general opinion on the Isle of Wight that "the children brought up in the house of industry turn out ill,"[66] an opinion perhaps partially explained by a report of 1834 that exposed their cramped and unhealthy living conditions.[67] Ratepayers on the Isle of Wight paid fines rather than take boys from the House as apprentices, and their payments created a fund that was used in part to send the boys to be apprenticed in Upper Canada.[68]

On the other side of the ocean, two children who wrote memoirs of their childhood experiences as apprentices in Upper Canada remembered a hard reality. Charles Adsett (who seemed to have lost all contact with two younger sisters adopted into local families) had his father to look out for him. For Charles, the worst aspect of his apprenticeship was that he had no status as a person. As a child, he was "rented twice to parties who rented the tannery [where he was apprenticed] like any of the chattels so rented," and as an adult, he had no say in the disposition of a business he had been running for some time.[69] Esther Chantler was passed from one family to another within the Quaker community north of Toronto without any outside supervision or any recourse when the first family treated her and her younger brother harshly.[70] The difficulties of funding single women and of supervising unaccompanied children kept Sockett from expanding either of these categories of emigrant.

SELECTING PETWORTH EMIGRANTS

Nothing better identified the Petworth emigrations as a project of relief under the pre-1834 poor law than the manner of selecting emigrants by nomination from all the different sponsors and parish administrations involved. Sockett was willing to vouch for the character and habits of emigrants he described as from his neighbourhood or as known to him. He probably meant to include most of the parishes where Egremont paid all or a significant part of the passage money and where Egremont's interest gave him a degree of control. Beyond this sphere, Sockett had only the tenuous assurance that many of his sponsors had heard of the scheme through some network of acquaintance with those already involved. Selection was settled locally according to the way a particular parish might handle its poor. In 1834, the Earl of Chichester set up emigration committees at Lewes and Brighton using Sockett's model, and he sent his emigrants in a Petworth ship under the Petworth superintendent. Even with all these connections and signs of trust, he requested Richmond to forward on to Lieutenant-Governor Colborne of Upper Canada a particular list of "his" emigrants.[71]

Certain constraints applied in all parishes. The Petworth emigrants were first of all voluntary migrants. Anywhere in the British Isles, assisted emigrants assessed the information available to them and at some point made their own decision to go.[72] However grim the alternatives at home, Petworth emigrants did choose to join the scheme and sail for Upper Canada. People might be prevailed on to leave their homes for all the wrong reasons, but unless they were tried and sentenced to transportation, they could not legally be forced to emigrate from nineteenth-century England. The voluntary principle was stated prominently in the failed Emigration Bill and in the Poor Law Amendment Act.

In the Petworth area as elsewhere, stories circulated of people who toyed with the idea of emigration and then melted away as the date of departure approached. Even assisted emigrants whose passage had been fully paid changed their minds at the very last moment and left for home. There would be no roast beef dinner, speeches, or gifts of Bibles to welcome them back, but they could decide not to go. Indeed, if they sailed to the colonies and returned destitute to their home communities, they were not left to starve. Proposals to deny a settlement (the acknowledgment of belonging to a parish that opened the door to public assistance) to returning assisted emigrants came to nothing. Sockett opposed including this penalty in legislation because he believed it would make emigration unpopular among the poor without achieving its object.[73] Talk of treating a wasted passage as a debt owed by the person who returned seems to have foundered for the same reason that stood in the way of denying settlement to people too poor to pay.[74]

Sockett went about selecting emigrants in his own area with confidence. Twenty-odd years on the Petworth vestry had taught him a lot about predicting the outcomes of giving aid to applicants for parish relief. He was familiar with the forms of rural poverty and saw many distinctions of character and skill. Under Sockett's leadership, the Petworth vestry worked on a case-by-case basis, responding in a pragmatic way to each new problem as it arose. Vestry members favoured those seen as worthy, gave them help more readily, and included small extras in their assistance, but under the old poor law and the laws of settlement a wide spectrum of the able-bodied labouring community could lay claim to parish aid.

Writing privately, Sockett could be quite blunt about the people he sent to Upper Canada. He summed up his experience "of the early workings of emigration in Sussex" for George Wyndham after Wyndham succeeded Egremont at Petworth. The people who did best in Upper Canada were the "many [who] told me they had been long *thinking of going*, but had not before had a chance – and these were the *solid*, good emigrants: those who has [*sic*] sent home the *good accounts*." In addition, "a good deal of scum floated on the top, just at the very last."[75] In the interest of filling his ships, he dealt philosophically with people whom his experience had warned him to avoid.

When in 1832 Sockett first circulated among parish officers his "Information to Persons desirous of emigrating from this Neighbourhood to Upper Canada," his invitation to join the Petworth scheme carried the single condition that the people be of approved character. The stipulation "of approved character" would probably help weed out those whom he did not want rather than serve as a precise direction. A passing reference to two candidates rejected on grounds of character in 1832 gives no clue to the reason.[76] Such matters were no doubt dealt with quietly with a word in the right place.

Some poor law unions, although never the Petworth committee, recorded two lists of potential emigrants: one of first-class labourers fit for any work, and a second of those able to work but not capable of the most physically demanding jobs. Every parish had workers who were limited in what they could do by injury or poor health.[77] Sir Charles Burrell complained in 1832 that farmers had an obligation to employ the "able hands" who were crowding the parish lists and were thus "depriving less able hands of such Parochial employ as repair of Roads when no longer able to do the heavier and more active work upon the Lands."[78] Unfortunately, Burrell did not comment on this distinction with reference to the selection of Petworth emigrants from his parishes of Shipley and West Grinstead. Sockett, however, was prepared to consider mitigating factors in matters of health and strength. He was quite ready to accept a man with a club foot who had a trade as a shoemaker,[79] and he took a few old people who had children able to support them in Upper Canada.

Other transactions reflected Sockett's balancing act between concerns for the overall reputation of the venture and business priorities, which led him to accept groups of emigrants whose reputations he did not know or did not choose to investigate. In 1837, Sockett had secured a contract providing for the contingency that he might not take up a whole ship, but he did in the end make up his numbers from the Isle of Wight. As superintendent, Brydone judged the Isle of Wight people harshly, ranking almost all of them below the other emigrants in terms of suitability for employment. The emigrants on the *Diana* sent from mainland parishes included two "naughty youths"; otherwise all were "well-behaved," "very respectable," or "most respectable." Half the Isle of Wight families were "dissipated"; the other half got a grudging "respectable." Brydone judged another twenty of twenty-six single men and all three single women from the island "not recommendable."[80] Perhaps they had questioned the authority of a superintendent from a different jurisdiction. Whatever really happened on the *Diana*, the Isle of Wight emigrants did not blend smoothly with the Sussex emigrants of that year.

In Petworth, Sockett and members of his vestry worked on the assumption that between them they had first- or second-hand personal knowledge of all the paupers in the parish. They did not give even a few shillings for rent without considering the character, conduct, and earnings of each candidate, and as we have seen, they put great emphasis on character in choosing emigrants. They also made exceptions. An intriguing minute of 1832 records a request to Carter and Bonus asking that they exchange passages and take a man on one of their ships sailing from London. This man had been tried and acquitted of "an offence against Mr. Sockett," an "obvious reason" that he could not go with the Petworth party.[81] Troublemakers talked into assisted emigration, perhaps (like William Shepherd) to avoid prosecution at home, might still cause problems for the organizers of their emigration.

Amid righteous comment from his fellow emigrants, an unidentified Dorking emigrant was jailed in Toronto in 1832 for breaking into stores (possibly on the ship). William West had a chequered career in his home parish of East Hoathly, and in 1834 he gave Brydone a bad moment at Lachine, where, after drinking and quarrelling, West had threatened to desert his large family and return to England. A search party found him hiding in some bushes with no worse consequences for the group than a slight delay in their departure.[82]

The Sharp family group caused Sockett more trouble than was recorded for any other. Their record in England underlines the bitterness some Petworth immigrants brought with them to Upper Canada. Edmund Sharp, an emigrant of 1833, attacked Hale fiercely in a private letter, and his brother-in-law, George Turner, "the black sheep of the [1833] party,"[83] made the family's accusations against Hale public by going to a newspaper. Sockett confided to Richmond "what we have not deemed it expedient to mention in a public manner" about Sharp and Turner. Before they left England, Sockett knew Edmund Sharp for an "extremely bad character" and Turner had narrowly escaped hanging for housebreaking.[84] A year later, Edmund's son David (who later emigrated in 1836) was jailed for a month for his part in displaying placards and parading an effigy of William Tyler, Egremont's land steward, around the Petworth market and the fair at Egdean.

In Dorking in 1832, Barclay presented three classes of emigrants without indicating any preference: single men, men with fewer than four children, men with four or more children. Two years later, Chichester presided at Brighton over a selection that focused on three questions: were the candidates receiving relief, how likely were they to apply again, and what were the chances that they would do well in Upper Canada. After checking the parish books and the costs of emigration, this committee decided to send only married people and their families. Four families and a single man had cost the parish £350: Martin, Kemp, and Perrin (families who sailed on the *British Tar*), Grafenstein (denied emigration because he was single), and Patching (a family who did not emigrate with the Petworth committee). In a dramatic last-minute appeal, Grafenstein stopped Chichester on his way out of the town hall and persuaded him to go back and reinstate his name.[85] Enthusiasm could also carry the day in less august circles. The young orphan John Luff kept after the overseer of the parish of Bury until he agreed to send Luff to Upper Canada on a Petworth ship.

In parishes where there was no ready sponsorship, would-be immigrants might still prevail for negative reasons. On the Isle of Wight in 1831, requests for assistance came from single labourers working for the parish. Even though government aid was not forthcoming, magistrates thought it "imprudent to neglect an application for the means of emigrating presented by a class of persons who were found most turbulent during the late agitations."[86] In other parishes, paupers prevailed using the weight of their poverty, bargaining with the understood "right" to assistance that so annoyed poor law reformers.[87] When the farmers of the parish of South Bersted sent three families to Canada in 1832, one of their number refused to allow his fellow sponsors any credit for benevolence. These people had asked for assistance, and as they were very poor, sponsors had raised the money to be rid of them.[88] Variations on these stories must have been repeated in many other parishes, parishes where no one of standing had sufficient interest to send the letter that would have enabled Alexander Buchanan or his nephew to identify their people as assisted emigrants after they arrived at Quebec.

How poor were these immigrants? If Slements, Sopp, Pullen, and Ayling had emigrated on a Petworth ship instead of staying home, they would by reason of the size of their families have been among the poorest passengers. With aid from the parish in assembling their outfit, their families would have presented a "decent" appearance. Their landing money would have been sufficient to rent accommodation in Toronto of a better standard than the minimal shelter and filthy conditions of the government sheds where the destitute congregated, and if they arrived in a year when the Canadian government offered rations as well as transport inland, they might even have arrived at their place of first settlement with a small sum in hand.

According to the *Portsmouth Herald*, the amounts deposited with the Petworth Emigration Committee to transfer on behalf of single emigrants and families ranged in 1832 from £1 to £25, depending on the size of the family and the proportion of the outfit they had been able to supply themselves. This same report stated that those able to realize something from their "cottages, and little property" (by bargaining with their remaining right of occupancy and selling their possessions) might have from £50 to £70.[89] Reports of money spent between Quebec and Toronto indicated that some Petworth emigrants carried cash in addition to the money entrusted to the committee by them or on their behalf. With reference to both 1832 and 1833, Sockett explained that sums transferred to Toronto by the committee on behalf of individuals had ranged from £1 to an exceptional £65 sent by a man who had been a small farmer (probably John Barnes).[90] In addition to the Barnes family, a few other Petworth emigrants received goods or small sums of money from home in the years after they emigrated – amounts up to the £20 sent with Brydone by Caroline Dearling's family to help her complete a land purchase.[91] Sums transferred by the committee through the Canada Company in April of 1835 and 1836 and specified for payment to "sundry Petworth emigrants" on arrival in Toronto amounted to £1,120 and £1,309 respectively.[92] Although an average does not tell anything of individual circumstances, a group of poor emigrants who commanded an average amount of over £4 per person on arrival at Toronto was in good shape by contemporary standards.

The great majority of people on Petworth ships, however, had been judged in their own parish as in need of assistance to emigrate. Sockett included a few people, usually single people, who were able to pay their own steerage passage, but this was an assisted emigration and we know that before they emigrated many of the emigrants had help from their parish for any one of numerous reasons – injury, illness, temporary unemployment, or numerous children. Parish records for some of this aid have survived, and the poor law commissioners included a question about past assistance on the form completed by parishes applying for a loan.

The evidence available to us indicates that the working poor rather than the destitute emigrated on Petworth ships. There were of course paupers of the class considered to be able-bodied beggars in the parishes sending Petworth emigrants. There were also families locked in poverty so deep that it was constant and continued from one generation to the next, families whose local reputation would determine whether they were regarded as beggars or struggling recipients of parish help.[93] In 1832, Dorking-area sponsors were reportedly disappointed that they could not persuade many such hard-core paupers to leave. The reason given was often heard in contemporary discussions of parish emigration: "This class of persons naturally prefer an idle but certain dependence on the parish at home, to an uncertain independence abroad, to be procured by industry and good conduct."[94] Although the judgment implied in this statement may be unfair, the decision to emigrate, if not taken in total despair, required energy and courage.

The greatest assets that Petworth emigrants brought to Upper Canada in addition to their hopes and ambitions were their work experience and their skills. The fields of the Petworth area bore crops familiar on the other side of the ocean. In this region, as in Upper Canada, wheat was the main cash crop on farms where crops such as turnips, beans, oats, and barley and livestock also had a place.[95] While farming men arriving on Petworth ships found that they had to adapt to new conditions, they had already learned the use of tools such as scythe or flail and acquired a manual dexterity that one contemporary observer compared to the skills of a swordsman.[96]

Most pioneer families in Upper Canada expected to clear and bring into cultivation a 50- or 100-acre farm with only occasional outside assistance. George Sockett, himself a gentleman farmer and the son of Thomas Sockett, had one full-time hired man and did not take on the Edward Longley family, a family hand-picked by his father to serve him. Explaining to them that he had no room to put them up, he found Longley temporary work with a neighbour; in fact, he probably could not afford to hire them.[97] In 1838, Benjamin Smith's farm near the long-settled village of Ancaster had nine or ten workers (including Smith himself), perhaps seven full-time and two or three seasonal helpers. Smith had obtained a location ticket for this land in 1794. By 1838, he had extended his farming operation from the original 150-acre home farm onto adjacent lands.[98] Immigrants had left behind the labour-intensive practices of Dean Farm, but if they could afford it, Upper Canadian farmers hired help by the year or for the harvest. On farms where the land was already cleared, farming men like Henry Miles could fit in quickly. Arriving in summer, their first job was often the familiar one of mowing hay. And, as we will discuss more fully in Chapter 6, there were employers in Upper Canada willing to provide families with housing, garden space, and even livestock in order to obtain the services of farming men such as were sent by the Petworth committee.

An 1835 list of emigrants on the *Burrell*, probably drawn up by Brydone, demonstrates an awareness of the demand in Upper Canada for men with farming skills.[99] Most of the men on this list who were "for employment" were described as farming men; only a few were labelled as agricultural labourers. The distinction was unrelated to character. The young agricultural labourer James Hilton was a "steady man, very respectable," while Edward Burch and Daniel Smith, two farming men in their forties with five and six children, were characterized respectively as "very discontented and impudent" and "a most impudent & insolent man." Two of the agricultural labourers were described as ex-soldiers from the 1st Footguards, and others were recommended as "able-bodied." As the terms were used on this list, agricultural labourers were understood to be only suitable to work at tasks requiring unskilled, manual labour. Farming men were more knowledgable and more versatile. If they had unusual skills, they expected to use them in Upper Canada. Thus Brydone singled out George Poland as "handy with carpenter's tools" and J. Ford as a "farming man and gardener."

A Canadian perspective on the term agricultural labourer gives insight into why the emigrants selected to sail on Petworth ships were welcomed by prospective employers. In the early 1840s, the authors of official reports responded to an influx of predominately Irish immigrants "unacquainted with the ordinary duties of a farm servant and unfit for any work beyond the use of spade and pick axe" by making a more formal distinction between farm servants and mechanics and "mere" or "common labourers."[100] Six years after he was appointed chief emigrant agent for Upper Canada, Anthony Hawke reviewed his experience of the labour market: "I have never experienced any difficulty in getting work for good farm servants – unless incumbered [*sic*] with large families – and at this time [early September] any man who can reap or mow can get work for a short time." Hawke warned that unskilled labourers could not get permanent work in Upper Canada. The canals under construction on both sides of the border in the 1830s absorbed large numbers of labourers and a "great many journeyman mechanics such as masons, carpenters & smiths." When the work was finished, they had to move on. "The mere labourers on each side of the line have always been a fluctuating population."[101] Some single men among Petworth immigrants who were sent to work on the canals may have become part of this mobile workforce. Those with farming skills had a better chance of settling down after a season at a canal site.

With rapid population growth and expanding settlement at the beginning of the 1830s, Upper Canada was a good destination for Petworth emigrants from the building trades. In some new communities, anyone at all familiar with carpentry must have been sure of work, and bricklayers like John Barnes in Toronto or Richard Neal in Dundas found ready employment from people wealthy enough to want a brick house. Egremont's patronage had given Sockett the luxury of being able to take some chances with people, and Petworth emigrants found in urban Upper Canada a small but sophisticated market for specialized talents. Hale reported a need for sign painters in Toronto after he arrived in 1833. John Worsfold, an emigrant of 1832, wrote that it was much easier to start in business in Upper Canada than at home and proposed that a friend join him in a partnership in a painting business. Before testing the market for "graining and flatting"[102] in Hamilton, however, Worsfold had taken a share in a farm with two other Petworth emigrants, a move he appeared to regard as a form of insurance to fall back on if his business venture did not succeed. Men like Worsfold had the versatility to survive the ups and downs of a colonial economy.

THE WRITER OF THE ARTICLE in the *Montreal Herald* quoted at the beginning of this chapter was trying to generalize from the reputation that the Petworth emigrations had gained in Upper Canada to counter the often-justified suspicions that many colonists harboured about the motives of those who sponsored assisted emigrants. In doing so, he mangled the arguments of the report of the poor law commissioners he cited as his authority. The commissioners criticized counties like Sussex and Hampshire for creating pauperism by supplementing wages from the parish poor rate. He used their records of high poor rates to bolster the argument for assisted emigration based on redundancy: people in the receiving colony could feel comfortable because in an overcrowded labour market sponsors would gain even if they sent good workers. Sockett promoted emigration on these grounds. The poor law commissioners, however, believed that work could be found for agricultural labourers in other regions of England. They intended to close the door on the option of using parish assistance to send good workers abroad.

Old ideas proved hard to shake and change came only slowly. To the extent that Petworth immigrants represent other parish-aided immigrants, they represent those of their own time and earlier, when parish relief was available to the working poor. This distinction between parish emigrants sent according to the standards of the old poor law and those of later years is often lost. In discussing parish emigration to Upper Canada, Rainer Baehre makes a common assumption in dismissing all 1830s emigrants to the Canadas who were "initially parish assisted" as "by definition destitute."[103] The Petworth committee had the reputation of sending as parish-aided emigrants "men of excellent character, and such as were likely to do well anywhere."[104] The fact that good labourers among the working poor could be described as paupers has been lost, overshadowed in the years since 1834 by a different concept of who was eligible for relief. As the rules of the new poor law took effect, the meaning of the word "pauper" narrowed to apply only to the destitute.[105]

Studies by Eric Richards and Robin Haines of emigrants assisted to go to Australia in the years following the Petworth emigrations suggest that similar kinds of people continued to be assisted to emigrate with aid from sources other than the parish, while parish-aided immigrants sank on the social scale. In ranking poor emigrants going from Britain to Australia by degrees of poverty, Richards places parish emigrants on the bottom rung of the ladder of poverty and goes beyond destitution as a characteristic to equate "redundant" with "broken down." He quotes a governor of the 1850s to the effect that colonists did not believe that parish paupers could be "a fair sample of the rural population of the United Kingdom."[106] Haines's account of the more typical assisted emigrant from an agricultural community in the south of England to Australia in the 1840s and 1850s describes rural labourers who seem very similar to Petworth emigrants – versatile, often combining farming experience with other work, and with wages too low to finance their own emigration.[107] They received a passage under a program financed from territorial revenues in Australian colonies rather than by an Egremont, and as time passed, the money raised locally for their outfit came from sources other than the poor rate. Although Haines compares these emigrants to emigrants who went to North America on their own,[108] it is clear that these are the people who should be compared with Petworth emigrants, not the unfortunates sent as parish paupers.

Family records have not survived to unravel all the multiple reasons why one labourer chose to take advantage of sponsorship under the Petworth committee and not another, why Henry Miles left his work at Dean Farm to emigrate to Upper Canada and John Miles did not. In his published writings, Sockett wrote about emigrants such as William Jackman, people who left England because they did not think that they could improve their lot at home however well or hard they worked.[109] Family research has revealed that Jackman was a labourer descended from a family that over previous generations had declined in status from farmers to smallholders.[110] He emigrated in a bid to mend his own circumstances and provide for the future of his children. His eldest son stayed back at first and then followed his father to Upper Canada in later years.[111] A successful family emigration followed by the chain migration of other family members was exactly the outcome Sockett had worked so hard to achieve.

There is, however, more to the Jackmans' story. This family was a typical Petworth success story in another way. The Jackmans got a start in Upper Canada in 1836 thanks to a plan that was tailored to meet the needs of parish emigrants. Under the terms of the plan, emigrants were given temporary possession of five-acre lots. Sockett showed considerable trust in the goodwill of authorities in Upper Canada by sending large families with only an understanding that they would receive additional help. He also saw to it that his people were well positioned to obtain whatever aid was available. Petworth emigrants arrived at Toronto early in the emigration season, in a group, with a superintendent to negotiate on their behalf, and accompanied by reminders of prominent sponsorship sent from the Colonial Office to the lieutenant-governor.

Sockett did not share the unrealistic expectations of some emigrants who hoped for individual attention from the hard-pressed agent at Toronto, but he did everything possible to give his group its own identity and to associate his immigrants with Egremont's name. The article in the *Montreal Herald* is one piece of evidence that he succeeded in using the recognition accorded Egremont's name to gain his people a reputation of their own and to set them off from any bad publicity that might attach to parish emigrants in the Canadas. If, as seems likely, Sockett was behind the insertion of the *Herald* article in the *Brighton Gazette,* he also used favourable reports of his scheme in the Canadas as part of his campaign to attract good candidates in England.

CHAPTER 4

"TROUBLE IN TRAVELLING": TRAVELLING AND FINDING A FIRST HOME IN THE CANADAS

I dare say you have heard bad accounts of Canada, from the Petworth
Party, for I know that they wrote home in the midst of their trouble in
travelling, before they know what it was, or had time to get situations.
William T. Upton, Niagara District, Upper Canada,
to George Warren, Petworth, 16 September 1832

Immigrants from Britain to Upper Canada sailed to New York or to Quebec. The
wealthy often chose New York for the greater comfort and speed of the American
ships. If their destination was the western end of the province, they used the Erie
Canal. In his first annual report as chief emigration agent for Upper Canada, Anthony
Hawke offered as proof that his province was attracting emigrants with capital his
claim that as many as one-quarter of the immigrants of 1833 had arrived through
New York and the Erie Canal. The Petworth immigrants did not fall into this category and had to make do with a passage to Quebec.

The Petworth committee chose Quebec as a port of entry and Toronto as the
place where its superintendents would hand their charges over to local authorities.
Immigrants travelling from Montreal to Toronto in the 1830s used two routes. The
route via Bytown (renamed Ottawa in the 1850s) and the Rideau Canal was easier
on the traveller and quicker and thus the first choice of Sockett and his superintendents. Although this route opened at the end of the 1832 season, it was ready too
late for Sockett's immigrants. In 1833 and again in 1836, Petworth superintendents
arrived in Montreal to find the Rideau Canal temporarily blocked and this route
of no use to them. Thus, the Petworth immigrants of 1832, 1833, and 1836 toiled up
the St Lawrence to Prescott in open Durham boats (see map 6). A traveller from
Portsea, near Portsmouth, wrote of the Petworth immigrants who went via the St
Lawrence. Although the actual time might vary, he believed that two weeks should
be allowed for the journey from Montreal to Toronto if it was to be made as cheaply
as possible in bateaux and Durham boats.[1]

Just as Sockett had determined that they would go to Toronto via Quebec, many
Petworth emigrants had their destination within the province chosen by the
lieutenant-governor and officials within the Crown Lands Office. Some of the immigrants chose to settle in and around Toronto. Those sent further west took advantage of water routes opened by the recent completion of two canals. Petworth

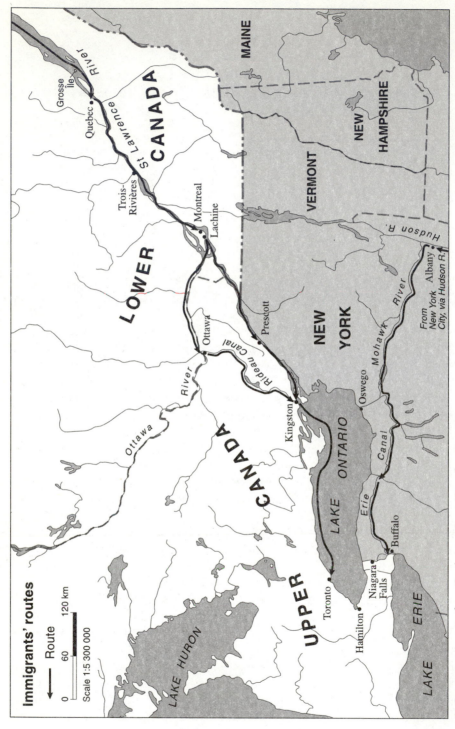

6 *Immigrants' routes from Quebec to Upper Canada, 1832–1837*

immigrants sent to the "head of the lake" (Lake Ontario) used the Burlington Bay Canal, which brought regular steamboat service to Hamilton. From Hamilton, they fanned out into the Gore District, settling particularly in communities on the central and upper Grand River valley and in Woodstock. A second contingent sailed through the Welland Canal, which gave immigrants ready access to Lake Erie. The main port they used on Lake Erie was Kettle Creek (Port Stanley). Port Stanley was an entry point for the London and Western Districts.

Travel within Canada was difficult at best in the 1830s. The troubles of William Upton and his fellow Petworth immigrants were compounded by the numbers of other immigrants travelling with them. During a short emigration season that peaked between May and July, hundreds of immigrants converged on facilities that were little used at other times of the year. By the official count, arrivals at Quebec almost doubled from 1829 to 1830, climbing from 15,945 to 28,000, and their numbers jumped again to over 50,000 in 1831 and 1832 when Upton arrived. Emigration agent Alexander Buchanan reported 26,500 of these emigrants travelling to destinations in Upper Canada in 1831 and 35,000 in 1832. Upper Canadian sources set arrivals from Quebec and Montreal at over 30,000 in 1831; they stopped counting during the cholera epidemic of 1832, with their figures incomplete and emigrants still arriving in numbers.

The year 1831 was the first in which parish-aided immigration was large enough to be noticed in the annual reports of the governors of Upper and Lower Canada. Official figures for Quebec arrivals in 1832 record only modest increases for total arrivals and parish-aided arrivals over 1831. Total arrivals for all of North America were up in 1832, and during the latter part of the season Buchanan compiled his records under the particularly difficult circumstances of the cholera epidemic. Once his office and the officers of the emigrant societies at Quebec and Montreal suspended their attempts to distinguish degrees of need among those applying for a free passage up the St Lawrence, they had no practical reason to identify parish emigrants.

Cholera had spread across Europe from the east. The disease reached Britain in 1831 and was confirmed in London early in 1832.[2] The immigrant ships of 1832 brought it to North America. Apart from their own fears, the immigrants of 1832 had to cope with the fears of the people they encountered. They met closed doors, inflated prices, and a reluctance among employers to hire people off an immigrant ship. In any year, officials in Quebec, Montreal, and the towns along immigrant routes had no choice but to send many immigrants further inland at the expense of charities or government; the alternative was numbers of people with no means of support collecting in these towns.[3] In 1832, the Montreal Emigrant Society forwarded more than twice as many destitute immigrants to Upper Canada as in 1831.[4] Immigrants who might have stopped in Lower Canada or eastern Upper Canada were pushed on westward.

Petworth immigrants who chose Upper Canada were part of a larger trend in settlement patterns. In the 1820s, many of the immigrants arriving at Quebec had travelled on to the neighbouring states of Ohio, Michigan, New York, and Pennsylvania. In 1831, Sir John Aylmer, the governor of Lower Canada, speculated that, allowing for the two-way traffic between the Canadas and neighbouring states, the

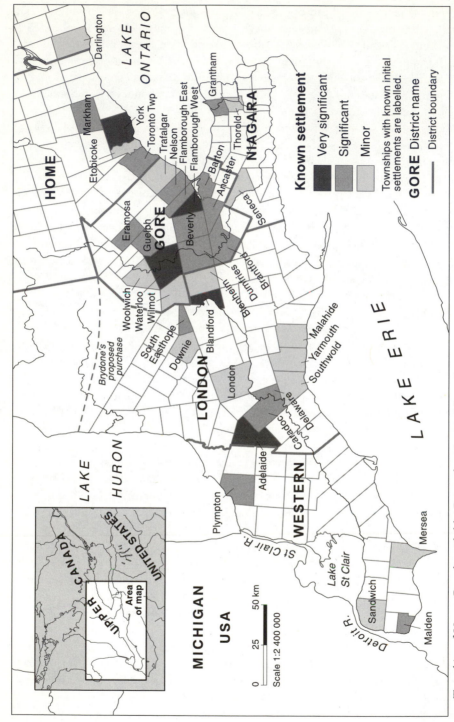

7 *Townships of Upper Canada settled by Petworth emigrants, 1832–1837*

number of immigrants who became permanent residents was perhaps equal to the number recorded arriving at Quebec. Buchanan was more specific: the Irish and Scots generally stayed in the Canadas. He predicted that before long the English would stay also because they "will soon find out that the gold-tinged paradise of the aguish [fever prone] Prairies of Illinois, or Michigan, are not to be put in comparison with the fertile and more convenient portions of these provinces."[5]

The scene for the reception of Petworth immigrants in 1832 was set by the events of 1831. In Lower Canada, Aylmer adopted a wait-and-see attitude. Justifying his inaction on the grounds that pauper emigration had been insignificant before 1831 and, by implication, might not be repeated, he left local charities struggling to provide for the sudden increase in sick and needy immigrants.[6] Emigrant and charitable societies in Quebec and Montreal attempted to find work for the able-bodied, but the tried-and-true solution was to forward unwanted immigrants upriver. The majority were sent to Prescott and Brockville over the border with Upper Canada.

In his annual report for 1831, Buchanan sounded embarrassed by Aylmer's failure to respond to the situation. Buchanan wanted to keep more British settlers in rural Lower Canada, but he encountered problems and ended by forwarding most of those who applied to him to Upper Canada. Although Buchanan had spoken and written in favour of pauper emigration – particularly from Ireland – and would continue to do so, his recommendations always included supervised settlement.[7] In 1831, he was defensive and anxious to forestall criticism. He claimed that the 4,931 parish emigrants tallied in his office were fewer than the numbers given in reports circulating around Quebec. He also insisted that they had arrived in better shape than these reports suggested. His own opinion on the first large parish emigration to the Canadas surfaced in a dry comment: it was "fortunate" that shipping had not been found to bring everyone in the agricultural and labouring communities who wished to come, "as from the want of necessary facilities for their reception, considerable disappointment must have been the consequence."[8]

In Upper Canada, Lieutenant-Governor Sir John Colborne had embraced the idea of parish-assisted emigration as it was described in accounts of Howick's Emigration Bill. Taking the home government's intention to participate as a given, he concentrated on two issues. His efforts to prevent too many immigrants from congregating in lakeside towns drove the policies that will be discussed in this chapter; his search for ways to encourage desirable immigrants to settle permanently in the province belongs to the discussion in Chapter 5. Colborne was particularly concerned to keep family men as permanent settlers. Immigrants, he explained, must travel inland. Mechanics and labourers arriving in large numbers and at one time could not be absorbed in the immediate vicinity of Upper Canada's ports. Farmers in settled districts near these ports preferred to hire workers already acclimatized to North American ways. Yet many immigrants did not bring enough money to carry them through to Upper Canadian communities where they would find year-round work.

In 1831, Colborne turned to the commissioner of crown lands, Peter Robinson, in his search for a way to prevent congestion along immigrant routes in Upper

Canada. Since his appointment in 1828, Robinson had relied for sales of crown lands mainly on deputy surveyors, who also reported to the surveyor general. With the increase in immigrant traffic, he began to hire more of his own agents. Although their contracts were temporary, being only for the immigrant season, Robinson developed a core of agents who were reappointed from year to year. He stationed them along the main travel routes and authorized them to smooth the immigrants' way, if necessary, by paying the fare for the next leg of their journey. Agents in lakeside towns directed immigrants wanting to buy crown lands to inland agents, who also reported to Robinson. As well as providing information and selling land, crown lands agents soon found themselves dealing with the casualties of immigration: orphaned families, the sick, and those stranded when their money ran out.

THE JOURNEY FROM THE GULF OF ST LAWRENCE TO TORONTO

The journey inland from the Gulf of St Lawrence to Toronto broke naturally at several points. Immigrant ships had to stop at the Grosse Île Quarantine Station for inspection and permission to proceed. At Quebec, Buchanan would name an arriving Petworth ship in his weekly report to the governor, but he had little to do for immigrants who after 1832 did not even get off the ship. Superintendents arriving at Quebec went ashore and sent off notice of a safe journey and a report to the Petworth committee. The next stop was Montreal, where all the immigrants left the ship that had brought them from Portsmouth. A short trip through the Lachine Canal took them to Lachine, the starting place for the journey to Upper Canada.

Petworth immigrants who travelled up the St Lawrence had their arrival recorded at Prescott. The agent here often had difficulty obtaining the records of steamboat passengers, records he relied on to compile the year's immigration data. Another agent at Bytown also depended on shipping firms for his statistics. Immigrants who transferred from the St Lawrence bateaux to a steamboat at Prescott normally changed again at Kingston. For those coming from Bytown, Kingston was the Lake Ontario terminus of the Rideau Canal. The last stage of the journey, from Kingston to Toronto, was well served by large steamboats. All Petworth immigrants travelled on one of these two Canadian inland routes, although many wrote home recommending that friends and relatives use the American route through the port of New York, Albany, and the Erie Canal.

For Petworth emigrants who had enjoyed carefully chosen and well-supplied ships, the risk factor of travel increased on inland waters and on land. During the first five years, the only casualties on the high seas among the emigrants were four infants whose lives must have been uncertain even at home. The *England* in 1832 had a close brush with disaster off the Island of St Paul in the St Lawrence estuary, and Sockett wrote in support of a growing demand for a lighthouse. Seventeen emigrant ships were wrecked with a loss of 731 lives in 1834 before steps were taken to improve navigation aids, but Petworth ships had no further problems.[9] As they sailed up the lower St Lawrence, passengers in cabin and steerage examined the river banks with some anxiety. The pretty sight of sun glinting off tin roofs in a foreign-looking landscape did not compensate for the barrenness of the hills and a cold, late spring. Brydone in 1834 reported the relief among the farming people when they caught sight of the more hospitable and fertile lands of the Île d'Orléans just above Quebec. Ready for the first time to give an opinion, they told him: "This will do."[10]

Other than the pilot who saw them up the St Lawrence, Petworth superintendents had their first contact with officialdom at the Grosse Île Quarantine Station downriver from Quebec. The station, hastily established in 1832 as a defence against cholera, was staffed by the British army during all the years that Sockett sent ships.[11] The knowledge that quarantine had failed to contain the disease in Europe gave little hope that the Canadas could be sealed off, and quarantine officers were as anxious to keep the healthy moving as to hold back the sick. James Rapson wrote that the *Lord Melville* was detained by quarantine officers for a short four hours in 1832. In 1833, a year when the Canadas had no cases of cholera, Hale had to land emigrants and baggage on the island. He had his people off the island within seven hours, and the *England* left the anchorage at midnight the same day.

The *British Tar*, with twelve cases of measles, arrived at Grosse Île on 23 May 1834 after a crossing of thirty-five days. The ship was met by the harbour-master, who carried a copy of a proclamation issued on 27 March 1834 by the Executive Council of Lower Canada. This proclamation declared hospitalization at Grosse Île mandatory for all cases of five communicable diseases: Asiatic cholera, fever, smallpox, and severe cases of scarlatina (scarlet fever) or measles. Although the inspecting physician ordered the *British Tar* to fly the dreaded "Yellow *Quarantine* Flag," Brydone did not expect a long delay. Because he was short of hospital space ashore, the Grosse Île doctor left recovered and mild cases in Brydone's care, taking only the Bartons' son, whose case of measles was complicated by a previous illness. The immigrants washed clothing, bags, and bedding. As they were also told to empty the straw and chaff from their mattresses overboard, they slept on bare boards and looked forward to a quick departure. Three days passed before the order came to land.[12] In addition to taking all their clothes and bedding from the ship, they were obliged to bring, and open, chests and casks from the hold.

A naval man himself, Brydone got on well with Captain Henry Reid, the military commander at Grosse Île, and spent a pleasant evening dining with him. He had no desire to blame the presiding officers, whom he believed to be as helpful as possible in the circumstances, but he was highly critical of conditions on the island. He saw no need to land immigrants from healthy ships when they might be inspected on board. The landing place put immigrants at risk from wind and wave. The rule requiring them to remove their luggage from the hold added to their distress. On the island, the immigrants had no choice but to wash themselves and their clothing in coves where dirt and refuse swirled in the eddies. The Petworth women and children spent the night in an open shed, separated by a pile of boxes from others of the over 1,800 people on shore that night. Writing privately to Sockett, Brydone described these others as "chiefly of the lowest description of Irish." There was no shelter for men and no food distributed until morning, when Brydone brought ship's biscuits and cheese from the ship. It was impossible, Brydone wrote, "to describe, how sorry I was, to see a cleanly and healthy people, mixed, as they were in the dirt, and filth, of thousands."[13] By 5:00 p.m. the next day, the ship was fumigated and immigrants and luggage were back on board, only to wait another three days for clearance. Once it was given, they reached Quebec on 1 June.

At Quebec, another afternoon and then a night slipped by, lost to visits by the harbour-master and officers of customs and quarantine and a change of pilot. After blowing favourably for days, the wind changed and trapped the *British Tar* in Wolfe's Cove. Brydone was forced into the indignity of having his sailing ship towed by a steamboat the 180 miles to Montreal. An immigrant on the *Lord Melville* had thought it a grand sight to see the steamer *John Bull* with six ships in tow, one on each side and four strung out behind.[14] Brydone did not share this sentiment, and he objected to paying half passage for the people on the ship in addition to towing charges.[15] Losing the wind and the nine-day delay had cost an extra £135 – all, Brydone fumed, for a few cases of measles, a disease he later found rampant in Quebec and Montreal, which they reached at last on 5 June.

Against this expense, he was spared the cost of the emigrant head tax that Sockett included in his ten-pound fare. At the suggestion of the Colonial Office, the provincial legislature had imposed a tax in 1832 of five shillings per adult passage. The tax was intended to recover some of the costs of facilities built to house sick and indigent immigrants. In 1833, Hale had been sent off from Portsmouth Harbour without a certificate of inspection and may have had to pay a double tax.[16] Brydone delayed his departure from Portsmouth for a day and incurred an extra towing charge over this paperwork in 1834, only to find on his arrival at Quebec that the tax had been allowed to lapse.[17] When the emigrant tax was reimposed in 1835, Sockett wrote to the under-secretary at the Colonial Office, while Brydone elaborated their case in a letter to the governor of Lower Canada. They asked for an exemption for Petworth ships arriving with healthy immigrants. Lord Egremont, they argued, had already incurred the costs of preventive measures. The committee's ships were painted before departure and kept clean. Brydone had a full medicine chest at his disposal, and he did not allow the immigrants to stop at Quebec or to linger in Montreal on their way to Upper Canada. Sockett and Brydone thought it very unfair that Egremont should be asked to pay a tax in support of facilities his immigrants would never use.[18] In this correspondence, they added their voices to a chorus demanding changes at Grosse Île. The tax remained, but Brydone reported favourably on revisions to the quarantine regulations. In 1837, the immigrants on the *Diana* were excused from landing because of the clean appearance of ship and people.[19]

In Quebec and Montreal, the Petworth committee worked with some of the most influential merchants in the country. It maintained an account with Peter McGill, who advanced money to the Petworth superintendents and whose company received and sold surplus stores from the Petworth ships. The committee also engaged William Price at Quebec and the forwarders John McPherson and Lemuel Cushing on the route beyond Montreal. These large concerns had the resources to assist in transshipping luggage and the empty warehouses to accommodate the immigrants and keep them together while they waited for the next conveyance. By dealing directly with these merchants, Sockett's superintendents got better service and the use of better facilities than if they had applied for these at the emigrant offices.

The Petworth superintendents were charged with keeping their people together and therefore tried to hurry them through the distractions of Quebec and Montreal. Several Petworth immigrants got drunk in 1832 celebrating their arrival at Quebec, and one drowned in the harbour; thereafter the superintendents did not let them ashore. They could not avoid letting the immigrants spend some time in Montreal, however, and with or without permission, a handful remained in Montreal after the others left for Lachine.

Thanks to their Petworth connection, the 1832 emigrants who were delayed for three days at Lachine stayed in a storehouse. William Phillips was not so lucky in 1833. His party of immigrants spent a Saturday night sitting in the two large Durham boats that had brought them from Montreal. Sunday night found them in makeshift tents beside a fire built with stolen wood.[20] In 1833, Hale distributed ten days' provisions at Lachine as a practical incentive to collect his people. A year later, Brydone took eight days' provisions from the ship for the shorter journey to Toronto via the Rideau Canal. His immigrants slept in McPherson's Lachine warehouse.

In deploying Robinson's agents in 1832, Colborne was hoping to treat the St Lawrence corridor as a single route. His plan to put an agent at Quebec to meet the ships of incoming immigrants ran into indignant opposition from Buchanan. Far from tolerating an agent of Upper Canada on his turf in 1832, Buchanan declared himself astonished and distressed by Colborne's proposal and, for his own part, pressed the Colonial Office to put him in charge of both provinces.[21] Colborne countered with equal annoyance. He believed Buchanan "a very zealous obliging good natured man, but he is forward, vain, self interested, and full of his own importance." He must be, Colborne thought, if he imagined any good could come of his interfering from a distance of 600 miles in the work of agents whose success had depended on local knowledge.[22] Through the Crown Lands Office, Colborne retained personal direction of the agents in his own province, and he made it clear that Buchanan must apply to him for information.[23]

Despite Buchanan's use of the title chief agent for the superintendence of emigrants in Upper and Lower Canada, relations between Buchanan and Colborne were patched over by dividing their jurisdictions.[24] Buchanan restricted his direct intervention in immigrant settlement to the Eastern Townships of Lower Canada. Colborne did not station an agent at Quebec and agreed to pay a part of Buchanan's salary to cover his services in providing information on Upper Canada to arriving immigrants. Although Anthony Hawke was assigned to Lachine in 1832 as an agent for Upper Canada with orders to consult with Buchanan and the Montreal Emigrant Committee, his instructions specified that he not concern himself with Montreal. His main attention was to be directed to Lachine and to the portion of the route between Lachine and Cornwall.[25]

From Lachine, immigrants travelling the St Lawrence route entered a thirty-five-mile stretch of navigation to Prescott that was interrupted several times by rapids.

Petworth immigrants writing home described it as the most difficult part of their journey. The emigrants of 1832 watched timber rafts from Upper Canada travelling downriver "nearly as fast as a horse could gallop." Moving upriver was a different story. Military engineers had opened navigation for bateaux with four short canals built between 1779 and 1783, and these waterways had been expanded at the beginning of the nineteenth century to accommodate the larger Durham boats. In calm water on the stretch between Lachine and Prescott, Petworth immigrants in Durham boats sailed or were towed by steamers. At the rapids, many passengers, and in some places all of them, had to walk or hire wagons while the boats were polled by the boatmen or drawn by oxen.

Where the water was fastest, emigrants wrote of eight or ten yoke of oxen or teams of as many horses. Accidents and near accidents were frequent – "the boat being over burthened began to draw the oxen back the drivers jumped in and chopped the rope and then they were driven back like the wind" – this a boat with children still on board – "wife with us saw it and I thought it would have frightened her into fits."[26] Accommodation was uncertain: a few inns for the sick or the fortunate, a tavern to get dry (as people remembered, it always seemed to rain), sometimes the chance of huddling on the steamer, sometimes camping out. From Prescott, immigrants sailed in steamboats that linked with Kingston and the regular steamers that served Toronto. This part of the journey was accomplished with regular schedules and in relative comfort.

As letters began to come in from his 1832 emigrants, Sockett was alternately satisfied with good reports of the country and disturbed by frequent accounts of great hardships in travelling up the St Lawrence. He feared that British emigration would be diverted to the United States. To lend urgency to his request to Richmond to call the attention of government to the St Lawrence rapids, Sockett enclosed a copy of a letter from James Rapson. He did not publish this letter, which he described as the "*least* encouraging" received to date.[27]

At Montreal, Rapson's party from the *Lord Melville* had carried the new mother Jane Penfold onto a Durham boat on a chair and found space for her in a leaky cabin. Rapson, suffering acutely, probably from neuralgia, was with the others, "stuffed in so thick we were not able to sit down, and were obliged to stand."[28] They spent the first night of the eight-day trip to Prescott still standing on the boat and the second sleeping outdoors. They had no access to their provisions during the day and paid the inflated price of two shillings for a loaf of bread. Although the steamboat the *Sir James Kempt* would eventually land them at York, a misunderstanding over fares saw them stranded for two days and two nights on the wharf at Kingston before local authorities intervened to rescue them. Between Kingston and Toronto, a storm forced the boat to take refuge in Cobourg. By the time they reached York, Rapson reported that some of the people were indeed penniless.[29]

Although Rapson's might seem like a worst case, the Rapsons and other emigrants from the *Eveline* and the *Lord Melville* were fortunate in travelling upriver just ahead of the first cases of cholera. The form of cholera brought to the Canadas in 1832 struck hard and fast. By the end of September, 3,451 cases had been reported in Quebec and close to 2,000 in Montreal. People died within three or four days, sometimes in hours, and the medical profession was deeply divided on both cause and possible treatments. Boards of health with uncertain legal authority attempted to enforce measures to preserve public health when there was no agreement on the efficacy of different methods; there were too few doctors, inadequate hospitals, and a population that feared hospitals as a place of death. The first confirmed cases were identified at Quebec on 6 June and in Montreal three days later. At the beginning of the epidemic, each of these cities reported over one hundred deaths a week. The transportation system temporarily collapsed as boatmen fled from the river, but not before the disease reached Upper Canada.[30]

Vivid accounts survive from two members of the families of the brothers Moses and Nathaniel Chantler. Although from the Dorking area and known to Petworth emigrants, the Chantlers did not travel under the Petworth committee and arrived on the *Brunswick*.[31] After leaving Montreal on 14 June, Nathaniel fell sick at Cedars, the first set of rapids above Lachine. On a local doctor's advice, the family hired a wagon to take him to the next small canal at Coteau du Lac. When they arrived, it was so apparent that he was dying of cholera that "we was not alowed even a shed everyone was afraid of us would not open doors when we went to buy milk ... as a last resort our dying father was laid on the wharf on a bed with no shelter but a cart turned over it." A lifetime later his daughter recalled scenes "stamped on my memory," her mother and cousin tending the dying man by lamplight, the storm that came up, and the frightening rocking of the barge where they sheltered next: "What must have been the feeling of that dear Mother a dying husband and five little children in a strange place where every one was afraid of us."[32]

Moses Chantler took both families in a steamboat from Coteau to Cornwall. Here they met with kindness from the captain and the cook. At Cornwall, they had to disembark to pass the fourteen miles of the Long Sault Rapids. Moses's daughter Ann also died of cholera, in a barn where the family camped. Nathaniel, who had been seen by a doctor, was buried in a cemetery, and as a head of family, his death became a matter of record. Ann was too far from the nearest doctor at Prescott, and her family buried her themselves in a field by the river, one of the early cholera victims in Upper Canada and one of many whose death was probably never officially recorded. [33]

Nathaniel's family might never have reached York without Moses, who located their boat and prevailed on the boatmen to continue with the baggage to Prescott. In Prescott, one of the Upper Canadian towns hardest hit by cholera, they apparently avoided the emigrant shed hastily erected by the town on Drummond's Island, and they reached York on 30 June without further incident. At York, Colborne and his wife were leading local efforts to provide for victims of cholera. Lady Colborne and her sister took a personal interest in Nathaniel's family. They found work for his wife, Sophia, and after she too died of cholera, they maintained their contact with her children until their Quaker uncle had placed all five with Quaker families to the north of York in the Newmarket area.[34]

Early in 1833, Sockett returned to the subject of the journey from Montreal in his correspondence with Richmond: "The complaints about the difficulties, and even suffering, attendant upon ascending the rapids above Montreal, are very numerous; are to be found in almost every letter; and the route by N. York [the Port of New York] is *strongly* recommended to those who shall follow them by most of the emigrants ... but though I have not *printed* these recommendations, yet the letters containing them have been much read, & they will have their effect."[35] Sockett warned of a loss of business for British shipping, of a potential loss to the colony if emigrants were deflected to settle in the United States, and, delicately, of the greater costs to the committee of an American route. Sockett also wrote of his concerns to the directors of the Canada Company. They had received many similar reports, and they were probably Sockett's source for early information on the Rideau Canal. He checked costs and decided that this route was the answer to his dilemma.[36] He made haste to publicize the Petworth committee's plans to use the Rideau in 1833.

For Upper Canadians with any interest in inland trade or bulk goods, the 1830s was an era of canal promotion. They had watched in dismay the phenomenal success of the Erie Canal, completed from New York to Buffalo on Lake Erie between 1817 and 1825. When the engineers of the British Ordnance Department laid out the Rideau Canal as a Canadian waterway from Montreal to Kingston, military considerations dictated that it should be inland, away from the St Lawrence and the American border. Navigation on the Ottawa River was improved by canals circumventing rapids between Carillon and Grenville in the years 1819–34. The locks and canals that linked stretches of navigable water between Bytown (Ottawa) and Kingston were completed between 1825 and 1832. In all, this 123-mile (198 km) waterway added 50 miles (80 km) to the journey from Montreal to Kingston and required the use of a multiplicity of locks. Except to ship locally, merchants found the Ottawa–Rideau route too circuitous. For poor immigrants who had to use water routes as the cheapest form of transport, the opening of the Rideau system was a boon.[37]

Hale, however, arrived in the spring of 1833 to find the Rideau Canal closed by winter damage. Buchanan might write in his official report that travel on the St Lawrence system had been improved – he probably referred to his success in making a better deal with immigrant carriers – but Petworth immigrants still faced a tedious journey. William Phillips slept outdoors for six of the eight nights he spent between Lachine and Prescott. When his party found a village and houses at nightfall, he described "begging hard" to pay to sleep on the floor using their own bedding.[38] Hale reported that his immigrants were towed in Durham boats by a steamer from Lachine to the Cascades and then walked from there to the Cedars. The rain forced the party to stop for the night and he found space for his people at an inn. He and Dr Clay from the *England* went on ahead by wagon, and some of the single men chose to walk. Rhoda Thair gave an immigrant's perspective. She wrote of a 4:00 a.m. start and of being wet through all day. All the men were "obliged" to walk, she noted, adding, "Sailors and Captain very cross, threatened us much." The immigrants told Hale of this — he reported "much murmuring" about "the discomforture of this part of the trip" — and he arranged for the women to go on board a steamer for the remaining distance to Cornwall. This night the people were "mostly accommodated in the [steamer's] Fore-Cabin and on the Deck."[39] Phillips said the cabin would have been comfortable but for their wet clothes.

On 26 June, three days after leaving Lachine, Hale and the *England*'s immigrants reached Cornwall and the Long Sault Rapids, where everyone had to get out of the boats. The men walked and Hale hired wagons for the women and children, who then jounced over the bad road around the rapids with the minimal comfort of spring seats.[40] Thair's comment that Hale "was three parts of his time tipsy" makes suspicious his report for the 26th that the spirits were "plundered." They resumed travel by water on the 27th. Hale, who had spent the night at an inn with the doctor and his patients, passed the Petworth Durham boats and saw from the deck of his steamboat that the passengers had been landed again to walk. His whole party reassembled in Prescott, where his immigrants slept in McPherson's "shed." On the morning of 29 June, they boarded the *United Kingdom* for an uneventful trip to Toronto.[41] John Patton, the emigrant agent at Prescott, supplied Hale with a paper certifying that he had seen the immigrants sent in Hale's care "and that I find from conversing with many of them that they are generally healthy and contented."[42]

Sockett's local credibility in Sussex was hurt when the more comfortable trip he had promised on the Rideau waterway failed to materialize. Although Hale went home as instructed through the Rideau and Ottawa River canals and reported very favourably on both comfort and cost, Sockett was still sceptical.[43] In 1834, he sent Brydone additional instructions to come home via the Erie Canal and New York in order to compare the cost of that route and to see if there were agencies along the canal that could be used to keep the emigrants together and on their way to Upper Canada. He was to inform himself on all three routes and bring back with him "every book map plan, every document of every kind that for love or money you can lay your hand upon."[44] As Brydone's report on the American route was accompanied by his very positive account of travelling via the Rideau Canal, Sockett abandoned all thought of sending immigrants through the United States.

In all, Brydone took three parties of emigrants from Montreal up the Ottawa River to Bytown (Ottawa) and from there through the Rideau waterway to Kingston — in 1834, 1835, and 1837. The journey took seven days in 1834. Warnings of ague and fever in low and swampy areas of the Rideau Canal led Brydone to take a good supply of quinine that year, but to his relief he had no need to use it. Although the emigrants were towed by a succession of steamboats, they remained in the same craft. And Brydone was especially pleased with this barge. It was new and better appointed than the Durham boats on the St Lawrence. It had a full deck and a cabin reached by a stairway leading up from the deck. He was able to put most of the women, girls, and children in this cabin, where they could sleep in fixed beds. The remaining women and children went below deck. Brydone grouped them at one end, with the married men in the middle and at the other end the single men, who had their own hatchway to reach their berths. On this boat, "the whole party had ample room for sleeping, in the night, and protection, and shelter, either from bad weather, or the heat of the sun, by day, and felt perfectly comfortable; being, as nearly as possible, in the same relative position, which they had been accustomed to in the *British Tar*, and from which they might easily fancy themselves not yet removed."[45] Although these people travelled with much less stress than those on the St Lawrence, a comparison with Brydone's account of his own style of travel on the same journey makes clear that the immigrants' "perfect comfort" had class connotations.[46]

Brydone's 1834 reports on the Ottawa–Rideau route were not consistently favourable. He noted delays of half a day at Lachine and twenty-four hours at the end of the Grenville Canal, disruptions in traffic caused by steamboats running aground. Navigation was difficult through the private lock at Sainte-Anne-de-Bellevue (Vaudreuil in Brydone's *Narrative*) at the entrance to the Lake of Two Mountains, and a further delay at Carillon was only avoided when the people agreed to take the place of the horses that should have been ready to draw their boat through the two-mile canal. Despite these minor hitches, Brydone had a pleasant time on the Ottawa River and enjoyed the local hospitality. The Rideau navigation system inland from Bytown up the Rideau River and through connecting lakes to Cataraqui River and Kingston had been expressly designed for steamboats, but Brydone found the waterway still primitive, or, as he put it, "in its infancy." Directing traffic through any of the forty-nine locks was still on occasion a matter of trial and error. In some places, the channel was narrowed by stumps or partially blocked by floating trees. Floating islands in one lake snagged the boats in tow. In addition, he thought the steamboats underpowered to pull the number of craft they had in tow. Brydone confidently expected these problems to be temporary. With various causes of delay removed, a journey that was already a great improvement on the old route would be significantly shortened. Despite the detour involved, the Rideau Canal remained an important route for emigrants until improvements on the St Lawrence were completed in 1848.

The Petworth immigrants of 1835 had perhaps the easiest journey of any. They made the trip from Montreal to Toronto via the Rideau in a mere six days. In 1836, the Rideau Canal was closed for repair when the emigrants from the *Heber* arrived in Montreal, and they had to toil up the St Lawrence. They had nothing good to report. The Jackmans, who were among this group, wrote a familiar tale of travel "in open boats, exposed to the heat of the sun by day, and to the rain, cold and fogs by night." Apparently, prices for food remained as high as the market would bear. In 1833, some immigrants would regret that they had left unwanted food behind in their berths on the *England*. Three years later, Lydia Hilton warned members of her family who had joined that year's emigration to draw out their full allowance on the ship (except for the biscuit) and to set up their own store. If she had done this in 1833 and kept her own supply for the journey around the rapids, all would have been well. By 1836, however, the route through the Rideau Canal had become well known, and Sockett did not have the same fears for his credibility as in 1833. He printed both the Jackmans' and the Hiltons' letters and allowed Brydone's *Narrative* to stand as his account of his preferred route.

From Kingston to Toronto, the steamboats used by Petworth immigrants of different years included the *United Kingdom*, the *Great Britain*, and the *William IV*. These large steamers were all of recent construction and capable of carrying several hundred people at peak times.[47] Once in Toronto, the immigrants scattered to find lodgings for themselves. Brydone would have preferred to keep them together, but he had to agree that the open emigrant shed at Toronto "was calculated only, for the most destitute description of Emigrants, and but ill suited to our people, (who were rather of a better class)."[48] Except at Grosse Île, where they had no choice, the Petworth immigrants avoided the emigrant sheds of Canadian towns as they did the emigrant hospitals. The only record we have of hospitalization is of the Barton boy on Grosse Île (he was returned to the ship in improved health). In other cases, the superintendent or the immigrants themselves hired lodgings for the sick, as was done for women in labour.

TRAVEL FROM TORONTO ON

Petworth immigrants who did not stop in the Toronto area went mainly to the Gore, London, or Western districts (see map 8). The Buchanans, both uncle and nephew, attempted to report the distribution of immigrants within the upper as well as the lower province. Despite highly suspect figures, their compilations provide a helpful backdrop to the travels of Sockett's immigrants. Although they seem to have had a common source in the figures given the agents of Upper Canada by steamboat companies, there is sometimes disagreement between the Buchanans' report and the occasional references to the distribution of immigrants in official reports originating in Upper Canada. Upper Canadian agents collected data closer to their source, but in these years their reports were not given in any consistent form and they defy tabulation.

As soon as they arrived in Toronto, Sockett's superintendents contacted the lieutenant-governor and the Crown Lands Department and deferred to them in any further action. They also signed over to the immigrants the credit notes sent through the Canada Company on their behalf. Rents in Toronto were high, and although they were not destitute, most Petworth immigrants were poor and had to decide quickly where they would go and what they would do. Employers looking for artisans with particular skills met the steamboats. Other employers might seek out the immigrants because they too were from Sussex. A few of the immigrants had relatives to help them find a place. If they did not get work right away, families especially had to be sent on quickly. Many of the immigrants who arrived in Toronto had days or even weeks of travel and temporary accommodation ahead of them before they found jobs and places where they could settle with security for their first winter in Upper Canada.

In 1832, Colborne had clear objectives for the settlement of townships in his new surveys, including those in the London and Western districts that received Petworth

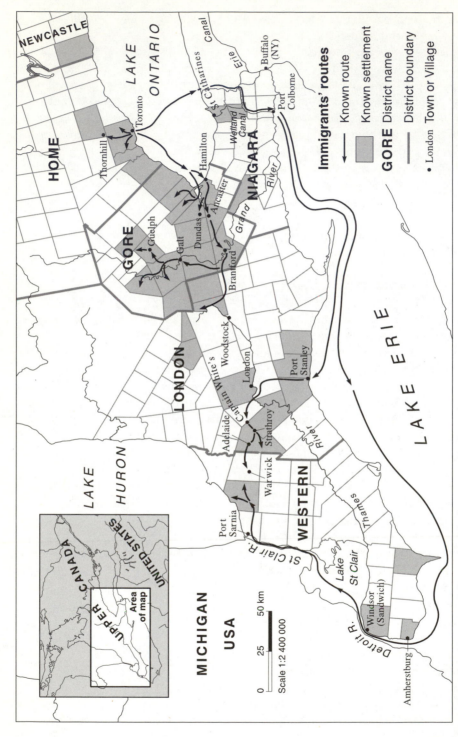

8 *Immigrants' routes into the interior of Upper Canada, 1832–37*

immigrants. He wanted to develop a transportation system that would draw settlers to Upper Canada rather than to the neighbouring states and to introduce a balanced population of educated leaders and labouring followers. The cholera epidemic forced his hand, causing him to act more quickly than could be done smoothly with the material and administrative resources available to him. At the end of the 1832 immigration season, Colborne's private secretary feared for his health and worried that he had "worked himself to an absolute skeleton."[49] If he and his agents failed to save the main St Lawrence and Lake Ontario towns from the full impact of the epidemic, they had better success with the immigrants they were able to get out into the countryside. Their efforts contributed substantially to a secure beginning for many of Sockett's immigrants and to a positive start to his scheme.

At the end of the 1832 season, Buchanan estimated that 6,000 immigrants had travelled inland from Hamilton, 3,000 had gone to the Niagara District, and an astonishing 8,500 had gone to distant townships reached from the north shore of Lake Erie and Lake St Clair. Although the Welland Canal had been opened three years earlier, 1832 was the first year in which immigrant travel west of Toronto was sufficiently organized for him to obtain numbers for his annual report. Upper Canadian sources recorded assistance in travel to as many as 4,000 of the immigrants sent via Lake Erie. Perhaps half this number were located in an assisted settlement in Adelaide and Warwick townships under the superintendence of crown lands agent Roswell Mount. The proportion of immigrants going to the western end of the province was never as high again in the six years of the Petworth emigrations.

Sockett wrote that some of the 1832 emigrants were employed on public works, but he did not give numbers or location. They may have worked improving one of the Lake Erie harbours, but their numbers cannot have been large. The promises of Howick and the emigration commissioners of certain work for all immigrants did not reflect the realities of Upper Canada. Employment with public works was not necessarily more certain than employment with private employers. The list of projects voted by the House of Assembly was impressive, but many of these projects were put forward on local initiatives with totally inadequate funding. During the cholera epidemic of the summer of 1832, Colborne experienced the difficulty of having to break up temporary settlements of new emigrants crowded in sheds, shanties, and even tents in the ports of arrival, and he had every reason not to recreate these conditions on a construction site, even if he had had a suitable project ready. The lieutenant-governor fell back on his own preferred initiatives and sent new immigrants far out into the countryside. Although immigrants had a better chance of being hired privately in these distant settlements, there was no big scheme of public works to absorb the excess. The Adelaide settlement grew out of this dilemma.

In 1832, harried officials in Toronto managed to record 22,000 arrivals in a town with a settled population of from 5,000 to 6,000. Immigrants from the *Eveline* described travelling upriver a few days ahead of reports of cholera cases. The timing of the arrival of the *Lord Melville* immigrants in Toronto suggests that they could have been on the steamer *Great Britain*, which brought the first cases of cholera to the town.

Colborne decided that quarantine was impossible. Arriving vessels were inspected, and then immigrants were dispersed with all possible speed. If necessary, they could be looked after in hospitals established by means of district grants. This decision put a huge burden on the officers of the Land Department and the emigrant societies that assisted them. Under Robinson's supervision, James Fitzgibbon, secretary of the Strangers' Friend Society at York, was given the task of providing transport.

In the urgency of the moment, Fitzgibbon paid above standard charter rates in 1832. He also provided provisions for the Petworth immigrants' journey beyond Toronto, setting a precedent with these early vessels that was continued through the season. John Stedman, an emigrant from the *Eveline*, complained that Fitzgibbon bundled "all them that was sent out by the parishes" onto three schooners with such haste that some people were separated from family members and others (like Stedman himself) from their possessions.[50] The immigrants had expected all three schooners to head to a common destination, but in fact two went to Hamilton while the third, with superintendent Goatcher on board, sailed out into open water for the Welland Canal, Lake Erie, and Kettle Creek (Port Stanley).

The completion of the Burlington Bay Canal had opened Hamilton to immigrant traffic. A gazetteer quoted by Sockett in 1833 claimed that the town's population had recently doubled; two years earlier, a traveller would never have seen a steamboat, now they arrived three times a week on a regular schedule.[51] Although Petworth immigrants of various years settled in the nearby towns of Dundas and Ancaster, as well as in Hamilton, more travelled inland by wagon to communities in the present-day counties of Wellington, Waterloo, and Oxford.

Some of the Petworth immigrants who came to Hamilton in 1832 had their destination chosen by Fitzgibbon, but others came this way deliberately with the intention of buying land in the Huron Tract. Before his immigrants sailed, Sockett had approached the London directors of the Canada Company about land. Although he seemed unaware that any poor man able to buy from the Canada Company had more resources than most of the poor men sponsored by his committee, the directors, or their secretary, were suspicious. A letter sent on behalf of the directors to the company's Canadian commissioners about the Petworth scheme warned that they knew nothing certain about these immigrants. The directors "understand it to be Lord Egremont's wish and intention that they [the immigrants] should settle together on the Huron Tract, they will no doubt please themselves on this point when they arrive. Many of them have money at their command which it is proposed to lodge with the company to be paid to them individually at York."[52] On further negotiation, these expectations of wealth were scaled down and arrangements were made to send lump sums in the names of the superintendents. Emigrants from Lodsworth and Lurgashall, however, still planned to settle in the Huron Tract, and they made their way to Hamilton with this intention.

The commissioners of the Canada Company were prepared to make travel arrangements from Quebec for emigrants who purchased lands in the Huron Tract. From Hamilton, they offered a wagon service which connected to their own Huron

Road and took settlers to any of the points along the road to Goderich on Lake Huron.[53] Rapson had not understood that the company was interested only in settlers with the means to purchase its land. He waited at Hamilton with his family for nearly two weeks, expecting the company to forward them the next stage on their journey. Without the protection of a superintendent, he was exposed to inflated prices for food and necessities in a town full of waiting emigrants. When the wagons finally arrived, he had his goods loaded before he discovered that the fee was beyond his means and did not include provisions. He unloaded his possessions, and in company with several other Petworth immigrants, made his own way to Guelph. Rapson himself had recovered his health, but he reported several members of his family "poorly" after the hardships of travel. Those who were well had lost so much weight that their clothes were too big for them.

Although many immigrants on later Petworth ships followed the 1832 pioneers to the hinterland of Hamilton, none seem to have gone in the footsteps of the families from the Lodsworth area who accepted the Canada Company offer and set off up the Huron Road to their land. When cholera struck these families, they halted and camped near Fryfogel Inn just east of Stratford. This was where twelve of the party of thirty-two died. John Capling wrote of eight days in which he lost his wife and five children "and what was more hard for me I was obliged to wrap them up in the rinds of trees and dig holes and put them in myself."[54] Capling's moving letter also revealed a familiarity with disease and death. Through his tragedy, he could see advantages in his new home: "… but it is all owing to the afflictions the Almighty was pleased to send upon us for I can see good prospects for a good living to be got."[55] Survivors, including Capling himself, established themselves on company lots in North and South Easthope. Nevertheless, perhaps it was because their experiences were so extreme that other Sussex families did not follow.

The immigrants travelling with superintendent Goatcher on the schooner sent to Lake Erie led the way for later Petworth emigrants who would join them in the London and Western districts even after the Upper Canadian government ceased to subsidize the Adelaide settlement. We are not sure how many Petworth immigrants travelled this far west in 1832, but at least four arrived on foot. John Stedman wrote the story of how a pursuit of his luggage determined his destination. He had grown impatient and decided to walk from Cobourg to Toronto after his steamboat sheltered there from a storm on the lake. He arrived in Toronto and applied at the emigration office only to find that the schooner with Goatcher and his boxes had left two hours earlier. He and three companions set off on a 170-mile journey, carrying a letter from the emigration office that served as a voucher at taverns along the road. By the time the schooner reached Port Stanley, Stedman had been there for a week and had found work for the winter with an area farmer.[56]

Goatcher's contingent of Petworth immigrants from the *Eveline* probably arrived at Port Stanley on the schooner *Canada*, despatched from York on 19 June with 120 emigrants in the charge of a superintendent.[57] The schooner took them through the Welland Canal to Chippawa. William Phillips (Jr) wrote home that he had climbed down the staircase behind Niagara Falls. Referring to some shared source, he assured readers at home that any wagon turned in the space behind the Falls must have been a small one. He was not able to see Buffalo during the six days they waited for a favourable wind on Lake Erie, however, for American authorities prevented their crossing the river.

All along the way, these immigrants were stopped for frequent medical inspections. At Port Stanley, the Petworth immigrants encountered the quarantine rules that were being enforced on travellers by local authority in many of the towns of Upper Canada. Because Mary Ann Hilton was "sea sick," they were held on the far side of the river from the village; food was brought to them as well as lumber to build shanties.[58] These Petworth immigrants must have been among the first that John Bostwick, the agent at Port Stanley, forwarded by wagon to Roswell Mount, the agent for the Adelaide settlement.

Mount held a large party of Petworth immigrants in a camp of their own for the better part of a month. After that, they waited, camped on land belonging to Captain Marvel White in Lobo Township on the road to Adelaide, while Mount made preparations for placing them on their assigned lots. At the end of July, they loaded their possessions on wagons to go from Lobo to Mount's depot on Bear Creek in Adelaide. A final, very rough wagon ride over bush roads saw them onto their individual lots. At some point during the summer, these immigrants from the *Eveline* were joined in the Adelaide settlement by immigrants from the *Lord Melville* and perhaps a few from the *England*.

The last ship to arrive in 1832 was the *England*. We do not know where most of this ship's immigrants chose to settle, only the destination of the people sent by the parish of Wisborough Green. The decision to charter the *England* seems to have been sparked by letters from James Knight, identified by Sockett as a former maltster and innkeeper at Wisborough Green. Knight had gone to Athens County, Ohio, with a party of English settlers after financial reverses at home. There, in addition to keeping a public house and a store, he was acting as an agent for the Courtauld family and promoting settlement on their estate. Sponsors in Wisborough Green arranged for Hale to take six families and three single men from their parish across the border to Knight's settlement.

Despite arriving in the Canadas in mid-June when cholera was raging, Hale conducted this party safely from Montreal to Lake Ontario and across Lake Erie to Cleveland, where American authorities turned their vessel back to Upper Canada. Hale found another way ashore, hired wagons for Pittsburgh, and from there took his immigrants down the Ohio River to Marietta, a relatively short distance from Athens and Nelsonville. Knight described the people from Wisborough Green as arriving happy and "stout hearted ... tho worn down with fatigue," and he gave Hale full credit for bringing them to their destination through the height of the cholera epidemic. Two women from Wisborough Green, both mothers of families, died within two weeks of arrival. The account of their deaths from a sickness that struck others as well as the Sussex immigrants did not give the cause or suggest that it might have been cholera. The rest of the Wisborough Green party stayed in Knight's settlement for only a few months and then moved to the town of Lancaster, Ohio.[59]

Until 1833, reports sent from Upper Canada on the numbers and distribution of immigrants were the responsibility of Colborne's civil secretary. In January of that year, Colborne moved Hawke from Lachine back to the Crown Lands Office in Toronto and made him responsible for all aspects of emigration not immediately connected with the sale of crown land.[60] Although the reports prepared by Buchanan and Hawke do not allow for direct comparison, they differed significantly in the proportion of new immigrants assigned to the western part of the province in 1833. Buchanan's estimate for the Gore, Niagara, London, and Western districts was 7,480, a number approaching half his total for the upper province. Hawke believed that only one third of the immigrant population of that year located in places west of Toronto and the Home District. The experience of Petworth immigrants suggests that the discrepancy may have in part been the result of some immigrants giving one destination as they travelled up the St Lawrence and then changing their minds before they reached their original goal.

The Petworth immigrants of 1833 lived the dilemma common to immigrants everywhere of arriving to find their information sadly out of date (in this case, letters written only a year earlier and published by the Petworth committee shortly before they had left England). They arrived expecting aid similar to that given in Adelaide in 1832. Once they realized how little the government would do to support them as settlers of a remote township, many of them decided to cut short their journey. Mary Barnes, an immigrant of 1832, gave an insider's view. She wrote sympathetically of the newly arrived immigrants as "all over the place at present, not knowing what to be doing."[61]

One party of immigrants who left the Petworth area on the *England* in 1833 had their way chosen for them by James Rapson. Rapson had gone ahead in 1832 and spent the winter near Galt, where he was waiting for the party, which included his brother and sister and their families, to arrive. Letters to Phillip Rapson in Lodsworth described the family reunion in Upper Canada. The group of five families had taken advantage of the offer Sockett made in 1833 and thereafter to cover the cost of about 50 miles of additional water transport to points on Lake Ontario as far as Hamilton, but William and Rhoda had been unable to get a letter to their brother James to warn him of their arrival. On 5 July, James told his father, "I saw William coming, near a quarter of a mile before he came to our house; and he held up his hat. I knew him, but I could not believe my eyes for some time."[62] Rhoda Thair, picked up the story: "Wm and George went on, and James came to meet us, we got here just as it was dark ... met the children about a mile from home, without any shoes or stockings, they all go so here ... The next day, poor Hannah (her niece) came in, did not know that we were here, she looked very hard, and at last begun crying before she could speak."[63]

The Petworth immigrants of 1833 who did not have relatives planning their reception were fortunate in finding a strong job market in Toronto. Hale described Toronto as the "most certain field of employment" for steady, sturdy men. He listed a range of possibilities open to people with occupations other than agriculture. Potential employers were looking for bricklayers and brickmakers, shoemakers, tailors (also wanted in Hamilton and Dundas), coopers, "lads of good behaviour capable of taking care of Horses as Gentlemans servants," gardeners (if capable of agricultural labour), and engravers. Sign painters also did well, and not far from Toronto there were openings for moulders of cast iron.[64]

On 17 July 1833, George Gurnett reported in his *Courier of Upper Canada* that the "fine, healthy, well clothed, and well behaved body of people" sent by the Petworth committee had no difficulty finding work. He reported that many "fine young women" among Egremont's immigrants had respectable places and that boys, young men, labouring men, and mechanics had all found work within three or four days of arriving on 1 July.[65] Gurnett had reason to follow the Petworth immigrants more closely than any other newspaper owner in Toronto because his uncle was Egremont's steward and he himself came from Horsham, just a short distance to the northeast of Petworth. He also had hopes of making his newspaper office an employment centre where Torontonians could hire Sussex emigrants. In an advertisement run in his paper in 1833, he and Hale proposed to act as finders for employers wishing to place requests for the kinds of workers Hale might bring from England in the next immigration season.[66] Although this plan seems to have fallen through, Gurnett hired Petworth immigrants for himself or on behalf of his friends in 1833, and in 1834 he met their steamboat again, looking for a particular trade.

At first, perhaps three-quarters of the Petworth immigrants who arrived in Toronto in 1833 joined together in making a request for land. They approached Colborne through Hale, asking to be assigned lots as close to the Adelaide settlement as possible. Colborne suggested Plympton, the next township west of Warwick on the shores of Lake Huron. Although on the line of the Egremont Road (a road laid out from Lobo Township to Lake Huron and named for Egremont) and geographically close to Petworth immigrants of 1832, this township was separated from settlers in Adelaide by vacant lands. For much of the distance between the village of Adelaide and Errol on Lake Huron, the Egremont Road was still a slash through the forest. Men on horseback used it at their peril; no one considered taking a wagon.[67] Immigrant families could not reach Plympton from this direction. The route chosen by the government was by water, through Lake Erie, Lake St Clair, and the St Clair River.

Later in the summer, after things had gone wrong, Hawke wrote to Sockett about these difficult days. Hale, he said, had told Colborne that the Petworth immigrants had sufficient funds of their own or from sponsors to manage without government aid. Hawke had obviously doubted that this was true. While the schooner *Trafalgar* chartered by government at a cost of ninety pounds waited at the dock in Toronto, Hawke had gone on board to try to speak personally to every head of family. He had wanted to be sure that the immigrants understood that they would get only minimal assistance to settle in Plympton. He informed Sockett that he had taken particular care to explain that they must buy their own food on the journey, and he claimed that as a result of his warnings 154 of their number had remained behind (a count that must have included the people going to join James Rapson). Another few of those who actually sailed for Plympton had been "tempted away" by high wages as they had passed through the Welland Canal. Perhaps no more that 35 or 40 Petworth immigrants had completed the journey to Plympton.[68]

Hale also wrote to Sockett justifying his actions. As Colborne had been unable to pay Hale's expenses, the decision to continue his journey to Plympton had rested with Hale. They had talked in terms of a large party, and Hale had had the impression that the governor had wanted him to go. He had drawn extra money on the committee's account with Peter McGill and had gone ahead with his plans to sail with them even after the numbers dropped. Where his actions became murky was in the matter of rations for the people travelling with him. According to the immigrants, Hale had purchased these rations himself. He seems to have seen himself as their agent and deducted the cost from the money due to them; they assumed that he had supplied food on behalf of the committee as he had until they had reached Toronto.

The immigrants bound for Plympton were on the schooner for ten days before being put off at a different location from the one intended. Strong winds prevented the vessel from getting out of the St Clair River and into Lake Huron. Rather than delay to wait for favourable conditions, the captain had decided to leave the immigrants at the landing place on the river nearest the lake. He had set them ashore at an Indian reserve (near Sarnia) and sent word to Henry Jones, the crown land agent who was to arrange their location. Hale left his immigrants in a storehouse at the wharf to await Jones's arrival and sailed back to Toronto with the schooner.[69] Hale's account with the Petworth committee for his party's expenses to Toronto, and his own during the remainder of his stay in Upper Canada, was over £300.[70]

For the 1834 emigration, Colborne and Hawke had regrouped after the problems of the previous year and put in place a new plan to send Petworth immigrants to Woodstock. Apprehensions of a new epidemic of cholera may explain why these immigrants were moved through and out of Toronto within five days of their arrival.[71] Superintendent Brydone stated that the 1834 immigrants had the option of finding jobs for themselves in Toronto, but they were given little opportunity and were offered attractive incentives to stay with him. His immigrants seem to have escaped the cholera epidemic of that year. The disease was not recognized in Montreal until 11 July and did not reach Upper Canada until the middle of the month. Thus, although they endured a prolonged and uncomfortable delay at the Grosse Île Quarantine Station, Brydone's party travelled safely in advance of the outbreak of the disease, which did not reach Woodstock during the summer. Brydone used Hawke's Toronto office to apprentice a few boys and make travel arrangements for the rest of his group as recommended by the lieutenant-governor.

In Brydone's *Narrative* for 1834, we have our best account of the distribution of a body of Petworth immigrants to their first destinations in Upper Canada. A group of the single men were sent to the Welland Canal and from there to construction jobs on the Grand River Canal or at the Port Stanley harbour. Men could earn from two to three pounds a month on public works that summer. Brydone chose "such of the young men as I thought fit, and were willing," and Colborne authorized a free passage on the schooner *Superior* via the Welland Canal. As is the case with the great majority of single men who travelled apart from a family, these young men disappear from view; we have found no reports of their arrival at their intended destination or of what happened to them at the end of the construction season.

Most of the remaining immigrants of 1834 settled initially in an area no more than two or three days' travel from Hamilton. A party one hundred strong went by steamboat from Toronto to Hamilton, and by wagon from Hamilton to Woodstock, under Brydone's supervision. At Colborne's request, Brydone included a twelfth family in addition to the eleven sent by the Petworth committee.

Colborne and Hawke were confident that even a large party of immigrants of the type sent by the Petworth committee would find work immediately in Woodstock. This community had grown to a sizeable village so rapidly that it still lacked an official name. (Contemporary sources give the destination of Brydone's party as Blandford [Township] or as the Blandford town plot.) Colborne and Hawke, however, were less confident that these families would flourish if they had to depend entirely on wage labour. They thus offered the additional resources of temporary possession of five-acre lots and log houses built at government expense.

Brydone claimed travel expenses of £110 currency for the party's journey from Toronto to Woodstock. Although these expenses were paid by the Crown Lands Department of Upper Canada, Brydone made a full report to the Petworth committee, beginning with his arrival at Hamilton on 19 June. For a time, he had thought his immigrants and their possessions might be stuck on the wharf. Rear-Admiral Henry Vansittart (who later employed Petworth immigrants) had hired a train of twenty-one wagons the day before and had left for Woodstock, depleting the available transportation resources. With the help of William Cattermole, a part-time agent for the Crown Lands Department, Brydone found the wagons he needed and a night's accommodation for his people. A few women slept in Cattermole's inn and the remainder bedded down on hay and straw in the barn.

The next day, the Petworth party set out for Blandford Township, a two-day trip from Hamilton. Brydone had fourteen wagons, four for fifty women and children and ten for luggage. Three or four families were assigned to each of the wagons. While his emigrants were on the road, Brydone used his discretion in buying tea for the women and milk for the children in addition to the bread, cheese, and beer specified by the lieutenant-governor (perhaps standard cold fare). Such a large party could not be accommodated over night on the road. Brydone explained to Sockett that he would have had to divide it into two contingents even if five or six wagons had not fallen far behind on the first day.

The landlady at Van Norman's Inn, "an American," was quick to take advantage of these large convoys of wagons. Brydone was not deceived by her fussing over the boys and taking quilts out to the barn to cover them. She snatched these coverings back as soon as Brydone made clear that he would not pay for them as beds. The next day, he relented and accepted her overcharging for the children's milk for the sake of Mrs West, whom he left behind at the inn to have her baby. She was attended by one of the Voice girls and a local midwife. Brydone and his wagons arrived in Woodstock the next day; the wagons that had fallen behind, in the charge of one of the Uptons, arrived a day later.[72] By then, the first arrivals were already being hired in and around Woodstock.

Petworth immigrants of 1835 to 1837 arrived in a province where the bright economic outlook of the beginning of the decade had dimmed. Hawke's annual reports for these three years painted a gloomy picture. In 1835, he wrote that he doubted that half the immigrants Buchanan had reported as having settled in Upper Canada were still in the province. The 4,500 who remained, he suggested, would do no more than replace immigrants from 1834 who had given up on the Canadas and joined the exodus over the border. Buchanan's figures for the total numbers of immigrants going from Quebec to Upper Canada rose steadily from 1835 to 1837. Although neither Buchanan nor Hawke speculated on the proportion, a great many of the immigrants of 1836 and 1837 must also have found their way across the border on a temporary or permanent basis. Undoubtedly a number of Petworth immigrants went with them, although families with assistance and those with friends or relatives already in the province had more reason to remain that did the general immigrant population. In these years, Hawke excepted those joining family members in the province from his warnings that poor emigrants should not be forwarded to him in expectation of certain work and good wages. Thanks to considerable publicity, Petworth immigrants might also expect to be hired on the strength of the reputation of the group as well as through individual recommendations.

The travels of Petworth immigrants in the years 1835–37 are not nearly as well recorded as those of the first three years. Sockett was content with Brydone's 1834 Narrative, and the absence of new government initiatives meant less attention in Canadian records. For the period after Sir Francis Bond Head replaced Colborne as lieutenant-governor at the beginning of 1836, official records of Petworth immigrants become still more scanty. In 1835 and 1836, Hawke extended the plan to give small lots of up to five acres to three Grand River communities, Brantford, Paris, and Cayuga (in the case of Cayuga, he specified the township rather than the village). In each of the three years from 1835 to 1837, Petworth families travelled by steamboat to Hamilton and then by road to Brantford or Woodstock. In 1835, Hawke reported 160 "Egremont settlers" forwarded at public expense to Brantford.[73]

A list of 1835 includes the information that some heads of families on the Burrell had a destination picked out and a few had employment waiting. One intended to go to Montreal and another planned to join his sons who had settled in the United States. The destinations of the others suggest where Petworth immigrants of these years may have settled: Thornhill, St Catharines, Ancaster, Hamilton, Brantford, and Guelph.[74] Woodstock should also be added to the list, as settlers from the ships of

1835 and 1836 found their way there. In 1837, Hawke wrote to John Hatch in Wood-stock to plan for the reception of eight or nine Petworth families.[75]

The limited evidence we have collected indicates that Petworth immigrants with needed skills were still able to find work in Upper Canada in 1836 and 1837, although they may have had to travel farther than the government was willing to take them in these years. In 1836, Lydia Hilton wrote that her family and that of John Barnes were the only families to stop in Toronto. She might have added that the Hiltons and the Barnes each had a son already established in Toronto with an employer in a position to help them find work. Other families were sent on to Brantford by the government, but the Jackmans complained that they had to pay part of their own expenses. They were probably expected to provide their own food on the journey from Toronto. The Coopers had to pay their own way from Hamilton to Adelaide. Ann Mann's family group travelled as far as Brantford and then paused there for five weeks, perhaps waiting to earn enough money to continue on to the Adelaide set-tlement by land. Such letters give the impression that emigrants of 1836 and 1837 may have found they needed to go west of Brantford to find permanent work. With travel within the Canadas in mind, immigrants wrote to those in England planning to follow with warnings against bringing too much bulky luggage. Luggage was expensive to transport beyond Montreal, and the farther inland people went, the more difficult travel became. These writers sometimes offered to meet family members, with or without a wagon, to see them over a final portion of the journey.

ALL INDICATIONS are that the initial destinations of many Petworth immigrants within Upper Canada were strongly influenced by the travelling assistance they were given. As the boundaries of settlement expanded in the 1830s, there was a general movement inland from the lakes and major rivers to open new townships. The town-ships in which records of Petworth immigrants can be found are best explained in terms of assistance. Sockett's immigrants, for instance, travelled past the ports on Lake Ontario that led inland to Peterborough and the Kawartha Lakes and to a number of townships where Colborne and the Crown Lands Department were locating both settlers of means and assisted immigrants. Sockett had decided that his immigrants were best to settle in the Toronto area or farther west. He reinforced his opinion by sending his superintendent, and the order on the Canada Company for cash pay-ments, through to that destination.

Assessing the immigration of 1832, Sockett wrote that "they have taken up excel-lent positions, both for their own benefit and to attract others to join them."[76] In all the years of the scheme, Sockett's policy of sending his party through to Toronto meant that very few settled east of that city. In the particular circumstances of the cholera epidemic of 1832, Colborne's government intervened strongly in distribut-ing arriving immigrants. Colborne offered the Petworth immigrants free transport through agents of the Crown Lands Department to Hamilton and Port Stanley and also gave them further assistance in 1832 to settle in Adelaide Township or to find work nearby. The extraordinary number of immigrants sent to the London and Western districts in 1832 is a prime example of assistance influencing settlement. An artificial community like that created by the government in Adelaide proved itself by attracting additional settlers. Petworth immigrants continued to join family and friends in Adelaide even though they were not given the same help in later years. In Plympton, at least so far as Petworth immigrants were concerned, the government failed to create enough of a community in 1833 to draw settlers of later years.

Not all Petworth immigrants followed the advice of government agents. In each year, there were also people whose previous occupations made urban settlement attractive to them. In 1832, for instance, the Goldring family from the coastal parish of South Bersted chose to stay close to Toronto and to Lake Ontario in order to earn a living in familiar ways. Nevertheless, in 1832 and again in 1834, free transport and assistance were strong persuaders to take the advice of the governor and go farther west. In 1833, however, Hawke's advice helped to convince many Petworth immigrants that their best chance of employment was in the city, and 1833 seems to have been the only year of six in which a high proportion of Petworth immigrants found their first job in Toronto and its environs. In 1834, Brydone reported that he left only a few young apprentices in Toronto. A quick departure and the presence of a number of immigrants from East Sussex who had no relatives in the province help to explain the large group who remained together in 1834 to start a new "Petworth" community in and around Woodstock.

By 1835–37, the immigrants reporting that they had found work in Toronto and the surrounding area usually had family or an acquaintance already established in the local community. Other Petworth immigrants found their own way to the Adelaide area and the Western District (and to Michigan) in these years, but our results in tracing individuals suggest that these people also were chain migrants following relatives or people known to them.

Many Petworth immigrants settled in the Gore District in 1832, and in every year after 1833, the largest number of Petworth immigrants settled for the first time in that district. Places like Hamilton, Ancaster, Dundas, and Guelph attracted Petworth immigrants wanting to work at a trade. In newer communities, there were opportunities to combine wage labour with the occupation and cultivation of enough land to raise food for a family. Townships on the middle and upper Grand River offered Petworth immigrants good opportunities for employment. Those who chose to become farmers had good prospects of acquiring land within the first generation. Hawke had designed his five-acre-lot plan for immigrants sent by English parishes if not for the Petworth immigrants. He must have been especially anxious that Egremont not experience any problems or hear a repetition of the criticisms of the scheme that reached England in 1833. He judged that these south-of-England labourers would do best under these conditions, and by 1834 there were enough parish-aided immigrants in Upper Canada for him to base his opinion on his observation of families who had settled comfortably.

Sir John Colborne,
lieutenant-governor of Upper
Canada, 1828–1836
James Scott after William
Fisher, *Field Marshal Lord*
Seaton, 1864
Toronto Reference Library,
T14945

Sir Francis Bond Head,
lieutenant-governor of Upper
Canada, 1836–1838
Charles Turner after Nelson Cook, *His*
Excellency Sir Francis Bond Head, 1837
Toronto Reference Library, T31830

Toronto: Maitland's Wharf, Toronto. Brydone stayed at the Ontario House Hotel seen in the background.

Edward John Roberts after William Henry Bartlett, *Looking north from Maitland's Wharf at the foot of Church Street* (1838)
Toronto Reference Library, T32137

Toronto, Front Street West. Brydone's 1834 immigrants found their own accommodation rather than use the immigrant sheds on the extreme left of the picture.

John George Howard, *Toronto, Front Street West* (1834)
Toronto Reference Library, T14945

Petworth immigrants of 1834 travelled from Toronto to Hamilton on the Queenston.

After an 1827 sketch by Captain Van Cleve, *The Steam Boat Queenston*
AO, FII94, Acc 9379

A settler's clearing and cabin

Henry Francis Ainslie, *Settler's House*
NA, C544

Woodstock in 1840
Sketch by Henry James Warre
NA, C17667

Brantford in 1840.
Sketch by Henry James Warre.
NA, C17694.

Both Woodstock and Brantford were involved in Colborne's five-acre-lot plan.

The Petworth Emigration Committee

will engage a SHIP, to sail from *Portsmouth* to *Montreal* early in April next.

———————◆◆◆———————

Mr. BRYDONE, Surgeon, R. N. who conducted the Party that went out in the Ship "BRITISH TAR" last year, has engaged to take charge of those who may go out, under the management of the Committee this season.

Mr. Brydone will be commissioned to purchase Land for the EARL OF EGREMONT, in UPPER CANADA, it is therefore necessary that he should get to that Country, as early as possible, in order that the operations of clearing and building, may be forwarded before the season is too far advanced.

Persons disposed to take advantage of this opportunity, must apply to *Mr. Phillips*, Library, Petworth; or to *Mr. Kennard*, No. 20, Penny Street, Portsmouth, without delay.

Petworth,
Feb. 24th. 1835.

———————◆◆◆———————

J. Phillips, Printer, Petworth.

Broadside announcing the Petworth Emigration Committee's plans for a settlement in Upper Canada, February 1835

English immigrants

From left to right, Mark, Thomas, John, Charles, and Eli, five sons of Ann (Downer) and Samuel Mann
Courtesy of Margaret Parsons

From left to right, Amina, Priscilla, Mary Ann, and Elizabeth, four daughters of Moses and Sarah (Hoad) Chantler
Courtesy of Elizabeth R. Gillespie

Descendants of James and Sarah (Redman) Harper. The occasion is believed to be a celebration of the seventieth anniversary of the family's arrival in 1832.
Courtesy of Flamborough Archives Photograph Collection

CHAPTER 5

"DOMICILES OF THEIR OWN": ASSISTED SETTLEMENT IN UPPER CANADA

It is from amongst the poorer classes of Emigrants that we are to look for
Pioneers to open the Wilderness ... it is highly indispensable to encourage
the Labouring farmer families to obtain *domiciles of their own* as soon as
possible after their arrival and not to keep them in that unpleasant state of
migration and dependence for shelter which must inevitably be the case if
they are not enabled to avail themselves of settlement.

A.C. Buchanan, Report on Emigration for 1833[1]

Petworth immigrants lived the adventure of immigration in all the messy details of
individual personality and circumstance. Their collective experience in successive
years is reflected in the debate between Lieutenant-Governor Sir John Colborne and
officials at the Colonial Office on the subject of poor immigrants. Colborne wanted
to continue assisting some among the families who arrived healthy but handicapped
by poverty and young children. He thought this assistance necessary to prevent great
misery and to attach useful settlers to the province. The Colonial Office wanted to
get out of the business of assisting settlement. Its officials believed that assistance
schemes were not a good use of crown lands or revenues, and in the spirit of the
administrative reforms of the times, they sought to keep the focus on the big picture in discussing the proper relationship between government and the poor.[2]

Perspective played an important part in deciding how necessary assisted settlement might be for poor arriving immigrants. Those involved in giving the kind of
assistance championed by Colborne and Buchanan knew that poor immigrants faced
high hurdles in getting settled as farmers, the primary occupation in Upper Canada.[3]
They saw an overlong exposure to the stresses of the "unpleasant state of migration"
– the hardships and uncertainties described in Chapter 4 – as a serious threat to family stability. The option of assisted settlement gave them a way to help families find
a place in a community where they could begin to feel that they had a home. They
believed that assistance could be a deciding factor between success and advantage
to the province or failure.

From the more distant perspective of the Colonial Office, Upper Canada seemed
to be receiving all the immigrants it needed. Colonial under-secretary Howick's conclusion that no public body should be asked to take responsibility for the selection
and sending of emigrants had the unspoken corollary that selection must be left to
the harsh realities of the marketplace. Officials in the Colonial Office did not want

to discourage emigration, but they certainly did not want to encourage unsuitable migrants by perpetuating a belief that they would receive substantial help on arrival. They looked at future implications; Colborne and his agents in the Crown Lands Department of Upper Canada dealt with actual people and their immediate and very pressing problems.

The experience of Petworth immigrants on the individual level is not conclusive proof that assistance was essential to their success as immigrants. We have examples of families who did well on their own and no way to prove that others who did well with government assistance might not have managed in the long run without it. On the question of community formation, however, hindsight favours Colborne. His two major initiatives in assisting Petworth immigrants are associated with Adelaide Township and Woodstock, two communities where the memory of a connection to the Petworth scheme lives today.

Apart from a log house on each lot to provide shelter (which the Quebec agent Alexander Buchanan identified as crucial), the assistance given Petworth immigrants in the two settlements of Adelaide and Woodstock was very different – as were the settlements themselves. Adelaide was a new settlement being created in the bush. Woodstock was also a new community, but it was in an area of previous settlements and the immigrants were placed on the fringes of a rapidly expanding village. Both communities, however, in the opinion of people in the Crown Lands Department, received the aid they needed to enable them to get a start in establishing themselves as permanent settlers in Upper Canada.

Government assistance had played a larger part than most contemporaries of the Petworth immigrants knew in the successes that bolstered the belief that Upper Canada was a good country for the poor man. When Colborne arrived in Upper Canada in 1828, he found a lively tradition of government-assisted settlement that had evolved over time to meet different needs. This tradition had an informal counterpart in the aid that private sellers sometimes gave to find purchasers or to attract the first settlers who would give value to their remaining wild lands. In the latter part of the eighteenth century and the beginning of the nineteenth, crown lands in Upper Canada had been dispensed freely as a means to an end – as a reward for military and other services to the government or as an incentive to attract settlers to particular areas. This was the expectation that Howick sought to change in 1831 when he introduced sale by auction and a policy of maximizing the monetary return to the government when crown lands were sold.

The pattern of government aid to new settlers in the territory that became Upper Canada had been set for loyalist refugees who had a strong claim for compensation for the land and property they lost as a result of the American Revolution. The grants of land they received were free, unencumbered by the fees imposed on "free" crown lands later in the eighteenth century, and the British government helped loyalist settlers to take up these land grants with transport, temporary accommodation, food, farm implements, tools, seeds, and sometimes clothing.[4] Their children still claimed a right to grants of land in the 1830s when the Petworth immigrants arrived.

The next wave of settlers crossed the border as "late loyalists" or arrived on ships from Britain in the late eighteenth century. They did not have the same initial claim on the government, but they wanted land and the sparsely settled colony could best provide for needy immigrants by helping them become frontier farmers. Marianne McLean has traced the fortunes of nine emigrant parties from Glengarry, Scotland, who settled in Glengarry, Upper Canada, between 1784 and 1816. Most of them had assistance in some form after they arrived, but the last party is the first she describes as assisted emigrants, sailing from Scotland in 1815 on a ship supplied by the Colonial Office.[5]

Assisted emigrations and settlements initiated by the Colonial Office between 1815 and 1825 began in the shadow of the War of 1812–14. Initially, the main objective of assistance was to attract, and attach to the land, a population able to defend the colony from any future American invasion. The generous first plan of 1815 was derailed by Napoleon's hundred days, and a second in 1818, aimed at capitalists willing to bring at least ten families, was discontinued after one season because of a poor response. Although Bruce Elliott's account of the chain migration that followed a single ship carrying Tipperary Irish in 1818 is a striking reminder of what a small beginning could do, the organizers of assisted emigration looked for a more immediate result.[6]

The largest scheme of assistance motivated by issues of defending a British possession was for the benefit of discharged soldiers, including the two groups who founded the Perth and Richmond military settlements in the Bathurst District. The soldiers located in the Bathurst District paid for their land indirectly by pioneering sites chosen for strategic importance rather than for the fertility of the soil or for an advantageous position. Their settlements were intended as a barrier between the border and the route laid out for the inland Rideau Canal. In these settlements, supervision and assistance were provided by the Military Settling Department under the governor of Lower Canada.[7] (The few former soldiers among the Petworth immigrants were some of the last to be given free land grants in Upper Canada on showing their discharge papers.)

In 1820–21, as a means of relieving conditions at home, the Colonial Office supported the sponsors of emigrants from weaving districts of Lanark and Renfrewshire. The initiative came from would-be economic migrants and from local sponsors who feared unrest among men put out of work by machines. Despite receiving inferior land, these Scottish weavers did make homes in the Lanark settlement of the Bathurst District with aid supervised by the Military Settling Department.[8]

During the rest of this decade, Robert Wilmot Horton used his position as undersecretary in the Colonial Office to develop the idea of assisted emigration in association with assisted settlement as a solution to a "surplus population" at home. Horton, however, chose as his candidates Irish Roman Catholics from a turbulent area in the hinterland of Cork, immigrants viewed with considerable alarm in Upper Canada. To win the cooperation of executive members of the Upper Canadian government, Horton gave them authority over the settlement (the Military Settling Department at Quebec was disbanded in 1822) and appointed Peter Robinson, one of their number, as superintendent of the Irish settlements.[9] Robinson's first settlement of some 560 emigrants in the Bathurst District in 1823, however, had mixed results and generated some negative publicity as a result of bad feeling between old and new assisted settlers. The Upper Canadian government responded by sending Robinson's 1825 emigrants, a party some 2,000 strong, to open up a promising region in the Newcastle District that had previously failed to attract settlers.[10] Robinson's second settlement, for which Peterborough was given his name, was the experiment Horton and his followers declared an unqualified success. Because they made the difficult journey to a thinly settled area chosen for its promising location, these settlers received better locations than had been given most of those who had gone to the Bathurst District. Their settlement in Peterborough-area townships proved once again that poor British immigrants could create a community if "enabled" by assistance.[11]

Little else happened in the field of government-assisted settlement between 1825 and 1831. The issues that stood in the way of assisted settlements were their cost and the fact that the institutions responsible for their authorization received no tangible return. In 1830, John Richards addressed the dilemma of assisted settlement as part of his one-man commission on land and settlement in British North America. Although Colonial Secretary Goderich, Under-secretary Howick, and their officials were more interested in what Richards reported about land policies, he did have some perceptive things to say about frontier settlement. On the one hand, he wrote, "it is only the poorest classes who will lead the way into the woods."[12] On the other, he recognized that any large settlement of immigrant paupers must be costly to someone. In the examples he gave, inexpensive settlers were not pioneers but people sent to a thinly settled area where the initial infrastructure of roads and supplies was already in place. In outlining how to provide for a large influx of assisted immigrants, Richards drew on his own experience with a private colonization company in the United States and had no new direction to offer. His proposal for an assisted settlement in the wild lands of New Brunswick differed little in essentials from assisted settlements formed by previous governments in British North America.

In 1831, Colborne believed in common with many others that the British government was preparing to take responsibility for finding the money for pauper settlements. He interpreted the arrival of large numbers of parish immigrants in Upper Canada in the light of reports of the Swing disturbances and of the proposed Emigration Bill and the parliamentary debates surrounding its introduction. The bill promised supervised emigration and settlement under the direction of emigration commissioners. Colborne jumped to the conclusion that 1831 was "a first trial, made for the purpose of relieving parishes at home," and that the government intended him to make good on his end of the promise.

Colborne turned to Robinson, who had been appointed commissioner of the newly created Crown Lands Department in 1826, to provide the land and supervision that would give desirable families the kind of stake in the province that more affluent immigrants could purchase. Fifty-acre lots were set aside in two selected areas: one in Newcastle District townships reached through Peterborough, and the other north of Toronto on Lake Simcoe. In addition to extending generous credit for purchase, Robinson's agents in charge of these two settlements arranged transport, built log huts, and supplied income by hiring immigrants to work on the roads into the settlements. In 1831, 471 families were located on these terms in the Newcastle District and 108 in the Home District. In his report to the colonial secretary, Colborne explicitly linked parish emigration and assisted settlement. He predicated his opinion that parishes might safely go ahead with plans to remove their surplus population to Upper Canada on the basis of the "experiment of this year of sending destitute emigrants on land, and giving them some assistance."[13]

Officials in the Colonial Office did not interest themselves much in the details of Colborne's assisted settlements, as they hoped to phase out such settlements within a year or two. The dispatch from the Colonial Office to Colborne in October 1831 on the subject of the sale of colonial lands anticipated the thinking that would dominate the emigration commissioners' report. Colborne was informed that using public revenues to locate and maintain pauper emigrants would "involve an expense which could not be met" and would be "utterly inconsistent with and destructive of the whole plan of disposing of land by public sale."[14] In the future, all sales of crown lands in Upper Canada were to be by auction and to the highest bidder. Land was for immigrants able to purchase. Pauper immigrants must labour for wages, preferably for private employers but if work could not be found, then for government.

Assisted settlements fitted too nicely into Colborne's vision of Upper Canada for him to abandon the idea easily. Artisans and labourers were as important as middle-class settlers to the fully rounded "British" communities he hoped to create, and he recognized that labour and services should be available from the beginning to keep middle-class families in the bush. He was also deeply concerned that the number of labouring families who did not find adequate employment during their first summer might be much larger than officials sitting in the Colonial Office imagined.

At the start of the 1832 emigrant season, Colborne replied to the new Colonial Office policy on poor immigrants. He believed that "the system of maintaining emigrants for a few months on land which they may purchase on credit ... [is] the best mode of settling this country," if – and this qualification was very important – funds could be found to supply them with provisions.[15] Colborne did not have much hope of funding from Britain. He knew that the British Parliament would not vote money as it had for Robinson's Irish emigrants, and his suggestion that the money might come from funds "raised by parishes desirous of removing their redundant population" died as he made it. His predecessor, Sir Peregrine Maitland, had dipped into the Military Chest to make up amounts not covered by direct votes of the British Parliament, but Howick had cut off this source when he became under-secretary. The option Colborne explored involved using the territorial revenue of Upper Canada, an option made possible by the recent increase in sales of crown lands.[16]

UPPER CANADA: GOVERNMENT ASSISTANCE TO PETWORTH IMMIGRANTS

Instructions sent to Colborne in February 1832 recognized the uncertainties of a laissez-faire policy. They acknowledged the possibility that not all immigrants who arrived in Upper Canada would be hired by private employers or given jobs on public works. The lieutenant-governor was given qualified permission to hire immigrants who could not be employed in any other way for clearing and cultivating selected crown lands. The policy was clearly described as a last resort, and pointed reference was made to the gratifying economy with which Colborne had managed the reception of immigrants in 1831. He was to offer the land these immigrants had improved for sale at a higher price than wild lands. A few of the immigrants might be given land on credit; the details were left to Colborne.[17]

Peter Robinson in the Crown Lands Department prepared his first notices for sales of crown lands in 1832 in January. These notices included information for indigent immigrants. After describing sale by auction according to the terms set down by the colonial secretary, he added that fifty-acre lots in selected townships would be made available to indigent immigrants by private sale. Purchasers in the auctions would have to pay a quarter down and would have three years' grace before they would have to make the first of three instalments on a price of five shillings an acre and begin to pay interest. By May his notices indicated which townships in the Bathurst District and on Georgian Bay would have fifty-acre lots. Once a lot was assigned, government agents would arrange for the building of a small log hut and would employ immigrant settlers in opening roads into these settlements.

Roswell Mount's name and his agency in the Western District were added to Robinson's notice in May.[18] He would soon become responsible for the large assisted settlement in the townships of Adelaide and Warwick, which would become home to a number of Petworth immigrants, but as late as 18 June a separate notice for his agency made no mention of aid in travel or settlement. This notice directed emigrants "with means" to Mount at his base in the Township of Caradoc. Payment for lots in Mount's agency was deferred for three years, presumably because of the remote location, which according to the Surveyor General's Office was 225 miles by stagecoach from Toronto.[19] The price was to be the average of land sales in the area. Petworth immigrants described the terms of purchase for their lots much as they were set out in Robinson's notice except that they reported a price of two dollars an acre. This was the price charged indigent immigrants assisted as settlers, and in the Adelaide settlement it was applied to lots of one hundred acres.

Before cholera broke out in July, Colborne had tried to comply with his orders. Crown lands agents were instructed to explain the terms on which indigent immigrants occupied fifty-acre lots. Applicants must understand that the local government was not able to give direct assistance such as food, household utensils, or farm implements. They would receive only the wages they earned on the roads that were being opened into these settlements.[20] After cholera struck in Quebec on 8 June, however, hordes of poor immigrants were hastily forwarded from Quebec and Montreal. As news of cholera in the Canadas spread, American authorities made every effort to close off the border, thus forcing Upper Canada to find places for all immigrants, sick or well. Colborne must surely have felt that the time had come for a policy of last resort. He saw no alternative to opening more crown land to indigent immigrants and to increasing the aid given to them.

James Fitzgibbon of the Strangers' Friend Society followed official policy in hastening Petworth immigrants from the *Lord Melville* and the *Eveline* out of Toronto with all possible speed. Other agents tended to follow suit. The last stopping point in Upper Canada was Roswell Mount's agency at the western extreme of Colborne's chain of agents. There, groups of immigrants forwarded by water to Port Stanley arrived in successive waves until late in the season – perhaps as many as 3,500 in all. Mount estimated that about 400 of these immigrants had been sent from England by Egremont's committee.

Courtesy of the Duke of Richmond, the Petworth immigrants of 1832 were preceded on their travels in Upper Canada by an effusive letter signed by Colonial Secretary Viscount Goderich himself asking that no pains be spared for emigrants so munificently supported by the Earl of Egremont. Beginning with Fitzgibbon, harried agents put aside considerations of cost in favour of results. Copies of this letter were sent to the agent at Port Stanley and to Roswell Mount.[21] The letter spoke to Mount's considerable ambition. No one was more determined than he that Egremont's protégés should send good reports back home of their treatment in Upper Canada.

The first Petworth immigrants arrived at Mount's agency from Port Stanley before Mount was ready to take them to their lots. They seem to have been the only immigrants he sent to Captain Marvel White's in Lobo Township, where Mount had them looked after for nearly a month. Despite the multitude of problems caused by the sudden influx, he sent doctors to look after their sick and messengers to carry medicines. In early August, he hired established settlers with their teams of oxen to bring the Petworth immigrants from Lobo and Woodhull's Mills to his depot on Bear Creek (Sydenham River).[22]

The road that would be named for Egremont had been surveyed to run east–west. Village sites for Adelaide and Warwick were laid out on the road, which served as the base line of lots on either side of it. According to the original plan, the Adelaide settlement would be reached by this road, with Lobo as the entry point. Mount soon found supplies from this direction insufficient. He decided to establish his main depot in Caradoc and to bring supplies north from the front townships rather than west from Lobo. He thus opened his own road from the Caradoc depot. This would be the road travelled by the majority of immigrants going into the settlement. It led to an intermediate depot at the twelve-mile point, the one at Bear Creek, and to his final supply point on the village plot of Adelaide. The Bear Creek depot, on the line between the fourth and fifth concessions of Adelaide, was at or very near the present site of Strathroy. Six miles beyond Bear Creek, Mount's road met the Egremont

Road at Adelaide Village, which became the base for a predominantly Irish community. The Bear Creek depot served a second community where there were more English settlers, settlers whose numbers included many others besides the Petworth immigrants and who are also associated with a community at Katesville.[23]

The name of the Egremont Road commemorates Sockett's immigrants in the Adelaide and Warwick area. If his hopes to rename Adelaide Township for Egremont had been realized, the Petworth scheme might be better known in Ontario.[24] A number of these families spent the rest of their lives in Adelaide Township or moved relatively short distances away in the same general area. Their children intermarried. Although the focus of our research was on the first settlement at Adelaide, we have turned up a number of chain migrants assisted by the Petworth committee in later years (see Table 5.1 on pages 152-3).

The largest cluster of Petworth immigrants were located on lots on the fourth and fifth concessions of Adelaide Township. Mount appears to have tried to reserve these lots – which were conveniently located in relation to his depots – for immigrants ready to settle immediately. Petworth immigrants whose plans were undefined were located on more remote lots. So far as we have been able to trace them, the actual settlers among the Petworth immigrants were assigned lots in Adelaide Township and placed relatively close together around a depot on the fifth concession. A map kept by Mount in 1832 and 1833 records a number of these locations and offers us the best chance of tracing the persistence of Sockett's people, as we need simply use conventional methods that rely on being able to associate names with property. Table 5.1 shows a cluster of Petworth immigrants from the 1832 ships who are either named on these two concessions on the location map or are connected in some way with those who are. Six of these heads of family were sent by Kirdford and three by Wisborough Green. Most of the others can be positively identified as sent by parishes similarly within Egremont's sphere of influence in West Sussex.

Mount's achievement on behalf of Petworth and other immigrants came at a high price. By August 1832, Robinson was beginning to realize the scale of his operation and sent cautionary instructions. Mount had supplied the Petworth immigrants with rations on credit, and Robinson was very concerned that this favour to Egremont's people would create a precedent in the settlement, as indeed it did. Robinson understood Mount's urgency to open the supply route from Caradoc, but once he had this road, Robinson ordered that, apart from two or three experienced axemen needed to lead the way, Mount hire only immigrants for road work. Mount was reminded that the settlement's roads were intended to give immigrants employment near their lots.[25]

In Robinson's Peterborough settlement, which was otherwise the model for Mount's, Horton had paid for rations until the harvest of the settlers' first crop. Robinson knew that forcing immigrants onto the roads was unpopular with his agents, and he knew why. New immigrants from Britain were at their most ineffective chopping out bush roads. Their inexperience wasted time and money, and they wore themselves out before they had properly recovered from their journey. Despite writing the order dictated by Colonial Office policy, Robinson may in his heart have approved of Mount's efforts to maintain the price of provisions at a level that allowed many immigrants to concentrate on getting their land ready for the all-important first crop.[26]

As few names of Petworth immigrants appear on the road work accounts, it seems that most of those who wintered in the settlement were well enough established to continue clearing their own land. Not all immigrants were as fortunate. After Mount left for York to take his seat in the House of Assembly, his assistant, Bella Brewster Brigham, kept on opening roads in order to support those with no money to buy food. Brigham reduced the daily wage once and then a second time, and he still found himself with too large a workforce. In March, Colborne issued a firm order to stop work on the roads, only to relent and to allow more money to be spent in April employing the more destitute. Mount described the classes of settlers most affected as commuted pensioners of the army and navy and immigrants who had arrived late in the season. The pensioners seem to have been the ones responsible for reports of instances of near starvation.[27]

Policies that enabled many immigrants to settle immediately on their lots were responsible for the achievements of those Petworth immigrants who wrote to England of having a house and of looking forward to a crop the next spring. The daughter of a large family, a couple without children, and single men who expected family to follow all wrote to this effect. Mary Holden, who had come to Adelaide with her widower father and younger brothers and sisters, took possession of a "warm house" in October after weeks of makeshift camping. At a cost of three pounds ten shillings for each house, Mount had brought in experienced labour to erect the shell of a log house, sixteen feet square and nine feet high with the doorway cut out, and to give it a shingled roof.[28] Mary's father had planted two acres of wheat despite being very ill with ague. "We expect to find very hard times this winter," she confided, with ten miles to travel for flour and other provisions, but her father had a vision of doing well on his own land in a few years' time.[29]

Encouraging family members to come out in the Petworth emigration of 1833, William Phillips enthused, "William Cooper, and Edward Boxall, and his wife, and I lives together, and works on our own land: we shall sow 6 acres of wheat this fall, and more in the spring."[30] Cooper had built his own log house sixteen feet by twenty-two, had wheat planted on two acres, and planned to have four more acres ready for spring planting. Catherine Boxall was immersing herself in pioneer tasks in a cabin still without floor or chimney. She had made soap, maple sugar, and starch, and had bought deer fat from Native people to make candles. She was baking bread in an iron pot, and she could recommend a nice black-squirrel pudding.[31] Several Petworth immigrants who sent letters from the Adelaide settlement during the first autumn and winter mention the clearing done on their first two acres, and some of these had already been planted with wheat.

Other letters reveal more of the risks and hardships of a new settlement. James Rapley, a widower, had died, leaving several orphaned children. Henry Smart reported to Rapley's relatives in England that three of the children were in service and that the

Table 5.1
Petworth Immigrants, Adelaide Township, Fourth and Fifth Concessions

Name	1831–33 Map	1851 Census Adelaide	Death or Removal (d = died)	Family Links
1832 Arrivals				
BACHELOR Benjamin	w½ lot 17 con 4SER	no	to Warwick c. 1840	
BAKER William	no	E½ lot 4 con 3NER		
BOXALL Edward, wife	E½ lot 21 con 4SER	same place	not in Adelaide 1871	
CARVER George	E½ lot 16 con 5SER	no	m 1842 London?	
COOPER William[1]	w½ lot 21 con 4SER	no		brothers James & John came later
DOWNER John	no	w½ lot 14 con 5SER	d 1886 Adelaide	Rapley
EVANS David	no	no	to Delaware	Hilton
GOATCHER Stephen	lot 20 con 5SER	no	returned to England	
HILTON Charles & family	E½ lot 14 con 4SER	son Alexander on same	d 1851 Adelaide	Humphreys, Rapley, Parker, Evans, Peacock
HOLDEN Thomas & family	E½ lot 19 con 4SER	same place	d 1854 Michigan	Downer, Mann, Joiner, Pannell, Cooper
JOINER James, wife	E½ lot 12 con 5SER	son Robert on same	d 1844 Adelaide	Holden
MANN Charles	w½ lot 19 con 4SER	no	to Delaware/Westminster	
NAPPER James & family	w½ lot 13 con 4SER	son Charles on same	d 1875 Petrolia son Charles to Michigan	Downer
PANNELL William	? w½ lot 22 con 3SER	same place	d 1882 Adelaide	Holden
PARKER James & family	E½ lot 15 con 4SER	same place sons on lot 16 con 4SER	d 1864 Adelaide	Napper, Hilton
PHILLIPS William Jr (See father below, 1833)	w½ lot 15 con 4SER	no	d 1889 Warwick	Pullen
RAPLEY Charles & family	E½ lot 19 con 5SER	E½ lot 14 con 5SER	d 1862 Adelaide	Mann
RAPLEY James & family	w½ lot 19 con 5SER	son William on same son David on E½ son Thomas pt lot 17 con 5	d 1832 Adelaide	Hilton, Downer

THOMAS Thomas & family	E½ lot 18 con 4SER	same place	d 1868 Adelaide	
TICKNER William	E½ lot 17 con 5SER	son David on same	d 1877 Lobo	
1833 Arrivals				
COOPER William[1]	no	no	no	
HASTED Frederick[2]	no	no	d 1868 Sarnia	Holden
PEACOCK Charles	w½ lot 12 con 5SER		to Delaware	Hilton
PHILLIPS William Sr	no	no	to Warwick with son	
ROBINSON George	no	no	to Delaware by 1833	
Later Arrivals (year of arrival in brackets)				
COOPER James (1836)		w½ lot 21 con 4SER	d 1883 Adelaide	
COOPER John (1844)		SE¼ lot 19 con 2SER		
HUMPHREY John[3] (1842)		no	to Delaware	
JOYES Luke (1836)		no	some family to Westminster	
[Family of] MANN Samuel Sr (1836), who died en route in Montreal, 1836				
son Samuel Jr (1835)		lot 8 con 4SER		
son Thomas (1835)		pt 18–19 con 4–5 Lobo	d 1882 Michigan	Holden
son John (1835)			to Metcalfe?	
son Mark (1835)		E½ lot 14 con 5	d 1904 Adelaide	Rapley
son Noah, family (1836)		no		
PULLEN Richard[4] (1837)		Caradoc	d 1872 Delaware	
RICH James (1837)		Caradoc		Hilton
RICHARD Charles (1836)		no	to Ekfrid	
SEDGEMAN Charles (1844)		¼ acre, w½ lot 19 con 5SER		Parker

SOURCES: AO, Map Collection, RG 1-100, C 103; NA, RG 31, Canada Census, Adelaide Township 1851, microfilm C-11737; and project files.

[1] This William Cooper came from Burton, Sussex; see also William Cooper who arrived in 1833, from Tillington.

[2] Frederick Hasted was not Petworth-assisted, but was part of the community in Sussex and in Adelaide.

[3] John Humphrey was from Lurgashall; this is not John Humphries from Wiltshire whose name appears on the early map, but is not a Petworth emigrant.

[4] A different Richard Pullen arrived in Adelaide in 1832 and appears on the early map. His daughter married William Phillips Jr and they all removed to Warwick Township.

other four, who were working on their land, had good prospects if they could get through this first winter (they did keep their lot). Mesheck Randall died soon after he drew his lot. Isaac Randall, who inherited it, went to Michigan and eventually sold it.

In the first stage of a bush settlement, a location ticket for a lot in itself represented little equity. Frederick Hasted, a small-scale speculator with connections to Sockett and the Petworth immigrants, reportedly bought the rights to a lot assigned to Charles Mann for an amount described in one place as four dollars and a musket valued at six dollars and in another as two pounds fifteen shillings. After improvements had been made on it, the lot sold for five hundred dollars and then for six hundred, but Mann saw none of this increase in value.[32]

Not all Petworth immigrants were as determined as Thomas Holden to have a farm. Although Henry Smart found his friends from the parish of Kirdford housed on their lots in Adelaide, "nearly altogether," he noted that they had been still "pretty much in the bush" when he had arrived in the winter of 1832–33 to draw land. Mount, who must have been aware of Smart's indecision, located him in Warwick Township, and Smart returned to his job in Ancaster. His final advice to friends in England was to come to him at Ancaster for the first year, as the hardships would be less than if they went straight to the bush.[33] After several years' experience as an emigration agent, Anthony Hawke was also of the opinion that the work of a new settler was harder than that of any labourer in England.

In Toronto in the Crown Lands Department in the winter of 1832–33, officials were beginning to tally the cost to government of this new settlement. Controlling expenses and accounting had been Robinson's weak point as supervisor of the Irish immigrations. As a former fur trader, militia officer, and entrepreneur, he was well qualified to establish a backwoods settlement, but he lacked the background and interest needed to supervise the difficult bookkeeping of the Crown Lands Department or to reform its antiquated accounting system.[34] In addition, he was in poor health as a result of a fever contracted in 1825, and in the very busy summer of 1832, he had left Mount to act without supervision.

Mount was an experienced surveyor, but 1832 was his first year in charge of immigrants. He and other crown lands agents followed the surveyors' practice of making up accounts at the end of the season after field work was completed. Colborne approved Mount's account in October, and to his later embarrassment, he reported to the Colonial Office under the impression that this was a final account. Over the winter additional bills from the Adelaide settlement kept coming in – large bills for road work, which continued into March 1834, and, still more annoyingly, bills for supplies sent to the settlement on contracts that Mount had negotiated in the name of the government without a shadow of authority.[35] These supplies exemplified Mount's dilemma. The success of his settlement depended on people who could not pay the inflated prices caused by their sudden influx, hence his decision to bring in food and other supplies to sell at cost and on credit.

Too unwell to go to see for himself, Robinson sent Alexander McDonell from Peterborough to Adelaide to investigate Mount's settlement. McDonell had been

Robinson's assistant in 1825 and was one of his most experienced agents. He concluded that Mount's immigrants could have been given cheaper food and cheaper houses. He faulted Mount for operating on too grand a scale, hiring too many people, and spending too much money, but he admired his zeal and energy in such difficult circumstances. He judged the weaknesses in Mount's administration to be the result of inexperience, not dishonesty.[36] Robinson and McDonell knew at first hand the weight of a whole settlement of dependent people, and Robinson urged Colborne to release the money for Mount to pay his suppliers.

Colborne was not quite ready to let Mount off the hook and he was anxious to prevent a recurrence. He separated responsibility for immigrants from Robinson's other duties and brought Anthony Hawke to Toronto in the spring of 1833 to take over. Hawke, who had been stationed at Lachine in 1832, had no backwoods-settlement experience corresponding to Robinson's and McDonell's. He felt none of Robinson's sympathy for Mount, clearly finding the manner in which Mount defended his actions arrogant and self-interested, and he was anxious to prove himself by imposing fiscal responsibility on agents like Mount. Mount's suppliers, anxiously waiting for payment and fearing bankruptcy, had won a hearing from Robinson but found themselves appealing to Hawke. Hawke referred them back to Mount and tried to distance government from the transactions.[37] The affair ended for Mount with his death from illness in Toronto in January 1834 at the age of thirty-seven.[38]

Colborne assumed responsibility for the spending of 1832. He toured the Western District early in 1833 and made the best case possible in writing to the Colonial Office. He emphasized that the province had gained a valuable population of immigrants who would otherwise have been lost to the United States. In addition to his own report, he sent detailed reports from Mount, who painted a glowing picture of a successful settlement that had taken shape in the wilderness during a few short months.

By the spring of 1833, Mount claimed to have settled close to 2,000 people in Adelaide and Warwick, the two townships in his agency opened to indigent immigrants and discharged soldiers. He estimated that another 450 who had drawn locations from him by the spring of 1833 were living and working in other Upper Canadian communities.[39] The discrepancy between the numbers of immigrants Mount reported arriving through Port Stanley and the numbers he said he located in the Adelaide settlement amounted to 1,000 or more, people who might have still been in the area or who had moved on from it. Several of these unaccounted persons were Petworth immigrants who had stayed close by, having found employment in more-settled townships, particularly in Delaware and Caradoc, where Mount had personal connections.

The venture closest to Mount's in terms of size and cost was Robinson's settlement at Peterborough, and Mount's initial population figures were not out of line with Robinson's results. Robinson, Mount, and others experienced in backwoods settlement knew that a high turnover in the original population was expected. They skated around the number of settlers at work outside the settlement or absent without reporting, as they had no way to know who would return. The positive factors they could report were progress in clearing and the creation of a viable nucleus for

future settlement. In the spring of 1833, Mount reported that immigrants in his settlement had cleared close to 3,000 acres and had half of that amount in crop. In the
near future, their community would have amenities such as saw and grist mills.[40]

Such reports could not balance the hard fact that the immigration of 1832 had
sucked up all the surplus territorial revenues. The £20,000 balance that Colborne
had reported at the start of the 1832 season vanished in paying for the immigrant
settlement of that year and the cholera epidemic.[41] When Hawke finished tallying
just the expenditures of Robinson's department for this period, calculated from the
spring of 1832 to the spring of 1833, he arrived at a sum of £18,826 provincial currency.[42] Yet Colborne, who was responsible for the spending, could not give a monetary value to his very considerable achievements.

Although Colborne was convinced that his policies had saved many lives, he had
no means of proving what might have been. He could not demonstrate how many
people had been saved from cholera by forwarding more immigrants to Mount than
he was ready to receive. Nor could he put a figure on the costs arising from the
understandable fears of the existing population. Hawke, on the basis of personal observation at Montreal, Lachine, and Prescott, believed that food, medicine, and shelter
supplied at Prescott on Colborne's orders had saved the lives of hundreds. Government had had to step in if these people were to "find a resting place somewhere"
in a province caught up by the dread of cholera.[43] But the urgency of first-hand experience was lost on London. The best financial justification Colborne could muster
was his settlement's contribution to the increased value of crown lands in the two
townships it opened and in others nearby. This future return to government from
these lands, however, could not be assigned a time frame or even an estimated value.

The short-term picture seen from the Colonial Office was of a project launched
by the governor where costs had run out of control. Mount had taken promissory
notes from immigrants for their houses and rations. Robinson does not seem to have
tried to collect. Such notes were almost meaningless in assisted settlements where
new immigrants signed on trust and cash was scarce. If they ever paid for a deed,
many such immigrants took years to do so, and many others moved away without
completing a transaction. Four years later, Hawke wrote that to his knowledge the
only payments made on the lots given indigent immigrants in Mount's settlement
had come as a result of occasional sales made to more affluent settlers who wanted
a clear title.[44] In 1829, John Galt had been recalled to London by the directors of
the Canada Company, having lost his job as their first superintendent after he let an
ambitious program of development run far ahead of returns.[45] Colborne was not in
danger in 1833 of a similar fate, but he must have known that, cholera or not, his
particular program was doomed. Immigrants in 1833 would feel a pinch because of
the need to limit expenses to make up for some of the spending of the year before.[46]

The experience of Petworth immigrants sent to Plympton in 1833 reveals just
how drastically Colborne had had to draw back from locating immigrants on the
model of Robinson's Peterborough settlement.[47] They arrived in Toronto expecting the assistance described in letters sent from the Adelaide settlement, and they

petitioned to join the Petworth immigrants there. Hawke knew their expectations and he visited heads of families personally, trying to make sure that they understood that all that the Crown Lands Department could offer them in 1833 was a location on lots in an even more distant township with very little support.

Hale's journey with the Petworth immigrants who chose to go on to Plympton has been described in Chapter 4. According to Hawke, they were promised temporary shelter in a shed built for their use on arrival and location on fifty-acre lots to be sold to them on credit, with three years to pay the first instalment. They would be allowed to leave their land to work as opportunity arose, but they must bring it into cultivation without relying on provisions or any other further aid from government. Again according to Hawke, Hale had said that, with the money he had to distribute and the money the immigrants brought in their own possession, they had enough resources to accept these terms.[48]

The Petworth passengers who arrived in Plympton in 1833 on the schooner *Trafalgar* had reason to be edgy and defensive. First, there had been the problem with Hale and the rations. Then, because the schooner captain was unable to enter Lake Huron as planned, he left them on 14 July at the Rapids, the landing place for the Indian reserve at the north end of the St Clair River. At this juncture Hale sailed off, leaving his immigrants to await the arrival of Henry John Jones, the agent for Plympton. Robinson's letter to Jones had been delayed, and Jones had only about five days' warning of their arrival. Finding the party much smaller than described, Jones decided to dispense with building an immigrant shed and would later assure Robinson that the group had been adequately housed in his storehouse (probably at Port Sarnia, now Sarnia).

Jones had been in Upper Canada for three years, his experience an uphill battle to make a viable proposition of his father's failing Owenite community settlement of Maxwell in Sarnia Township. He was in transition from a role as deputy leader of a socialist experiment to one as a struggling but well-connected backwoods landowner, and he had only recently been appointed as land agent. Mount, admittedly with more resources and encouragement, had seen indigent settlers as an opportunity. Jones saw more of his father's "ragged regiment" and confided to his diary that the Petworth immigrants were a "discontented poor set."[49] In favouring the Welshman who came with the Petworth immigrants as "by far the best of the party," he may also have been indulging in the national prejudices that ran through so many reports on the relative merits of English, Scottish, Welsh, and Irish immigrant settlers.

Once Jones had written off those Petworth immigrants who had skipped over the border into Michigan, and dealt with the discharged soldiers who were in everyone's bad books, the others did not look so bad. Single men worked for a short time for the contractor who was opening a road through Plympton and then scattered in search of better-paid harvest work. The married men were more troublesome, claiming that Hale and "the government" had promised work at twelve dollars a month with rations for them and their families. Jones could not meet their expectations, and without rations for their families they were unwilling (or perhaps really could not manage) to work on the road for the same wages as single men. After the soldiers left, the other married men found harvest work with local farmers and took possession of their lots. This party was by now small enough to fit into two abandoned log houses, which the immigrants repaired with materials supplied by Jones. He concluded his report by saying that they would make good settlers.[50] Land in Plympton was originally offered to indigent immigrants at ten shillings an acre, but it was later reduced to the same five-shilling rate as in Adelaide and Warwick.

Petworth immigrants made public complaints against Hale only after they settled in Upper Canada. During their travels, the immigrants had almost no one to turn to except government agents whose time for such matters was taken up with cases far more serious than theirs. Hale and Jones had singled out George Trussler as the worst complainer, but it was George Turner (an immigrant whom Sockett characterized as having narrowly escaped the hangman) who sparked public controversy with his visit to the editor of the Sandwich *Canadian Emigrant*. The resulting article, printed in an obscure paper on the western boundary of Upper Canada, was picked up and reprinted from one newspaper to another across the province and across the ocean until it reached Egremont's hands.[51] A succession of editors had a field day with the story. They squeezed the full shock value that the use of Egremont's name gave to Turner's accusations and covered themselves by printing the official response supplied mainly by Hawke (although he did not use his name).[52]

Turner made charges common among immigrants dissatisfied with those who took charge of their travel. Hale, he said, had enriched himself at the expense of immigrants in his charge and had been constantly drunk. For those who sponsored the journey, such charges might be seen as an annoyance on an otherwise successful trip. For immigrants with as little money as Turner, the consequences were serious. Blaming Hale, he claimed that he had spent all his money to feed his family between Quebec and Plympton. Now he could not afford to take his family on to the lot due to him as a pensioner and former soldier.

Newspaper owner George Gurnett made his own inquiries and reported the result in the *Courier of Upper Canada*. Gurnett did not think that Hale had robbed the shipboard supplies provided by Egremont's committee. Nevertheless, he described as contemptible Hale's conduct in encouraging the Isle of Wight boys to spend their landing money during the voyage in buying unnecessary treats from him. If Hale did not come out well, neither did his accuser. Gurnett found that Turner, who claimed that he had been promised a house in Plympton and work at four shillings a day with rations, was one of a group of "turbulent fellows" who had been troublemakers from the start. Hale was indirectly condemned when he maintained his silence after Gurnett's piece appeared. Turner, however, rose to the challenge. After reading what Gurnett had written about him, he returned to the office of the *Canadian Emigrant* to swear an affidavit reaffirming his charges. The editor promised to forward to Egremont his document and those he offered to obtain from other Petworth immigrants.[53]

Although Turner's accusations were by now old news outside his own district, the editor of the *Emigrant* contributed some thoughtful comments that reflected Colborne's dilemma in trying to provide a backwoods home for indigent immigrants without adequate resources. In 1833, Mount estimated that in a settlement like the one he established at Adelaide a couple with four children needed aid in provisions and kind to the amount of £25 currency. Writing several years later, Hawke gave a similar opinion: an immigrant family taking up a remote and uncleared lot needed £25 to £30 to see them through to their first crop.[54] The fate of the Petworth immigrants sent to Plympton in 1833 was a typical result of sending poor immigrants to the frontier with insufficient resources. A few might do all right in the end, but the initial reports sent home were discouraging and too few immigrants persisted to form a community capable of attracting chain migrants. At the end of 1833, Colborne was as committed as ever to planting settlers in the place of trees, but he clearly needed a new approach.

REDUCED ASSISTANCE AND THE FIVE-ACRE-LOT PLAN

The new approach Colborne adopted was to provide much smaller lots of only five acres, the size of park lots laid out as part of a new townsite in Upper Canada. In 1833, there were several plans under discussion involving lots of this size. The suggestion could have started with Isaac Buchanan, the British consul at New York and the brother of Alexander Buchanan, or it might have been made to Colborne by someone else. Many colonizers of the school of Robert Wilmot Horton were still seeking the key that would reduce costs to a level acceptable in Britain. In 1833, Colborne sent the Colonial Office an ambitious plan that was based on five-acre lots and involved settling 10,000 parish emigrants a year for ten years. Under this plan, immigrants would be paid wages for clearing land and the sales of cleared land would finance the next year's immigrants. The newest element in this plan was the use of lots too small to become a farm. Commenting for the Colonial Office, R.W. Hay and James Stephen were rightly sceptical about the scale and viability of the plan, but they did allow that a small trial might be made.[55] Trials based on lots this size never introduced large numbers of immigrants, but Colborne did turn to variations of the plan in three quite different sets of circumstance.

The British army had offered emigration in exchange for commutation of their pensions to ex-servicemen supported through the Chelsea Hospital. After many had died, Colborne had arranged for others who were destitute to be supported at Penetanguishene; the five-acre lots assigned some of these men were only expected to reduce the cost of their maintenance. A second plan involving the availability of five-acre lots in Nottawasaga and Sunnidale townships in 1834 was closer to Colborne's large plan but was offered only to settlers in the difficult circumstance of having arrived too late in the season to provide for themselves. Nottawasaga had better land than Sunnidale and did attract settlers, but the recession of 1835 brought this attempt at planting a self-sufficient settlement to an inglorious end. Purchasers did not materialize, and Hawke was forced to incur more expense keeping the land from reverting to wilderness than he earned by leasing it.[56] Petworth immigrants were not involved in either of these plans.

Under a third five-acre-lot plan pioneered by Petworth immigrants in Woodstock in 1834, families were located on small lots near a quickly developing community.

As they constituted all but one of the original twelve families, Petworth immigrants may have been sent to Woodstock partly to make sure that Egremont did not hear bad reports of his emigrations for a second year in a row. (Table 5.2 lists the eleven Petworth families in column 1.) Whether or not this was a factor, the plan had a local justification. Anthony Hawke, now the emigration agent at Toronto, claimed credit for devising it as he listened to the complaints of middle-class settlers who had either purchased large land grants or claimed them for military service. These people had money to hire workers and were clamouring for Hawke to provide them with labourers and tradesmen. Many of them were of the same English background as Petworth immigrants.

Hawke's plan was to give suitable immigrants temporary possession of five-acre lots and to build them a log shanty. As the period of time for possession was variously described as three and five years, and as an option to purchase was not clearly spelled out, Hawke and Colborne seem to have expected that the immigrants would use their savings to buy land to farm at the first opportunity.[57] Their first resource was to be readily available work. The house provided shelter and a sense of security and the land made saving possible. A single man working for a farmer or master got his housing and board as part of his pay. Labourers who saw their summer earnings melt away for the winter support of a family grew discouraged. Five-acre lots were big enough to enable families to save the maximum amount out of seasonal earnings by raising their own food, and they gave occupation to all members of the family at all seasons.

The total area of the original park lots laid out for the original twelve families in Woodstock was less than the hundred acres of a single lot in the Adelaide settlement where some 2,000 people were located in a single season. Nevertheless, the value of assistance that the government gave in Woodstock was sufficient to establish a community able to attract chain migrants. In Woodstock, Hawke had all three elements essential to his plan: Colborne was willing to commit public money and anxious to encourage Egremont's scheme; Woodstock employers could afford to hire; and Petworth immigrants had the skills that were in demand and a background of wage labour. Like all Colborne's plans for settling families, this one was posited on an appropriate mix in the immigrant population of half-pay "officers of the Navy and Army, and capitalists, and a proportion of indigent emigrants."[58]

In 1835 and 1836, Hawke extended this plan to parish immigrants sent by other emigration "societies" and geographically to the villages of Brantford and Paris and the Township of Cayuga, and he continued with it for one more year, in 1837.[59] Brydone, the Petworth superintendent, took parties of Petworth immigrants to Brantford in 1835 and 1836. In both years, but particularly in 1836, Petworth families also went to Woodstock and perhaps to Paris. In 1837, Hawke wrote to the Woodstock magistrate John Hatch to have lots laid off for another eight or nine large families sent by the Petworth committee, but we have not been able to locate the families in and around Woodstock that came on the *Diana* in that year.[60]

The Grand River communities that Hawke added to the plan shared with Woodstock a period of very rapid growth. The *Hamilton Mercury*, reporting in 1833 on the

remarkable emergence of Blandford Village (Woodstock), described several gentlemen "of fortune and respectability" who were planning to build brick houses and
had expressed a need for carpenters, labourers, blacksmiths, and wagon makers.[61] Cornelius Voice, a carpenter and joiner by trade from Billingshurst, wrote from Woodstock that three stores and fifty frame houses had gone up in less than two years. Similar
stories of very rapid expansion can be collected from the other sites Hawke selected
for the five-acre-lot program. Such specific requirements kept the scheme small.
Including 1837, Hawke recorded upward of sixty families, primarily parish-aided
immigrants and roughly half of them sent by the Petworth Emigration Committee.

Woodstock has by far the best records of the sites receiving Petworth immigrants
under this plan, and it seems to have been the most successful from the point of view
of the immigrants settled there. These immigrants enjoyed an advantage that those
in Brantford may have lacked – a more desirable location in the future town than
assisted immigrants might normally expect. Andrew Drew, one of the first founders
of Woodstock, had bypassed the town plot originally surveyed by the government
and built the church and laid out lots on his own property at the east end of the
present town. As the land was empty, surveyor Peter Carroll was sent instructions
from the surveyor general's office on 19 June to extend the existing survey of the
original town plot by laying out three- to five-acre lots on part of an adjoining hun-
dred-acre government reserve. In correspondence concerning Petworth, the site was
identified as the town plot of Blandford Township.

In 1834, Brydone left eighty members of twelve families and fourteen single men
at Woodstock in the charge of John Hatch, one of two local magistrates. Hatch provided some initial rations and medical attention, helped to match immigrants with
employers, and oversaw the move from the barns to huts.[62] The hiring of both single and married men proceeded quickly. Henry Heasman, who apprenticed himself to a blacksmith, wrote: "Jack is as good as his master here. Masters are glad to
get servants, and come to hire them: no running after masters." Brydone explained
in more formal language. He had "several applications" the first day for labourers
and mechanics. On the second day, employers began asking for female servants and
little girls and even offering to hire them on the spot.[63]

Potential employers waited a day to look the Petworth immigrants over before
hiring female servants to live and work in their houses. They liked what they saw.
Petworth letter-writers were delighted to find ready work for children in Upper
Canada and sent their older girls out to service as a matter of course.[64] John Gamblen, however, considered a wife in the home as a sign of prosperity. Ann "enjoys
her health a deal better than in England," he wrote, "for she is not obliged to work
so hard ... Here is a great plenty for her to do, but I will not suffer her to do it while
I can get a good living without her help. We have plenty of gentry here at Blandford – they strive their utmost to get her to work but their labour is all in vain."[65]

On 7 July 1834, Carroll inspected the huts built by the crown lands contractor,
James Henderson of Toronto, and supervised the emigrant families in drawing for
lots. Brydone paid a brief return visit to Woodstock a few days later and left a picture

of Colborne's latest attempt at community planning working at its best, a picture confirmed and supplemented by immigrant letters. Brydone reported full employment (even the organist Barton had found other jobs), and both he and the immigrants reported high wages – the crucial elements of the plan. As a sign that they were fitting into the community, Brydone let Sockett know that Petworth immigrants had formed a choir for the first service in the new church.

Within a month after their arrival, the families were moving out of the cramped quarters in Hatch's barn where, in the laconic words of William Voice, there had been "plenty of company." Touring the log houses, Brydone was pleased to see several with "regular roofs, instead of the one-sided lean-to appearance of the shanty." Thomas Ditton had caused a local stir by obtaining straw and thatching his; others had either done the work themselves or paid the contractor a small advance from their earnings.

The Voices, a family of carpenters and joiners, wrote home describing what could be done to make a home of a log shanty: "some round trees put on one another" and erected without window or door openings or chimneys. To make theirs "very comfortable," the Voices had cut out a front and back door and had added "two great sash windows, a brick chimney, and oven at the side of the chimney." The roof was shingled because, as they explained to their English relative, neither tiles nor slate for roofing were to be found in Upper Canada.

The four adult men in the Voice family cleared their five acres in the first year and reached more quickly than most families the point of trade-off between a more comfortable lifestyle on their lot and the vision of becoming a farmer. "Provisions are as handy here, as you have at home," William wrote; "we live about half a mile from the village, a new church is as near to us as you have to you [in Ashington, Sussex]." Elizabeth Voice and her daughter Elizabeth made maple sugar, soap, and candles in Woodstock as Catherine Boxall did in Adelaide Township, but they were also able to purchase a range of goods similar to those they had known in English village stores. Although they paid a bit more for footwear than in England and clothing was "rather dearer," there was a market for their sewing skills making men's clothes, when they had time for the work. A year later, their cows, pigs, and fowl had multiplied and Elizabeth senior was making twenty pounds of butter a week. On the negative side, there was no more land to clear on their lot and two of the Voices' boys were already restless, investigating the possibilities of going further up country where "they are giving out land to get inhabitants."[66]

Letters giving favourable reports of Woodstock drew later Petworth immigrants who in turn sent their own good reports. The family of Cornelius Voice moved on from Woodstock, but Ham Voice, also from Billingshurst, came in 1836 and settled on Cornelius's lot. The Voice families seem to have been related. Their experience suggests there was succession on some of the lots originally laid off in 1834 as Petworth immigrants of one year moved on and those of another year came in. But the succession might also be from one Petworth emigrant family to another.

Table 5.2 shows the occupation record of lots assigned to Petworth immigrants in 1834. It does not account for Petworth immigrants of later years who came to

Woodstock either to occupy lots we cannot trace or to settle without this incentive. In addition to the Petworth immigrants who settled within the boundaries of present-day Woodstock, others moved out from Woodstock or settled initially close by in Blandford Township or in the surrounding townships of Blenheim, Zorra, and Oxford. As in the Adelaide settlement, evidence of intermarriage between the children strengthens the impression of a sense of community among this cluster of people sent under the auspices of the Petworth Emigration Committee.[67]

When Peter Carroll went back to inspect the lots he had laid out for Brydone's immigrants, he found some lots "partially" or "mostly" cleared and others "all improved." His notes show that Thomas Ditton, James Budd, and Ham Voice had all built new houses.[68] In 1842, these men and seven other Petworth immigrants of various years joined with other occupants of lots on the government reserve in a successful petition to stay and to purchase. According to local lore in Woodstock, the reserve was known informally for a time as Brighton, a name attributed to the presence of several Petworth families from Brighton in East Sussex. After Woodstock became the district town of Brock in 1840, and as it expanded to amalgamate its east and west ends, these lots became a prime location. As in the Adelaide settlement, we have not made a point of following the Woodstock settlers past their initial location, but some of the information we collected in the course of identifying Petworth families suggests intriguing possibilities for future research.

Families who stayed in a village might be as ambitious for their children as those who acquired farmland. In 1838, James and Mary Budd had only their three youngest children at home. James's nephew was apprenticed to a cabinetmaker and his eldest son to a blacksmith, trades that these two men were following in 1851. The next two sons, about fifteen and thirteen in 1838, were apprenticed to a tailor. James Budd himself worked as an agricultural labourer. He died in 1850, too early to be included in the gazetteer prepared the following year, but this source shows that Thomas Ditton, James Denman, James Lannaway, and Thomas Perrin all worked as labourers. Henry Harwood Sr, who moved from Woodstock to Ingersoll, gave his original occupation of shoemaker when he was enumerated at the age of eighty for the 1851 census. The suggestion of this evidence is that parish-aided immigrants who came as middle-aged parents with young children needed all their energy just to get established. Social advancement was the work of the next generation.

Although we may speculate about why we know less of the Petworth immigrants sent to Brantford in 1835 than of those sent to Woodstock in 1834 – records may not have survived, immigrants may have dispersed from a less desirable location – we can be clear about one factor. Petworth immigrants received less assistance after Sir Francis Bond Head replaced Colborne as lieutenant-governor at the beginning of 1836. The fact that Petworth immigrants received at least some aid in settling under Head is a tribute to the power of Egremont's name and the goodwill that this and similarly well-organized parish emigrations had garnered.

In 1834, Brydone and Hatch exercised considerable discretion in spending on the Woodstock venture, and Brydone's bill for travel expenses of £110 currency was passed

Table 5.2
Woodstock Government Reserve: Occupation Record of Petworth Immigrants

Government Reserve, Assigned 1834	1841–52 Locations[1]	Death or Removal (d = died)	Family Information (m = married; dau = daughter)
Barton, John? (labelled Barnabas Burton) lot 2 range1 [N side Barwick St]	occupied by James Thompson 1841[2]		
Coleman, George lot 3 range 2 [N side Admiral St]	occupied by Donald Gunn 1841[2] Coleman signed a petition E Oxford 1835	d 1836 Woodstock	wife Sarah d 1845 Woodstock dau Lucy m Henry Harwood Jr son George m Elizabeth Voice
Denman, John not on first map [emigrant of 1836]	lot 5 range 3 by 1841, occupancy approved March 1842[3] labourer, 1852 Gazeteer Woodstock	d 1852 Woodstock	dau Charlotte m James Budd Henry Denman m Mary Perin
Ditton, Thomas lot 2 range 3 [N side Henry St]	Henry St 1841, Vincent St 1848 occupancy approved March 1842[3] labourer, 1852 Gazeteer Woodstock Thomas Jr sold lot 2 range 4 in 1849	d 1851 Woodstock	sons Thomas & Francis 1851 census Woodstock son Thomas d Woodstock 1854 son William d Goderich 1847/8
Gamblen, John lot 2 range 2 [N side Admiral St]	occupied by Warman Barnard 1841[2]		William Gamblin in Woodstock 1851 (connection unknown)
Green, William lot 5 range 2 [N side Admiral St]	occupied by John Shaw 1841[2] Green signed a petition in E Oxford 1835 carpenter, 1852 Gazeteer Woodstock		Mary Ann Green d 1847 Woodstock (possibly wife)
Harwood, Henry (Sr) lot 1 range 2 [N side Admiral St]	occupied by Williams Sims 1841[3] Harwood occupied lot 1 range 1 by 1841[3] Harwood a shoemaker in Woodstock 1851	d 1879 Ingersoll	Henry Harwood Jr d 1885 E Zorra William Sims d 1857 Woodstock
Holden, John not on first map [emigrant of 1837]	lot 3 range 4 by 1841, occupancy approved 1842[3] mortgaged 1843 patent to mortgagor 1844		

Name / lot	Acquisition & occupancy	Family / connection
Kemp, Ann lot 3 range 3 [N side Henry St]	lot acquired 1838 by James Lanaway [emigrant of 1838] Lanaway occupancy approved 1842[3] Lanaway, labourer, 1852 Gazeteer Woodstock	Ann M. Kempt m Thomas Wagstaff 1853 Woodstock (connection unknown) son Harry Kempt d 1851 Woodstock James Lanaway d 1890 Woodstock
Martin, William lot 1 range 1 [N side Barwick St]	Barwick St, 1841, occupancy approved March 1842[3] Vansittart St, 1843 lot acquired by Henry Harwood 1844	wife Jane d 1835 Woodstock William Martin d 1854 Woodstock, possibly son
Perrin, Thomas lot 4 range 2 [N side Admiral St]	Admiral St, 1841, occupancy approved March 1842[3] acquired soldiers' grant Warwick Sept 1842 Vansittart St, 1844 labourer, 1852 Gazeteer Woodstock	dau Mary m Henry Denman dau Ann m Charles Pascoe[2] Christopher Perrin settled on Warwick lot (connection unknown)
Sims, William [emigrant of 1835]	see Harwood, Henry, above	
Snelling, Henry lot 4 range 1 [N side Barwick St]	lot acquired by William Martin by 1841 Martin's occupancy approved 1842[3]	
Voice, Cornelius lot 3 range 1 [N side Barwick St]	occupancy of Ham Voice approved March 1842[3] [Ham Voice emigrant of 1836]	Ham Voice d 1861 Blandford Cornelius's son George in St Marys 1871 Sara Foice age 77 in E Zorra 1871 (connection unknown)
West, William lot 1 range 3 [N side Henry St]	lot acquired by James Budd, 1841 Budd's occupancy approved 1842[3] lot patented by Henry Budd, 1847 Henry Budd, carpenter, 1852 Gazeteer Woodstock John Budd, blacksmith, 1852 Gazeteer Woodstock	son Edward West m in E Zorra 1868 James Budd d 1850 Woodstock

SOURCES: OMNR, SR 24, Part of the Town Plot of Blandford, showing the part surveyed for Petworth Emigrants, by Peter Carroll, 12 July 1834, endorsed with "A 65" and "613"; AO, Map Collection, RG 1-100, C-69, Plan of the Town of Woodstock, County of Oxford, in the Township of Blandford, London District, endorsement "A 65," 22 January 1841, showing the 5-acre lots surveyed June 1834 for Petworth emigrants, with additions probably dating 1844-49; NA, RG 1, L 3, Upper Canada Land Petitions, vol. 242, bundle "H," no. 52, mfm C-2097; AO, RG 1, C-IV, Woodstock Township Papers, mfm MS 658 reel 528; and project files.

1 Street name may be "different" from 1834 because of where the house was located on the lot.
2 Non-Petworth names in the immediate vicinity.
3 On 19 March 1842, the government approved the request of a group petition (NA, RG 1, L 3, as above) from the government reserve near Woodstock, to "allow them to remain in their present occupancy" and purchase their lots.

without question. A year later, Hawke sent Brydone with 160 of the immigrants from the *Burrell* to Brantford, a place where "labourers are much in demand."[69] Brydone hired thirteen wagons at Hamilton, one less than the year before, so perhaps not all the 160 went all the way to Brantford. In Brantford, Brydone handed over supervisory duties to the surveyor Lewis Burwell. Burwell laid out lots and rented houses for the immigrant's temporary accommodation until they could occupy the lots. He had also had at least six shanties built at Brantford at an unknown location before Brydone arrived, and he had others run up in the course of the summer, but we have no direct evidence placing Petworth immigrants in these shanties.[70]

In 1836, we have no direct evidence Petworth immigrants occupied government shanties. The Jackmans, who reported reduced assistance in reaching Brantford, wrote of shared accommodation. In their second place in the first few months, they were "pretty comfortable" in the downstairs of a house that they rented jointly with "Master Ford" for three shillings a week. Jackman was working with Ford and another Petworth immigrant clearing land, but as he did not explain what land this was, we do not know if they had government lots.[71] In contrast, there are the instructions Hawke sent to Hatch about preparations for Petworth immigrants in Woodstock in 1837. Hawke set precise limits to each category of aid Hatch might give: three-acre lots were suggested; Hatch was not to spend more than fifteen dollars on a shanty (and there was no contractor from Toronto); and rations were to be for three or four days while immigrants looked for work.[72]

As individuals, the Petworth immigrants sent to Brantford gained enough from their assistance to keep the program going for three years, but there is no evidence in Brantford – as there was in Woodstock – of the formation of a community of Petworth immigrants within the larger community of the future town. Although the situation is less clear than with Adelaide and Plympton townships (we may be dealing in part with the loss of relevant records), the contrast between Woodstock and Brantford suggests once more that government had to provide assistance of substantial value to get this result.

Some Petworth families undoubtedly regarded Brantford as a staging post, the farthest destination for which government would pay transport and perhaps a place where they regrouped and earned some money before continuing on their own. The Manns seem to fall into this category and may have left England intending to go to the Adelaide settlement. Other Petworth immigrants may have been caught up in a more general westward movement of recent immigrants through a province troubled by recession and travelled on to Michigan or other western states where they expected cheaper land and greater opportunity.[73]

The Jackmans seem different in that they gave no sign in their letter home that they intended to move. At least in October 1836, the Brantford area did have a Petworth community. William and Sarah wrote cheerfully of immigrants of both 1835 and 1836 settled nearby who were from the neighbourhood of Goring, their former home on the Sussex coast. They anticipated, however, that their son would hear gloomy reports from James Gates and Thomas Grinyer, who had left for home "as soon as they got here" when they had not found work right away. The Jackmans warned their son not to believe "every letter that comes home from Canada"; Canada "is a great deal better for young men than at home." Three of their younger children had places. William had found work immediately, much better paid than in England, "and need not work so hard." Shortly, Sarah would die and William would move on; only concentrated family research has traced him from these beginnings in Brantford to a frontier farm in faraway Wawanosh Township, where he acquired title to 150 acres in 1847.[74] Other Brantford immigrants await similar attention.

After the 1837 Rebellion, Hawke was asked about reviving the five-acre-lot plan in Canada West (formerly Upper Canada). He was interested at first, but he concluded that there no longer was the necessary combination of people and circumstances.[75] Although the expense would be less than if immigrants were placed as farmers on more distant, crown lands, there would still be the problem of the government's spending having no measurable return, and he doubted that such funds would be found. He also doubted that the particular combination in Woodstock of wealthy settlers of the officer class and trained English labourers could be replicated in the 1840s. Edward Heming, who had sailed as a cabin passenger on the *Lord Melville* in 1832, and Sockett's son George, who had received his discharge from the army and settled nearby in Eramosa Township in 1833, had typified a form of emigration "mania" that passed as quickly as the brief, booming prosperity it had helped to fuel. Hawke did not cite the Petworth example, but immigrants of the sort sent by the committee were not coming from England in the same numbers. In the new conditions of a new decade, the typical labouring immigrant who occupied Hawke's attention as emigration agent was the unskilled worker arriving from Ireland.

SETTLEMENT STRATEGIES OF PETWORTH IMMIGRANTS

The most detailed information about Petworth immigrants who forged out on their own is contained in the letters they sent to family and friends back home.[76] As many of these survive only in the form published by Sockett, his needs for promotion have to be taken into account in comparing the letters of different years. His first published collection presented "a chronological series from the day of the sailing ... down to the last letter [received]." He used the immigrants' letters to tell the story of emigration, and he added a long appendix containing useful information on Upper Canada. The letters of 1833 were literally continuations, six instalments brought together in a single volume at the end of the year. A year later, Sockett printed at least two letters of 1834 from Woodstock as the kind of reminder that he liked to keep circulating in the neighbourhood. His main publications for 1834, however, were his own *Letter to a Member of Parliament* and Brydone's *Narrative*. In 1835 and 1836, Sockett's ships filled easily, and his attention was taken up with plans to buy land in Upper Canada for a distinctly Sussex settlement.

The 1837 season called forth a new and vigorous publicity campaign in which Sockett published letters with dates right up to January 1837. Bad reports from Upper

Canada, compounded to some degree by troubles with the poor law commissioners, had meant sharply reduced applications at the beginning of the emigration season. At this juncture, Sockett was less concerned with narrative and more with reassuring his readers about the variety of options still open to Petworth emigrants in Upper Canada. Two pamphlets of his own included letters from agricultural immigrants, tradesmen, and people who combined a trade or part-time work with farming or with cultivating a few acres. He included families assisted by government and others who had made their own way. He also included immigrants whose letters he had printed in earlier collections, people who were still doing well after two, three, or four years in the country, and he included evidence of chain migration. Sockett's hand is also evident in a third pamphlet issued from Chichester in 1837. This pamphlet adds two previously under-represented areas to his collection: the parish of Walburton in West Sussex and the area around Thornhill, north of Toronto in Upper Canada.

An interesting aspect of the five-acre-lot project is that Hawke and Colborne seem to have been trying to recreate those conditions under which English parish-aided immigrants – like those sent by the Petworth committee – had done best on their own. In the quotation at the head of this chapter, Buchanan had in mind a settlement like the one in Adelaide Township. A number of Petworth immigrants used the offer of assisted settlement to advantage, but Petworth immigrants were often prepared to forgo or delay ownership of land if a more attractive opportunity beckoned.

Their own stories suggest that, on first arriving, these south-of-England immigrants saw a job as the most important security. They had a background of wage labour, they knew all about winter unemployment, and the baptismal records of their children indicate that many of them had moved short distances in the past to find work. Some continued in this way of thinking. After four years in Nelson Township working for different employers, George Boxall planned to sell the house he owned in order to rent a better one with ten acres attached to it. Other Petworth immigrants put down roots as farmers, but even among this group not all were willing to pioneer in the back country. A decision to go to the frontier was often based on an assessment of the combined strengths of members a family, or perhaps of related families, who could support each other.

The majority of Petworth families, without assistance or with assistance only in travel, seem to have had their best chance of finding compatible work in communities and on farms that were past the first stage of frontier development but were still growing. Brydone relayed to Sockett in 1834 the lament of a miller he interviewed in Wilmot Township. This man would have liked to have hired Brydone's immigrants "but feared he was too far in the bush to expect that." He assumed that they would take more desirable places closer to established communities.[77]

As a group, the Petworth immigrants enjoyed a good reputation. Goatcher wrote home in 1832 that Upper Canadians "like the English." Although Canadian farmers had the reputation of hiring only single men,[78] Petworth families discovered a number of possibilities. An incidental side effect of regulations issued in 1832 and 1833 making residence a condition of patenting lands held on location tickets helped some of them find a place, as owners sought settlers who would substitute for them as residents on these lands.[79] In 1833, John Elmsley, an executive councillor and prominent speculator, employed five Petworth families from Wiltshire to improve properties in an area he wished to open for sales. He gave a form of assistance by providing housing for the women and children while the men went to prepare the lots for their reception, and he may have paid for labour in land.[80] More typical employers of Petworth families looked for one family only. These employers were speculating on a smaller scale, or perhaps they were opening a country property or hoping that a family would fill all their needs for farm work and house work. Some may have taken on a family in desperation as the only way of keeping the services of a man they wanted. On the strength of opinions expressed in their letters, the Petworth immigrants seem to have preferred earning a wage to farming on shares (sharing in both risks and profits), though they did both.

A William Robinson wrote Sockett with grandiose plans for his "estate" in Delaware Township. He requested two additional farming families, a well-recommended servant woman, a boy with farm experience, and mechanics or tradesmen whom he would place on village lots at a nominal rent, and above all he wanted "good old English manners and habits." In actual practice, Robinson seems to have hired only one Petworth family at a time and to have offered considerable inducements to attract and keep them in his remote township. In 1836, he offered George Older thirty pounds per annum, housed his family in his own house while a cottage was built, and agreed to provide a house, fuel, the keep of a cow year-round, and land for a garden or other purposes.[81]

Married and single immigrants delighted equally in the value that a labour scarcity gave their services in Upper Canada. The fact that farm labourers ate in the house, ate well, and sometimes ate before the family was a source of great satisfaction. Married settlers also had stories of employers anxious to attract the kind of workers they wanted, both farm labourers and people with a trade. Mary Hills wrote in 1836 to the Drewitt family, her family's sponsors, to tell them of her experience in West Flamborough. Her children were working for the adult children of her new employers. The Hills had been taken in when sick, given medicine, "a nice little house close by a beautiful stream of water," twelve dollars a month for George, fuel, milk, and "so many good things from the house, that we have been able to save twelve dollars since we have been here." They had acquired two pigs during this first summer, and they had the promise of fenced ground for a garden and orchard and a cow in the spring. Once the farm acquired poultry, Mary was to have half for their keep. In this case, the relationship seems to have gone beyond an effort to retain compatible servants. Mary's daughter, Ellen, worked as a servant in the house but her employer was teaching her to write.[82] Several other Petworth immigrants also wrote appreciatively of more relaxed working conditions in Upper Canada.

William Upton wrote home in 1832 saying that a man with a wife and no children was better off in Upper Canada than a single man, "as there are so many situations for them in gentlemen's families: the woman as housekeeper; and the man as indoors servant."[83] The Barnes family demonstrated when they immigrated in 1836 that even a couple with children could find this kind of work. John Barnes, a brick-layer, was employed with his son as helper by Charles Matthews, one of the origi-nal masters at Colborne's Upper Canada College. Matthews housed Barnes's wife and daughter in his empty quarters at the college while the father and son put an addition on his country cottage. In the winter, Matthews moved into the house at the college and kept the family on to look after it, and him, with the promise of more work for Barnes in the spring. Barnes wrote about all this at length to his brother in England, hoping that his brother would accept Matthews's offer to farm his land outside Toronto on shares. Barnes's letter was part of a three-way corre-spondence between Toronto, England, and New York State, where other brothers had settled. His first plan had been to go to them, but now, reluctant to leave his happy situation in Toronto, he tried to bring family to join him there.[84]

In 1838, Brydone informed Sockett that "very many" labourers who went to Upper Canada from Sussex are now "*proprietors* there of from 20 to 50 acres of land."[85] Fifty acres was enough for a subsistence farm, but twenty suggests some other source of income or an unusually favourable location. A Guelph observer reporting to the Canada Company in 1840 described immigrants from Scotland or the north of Eng-land as more likely to persist as farmers than those from the south. He criticized poor English immigrants for sending their sons out to work as servants for high wages: "generally speaking, English families do not hold together long enough to ensure suc-cess [as farmers on land purchased from the Canada Company]."[86] From a different point of view, he could have been observing immigrants who had more flexible strate-gies for earning a living and were willing to see success in several different outcomes.

As they had in England, Petworth immigrants in Upper Canada changed their occupations to fit the economic climate or made a living by following more than one occupation, according to the season. The memoir of Charles Adsett, who began his life in Upper Canada as a young apprentice, suggests a loyalty to an area rather than to any one community or one piece of land. He moved frequently and changed occupations a number of times, but apart from a nine-month stint in Michigan, his life was spent in the general area of Galt and Guelph. If opportunity offered, Adsett preferred his trade as a tanner and the life of a small businessman to farming.

Another characteristic of Petworth immigrants that might extend to other immi-grants of their time from the south of England was the strength of extended fami-lies. Family members already in Upper Canada were a great resource. Charlotte Willard encouraged her sister in Dorking to come: "you will not have the care on your mind that we had, not knowing where to go to, or what we was going to do, for you know that we tried the road for you."[87]

Chain migration sometimes spread over several years. There were Hiltons on Pet-worth ships in 1832, 1835, and 1836. In 1837, Grandmother Hilton, in her late sev-enties, set out to join her children in Upper Canada. When George and Lydia Hilton arrived in Toronto in 1836, they were met at the wharf by their son James's employer, who perhaps looked for them with news of work for Toronto alderman George

Denison. James, who followed in his master's "four wheel chaise" to collect his parents, took them to an inn for a night and a day of celebration. George and Lydia sent the oldest three of the children who accompanied them from England into service. The parents and remaining children had the use of a house and three acres of land on Denison's farm on the outskirts of the city. In addition, Denison paid George Hilton sixteen dollars a month.[88]

Community ties also served new immigrants well. The aptly named Mark Messenger greeted immigrants from his home parish of Walberton. He took John Ayling into his own home when he first arrived and seems to have been the one who found Walberton immigrants jobs in the area of Newmarket and Holland Landing. Like John Barnes from Petworth, people from Walberton kept in touch with a small colony from Walberton settled in the state of New York along the route of the Erie Canal, as well as with those at home.

In other cases, Petworth immigrants lived cooperatively for a space of time. When James Rapson's family arrived in 1832, they banded together with other Petworth immigrants to buy 48 acres near Guelph and build a house. This household of sixteen people shared expenses. The Rapsons next move found them sharing 200 acres in Waterloo Township with James's brother's and sister's families and the Dearlings. Each family occupied its own 50 acres, but the relationship involved considerable trust. Rapson made the purchase and had deeds "taken off" for the others.

David Sharp, who arrived from England with a "bad character" and a record of constant poor relief, showed another side to his personality in a letter describing a similar cluster that formed around him. Writing from Sandwich in the Western District in the summer of 1836, he reported a household swelled by other immigrants from the *Heber*. In addition to his own young family, he was sharing his living quarters with his recently widowed sister-in-law, his uncle Thomas Sharp, William Sageman and his family, and two single young men. He wrote that "we have all been in one house together ... [for over a month] except George Turner and his family, who are but a little way from us, so that we can attend to one another at a few moments notice, if required." Despite cramped quarters and the heat of high summer, Sharp saw proximity as a comfort.[89]

Petworth immigrants writing home were careful to be specific about opportunities; in this respect their letters differ markedly from middle-class writing purporting to speak for the labouring emigrant, which dealt almost entirely in generalizations. If Petworth immigrants wrote of good openings for tradesmen, they almost always specified which trades, and they might name the people they thought would do well. They also made it clear whether they were sending a general opinion about work to be found in their area or whether they were willing to look for specific employment for the people they invited to come. Similarly, if they wrote suggesting that others come, they stated what assistance they would offer. This assistance might be very generous – a share of their lot in the case of those who had land – but such promises were made with thought and spelled out with some care.

William Courtnage, an 1832 emigrant writing in January 1837, was typically precise. He answered James Enticknap's inquiries with assurances that blacksmithing was a good trade with high wages in Upper Canada – "we would be happy to see him here, and his wife, and family, for I know he would do well here" – assurances but no invitation. In the same letter to his brother and sisters, he explained that he and Edward Berry, who was currently his neighbour on rented fifty-acre lots, "have been talking a good many times of going further up the country to buy us some land, but if you are coming, we will wait till you comes, if you comes in the spring, and go altogether." His invitation was coupled with a stream of advice about the voyage, about the country, and about what they should bring, and ended with renewed hopes that they would "take good courage and come." His message for his father was short and simple: "If my father will come with you, I will take care of him as long as he lives, and I live, and my brother George."[90]

AS AID TO EMIGRANTS and immigrants was cut back during the 1830s, government officials, sponsors, and the people themselves began to put more emphasis on personal connections, on people in the colony who could provide assistance. Hawke in 1836 wanted labouring immigrants to be discouraged from coming to Upper Canada unless they came to join friends or family willing to help. After Egremont died and his son George Wyndham reduced the assistance offered Sussex emigrants, Sockett changed the emphasis in his selection to favour people who planned to join immigrants established in Upper Canada.

In the case of the Petworth emigrations, assistance provided by sponsors and parishes in England introduced the idea of emigrating to a labouring population in a number of parishes where there had been little if any previous movement to Upper Canada. Further assistance in Upper Canada encouraged many Petworth immigrants to find their first home farther inland than they would otherwise have gone. For sponsors such as Sockett and Egremont and for Colborne with his agenda for settlement, part of the intention of assisted emigration was to plant the seeds of chain migration. Chain migration by its nature tended to be less venturesome. For the migrants, family might offer a warmer welcome than any government, but it was a welcome that depended on individuals and on their willingness and ability to match wishes with action. In this setting, immigrants relied on the goodwill and often limited resources of those who received them. The wider literature of emigration contains many examples of immigrants who felt that they had been misled by those who urged them to come. The Petworth immigrant letters provide examples of new immigrants who weighed what they could offer before sending a letter.

CHAPTER 6

"NOTHING WILL BE DONE BY THE GOVERNMENT": FAILED PLANS FOR ASSISTED SETTLEMENT AND THE ENDING OF THE PETWORTH SCHEME

> The Late Earl of Egremont would have made a considerable purchase in Upper Canada and proceeded to settle emigrants upon it, if the Government had been disposed to afford him any facilities, and Colonel Wyndham has the same feeling on the subject.
>
> Sockett to [Elliot], 5 November 1838[1]

> We must always have poor People and many idle Persons ... The government should take up Emigration. The very little we can do towards it is of no consequence, beyond being a Charity to a few Individuals ... and be assured that nothing will be done by the Government 'till the pressure become great.
>
> Wyndham to Sockett, 10 November 1840[2]

With the benefit of hindsight, 1834, the mid-point of the Petworth emigrations, appears as the pivotal year for this venture. The passing of the Poor Law Amendment Act in England that summer set the conditions of the power struggle that ensued, as the poor law commissioners sought to bring the Petworth Union into conformity with their rules.[3] By 1837, the commissioners had broadened their attack to challenge Sockett's control over the standard of comfort on the Petworth Emigration Committee's ships and the resulting costs of his scheme. They insisted on their rules and their standards. Egremont's death cut short the war of wills between Sockett and Assistant Commissioner Hawley, but not before Sockett had expressed doubts that he could continue to assume the risk of chartering ships if he could not count on the poor law commissioners approving loans to parishes sending emigrants under his committee.

The year 1834 also marked the beginning of a second initiative on Sockett's part, this time concerned more with Upper Canada and immigration than with England and emigration. Sockett had created the Petworth Emigration Committee to fill the vacuum in sponsorship and supervision that resulted when the Emigration Bill of 1831 died on the order paper. Aware by 1834 that the government had no commitment to assisted settlement in Upper Canada beyond Colborne's personal enthusiasm, he turned to Egremont a second time, urging him to use his private fortune to fill a role abandoned by the government. Egremont agreed readily to Sockett's proposal that he purchase wild land in Upper Canada and assist his emigrants to settle these lands. This second part to Sockett's scheme would founder against a familiar rock. Officials in the Colonial Office were unwilling to bend their self-imposed rules even slightly in his direction. Just as his emigration scheme reflected his differences with the poor law commissioners, so the downward trajectory of his project of assisted settlement revealed a widening gap between his expectations and the intentions of both the government and those in charge of the Colonial Office.

As he could not foresee the future, Sockett was all optimism in the autumn of 1834. He had a number of reasons to feel confident. A scare over Egremont's health in the autumn of 1833 had had a happy outcome. He wrote to the Duke of Richmond in January, telling him that "Lord E's recovered health assures me of the same support as heretofore in promoting emigration."[4] During the early part of the year, he lobbied hard for government security for loans raised by parishes to send emigrants. He welcomed the emigration clauses in the Amendment Act as freeing the funds for a steady stream of emigrants on the annual Petworth ships, and he was convinced that his sponsors would respond positively. Sockett also believed that he had solved the two nagging problems that had given him the most cause to worry about his own scheme. He had found the superintendent he sought in Brydone, and the Rideau Canal route had proved to be a viable alternative to the St Lawrence River with all its hardships and hazards. The time seemed right to branch out in a new direction.

When he launched the Petworth emigrations in 1832, Sockett had had no strong preconceptions about the best course for his emigrants to follow in Upper Canada. Perhaps as a result of relying so heavily on the Canada Company for information, he seems to have been overly sanguine about their likelihood of acquiring land in 1832; Colborne, it should be noted, cited the Petworth immigrants as one of two large groups who had arrived expecting land and the means to bring it into cultivation. But Sockett in 1832 also had assurances from the secretary of Richmond's Emigration Commission that "persons willing to work and nonetheless unable to find a private engagement on their arrival in Canada may rely on being offered employment on some public work until they may have a preferable opportunity of disposing of their labour."[5] He had always expected that some of his people would seek employment rather than land, and in 1833 he was "inclined" towards this option. As work in Upper Canada was "abundant," he believed "on the whole" that a scheme entailing the expectation that immigrants would work would be cheaper for the sponsor and better for the immigrant. At this time, he repeated the standard argument for this approach. Poor immigrants would exert themselves more if they had to find a job than if they were kept dependent in an assisted settlement. He offered letters written by Petworth immigrants as evidence of the "complete success of many of the families thus sent out."[6]

In 1832 and 1833, Sockett thought he was doing everything that was necessary and more by planning supervision beyond Quebec and all the way to Toronto. In 1834, he was successful in attracting some "very respectable" emigrants to the *British Tar*, and he believed that Brydone's name as superintendent helped to confirm their plans, but others of this class hung back, reluctant to go now that they knew that the emigrants of 1833 had not been offered the assistance to become farmers given in 1832. As well as carrying fewer people from Sockett's core area, the *British Tar* in 1834 carried a smaller percentage of children and families than any other Petworth ship.

AN ATTEMPT TO ASSIST SETTLEMENT IN UPPER CANADA

Sockett urged Egremont to buy land for an Upper Canadian "estate" in order to encourage good settlers with "useful" families. Presumably these settlers were to be from parishes deferring to Egremont, although Sockett never specified and would undoubtedly have left his superintendent free to make exceptions Sockett's concern was for emigrants "rather above the common labourer" – these must have been the people writing the "good" letters. They had higher expectations and, Sockett explained, they wanted land and more security than he could offer. They held back from emigrating because they did not have the means to purchase a small lot or to support themselves for the first two or three years in Upper Canada.[7]

With his proposal to buy land, Sockett crossed over from the ranks of the emigration enthusiasts to those of the colonizers. Apart from his desire to attract a certain type of emigrant, Sockett was personally caught up in the venture. The settlement he proposed to Egremont had its origins in the ambitious projects of private colonizers and big land companies. His own contact among British owners of Canadian estates was Sir Robert Pilkington, a high-ranking military engineer who was also an absentee landlord of some 15,000 acres purchased from Joseph Brant on the Grand River. Pilkington had served in Upper Canada under Lieutenant-Governor John Graves Simcoe in the 1790s and had not been back since 1802. He nonetheless maintained a sporadic interest in his Canadian estate and its north-of-England settlers.

His persistence on behalf of his son George, as revealed in his surviving correspondence with Richmond, suggests that Sockett probably made contact with Pilkington hoping to help George when he decided to emigrate in 1833. George settled on a farm in Eramosa Township, near Guelph and not far from Pilkington's lands. Along with some advice for George, the elderly Pilkington may have given Sockett a rather rosy picture of his estate. In reality, it was thinly peopled by settlers who laboured under a variety of difficulties.[8]

In his proposal to Egremont, Sockett laid out a plan for the creation of a village and farming community on 10,000 to 15,000 acres of wild land in Upper Canada. Like many such plans, it had too much of England in it. His imagined community was too tidy, and he was too clearly unaware of the difficulties of varying from such norms as the 100- and 200-acre lots that surveyors ran across most uncleared land. More seriously, Sockett did not take into account the proposed community's distance from a settled source of supplies, and he assumed that settlers assisted for the first three years would be willing to pay back their debts in the form of increased rent for leased land, a dangerous assumption in Upper Canada, where settlers expected to buy – not rent – if they paid out money.

The core of Sockett's village was to be a small church and school (these might be the same building "*at first*"), with a storehouse, barns, and workshops. Single men would be employed by the owner (Egremont), working in the village and making preparations for new arrivals, preparations that would include clearing and erecting "proper log houses" and the necessary outbuildings on lots to be leased by families.

Calculating on land costing ten shillings an acre, Sockett suggested an initial investment of one pound an acre – it would be higher if the purchase was smaller. With assistance to settlers and a considerable outlay for roads, bridges, and a saw and grist mill, he warned that there would be little or no return in the first four to five years. In the meantime, the owner would have as security for debts incurred by the emigrants the increased value of land that was all or partly cleared and within a developed community. He predicted the creation of a profitable estate that would also make a valuable public contribution.[9]

Sockett himself may have realized that his vision was unrealistic. He turned to Brydone, who in a varied career had farmed in Scotland before studying medicine and joining the navy.[10] In 1834, he sent Brydone on a fact-finding tour in Upper Canada after his supervisory duties were completed, and over the next few years Brydone worked with Sockett's plan to bring it closer to actual experience in the colony.

Although Brydone's instructions and report as edited for his *Narrative* at the end of 1834 did not mention plans for a purchase, or plans to make this purchase from the Canada Company, his travels in 1834 took him to company lands, and his report made frequent reference to the company and to people associated with it in different ways. The two loops of Brydone's exploratory journey were centred on Guelph and Goderich, two communities founded by John Galt while he was still the superintendent of the Canada Company. Galt in his turn owed a debt to earlier Canadian colonizers such as his fellow Scot, William Dickson, who had developed the township of Dumfries and named the principal village of Galt in John's honour.[11]

In 1834, after leaving his party in the care of the Woodstock magistrate John Hatch, Brydone travelled through Guelph as part of his investigation of townships on the upper portion of the Grand River. He spent some time with David Gilkison, visiting his mill at Elora and discussing his plans for developing a family property of some 14,000 acres in Nicol Township (a township adjoining Woolwich).[12] He also intended to meet with Adam Fergusson, who had recently purchased land in the same township and was pressing forward with plans for a Scottish settlement at Fergus. Fergusson had himself toured New York State and Lower and Upper Canada in 1831 and 1833, and his publications had caught Sockett's attention. A violent storm prevented Brydone from making this visit and there was no further mention of consulting him, although Sockett did have John Phillips of Petworth reprint a newspaper account of Fergusson's budding settlement as part of his own promotion.[13]

For the second phase of his journey, Brydone made his way westward, stopping in Waterloo Township to visit the Rapsons. He travelled through some difficult and unsettled country before linking with the Canada Company's road to the Huron Tract. En route to Goderich, Brydone stayed at the taverns the company had provided for travellers. In Goderich, he enjoyed the hospitality of the already legendary "Tiger" Dunlop and heard about Dunlop's plans for a steamboat on Lake Huron based at Goderich Harbour.[14]

On his way south from Goderich to Lake Erie, Brydone stopped at Captain White's in Lobo Township with a view to visiting the Petworth immigrants in the

Adelaide settlement. Here he was told that the road (soon to be named for his patron) was impassable and that no guide was available to take him through the woods along the concession lines. Rather than delay his journey, he settled for a conversation with one Petworth immigrant and good reports at second hand of others. His length of stay left him no time to inquire about the newly opening townships between Adelaide and Lake Huron. With better sources of information, he might have learned that Henry John Jones's settlement at Maxwell was in great difficulty by 1834. In this thinly settled area, most purchasers active on a large-scale area acted as speculators rather than as colonizers. They bought land in scattered parcels and trusted mainly to future settlement around their lots to add value to their properties.[15]

Reaching Lake Erie, Brydone visited Thomas Talbot at Port Talbot, where in his host's hospitality he found a welcome relief from the "privations and toils" of the forest. Backtracking to visit London, Brydone remarked on the extent of the clearing and the prosperity of this region: "were it not for the rail fences, and the want of hedges, one might imagine himself in some well cultivated district in England." In London, he discussed employment opportunities for "a superior class of mechanics and labourers" with the crown lands agent.[16]

Brydone's route back to Toronto took him through Woodstock (where he checked on his settlers) and Brantford. As instructed by Sockett, he returned to England via the Erie Canal, referring Sockett for additional information on this route to Upper Canada to Andrew Picken's *The Canadas*. Picken's sources brought Sockett full circle back to companies with land to sell in the Canadas. Picken used material supplied to him by Galt himself and by Nathaniel Gould of the British American Land Company, which was opening up lands in the Eastern Townships of Lower Canada.[17]

Sockett may have included Brydone's account of his western trip in the published *Narrative* with a view to a project to form a joint-stock Sussex Canadian association to invest in Canadian lands. After a grumpy response from Richmond, who did not hold with joint-stock companies, Sockett let this proposal drop.[18] So far as Sockett's object was concerned, Richmond had added somewhat as an afterthought that Egremont "will find no difficulty in purchasing land in Canada."[19] Richmond had left office in the summer of 1834, he was out of touch, and his confidence in this matter was unwarranted. He was, however, correct in thinking that Egremont's backing was sufficient for Sockett's purposes.

Sockett began with enquiries to the Canada Company. He wrote to the directors to ask for prices and terms for buying a block of land and inquired specifically about land that Brydone had seen on his tour of the Huron Tract. This letter demonstrated that he was listening to Brydone and that he knew more about the company than he had in 1832. He now incorporated the idea of selling lots to his settlers, as well as renting, the first of several modifications that would bring his plan closer to Upper Canadian practice. For this audience, Sockett described potential emigrants who were reluctant to work for others and aspired to independence. The company's Canadian commissioner, Thomas Mercer Jones, buoyed by heady visions of other large landed proprietors following Egremont's lead, offered in 1835 to meet Brydone in Toronto.[20] If they did meet, no concrete proposals emerged for discussion.

The plan for a settlement that Sockett and Brydone actually pursued in 1835 was on a scale quite different from the one Sockett had projected a year earlier. The 1834 proposal had envisioned a property about the size of Pilkington's, 10,000–15,000 acres; in 1835, Brydone negotiated for a tract of 60,000 acres, the size of a township in Upper Canada, and asked to have additional land held in reserve. The area proposed was roughly equivalent to Mount's Adelaide settlement, although Sockett intended to take several years to open it and to proceed more cautiously. Creating a settlement on this scale depended on an accommodating attitude in government.

Sockett appears to have been driven to seek land in a remote location because there was no suitable tract available in more-settled townships. In addition, his own ambitions grew between the 1834 and 1835 seasons of emigration as a direct result of the passing of the Poor Law Amendment Act and its emigration clauses. Sockett believed that legislation to facilitate borrowing by parishes gave his emigration scheme the solid foundation it had lacked in the earlier years, when sponsors had had to make unsecured loans to their parish. The Petworth committee's experience in 1835 and 1836 supported his confidence. Sponsors pressed the poor law commissioners to process applications quickly lest they lose a place on the Petworth ship.[21] The reputation of the Petworth committee was spreading, and Sockett had an inquiry from as far away as Nottinghamshire. He declined taking this family because of the distance from Portsmouth, but he treasured the letter.[22] In 1836, he had more applicants than he could take on the *Heber*, a larger ship than the *Burrell*, which had sailed the year before.

Because Sockett's reasons for wanting a bigger settlement lay at home rather than in Upper Canada, it is necessary to backtrack in order to link them to Brydone's new mandate for buying land in 1835. At the upper level of government in England, the conservatives' brief interlude in power over the winter of 1834–35 made little difference to Sockett's emigration plans. On behalf of the new colonial secretary, Lord Aberdeen, R.W. Hay wrote from the Colonial Office to inform Sockett that he might rely on Colborne for every assistance "consistent with impartiality and with the general rules established in the colony."[23] Sockett probably expected no more, although he probed further just in case Aberdeen planned to implement policies more favourable to assisted emigration. Hay replied that there would be no public aid for female emigration to Canada (as there had been to Australia) and that Aberdeen would not – Hay said could not – frank printed papers connected with emigration for free postage from Sussex. Sockett, who had funds for a purchase in hand and the precedents of many large purchases by private British interests in mind, saw no obstacle in the negative tone of this letter.

While Sockett saw long-term possibilities for a sustained stream of emigration in the provisions of the Poor Law Amendment Act, the magistrates among his sponsors had a short-term interest in defusing potential unrest. Richmond was one who predicted disturbances possibly worse than those of 1830. After succeeding Egremont as lord lieutenant of Sussex in July 1835, he made plans to be present personally to deal quickly with any new disturbances in West Sussex.[24] His worst fears were soon quieted, but as lord lieutenant, he received correspondence that detailed local incidents where protest had spilled over into violence, and told him that local people feared arson and other forms of reprisal. The Petworth emigrations served as a preemptive move in 1835 and 1836 in the former Yapton Gilbert Union, where authorities knew that the poor law reforms that took away the "right" to work for the parish enshrined in Gilbert's Act would bite hard. Disturbances in the three parishes in the union had been serious in 1830, and reports reached the poor law commissioners that defiant labourers in Yapton and Felpham had intimidated parish officers and were idling in the gravel pit for their parish pay.[25]

In 1835, Sockett recorded fifty-six emigrants on the *Burrell* sent from the three parishes of Felpham, Yapton, and Walberton. These parishes, which had constituted the disbanded Yapton Gilbert Union, were now administered as part of Westhamptnett. Egremont undoubtedly took account of the local situation when he made the "benevolent" decision to assist with the passage of emigrants from Felpham despite his slight connection with the parish. In Walberton, Richard Prime, the major landholder, represented the lesser magistrates among Sockett's sponsors who felt personally threatened by unrest. In 1830 Prime had been left to cope on his own and had temporized with the local labourers. Upon the introduction of the new poor law, he recommended a plan favoured by Sussex magistrates, to introduce the new rules in very gradual stages so that no large number of people were adversely affected at any one time.[26] His concerns ignored, he sent eleven emigrants from Walberton in 1835 and eleven single men and one woman on the *Heber* in 1836.

Sockett's relations with the new poor law commissioners and their secretary, Edwin Chadwick, never easy, were at their best over arrangements for the 1835 emigration. Although less concerned with possible unrest than with negotiating boundaries for poor law unions, the commissioners still had West Sussex to organize. They were hoping to accommodate Egremont and win over the people around him, and they put no real obstacles in Sockett's way. At the parish level, the financial provisions of the new poor law worked to Sockett's advantage, although not without irritations.

Sockett spent March of 1835 fuming that he was being held back when it was most important to act quickly.[27] Parish officials, unaccustomed to outside direction, had trouble with the new and cumbersome procedure for applying for parish loans and often stumbled through the application process. Once they figured out what was expected, held the required meetings, and filled out three sets of forms to the commission's satisfaction, they might still encounter frustration or delay. People in Wisborough Green did everything right only to be told to look locally for £35 of the £85 they had requested because the Exchequer Loan Commission worked exclusively in increments of £50. The commissioners, however, did not allow these problems to interfere with the sailing of the *Burrell* or with that of other ships facing similar delays. Chadwick, their secretary, could not dispense with elements of the application system such as the parish meeting, but the commission did agree to sanction loans even if they had not received the final forms.[28] Parishes supplied the details of names and ages, destination, occupation, and previous assistance of their emigrants after the event or perhaps not at all. With this degree of flexibility, Sockett got his ship off in April as planned.

Brydone sailed from Portsmouth in 1835 carrying with him Egremont's authority to purchase land and make initial preparations for the reception of settlers in 1836. Sir Charles Burrell, who saw a good omen in the ship chosen, made available an additional sum of up to £5,000, having his landless younger son Walter in mind.[29] The decision to seek a block within crown land seems to have been made before Brydone left England. He left his people in Brantford at the very end of June, spent five days in Toronto and another few visiting friends in Niagara, and then set out on another round of tours of inspection.

In presenting his mandate to Colborne, Brydone returned the focus to emigrants "who have not means to support themselves for the first few years without assistance." He then rearranged Sockett's priorities for the settlement in an obvious attempt to offer a more realistic outline: the saw and grist mill now came first, followed by a store, a schoolhouse, and "ultimately" a church. The size of purchase he proposed would mean going beyond the boundaries of existing settlement. Colborne recommended two sites and sent Brydone off armed with letters of introduction.

The first block Brydone explored was a triangular portion of unsurveyed land between the northern boundary of the Huron Tract and the southern limit of lands still held by Native people. His starting point was Goderich, which had been the most distant point he had reached in 1834. Accompanied by a professional surveyor and a small survey party, Brydone made his first venture into unexplored country on a tour of inspection that lasted from 21 July to 3 August. His party followed the northern boundary of the Huron Tract, which would form the southern limit of the proposed purchase, and the line that defined the boundary with aboriginal lands to the north. They then struck out into the interior and followed the banks of the Maitland River, trying to establish the course of various creeks, noting possible mill sites, and checking exposed soil and the growth of trees.[30] The land near the lakeshore was of disappointing quality, but as they went inland, it improved significantly. Brydone held off from making a commitment until he had looked at the second district recommended by Colborne (see map 7).

After a return visit to Toronto, Brydone left on 16 August on this second tour, which lasted until 9 September. The object of his journey was Balsam Lake and the new townships being laid out around it. Balsam was one of the chain of Kawartha lakes north of Lake Ontario. The promise of that region lay in its location, along the line of water transport under survey that summer from Peterborough to Lake Simcoe – a section of the future Trent-Severn Waterway. On this more populated route, Brydone took his time and made good use of introductions to government officials, of opportunities to confer with leading citizens, and of his own connections with Scots in the area. He travelled by way of Yonge Street and then the steamboat that went from Holland Landing into Lake Simcoe. Finding the Talbot River leading out of Lake Simcoe clogged by water lilies and fallen trees, he abandoned the boat he had hired and continued on foot. Members of a road party under Wesley Richey of the Crown Lands Department guided him to the surveyors John Huston and John Smith, who were working on the west and east sides of Balsam Lake.

By his own account, Brydone had an enjoyable trip but he did not see land that he could recommend. Admiral Vansittart, who had preceded Brydone to Woodstock by a couple of days in 1834, made a large purchase here. Brydone was more cautious or more knowledgable. Although the Laurentian Shield was not known as such in 1835, this was the landscape described in Brydone's notes. He concluded that "although the scenery be pretty [land in this neighbourhood] is not suited as a general settlement for the poor man."[31] After rejecting these townships, he returned to Toronto via Peterborough, Rice Lake, and Cobourg with his mind made up.

Brydone opened negotiations with Colborne for the tract north of Goderich on Lake Huron early in September 1835. His proposal followed Sockett's plan to purchase on a scale that could only be accommodated by buying from government. Brydone offered to make an outright purchase of about 60,000 acres fronting on Lake Huron and bounded by the Canada Company to the south and the Indian Territory to the north. It was to include the Maitland River. At the direction of the Petworth committee, he asked the government to give them a three- to five-year option to purchase on the same terms an adjoining tract of some 40,000 acres.

Brydone bargained with Colborne in the knowledge that the lieutenant-governor would look favourably on this "work of charity." He also knew that his proposed purchase dovetailed with Colborne's plans to develop the eastern shores of Lake Huron, and he had no doubt that Colborne would agree that a more rapid improvement would result than could be hoped for without "some influential first settlement."[32] He hoped to use this knowledge in the negotiations by emphasizing the difficulties of his chosen site north of Goderich before he made a specific offer. The land near the lakeshore where the village must be built, Brydone wrote, was inferior for farming, and in such a remote location the costs of clearing and fencing and of building roads and bridges would be high. Furthermore, there was no access road through the Township of Colborne. He asked that the governor use his influence with the Canada Company to hasten the opening of communications. All in all, he thought the price should not exceed one dollar an acre, half that for intervals of inferior land, and no charge for swamps unfit for cultivation. He also wanted a concession similar to one granted to the Canada Company: government should commit one-quarter of the purchase money to building roads and bridges within the tract. Colborne's counter-proposal restricted the sale to the 60,000 acres of the initial purchase and included a price of five shillings an acre.

The negotiations between Brydone and Colborne in 1835 stalled at this stage because Colborne did not have the authority to sell except by auction, and an auction had to wait for an official survey – an eventuality Sockett and Brydone had not foreseen. All Colborne could do was to promise a survey and a favourable reference to the Colonial Office recommending special consideration for Egremont's purchase.

Brydone was unable to implement Sockett's plans to have the site ready to receive immigrants early in 1836, plans he had relayed to Petworth immigrants in Brantford and Woodstock. His instructions had been to put in a mill dam in the fall of 1835, to have land cleared over the winter, and to build a mill in the spring. As none of these preparations were possible, Brydone went on to Montreal where he had business with Peter McGill.

McGill used this opportunity to try to sell Brydone land belonging to the British American Land Company. Brydone travelled through Nicolet en route to New York and the ship that would carry him back to England, and made a cursory inspection of townships held by the company.[33] He described the scenery as "beautifully pictoresque and romantic" and found several locations attractive to a gentleman "of moderate independence ... desirous of combining ornament with profit."[34] The land he passed, however, was of uneven quality and early frost warned him that winter everywhere lasted a month to six weeks longer than in Upper Canada. Returning to his mandate, he concluded that, for the poor settler, "I do not consider these Townships, of half the value ... in an agricultural point of view, as the Tract, which I had selected, on Lake Huron."[35]

After Brydone arrived back in England in the fall of 1835 with his site chosen but his purchase incomplete, action shifted from Upper Canada to England and from Brydone and Colborne to Sockett and Charles Grant, first Lord Glenelg, colonial secretary since the Whigs and Melbourne had returned to power. In the Colonial Office, attention on the Canadas was focused entirely on the deteriorating political situation. Political tensions and the rising temperature of public protest had grabbed attention from land policy and economic development. During the summer of 1835, Archibald Acheson, the second earl of Gosford, had been sent to Lower Canada as governor-in-chief and the head of a commission of inquiry into the political impasse between the executive and the legislature of that province. The Legislative Assembly of Lower Canada was refusing to pass supply bills, and the salaries of government officials (including emigration agent Alexander Carlisle Buchanan) had not been paid for nearly three years. The British government hoped that Gosford would be a moderating influence but his mission failed in its main objectives.[36]

In Upper Canada, the sale of crown lands to the Canada Company had assured funds for a civil list, a fixed annual sum appropriated to paying the salaries of political, administrative, and judicial officials. Thus, the salaries of the executive were not at issue in Upper Canada as in the lower province, but reformers in the House of Assembly were demanding an end to the executive's discretionary spending of unallocated territorial revenues (the revenues Colborne had used during the cholera-plagued immigration of 1832). Members of the Assembly had been examining the spending of the Crown Lands Department since 1832, and a committee on grievances headed by radical leader William Lyon Mackenzie was working on its inefficiencies.[37] A long, acrimonious battle to wrest control of land revenues from the Colonial Office was entering a final phase at the time that Sockett proposed his purchase.[38]

Officials in the Colonial Office feared that Sockett might became an involuntary player in the politics of Upper Canada. The last thing they wanted was to call additional attention to well-publicized grievances by facilitating a large land purchase by a prominent British nobleman, but they considered it impolitic to explain their reasoning to Sockett. He was given no hint of the contents of an internal memorandum setting out why the Colonial Office was willing to forgo Egremont's investment in Upper Canada.

The case against special consideration for Egremont's purchase revolved around the issues of territorial revenues and the widespread complaints about abuses in the use and misuse of crown lands articulated by Mackenzie's committee on grievances. Bending the rules for Egremont would give the members of the Upper Canadian Assembly the clear issue they sought. Were the "public mind in that Province in a healthful tone," the sale might proceed without incident. In the present state of affairs, it was inexpedient to offer "a fresh handle to the seekers of grievances within the Province." The people of Upper Canada should therefore be left to suffer "the risk of any diminution of the benefit which they would otherwise obtain from the immigration of Lord Egremont's settlers."[39]

This last sour comment was never intended for Sockett's eyes. The original draft of the letter to him had, however, included a partial explanation: "Without entering into a detail of circumstances with which you are probably well acquainted through the medium of the public journals, it is sufficient to observe that under the present aspect of public affairs in the Province, his Lordship would not feel justified in offering to the Petworth Emigration Society, any advantages in the acquisition of land, beyond those which are held out to other purchasers."[40] This paragraph was deleted before the letter was sent to Sockett. The version he actually received coupled expressions of high regard for Egremont's contributions to emigration with a bland statement that the colonial secretary would not allow any departure from the ordinary rules of purchase.

Sockett was used by now to receiving word that no exceptions could be made to regulations governing sales of crown lands. With no hint that this new refusal reflected a hardening attitude towards purchases like his, he seemed satisfied by a promise that a survey of the block on Lake Huron would be ready in time for his plans to go forward in 1836. He was further encouraged by the continued strong demand for places on his ship. His plan flourished while Hawley and the poor law commissioners found few candidates in his district for their rival scheme of sending the families of the unemployed as internal migrants to Manchester.[41]

In April 1836, Brydone sailed for Upper Canada carrying instructions to renew the offer for the block on Lake Huron and to prepare it for the reception of immigrants the following season. On arrival, he found a province in economic difficulties so serious that he began to doubt his mission.

Hawke's report on the emigration of 1835 to Upper Canada was full of gloom. He blamed the reduction in immigration on news reaching Britain of the immigration of 1834, which had been marred by shipwrecks in the Gulf of St Lawrence and a cholera epidemic in both provinces. In England, he wrote, rural people saw improvements in their prospects at home at the same time as they received bad reports from North America. In the United States, immigrant numbers were also down.

Hawke was not, however, without hopes that the situation could be turned around, and he pinned these hopes on the region north of Goderich on Lake Huron where Brydone proposed to locate Egremont's settlement.

In a long memorandum written for the new lieutenant-governor, Sir Francis Bond Head, Hawke explained his hopes and Colborne's for this region. His report on the immigration of 1835 had reflected his fears that Upper Canada was becoming a conduit to the western United States. To counter this trend, he proposed a government purchase of the aboriginal lands north of the Huron Tract. He wanted land there to be sold to poor settlers at prices competitive with land in nearby Michigan. To give a further edge to Upper Canada, Hawke recommended turning a portion of the profits from land sales back into developing the tract.[42] He had probably discussed these plans with Brydone. If he did, both men would have seen mutual advantage in Egremont's purchase and improvement of a portion of the triangular strip between the Indian lands and the Huron Tract.

With Colborne's departure, Brydone lost an important supporter. He left no record of his impression of Head, or of Head's politically motivated interventions in the election of June 1836, but he was greatly concerned about the deepening recession, which convinced him that the moment had passed for buying a large and remote tract of land. A province heavily dependent on agriculture was gathering in a meagre harvest in 1836.[43] Hawke advised Head early in the season that the government should subsidize travel from the St Lawrence to Upper Canada for new immigrants only if they had relatives or friends in the province ready to help them. Farm jobs that might normally have gone to new immigrants were being taken by back-country settlers forced out of the bush to look for work.[44] Brydone had himself observed the exodus to the United States in 1835, and he had repeated the common opinion that the high price of land was pushing new settlers over the border.[45] He resumed negotiations to purchase the block north of the Canada Company's Huron Tract as set out in his instructions, but he wrote to Head without enthusiasm.

The proposal Brydone presented to Head in September 1836 was trimmed down from the year before. He now requested 25,000 acres with a six-year option on a further 45,000. He also tried for a lower price without going so far as to suggest a figure. In making his case, he repeated the opinion which now "prevailed" in the colony that government must reduce the price of land. The province was in worse shape economically than in 1835, and development in Goderich (the only town near his land) was stalled if not actually regressing. Whatever might be thought of the potential advantages of the purchase, the settlement was a less attractive prospect than it had been a year earlier. In addition to a less certain value, the costs of its establishment could only be higher in 1836, "much exceeding what may be anticipated by the sanguine projector of the plan."[46] This remark, as close as Brydone came to direct criticism of his friend's plans, seems to have represented his last word in 1836.

On the other side of the Atlantic in Petworth, the poor law commissioners' careful policy of putting new rules in place during seasons of full employment proved generally effective in Sussex. Occasional incidents – noticed by the national press because of the size of the crowd or a violent act – were contained by local authorities. The commissioners judged this county ready in June 1836 for their order that local unions cease giving relief to able-bodied applicants in their homes and insist that they enter a workhouse. With this order, the lines were drawn between the poor law commissioners and the guardians of the Petworth Poor Law Union.

The poor law commissioners had no power to influence employers other than what they they could do indirectly by setting rules for poor relief. They believed that farmers in parishes like Petworth laid people off and provided outdoor relief – parish support in the home – as the cheapest way of maintaining the large agricultural labour force they needed at only certain times of year. They hoped that farmers, who were also ratepayers, would think differently if they had no alternative for laid-off workers but the more expensive option of supporting them and their families in a workhouse. The Petworth guardians, with Egremont's silent backing, clung to their opinion that it was against common sense to "break up the little Establishment, the Cottage Comfort, and the Spirit of the Pauper" and force whole families into the workhouse when a few weeks of less costly outdoor relief would keep most of them independent.[47] They used what expedients they could to ease the burden and took one, two, or three children into the workhouse from families like those of the four labourers whom Sockett brought to give evidence to the Select Committee on the Poor Law Amendment Act in 1837.

The Sussex labourers in Sockett's district did not benefit from the upturn in the English rural economy noted by Hawke. As they lost their parish aid at a time when their wages were not keeping pace with price increases, the only way they could avoid the workhouse was to lower their standard of living or to leave. In Sockett's opinion, the desire to emigrate evident in his neighbourhood in 1836 was "clearly traceable to the operations of the Poor-Law Amendment Act" on labourers' wages. Egremont had sponsored fifty individuals from Tillington, and Sockett thought that just as many would have gone from every other parish in the Midhurst Union "had there been a Lord Egremont in each to defray the expense."[48] Sockett knew that less scrupulous employers used their labourers' fear of the workhouse to reduce wages. He described deserving family men working for starvation rates as low as five or six shillings a week. People who could obtain neither work nor relief were complaining bitterly to him that emigration was also out of their reach. Humanitarian reasons for expanding his scheme were, in his opinion, stronger than ever under the new law.

Sockett chose to take a public stand against the impact of the commissioners' ruling against outdoor relief for large families in 1837. So long as Egremont lived and local opinion ran against the new law, Sockett's influence was enhanced by his decision not to stand for election as a Petworth guardian and by the free hand this gave him to use Egremont's charity against the intention of the commission. Just as Hawley chose to report on employment in the district during the harvest season when everyone was at work, Sockett selected the unemployment in winter months for special attention. Over the winter of 1836–37, he had many occasions to exercise charity as snow and bad weather brought unemployment, a flu epidemic, and much distress to his district of Sussex. His letter in the *London Standard* in February 1837 must have been seen by some; his testimony in March to the select committee was printed verbatim in *The Times*.[49] Although Sockett was not always a match for the lawyers questioning him for the government side, he held his own and he was the first of a number of witnesses whose combined testimony caused even the large majority of the committee members in favour of the Poor Law Amendment Act to lean slightly in the direction of more discretion in granting relief.[50] He came home from London to a hero's welcome.[51]

Hawley, a strong supporter of Chadwick's hard line, reacted with great bitterness and singled out his clerical opponents when he came to write up his reaction to the committee.[52] Relations between Sockett and Hawley, which had been bad before, were now poisoned, with the result that the poor law commissioners began to harass parishes such as Balcombe to prevent them using a Petworth ship. Richmond also came in for a large share of the bitterness stirred up against the new law.[53] His critics had misunderstood his championing of the poor labourer and the direction of his campaign to introduce central supervision of the poor laws, and Richmond's memory of this was that "no man had been more personally abused than he for taking that office [of chairman of a board of guardians]."[54] Caught up in the politics of the Westhamptnett Union, Richmond had no time for emigration in 1837.

Sockett, practical as always, used the sailing of the *Diana* in 1837 to give the opportunity of escape to several very large families from his neighbourhood. Although he got these families off, his difficulties in filling this ship must have given him pause in planning for Upper Canada. We have no evidence that Brydone tried to advance Sockett's plans for purchase during his stay that year in Upper Canada. Everything he learned over the summer must have reinforced the pessimistic view of the plan he had held in 1836.

In 1837, Upper Canada was reeling from the effects of a financial crisis that had begun in Britain and the United States in 1836 and spread to the Canadas. Lieutenant-Governor Head added to the financial problems of the province by insisting that its bankers follow a different course from those pursued in the United States and Lower Canada. These woes compounded the agricultural recession brought on by the bad harvest of the year before.[55] In the political realm, the opposition to the conservative-dominated local government, elected in 1836, was growing more strident and threatening.

In addition to outlining the political and economic factors that bore on the whole population, Hawke, in his emigration report for Upper Canada in 1837, described a change in the character of immigrants arriving from Britain. If perhaps one-sixteenth of the immigrants arriving at Quebec in 1834 had been paupers assisted by landlord or parish, the proportion had risen to one-fifth two years later in 1836. By 1837, it amounted to nearly one-quarter of the total. In addition, many others had arrived claiming that the cost of the passage had exhausted their funds.[56] Such "independent" immigrants, if they told the truth, were less well off than those sent by the

Petworth committee. Writing of the province in 1837, Head himself described the plight of the poorest immigrants, "the last year's crop of potatoes having failed – the public works being arrested – and the province being invaded by a number of emigrants, who were roaming about without the means of obtaining food or employment."[57]

Hawke's 1837 report made note of "mere" labourers who came chasing the illusion of high pay in Upper Canada when he had no work to give them. His pessimism in part reflected his exasperation with the mindless and misleading reports sent to Britain by Buchanan and Head. They were responsible for some wildly inaccurate calculations of the number of men to be employed on proposed public works – works that with the exception of the Cornwall Canal would remain idle for lack of funds in 1837. In his annual report for 1836, the younger A.C. Buchanan had anticipated "no difficulty in obtaining settlement and immediate employment for 20,000 persons of the labouring class during 1837." The following spring, Head sent a circular to the boards of guardians in England forecasting "an unusual demand here for artificers and labourers."[58] In Sussex, Hawley's plans to send migrants to Manchester were on hold because of the recession there, and he promised to send a copy of Head's letter to all poor law unions in his district. In Upper Canada, Hawke reported a strong backlash against parish immigration in Upper Canada simply on the strength of reports of Head's circular. With a bit of exaggeration, he stated that there were no pauper immigrants taking jobs from Upper Canadians because he knew of none sent by the commissioners.[59]

On 14 September 1837, Brydone wrote from Toronto giving Head formal notice on behalf of his principals that he did not intend to renew his proposal to purchase land north of Goderich "under the existing circumstances of the province."[60] Less than three months later, at the beginning of December, Mackenzie's hastily assembled rebels marched down Yonge Street in a failed attempt to take Toronto, and a few days later Charles Duncombe led a doomed rising in the Brantford area.[61]

Sockett may have hesitated as late as September to finally abandon his plans because he was still receiving favourable letters from Petworth immigrants in Upper Canada. Hawke's gloomy predictions about lack of work for emigrants were not aimed at them. Looking back from 1839, Hawke admitted that he had never had problems finding work for the skilled farming man if single,[62] and from 1834 he had had five-acre lots to offer Petworth families. A generally bleak picture for the mass of those who arrived poor and unskilled did not mean that there were not individual employers with money to hire someone who fitted their needs. The Hilton family sailed on the *Diana*, and with the help of a son in Toronto, George and his older children found work immediately. The Pullens also came on the *Diana* and brought seven young children (their eldest daughter died on the way over). They had no relatives or friends where they settled in the London District of Upper Canada, yet by the end of the year they had found not one but two employers willing to house their large family over the winter. Discovering that their first place had been too far into the bush for their taste, they had moved closer to the village of Delaware and its church. Richard had "constant" work and Frances assured her sister "that we get a better living than we should in England, if it is so bad as when we left."[63]

1838 AND AFTER

In 1838, even Sockett admitted that people in his neighbourhood would not go to Canada. The Petworth committee sent only a single family. Letter-writers among Petworth immigrants discouraged their friends and relatives at home more with tales of military exploits than with concerns about their finding work.[64] The letters Sockett published about the events of the 1837–38 Rebellions were written from the Adelaide settlement, chosen perhaps as the most coherent accounts or perhaps because the Adelaide militia was actively involved in defending the border against patriot raids in 1838. Frederick Hasted, a colourful character from Arundel who kept in touch with Sockett on the subject of his immigrants, may have supplied more than one of these accounts, as he said he acted as a scribe for his fellow immigrant settlers. Hasted was probably glad of the opportunity to get out of the bush afforded by work for a baker who supplied British troops stationed in London, and Charles Rapley delighted in the adventure of militia service and in his daily pay of one shilling and one pence English money (sterling) as head drummer.

Other letters, particularly those written by women, give a better idea of what was keeping people home in England. James Cooper, as the farming head of a large family, was relieved that he had escaped being recruited by the Adelaide militia and had no regrets about missing a long, hard march across half-frozen swamps to Amherstburg. Frances Pullen had seen the "awful sight" of captured prisoners driven on foot past her house and had heard stories of the bodies of dead invaders being thrown into a pit "like logs." Although she left no doubt that her sympathies were with British soldiers, her fervent thanks to the Almighty that Richard had not been called out for militia service reminded her family of the possibility that he too might have been killed.[65] Obed Wilson's mother, Maria, in Bassingbourn near Royston in Cambridgeshire, reported on the dual effect of dramatic newspaper reports and her son's failure to write. After finally receiving a letter from Obed in 1838, she wrote back: "I never Expected to hear from you again for I quite thought you wair Dead."[66] Maria was a protective mother and Obed her youngest child, but her reaction is a reminder that the Canadian rebellions, given that armed rebels were engaging regular soldiers in battle, must have appeared as true rebellions in English cottages. The Royston area of Cambridgeshire had seen significant disturbances in 1830, but rioters had not carried guns during the Swing disturbances and the single reported fatality had been an unarmed Wiltshire man shot by the local yeomanry.

Sockett himself remained enthusiastic about Upper Canada and ready to believe that the interruption to emigration in 1838 was temporary. A year later he claimed that local people who were dead set against emigrating to Canada in 1838 had changed their minds again in 1839. He was quick to publish an encouraging letter from William Phillips. Phillips had written that "there never was a better time to come to Canada than the present: for the late disturbance has kept back emigration for the last two years, and hundreds have left the province and gone to the United States, so that there is a good chance for emigrants of all classes."[67] As opinion changed among potential emigrants, Sockett was unable to find sponsors to match their expenses.

Egremont's death in 1837 affected everyone on the estate the earl had presided over for more than seventy years. Reportedly quite paranoid in his last months, Egremont had dismissed his old servants for new ones and turned on some of the people closest to him.[68] On his deathbed in November, he was attended by the Petworth curate rather than by Sockett, who, according to rumour, had been denied entry to the house.[69] Egremont was angry with Sockett for not giving active support to General Henry Wyndham, his second son, in the election that summer. Sockett's fall from favour may have had as much to do with the politics of Egremont's family as with Sockett's efforts to stay neutral on Henry's candidacy. Sockett had long disapproved of Henry's conduct, but as Egremont's life drew to a close, he may have been forced to take sides with Henry's older brother, George. Sockett must have found all aspects of the situation distressing, but it did not affect his status or his income.[70]

Colonel George Wyndham, later first Lord Leconfield, was initially overwhelmed by the problems of putting to rights an estate his father had neglected in his later years and of having to maintain it on a lower income than his father's.[71] The customs of estates like Petworth allowed the new owner the option of changing anyone on his father's staff, and the staff members in turn could leave without prejudicing their references. Wyndham himself soon recognized that he did not have the stamina or desire to carry out his aspirations to make an efficient business of Petworth House and its lands. He was not good with people or with handling the responsibility of hiring and firing. During his first few months in control, he leaned heavily on Sockett, who was soon involved in managing the house, the stables, and the park.[72] Sockett saw an opportunity to end the abuses that had crept in as Egremont had aged, but his advice was conservative and he leaned towards the people he knew. In between supervising decorators for Mary Wyndham and finding good homes for his former patron's too numerous donkeys, Sockett used his influence with Wyndham to secure the shaky position of Egremont's former estate agent and to find work for Brydone. He persuaded his new patron to take Brydone as his secretary during inspection tours of his estates in Yorkshire and in the counties of Clare and Limerick in Ireland in 1838 and again in 1839.[73]

If the changes Wyndham introduced were less than he had at first intended, he did want change and he wanted to make his mark as a landowner of his own generation. Despite his respect and affection for his old tutor, he began to assert a different point of view on the subject of poor relief and emigration early in his new relationship with Sockett (see Appendix A). Hawley received an introduction to Wyndham from Richmond in 1838, and his hopes that Wyndham would be persuaded to establish a better spirit in the Petworth Union bore fruit. Under this new leadership, Hawley soon reported a greater willingness on the part of the union to conform to the commissioners' directives.[74]

Wyndham's views on emigration took longer to formulate. In this as in other matters, he was most receptive to Sockett at the outset, and he seems to have accepted the view that assisted emigration and assisted settlement were linked. According to Sockett, in 1838 Wyndham was willing to buy land either in Australia or in Canada if this would allow him to get rid of excess population on his estates in Ireland. Wyndham himself wrote to the prime minister, Lord Melbourne, inquiring about the truth of rumours that Lord Durham's mission to the Canadas might lead to a revival of old policies towards government-assisted settlements or, at least, of grants of land to capitalists willing to form their own settlements.[75]

In a separate correspondence, Sockett tried to find out from the colonial secretary what might happen as a result of Durham's mission. The reply came from Thomas Elliot, who had first corresponded with Sockett in his role as the secretary to Richmond's Emigration Commission. Although Elliot refused in his official capacity to make any commitments in advance of Durham's report, his correspondence indicated that he saw the subject in the same light as he had in 1832. He lectured Sockett that only the cost of transport held emigrants back from going to North America. Once in the colony, they were "as well, and better disposed of as labourers than as settlers upon land." He advised that Wyndham, or any other landlord considering either assisted emigration or buying land in the colonies, should not see the two actions as linked. He might wish to undertake both activities but he should regard the purchase of land in Upper Canada as an investment, not as "an indispensable part of emigration."[76]

In Sussex in 1838, emigration sprang to Wyndham's mind as a way of dealing with his personal problem of having to reduce the staff of Petworth House. As the Canadas in January 1838 were not "in that state to invite settlers there," he raised the question of Australia with Sockett.[77] Even in 1838, Sockett preferred Canada over Australia for people made redundant at Petworth House, but he called Wyndham's attention to a government announcement that agricultural labourers would be sent to Australia.[78] Because of the timing of Wyndham's interest, Sockett, who had spent several years studying Upper Canada, ended by making a quick purchase in Australia sight unseen. He bought several hundred acres for Wyndham from the South Australia Land Company and seems to have made a small investment himself.[79] An agent, Frederick Mitchell, was outfitted at Wyndham's expense, given instructions prepared by Sockett, and sent to Australia in the spring of 1838, taking with him some tiresome Ayliffe (Illive) relatives of Wyndham's mother as remittance men.[80] South Australian land was a popular speculation at the time, but this investment turned sour and led nowhere from the point of view of systematic emigration from Petworth. Over the next few years, Wyndham sent only a trickle of emigrants from Sussex to Australia, apparently allowing those who qualified a free choice between this destination and Canada.

The emigration that most engaged Wyndham's attention was that from Ireland. The passing of poor law legislation for Ireland in 1838 turned the attention of landlords there to assisted emigration as an alternative to supporting paupers with a claim as residents on their lands.[81] While he waited to learn what Durham would say about assisted emigration, Wyndham allowed Sockett to talk him into chartering an emigrant ship from Ireland to be organized under Brydone's direction by the Ennis Emigration Committee and to use the Petworth model.[82]

Although a collection of very disparaging references to Irish emigrants can be gleaned from Sockett's writing, his actions in 1839 make clear that he condemned the manner in which they were sent, not the people themselves. Despite his goodwill, Brydone's hard work, and the hiring of an effective superintendent, Charles Rubidge, a former naval officer settled in the Newcastle District near Peterborough, the sailing of the *Waterloo* was problematic.[83] Warnings given Brydone that the scheme would not transplant easily and that many emigrants would drop out at the last minute proved accurate.[84] Canadian newspapers circulated rumours that Rubidge's people had absconded to the United States after landing, and although he countered with evidence that many of them were working where he placed them in the Cobourg area, the reports were damaging nonetheless.[85] Most damaging of all from Wyndham's perspective, emigrants on the *Waterloo* travelled at an estimated cost of just over twelve pounds seven shillings per passage,[86] surely a record for assisted Irish emigrants and an experiment he had no intention of repeating.

Wyndham is remembered by historians of emigration as an absentee landlord who assisted emigration from Ireland. In all, he sent roughly the same numbers from his Irish estates as the Petworth committee had sent from the south of England under Egremont.[87] His participation was, however, a better measure of the scale of Ireland's population problem than of his interest. Brydone handled correspondence from Petworth and acted as a spokesperson when necessary, but after 1839 Wyndham transferred responsibility for sending Irish emigrants to his Irish agent, Thomas Crowe. Crowe sent emigrants from Shannon to Quebec as individuals with no superintendent and no support other than a small gift of landing money. In 1840, Wyndham advised Crowe to be certain to assist only people whose going would be a positive advantage to the estate.[88] A year later, writing about people who had been given notice, Wyndham instructed Crowe that they could be sent to Canada if they asked but that they should not be encouraged: "It will be less expensive to give them something to go away [within Ireland]."[89] Within three years of Wyndham taking over from Egremont, assisted emigration directed from Petworth House had caught up with the trends Hawke noted in immigration to the Canadas in 1837. The immigrants sent by Wyndham were Irish, very poor, and assisted only as far as Quebec.

More optimistic than most about the future of Canada, Sockett still dreamed of establishing a settlement in 1838 and 1839, and he linked his hopes for it with his hopes for Brydone. He speculated that Brydone might move to Upper Canada as superintendent of an estate there until his sons grew old enough to take over and he could return to England. While Brydone was very anxious to find a place with Wyndham, he confided to Sockett that his wife did not want to go to Canada and that he would prefer Yorkshire to Ireland. (Brydone in fact rose in Wyndham's service to be land agent at Petworth with a large house in the town. His two sons worked for the Petworth estate as did a grandson, Robin Brydone, who supplied a later Lord Leconfield with some of the information used in this book.)

In 1838, Brydone wrote admiringly to Sockett of the way the latter rose to a challenge, how his spirits and health seemed best when he was busiest.[90] Over the next two years, Sockett directed some of this energy towards buying land for a settlement. An approach from Thomas Rolph in 1839 showed that Sockett also kept the door open to take advantage of renewed interest in emigration in Sussex. Rolph was in England that year representing the Canada Emigration Association, an association formed to sell land in the Canadas, and he convinced Wyndham to invite him to Petworth.[91] Sockett's enquiries did not lead him to encourage the connection, and Sockett let it drop after giving Rolph the forum of a speech at his annual audit dinner.[92] Instead, Sockett and Brydone investigated possibilities offered through Brydone's acquaintance with Anthony Hawke, Upper Canada's emigration agent.

Hawke's involvement in land sales during the years that he was emigration agent has not received the same attention as Buchanan's in Lower Canada, but he was busy on Wyndham's behalf trying to find a large enough block in a single location. Sockett collected new information from the land companies and gave some thought to a small purchase to serve as a "nursery" for emigrants who might afterwards be sent farther afield. Although Brydone once sent off an authority to purchase from Wyndham, nothing came of this transaction because Hawke received Brydone's authorization after the land in question had been sold to others.[93]

Brydone had succeeded in convincing Sockett that location was more important than size, and the tracts they considered in 1839 and 1840 were smaller and closer to earlier settlements than the tract north of Goderich that Sockett had tried to buy for Egremont. None of these prospects appealed to Sockett as much as General Pilkington's property on the Grand River. Pilkington had died in 1834, and Sockett had been offered an option on his land in 1835. He abandoned it because he expected the estate to be tied up in Chancery for years. In 1839, Pilkington's executor approached him unexpectedly, writing that he would be in a position to sell within the year.[94] Brydone began serious discussions concerning the purchase of some 15,000 acres in Pilkington Township in 1840 only to have Wyndham bring his negotiations to an abrupt halt and cancel a proposed trip to North America that was to have included an inspection of the land in Pilkington Township. The only land Sockett ever acquired in Upper Canada was a 200-acre lot that he purchased himself in Eramosa Township near Guelph and intended for his son George.[95]

The possibility of reviving Egremont's emigration scheme came to an end with Wyndham's statement that he had "no intention of buying a single foot of land in Canada." He had made up his mind that these "distant things" produced only "vexation and trouble."[96] Sockett must have had warnings that Wyndham's mood was changing. Wyndham, easily aggrieved, had become resentful of the cost of assisting emigration.

The declaration of bankruptcy by the South Australian commissioners in 1839 was a major setback, bringing Wyndham to the realization that he had sunk £3,800 into

Australia with little to show for it.[97] Assisted emigration to the Canadas provoked irritation of a different sort by exposing Wyndham to public criticism. In a despatch to the colonial secretary concerning Irish emigrants sent by Wyndham from County Clare to Quebec in 1840, Governor Thomson of Lower Canada chose to assume that "it could not have been his [Wyndham's] intention to throw these people on the charity of the government."[98] Thomson forwarded the emigrants to Charles Rubidge, Wyndham's 1839 superintendent in the Newcastle District.[99] The first Wyndham heard about the governor's actions was a request for reimbursement of the cost.

This incident demonstrated the differences between Egremont's and Wyndham's attitude to assistance. Egremont's benevolence was humanitarian but also part of a larger-than-life image that had been deliberately cultivated. Sockett was well aware that Egremont liked to excel and to have the excellence of his projects recognized. Having undertaken the Petworth emigrations as a measure to deal with a "surplus population" of labourers, Sockett set out in 1832 to make them "the best example of a well-conducted emigration during these years."[100] Wyndham did not want to be compared with his father, and he deeply resented being singled out for an implied criticism not attached to other aristocratic landlords who sent emigrants abroad. His reaction was that he would not send emigrants again if sending them entailed an obligation to provide for their "future wants."

A conciliatory response from the Colonial Office included assurances that Colonial Secretary Lord John Russell personally supported the idea that government should share the burden of assisting emigration. This letter, however, gave Wyndham the clear answer that "neither Parliament, nor the Provincial Legislature have placed any funds at the disposal of government which could be applied in this manner."[101]

Sockett recognized Wyndham's decision against investing in Canada as final, and he did not even consider trying to continue a project of assisted settlement in Upper Canada that had lost government support some time before. He did, however, manage to continue limited assisted emigration from the district around Petworth and parishes in the Sutton Union. We know of roughly a hundred people, families and individuals, who were sent by the Petworth committee from London to Quebec and Montreal on Carter and Bonus ships between 1838 and 1845. In 1843 and 1844, Phillips printed information promoting these emigrations, including a list of parishes where Wyndham would contribute a percentage, and the committee followed past procedures in sending out messengers to post notices and printing emigrant letters.[102] The committee sent its largest numbers in 1844, which was a hard year in rural England. As it was not chartering ships, the committee did not recruit beyond Wyndham's sphere of influence. Most of the emigrants were chain migrants forwarded at their own "ernest desire."

We have found no reference to the Petworth Emigration Committee after 1845, the year committee member William Knight died. Although Sockett's name appears on a resolution of the Petworth vestry requesting sanction of a loan for emigration from the poor law commissioners in 1850, the only visible link with the past was the use of a Carter and Bonus ship.[103]

CHAPTER 7

CONCLUSION: THE PETWORTH EMIGRATIONS AND ASSISTED EMIGRATION

The practical outcome of Thomas Sockett's scheme of assisted emigration was to provide over 1,800 people with a new start in Upper Canada. Although Sockett's energy and efficiency and Egremont's generosity carried the benefits of the plan beyond Petworth, the Petworth emigrations reflect the limitations of parish-aided emigration when it was organized according to the old poor law. An emigration scheme tied to local patronage was open to some and not to others, and the size to which it could grow was limited by its reliance on individuals and individual initiative. In the hands of a man like Sockett, however, there were definite advantages to a local scale of operation. The Petworth Emigration Committee made good use of its discretionary powers and tailored the scheme to the needs of a well-defined group of people. The assistance it offered, together with the official interest the scheme attracted, meant that emigrant families sent by the Petworth committee had improved prospects in Upper Canada.

Our research for this book and for the collection of letters in *English Immigrant Voices* confirms Sockett's conviction that many Petworth immigrants were better off in Upper Canada than in England. With the benefit of hindsight, we know that some, especially those who emigrated as children or young adults, would succeed in moving up the social and economic scale. We have not identified all Petworth immigrants in Upper Canada, but repeated migrations from the same places and chain migration within families are evidence that any negative reports reaching England were outweighed by encouraging news.

As a case study in parish-assisted emigration, the Petworth emigrations serve as a rare example in which the records are unusually complete at all stages of emigration. The wide range of parishes contributing to the Petworth emigrations provide examples of many kinds of sponsorship and of the occupations and family circumstances of the rural labourers who were suffering most from low wages and seasonal unemployment. Petworth emigrants are representative of the working people seen as "redundant" in rural parishes in areas implicated in the Swing disturbances at the beginning of the decade. The arrangements made for their assistance to emigrate were more extensive than the norm, but they differed in degree rather than in kind. Once in Toronto, the emigrants travelled, or were assisted to travel, to communities attracting many of the English emigrants who came to Upper Canada on their own in these years. Their experiences finding jobs and getting established in their places of first settlement offer examples of different options open to them and to people like them.

The stories of Petworth immigrants on their first arrival in Upper Canada demonstrate that the key to their successes was the versatility of their settlement strategies. English immigrants of the class of officers and gentlemen drawn to Upper Canada in the 1830s by prospects of land ownership stood out because of their difficulties in earning a living from their large land grants and in fitting into North American society. Parish immigrants like those on Sockett's ships were well adapted to immigrate to Upper Canada at a time when the best opportunity open to them might be either as farming settlers or as wage workers. By contrast with more articulate middle-class immigrants, they integrated so successfully that their contribution to building the province has been largely overlooked.

The impact of the Petworth emigrations on communities both in England and in Upper Canada is a more open question than their success in improving individual lives. Sockett believed that the numbers he sent out of the Petworth area helped to reduce unemployment, but just as William Hawley could not prove that the new poor law was the single factor responsible for reducing the numbers out of work, so there were always too many other local factors involved for Sockett to make a clear case for the contribution of emigration. In Upper Canada, the exact significance of the Petworth immigrations is equally difficult to measure. The immigrants made a recognized contribution to the growth of areas around Strathroy and Woodstock, but they never congregated in sufficient numbers to lay claim to a community. The departure of Petworth emigrants probably had some localized impact on employment and on the numbers of children living in poverty in 1830s West Sussex, and if the immigrants and all their descendants could be counted, their contribution to settling and developing Ontario would be substantial; but these emigrations were not on a scale to give an identifiable turn to the course of events in either country.

In the tradition of schemes of assisted emigration from Britain to Canada, the Petworth emigrations belong to a period of transition, representing a shift from the plans of the 1810s and 1820s, which linked assisted emigration and assisted settlement, to a different concept developed in the 1830s and 1840s that assumed that labouring emigrants were best to start out in the colonies as wage workers. Robert John Wilmot Horton was the champion of the first plan of proceeding; colonial theorist Edward Gibbon Wakefield publicized the second.

The Tory paternalism represented by Horton and his chief, Colonial Secretary Lord Bathurst, was a good fit with that of Sockett and Egremont. The Petworth immigrants located in Adelaide Township were placed in an assisted settlement of the old style. Continuity was assured by Peter Robinson, who had been Horton's superintendent before he was appointed as commissioner of crown lands. Even this settlement, however, was different from those of the 1820s in depending on the good-will of Lieutenant-Governor Sir John Colborne. Unlike the earlier schemes in which government had aided settlement as well as emigration, assisted settlement was not part of the responsibility of sponsors sending emigrants in the 1830s. For the first two years he sent emigrants, Sockett held an assumption, also shared by Richmond's Emigration Commission and its secretary, T.F. Elliot, that if the government of Upper Canada did not provide land, it would provide work for new immigrants who did not immediately find private employers. When he realized that his immigrants could not count on the security of an offer of land or work backed by the government, Sockett tried to provide it privately with his failed plan to purchase a block of land on Egremont's behalf.

The assistance given to Petworth families on five-acre lots between 1834 and 1837, a plan began under Colborne and allowed to continue in a reduced form for a couple of years under Head, eased Sockett's concerns in sending large families. It is of interest in the study of English immigration because it appears to have reflected the strategy of English parish-aided immigrants who succeeded on their own. It was too small in size and too short in duration, however, to represent a significant trend in assisted emigration.

The approach to assisted emigration to British North America adopted in 1831 and 1832 in the Colonial Office and by Parliament was not Wakefield's – he, for instance, advocated the selection of the immigrant labourers most likely to succeed – but his very effective publicity fed off propaganda in favour of poor law reform and reinforced decisions already made about immigration to British North America. The government did not entirely abandon poor emigrants destined for North America, but the emigration agents in British and North American ports, and after 1840 the Colonial Land and Emigration Commission, acted mainly in the role of advisers informing and warning emigrants on the one hand and making recommendations to government on the other.

Assisted emigration to North America never developed the framework of official regulation created in the 1840s and 1850s to select and send emigrants to Australian colonies willing to pay an assisted passage. As the later history of the Petworth Emigration Committee shows, rural parishes remained receptive during the 1840s to requests for aid to join friends or relatives in Upper Canada, and the poor law commissioners continued to approve loans for this purpose. As aid to the able-bodied poor was curtailed and the regime of the workhouse enforced, however, the pool of people eligible for this category of assistance shrank. If they needed assistance in the 1840s or 1850s, growing numbers of rural emigrants from the south of England chose Australia over Canada.

In Upper Canada, proposals for the assisted settlement of immigrants sent from Britain did not grow much beyond the planning of the 1820s. When emigration enthusiasts of the old school such as Horton, Buchanan, or Colborne suggested expanded schemes for assisted settlements on lots of whatever size, they did not progress much beyond a vision of simple multiplication. Their plans for the reception of thousands were modelled on experiments with tens and hundreds. The same criticism might be made of Sockett's hope that government would encourage the replication of his and Egremont's scheme on estates and in parishes throughout England. Practical politicians looked at such a possibility on three different occasions in the twenty years between 1827 and 1847 and concluded each time that it would not work. Schemes of this nature were discussed in 1827, when Horton submitted the third and final report of his emigration committees; in 1831–32, and again in the famine year of 1847, when a House of Lords' committee on colonization from Ireland brought out Brydone, Rubidge, and Robert Carter of Carter and Bonus to testify on what were by then distant projects of assistance.[1] Difficulties were expressed most simply in terms of the cost of giving adequate assistance to so many. A few politicians such as Howick thought through the problems of scale. They could not envisage an administration that could overcome the inherent conflict of interest between sponsors – who paid to send people outside their jurisdiction – and those in the colony who dealt with the immigrants assisted to leave.

The attitudes of politicians and administrators were crucially important to the future of parish emigration in the 1830s because most people looked to government for leadership. Egremont's self-sufficient isolation was unusual; other sponsors who took advantage of his scheme were more aware of changes in the general climate of opinion and more influenced by them. The strongest incentive to start a parish emigration was a belief that the government might give financial support. Any public sign that seemed to promise increased government involvement in assisted emigration resulted in a surge of activity, such as occurred in 1831–32 and again in 1835–36. After the Canadian rebellions, Lord Durham's mission to the Canadas in 1838 struck a cord with sponsors such as Wyndham, though by then his hopes were attached to Ireland and the recent introduction of a poor law there.

The hopes of sponsors that government would take over parish emigration were dashed in part because the ruling classes in Britain equated poor immigrants with able-bodied applicants for poor relief at home. Legislators who believed in the discipline of the marketplace for labourers competing in the crowded job markets of England had little sympathy for workers unemployed in the empty colonies of North America. They let attitudes formed at home shape what was done in the colonies without serious consideration of the many differences between the two economies. The Whig policies on assisted emigration to British North America, which were developed under Howick's direction and made public by Richmond's Emigration Commission, had a very narrow base. Howick and his fellow commissioners looked only at parish-aided emigration. At home, they focused on rural parishes in the counties beset by Swing disturbances, and in Upper Canada they examined only the events of 1831, the first year a lieutenant-governor singled out parish-aided immigrants in his reports. They gave great weight to Colborne's statement that the immigrants of that year had been absorbed without diminishing the high wages paid for labour in Upper Canada, and ignored his opinion that assistance was often necessary to secure a permanent settlement, particularly for families. In subsequent years, these laissez-faire policies towards poor immigrants were continued long after the truism that all who were sober and industrious were certain to find work in Upper Canada had outlived any validity it may have had in 1831.

Attempts made in the Colonial Office during the 1830s to extricate the office from an expensive responsibility for poor immigrants after they arrived in Upper Canada were both impelled and encouraged by Parliament. By the end of the decade, control of the territorial revenues in Upper Canada – which under Colborne had absorbed much of the cost of aid to new immigrants – was being allowed to devolve from the governor and his Executive Council to the Assembly; therefore, it seemed logical to Colonial Office officials to transfer responsibility for arriving immigrants. For their part, colonial legislators in Upper Canada had other plans for territorial revenues, and they protested vigorously when saddled with the problems of people whose arrival they could not control.

The network of crown lands agents and temporary assistants that under Colborne and Peter Robinson had helped poor immigrants find work and get settled was a casualty of change. This network had reached far inland to the new settlements of Upper Canada. Only a few of these people were kept on under Colborne's successor, and Head pressed local communities to take responsibility for the casualties of immigration in all but a few towns on the principal routes. Under his regime, Anthony Hawke's instructions to the remaining emigration agents on the subject of relief to the able-bodied were as stringent as those sent from the Poor Law Commission to English parishes. After the reorganization within government occasioned by the union of Upper and Lower Canada in 1840, Alexander Carlisle Buchanan's nephew of the same name achieved his uncle's goal of becoming the chief emigration agent for both provinces in fact as well as in name, but the duties of the agents who reported to him from Canada West were restricted to the main points of entry.

In the late 1830s, people in Upper Canada were only beginning to think about institutionalizing the able-bodied poor. The first workhouse in Toronto was opened with Head's encouragement in 1837. Emigration agents in Quebec and Montreal in Lower Canada, or in Prescott, Kingston, or Bytown in the upper province, had no viable alternative to forwarding a certain number of immigrants further inland at government expense. Any further aid to the physically able was given grudgingly. Just as people in rural English parishes had felt overwhelmed by the numbers of poor labourers and feared their distress, so in Upper Canada people reacted against a great increase in the numbers of immigrants who arrived poor and unskilled.

At the beginning of the 1830s, Colborne had enthusiastically welcomed the prospect of government-aided parish immigration. He believed that, with help from his administration, English parish immigrants could play an important part in achieving his goal of expanding the boundaries of settlement in Upper Canada and establishing a permanent and prosperous population, one distinctly British in character.

During the cholera epidemic of 1832, the plans intended to provide for an orderly expansion of settlement became instead a lifeline for immigrants sent forward from towns such as Prescott, Kingston, and Toronto. Some Petworth immigrants died of the disease, but the great majority survived their short stays in the towns where the disease spread so alarmingly, and many benefited from assistance by government agents in the hinterland who helped them find jobs, gave them temporary employment, or assisted them as settlers.

After 1832, Sockett in England maintained his standards and controlled costs by restricting his annual emigrations to the one ship he and his committee could manage personally. The lieutenant-governor and his executive in Upper Canada had no way of limiting numbers. Men such as Roswell Mount, whose experience was in organizing land surveys, had found themselves in charge of tens and hundreds of dependent immigrants in 1832. The primitive administration Colborne cobbled together from the Crown Lands Department and emigrant societies achieved a credible result in moving and settling as many immigrants as it did, but Colonial Office officials were correct in surmising that the operation had run out of control with few, if any, checks on the actions of individuals. These officials and their political masters in Lord Grey's administration tried to impose control according to the principles that would drive the new poor law legislation. One way they dealt with the numbers of people seeking aid was to define need more narrowly and thus to force those judged able to look after themselves.

Although the most important policy decisions were made in England in 1832 before the Colonial Office knew the costs of the emigration of that year, a desire to prevent a similar expenditure shaped the implementation of those decisions in Upper Canada. Restrictions on aid to arriving able-bodied immigrants took effect in the years at mid-decade when the Petworth people with their farm training and useful trades were becoming members of an elite among labouring immigrants, set apart in immigration reports from the mass of common labourers. Succeeding Colborne, Head tried to bring the principles of poor law management to the poor of Upper Canada. Rather than improve Colborne's budding immigrant service, Head largely dismantled the inland stations and severely restricted services offered to able-bodied immigrants at Upper Canadian ports of entry. He was recalled early in 1838 and so did not stay to see the results of his actions in a year of heavy immigration.

The Irish famine immigration of 1847, the only immigration disaster in the history of pre-Confederation Canada worse than the cholera epidemic of 1832, lies outside the boundaries of this case study. By the beginning of the 1840s, however, thoughtful administrators saw the seeds of serious troubles. Ten years after Colborne had enthusiastically welcomed the prospect of government-supported parish immigration, Governor General Poulett Thomson contemplated a mass influx to Quebec of unskilled workers. He could offer some succor to the sick and dying, but he had no administrative tools at his disposal to integrate those who would have to make a living as common labourers. They did not have the training to obtain year-round work in the Canadas, and they entered an overcrowded labour market where they would face the problems of seasonal unemploment without the social networks that might help native-born workers to cope.[2] Far from valuing the assisted emigrants among them, he heartily wished that they had never been sent to his jurisdiction.

Part Two

A LIST OF PETWORTH EMIGRANTS, 1832–1837

Edited by Mary McDougall Maude
Compiled by Wendy Cameron,
Sheila Haines, Leigh Lawson,
and Brenda Dougall Merriman

Editors' Introduction

This list was begun as a compilation of all those emigrating from England to Upper Canada under the sponsorship of the Petworth Emigration Committee. We hoped through this means to build a snapshot picture of individuals and groups at the point at which they emigrated. We wanted to find out who was emigrating, how old they were, what family they went with. We wondered about what family followed, how large the units travelling together were, whether families were accompanied by unrelated people. We wanted to know from whence they came, where they first settled, what their occupation was in England, and whether they did the same kind of work in Upper Canada. We also were interested in finding out what we could about religious affiliation. With these objectives in mind, we designed the fields that would be included in our database.

We concentrated initially on collecting the information in the form in which it was recorded – to keep intact that snapshot record. The first sources we used were some scattered lists we found of emigrants sent by the Petworth Emigration Committee. These lists were incomplete, but some of them did list emigrants by name and age. Others gave the name of the head of household and noted "single man," "single woman," or "and family." The parish sponsoring the emigrant was often found. Other useful sources were the collections of letters from emigrants published by Thomas Sockett as an encouragement to others to emigrate. These letters contained a wealth of information about those who had emigrated and their families, but it was information that was sometimes hard to decipher. In the case of a couple emigrating, letters might be signed by either one or both. References were cryptic; first names were used and the terms mother, father, aunt, or uncle could be used to refer to the writer's birth family or to his or her family by marriage.

Our horizons soon expanded, however, as holes in the data appeared and other possible sources – sources not related to the emigration *per se* – were uncovered. We turned to parish records to identify the individuals on the list and to add to the list when we knew certain parishes had acted as sponsors. On doing so, we were quickly faced with the decision of whether to collect other material on our people: should we note the older children who did not emigrate, children who died as infants, and other family material. We decided that we should be inclusive rather than exclusive, since all this information gives a much fuller view of the emigrants and of who they were, and is invaluable to genealogists. We also published an abbreviated version of the list and circulated it in the south of England and in Ontario. We asked descendants of the original emigrants to get in touch with us if they had information about their ancestors and especially if they had or knew of any documentary material. Many descendants did write or phone us, and they shared their research and family treasures with us. And all the pertinent information we added to our database.

As our research progressed, our chronological limits seemed too narrow in terms of the material that was coming forward. Some people had emigrated from these parishes in the southeast of England in the late 1820s; others had emigrated on into the 1840s and even 1850s. It was not always easy to determine from some of the sources whether emigrants were sponsored by the Petworth committee. We had numbers and parish names for the years 1832–36 from Thomas Sockett's chart of emigrants, but when we followed these up, it was not always clear whether individuals found in parish records as emigrating to Canada did so under the auspices of the committee. Rather than discard all those who were not proven to be Petworth people, we decided to keep the probables and the possibles on our database. All are emigrating from a small area in a very few years. All those sponsored are from a similar economic background. Together they present a fascinating picture of one wave of migrants.

We also have included on the database and in the list a few emigrants (such as the Chantlers) who we know were not sponsored by the committee; these people wrote letters that added greatly to our knowledge of the emigration and come from the same area at the same time. Their status is noted in the list and they have been excluded from our tabulations.

Published here are the entries in our database for those emigrating in the years 1832–37. The list reflects the way it was constructed. At its base is the emigration and the data recorded at the time of emigration. Added to that base is the information received from non-emigration sources; this information is primarily genealogical in nature and covers a much greater period of time. The information on our database has been organized by county and parish; Table P-2.1 table presents the numbers of emigrants sent by the different locations. The parishes responsible for sending most of the emigrants – those from Sussex, Surrey, and the Isle of Wight – and the numbers sent are illustrated in Map P-2.1.

KEY TO THE LIST

The list is organized, as shown below, with line divisions | used to indicate different kinds of data. The field names included in the list are in italics.

> **Name of emigrant** | age at emigration, birth, baptismal dates, death date | *Spouse*: name of spouse, marriage date and place | age of spouse at emigration, birth, baptismal dates, death date | *Children*: names of children, birth dates, baptismal dates, death dates (marriages) | information on religion | *From*: parish sending emigrant | *To*: place in Canada of first settlement; later places of settlement | *Occupation Eng*: | *Occupation Can*: | year of emigration | ship (for 1832 emigrants only) | *Assistance*: people or organizations who enabled the person or family to emigrate | Other data of interest
>
> SOURCE: sources of information in brief

Name of emigrant   Where possible we have listed families under the name of the head (given in boldface) as it was recorded at the time. Almost all heads of households were men; we found that women were listed as heads of households only when they were widows or unmarried women. Variant spellings are indicated in parentheses.

Age   When the emigrant's age is given in years in this list with no source following it in parentheses, it represents his or her age at the time of emigration. Where we have found birth or baptismal information, we have included it. In a few instances, we note an age found in census data, always indicating the source. N.B., if no place of baptism is given, it was the same as the parish of settlement (noted in the field *From*).

Spouse   The wife's given name is sometimes specified in lists of emigrants, but women's birth names are never included. These have been added from parish records. Because of the usefulness of the information for sorting out families, we have included names of wives or husbands who died before the family emigrated, as well as information on marriages contracted in Canada.

Age   If the age of the spouse is given, it represents the age at the time of emigration as recorded in the sources. Birth, baptismal, and death dates are given when we have found them.

Children   Lists of emigrants sometimes gave the number of children, and sometimes provided names and ages. We have included this data on our list when we had it. When an entry reads: "4 children emigrated," it means that the list of emigrants included this information. We have tried to complete the information on the family through research in the parish records; an asterisk after a name indicates that that person did not emigrate. *Note* that if the place of baptism is not given, it took place in the parish from which the family emigrated. Information on children born in Canada is noted if known.

Religion   The information collected here was incomplete. Most of the emigrants belonged to the established Church of England, but some proved to be Baptist, Methodist, or Quaker. In England, the fact that a couple was married in the Church of England does not necessarily indicate a religious affiliation because it was a legal requirement. Baptism in a parish was proof of a person's existence and right to parish relief. In the back concessions of Upper Canada, settlers were likely to attend whatever services were available to them. We decided, therefore, to note only where there was evidence of a religious affiliation other than Church of England, and the source is generally noted.

From   This field presents the sponsoring parish – or parish of settlement – in England. Often, but not always, the family also lived in this parish. If no place of baptism is given for the parents or the children, they were baptised in this parish.

To   Immigrants are listed for the most part at their first home in Canada. Many, however, moved on to another site within a few years, and when possible we give some indication of where they went.

Occupation Eng   Lists of emigrants sometimes indicate the occupation of the head of household in England, and baptismal records of children sometimes give the occupation of the father; "out of employ" is sometimes noted in the records. A majority of the emigrants were agricultural labourers, a group that suffered from unemployment, both permanent and seasonal, in the southern counties in England at this period. Those who had received parish relief were sometimes noted in parish records.

Occupation Can   This field gives the emigrant's occupation in Canada.

Year   The year of emigration.

Ship   Petworth emigrants sailed on three ships in 1832: *Lord Melville*, *Eveline*, and *England*;

we specify which ship an emigrant travelled on in that year if we know it. Only one ship was chartered by the Petworth Emigration Committee in the other years covered: 1833, *England;* 1834, *British Tar;* 1835, *Burrell;* 1836, *Heber;* 1837, *Diana. Note:* There are no passenger lists for ships of these years found in government records.

Assistance   Any information we have about who assisted the individuals or families to emigrate is located here. The Earl of Egremont is, of course, the most prominent of the names found in this field, but other landlords and the parishes themselves are noted. The number of "passages" paid for was often recorded, a passage representing the amount required to cover all costs for one adult or two children to travel from Portsmouth to Toronto, Upper Canada.

Other data   Family links, comments that Sockett or others noted about emigrants, and sundry other details are noted in this field. Many of the emigrants in this list bear names commonly found in Upper Canada at the time; information about an individual in Canada who *may* be the Petworth emigrant is given here.

Sources   The sources of information for the entries are noted here. Printed and archival sources are found in the bibliography; information has also been supplied by descendants and other correspondents and is recorded in the project files. Abbreviations of sources are listed at page 295.

Italic entries   Italics have been used to mark off subsidiary entries of adult children who emigrated with their parents but who immediately married and set up their own households on arrival in Canada. For these people, we simply have more information than could be accommodated under the main entry, but they are counted as part of the original household unit.

Asterisks   Asterisks following the names of children or a spouse indicate that those persons did not emigrate to Canada.

Boldface   Boldface has been used within entries to indicate that someone is found elsewhere on the list, and it therefore acts both to refer readers to related entries and visually emphasizes the interrelationship of this group of emigrants.

Letters   If a letter from a Petworth emigrant is noted in the sources, it will be found in *English Immigrant Voices.*

Table P-2.1
Number of Emigrants Identified in Part 2 Sent sent by Parishes or Areas, 1832–1837, by County[1]

	Date Unknown	1832	1833	1834	1835	1836	1837	Subtotal	Total
Parish unknown	7	29	16	23	19	3	68		165
Subtotal – unkn	7	29	16	23	19	3	68	165	
Cambridgeshire	1								1
Bassingbourn	1	21							22
Subtotal – Camb	2	21						23	
East Sussex									
Brighton		2		27		2			31
East Hoathly				15					15
Hellingly				8					8
Kingston by Lewes				10					10
Lewes				3					3
Rodmell (and Lewes)				4					4
Seaford				3					3
Subtotal – ES	0	2		70		2		74	
Isle of Wight			1	7					8
Brightstone (Brixton) IOW				1					1
Calbourne, IOW				1					1
Carisbrooke, IOW			3	2			11		16
Chale, IOW							1		1
East Cowes, IOW							1		1
Godshill, IOW			1	1					2
Little Chessel, IOW							4		4
Newport, IOW				9	1		53		63
Node Hill, IOW							5		5
Northwood, IOW			1						1
Shalfleet, IOW							3		3
West Cowes, IOW			1						1
Whippingham, IOW				1			2		3
Whitwell, IOW							1		1
Yarmouth, IOW			2						2
Subtotal – IOW	0		9	22	1		81	0	
Hertfordshire									
Ware					10				10
Subtotal – Herts	0				10			10	
Norfolk									
Attleborough						1			1
Subtotal – Norfolk						1		1	

Table P-2.1 (continued)

	Date Unknown	1832	1833	1834	1835	1836	1837	Subtotal	Total
Somerset									
Bath					11				11
Subtotal – Somerset	0				11			11	
Surrey									
Capel		14							14
Chiddingfold		2							2
Dorking	11	86	1						98
Dunsfold			10			6			16
Epsom	1								1
Hascomb (nr Godalming)		1							1
Haslemere		9	11						20
Subtotal – Surrey	12	112	22			6		152	
West Sussex									
Aldingborne	1								1
Angmering	2	10		3					15
Arundel		2			2	9			13
Ashington		1							1
Beeding, Upper			5						5
Bepton					13				13
Billingshurst		3		9		20			32
Boxgrove		4							4
Burpham						8			8
Burton		3							3
Bury		1	3						4
Chichester		6	9						15
Climping					18				18
Cocking						10			10
Cuckfield (and Hurst.)				1					1
Donnington		2							2
Easebourne						7			7
East Lavant					2				2
Egdean				1					1
Felpham		21			44				65
Fernhurst	2	16	22						40
Findon					35				35
Fittleworth		2							2
Goring					11	22			33
Graffham/Woolavington						6			6
Heene					10				10
Heyshott							16		16
Horsted Keynes					10				10
Iping		1							1
Kirdford	3	45	1						49
Linchmere					8				8

Table P-2.1 (continued)

	Date Unknown	1832	1833	1834	1835	1836	1837	Subtotal	Total
Littlehampton		1							1
Lodsworth		19	15		3	6			43
Lurgashall		58	4						62
Merston		1	3						4
Northchapel		25							25
Nyetimber, Pagham		4							4
Oving	1								1
Petworth	2	47	22	5	10	33	7		126
Pulborough		11	2	4		5			22
Rusper	3								3
Shipley		6			15				21
Singleton	1	1							2
South Bersted		32		1	1				34
Stedham		1							1
Steyning					3				3
Sullington		9			8				17
Sutton		6	1				1		8
Thakeham		4							4
Tillington		15	1	2		47			65
Walberton	13	2			11	17			43
Warnham				1					1
Washington		1		1					2
Westbourne		1							1
West Grinstead				2	11	1			14
Wisborough Green	1	80			14	22			117
Wiston				1	2	1			4
Woolbeding							8		8
Worthing	1	1		8					10
Yapton		1			12				13
Subtotal – WS	30	443	88	39	243	207	40	1090	
Wiltshire									
Chicklade			1						1
East Knoyle						2			2
Subtotal – Wilts			1			2		3	
London		5							5
Scotland?					1				1
TOTAL	51	612	136	154	285	228	181		1647

NOTE: Unspecified family units counted as 5. Parishes sending 25 and over are in italics.

[1] Some late additions not tabulated.

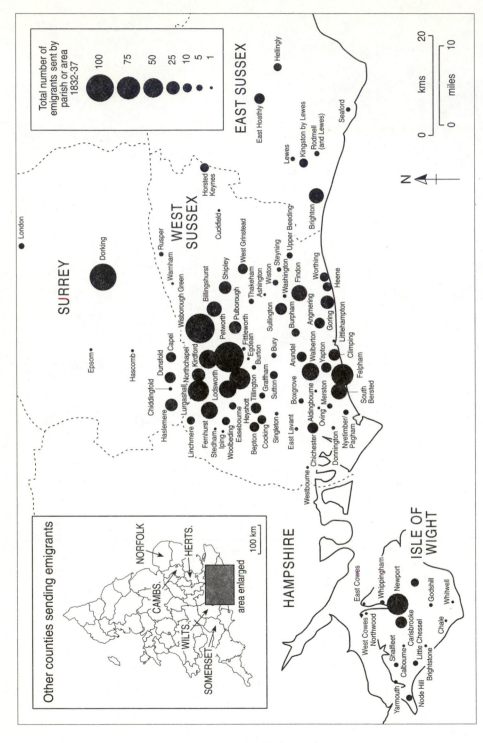

P-2.1 *Number of emigrants from Sussex, Surrey, and the Isle of Wight, 1832–1837, as identified in Part 2*

Emigrants on Petworth Ships, 1832–1837

Anonymous | *From*: Petworth, West Sussex ? | *To*: West Flamborough; they have bought land at West Flamborough | 1837 | She appears to have a large family with her including her parents and a daughter or a sister named Emily, but she is unmarried.
Source: *Letters from Emigrants … in 1832, 1833 and 1837*, 8–12

Able, Christopher | *From*: Dorking, Surrey | *To*: Nov 1832: visiting Geneva, Ontario Co., NY | 1832 | Lord Melville | Superintendent of Dorking Society emigrants. Visiting James Tewsley, a Dorking farmer who emigrated to New York State in the spring of 1832 and was working at Geneva in Ontario County.
Source: *Letters from Dorking*, 28; wsro, pha 137

Adsett, Thomas | 33, bap 9 Jun 1799, d 21 Apr 1870 Woolwich Twp | *Spouse*: (1) Sarah Scutt, m 18 Oct 1824 Petworth, bap 12 Feb 1805 Bignor, d of scarlet fever shortly after arrival | (2) Matilda Penfold, m in Canada, bap 12 Jun 1819, d 24 Apr 1896 | *Children*: 4 children emigrated: Charles bap 18 Jun 1826, d 1908; Sarah 2-½, bap 15 Nov 1829; Emma 7; Harriett 7 weeks, bap 11 Mar 1832, d of scarlet fever shortly after arrival | Methodist (1851 census) | *From*: Northchapel, West Sussex | *To*: Galt, Dumfries Twp; Woolwich Twp (1851) | *Occupation Eng*: Labourer working for Earl of Egremont under Upton, Dec 1830 | *Occupation Can*: Farm labourer and farmer | 1832 | Lord Melville | *Assistance*: Earl of Egremont | Matilda was a daughter of Jesse **Penfold**.
Source: *Emigration: Letters* (1833), 18–19, 45–46; *No. 2 Continuation*, 12–13; *No. 4 Continuation*, 25–6; *Continuation of Letters from Sussex Emigrants … Written in 1836* [1837], 10–11; Brighton Reference Library, Sussex Pamphlets, Box 38, "*Autobiography of Charles Adsett 1826–1908*"; wsro, pha 137; pha 8557; par 130/1/2/1, par 142/2/1, par 149/1/3/1, par 201/1/1/3, par 202/2/2; ao, Waterloo Co., Woolwich Twp, Winterbourne Pioneer Methodist Cemetery; Wellington Co., Howitt/Kirklands Memorial Cemetery; na, rg 31, Canada Census, 1851 Woolwich Twp, p23

Anscomb, (Mrs) Ann | 60 | *Spouse*: James Anscomb* | 1835 | Sons **Benjamin** and **William** emigrated; also possibly David.
Source: wsro, par 9/1/2/1, par 106/1/1/3, par 168/1/2/1; pha 142; Correspondent Ron Cox; na, rg 31, Canada Census

Anscomb, Benjamin | 26, bap 6 Nov 1808 Horsham; d 4 Apr 1886 Paris, Ont | *Spouse*: Elizabeth Grinstead, m 20 Feb 1830 Pulborough | bap 22 Sep 1805 Pulborough | *Children*: 1 child emigrated: Eliza bap 15 Jun 1834; b in Canada: George, Thomas, Clement | Church of England | *From*: Shipley, West Sussex | *To*: Brantford, 1845, 1851; then Burford Twp 1857, 1861; North Walsingham Twp 1871 | *Occupation Eng*: Farming man | *Occupation Can*: For employment | 1835 | *Assistance*: Sir Charles Burrell and parish | Both signed marriage register with a mark.
SOURCE: WSRO, PAR 106/1/1/3, PAR 153/1/3/1, PAR 153/1/1/1, PAR 168/1/2/1; PHA 142; Correspondent Ron Cox; NA, RG 31, Canada Census, 1851, 1861, 1871, 1881, 1891

Anscombe (Anscomb), William | b 17 Mar 1813, bap 7 May 1815 Ashington, West Sussex, d 1902 poor house, Woodhouse Twp, Norfolk Co. | *Spouse*: (1) Emily E. **Viney**, m c1836 in Canada; (2) Emily Saxby, m 2 Nov 1845 | *Children* b in Canada: Emily b 8 Aug 1836, Louis or Louisa Jane b c1840 (m Richard Jones 1861), Mary Rose b c1848, Lorenzo b c1850, James Charles b Oct 1857 | *From*: Shipley, West Sussex ? | *To*: Brantford; in Burford Twp 1857, 1861; North Walsingham 1871 | 1835 ? | Probably emigrated at same time as mother and brother **Benjamin**. A second married couple is in William's household in 1842.
SOURCE: AO, RG 21, Gore District Census and Assessments, 1842 Brantford Twp; Correspondent Ron Cox; NA, RG 31, Canada Census, 1851, 1861, 1871, 1891

Ansell, Mary | bap 25 Sep 1825; b Pulborough Poor House, illegitimate daughter of Sarah Ansell; Henry Rugman cited as father (Bastardy Bonds 1762–1835) | *From*: West Grinstead, West Sussex | 1836 | *Assistance*: Discharged as a pauper child from Pulborough Workhouse Dec 1835 | "With her father to West Grinstead for America." The banns of marriage were called between Sarah Ansell & Henry Rugman in Pulborough in Nov 1824 but no marriage seems to have taken place.
SOURCE: WSRO, PAR 153/31/5, PAR 153/34/2

Arnold, Charles | bap 25 Dec 1819 | *From*: Newchurch, Isle of Wight | 1834 | *Assistance*: Parish/House of Industry | Admitted to House of Industry 5 Oct 1833; discharged 16 Apr 1834 "to Canada." Orphan.
SOURCE: IOWRO, Z/HO/L5; Index of Baptisms, Marriages, and Burials

Arnold, John | 32 | Single | *From*: Dorking, Surrey | 1832 | Lord Melville | *Assistance*: Dorking Emigration Society
SOURCE: *Letters from Dorking*, 10

Ayling, John | 19, bap 5 Apr 1818 | *Spouse*: Sarah White, m 5 Nov 1842 in Canada | *Children* b in Can: Mary Ann 8, Eloses(?) 5, Sarer 1 (in 1851 census) | Congregationalist (1851) | *From*: Walberton, West Sussex | *To*: Thornhill, York Co. | *Occupation Eng*: Bricklayer | *Occupation Can*: "Farming, mowing and a shoveling about" | 1836 | *Assistance*: Richard Prime and parish
SOURCE: GB, Parl. Papers, *Select Committee … Poor Law Amendment Act …* App. to 12th Report, 1837; *Letters from Sussex Emigrants*, 8–9; WSRO, PAR 202/2/3; NA, RG 31, Canada Census, 1851 Vaughan Twp, p 321; AO, RG 80-27-1, vol 11, Home District marriage register, p105

Bachelor (Batchelor), Benjamin | poss bap 5 Dec 1813 | *From*: Kirdford, West Sussex | *To*: Adelaide Twp lot 17 con 4; Warwick Twp lot 16 con3 | *Occupation Can*: Farmer | 1832 | *Assistance*: Earl of Egremont and parish | Son of William & Anne Bachelor. A Benjamin Bachelor, Baptist, married Elizabeth Hobson 30 Jun 1853 in Warwick.
SOURCE: *Emigration: Letters* (1833), 31–2; WSRO, PAR 116/1/2/1; Misc. Paper 1031; *Middlesex County Marriages and Baptisms, 1848–1858*; NA, RG 31, Canada Census, 1861 Warwick Twp, p24

Baker, William | bap 26 Feb 1809 | May have attended dissenting meetings (see his letter of 13 Mar 1833, *No. 2 Continuation*) | *From*: Kirdford, West Sussex | *To*: Adelaide lot 18 con 5 | *Occupation Eng*: Labourer | *Occupation Can*: Farmer | 1832 | *Assistance*: Earl of Egremont and parish | Brother of Jane **Smart** (née Baker).

SOURCE: *Emigration: Letters* (1833), 41; *No. 2 Continuation*, 15–16; WSRO, Misc. Paper 1031; PAR 116/1/1/6

Ballison, Thomas | *From*: Attleborough, Norfolk | *Occupation Eng*: Soldier | 1836 ?

SOURCE: PRO, CO 385/10

Barberry (Burberry), John | d 17 Feb 1864 | *Spouse*: Rebecca Peskett, m 20 Jun 1815 Wisborough Green, poss bap 8 Jul 1792 or 22 May 1796 Billingshurst, d 16 Oct 1832 Nelsonville, Ohio | *Children*: John b 1 Dec 1816, bap 9 Feb 1817; Thomas b 19 Sep 1818, bap 15 Nov 1818; James b 10 Apr 1820, bap 11 Jun 1820; David bap 11 Nov 1821; Elizabeth bap 8 Jun 1823; Stephen bap 3 Dec 1826; Sarah bap 27 Jan 1828; George bap 17 Oct 1830 (all bap Loxwood in parish of Wisborough Green) | *From*: Wisborough Green, West Sussex | *To*: Nelsonville, Ohio | *Occupation Eng*: Fellmonger / glover | 1832 | England | *Assistance*: Parish and landowners

SOURCE: *Courtauld Family Letters* I: xxi; WSRO, PAR 21/1/1/5, PAR 210/37/11(3), PAR 210/1/2/1; Correspondent Virginia Curulla

Barlow, Barnabas | *To*: Blandford ? | 1834

SOURCE: AO, RG 1, C-IV, Township Papers, Town of Blandford

Barnes, John | 34, bap 31 May 1801 | *Spouse*: Charlotte [Woodford, m 18 Aug 1822 Kirdford? IGI only] | 34, bap 24 Apr 1803 | *Children*: 4 children emigrated: Henry 14; Emma 11; John 4, bap 7 Oct 1832; Ellen 6 months, bap Apr 1836 | *From*: Petworth, West Sussex | *To*: Toronto | *Occupation Eng*: Bricklayer | *Occupation Can*: Bricklayer | Hired by the Reverend Charles Matthews to enlarge a cottage. Matthews, a master at Upper Canada College, employed the family in his Toronto home. | 1836 | *Assistance*: Earl of Egremont, parish (outfit, £25.10.0), and Poor Law Commissioners

SOURCE: *Continuation of Letters from Sussex Emigrants ...Written in 1836* [1837], 12–15; *Continuation of Letters from Sussex Emigrants* (1837), 1–5; PRO, MH 12, 13060; WSRO, PAR 116/1/2/1, PAR 116/1/1/6, PAR 149/1/2/1, PAR 201/37/13

Barnes, John | 31 | *Spouse*: Elizabeth Bevis, 24, m 4 Aug 1833 Northwood, Isle of Wight | *Children*: 3 children emigrated: Jane 5, d of Elizabeth Bevis bap 27 Nov 1831; Elizabeth 2-1/4, bap 28 Sep 1836; Marianne 9 months, bap 28 Sep 1836 | *From*: Newport, Isle of Wight | (House of Industry) | *Occupation Eng*: Agricultural labourer | 1837 | *Assistance*: Parish, House of Industry; 3 passages | Elizabeth had been apprenticed by the House of Industry "to husbandry" in 1828. Her parents were "unknown." She was back in the House of Industry in 1829 "a bad girl." The address at the time of the baptism of the children was the House of Industry. Remarks on abstract of IOW emigrants: "Dissipated." Burials in Toronto included Elizabeth Barnes age 25 on 20 Feb 1835, Mary Anne age 1 year 4 months on 23 Dec 1837, and Elizabeth age 4 on 13 Apr 1838.

SOURCE: IOWRO, Z/HO/44; Z/HO/MI; Index of Baptisms, Marriages, and Burials; *Sussex Family Historian* 1, no. 2; WSRO, PHA 140; *The Cathedral Church of St James (Anglican), Toronto, Ontario; A Transcription of Records of Burials, 1807-1850*.

Barns (Barnes), William | d 1832 Toronto | *Spouse*: Mary, "clever managing woman" | *Children*: 6 children emigrated | *From*: Tillington, West Sussex | *To*: York, Upper Canada; Postal address: Cooper's Black Horse Tavern, Church Street, York | *Occupation Eng*: Bailiff to various people, then farmed on own account unsuccessfully; depressed, "events seem to show

that he is not competent to manage his own affairs" | 1832 | Robbed of all his money
£60–£70; Sockett forwarding £20; man who robbed him in jail Port Hope.
SOURCE: *No. 5 Continuation*, 35; *Brighton Guardian*, 16 Oct 1833; Letter from James Cooper,
May 1838, *Brighton Herald*, 25 Aug 1838; WSRO, Goodwood Ms 1460, f34; Misc. Paper 1219;
PHA 137; AO, F129, Canada Co. Papers, A-6-2, p 313, John Perry to Commissioners, 20 Sep
1832

Bartiett (Bartlett), George | *Spouse*: Wife | *Children*: 4 children emigrated | *Occupation Eng*:
Shoemaker | 1837 | *Assistance*: 4 passages
SOURCE: WSRO, PHA 140

Bartlett, George | *Spouse*: wife | *Occupation Eng*: Agricultural labourer | 1837 | *Assistance*:
2 passages | Remarks on abstract of PEC emigrants: "Most respectable" family.
SOURCE: WSRO, PHA 140

Bartley (Barteley), William | 40 | *Spouse*: Mary | 37 | *Children*: James 12, Caroline 10, George
8, Godfrey or Alfred 3-½ | *From*: Carisbrooke, Isle of Wight | *Occupation Eng*: "shoemaker:
no employ" | 1837 | *Assistance*: Parish, House of Industry | Admitted to House of Industry
22 Mar 1837; discharged 26 Apr 1837. Remarks on abstract of IOW emigrants: "Respectable."
SOURCE: IOWRO, Z/HO/44; Z/HO/L5; Index of Baptisms, Marriages, and Burials

Barton (Burton), John | *Spouse*: Wife | *Children*: 3 children emigrated | *To*: Blandford (town
plot) | *Occupation Can*: Schoolmaster and parish clerk | 1834
SOURCE: Brydone, *Narrative*, 41; WSRO, Goodwood Ms 1476, f277; PHA 139

Barton, John | Single | *From*: Hellingly, East Sussex | *Occupation Eng*: Labourer, had been
on parish relief | 1834 | *Assistance*: Parish, Earl of Chichester, Thomas Calverley
SOURCE: ESRO, PAR 375/12/5, PAR 375/31/2/6, PAR 375/31/2/7

Bassam, J. | *Spouse*: Wife | *Children*: 1 child | 1834 | He was head of one of the messes in
the middle steerage on the ship. Disembarked at Montreal as intended.
SOURCE: Brydone, *Narrative*

Batchelor. See Bachelor

Bennett, Richard | 35, bap 2 Mar 1797 | *Spouse*: Elizabeth Kemp, m 27 Oct 1816 | *Children*:
(no children found) | *From*: Boxgrove, West Sussex | *Occupation Eng*: Sawyer | 1832 ?
SOURCE: WSRO, PHA 137; PAR 27/1/1/3, PAR 27/1/3/1

Berry, Edward | 14, bap 21 Jan 1821 | *From*: Findon, West Sussex | *To*: Niagara area | *Occu-
pation Eng*: Labourer | 1836 | *Assistance*: Loan from Hugh Penfold, churchwarden, and
backed by Poor Law Commissioners. | This may be the Edward Berry mentioned in WSRO,
PAR 5/37/5, and PHA 142. Not a brother of William. Son of Phyllis Berry, he was born in
the poorhouse of a "labourer's daughter."
SOURCE: *Continuation of Letters from Sussex Emigrants*, 6–8; PRO, MH 12, 13128, WSRO, PAR
84/1/2/1

Berry, Isaac | bap 26 Jun 1796 | *Spouse*: (1) Sarah Madgwick*, m 2 May 1819, d Mar 1827;
(2) Emma Curtis, m 25 Jan 1828 | *Children*: 5 children emigrated: Isaac bap 9 Jan 1819;
Sarah bap 5 Apr 1822; George bap 6 Feb 1824, d 1832 York; Emma Pamela bap 9 Nov
1828; Barbara b 1 Aug 1830 | *From*: Fernhurst, West Sussex | *Occupation Eng*: Brickmaker,
labourer | 1832 | *Assistance*: W.H. Yaldwin and parish | Asked for the Lord Melville as
Mrs Berry had lived as a servant with Mrs Penfold. Isaac and his first wife had 3 children
who may well all have emigrated with Isaac and Emma.
SOURCE: WSRO, PHA 137; PAR 82/1/1/5, PAR 82/1/2/1, PAR 82/1/3/1

Berry, William | 34, bap 2 Mar 1800 | *Spouse*: Hannah Charman, m 1821 Washington, West
Sussex | 35 | *Children*: 6 children emigrated: Eliza Ann* bap 14 Apr 1822, Charlotte bap

30 Jun 1822 (Washington), Henry bap 28 Apr 1824, Reuben bap 21 Nov 1830, Edward bap 31 Mar 1833, Louisa bap 5 Jun 1835 | *From*: Findon, West Sussex | *Occupation Eng*: Labourer | 1836 | *Assistance*: Loan from Hugh Penfold, churchwarden, backed by Poor Law Commissioners | List in MH12 also lists sons aged 9 and 7 as emigrating. Charlotte probably did not emigrate.
SOURCE: PRO, MH 12, 13128; WSRO, PAR 84/1/2/1, PAR 205/1/2/1, PAR 205/1/3/1

Biggs, John | 19 | *From*: Petworth, West Sussex (Hesworth) | 1832 ? | On 29 Mar parish entry noted John Biggs was not going but James Biggs was. On 3 Apr, "Biggs does not go." John or James?
SOURCE: WSRO, PHA 137

Birch (Burch), Edmund (Edward?) | 42, bap 20 Sep 1789, bur 11 Oct 1842 Thornhill | *Spouse*: Mary Caiger, m 3 Jan 1809 | 40 | *Children*: **Edmund** bap 28 Apr 1811; **James** bap 14 Feb 1813; Henry* bap 5 Nov 1815; Charles bap 20 Jan 1818, bur 30 May 1843 Thornhill; Mary Ann bap 4 Feb 1821; William bap 30 Jun 1823; George bap 22 Jul 1825; Emma bap 6 Jul 1827, bur 28 Feb 1847 Thornhill | *From*: Walberton, West Sussex | *To*: Thornhill, York Co. | *Occupation Eng*: Agricultural labourer | 1835 | *Assistance*: Richard Prime and parish | Father of **Edmund** and **James**. Five children emigrated with him. There is no record of Henry emigrating. Described as "A very discontented and impudent man."
SOURCE: *Letters from Sussex Emigrants*, 6–7, 7–8, 8–9; GB, Parl. Papers, *Select Committee … Poor Law Amendment Act … App. to 12th Report, 1837*; WSRO, PAR 51/1/2/1, PAR 202/2/2, PAR 202/2/3, PAR 202/1/2/11, PAR 202/1/1/3, PAR 202/1/2/3; PHA 142; ADT, Thornhill, Holy Trinity Church Registers

Birch, Edmund | b 26 Jan 1811 | *Spouse*: Sarah, m in Canada | 37, b England (1851 census) | *Children* b in Can: Henry bap 24 Dec 1839, Edwin bap 15 Aug 1841, Robert Thomas bap 14 Jan 1844, Marianne bap 28 Sep 1848 | *From*: Walberton, West Sussex | *To*: Thornhill, York Co.; in 1850 lot 9 con 4 Vaughan Twp | *Occupation Eng*: Agricultural labourer | 1832 | Son of **Edmund** and Mary. Name given as Edmund Birch in the parish register.
SOURCE: *Letters from Sussex Emigrants*; WSRO, PAR 202/1/2/3; NA, RG 31, Canada Census, 1851 Vaughan Twp; ADT, Thornhill, Holy Trinity Church Registers

Birch, James | bap 14 Feb 1813 | *Spouse*: Frances **Viney**, m in Canada, bap 14 Apr 1816 Climping | *Children* b in Can: Martha bap 18 Sep 1836, bur 17 Sep 1837; James bap 23 May 1838; Mary bap 26 Dec 1840; Emily; Richard b c1845 | *From*: Walberton, West Sussex | *To*: Thornhill, York Co.? | 1832 | *Assistance*: Richard Prime and parish | Son of **Edmund** and Mary, brother of **Edmund**. In 1836 he was working as a labourer and located on Yonge St in Markham.
SOURCE: *Letters from Sussex Emigrants*, 6–7; WSRO, PAR 51/1/2/1, PAR 202/2/3; ADT, Thornhill, Holy Trinity Church Registers

Bishop, James | 58, b 14 Apr 1784, bap 22 May 1785 Carisbrooke, Isle of Wight | *From*: Northwood, Isle of Wight | *Occupation Eng*: "out of employ" | 1833 | *Assistance*: Parish/House of Industry | Admitted to House of Industry 16 Apr 1833; discharged 25 Apr 1833
SOURCE: IOWRO, Z/HO/L5; Index of Baptisms, Marriages, and Burials

Blandford, Charlotte | 19, b 3 Mar 1819, bap 17 Mar 1819; d of Elizabeth Blandford and James Wearn | *From*: Newport, Isle of Wight | (House of Industry) | *Occupation Eng*: Servant: had "left her place" | 1837 | *Assistance*: Parish, House of Industry
SOURCE: IOWRO, Z/HO/44; Z/HO/L5; Index of Baptisms, Marriages, and Burials

Bloes (Blows), William | *Spouse*: Elizabeth Warboys, m 11 Mar 1824 | 70 (1871 census) | *Children*: Isaac* bap 14 Feb 1827; bur 30 Apr 1827, aged 3m; Isaac bap 8 Feb 1829; Sarah

Ann b 4 Jun 1832 Montreal on the ship, bap 19 Jul 1835 Dundas; b in Can: James b 18 Nov 1835 [1834?], bap 19 Jul 1835 Dundas | *From*: Bassingbourn, Cambridgeshire | *To*: Dundas | *Occupation Eng*: Labourer – digging gravel in 1831 | 1832 | *Assistance*: Charles Beldam and vestry | The 1842 census noted 1 child born in England and 5 born in Canada. SOURCE: Letter from Simeon Titmouse; *Emigration: Letters* (1833), 19–21; Cambridge County Record Office, P11/1/4; P11/1/10; P11/12/5; P11/12/6; Ancaster Anglican Parish Registers; NA, RG 31, Canada Census, 1842 Ancaster Twp; 1871 Hamilton, St Andrews Ward, 2: 118

Blunden, alias Mitchell, Jas. | 22 | Single | *From*: Dorking, Surrey | 1832 | *Assistance*: Dorking Emigration Society
SOURCE: *Letters from Dorking*, 10

Blythman, James | bap 31 Aug 1817 | *From*: Dunsfold, Surrey | 1833 | *Assistance*: Vestry
SOURCE: SRO (GMR), PSH/DUN/8/2

Booker, George | 19, bap 27 Jul 1817, d 6 Aug 1898 Rainham Twp, Haldimand Co. | *Spouse*: Ruth **Leggett** m 25 May 1839 Thornhill, Ont | 19, bap 25 Jan 1818 Walberton, d 6 Mar 1899 Rainham | *Children* b in Vaughan Twp: William M b 1 June 1840, Thomas b 30 Nov 1841, Nancy Ann b 14 Sep 1844, Mary b 29 Dec 1845, George A. b 6 May 1848; b in Rainham: James Calbert b 17 Feb 1851, Charles b 13 Oct 1853, Jane b 27 July 1856, Mary b Feb 1860, Henry b 7 May 1861 | *From*: Walberton, West Sussex | *To*: Thornhill, later Rainham Twp | *Occupation Eng*: Agricultural labourer | *Occupation Can*: Farmer | 1836 | *Assistance*: Richard Prime and parish | George and Ruth Booker are buried in Old Disciples cemetery, Rainham Centre.
SOURCE: GB, Parl. Papers, *Select Committee … Poor Law Amendment Act …* App. to 12th Report, 1837; *Letters from Sussex Emigrants*, 8–9; WSRO, PAR 202/2/3; AO, RG 80-27-1, vol 10, Home District Marriage Register, p 390; Correspondent Helen Fortney

Botterell, Rev. | Wesleyan Methodist | *From*: Newport, Isle of Wight | 1835 | Going as missionary to Upper Canada. A Rev. E. Botteral, Wesleyan Methodist minister of Shipton married M.A.J. eldest daughter of George Henderson and widow of Thomas Renfrew of Shipton in Quebec 14 Aug 1838 (*Christian Guardian* 15 Aug 1838: Wilson, *Ontario Marriage Notices,* 43). An Edmund Botterel, b 1811 Cornwall UK, d 26 Oct 1893 Montreal, ordained IOW Methodist minister, served in Quebec, Ontario, PEI, Newfoundland, and Nova Scotia.
SOURCE: *Hampshire Telegraph*, 30 Mar 1835; *Christian Guardian*, 8 Nov 1893; UCA, Clergy Files

Bound, John | *From*: Newport, Isle of Wight | *Occupation Eng*: Agricultural labourer | 1837 | *Assistance*: Parish, House of Industry | Remarks on abstract of IOW emigrants: "well behaved during voyage and subsequently."
SOURCE: IOWRO, Z/HO/44; WSRO, PHA 140

Bowley, George Arland | 19, b 1815 Climping , Sussex; d c 1886 Bradford, Ont | *Spouse*: Nancy DeVall, m 17 Sep 1839 Chinguacousy Twp, Peel Co, b 1819 Etobicoke, York Co., d 26 Mar 1906 Toronto | *Children*: b in Can: Thomas A. b c1840 (m Elizabeth Anne Devall), Eliza Ann b c1844 (m Thomas Bulleyment), Elizabeth b c1846 (m Joseph Mulligan), Mary Jane b c1849 (m James Donaldson), Martha Alice b 18 Mar 1853 (m (1) John Mulligan, (2) Frederick Tracey), George Inkerman b c1855, William b c1858 (m Elizabeth J. Davis), Frederick Rufus b c1860, John Wesley b c1863 (m Elizabeth Young), Susannah b c1867 (m Frank Brooks) | *From*: Felpham, West Sussex | *To*: Peel Co | *Occupation Eng*: Agricultural labourer | 1835

SOURCE: GB, Parl. Papers, *Select Committee … Poor Law Amendment Act …* App. to 12th Report, 1837; Correspondent Thomas A. Ryerson

Boxall, Charles | b 14 Mar 1799, bap 7 Apr 1799, d 1832 | Single | *From*: Tillington, West Sussex | 1832 | *Assistance*: Parish, and Earl of Egremont | Drowned at Montreal after drinking.
SOURCE: *Portsmouth, Portsea, and Gosport Herald and Chichester Reporter*, 22 Jul 1832; WSRO, PAR 197/12/1, PAR 197/1/1/4, PAR 197/31/5

Boxall, Edward | bap 25 May 1790 | *Spouse*: Catharine | d 26 Oct 1857 aged 67 | *From*: Petworth, West Sussex | parishioner of Petworth, resident at Coldwaltham | *To*: Adelaide, Upper Canada, with William Cooper | *Occupation Eng*: Soldier, 36th Regiment of Foot | *Occupation Can*: Farmer | 1832 | Eveline | *Assistance*: Earl of Egremont and parish | 100-acre grant as discharged soldier; living on E ½ lot 21 con 4SER Adelaide in 1851.
SOURCE: *Letters: Emigration* (1833), 8; *No. 1 Continuation*, 7–8; WSRO, Goodwood Ms 1460, f35; PHA 137; PRO, CO 42/424, ff.391-1v; CO 42/425, f.348; AO, Middlesex Co., Adelaide Twp, 4th line cemetery, Mt Zion Old Methodist; NA, RG 31, Canada Census, 1851 Adelaide, p5

Boxall, George | *Spouse*: Mary Tilley, m 24 Dec 1829 Petworth, bap 24 Jan 1807 Thursley, Surrey | *Children*: Alfred, bap 5 Dec 1830; 3 children by 1836 including James Andrew b 2 Apr 1836 bap 10 Jul 1836 | *From*: Fernhurst, West Sussex | *To*: Nelson Twp, Upper Canada; Mr Jacob Truller's, Nelson Twp, Co. of Halton, Gore Dist; then Mr George Chisholm's, Nelson Twp | *Occupation Eng*: Agricultural labourer | *Occupation Can*: Sawyer | 1832 | *Assistance*: W.H. Yaldwin and parish, 2½ passages | Emigrated with William **Tilley**, Mary's brother. Living on Agnes St, Toronto, in 1850.
SOURCE: *Emigration: Letters* (1833); *Continuation of Letters from Sussex Emigrants … Written in 1836* [1837], 18–19; WSRO, PHA 137; PAR 82/1/2//1, PAR 149/1/1/2, PAR 149/1/3/1/; EP 1/24/46B; Toronto Directory 1850; AND, St Luke's, Burlington

Boxall, William | 47 | *Spouse*: Harriet Hall, m 30 May 1816 | 40 | *Children*: Mary Ann 19, bap 26 Apr 1818 Lodsworth; Jane 17, bap 5 Dec 1819 Lodsworth; Clara 13, bap 29 Oct 1823 Lodsworth; Emily, bap 20 Jan 1826 Lodsworth; Rhoda 9, bap 20 Dec 1827 Lurgashall, d 1871 (m John **Budd**); William 4, bap 17 Jun 1832 Lurgashall; John 1, bap 17 May 1835 | *From*: Tillington, West Sussex | *To*: Blandford, Oxford Co. | *Occupation Eng*: Labourer. Worked in Petworth Park under Lawrence – succeeding his father; had 4s a week from the Parish. | 1836 | *Assistance*: Earl of Egremont, and parish | Not brother of George.
SOURCE: Letter from James Cooper, May 1838, *Brighton Herald*, 25 Aug 1838; WSRO, PHA 6572, c 1830; PAR 128/1/2/1, PAR 128/1/5/1, PAR 130/1/2/1, PAR 197/1/2/1, PAR 197/1/5/1

Bridger, Miram | *From*: Lodsworth, West Sussex | 1832 ? | Lived at Lodsworth, belonged to Selham.
SOURCE: WSRO, PHA 137

Bright, John | *Spouse*: Wife | *Children*: 3 children emigrated | 1832 | *Assistance*: 3 ½ passages
SOURCE: WSRO, PHA 137

Bristow, Edward | b 2 Mar 1807 Shipley, West Sussex, bap 5 Apr 1807 Horsham, d 25 Sep 1884 Woolwich Twp | *Spouse*: Hannah Streeter (Streater), m 31 Jul 1827, b 2 Jul 1808, bap 2 Oct 1808, d 2 Aug 1873 Wallace Twp | *Children*: Fanny bap 16 Dec 1827 (m Henry Peterson); Edward bap 10 Jan 1830, d 1893 (m Nancy Allison); Hannah bap 15 Jan 1832; b in Canada: John b 6 May 1833; Sarah b c1834, d 17 Mar 1893 (m James Eisenhauer); Ann b c1836; Walter b 1838 (m Margaret Harris); Mary b c1840; Allan b 17 Oct 1843 (m

Hannah Andrew); William b 8 Feb 1846 (m Amanda Harris); Elizabeth b c1849 (the last six b in Woolwich Twp) | *From*: Shipley, West Sussex | *To*: Woolwich Twp, Waterloo P.O., Gore | (David Musselmans) | *Occupation Eng*: Labourer | 1832 | Lord Melville | Hannah was a sister of **George** Streeter and **Sarah** Streeter, who married Edward's brother **John**.

SOURCE: *No. 6 Continuation*, 41–2; WSRO, PAR 168/1/1/5, PAR 168/1/2/1, PAR 168/1/3/1; Correspondents Virginia Sande; Roger Miller

Bristow, John | 32, bap 29 Apr 1799 Shipley, West Sussex | *Spouse*: Sarah Streeter, m 1 Jan 1829, bap 8 Jan 1804, d 25 Nov 1858 Elmira | *Children*: Sarah b 31 May 1829; Elizabeth b 30 Jun, bap 24 Jul 1831; Edward b 31 Jul, bap 18 Aug 1833, d 12 Apr 1920; b in Woolwich Twp, Can: Hannah b c1838; Mary b c1839; Nancy b c1841; John b c1845; Lucy b c1846; Henry b 17 Jul 1850, d 3 Oct 1862 | *From*: Shipley, West Sussex | *To*: Woolwich Twp, Waterloo | *Occupation Eng*: Farming man | 1835 | Brother of **Edward**. "Very steady man & wife for employment."

SOURCE: WSRO, PHA 142; Correspondents Virginia Sande, Roger Miller

Bristow, John | 30 | *Spouse*: Hannah Boniface, m 9 Apr 1825 Shermanbury, bap 30 Dec 1804 | *Children*: John bap 8 Jun 1825, James bap 18 May 1828, Rebecca bap 15 Aug 1830, Henry b c1833; b in Canada: William b c 1835, Allen b c1837, Carolyn b c1839, Isaac b c1841, Peter b c1843, Edwin b c1845, Frederick b c1847 | *From*: West Grinstead, West Sussex | *To*: Blandford Twp (1851) | *Occupation Eng*: Farming man | 1835 | *Assistance*: Parish granted £35 on 17 Mar 1835 | Had a broken arm at end of 1834; on parish relief. "Very steady man & wife for employment."

SOURCE: WSRO, PHA 142; PAR 95/1/1/4, PAR 95/1/2/1, PAR 95/12/1, PAR 95/38/1, PAR 167/1/3/1; NA, RG 31, Canada Census, 1851 Blandford Twp, p31

Brooks, Eliza | *Spouse*: Penfold, m in Canada between 1832 and 1833 | *From*: Thakeham, West Sussex (or Sullington) | *To*: Guelph | 1832 | Married Penfold (possibly William) 7 days after his wife, her sister, died.

SOURCE: See letter from George and Ann Hills, *No. 2 Continuation*, 13–14

Broughton, George | 19, bap 25 Aug 1813 | Single | *From*: Dorking, Surrey (Ram Alley, next to White Horse) | 1832 | *Assistance*: Dorking Emigration Society | Brother of **Richard**.

SOURCE: *Letters from Dorking*, 10; SRO (GMR), PSH/DOM/3/1

Broughton, Richard | 20, bap 11 June 1809 | Single | *From*: Dorking, Surrey | 1832 | *Assistance*: Dorking Emigration Society | Brother of **George**.

SOURCE: *Letters from Dorking*, 10; SRO (GMR), PSH/DOM/3/1

Budd, Edward | 17, bap 28 Aug 1817 | *From*: Felpham, West Sussex | *Occupation Eng*: Agricultural labourer | 1835 | *Assistance*: Parish and Earl of Egremont | Brother of **William**.

SOURCE: GB, Parl. Papers, *Select Committee … Poor Law Amendment Act …* App. to 12th Report, 1837; WSRO, PAR 81/1/2/1

Budd, James | 48, bap 2 Nov 1788 Angmering, d 8 Apr 1850 | *Spouse*: Mary Carter, m 11 Jun 1818, 43, bap 2 Mar 1800 Treyford | *Children*: Henry Budd 19 (son of James's twin brother), bap 19 Mar 1815; John 17, bap 20 Nov 1819, d 18 Oct 1898 (m (1) Charlotte **Denman** 7 Oct 1841, 6 children by 1851, (2) Rhoda **Boxall** after 1856, 3 children, (3) Mrs Heath 1873); James 13, bap 20 Apr 1823; George 11, bap 30 Jul 1826; Joseph 8, bap 15 Jan 1829; Mary 8, bap 15 Jan 1829; Barbara Ann 5, bap 18 Sep 1831 | *From*: Cocking, West Sussex (and Bepton) | *To*: Blandford, Oxford Co. (town plot) | *Occupation Eng*: Agricultural labourer | 1836 | *Assistance*: £100 loaned to parish by Charles Caplen, linen draper

of Midhurst | "sent in great distress"; Mary Carter was sister to Harriet Carter, wife of James **Cooper**. In 1847, James Budd sold his blacksmith shop and business in Woodstock.
SOURCE: *Continuation of Letters from Sussex Emigrants*, 11–12; Letter from James Cooper, May 1838, *Brighton Herald*, 25 Aug 1838; PRO, MH 12, 13029; WSRO, PAR 17/1/2/1, PAR 53/1/2/1, PAR 199/1/1/1; AO, RG 80-27-1, vol 2, Brock District marriage register, p13; Oxford Co., Old St Pauls burial register; NA, RG 31, Canada Census, 1851 Woodstock, p79; Woodstock *Sentinel-Review and Dominion Dairyman*, 18 and 21 Oct 1898; *Woodstock Monarch*, 20 Apr 1847

Budd, William | 24, bap 1 Jul 1810 | *From*: Felpham, West Sussex | *Occupation Eng*: Agricultural labourer | 1835 | *Assistance*: Parish and Earl of Egremont | Brother of **Edward**.
SOURCE: GB, Parl. Papers, *Select Committee ... Poor Law Amendment Act ...* App. to 12th Report, 1837; WSRO, Goodwood Ms 1501, f1; PAR 81/1/2/1

Bull, Benjamin | 20 | *From*: Carisbrooke, Isle of Wight | 1833 | *Assistance*: Parish, House of Industry | Admitted to House of Industry 12 Dec 1832; discharged 25 Apr 1833.
SOURCE: IOWRO, Z/HO/L5; Index of Baptisms, Marriages, and Burials

Bull, James | 18 | *From*: Whitwell, Isle of Wight | *Occupation Eng*: "out of employ" | 1837 | *Assistance*: Parish, House of Industry | Admitted to House of Industry 25 Apr 1837; discharged 26 Apr 1837. An Elizabeth Bull aged 13 was discharged 24 May 1838 "to Canada."
SOURCE: IOWRO, Z/HO/44; Z/HO/L5; Index of Baptisms, Marriages, and Burials

Burberry. See Barberry

Burch. See Birch

Burchell, (Mrs) J. | Married | *From*: Arundel, West Sussex | 1832 | England | Sailed with party from Wisborough Green; emigrated with her husband and some relatives.
SOURCE: WSRO, Goodwood Ms 1460, f115.

Burgess, (Mr) | 1833
SOURCE: *No. 4 Continuation*, 30–2

Burningham, Henry | b 14 Dec 1812 | *From*: Petworth, West Sussex | 1836 | In the autumn of 1835 proceedings were initiated by C. Murray for the Earl of Egremont against Henry Burningham for "trespass in His Lordship's Home Park." In Apr 1836 was noted "this defendant went to Canada and not further proceeded with." There is evidence that he did not sail but returned from the ship. He was seeking poor relief in Petworth in 1846.
SOURCE: WSRO, PHA 4458, Accounts of William Tyler & Charles Murray with Earl of Egremont 1835/36, Apr 1836; PAR 149/1/2/1; PRO, MH 12, 13060, 13063

Burstead, William | 23 | *From*: Boxgrove, West Sussex | *Occupation Eng*: Sawyer and carpenter | 1832 ?
SOURCE: WSRO, PHA 137

Burton. See Barton

Capelain (Caplain, Capling?), James | *From*: Lurgashall, West Sussex | 1832 | *Assistance*: W.H. Yaldwin, Earl of Egremont and Parish | PEC sent letters to Canada Co to forward to James and John Caplain.
SOURCE: WSRO, PHA 137

Capling (Caplin, Caplain, Capelain), John | b 1788, bap 26 May 1788 | *Spouse*: Jane Booker, m 20 Nov 1811, prob bap 14 Nov 1793 (daughter of Oliffe), d 1832 of cholera | *Children*: 11 children emigrated: George bap 25 Oct 1812; Thomas bap 28 Aug 1814; [Caroline?] John bap 20 Sep 1818 (m Elizabeth Fryfogel); William bap 18 Mar 1821; Mary bap 23 Mar 1823, d of cholera 1832; James bap 29 May 1825; Stephen bap 17 Sep 1826; Edmund bap 7 Sep 1828; Jane bap 27 Jun 1830; Charlotte bap 25 Mar 1832; 3 youngest children also d of cholera 1832 | *From*: Lurgashall, West Sussex | *To*: South Easthope Twp, lot 13 con I (100 acres) | *Occupation Eng*: Labourer of Lurgashall receiving £1.10s in Nov 1830 | *Occupation Can*: Labourer; farmer | 1832 | Eveline | *Assistance*: Earl of Egremont, W.H. Yaldwin, and parish | Purchased 100 acres from Canada Co.; George also acquired 100 acres from Canada Co., N. Easthope Twp, lot 13 con 12. Both mortgaged until 1854. (Jane not a sister of George or Lydia Booker Hilton.)

SOURCE: *Emigration: Letters* (1833), 16–17; WSRO, Goodwood Ms 1460, f113; PAR 130/1/1/3, PAR 130/1/1/4, PAR 130/1/2/1; PHA 137; PHA 8557; NA, RG 31, Canada Census, 1851 North Easthope, p19; A.J. Capling, *The Capling Family* (n.p. 1988); letter from Beatrice and Harold Cosens

Capling, George | *b 8 Oct 1812, bap 25 Oct 1812, d 20 May 1891* | *Spouse: Mary* **Morley** *(daughter of Nathaniel and Sarah), m in Canada, b 4 Dec 1814, d 4 Mar 1896* | *Children: Elizabeth b 1833, Jane b 1835, Sarah b 17 Oct 1837, Charlotte b 1839, Johnathon b 14 Oct 1839 (sic), Susannah b 10 Oct 1842, Joshua b 1843, William b 28 Jan 1847, Stephen b 1848, George b 20 Dec 1850, Noah b 1851, Mary b 1854, Daniel b 21 Nov 1856, Edwin b 1859* | *From: Lurgashall, West Sussex* | *To: Shakespeare, Ont.* | *Occupation Can: Farmer* | *1832* | *Assistance: W.H. Yaldwin, parish, and Earl of Egremont* | *Son of John Capling Sr.*

SOURCE: *Perth County Archives, Capling file, Correspondents Nancy Graden, Harold Cosens; WSRO, PAR 130/1/1/4, 130/1/2/1; UCA,, Wesleyan Methodist baptismal registers, North Easthope 1: 57, 1: 58, 1: 547*

Carey, Philip | 20 | *Spouse*: Mary Golds, m 19 Apr 1835 "with consent of parents" | *From*: Washington, West Sussex | *Occupation Can*: For employment | 1835 | Married just before the ship sailed.

SOURCE: WSRO, PHA 142; PAR 211/1/3/1

Carter, Richard | *Spouse*: Wife | *To*: York, Upper Canada | 1832 ? | Seen by William Cooper of Burton, West Sussex, at Little York.

SOURCE: *Letters: Emigration* (1833), 8–9

Carver, George | bap 10 Jul 1791 | single | *From*: Sutton, West Sussex | *To*: Delaware Twp, Middlesex Co., London Dist. | 1832 | *Assistance*: Earl of Egremont | The 1842 census for Delaware lists a George Carver age 66 and wife Jane age 57.

SOURCE: WSRO, Goodwood Ms 1476, f278; WSRO, PAR 191/1/1/3; NA, RG 31, Canada Census, 1851 Delaware Twp, p53

Chalcraft, Matthew | b 2 Aug 1804, bap 30 Sep 1804 | *Spouse*: Charlotte [Finfield], m 30 Oct 1830 | 26 | *Children*: 3 children emigrated: Mary Ann 5, bap 15 May 1831 Midhurst; George 3, bap 28 Apr 1833 Duncton; Maria 1 ½, bap 25 Dec 1834; born in Canada: Charles 13, Charlotte 11 (in household of William Chambers), Susannah 9, Susan 6, Richard 4, Rhoda 1 (1851 census) | *From*: Tillington, West Sussex | *To*: Blandford, Oxford Co | *Occupation Eng*: Labourer | 1836 | *Assistance*: Earl of Egremont and parish | Matthew was cousin to Clara Chalcraft, wife of George **Goble**.

SOURCE: WSRO, PAR 69/1/2/1, PAR 138/1/2/1, PAR 197/1/1/4, PAR 197/1/2/1, PAR 197/1/3/1/, PAR 197/12/1; Letter from James Cooper, May 1838, *Brighton Herald*, 25 Aug 1838; NA, RG 31, Canada Census, 1851 Blandford, p47

Chalwin, Robert | bap 28 Feb 1813, d 1832 of cholera | *From*: Lurgashall, West Sussex (Crossways, Navant Hill) | 1832 | *Assistance*: Earl of Egremont, W.H. Yaldwin, and parish | Son of Robert and Elizabeth (nee Caplin). In 1826 Robert was cared for by Luffs on the parish poor rate. One of a large family of children; may have emigrated with John Caplin, his uncle.

SOURCE: AO, F129, Canada Co. Papers, A-6-2, pp314–16, John Perry to Commissioners, 25 Oct 1832; *Emigration: Letters* (1833), 16–17; A.J. Capling, "The Capling Family"; Correspondent Roger Chalwin; WSRO, PAR 130/1/2/1

Chantler, Moses | b 7 Nov 1793 | *Spouse*: Sarah Hoad, m 28 May 1812 Shipley, bap 20 Apr 1794 Shipley | *Children*: William Nathaniel* b 14 Oct 1813 Abinger Mill, Surrey (emigrated 1840); John b 3 Jun 1816 Abinger Mill; Elizabeth b 22 Oct 1818 Abinger, Mill; Charles b 26 Feb 1821 Abinger Mill; Ann b 11 May 1823 Ockley, Surrey, d 1832 on voyage down St Lawrence; Robert* b 19 Mar 1825 Ockley, d 26 Nov 1825; George b 6 Oct 1826 Findon; Mary Ann b 26 Nov 1828 Findon; Emma b 14 Jan 1831 Ockley; b in Canada: Piscilla [sic] 19 and Amine 14 (1851 census) | Quaker | *From*: Ockley, Surrey | *To*: Newmarket area, then St Vincent Twp | *Occupation Eng*: Miller | *Occupation Can*: Miller | 1832 | *Assistance*: £100 borrowed from Joseph Sayers, on behalf of the Friends at 5% (repaid Dec 1833). | Brother of **Nathaniel**. Sailed on the *Brunswick*, not with PEC.
SOURCE: WSRO, MF 676, A Register of Births of the People called Quakers Belonging to the Monthly Meeting of Horsham & Ifield, Sussex; MF 675, A Register of Births belonging to the Quarterly Meeting of Sussex 1796-1836; PAR 168/1/1/4, PAR 168/1/1/5; Religious Society of Friends (Quakers), Dorking Preparative Meeting, 1) List of members of the Dorking, Horsham, and Guildford Monthly Meeting in the county of Surrey and Sussex 1837-1897; 2) Monthly Meeting Book of Dorking Meeting 1827-1834; 3) membership letter in File 158, Dorking Meeting Record; 4) Monthly Meeting, Ifield, 14 Aug 1833, Dorking Minute Book; 5) Monthly Meeting, Horsham, Dec 1833, Dorking Minute Book; NA, RG 31, Canada Census, 1851 St Vincent Twp, p 5

Chantler, Nathaniel | b 27 Jun 1780 at Cripplegate, Horsham, d 1832 near Coteau-du-Lac of cholera | *Spouse*: (1) Elizabeth Cong, d Jan 1817 Horsham; (2) Sophia Rowe, m 14 Sep 1819 Wotton, Surrey, d 1832 Toronto of cholera | *Children*: 5 children emigrated: Esther (Hester) Mary b 28 May 1820 Broadmoor, Wotton, Surrey; Joseph b 18 Feb 1822 Broadmoor; Henry b 11 Nov 1823 Broadmoor; Alfred b 2 Jul 1825 Broadmoor; Nathaniel Rowe b 27 Mar 1829 Coldharbour, Dorking | Quaker Meeting House | *From*: Dorking, Surrey | *To*: Yonge St, Toronto | *Occupation Eng*: Weaver; Sophia had been a straw milliner | 1832 | Brother of **Moses**. Sailed on the *Brunswick*, not with PEC.
SOURCE: *Letters from Dorking*, 25–7; SRO (GMR), typescript mss (uncatalogued), Esther Chantler Dennis to her children, c. 1896; WSRO, MF 676, A Register of Births of the People called Quakers Belonging to the Monthly Meeting of Horsham & Ifield, Sussex

Charman, Richard | *Spouse*: Wife | *From*: Sutton, West Sussex | *To*: York, Upper Canada | 1832 ?
SOURCE: *Emigration: Letters* (1833)

Chase, Mr | *From*: Epson, Surrey | *To*: York (area) ? | Mentioned in letter from James Helyer Sep 1833.
SOURCE: *No. 6 Continuation*, 43-4

Chase, William | bap 22 Dec 1799, d 17 Apr 1874 | *Spouse*: Lucy Gregory, m 12 Oct 1829 | bap 8 Jul 1810 at Sidlesham | *Children*: 2 children: Frank bap 8 Jun 1830, Fanny bap 10 Feb 1832; b in Canada: Edwin b c1841; Sarah A. b c1843 | *From*: Nyetimber (Nightimber), Pagham, West Sussex | *To*: St Catharines | *Occupation Can*: Labourer, lock tender | 1832 ? | *Assistance*: £5 deposit paid by Mr Goddard | He may be the Chase, farm labourer, living with E.F. Heming in 1832.
SOURCE: *Emigration: Letters* (1833), 30; *Sussex Advertiser*, 22 Feb 1836; WSRO, PAR 146/1/1/3, PAR 146/1/3/1, PAR 146/1/2/1, PAR 173/1/1/5; PHA 137; NA, RG 31, Canada Census, 1871 St Catharines, 1: 116; AO, RG 22/235, Lincoln Co. Surrogate Court, file 542

Chatfield, Benjamin | 36, named Aug 1798, bap 21 Oct 1801 | *Spouse*: Charlotte | 44 | | *From*: Yapton, West Sussex | *Occupation Eng*: Agricultural labourer; "soldier of the 1st foot-

guards and the Police. For employment" | 1835 | *Assistance*: Richard Prime and parish
SOURCE: GB, Parl. Papers, *Select Committee ... Poor Law Amendment Act* ... App. to 12th
Report, 1837; WSRO, PAR 225/1/1/3; PHA 142

Chivers? (Clemens?), Luke | 40 | Single | *From*: Findon, West Sussex | *Occupation Eng*:
Labourer | 1836 | *Assistance*: Hugh Penfold and Poor Law Commissioners
SOURCE: PRO, MH 12, 13128

Clear, Edward | 1832 | Seen at Montreal by Obediah Wilson.
SOURCE: *Emigration: Letters* (1833), 21

Clements (Clemens), Thomas | 49 | *Spouse*: Alice Ann | 46 | *Children*: 9 children emi-
grated: 5 sons aged 19, 15, 13, 9, 3 incl. Richard bap 8 Jun 1828, Thomas bap 16 Sep 1832;
4 daughters aged 17, 11, 7, 2 months incl. Elizabeth bap 21 Jun 1824; Catherine bap 8 Jun
1828; Eliza bap 13 Dec 1835 | *From*: Findon, West Sussex | *Occupation Eng*: Agricultural
labourer | 1836 | *Assistance*: Hugh Penfold and Poor Law Commissioners
SOURCE: PRO, MH 12, 13128 (children's names illegible); WSRO, PAR 84/1/5/1

Clowser (Cloudesly). See Sharp

Cobby, Benjamin | 30 | *Spouse*: Wife | *From*: Donnington, West Sussex | *Occupation Eng*:
Stonemason, sawyer (stone cutter), and polisher | 1832 ? | 2 passages
SOURCE: WSRO, PHA 137

Cole, Charles | 30, bap 17 Mar 1805 | *Spouse*: Harriet | 30 | *Children*: Charles 4 | *From*:
Yapton, West Sussex | *Occupation Eng*: Agricultural labourer; "soldier of the 1st Footguards"
"an able-bodied man for employment" | 1835 | *Assistance*: Richard Prime and parish
SOURCE: GB, Parl. Papers, *Select Committee ... Poor Law Amendment Act* ... App. to 12th
Report, 1837; WSRO, PAR 225/1/1/3; PHA 142

Cole (Coles), George | 20, bap 26 Jan 1817 | *From*: Walberton, West Sussex | *To*: Thorn-
hill, York Co. ? | *Occupation Eng*: Agricultural labourer | 1836 | *Assistance*: Richard Prime
and parish | Brother of **William**.
SOURCE: GB, Parl. Papers, *Select Committee ... Poor Law Amendment Act* ... App. to 12th
Report, 1837; WSRO, PAR 202/2/3; Letter from John Ayling, 24 Jul 1836, *Letters from Sus-
sex Emigrants*, 8–9

Cole, William | 21, bap 2 Apr 1815 | *From*: Walberton, West Sussex | *To*: Thornhill, York
Co. | *Occupation Eng*: Agricultural labourer | 1835 | *Assistance*: Richard Prime and Parish
| Brother of **George**.
SOURCE: GB, Parl. Papers, *Select Committee ... Poor Law Amendment Act* ... App. to 12th
Report, 1837; Letter from John Ayling, 24 Jul 1836, *Letters from Sussex Emigrants*, 8–9; WSRO,
PAR 202/2/3

Coleman, George Sr | b 1779 or 1780, d 26 Jul 1836 | *Spouse*: Sarah Pollard, m Apr 1800
Lewes, b c1775, d 13 Feb 1845 | *Children*: Ann Sophia bap 20 Jul 1800; John Friend bap
18 Jul 1802; Sarah bap 4 Mar 1804; Elizabeth Gaston* bap 30 Mar 1806, bur 15 Dec 1810;
James Friend bap 6 Mar 1808; Mary bap 24 Sep 1809; Daniel* bap 18 Aug 1811, bur 14
Mar 1833; Lucy Susannah bap 11 Apr 1813 (m Henry **Harwood** Jr in Can); George Peck-
ham b 31 Dec 1815 (m Elizabeth **Voice**); Jane bap 31 May 1818 | *From*: Kingston by Lewes,
East Sussex | *To*: Blandford (town plot) | *Occupation Eng*: Labourer | *Occupation Can*: Car-
penter | 1834 | *Assistance*: Possibly Earl of Chichester and parish | *Definitely did not go
to Canada; some of the other older children may not have gone.
SOURCE: AO, RG 1, C-IV, Township Papers, Town of Blandford; Oxford Co., Woodstock, Old
St Pauls Anglican Cemetery; Brydone, *Narrative*; Continuation of Letters from Sussex Emigrants, 9–11; ESRO, PAR 403/1/1/3; John H. Harwood, Bett Harwood, and Stuart Harwood,

Harwood History (privately printed, 1979); WSRO, Bishop's Transcript, EP/11/16/124B; "Sussex Marriage Licences for Archdeaconry of Lewes ...," *Sussex Record Society* XXV, 1772–1837

Coleman, George Jr | *b 27 Nov 1815, d 7 Oct 1883* | *Spouse: Elizabeth Voice, m in Canada 1834 or 1835, bap 28 Sep 1817, d 27 Jun 1873* | *Children: John 1836 (Ontario); Cornelius 1842 (Illinois); Daniel 1846 (Illinois); George 1848 (Illinois); Edwin 1852 (Illinois); Walter 1854 (Illinois); David 24 Mar 1863 (Kansas)* | *From: Kingston by Lewes, East Sussex* | *To: Blandford (town plot)* | *1834*
SOURCE: *Continuation of Letters from Sussex Emigrants, 9–11; Information supplied by Tony & Lesley Voice*

Coleman, William | b 3 Sep 1826 | 1834 | "Son of a sister of George Coleman."
SOURCE: John H. Harwood, Bett Harwood, and Stuart Harwood, *Harwood History* (privately printed, 1979).

Cook, Henry | *Spouse*: Wife | *From*: Dorking, Surrey | *Occupation Eng*: Labourer | 1832 | *Assistance*: Dorking Emigration Society
SOURCE: *Letters from Dorking*, 10

Cooke, Cornelius | 20 | *From*: Walberton, West Sussex | *To*: Toronto | *Occupation Eng*: Shoemaker | 1836
SOURCE: GB, Parl. Papers, *Select Committee ... Poor Law Amendment Act* ... App. to 12th Report, 1837; Letter from John Ayling, 24 Jul 1836, *Letters from Sussex Emigrants*, 8–9

Cooke, Mark | 20, poss bap 5 Apr 1829 Carisbrooke, Isle of Wight | *From*: Newport, Isle of Wight | *Occupation Eng*: Agricultural labourer | 1837 | *Assistance*: Parish, House of Industry | Remarks on abstract of IOW emigrants: "well behaved during the voyage and subsequently."
SOURCE: IOWRO, Z/HO/44, Index of Baptisms, Marriages, and Burials; WSRO, PHA 140

Cooper, Humphrey | bap 1 Mar 1792, Sutton | *Spouse*: Charlotte Boswell, m 12 Aug 1813 Tillington, b 13 Nov 1787, bap 9 Dec 1787, illegit. d of Mary Boswell | *Children*: 3 children emigrated (2 under 14): **William** bap 20 Apr 1814; Elizabeth bap 10 Apr 1816 (m Charles Child 6 Aug 1836); perhaps James Sayers was 3rd child | *From*: Tillington, West Sussex (Hill Top) | *To*: York | *Occupation Eng*: Shoemaker | *Occupation Can*: Shoemaker | 1832 | *Assistance*: Parish and Earl of Egremont | H. Cooper was listed as a boot and shoe maker at 8 Market Lane in the 1833/4 *Directory of Toronto*.
SOURCE: *Emigration: Letters* (1833), 17; WSRO, PHA 137; PAR 153/34/2, PAR 191/1/1/3, PAR 197/1/1/4, PAR 197/31/5

Cooper, James | bap 18 Nov 1792, d 12 May 1883 | *Spouse*: (1) Mary Lambert*, m 22 Sep 1817, d 1820, bur 7 Jun 1820; (2) Harriet Carter, m 18 May 1822 Lodsworth; (3) survived by 3rd wife, Harriet b 14 Apr 1802 Steep, Hants; d 6 Dec 1857 Strathroy | *Children*: Mary 18 (daughter of Mary), bap 25 Jan 1818; Harriett 14, bap 23 Dec 1822 (m George Pegley); James King 11, bap 18 Jul 1824; Emma 10, bap 26 Feb 1826 (m Thomas **Rapley**); Henry 8, bap 9 Sep 1827; Caroline 7, bap 15 Mar 1829; Sarah 6, bap 16 Jan 1831; William 3, bap 4 Nov 1832; George 1, bap 27 Oct 1834; Charlotte b 9 May 1838 in Canada. All but William and George were baptized in Graffham. | Wesleyan Methodist after 1839 | *From*: Tillington, West Sussex; was removed from Graffham to Tillington as a pauper in 1817. | *To*: Adelaide Twp; Woodcut Farm, lot 21 con 4SER | *Occupation Eng*: Baker or gingerbread maker | *Occupation Can*: Farmer | 1836 | *Assistance*: Parish and Earl of Egremont | James was brother of **William** and John, who emigrated in 1844. Harriet Carter is sister of **Mary** Carter, wife of James **Budd**.
SOURCE: Letter from James Cooper, May 1838, *Brighton Herald*, 25 Aug 1838; Letter from

J. Walden, *Sussex Advertiser*, 14 Mar 1836; WSRO, PAR 93/1/2/1, PAR 93/1/2/2, PAR 128/1/2/7, PAR 197/1/2/1, PAR 197/31/5, PAR 197/32/3/1; NA, RG 31, Canada Census, 1851 Adelaide agricultural schedule; *Strathroy Age,* 17 May 1883; *Christian Guardian*, 27 Jan 1858; Correspondent Eileen Whitehead

Cooper, Richard | 18, bap 17 May 1818 | *From*: Walberton, West Sussex | *To*: Toronto ? | *Occupation Eng*: Agricultural labourer | 1836 | *Assistance*: Richard Prime and Parish
SOURCE: GB, Parl. Papers, *Select Committee … Poor Law Amendment Act …* App. to 12th Report, 1837; WSRO, PAR 202/1/2/1; PAR 202/2/3; Letter from John Ayling, 24 Jul 1836, *Letters from Sussex Emigrants*, 8–9

Cooper, William | bap 6 Mar 1796 at Graffham/Woolavington | *From*: Burton, West Sussex | *To*: Adelaide Twp, Upper Canada | *Occupation Can*: Farmer | 1832 | Eveline | Brother of **James** and John, who emigrated in 1844.
SOURCE: *Emigration: Letters* (1833), 8–9; *No. 1 Continuation,* 5–6; WSRO, Goodwood Ms 1460, f35; PHA 137

Cooper, William | bap 20 Apr 1814 | *From*: Tillington, West Sussex | 1833 | *Assistance*: Parish £3 and taken to Portsmouth | Son of **Humphrey**
SOURCE: WSRO, PAR 93/2/2, PAR 197/12/1

Cosens (Cosins), Charles Sr | 59, b 1771, d 27 Dec 1846, bur Turner Churchyard, Tuckersmith Twp | *Spouse*: Ann Goodchild | 43, b 1786, d 3 Apr 1853, bur in Turner Churchyard | *Children*: 11 children emigrated: Hester 21; Cornelius 20; Thomas 18; Mary 18; Elizabeth 16; Caroline 15; Nathaniel 13, bap 30 Jun 1818 Fittleworth, d 19 Sep 1894; Francis William 11, bap 21 Dec 1820 Fittleworth; Ann 8, bap 14 Oct 1823 Slinfold; John 6, bap 10 Oct 1824 Slinfold; Jesse 5, bap 23 Feb 1827 Dorking, d 26 Jun 1878 in London Asylum; Mary Ann d 1832 | Charles, Ann, and Jane buried in Turner Cemetery, Wesleyan Methodist | *From*: Dorking, Surrey (Redland Farm) | *To*: Waterloo Twp | *Occupation Eng*: Agricultural labourer | *Occupation Can*: Farmer | 1832 | Lord Melville | *Assistance*: Dorking Emigration Society | Another daughter Jane m William **Tilt** and d in childbirth in 1832. Anna Cosens m Robert Landsborough in Canada. Thomas Cosens was listed in the 1851 census for Wilmot Twp with his wife Ann and 8 children between the ages of 14 and 3.
SOURCE: *Letters from Dorking*, 10; Letter from Ann Miller Cosens, 31 Mar 1833; AO, Huron Co., Tuckersmith Twp, Turner Cemetery; RG 21, Gore District Census, 1833, 1834; WSRO, PAR 86/1/2/1/, PAR 176/1/2/1; SRO (GMR), PSH/DOM/3/1; *Christian Guardian*, 19 Feb 1868; *Daily Telegraph* (Berlin), 15 May 1907; *Listowel Banner*, 12 Jul 1878; Correspondent Harold Cosens

Cosens, Charles Jr | 19 | *Spouse*: Ann Miller, m 20 Feb 1832 Dorking, 20, d by 1871 | *Children* b in Can: Henry, George, Charles, Mary and "expection of another" (all b between 1833 and 1839); 1871 census: Flacherd 26, Joseph 19, Jane 14, Albert 8 | Primitive Methodist (1871) | Charles has given up cricket & other "transitory trifles"; he has taken to "a religious course of life" (Sep 1839) | *From*: Dorking, Surrey | *To*: Waterloo Twp, Upper Block, Halton Co., Gore, later Blenheim Twp, Wallace Twp, Perth | 1832 | Lord Melville | *Assistance*: Dorking Emigration Society
SOURCE: *Letters from Dorking*, 14–15; Letters from Ann Miller Cosens 1833, 1839; SRO (GMR), PSH/DOM/2/2/3; NA, RG 31, Canada Census, 1871 Wallace Twp; Correspondents Eunice M. Brake, Harold Cosens

Cosens, Cornelius | 20 | *Spouse: Emily, b 1819 Kent UK, d 6 Mar 1872 age 52* | *Children: Edmond d age 19, poss Henry d 1865 age 31, Richard b c1841, Richard b c1841, Ruth d 22 Nov 1865 age 22, Mark b c1847, George b 13 Oct 1850, Jane b 14 Feb 1852, Mary Ann b 7 July 1853, Thomas*

b c1854, Isaac b c1856, Silas b c1858, Emily b 20 June 1860 | *Methodist* | *From: Dorking, Surrey* | *To: Waterloo Co. (12 miles from Guelph)* | *Occupation Eng: Blacksmith* | *Occupation Can: Labourer* | *1832* | *Lord Melville* | *Son of Charles Cosens*
SOURCE: *Letters from Dorking, 14–15;* NA, RG 31, *Canada Census, 1871 Elma Twp, 2:3; Christian Guardian, 27 Dec 1865; Canada Christian Advocate, 10 Apr 1872;* UCA, *Wesleyan Methodist baptismal registers, Elma Twp, 1:66, 2:207, 2:404, 2:405*

Cotton, James | 22, bap 25 Dec 1814 | *From*: Newport, Isle of Wight | *Occupation Eng*: Bricklayer; "No employ" | 1837 | *Assistance*: Parish, House of Industry | Admitted to House of Industry 10 Feb 1827 aged 11 years; admitted 25 Apr 1837; discharged 26 Apr 1837. Remarks on abstract of IOW emigrants: "well behaved during the voyage and subsequently."
SOURCE: IOWRO, Z/HO/44; Z/HO/L4; Z/HO/L5; Index of Baptisms, Marriages, and Burials; WSRO, PHA 140

Cotton, William | 20 | *From*: Newport, Isle of Wight | *Occupation Eng*: "no employ" | 1837 | *Assistance*: Parish, House of Industry | Admitted to House of Industry 25 Apr 1837; discharged 26 Apr 1837.
SOURCE: IOWRO, Z/HO/44; Z/HO/L5; Index of Baptisms, Marriages, and Burials

Courtnage, William | b 28 Mar 1799, d 1851 | *Spouse*: Ann Madgwick, m 5 Feb 1825 Thursley, Surrey, b 28 Apr 1806, bap 6 Jul 1806 Haslemere, Surrey | *Children*: Hannah b 28 May 1826, bap 25 Jun 1826 Fernhurst, West Sussex; James b 11 May 1830, bap 20 Jun 1830 Haslemere; b in Canada: John b 10 Nov 1832; Mary Ann b 1835; Thomas b 1839, Susan b 1840, Maria b 1843 | *From*: Fernhurst, West Sussex (and Haslemere) | *To*: Niagara | *Occupation Eng*: Weaver. Ann was also a weaver. | *Occupation Can*: Farmer; labourer | 1832
SOURCE: *Continuation of Letters from Sussex Emigrants, 6–8;* WSRO, PAR 82/1/2/1; SRO (GMR), PSH/THU/3/3; PSH/HME/1/5; PSH/HME/3/1; Correspondent Ralph Courtnage

Cox, James | 26, bap 27 Aug 1809 | *Spouse*: Harriet Tozer, m 9 Oct 1830, 26, bap 24 Dec 1820 (age 11 years) | *Children*: 2 children emigrated; Fanny 3, bap 9 Aug 1831, William infant, bap 14 Sep 1834 | *From*: Felpham, West Sussex | *Occupation Eng*: Agricultural labourer; "able bodied man for employment"; had been a pauper boy | 1835 | *Assistance*: Parish and Earl of Egremont | James probably brother of **John**.
SOURCE: GB, Parl. Papers, *Select Committee ... Poor Law Amendment Act ...* App. to 12th Report, 1837; WSRO, PAR 81/1/1/4, PAR 81/1/2/1, PAR 81/1/3/1; PHA 142

Cox, John | 23, bap 28 Apr 1816? | Church of England | *From*: Felpham, West Sussex | *Occupation Eng*: Agricultural labourer | 1835 | *Assistance*: Earl of Egremont and parish | Probably brother of **James**.
SOURCE: GB, Parl. Papers, *Select Committee ... Poor Law Amendment Act ...* App. to 12th Report, 1837; WSRO, PAR 81/1/2/1

Crockford, (Mrs) | 1833 | Cabin passenger | Wife of cabinetmaker settled in Montreal
SOURCE: WSRO, Goodwood Ms 1470, f179

Crossing, Charles | *From*: Isle of Wight | *To*: Montreal | 1834 | Left group at Montreal without permission.
SOURCE: Brydone, *Narrative*

Croucher, Thomas | *Occupation Eng*: Agricultural labourer | 1837 | *Assistance*: 1 passage | "Well behaved"
SOURCE: WSRO, PHA 140

Cull, Francis | *Occupation Eng*: Sailor | 1837 | *Assistance*: 1 passage | Remarks on abstract of PEC emigrants: "Most respectable."
SOURCE: WSRO, PHA 140

Curley, George | 18 | *From*: Newport, Isle of Wight | 1834 | *Assistance*: Parish, House of Industry | Admitted to House of Industry in 1831 (aged 15) by surgeon, Sir R. Bassett; discharged 12 Apr 1834 "to Canada."
SOURCE: IOWRO, Z/HO/BI, f81; Z/HO/L5

Curtis, William | *Occupation Eng*: Agricultural labourer | 1837 | *Assistance*: 1 passage | "well behaved"
SOURCE: WSRO, PHA 140

Dale, James | 45 | *Spouse*: Wife | 46 | *From*: Findon, West Sussex | *Occupation Eng*: Labourer | 1836 | *Assistance*: Hugh Penfold and Poor Law Commissioners
SOURCE: PRO, MH 12, 13128

Daniels, William | bap 4? Nov 1792 Easebourne, d 10 May 1876 Wilmot Twp | *Spouse*: Elizabeth Horton, m 30 Jan 1814 Petworth | *Children*: 5 children emigrated: Mary bap 5 Jan 1817 Lodsworth; Jane bap 11 Jun 1820 Easebourne; William bap 27 Jun 1824; Ann bap 1 Jun 1827 Petworth, Louisa Elizabeth bap 3 Apr 1831 | *From*: Tillington, West Sussex | *To*: Wilmot Twp | *Occupation Eng*: Labourer, drawing poor relief in 1832 | 1832 | *Assistance*: Parish and Earl of Egremont | The 1851 census of Wilmot Twp lists the following children: Elizabeth 16 (b Eng), Edwin 14 (b Eng), Hannah 13 (b U.S.), Charles 11 and Joseph 9 (b Canada).
SOURCE: *No. 5 Continuation*, 34–5; WSRO, PAR 75/1/1/5, PAR 75/1/2/1, PAR 128/1/2/1, PAR 149/1/2/1, 149/1/3/1, PAR 197/12/1, PAR 197/31/5; PHA 110; NA, RG 31, Canada Census, 1851 Wilmot Twp, p35; 1871 Wilmot Twp, 2: 4; AO, RG 80, Death registration 12725 (1876) and 16993 (1883)

Davies (Davis), Charlotte Maria | 19, b c1818, bap 10 Mar 1833 | *From*: Newport, Isle of Wight | *Occupation Eng*: Servant | 1837 | *Assistance*: Parish, House of Industry | Discharged from House of Industry, IOW, 26 Apr 1837.
SOURCE: IOWRO, Z/HO/44; Z/HO/L5

Davis, alias Watson, James | 22 | Single | *From*: Dorking, Surrey | 1832 | *Assistance*: Dorking Emigration Society
SOURCE: *Letters from Dorking*, 10

Davis, William | *To*: Hamilton, Upper Canada | 1832
SOURCE: T. Adsett, Galt, 25 Jun 1833, *No 4. Continuation*

Dearling, John | d 1842/43 | *Spouse*: Caroline Francis, m 20 Nov 1824 Selham, bap 14 May 1807 Lodsworth | *Children*: Phoebe bap 17 Apr 1825, Jane bap 9 Mar 1828, Caroline 2 bap 10 Oct 1830; b in Canada: Hannah, John; Charlotte b 30 Aug 1842 Waterloo Twp | British Wesleyan (1840 census) | *From*: Lodsworth, West Sussex (and Selham) | *To*: Waterloo Twp | *Occupation Eng*: Labourer | *Occupation Can*: Farmers | 1833 | *Assistance*: Perhaps W.H. Yaldwin | In August 1843 his estate was valued at £263.18.9.
SOURCE: *Brighton Guardian*, 16 Oct 1833; *Continuation of Letters from Sussex Emigrants ... Written in 1836* [1837], 1–3; *Letters from Emigrants ... in 1832, 1833, and 1837*, 1–2; *No. 4 Continuation*, 27–8; WSRO, Goodwood Ms 1469, f16, Hale to Lord Egremont's Emigration Committee, 2 Jul 1833, copy; PAR 128/2/6, PAR 165/2/2; AO, RG 22/318, Wellington District Surrogate Court files; UCA, Wesleyan Methodist baptismal registers, Waterloo Twp 1: 359; AO, RG 21, Gore District Census and Assessments, Waterloo Twp, 1840 census; KPL, Cambridge (Hespeler), New Hope Cemetery

Dell | *Spouse*: Wife | *Children*: 3 children under 14 | *From*: London | *Occupation Eng*: Shoemaker | 1832 ? | *Assistance*: Passage engaged by Mr Birch, £7 deposit paid for 3-½ passages.
SOURCE: WSRO, PHA 137

Denman, John | 40; bap 8 Nov 1795, d 18 Dec 1852 Woodstock | *Spouse*: Hannah Ede, m 18 Oct 1815; 39; possibly bap 27 Mar 1796 | *Children*: 8 children emigrated: William 19, bap 7 Jul 1816; Henry 18, bap 21 Jan 1819 (m Mary Parin/Perring 22 Sep 1842); Charlotte 14. bap 10 Feb 1822, d 1856 (m John **Budd** 7 Oct 1841); James 11, bap 8 Aug 1824; Sarah 9, bap 10 Jun 1827; Job 6, bap 28 Mar 1830; George 3, bap 4 Aug 1833; Harriette, bap 14 Feb 1836; b in Canada: David (Daniel?) bap 1838?; Mary bap 1840? | *From*: Billingshurst, West Sussex | *To*: East Flamborough Twp, and Woodstock | *Occupation Eng*: Agricultural labourer | 1836 | *Assistance*: Parish, Charles Farhall, and Poor Law Commissioners | Accompanied by Ann Fair's little girl. The 1851 census lists John (59, Labourer), Hannah, and 4 youngest (George also given as labourer) in Woodstock.
SOURCE: *Continuation of Letters from Sussex Emigrants ... Written in 1836* [1837], 15–16; PRO, MH 12, 13060; WSRO, PAR 21/1/1/5, PAR 21/1/2/1, PAR 21/1/3/1; AO, RG 80-27-1, Brock District marriage register, p13; Oxford Co., Woodstock, Old St Pauls Cemetery; NA, RG 31, Canada Census, 1851 Woodstock, p79; Correspondents John Sayers, Eileen Whitehead

Dighton (Diton, Deighton), William | 16 [11 in 1829], poss bap 8 Oct 1816 | *From*: Newport, Isle of Wight | 1834 | *Assistance*: Parish/House of Industry | Admitted to House of Industry, Jan 1829, with "bad leg"; discharged (27 Apr?) "to Canada."
SOURCE: IOWRO, Z/HO/L5; Index to Births, Marriages, and Burials.

Dilley, Elias | 21, bap 10 Dec 1815 Portsea, Hants, son of John and Mary | *From*: Newport, Isle of Wight | (previously Whippingham) | *Occupation Eng*: "no employ" | 1837 | *Assistance*: Parish, House of Industry | Admitted House of Industry IOW 20 Apr 1837; discharged 26 Apr 1837. Brother of **Hannah**.
SOURCE: IOWRO, Z/HO/44; Z/HO/L5; Index of Baptisms, Marriages, and Burials; IGI for Hants.

Dilley, Hannah | 20, bap 18 Jan 1814 Portsea, Hants, daughter of John and Mary | *From*: Newport, Isle of Wight (previously at Whippingham) | *Occupation Eng*: "out of employ" | 1837 | Parish, House of Industry | Admitted to House of Industry IOW 25 Apr 1837; discharged 26 Apr 1836. Sister of **Elias**.
SOURCE: IOWRO, Z/HO/44; Z/HO/L5; Index of Baptisms, Marriages, and Burials; IGI for Hants

Ditton, Thomas | d 1851 Woodstock | *Spouse*: Tabitha | *Children*: Thomas bap 3 Mar 1818 St Marys, Marylebone (London), d 20 Apr 1854 Woodstock (m Ann Lamport); William bap 1819 St Marys, Marylebone, d c1846 Goderich; Emma bap 1827 St Marys, Marylebone, d after 1861 (m (1) John Brown, (2) Charles Pope); Lucy bap 1827 St Marys, Marylebone, d after 1871 (m Bernard Sessions); Francis b 9 Feb 1828 Brighton, bap 30 Mar 1834, d 18 May 1881 Auburn, NY; Alfred b 28 Apr 1831, bap 30 Mar 1834, d 22 Feb 1874 Auburn, NY; Mary bap 14 Dec 1832; Ann b 28 Apr 1834 on *British Tar* (m Charles Pascoe) | *From*: Brighton, East Sussex (Claremont Place) | *To*: Blandford (town plot) | *Occupation Eng*: Porter, labourer | *Occupation Can*: Labourer | 1834 | *Assistance*: Hyam Lewis and James Collins, Earl of Chichester, parish, Brighton Emigration Committee
SOURCE: Brydone, *Narrative*; WSRO, Goodwood Ms 1476, f277; WSRO, PHA 139; ESRO, PAR 255/1/2/8; *Brighton Herald*, 19 Apr 1834; AO, RG 1, C-IV, Township Papers, Town of Blandford; Oxford Co., Woodstock, Old St Paul's Anglican Registers; RG 61, Woodstock Copybook of Deeds, 4015 (unprobated will of Thomas Ditton); NA, RG 31, Canada Census, 1851 Woodstock, p61; Correspondent Diane Khouri

Downer, John | b 9 Apr 1816 Kirdford, bap 5 May 1816, son of Avis Downer and James **Napper**; d 28 Mar 1885 | *Spouse*: Lucy **Rapley**, m 20 Nov 1843 Adelaide Twp, bap 8 Apr 1824, d 12 Apr 1905 | *Children* b in Canada: Annie b 9 Jun 1844, Charles Henry b 25 Jul 1845,

John Wesley b 15 Jan 1847, James Franklin b 14 Apr 1849, Avis Lucy b 24 Aug 1850, George William b 29 Jan 1852, Emma Jane b 21 Jul 1855, Jesse b 20 Jun 1857, Mary Collins b 15 Jan 1859, Martha Sarah b 11 Oct 1861, Ira Edward b 14 Apr 1864, Alexander David b 8 Feb 1866 (all b in Adelaide) | bur Adelaide Twp, 4th line cemetery, Mt Zion Old Methodist | *From*: Kirdford, West Sussex | *To*: Adelaide Twp | *Occupation Eng*: Agricultural labourer | 1832 | *Assistance*: Earl of Egremont and parish | Avis Downer was sent back to Kirdford from Wisborough Green in Oct 1815. The poor law authorities did not want the child born in Wisborough Green as it would have settlement rights, i.e. a claim on the poor rate.

SOURCE: WSRO, Misc. Paper 1031; Misc. Paper 2767; PAR 116/1/2/1, PAR 116/32/3/; Removal orders for Kirdford 1715–1866; AO, Middlesex Co., Adelaide Twp, 4th line cemetery, Mt Zion Old Methodist; RG 80-27-1, vol 16, London District marriage register, p171; NA, RG 31, Canada Census, 1851 Adelaide, p18; UCA, Wesleyan Methodist baptismal registers 1: 88, 96; Correspondent Jane Thompson

Drake, Henry Jenkins | 14, b 24/26 Sep 1823; bap ? Oct 1823, son of James (a private in 37th Regiment) and Anne (née Nobb), of Albany Barracks | *From*: Newport, Isle of Wight | 1837 | *Assistance*: Parish, House of Industry | Admitted into the House of Industry 10 Feb 1827 aged 3 years with Ann 50 and Charles 2 and George 9 months.

SOURCE: IOWRO, Z/HO/44; Z/HO/L4; Index of Baptisms, Marriages, and Burials

Drewett, Charles | *Occupation Eng*: Soldier | 1835 ?

SOURCE: PRO, CO 385/9, Pinnock to T. Sockett, Apr 1835

Dutton, Walter | 13, bap 16 Jan 1820 | *From*: Carisbrooke, Isle of Wight | 1833 | *Assistance*: Parish/House of Industry | Admitted to House of Industry 1 Dec 1832 "parents poor"; discharged 25 Apr 1833. Son of George and Mary Dutton of Albany Barracks, Sergeant 7th Regt.

SOURCE: IOWRO, Z/HO/L5

Eade, George | *From*: Petworth, West Sussex (Medhone Farm) | *Occupation Eng*: Farmer | 1834 | *Assistance*: Earl of Egremont

SOURCE: WSRO, PHA 8618

Edsall, William | 31 | *Spouse*: Mary Ann Wheeler, m 11 Oct 1823 | 32 | *Children*: 4 children emigrated; George bap 12 Mar 1826; Ellen bap 4 Nov 1827; Eliza bap 21 Feb 1830; Henry bap 25 Dec 1831; Louisa **Marshall** 17 to go with them. | *From*: Haslemere, Surrey | *Occupation Eng*: Labourer (William), tanner (Mary) | 1832 | *Assistance*: Peter Scovell, parish

SOURCE: WSRO, PHA 137, 28 May 1832; SRO (GMR), PSH/HME/2/3, PSH/HME/3/1

Edwards, Alfred | 20 | Single | *From*: Dorking, Surrey | 1832 | Paid his own way.

SOURCE: *Letters from Dorking*, 10

Edwards, Charles | *To*: Nelless Settlement, Niagara District | 1832 ? | Described in PHA 8618 as a "loose and runagate fellow"; suspected in Jul 1831 with Ned Lucas of setting fire to "the barn, part of the stable and a Hay Rick at Northlands" (part of the Rev. T. Sockett's premises).

SOURCE: Wm. T. Upton to George Warren at Petworth, 16 Sep 1832, *Emigration: Letters* (1833), 23-4; WSRO, PHA 8618

Edwards, George | 40, poss bap 26 Apr 1795 | *Spouse*: Esther | 39 | *Children*: George* bap 10 Dec 1820; James 13, bap 31 Mar 1822; Ann 9, bap 26 Mar 1826; Emma 8, bap 4 May 1828; William 6, bap 21 Mar 1830; Charles* bap 15 Apr 1832, bur 8 Mar 1834; Mary 2, bap 22 Jun 1834; Alfred 1, bap 14 Feb 1836 | *From*: Heyshott, West Sussex | *Occupation Eng*:

Agricultural labourer | 1837 | *Assistance*: Parish and Earl of Egremont, 5 passages | had cost the parish "about £25" last year | Possibly brother of **John** of Heyshott. Remarks on abstract of PEC emigrants: "Most respectable families."

SOURCE: PRO, MH 12, 13127; WSRO, PHA 140; PAR 101/1/2/1

Edwards, John | 35, poss bap 27 May 1792 | *Spouse*: Mary Crowter, m 20 May 1822 Donnington; 32 | *Children*: John 14, bap 11 Feb 1823 Donnington; Charlotte 12, bap 13 Dec 1824; William 10, bap 3 Dec 1826; Mary Ann 8, bap 1 Mar 1829; Thomas 6, bap 6 Jun 1831; Eliza 4, bap 24 Feb 1833; Charles 1-½, bap 17 Jan 1836 | *From*: Heyshott, West Sussex | *Occupation Eng*: Agricultural labourer | 1837 | *Assistance*: Parish and Earl of Egremont; had cost the parish "about £25 during last year"; 6 passages | Possibly brother of **George**. Remarks on abstract of PEC emigrants: "Most respectable families."

SOURCE: PRO, MH 12, 13127, 13061; WSRO, PHA 140, PHA 8557; PAR 68/1/2/1, PAR 68/1/3/1, PAR 101/2/1

Edwards, John | 23, b 3 Apr 1811, bap 5 May 1811 Calbourne, IOW | *From*: Newport, Isle of Wight | 1834 | *Assistance*: Parish, House of Industry | Admitted to House of Industry 21 Jan 1833; discharged 16 Apr 1834 "to Canada."

SOURCE: IOWRO, Z/HO/5; Index of Baptisms, Marriages, and Burials

Edwards, William | *From*: Sutton, West Sussex | *To*: Nelson Twp? | 1833 ?

SOURCE: *No. 4 Continuation*, 30–1

Elliott, Elias | *From*: Sutton, West Sussex | *To*: Niagara area; 12 miles back from Fort George | *Occupation Can*: Farmer | 1832 | An Elias Elliott, labourer, age 56, is listed in the 1871 census for Louth Township lot 18, concession 4 (NA, RG 31, Canada Census, 1871 Louth Twp); his wife was Ann Maria, age 43 and their children were Richard age 17, Hannah 15, Elias 13, John 10, Robert E. 7, George 4. An Elias Elliott, age 64, born in Sussex, died in Louth Twp 20 Jul 1878 (AO, RG 80, death registration 7772 [1878]).

SOURCE: *Emigration: Letters* (1833), 26; WSRO, Goodwood Ms 1476, f278

Elliott, James | 48, b England (1851 census) | *Spouse*: Mary | 55, b England (1851 census) | *Children*: John 28, James 22 (b England); Caroline 16, Maria 14, Thomas 12, Mary Jane 10, Henry 8, George 6, Louisa 5 (all b Canada) (1851 census) | *To*: Adelaide Township | 1833 | About 19 years ago (date of statement not recorded), "Lord Egremont Settler" James Elliot applied for W 1/2 lot 11 con 9 Plympton Twp, name mistakenly entered as John Elliot; Elliot assigned claim to brother-in-law James Littleworth who assigned it to William Longley.

SOURCE: AO, RG 1, C-I-1, Crown Lands Petitions, Longley; C-IV, Adelaide Twp Papers; NA, RG 31, Canada Census, 1851 Adelaide Twp, p75

Elliott, Phoebe | probably bap 25 Dec 1815 Lyminster | *From*: Bury, West Sussex | 1833 | *Assistance*: Parish

SOURCE: WSRO, PAR 33/12/1, PAR 131/1/2/1

Elliott, T. | *Spouse*: family | *To*: Plympton Twp ? | 1833

SOURCE: WSRO, Goodwood Ms 1469, f16, Hale to Lord Egremont's Emigration Committee, 2 Jul 1833, copy

Elliott, Thomas | *From*: Bury, West Sussex | 1833 | *Assistance*: Parish

SOURCE: WSRO, PAR 33/12/1

Elliott, William. See Lelliot

Enticknap, George | bap 25 Jan 1818 | *From*: Fernhurst, West Sussex | Brother of **Thomas**. Seen by Caroline and John Dearling, Jul 1836.

SOURCE: *Continuation of Letters from Sussex Emigrants ... Written in 1836* [1837]; WSRO, PAR 82/1/1/5

Enticknap, Thomas | bap 11 Jan 1810 | *From*: Fernhurst, West Sussex | Brother of **George**. Seen by Caroline and John Dearling, Jul 1836.
SOURCE: *Continuation of Letters from Sussex Emigrants … Written in 1836* [1837]; WSRO, PAR 82/1/1/5

Evans, (Mrs) | *Children*: "Expects to be confined very soon" | *From*: Lodsworth, West Sussex | *To*: Galt or Hamilton ? | 1833
SOURCE: *No. 4 Continuation*

Evans, Charlotte (Tribe) | *bap 9 Jan 1803, daughter of Henry and Charlotte Tribe* | *Spouse: Joseph Neuroke Evans, m in Canada, d 2 Apr 1867 Blenheim Twp* | *Children b in Canada: Joseph Jr, Connell, Jane, Charlotte, Ann, Hannah, Mary* | *From: Lurgashall, West Sussex (near Petworth)* | *To: Waterloo ?; Joseph Evans was evidently from Ireland and had a militia/military grant Jul 1832 E 1/2 lot 8 con 6 Medonte Twp (OLRI).* | *Occupation Can: Farmer's wife* | *1832* | *Eveline* | *Joseph Evans's will, dated 18 Mar 1867, did not mention real estate; his estate was valued at $578.*
SOURCE: *Emigration: Letters (1833), 17–18;* WSRO, MP 3191, *"Tribe Tribe";* PAR 130/1/1/4; AO, RG 22-221, *Oxford Co Surrogate Court, file 261.*

Evans, David | *Spouse*: Ann Hilton, m in Canada, bap 5 Oct 1817 South Bersted | *Children*: daughter born in Canada 1835/36, Charles bap 9 Sep 1842 Delaware | *From*: Angmering, West Sussex | *To*: Delaware | *Occupation Can*: Farmer | 1832 | *Eveline* | Ann was daughter of Charles **Hilton**.
SOURCE: *Continuation of Letters from Sussex Emigrants … Written in 1836* [1837], 3–7; WSRO, PAR 19/1/2/1, Correspondent Jane Thompson; AO, Church Records Coll, Delaware, Ekfrid, and Carodoc, Anglican register 1834–51

Ewens, John | 16, bap 26 Nov 1820, son of Rachel | *From*: Walberton, West Sussex | *To*: Toronto | *Occupation Eng*: Agricultural labourer | 1836 | *Assistance*: Richard Prime and Parish
SOURCE: GB, Parl. Papers, *Select Committee … Poor Law Amendment Act … App. to 12th Report, 1837; Letters from Sussex Emigrants, 8–9;* WSRO, PAR 202/2/3

Fair. See also Thair

Fair (Thair?) | daughter of Ann Fair | John Denman: "Remember me to Ann Fair: her little girl is very well, and grown very much since she left England." Denman was from Billingshurst, West Sussex.
SOURCE: *Continuation of Letters from Sussex Emigrants … Written in 1836* [1837]

Fallick, Peter | 13, b c1823, bap 29 Mar 1837 before emigrating | *From*: Newport, Isle of Wight | 1837 | *Assistance*: Parish, House of Industry | A John Fallick had emigrated in 1831. Remarks on abstract of IOW emigrants: "Unprotected."
SOURCE: IOWRO, Z/HO/44; Index of Baptisms, Marriages, and Burials; WSRO, PHA 140

Farley, William | 18; bap 29 Nov 1807 | *From*: Felpham, West Sussex | *Occupation Eng*: Agricultural labourer; Had been a pauper boy. | 1835 | *Assistance*: Parish and Earl of Egremont
SOURCE: GB, Parl. Papers, *Select Committee … Poor Law Amendment Act … App. to 12th Report, 1837;* WSRO, PAR 81/2/1

Farre, B. | 19 | *To*: Brockville (left at Montreal for Brockville) | *Occupation Eng*: Gentleman | 1835
SOURCE: WSRO, PHA 142

Fleet, Francis | *Spouse*: Mary | *Children*: 4 children emigrated: Frank bap 26 Aug 1810 St Andrews, Chichester; Elizabeth bap 20 Apr 1812 St Peter the Less, Chichester; Hannah bap 2 Jun 1816 St Peter the Less, Chichester; Sarah bap 6 Dec 1823 (Presbyterian) | *From*:

Chichester, West Sussex (North Street) | *Occupation Eng*: Cabinetmaker | 1832 | *Assistance*: Liberal subscription raised by several of the respectable inhabitants; to "America."
SOURCE: *Brighton Guardian*, 21 Mar 1832; WSRO, PAR 37/1/1/5, PAR 45/1/1/3, PAR 45/1/2/1; PRO, RG4, 2728 (MF 678)

Fletcher, Luke | *Spouse*: Wife | 4 children | *From*: East Knoyle, Wiltshire | 1836 | *Assistance*: Parish, Henry Seymour, and Poor Law Commissioners
SOURCE: Wilts. RO, 536/23

Flux, William | 28, b 9 May 1804, bap 21 May 1804, illegitimate son of James | *From*: Whippingham, Isle of Wight | *Occupation Eng*: "Out of Employ" | 1834 | *Assistance*: Parish, House of Industry | Admitted to House of Industry 11 Nov 1833; discharged 16 Apr 1834 "to Canada."
SOURCE: IOWRO Z/HO/L5; Index of Baptisms, Marriages, and Burials

Ford (Foard), Michael | 18 | *Spouse*: Sarah **Wakeford**, m in Canada, d 1854 | *Children*: George b 1841 Goderich, Michael Jr | *From*: Lodsworth, West Sussex | *Occupation Eng*: Agricultural labourer | 1835 | *Assistance*: Parish and landowners | "At a special meeting held at the Parish Church on the 20 day of March 1835 the following resolutions were agreed to – that Michael Ford should be allowed £5 out of the Parish rates ... to Emigrate to Upper Canada and ... [his] passage over to be paid by the Landowners in the Parish ..." Sarah is buried with her parents James **Wackford** (Wakeford) and Elizabeth Nash in Woolwich Twp; 2 sons were living with Wakeford uncles in Woolwich Twp in 1851.
SOURCE: WSRO, PAR 128/12/2, PAR 128/13/1/2; PHA 142; Correspondent Roy Marvel

Ford, Charles | *Spouse*: Amelia Cooper "from Frightfold" | *From*: Kirdford, West Sussex | *To*: London District | *Occupation Can*: Butcher | 1832 or 1833
SOURCE: *No. 6 Continuation*, 46–7, Letter from William Baker, 3 Nov 1833

Ford, John | 26, bap 13 Oct 1805 | *Spouse*: Clara Olliver, m 6 Nov 1830 | *Children*: 2 children emigrated: Fanny bap 30 Oct 1831, Ann bap 23 Jun 1833 | *From*: Goring, West Sussex | *Occupation Eng*: "Farming man and gardener" | 1835 | *Assistance*: Landlords of the parish | "For employment and have place in view."
SOURCE: WSRO, PHA 142; PAR 92/1/2/1/, PAR 92/1/3/1/; PRO, MH 12, 12905

Forster, James | *From*: Dunsfold, Surrey | 1833 | *Assistance*: Vestry
SOURCE: SRO (GMR), PSH/DUN/8/2

French, George | bap 23 Sep 1810, d 15 Mar 1863 | *From*: Yapton, West Sussex | *To*: Albion, Illinois (at time of death) | 1832 | England ?
SOURCE: *West Sussex Gazette*, 7 Apr 1864; WSRO, PAR 225/1/1/3

Fry, George | 20 | *From*: Whippingham, Isle of Wight | *To*: Toronto ? | *Occupation Eng*: "no employ" | 1837 | *Assistance*: Parish, House of Industry | Admitted to House of Industry 20 Apr 1837 (also admitted Jul 1830); discharged 26 Apr 1837. A George Fry from the Isle of Wight died age 44 at Toronto 10 Apr 1861 and was buried 14 Apr at the Necropolis cemetery.
SOURCE: IOWRO, Z/HO/44, Z/HO/L4, Z/HO/L5

Gaiger, William | 20 | *From*: Newport, Isle of Wight | *Occupation Eng*: "no employ" | 1837 | *Assistance*: Parish, House of Industry | Admitted to House of Industry 20 Apr 1837; discharged 26 Apr 1837.
SOURCE: IOWRO, Z/HO/44; Z/HO/L5

Gamblen (Gamblin), John | *Spouse*: Ann | *Children*: son | *From*: Brighton, East Sussex | *To*: Blandford (town plot) | *Occupation Eng*: Painter, previously at sea for 12 years | *Occupation Can*: Painter and labourer | 1834 | *Assistance*: J.H. Puget, Brighton Provident and

District Society | Brydone wrote: "Gamblen is a decided radical."
SOURCE: Brydone *Narrative*; *Brighton Gazette*, 23 Apr 1835; WSRO, Goodwood Ms 1476, f277; PHA 139; AO, RG 1, C–IV, Township Papers, Town of Blandford

Gates | *From*: Lewes, East Sussex ? | *To*: Ancaster | *Occupation Eng*: Shoemaker | by 1834
SOURCE: Letter from Henry Harwood, *Sussex Advertiser*, 8 Sep 1834

Gates, James | bap 9 Mar 1806 | *From*: Goring, West Sussex | *Occupation Eng*: Agricultural labourer | 1836 | *Assistance*: Levi Bushby | Not brother of William but a relation. Both James Gates and Thomas Grinyer had returned to Goring by December 1836.
SOURCE: *Continuation of Letters from Sussex Emigrants ... Written in 1836* [1837], 23–4; PRO, MH 12, 12905; WSRO Index; PAR, 92/1/1/5; Goring Census, 1861; *Brighton Guardian*, Dec 1836

Gates, William | bap 4 Apr 1817 | *From*: Goring, West Sussex | *Occupation Can*: Apprentice to a carpenter | 1835/36 | *Assistance*: Landlords of the parish; Levi Bushby | Related but not brother of **James**.
SOURCE: *Continuation of Letters from Sussex Emigrants ... Written in 1836* [1837], 23–4; PRO, MH 12, 12905; WSRO, PAR 92/1/1/5

George, William | *Spouse*: Sarah Star, m 15 Oct 1809 St Peter the Great, Chichester, poss bap 21 Sep 1787 Heathfield Independent | *Children*: Charles* bap 21 May 1814; James bap 24 Apr 1816; Edmund bap 27 Mar 1818; Thomas bap 5 Jul 1820; Frank bap 9 Oct 1822; Rebecca bap 29 Oct 1824; Charles bap 13 Jun 1826; Alfred bap 13 Mar 1827 | *From*: Chichester, West Sussex | *To*: Plympton Twp ? | *Occupation Eng*: Labourer/gardener | 1833 | *Assistance*: Guardians of the Poor £30; J.D. Newland and Mr Mason bookseller paid £45 – total of £75.
SOURCE: WSRO, Goodwood Ms 1469, f16, Hale to Lord Egremont's Emigration Committee, 2 Jul 1833, copy; *Portsmouth, Portsea and Gosport Herald*, 21 Apr 1833; WSRO, PAR 44/1/1/8, PAR 44/1/2/1

Goatcher (Goacher), Stephen | *Spouse*: Elizabeth Burchill, m 28 Oct 1806 Pulborough by licence | *From*: Pulborough, West Sussex (Nash Farm) | *To*: Adelaide Twp; by 17 Jan 1833 he is operating a dairy farm in Adelaide Twp near town of Adelaide, 14 acres cleared | *Occupation Eng*: Farmer | 1832 | Eveline | Superintendant of the party on the Eveline. His wife remained in England; apparently no children. He returned to England, possibly in 1833, and was in Pulborough in 1839.
SOURCE: *Emigration: Letters* (1833), 3–4; WSRO, Goodwood Ms 1465, f18; PAR 153/1/1/3; TDW/99

Goble, George | 54, bap 20 Feb 1780 | *Spouse*: Clara Chalcraft, m 16 Sep 1818 Upwaltham, 43, bap 5 Mar 1797 | *Children*: 4 children emigrated: Charles 13; Frederick 9; William 4; Joseph 2, bap 25 May 1834 | *From*: Tillington, West Sussex | *To*: Amherstburg 1838 | *Occupation Eng*: Soldier | 1836 | *Assistance*: Earl of Egremont and parish | In his army record he was described as "5' 7½" height, hair, brown, eyes, grey, complexion, fair" and "a very good soldier." He was removed as a pauper from Graffham/Woolavington to Tillington, 19 Feb 1829, with Clara his wife, children Charles and Fred; also removed from Lodsworth to Tillington 19 Dec 1833. Clara Chalcraft is a cousin of Matthew **Chalcraft**.
SOURCE: PRO, CO 385/10, 17, Pinnock to Sockett, 22 Mar 1836; CO 384/550, ff191–2, Letter from James Cooper, 26 May 1838; WO 97/523; WSRO, PAR 197/1/1/4, PAR 197/1/2/1, PAR 197/12/1, PAR 197/31/5, PAR 197/32/3/1, PAR 201/1/3/1

Goddard, John | bap 8 Mar 1807 | *From*: Angmering, West Sussex | 1832 | *Assistance*: Parish and Miss Susan Loud | According to *Portsmouth, Portsea and Gosport Herald* the people from Angmering went with PEC.
SOURCE: WSRO, PAR 6/1/1/3, PAR 6/12/1

Goddard, Robert | *Spouse*: Elizabeth Clements, m 16 Mar 1832 | *From*: Angmering, West Sussex | 1832 | *Assistance*: Parish and Miss Susan Loud
SOURCE: WSRO, PAR 6/1/3/1, PAR 6/12/1

Goldring, Henry | bap 18 Sep 1791 | *Spouse*: Mary Ann Rayner, m 8 Nov 1819, bur 28 Mar 1838 | *Children*: 4 children emigrated: Eleanor bap 25 Dec 1823, Samuel bap 18 Dec 1825, Emma bap 21 Dec 1828, Caroline bap 28 Aug 1831, George b c 1835 Toronto Twp (m Jessie Manson 1 July 1858) | *From*: South Bersted, West Sussex | *To*: Etobicoke Twp | *Occupation Eng*: Labourer | 1832 | England ? | *Assistance*: Parish | Brother of **James**.
SOURCE: *No. 3 Continuation*, 17–18; WSRO, PAR 19/1/1/5, PAR 19/1/2/1; AO, Church Records Coll., Mimico, Christchurch Anglican; RG 80-27-2, Toronto City marriage registers, vol 66, p12

Goldring, James | bap 26 Oct 1783 | *Spouse*: Sarah Pratt, m 20 May 1809 | *Children*: James S. bap 1 Apr 1810, d 21 Jan 1885 in gaol, committed there as a lunatic in May 1884; William bap 19 Apr 1812; Frances bap 19 Mar 1817; Eleanor bap 19 Aug 1821; Michael bap 9 Nov 1823; George bap 2 Oct 1825; Edward bap 1 Jun 1828 | *From*: South Bersted, West Sussex | *To*: Etobicoke Twp | *Occupation Eng*: Labourer | 1832 | *Assistance*: Parish | Brother of **Henry**.
SOURCE: WSRO, PAR 19/1/1/4, PAR 19/1/1/5, PAR 19/1/2/1; NA, RG 31, Canada Census, 1851 Etobicoke Twp, p5; *Toronto Mail*, 22, 23 Jan 1885

Goldring, James S. | *23, bap 1 Apr 1810* | *From: South Bersted, West Sussex* | *To: Etobicoke Twp* | *Occupation Can: "hired out for one year, for £20"; probably became a sailor* | *1832* | *Assistance: Parish* | *Son of James; either he or his father fined for smuggling (WSRO Add. Ms. 1476).*
SOURCE: *No. 3 Continuation*, 17–18; WSRO, *Misc. Paper 1705*; PAR 19/1/1/4

Goldring, William | *bap 19 Apr 1812, d 12 Apr 1891 Toronto* | *Children: William James, John Henry, Edmund, Richard, Charles, Francis, Fannie Jane, Harriett, Sarah, stepson George Henry Goldring* | *From: South Bersted, West Sussex* | *To: Etobicoke Twp, later Toronto* | *Occupation Can: Shoemaker, fisherman, later shipowner and wharfinger in Toronto* | *1832* | *Son of James. He was listed as a widower in the 1851 census, apparently married at least twice and his children were listed in his will; his estate was valued at $5600.*
SOURCE: *No. 3 Continuation*, 17–18; WSRO, *Misc. Paper 1705*; PAR 19/1/1/4; AO, RG 22/305, York County Surrogate Court, file 8414; NA, RG 31, Canada Census, 1851 Etobicoke Twp, pp7, 13; *Toronto Mail*, 13 Apr 1891

Golds, George | 37, bap 8 Apr 1798 West Grinstead | *Spouse*: Elizabeth Hobden, m 17 Aug 1828 Ditchling | *Children*: 3 children emigrated: Marianne bap 25 Jan 1829 Streat, East Sussex; George bap 13 Feb 1831 Ashington; Thomas bap 29 Sep 1833 Shipley | *From*: Shipley, West Sussex | *Occupation Eng*: Farming man | 1835 | *Assistance*: Probably Sir Charles Burrell. | "For employment. A quiet man & wife."
SOURCE: PRO, MH 12, 12989; ESRO, PAR 488/1/2/1; WSRO, PHA 142; PAR 9/1/2/1, PAR 95/1/1/4, PAR 168/1/2/1; Correspondent R.A. Golds

Grace, William | b 8 Nov 1812; "base-born" son of Mary Grace | *From*: Chicklade, Wiltshire | 1833 | *Assistance*: Parish
SOURCE: Wilts. RO, 1730/16; Chicklade Parish Register 1781–1812

Grafenstein (Graefenstine), Adolphus | "young" | *From*: Brighton, East Sussex, Workhouse | *Occupation Eng*: Porter, Brighton Town Hall | 1834 | *Assistance*: Hyam Lewis and James Collins, Earl of Chichester, Parish, Brighton Emigration Committee and possibly the Jewish community | All the evidence suggests it was Grafenstein who waylaid the Earl of Chichester at the Town Hall and asked him to intercede on his, Grafenstein's, behalf as

he had been struck off the list of prospective emigrants as a single man.
SOURCE: *Brighton Gazette*, 17 Apr 1834; *Brighton Herald*, 19 Apr 1834; Brydone, *Narrative*; WSRO, PHA 139

Graffam (Grantham), John | *Spouse*: Meliora (Milly) "Mille" Boulton, m 30 Jan 1810 Cranleigh, Surrey | *Children*: 3 children emigrated: Meliora b 22 Feb 1819, bap 21 Mar 1819; Charles bap 24 Feb 1822; William bap 4 Jul 1824 | *From*: Wisborough Green, West Sussex | (Loxwood) | *To*: Nelsonville, Ohio | *Occupation Eng*: Labourer | 1832 | England | *Assistance*: Parish and landowners
SOURCE: *Courtauld Family Letters* I: xxi; WSRO, PAR 210/1/2/1, PAR 210/37/11(3)

Green, William | b c1796 Whitchurch, Shropshire | *Spouse*: Mary Ann | *Children*: 3 children emigrated: 2 sons and 1 daughter; Mary Ann bap 20 Mar 1836 Woodstock | *From*: Pulborough, West Sussex | *To*: Blandford (town plot) | *Occupation Eng*: Whitesmith (tinsmith), colour sergeant 36th Regiment of Foot | *Occupation Can*: soldier 1837-9 | 1834 | *Assistance*: Parish and Earl of Egremont | Listed among names of paupers receiving parochial relief in Pulborough, Mar 1833-34. Noted as sent to Canada; had £42.5s.6d relief. Received a 200-acre military grant in Enniskillen Twp (lot 14 con 2).
SOURCE: Brydone, *Narrative*, 58, 63 (extract of letter from Green, 20 Oct 1834); PRO, MH 12, 13128; WSRO, PAR 153/12/3; NA, RG 1, L3, Upper Canada Land Petitions, vol 211a, G18/145; vol 213, G21/18; vol 214, G22/10; Oxford Co., Woodstock, Old St Pauls Anglican Registers

Grevatt, William | bap 8 Jan 1797 | *Spouse*: Jemima Steer*, m 30 Mar 1822, bap 20 Apr 1802, bur 9 Feb 1832 | *Children*: James* bap 1828, bur 5 Nov 1828; Eliza bap 21 Aug 1830 | *From*: Angmering, West Sussex | *Occupation Eng*: Agricultural labourer | 1832 | *Assistance*: Parish and Miss Susan Loud
SOURCE: WSRO, PAR 6/1/5/1, PAR 6/12/1

Grinyer (Greenyer), Thomas | bap 19 Jan 1817 Broadwater | *Occupation Eng*: Agricultural labourer | *From*: Goring West Sussex | 1836 | He and James Gates had returned to Goring by Dec 1836.
SOURCE: *Continuation of Letters from Sussex Emigrants ... Written in 1836* [1837], 23-4; WSRO, Goring Census 1861; PAR 29/1/2/1; *Brighton Guardian*, Dec 1836

Groggin (Gogger), Henry | *From*: Lurgashall, West Sussex | 1832 | Died of cholera in 1832
SOURCE: Capling, "The Capling Family"; *Emigration: Letters* (1833)

Habbin, Henry | 19 | *From*: Petworth, West Sussex | 1833 | *Assistance*: Earl of Egremont | Had applied to Duke of Richmond for position in Post Office – refused Mar 1833.
SOURCE: *Brighton Guardian*, 16 Oct 1833; *No. 5 Continuation*; WSRO, Goodwood Ms 155: f.80

Hacker, Thomas | *Spouse*: Wife | *Children*: 4 children under 14 | 1832 | *Assistance*: 4 passages
SOURCE: WSRO, PHA 137

Haines, Charles | bap 14 Apr 1811 Findon | *From*: Ashington, West Sussex (Frenchland) | 1832 | *Assistance*: Mr Hampton
SOURCE: *No. 2 Continuation*; WSRO, PAR 84/1/1/5

Hale (Hall), Frances (Francis) | b 8 May, bap 19 Jul 1799 Petworth | Single woman | *From*: Tillington, West Sussex | *To*: York (Toronto) | 1832 | *Assistance*: Parish and Earl of Egremont | Had 10s. for clothes from parish in 1830.
SOURCE: *No. 5 Continuation*, 34; WSRO, PAR 149/1/1/2, PAR 197/12/1

Hall, James | *Occupation Can*: shingle making, teaching | *From*: Singleton, West Sussex | *To*: Galt, Dumfriens Twp, Gore District | Mentioned by James Rapson in 1836 as still living at George Thair's; had returned to Singleton area by 1839.
SOURCE: *Continuation of Letters from Sussex Emigrants … Written in 1836* [1837], 10-11; WSRO, PHA 1068, letter of W. Phillips of Singleton

Hall, John | *Spouse*: Wife | *Children*: 13 children [all under 14] | *Occupation Eng*: Agricultural labourer | 1837 | *Assistance*: 8.5 passages | Remarks on abstract of PEC emigrants: "Most respectable family."
SOURCE: WSRO, PHA 140

Hambleton (Hamilton), James | 24, b 27 Jan 1812, bap 8 Mar 1812 | *Spouse*: single | *From*: Tillington, West Sussex | *Occupation Eng*: Agricultural labourer | 1836 | *Assistance*: Earl of Egremont and parish | Earl of Egremont and Parish; had been on poor relief | Brother to Emily (Emma) and to William, who emigrated in 1844.
SOURCE: WSRO, PAR 197/12/1, PAR 197/31/5

Hammond, C. | 55 | *Spouse*: – Overdean? | *Children*: 2 sons of 18 and 15 plus 6 other children | *From*: Bath, Somerset | *To*: Cobourg ? | *Occupation Eng*: Lieutenant, Royal Navy | 1835 | *Assistance*: Miss Mitford | Mrs Hammond's mother, Mrs **Overdean** (58 years old) was with them. "Mr H–" described as "poor blind man"; Mrs H as "healthy cheerful and active"; Mrs H's mother as "sensible woman." Maria **Parker**, their maid, emigrated with them.
SOURCE: WSRO, PHA 142; Letter from Sockett to Brydone [1835], in possession of Barbara Brydone Calder

Hammond, Edward | poss bap Apr 1809, illegitimate son of Henrietta | Single | *From*: Hellingly, East Sussex | *To*: Oakville | *Occupation Eng*: Labourer on parish relief | 1834 | *Assistance*: Assisted by parish, Earl of Chichester, and Thomas Calverley
SOURCE: Brydone, *Narrative*, 26; ESRO, PAR 375/12/5, PAR 375/31/2/5, PAR 375/31/2/7

Hammond, Henry | Possibly bap Aug 1815, illegitimate son of Harriet | Single | *From*: Hellingly, East Sussex | *To*: Oakville | *Occupation Eng*: Labourer on parish relief | 1834 | *Assistance*: Parish, Earl of Chichester, Thomas Calverley | Brydone reported that the 2 Hammonds "found employment" at Oakville, one at 40s./mo. and one at 50s./mo. with board and lodging. A Henry Hammond, sailor, was boarding with shoemaker John Ray in 1851.
SOURCE: Brydone, *Narrative*, 26; ESRO, PAR 375/12/5, PAR 375/31/2/6, PAR 375/31/2/7; NA, RG 31, Canada Census, 1851 Trafalgar Twp, p33

Handsfield, Thomas | b c1796, bur Mohawk Chapel churchyard, Brantford Twp | *Spouse*: Elizabeth Hills, m 12 Apr 1819 Goring, West Sussex, bur Mohawk Chapel churchyard | *Children*: Thomas bap 18 Sep 1825, Levi bap 15 Jan 1832, Ann bap 2 Aug 1835 | *From*: Goring, West Sussex | *To*: Duffs Corner, Ancaster; Brantford Twp about 1835 | *Occupation Eng*: Labourer | *Occupation Can*: Farm labourer | 1836 | *Assistance*: Probably Levi Bushby | Elizabeth was a sister of George **Hills**; Brother of William **Handsfield** and probably of Ann (Hansfield) **Miles**. Thomas served as sergeant in Ancaster militia in 1837.
SOURCE: WSRO, PAR 92/1/2/1, PAR 92 1/3/1; *Brantford Expositor*, articles by Jean Waldie, 19 Nov 1948, 12 Jan 1949; Correspondent Mary H. Knox

Handsfield, William | b c1801 | *Spouse*: Wife | *From*: Goring, West Sussex | *To*: Brantford | 1836 ? | *Assistance*: Possibly Levi Bushby | Brother of **Thomas** and probably of Ann (Hansfield) **Miles**.
SOURCE: WSRO, PAR 92/1/2/1, PAR 92 1/3/1

Handy, Richard | *Spouse*: Wife | *Children*: 2 children | *Occupation Eng*: Labourer | 1837 | *Assistance*: 3 passages
SOURCE: WSRO, PHA 140

Hard, William | *Occupation Eng*: Shoemaker | 1837 | *Assistance*: 1 passage | "Most respectable"
SOURCE: WSRO, PHA 140

Harper, James | b 25 Jan 1798, bap 11 Feb 1798 Ewhurst, Surrey; d 30 May 1877 East Flamborough Twp | *Spouse*: Sarah Redman | b 7 Feb 1801, d 8 May 1856 | *Children*: George b 19 Jul 1829 bap 13 Sept 1829, d 8 Jan 1904 (m Elizabeth English or Livingston); James b 19 Sep 1830 bap 16 Dec 1830, d 7 Dec l870 (m Mary Carson) (George and James bap Independent West St Chapel, Dorking); b in Canada: John Layers b 21 Jun 1833, d 21 Apr 1901 (m Christina McBeth); Lucy b 11 Oct 1835, d 16 Jun 1916 (m John Laking); William Joseph b 21 Jan 1838, d 20 Sep 1866; John Charles b 8 Aug 1840, d 17 Feb 1927 (m Elizabeth Worthington) | Congregational in England, Methodist in Canada | *From*: Dorking, Surrey | *To*: East Flamborough Twp, lot 13 range 8 | *Occupation Can*: Farmer | 1832
SOURCE: *Letters from Dorking*, 19, 35; Waterdown East Flamborough Heritage Soc. files

Harwood, Henry Sr | bap 16 Jun 1791 Rodmell, d 1879 Ingersoll | *Spouse*: (1) Sarah Wise*, m 8 Aug 1810 Iford, d 1818; (2) Sarah Holden, m 30 Jul 1842 in Canada | *Children*: William bap 16 Mar 1811, Henry bap 18 Apr 1813, Alfred bap 2 Apr 1815 (m Mary **West** 3 Oct 1839), Richard bap 7 Jun 1818 (all bap in Lewes); b in Canada: Sarah bap 20 Apr 1843, Rhoda b 4 May 1845, John bap 11 Aug 1847, Abraham b Oct 1852, Soffiah b 1859, Emily b 1863 | *From*: Lewes, East Sussex | *To*: Blandford, Oxford Co | *Occupation Eng*: Shoemaker | *Occupation Can*: Shoemaker | 1834 | *Assistance*: Mr Hurly (Lewes banker) and Mr Rogers
SOURCE: *Sussex Advertiser*, 8 Sep 1834; AO, RG 1, C–IV, Township Papers, Town of Blandford; John H. Harwood, Bett Harwood, and Stuart Harwood, *Harwood History* (privately printed, n.p. 1979); ESRO, PAR 403/1/1/3, PAR 412/1/2/1, PAR 413/1/2/1, PAR 414/1/2/1; AO, Oxford Co., Woodstock, Old St Pauls Anglican Registers; NA, RG 31, Canada Census, 1851 Woodstock, p57

*Harwood, Henry Jr | bap 18 Apr 1813, d 30 Nov 1885 | Spouse: (1) Lucy **Coleman**, m 11 Oct 1834 Woodstock, bap 1813, d 1852; (2) Ann Weber, m 9 Dec 1854 | Children: Henry b 12 Jul 1835 bap 1 May 1836, George b 16 Apr 1837 bap 24 May 1837, Sarah bap 3 Mar 1839, Jane b 1841, Mary b 1843, Richard b 1845, Frederick b 1847, James b 1848 (Lucy's children); Lucy Ann, Wellington Albert, Frank, Emma, Gertrude (Ann's children) | bur Baptist Church, East Zorra | From: Lewes, East Sussex | To: East Zorra (lot 25 con 11, 12th line) | Occupation Can: Brickmaker | 1834 | Assistance: Mr Hurley (Lewes banker) and Mr Rogers | Son of Henry Harwood*
SOURCE: John H. Harwood, Bett Harwood, and Stuart Harwood, Harwood History (privately printed, n.p. 1979); Sussex Advertiser, 8 Sep 1834; ESRO, PAR 414/1/2/1; AO, Oxford Co., Woodstock, Old St Pauls Anglican Registers; NA, RG 31, Canada Census, 1851 East Zorra Twp, p33; RG 22/221, Oxford Co. Surrogate Court, file 1524

Harwood, Philip | 33 | *From*: Yapton, West Sussex | *Occupation Eng*: Agricultural labourer | 1835 | *Assistance*: Richard Prime and parish
SOURCE: GB, Parl. Papers, *Select Committee ... Poor Law Amendment Act ...* App. to 12th Report, 1837

Haslett, William | bap 5 Mar 1819 | *From*: Petworth, West Sussex | *Occupation Eng*: Shoemaker | 1836 (or 1842 to New York) | Heber | *Assistance*: Earl of Egremont, parish, and Poor Law Commission | Brother of Frederick, Peter, Ann, Rachel, Jesse, Benjamin, and

John who emigrated c1844 and in 1850.

SOURCE: PRO, MH 12, 13060; WSRO, PAR 149/1/2/1; Correspondent Alfred Haslett

Haslett (Hastlett), William | b Sep 1808, d c1832 | Single | *From*: Kirdford, West Sussex | *Occupation Eng*: Labourer | 1832 | *Assistance*: Earl of Egremont | He was removed from Witley, Surrey, aged 5 weeks with his parents John & Elizabeth Haslett, 1 sister, Elisabeth, aged 3, & another, Mary, aged 1; sent back to Kirdford under Poor Law Settlement law, 22 Oct 1808. He died shortly after arrival in Canada, presumably of cholera.

SOURCE: *Emigration: Letters* (1833), 31–2; WSRO, Misc. Paper 1031; PAR 116/32/3, Removal orders to Kirdford 1715–1866

Hasted, Frederick | bap 11 Nov 1793 Arundel, d 1868 Sarnia | *Children*: 1 daughter born in UK [Mary Ann] (m William Holden) | Protestant in Canada | *From*: Arundel, West Sussex | *To*: Adelaide Twp, London Dist. | *Occupation Eng*: Hawker | 1833 | Had a varied career in Upper Canada and the USA; did not emigrate on a PEC ship.

SOURCE: *Letters from Emigrants* (1839), 2–5; Letter from James Cooper et al., *Brighton Herald*, 25 Aug 1838; AO, Pamphlet 1839 10; RG 22/273, Lambton Co Surrogate Court, file 166

Hatton, William | 24, bap 23 May 1813 | *Spouse*: Ann Salter, m 18 Mar 1833 Newport | 23 | *Children*: 2 children emigrated: William 4; Edith 1 | *From*: Newport, Isle of Wight | *Occupation Eng*: Agricultural labourer; "no employ" | 1837 | *Assistance*: Parish, House of Industry, 3 passages | Admitted to House of Industry, IOW, 21 Apr 1837; discharged 26 Apr 1837. Remarks on abstract of IOW emigrants: "Respectable."

SOURCE: IOWRO, Z/HO/44; Z/HO/L5; Index of Baptisms, Marriages, and Burials; WSRO, PHA 140

Hawkins, Charles | *From*: Pulborough, West Sussex ? | *To*: York, then Warwick Twp | 1832

SOURCE: Letter from James and Amy Parker, *No. 5 Continuation*, 38–40

Hayles (Hayless), Robert | 29, bap 15 Mar 1807 | *Spouse*: Jane Towell Hooper, m 27 Sep 1830 Newchurch | 32 | *Children*: 2 children emigrated: Theresa 5; Mary-Ann, bap Jan /Feb 1837 House of Industry | *From*: Newport, Isle of Wight | *Occupation Eng*: Tailor | 1837 | *Assistance*: Parish, House of Industry 2.5 passages | Remarks on abstract of IOW emigrants: "Dissipated."

SOURCE: IOWRO, Z/HO/44; Z/HO/L5; Index of Baptisms, Marriages, and Burials; WSRO, PHA 140

Heasman, Henry | bap 22 Jun 1814 | *From*: West Grinstead, West Sussex | *To*: Blandford | *Occupation Can*: Apprenticed to Mr Jones, blacksmith | 1834 | *Assistance*: Rev. W.P. Woodward

SOURCE: Brydone, *Narrative*, 55; WSRO, PAR 95/1/2/1; Letter from Henry Heasman, 19 Oct 1834, PRO, CO 384/39

Heather, George | b 6 Dec 1813, bap 8 Jan 1814 | *From*: Petworth, West Sussex | *To*: Eramosa | *Occupation Can*: Yeoman | 1832 | *Assistance*: Earl of Egremont

SOURCE: WSRO, PAR 149/1/1/2, PAR 149/1/2/1; *No. 4 Continuation*, 30–32; Letter from W. Baker, *No. 6 Continuation*, 46–475

Heather, John | *From*: Petworth, West Sussex | Mentioned in letter from James Rapson. Heather had a sister at Redhill.

SOURCE: *Continuation of Letters from Sussex Emigrants …Written in 1836* [1837], 82–3

Helyer (Hillier, Hilyer, Hillyer), James Sr | *Spouse*: Charlotte Goble, m 24 Dec 1808 Easebourne, bap 9 Dec 1787 Heyshott | *Children*: Ann bap 25 Nov 1812, **James** bap 3 Dec 1815, Eliza bap 19 Feb 1817, Jane bap 20 Jun 1819, Benjamin bap 25 Mar 1821, Elizabeth bap 2 Mar 1823, Henry bap 20 Mar 1825, Thomas bap 3 Dec 1826 | *From*: Haslemere,

Surrey | *To*: Toronto Twp near York | *Occupation Eng*: Labourer | 1833 | James Jr emigrated in 1832; his father was advertising for his whereabouts in 1833.
SOURCE: Letter from James Helyer, 29 Sep 1833, *No. 6 Continuation*, 43–4; SRO (GMR), PSH/HME 1/6, PSH/HME/3/1; WSRO, PAR 75/1/1/9, PAR 101/1/1/3

Helyer (Hillier), James Jr | bap 3 Dec 1815 | *From*: Haslemere, Surrey | *Occupation Eng*: Labourer | 1832 | *Assistance*: Peter Scovell, Kings Arms, Haslemere | Son of James **Helyer** Sr
SOURCE: WSRO, PHA 137, 28 May 1990); SRO (GMR), PSH/HME/3/1

Helyer (Hillier, Hilyer), John | poss bap 26 Sep 1813 Haslemere | *From*: Haslemere, Surrey | *Occupation Eng*: Labourer | 1832 | *Assistance*: Peter Scovell, Kings Arms, Haslemere | Drowned at Quebec.
SOURCE: *Portsmouth, Portsea and Gosport Herald and Chichester Reporter*, 22 Jul 1832; WSRO PHA 137, 28 May 1832; SRO (GMR), PSH/HME/3/1

Heming (Hemming), Edward Francis | b 28 Mar 1810, bap 9 Apr 1810 St Peter the Less, Chichester, d 19 Aug 1892 Bognor, England | *Spouse*: Eliza Sarah Jones, m 1 Nov 1832 Guelph | *Children b in Canada*: George Edward bap 4 Jan 1835; Charles Henry bap 22 Sep 1839; Howard Payne bap 6 Jul 1841, d 1911; Walter John bap 6 Jul 1843, d 1913; Edward Francis bap 1 Mar 1846, d 1867; Anna Marie bap 5 Nov 1848, d 1926 Petersfield Hants; Thomas Long b Sep 1850, d Jan 1854; all bap by Rev Palmer of St George's, Guelph | *From*: Bognor, West Sussex | *To*: Guelph Twp | Eramosa Road, 2½ miles from Guelph | Bought land Guelph Twp, Wellington Co., lots 3/VII, 4/VII, 8/VII, 10/XI, 8/VI, Division C | *Occupation Eng*: Gentleman farmer | *Occupation Can*: Gentleman farmer | 1832 | *Assistance*: Letter of recommendation from Dr Laird, a physician of Bognor, and Charles Murray, Egremont's steward | Son of Canon George Francis Hemming of Chichester and Anna Maria Payne. Said to have had a "well grounded Farmer's education" and some capital to invest. Cabin passenger. By 1851 he was a widower, back in England, at Stedham, West Sussex, with at least two of his chilren, Edward and Anna.
SOURCE: WSRO, MF 55 census for Stedham 1851; STM 19, PHA 137, PHA 9600, Brydone *Narrative*; *Emigration: Letters* (1833), 4–5, 30; AO, MU 1717, Mary Leslie Papers, George Sockett Business Papers, Accounts; *Historical Atlas of Wellington County* (1906); Guelph, St Georges Anglican Registers; Correspondents Richard Holt, Dennis Ruhl

Hendy, Richard | 24, b Titchfield, Hants. | *Spouse*: Charlotte Groves, m 8 Jul 1832 Brighstone, IOW, 23, bap 24 Apr 1814 | *Children*: 2 children emigrated: Richard 2 3/4, bap 17 Nov 1833; James 1 | *From*: Little Chessel, Isle of Wight | *Occupation Eng*: Agricultural labourer: at work "on the Cross Roads," on parish relief 1834 | 1837 | *Assistance*: Parish, House of Industry | Discharged from House of Industry, IOW, 26 Apr 1837. Remarks on abstract of IOW emigrants: "Respectable."
SOURCE: IOWRO, Z/HO/44; Z/HO/L5; Z/HO/L7; Index of Baptisms, Marriages, and Burials; WSRO, PHA 140

Hersee, C. | 31 | *Spouse*: Wife | *Children*: 5 children emigrated | *From*: Wisborough Green, West Sussex | *To*: Toronto | *Occupation Eng*: Wheelwright and farmer | 1835 | A Hersee family seems to have been in financial trouble in 1813/1814 when Mr Tyler, Egremont's steward, wrote to them giving a warning of distraining their goods for debt. Travelling with them were 17-year-old Jane **Turner**, a maid, 18-year-old Harriet, sister of Mr Hersee, and 13-year-old Edward **Knott**, an apprentice to Mr Hersee. A William Hersee, b in Sussex, d in Blenheim Twp 26 Feb 1871, age 67.
SOURCE: WSRO, PHA 142; PHA 2682; *Canada Christian Advocate*, 8 Mar 1871

Hetzel, William | *From*: Haslemere, Surrey | *To*: Toronto Twp ? | 1833 ?
SOURCE: Mentioned in letter from James Helyer, *No. 6 Continuation*, 43–4

Hewitt, William | 21; d 26 Dec 1866 Blandford Twp | *Spouse*: Sarah Burdett, m in Canada | *Children b in Canada*: Mary Ann, Elizabeth, Margaret, Augusta, William Henry, James Albert | *From*: Cocking, West Sussex | *To*: Blandford Twp, Oxford Co | *Occupation Eng*: Agricultural labourer | *Occupation Can*: Farm labourer; "hired for 5 months at $10 per month, board and lodging ..." | 1836 | *Assistance*: Charles Caplen, linen draper of Midhurst | Estate valued at $500.
SOURCE: *Continuation of Letters from Sussex Emigrants ... Written in 1836* [1837], 11–12; Letter from James Cooper, May 1838, *Brighton Herald*, 25 Aug 1838; PRO, MH 12, 13029; WSRO, PAR 53/1/2/1; AO, RG 22/221, Oxford Co Surrogate Court, file 241; NA, RG 31, Canada Census, 1851 Blandford Twp, p51

Hide, George | bap 18 Jul 1819 | *From*: Goring, West Sussex | *To*: He lives 25 miles away from Brantford | *Occupation Can*: "has a good place" | 1835/6 | *Assistance*: Landlords of the parish, Levi Bushby
SOURCE: *Continuation of Letters from Sussex Emigrants ... Written in 1836* [1837], 23–4; WSRO Index; PAR 92/1/1/5; PRO, MH 12, 12905

Hill. See also Hills

Hill, Charles | 30 | *From*: Northchapel, West Sussex | *Occupation Eng*: Agricultural labourer | 1832 ? | *Assistance*: Earl of Egremont
SOURCE: WSRO, PHA 110; PHA 137

Hill, Samuel Jr | 40, bap 27 Sep 1793 | Single | *From*: Dorking, Surrey | *Occupation Eng*: Labourer | 1832 | *Assistance*: Dorking Emigration Society
SOURCE: *Letters from Dorking*; SRO (GMR), PSH/DOM/1/7

Hillier. See Helyer

Hillman, Ellis | 17, b 4 Feb 1817, bap 16 Mar 1817, d 15 May 1909 Leamington | *Spouse*: Elizabeth Abbott, m 16 Nov 1841 in Canada, b 2 Feb 1822, d 22 Dec 1892 | *Children*: b in Canada: Thomas b 18 Oct 1841, Esther b 24 Feb 1844, Jonas b 27 Mar 1845, David b 6 Oct 1846, Peter b 23 Mar 1848, Mary b 26 May 1849, William b 19 Dec 1850, Abigail b 15 Dec 1852, Oliver b 5 Nov 1854, Lucinda b 9 Oct 1856, Ellis Jr b 10 Oct 1856 [sic], Ezra b 3 Oct 1860, Robert Lambert b 22 Oct 1862, George Amos b 30 Sep 1863 | Methodist preacher in Canada after 1841 | *From*: Wiston, West Sussex (Yew Tree House) | *To*: Essex Co, W ½ lot 18 con 2 Mersea Twp | 1834
SOURCE: WSRO, PAR 211/1/2/1; MF 495; Correspondents Agnes M. Kelcher, Gerry Hillman

Hills, George | *Spouse*: Ann Charman, m 20 Jul 1818 | *Children*: 6 children emigrated: Jane 12, bap 5 Sep 1819; George 10, bap 14 Oct 1821; Caroline bap 28 Sep 1823; John bap 1 Jan 1826; Ann bap 27 Jan 1828; Henry bap 7 Feb 1830 (all bap Warminghurst (Heath Common)); William b 15 Jul 1833 Ancaster | *From*: Sullington, West Sussex | *To*: Ancaster | *Occupation Eng*: Labourer | *Occupation Can*: Farm labourer | 1832 | Eveline | *Assistance*: Mr Hampton and Mr Gibson
SOURCE: *Emigration: Letters* (1833), 10–11; *No. 2 Continuation*, 13–14; WSRO, Goodwood Ms 1460, f36; WSRO, PAR 31/30/1, PAR 190/1/3/1, PAR 217/1/2/1; C. Pinch, *Anglicanism in Ancaster, 1790-1830* (Ancaster Hist. Soc. 1979)

Hills, George | *Spouse*: Mary Ann Ewens, m 13 Aug 1817 Arundel, bap 19 Mar 1792 Arundel | *Children*: 6 children emigrated: Lucy bap 1 Mar 1818; Eleanor bap 2 Sep 1821; Esther bap 17 Apr 1825; Emma bap 13 Jan 1828; Charles bap 26 Sep 1830; Mary Ann bap 12 May 1833 | *From*: Burpham, West Sussex (Great Peppering Farm) | *To*: Findon Place, West Flamborough, Upper Canada (near Dundas) | *Occupation Eng*: Farm labourer | 1836 | *Assis-*

tance: John and Frances Drewitt, tenant farmers of the Duke of Norfolk

SOURCE: *Continuation of Letters from Sussex Emigrants …Written in 1836* [1837], 17–18; WSRO, PAR 8/1/3/1, PAR 31/1/2/1

Hills, Hugh | 38 | *Spouse*: Sarah | *Children*: 7 children emigrated: Martha bap 26 Apr 1818; William bap 4 Apr 1820; Mary Ann bap 3 Mar 1822; James; Mary bap 3 Oct 1830; George bap 14 Apr 1832; Edward Hugh bap 7 Sep 1834 | *From*: Climping, West Sussex | *Occupation Eng*: Farming man and seaman | 1835 | *Assistance*: Parish; H. Hills was having regular parish assistance from Dec 1816 to 23 Apr 1835 (the last entry): "Pd for emigration" £14.11.6 | Described as "hard-working man, for employment; temper violent."

SOURCE: WSRO, PHA 142; PAR 51/1/2/1/, PAR 51/31/2

Hills, Thomas | 41, bap 17 Feb 1793 | *Spouse*: Ruth Irish, m 22 Jul 1816 | 40, bap 8 May 1796 | *Children*: 3 children emigrated; Frank bap 8 Dec 1816; Thomas bap 25 Feb 1826; Mary Ann bap 31 Jul 1819 | *From*: Felpham, West Sussex | *Occupation Eng*: Farming man; had been a pauper boy. | *Occupation Can*: For employment | 1835 | *Assistance*: Parish and Earl of Egremont | Ruth was sister of **James** and **Charles Irish**.

SOURCE: GB, Parl. Papers, *Select Committee … Poor Law Amendment Act …* App. to 12th Report, 1837; WSRO, PAR 81/1/2/1, PAR 81/1/3/1; PHA 142

Hills, William | *Spouse*: Wife | *To*: Ancaster ? | *Occupation Eng*: Farming man | 1835

SOURCE: WSRO, PHA 142

Hilman, Harriet | 16, probably bap 22 Apr 1821 Findon | *From*: Wiston, West Sussex | 1836 | *Assistance*: Parish, backed by Poor Law Commissioners | A single young woman going out with a family "by whom she was reared."

SOURCE: PRO, MH 12, 13128; WSRO, PAR 84/1/2/1

Hilton, Alexander | *b 12 Feb, bap 25 Feb 1816 South Bersted, d 12 Nov 1892 Strathroy* | *Spouse: Martha Humphries (of Ann Arbor, Mich), m in Canada 1841, b 1815, d 1 Mar 1885* | *Children b in Canada: Charlotte b 24 Apr 1842, Maria b 1 Mar 1844, Martha Jane b 25 Aug 1847, Rachel b 1849, Hattie, James* | *From: Sutton, West Sussex (or South Bersted)* | *To: Delaware, London District* | *Occupation Can: Carpenter and joiner* | *1832* | *Eveline* | *Assistance: Lord Egremont and parish* | *Son of Charles and Mary Ann Hilton; grandson of Old Sarah. Lived in Michigan for 4 years, returned to Delaware, moved to Adelaide and then to Strathroy.*

SOURCE: *Continuation of Letters from Sussex Emigrants …Written in 1836 [1837], 7–8;* WSRO, *PAR 19/1/2/1; NA,, RG 31, Canada Census, 1851 Adelaide, p12; AO, RG 22/321, Middlesex Co. Surrogate Court, file 4633; Strathroy Age, 5 Mar 1885; Strathroy Dispatch, 16 Nov 1892*

Hilton, Charles | bap 4 May 1794 Sutton; d 1851 | *Spouse*: Mary Ann Webb, m 22 Oct 1815 Broadwater | *Children*: Alexander bap 25 Feb 1816, Ann bap 5 Oct 1817 (m David **Evans**), Jane bap 19 Sep 1819 (m William **Rapley** 23 Mar 1838), Harriet bap 28 Oct 1821 (m David **Rapley** 23 Mar 1840), Charles bap 26 Oct 1823, James bap 12 Jun 1825, William bap 31 Aug 1828, Sarah Ann bap 13 Feb 1831 (m George **Parker**), baby b 6 Jun 1836 in Canada | *From*: South Bersted, West Sussex (Shripney) | *To*: Delaware Village, later Westminster Twp and Adelaide | *Occupation Eng*: Labourer | *Occupation Can*: Farmer; digging wells and cellars | 1832 | Brother of **George**; son of William and Sarah.

SOURCE: *Continuation of Letters from Sussex Emigrants …Written in 1836* [1837], 3–7; WSRO, Goodwood Ms 1476, f278; PHA 137; PAR 19/1/2/1; PAR 29/1/3/1; PAR 191/1/1/3; ADH, Adelaide, St Ann's registers, 1833–83; *Strathroy Age*, 1 Mar 1888; Correspondents Blake Rapley, Jane Thompson

Hilton, George | bap 10 May 1789 Sutton, d before 1851 census | *Spouse*: Lydia Booker, m 27 Oct 1812 Tortington, bap 22 Feb 1795 Tortington | *Children*: George; Martha (m Charles

Peacock 1841); **James** bap 1817; Henry bap 28 Jul 1822 Arundel; Friend bap 12 Jun 1825 Arundel; Charles bap 29 Jul 1827 Tortington, Charlotte bap 25 Apr 1830 Arundel; Emily bap 14 Jun 1835 Arundel, d 12 Jul 1835 | George and Charles "went to a meeting house in a wood, where there is hundreds go, for there is no churches built yet." | *From*: Arundel, West Sussex (and Tortington) | *To*: Toronto | *Occupation Eng*: Labourer | *Occupation Can*: Agricultural labourer, works for George Denyson, alderman, Lot Street, Toronto | 1836 | Son of Sarah & William, brother of **Charles**. Purchased land in Delaware Twp in 1845.
SOURCE: *Continuation of Letters from Sussex Emigrants ... Written in 1836* [1837], 3–7; WSRO, PAR 8/1/2/1, PAR 191/1/1/3, PAR 198/1/1/4, PAR 198/1/2/1; NA, RG 31, Canada Census, 1851 Delaware Twp, p31

Hilton, Henry | *Spouse*: wife | 1837 | *Assistance*: 2 passages | Remarks on abstract of PEC emigrants: "Most respectable" family.
SOURCE: WSRO, PHA 140

Hilton, James | 19 | *Spouse*: Barbara Bridger, m 20 Apr 1835 Arundel | *From*: Arundel, West Sussex | *Occupation Eng*: Agricultural labourer | 1835 | Son of **George** and Lydia. "For exmployment. Steady man. Very respectable."
SOURCE: WSRO, PHA 142; PAR 8/1/3/1

Hilton, Sarah (Overington) | "Old Mrs Hilton" | 75 in 1834 | *Spouse*: William Hilton*, m 12 Oct 1788 | *Children*: **George** bap 10 May 1789, **Charles** bap 4 May 1794, James* bap 4 May 1794, Thomas* bap 2 Oct 1796, Sarah* bap 17 Feb 1799, Henry bap 10 May 1806 (all bap Sutton) | *From*: Sutton, West Sussex | *To*: Strathroy | 1837 | *Assistance*: Earl of Egremont and parish | Some of her family went to Canada in 1832, others 1834, and in 1837 she was "accompanied by a married son [presumably Henry] and daughter and several grandchildren." Remarks on abstract of PEC emigrants: "Childen married and now all in Canada."
SOURCE: *Hampshire Telegraph*, 1 May 1837; *Brighton Herald,* 12 Aug 1837; WSRO, PHA 140; PAR 191/1/1/3, PAR 191/1/1/4

Hilyar. See Helyer

Hoare, John | *Spouse*: Wife | *Children*: 9 children | *Occupation Eng*: Farmer | 1837 | *Assistance*: 7 passages | Remarks on abstract of PEC emigrants: "most repectable" family.
SOURCE: WSRO, PHA 140

Hodge, Job | bap 27 Jun 1790 | *Spouse*: Jane Munday*, m 1 Jul 1821 Newport, d Nov 1833 | bap 26 Feb 1804 | *Children*: Joseph* bap 29 Jun 1823, d Jul 1823; William b 8 Jan 1825; Francis* b 4 Apr 1833, d 23 May 1834 in House of Industry | Independent Chapel | Francis was bap at the Meeting House, Barton Village | *From*: Newport, Isle of Wight | *Occupation Eng*: Labourer/pauper | 1834 | A Job Hodge went in 1834 but whether or not it was this man is unconfirmed. Jane was sister of Mary **Sheath** who emigrated in 1837.
SOURCE: IOWRO, Z/HO/44; Index of Baptisms, Marriages, and Burials

Holden, John | 19, bap 21 Feb 1813 | *From*: Washington, West Sussex | *To*: Delaware Twp, then Woodstock | *Occupation Eng*: Bricklayer | 1832 ? | *Assistance*: Mrs Goring | In 1843 he was still in Woodstock. A John Holden and his wife, Sarah, had a son, Henry Edward, baptized at Old St Paul's Woodstock in 1842.
SOURCE: WSRO, PHA 137; PHA 1068; PAR 205/1/2/1; Holden to his mother and father, 6 Nov 1833, *No. 6 Continuation*, 47–8; AO, RG 1, C-IV, Woodstock Twp Papers, Holden file

Holden, John | *Spouse*: Hannah Howick, m 1 Feb 1820 Kirdford | *Children*: 7 children: including Hannah bap 16 Sep 1821; Keziah bap 27 Jul 1823; John bap 17 Jul 1825; George bap 2 Sep 1827; Peter bap 31 Jan 1830; Charles bap 24 Jun 1832 (all in Northchapel) |

From: Northchapel, West Sussex (Fishers St) | *To*: Woodstock by 1841 | *Occupation Eng*: Agricultural labourer | 1837 | *Assistance*: 5.5 passages | Remarks on abstract of PEC emigrants: "Most respectable" family.
SOURCE: WSRO, PHA 140; PAR 116/1/3/1; PAR 142/1/2/1

Holden, Thomas | 64 (1851 census), d 20 Feb 1854 age 56 Michigan, bur 19 Aug 1854 4th line cemetery, Adelaide Twp | *Spouse*: (1) Ruth Richardson* m 19 May 1813 Thakeham, d 1829 Kirdford; (2) Ann Downer Mann (widow of Samuel **Mann**), m in Canada 20 Feb 1837 | *Children*: 7 children emigrated: Mary (m William **Pannell** 29 Jan 1833); Ann bap 31 Mar 1816 Thakeham; Ruth bap 26 Jul 1818 (m Thomas **Mann** 1 May 1837); Harriet bap 16 Jul 1820, d Jul 1880 Arkona (m (1) W. Paisley 1840, (2) M.L. Smith 5 Mar 1851); James bap 7 Jul 1822; Thomas bap 20 Feb 1824 (m Margaret Joiner 5 Oct 1846); Moses bap 8 Apr 1827 | *From*: Kirdford, West Sussex | *To*: Adelaide | *Occupation Eng*: Labourer, some poor relief 1830 | *Occupation Can*: Farmer | 1832 | *Assistance*: Earl of Egremont | Holden had purchased 100 acres at $2 per acre with 6 years to pay.
SOURCE: *Emigration: Letters* (1833), 45; *Letters from Emigrants* (1839); WSRO, Misc. Paper 1031; PAR 116/1/2/1, PAR 116/1/5/1, PAR 116/31/1, PAR 195/1/2/1, PAR 195/1/3/1; AO, Middlesex Co., Adelaide Twp, 4th line cemetery, Mt Zion Old Methodist; RG 8, 1-6-A, vol 16, London District marriage register, p174; NA, RG 31, Canada Census, 1851 Adelaide Twp, p15; *Strathroy Dispatch*, 14 Jul 1880; Correspondents Margaret Parsons, Jane Thompson

Hollis, John ? | *Spouse*: Jane | *Children*: 4 children emigrated: John, Jane, Mary, Sarah | *From*: Felpham, West Sussex | *To*: York, Upper Canada ? | *Occupation Can*: Tailor (1833) | 1832 | *Assistance*: £150 from sum borrowed by Felpham remained to be paid off in 1835
SOURCE: PRO, MH 12, 13198; *Sussex Advertiser*, 22 Feb 1836

Holloway, William | *Spouse*: Wife | no children | *From*: Brighton, East Sussex | *Occupation Eng*: Stone sawyer (stone cutter) and farmer | 1832 ?
SOURCE: WSRO, PHA 137

Holmwood, Charles | bap 10 Nov 1813 | *From*: Burton, West Sussex | *Occupation Eng*: Volunteer 1st class, Navy | 1832 ? | Brother of **John**; PEC made arrangements but not on its ship.
SOURCE: WSRO, Goodwood Ms 1470, f216

Holmwood, John | bap 20 Apr 1812 | *From*: Burton, West Sussex | *Occupation Eng*: Miller | 1832 ? | Brother of **Charles**; PEC made arrangements but not on its ship.
SOURCE: WSRO, Goodwood Ms 1470, f216

Holmwood, John Stephens | *Spouse*: Leah Hopkins, m 29 Nov 1808, bap 8 Jan 1782 Poling | *Children*: Jane Sarah bap 29 Dec 1809, Emma bap 20 Feb 1811, **John** bap 20 Apr 1812, **Charles** bap 10 Nov 1813, Leah bap 5 May 1815, Fanny bap 24 Jun 1816, Walter bap 10 Aug 1818, Henry bap 15 Nov 1819, George Stephens bap 4 Aug 1822, Robert Penfold bap 8 Oct 1824 | *From*: Angmering, West Sussex (Swills or Swillage Farm) | *To*: Dundas | *Occupation Eng*: Farmer | *Occupation Can*: Farmer | 1834 | *Assistance*: Sockett and Duke of Richmond | The family probably did not go on a PEC ship. John Jr and Charles emigrated in 1832. No direct evidence that Leah Hopkins and Fanny **Hopkins** were related.
SOURCE: *Brighton Gazette*, 10 Nov 1836; WSRO PAR 6/1/1/3; PAR 6/1/1/4; PAR 6/1/2/1; PAR 6/30/2; PAR 6/30/3; Goodwood Ms 1470, f 216

Hook, George | b 25 Jul 1815, bap 20 Aug 1815 | *From*: Wisborough Green, West Sussex | *To*: Nelsonville, Ohio | *Occupation Eng*: Labourer | 1832 | England | *Assistance*: Parish and landowners
SOURCE: *Courtauld Family Letters* I: xxi; WSRO, PAR 210/1/2/1; PAR 210/37/11(3)

Hopkins, Fanny | bap 8 Dec 1815 | *From*: Angmering, West Sussex | *Occupation Eng*: In 1829 Fanny was put out to work at 1*s* a week and clothes | 1832 | *Assistance*: Parish and Miss Susan Loud | No destination given but *Portsmouth, Portsea and Gosport Herald* (1832) said people went from Angmering with PEC.
SOURCE: WSRO, PAR 6/1/2/1, PAR 6/12/1

Hopkins, Mary | *From*: Lodsworth, West Sussex | 1832 ?
SOURCE: WSRO, PHA 137

Hopkins, Sarah | b 10 Oct 1802 | *Children*: 3 children emigrated: Emily bap 18 Feb 1826, Haise/Esau bap 29 Jun 1828, Isabella bap 8 Jul 1833 | *From*: Petworth, West Sussex | *Occupation Eng*: Laundress | 1837 | *Assistance*: Earl of Egremont and parish, 2.5 passages
SOURCE: PRO, MH 12, 13061; WSRO, PHA 140; PAR 149/1/1/2

Hornsby, William | 18 | *From*: Walberton, West Sussex | *Occupation Eng*: Agricultural labourer | 1835
SOURCE: GB, Parl. Papers, *Select Committee ... Poor Law Amendment Act ...* App. to 12th Report, 1837

Howick, George | 36; bap 10 Dec 1797 | *Spouse*: Mary | *Children*: 6 children under 14: Elizabeth bap 3 Mar 1822, Harriett bap 20 Mar 1824, George bap 22 Dec 1826, Jane bap 23 Nov 1828, Martha bap 20 Nov 1831, William bap 20 Jul 1834 | *From*: Bepton, West Sussex | *Occupation Eng*: Farming man, "poor" | 1835 | *Assistance*: Outfit £21.0.0; conveyance £75.0.0 (with W. Howick) | Brother of **William**. "For employment" "a quiet man & wife."
SOURCE: PRO, MH 12, 13028; WSRO, PHA 142; PAR 17/1/2/1

Howick, John | bap 19 Jun 1785 | *Spouse*: Ann Southerton, m 26 Apr 1806 | *Children*: John b 7? Jun 1806, bap 27 Jul 1806; William b 14 Nov 1809, bap 7? Jan 1810; Stephen b 5 Nov 1812, bap 3 Jan 1817, d 1 May 1902; Mary b 5 Mar 1817, bap 1 Jun 1817; Ann b 11 Nov 1819, bap 7 Jun 1821; Sarah b 1824, bap 19 Dec 1824, Loxwood, West Sussex | *From*: Wisborough Green, West Sussex | *To*: Sunday Creek, Ohio | *Occupation Eng*: Labourer | 1832 | Stephen emigrated in 1831. We do not know how many of the other children emigrated.
SOURCE: *Courtauld Family Letters* 1: xxi; WSRO, PAR 210/1/1/9, PAR 210/1/2/1, PAR 210/37/11, Correspondent Richard Howick

Howick, William | 31, bap 24 Jul 1803 Bepton | *Spouse*: Jemima Southerton, m 26 Feb 1827 Aldingbourne | *Children*: 3 children emigrated: Jemina bap 9 Mar 1828 Sidlesham, Mary bap 15 Nov 1829 Sidlesham, William bap 1 Dec 1833 Graffham/Woolavington | *From*: Bepton, West Sussex | *Occupation Eng*: Farming man | 1835 | *Assistance*: Outfit £15.0.0; conveyance £75.0.0 (with G. Howick) | Brother of **George**. "For employment."
SOURCE: PRO, MH 12, 13028; WSRO, PHA 142; PAR 1/1/3/1, PAR 17/1/1/2, PAR 19/1/1/4, PAR 93/1/2/1, PAR 173/1/2/1

Hubbin. See Habbin

Hunt, Edward | *From*: Dorking, Surrey ? | *To*: Hamilton | 1832 ?
SOURCE: *Letters from Dorking*, 37

Hunter, John | 29 | *Spouse*: Wife | 29 | *From*: Findon, West Sussex | *Occupation Eng*: Labourer | 1836 | *Assistance*: Hugh Penfold, churchwarden, and Poor Law Commissioners
SOURCE: PRO, MH 12, 13128

Huntley, W. | *Spouse*: Wife | *To*: Guelph | 1834 (returned to Can) | He had been in Guelph in 1832 and went back to England "to take a wife." Brydone visited them on 22 Jul 1834 at Guelph where they had purchased 200 acres.
SOURCE: Brydone, *Narrative*, 14, 15, 42; Letter from Martin Martin, *Emigration: Letters* (1833), 27-30

Ide, Thomas Jr | probably bap 4 Jun 1815 | *From*: Oving, West Sussex | Pre-1837
SOURCE: GB, Parl. Papers, *Select Committee … Poor Law Amendment Act …App. to 12th Report*, 1837; WSRO, PAR 145/1/2/1

Inwood, John | 30 | *Spouse*: Sarah Weller*, m 20 Jul 1817 Ockley, bur 11 Apr 1830 | *Children*: John Jr 13, bap 1 Nov 1818; Emily* bap 19 Mar 1820 | *From*: Dorking, Surrey (Back Lane, Holmwood) | *Occupation Eng*: Labourer | 1832 | *Assistance*: Dorking Emigration Society
SOURCE: *Letters from Dorking*, 10; SRO (GMR), PSH/DOM/3/1

Irish, Charles | 36, bap 14 Oct 1798 | *Spouse*: Mary Clark, m 4 Oct 1823 | 33, bap 10 Sep 1801 | *Children*: John 16 | *From*: Felpham, West Sussex | *Occupation Eng*: Farming man; "for employment" | 1835 | *Assistance*: Parish and Earl of Egremont | Brother of **James** Irish and Ruth (**Hills**). No record found of a son John; Mary Clark had a son William in 1821; presumably William Dyer **Reeves**, 13, who was travelling with party. John might have been Charles's nephew bap 15 Apr 1819.
SOURCE: GB, Parl. Papers, *Select Committee … Poor Law Amendment Act …* App. to 12th Report, 1837; WSRO, PHA 142; PAR 81/1/2/1; Information supplied by Rachel Fletcher

Irish, Henry | 21 | *From*: Felpham, West Sussex | *Occupation Eng*: Agricultural labourer | 1835 | Brother of **Thomas**; nephew of **Charles** and **James** Irish and Ruth (**Hills**).
SOURCE: GB, Parl. Papers, *Select Committee … Poor Law Amendment Act …* App. to 12th Report, 1837; Information supplied by Rachel Fletcher

Irish, James | 28, bap 27 Mar 1803 | *Spouse*: Amy (Emey/Emily) Sparshott, m 15 Dec 1827 | 26 | *Children*: 4 children emigrated: Amy 7, bap 10 Sep 1828; Elizabeth 5, bap 10 Jan 1830; Harriet 3, bap 24 Jun 1832; Ephraim infant, bap 18 Aug 1834 | *From*: Felpham, West Sussex (Flansham) | *Occupation Eng*: Farming man; "for employment"; had been a pauper boy | *Occupation Can*: Farmer | 1835 | *Assistance*: Parish and Earl of Egremont | Brother of Charles **Irish** and Ruth (**Hills**). W.D. **Reeves** travelling with him.
SOURCE: GB, Parl. Papers, *Select Committee … Poor Law Amendment Act …* App. to 12th Report, 1837; WSRO, PAR 81/1/2/1; PHA 142

Irish, Thomas | 19, bap 21 Jan 1816 | *From*: Felpham, West Sussex (Ankton) | *Occupation Eng*: Agricultural labourer; had been a pauper boy | 1835 | *Assistance*: Parish and Earl of Egremont | Brother of **Henry**; nephew of **James** and **Charles** Irish and Ruth (**Hills**).
SOURCE: GB, Parl. Papers, *Select Committee … Poor Law Amendment Act …* App. to 12th Report, 1837; WSRO, PAR 81/1/2/1; Information supplied by Rachel Fletcher

Jackman, William | bap 22 Jan 1797 Storrington, West Sussex; d 24 Aug 1869 Nile, Huron Co | *Spouse*: (1) Sarah Lillywhite, m 5 Apr 1818 New Shoreham, Sussex; bap 24 Oct 1801 Thakeham, West Sussex; (2) Barbara Smith 29 Apr 1839 Oxford Twp | *Children*: (1) Stephen* bap 7 Feb 1819 Ferring, West Sussex, d 11 May 1881 Toronto; Ann bap 28 Jan 1821; Mary bap 8 Dec 1822 West Tarring, West Sussex; Francis bap 18 May 1824, d 21 Mar 1892; Eliza* bap 11 Jan 1826, bur 9 Feb 1827; Edward* bap 10 Dec 1827, bur 28 Mar 1830; William* bap 1 Nov 1830, bur 18 Mar 1832; Henry William bap 11 Nov 1832, d 23 Oct 1893 Toronto; Ellen bap 30 Apr 1835; (2) Barbara Sarah b c1840, James Wawanosh b c1842 | Church of England (1851 census), Wesleyan Methodist (1861 census) | *From*: Goring, West Sussex | *To*: Brantford, later Oxford Twp, Wawanosh Twp | *Occupation Eng*: Labourer | *Occupation Can*: Labourer and farmer | 1836 | *Assistance*: Levi Bushby | Stephen and his family emigrated sometime after 1851. William eventually settled Nile, Wawanosh Twp, Huron Co. Sons Francis and Henry William became ship's captains.
SOURCE: *Continuation of Letters from Sussex Emigrants …Written in 1836* [1837], 23–4; WSRO, Ep IV/7/10 B; PAR 83/1/2/1, PAR 92/1/1/2, PAR 92/1/2/1, PAR 170/1/3/1, PAR 188/1/1,

PAR 188/2/6, PAR 195/1/1; PRO, MH 12, 12905; NA, RG 31, Canada Census, 1851 Wawanosh Twp, p9; 1861 Wawanosh Twp, p4; B.D. Merriman, *The Emigrant Ancestors of a Lieutenant Governor of Ontario* (Toronto: OGS 1993)

Jarrett (Jerratt), James | 21, bap 20 Jun 1813 | *From*: Yapton, West Sussex | *Occupation Eng*: Agricultural labourer | 1835 | *Assistance*: Richard Prime and parish
SOURCE: GB, Parl. Papers, *Select Committee ... Poor Law Amendment Act ...* App. to 12th Report, 1837; WSRO, PAR 225/1/2/1

Jay, Henry | *From*: Aldingbourne, West Sussex | before 1835 | Mentioned by Edmund Birch who had seen nothing of him.
SOURCE: *Letters from Sussex Emigrants*, 7–8

Jeater, James | 27, b 23 Dec 1805, bap 24 Jan 1806 | *Spouse*: Eliza | 29 | *Children*: 2 children emigrated: Israel 3, d 19 Feb 1913, bur Ripley Cemetery, Huron Twp (m Margaret Husband 32, 11 Jul 1860); Elizabeth 1, bap 13 Feb 1831 Dorking | *From*: Dorking, Surrey | (Mill Lane) | *To*: Halton Co. | *Occupation Eng*: Postman | 1832 | *Assistance*: Dorking Emigration Society
SOURCE: *Letters from Dorking*, 10; Correspondent Donald Tomlinson; SRO (GMR), PSH/DOM/3/1; AO, RG 80-27-2, vol 17, Halton Co. marriage register, p26

Joice. See Joyes

Joiner, James | b 22 Dec 1796, bap 1 Jan 1797 Petworth, d 22 Apr 1844 | *Spouse*: Margaret | d Sep 1886, age 90 | *Children*: 3 children | *From*: Kirdford, West Sussex | *To*: Adelaide Twp | 1832
SOURCE: WSRO, Misc. Paper 1031; PAR 149/1/1/2; *No. 2 Continuation*, 15–16; AO, Middlesex Co, Adelaide Twp, 4th line cemetery, Mt Zion Old Methodist; NA, RG 31, Canada Census, 1851 Adelaide, p15

Jolliffe, Jacob | 46, bap 15 Jul 1792 | *Spouse*: Mary | 40 | *Children*: 7 children emigrated: Alfred 16, b 28 Apr 1821, bap 13 Jul 1821; Henry 12, b 29 Aug 1824, bap 15 Oct 1824; Josiah 10; Mary Eleanor 7, b 29 Aug 1829, bap 26 Mar 1830; Hester 5, b 24 Nov 1831, bap 6 May 1832; Thomas 2, b 8 Mar 1835, bap 2 Aug 1835; Jane Margaret 11 weeks, b 6 Feb 1837, bap 12 Apr 1837 | Wesleyan Methodist Church, Wootten Bridge, IOW | *From*: Newport, Isle of Wight (previously Balams, Arreton, IOW) | *Occupation Eng*: Agricultural labourer | *Occupation Can*: Labourer (Jacob); mariner (Alfred) | 1837 | *Assistance*: 5.5 passages; Parish, House of Industry | Admitted to House of Industry 19 Apr 1837; discharged 26 Apr 1837 "for Canada." Alfred admitted to House of Industry 26 Apr 1837 and discharged same day. Remarks on abstract of IOW emigrants: "Respectable"
SOURCE: IOWRO, Z/HO/44; Z/HO/L5; Z/HO/L6; Index of Baptisms, Marriages, and Burials; WSRO, PHA 140

Jones, Abraham | 18 | 1832 ? | Mr White of Chiddingfold, Surrey, wished to substitute him for John Pennell who had gone to Horsham.
SOURCE: WSRO, PHA 137

Jones, (Mrs) Sarah Eliza (Cooper) | Children: Eliza Sarah Jones, m Edward Francis **Heming** 1 Nov 1832 | 1832 | Lord Melville | Spouse Thomas already settled near Guelph in Upper Canada.
SOURCE: *Portsmouth, Portsea, and Gosport Herald and Chichester Reporter*, 22 Jul 1832; WSRO, PHA 137; see *Brighton Herald*, 30 Jan 1830

Jordan, Frances | probably bap 10 Oct 1813 Walberton | *From*: Angmering, West Sussex | 1832 | *Assistance*: Parish and Miss Susan Loud
SOURCE: WSRO, PAR 6/12/1, PAR 202/2/3

Joyce (Joice), Thomas | *Spouse*: Rachel | *Children*: 5 children emigrated: Richard b 16 Apr 1819, bap 20 Apr 1832; Anna bap 25 Dec 1823; Sarah b 6 Aug 1826, bap 20 Apr 1832; George b 13 Jun 1830, bap 20 Apr 1832; Caroline bap 4 Mar 1832 | Church of England | *From*: South Bersted, West Sussex | *Occupation Eng*: Labourer | 1832 | England ? | *Assistance*: Parish | To Montreal; several children baptized together before the hazards of the journey!
SOURCE: WSRO, Misc. Paper 1705; PAR 19/1/2/1

Joyes (Joice), Luke | b 1809 | *Spouse*: Hannah Dennett, m 19 May 1834 Itchingfield, West Sussex | *Children*: Daniel 14 months, bap 11 Jan 1835 (m Hepzilla Aldah 1858); Frederick 3 months, bap 22 Nov 1835; b in Canada: Solomon b c1836; Richard b c1840 (m Lois Jane Anscombe 1861); William Henry b c1841; Robert b c1842; Anna M. b c1843 (m Samuel Rowelett 1860); Cyrus b c1847; Edward b c1854; Albert Emanuel b c1855 | *From*: Billingshurst, West Sussex | *To*: Nelson Twp, Gore Dist, later Hamilton, Brantford, and Westminster Twp | *Occupation Eng*: Agricultural labourer | 1836 | *Assistance*: Parish, backed by Poor Law Commissioners | Has had parish relief of £1.3.6. His going was resented by Charles Chitty, his employer, as he was losing a hard-working man.
SOURCE: *Continuation of Letters from Sussex Emigrants … Written in 1836* [1837], 16; PRO, MH 12, 13060; WSRO, PAR 21/1/2/1, PAR 113/1/3/1; NA, RG 31, Canada Census, 1861 Westminster Twp, p71; AO, RG 80-27-2, vol 1, Brant Co. marriage register, p81; *Middlesex County Marriage Register* (Agincourt, ON: Generation Press 1991); Correspondents Margaret Major, Ron Cox, Ken Cook

Joyes, Thomas | 21 | *Spouse*: Kezia Hopkins, m 4 Apr 1837 just before ship sailed | 19 | *From*: Petworth, West Sussex | *Occupation Eng*: Agricultural labourer | 1837 | *Assistance*: Earl of Egremont and parish, backed by Poor Law Commissioners | Remarks on abstract of PEC emigrants: "Most respectable" family. A Thomas Joys, labourer, b England, was in Nelson Twp in 1842.
SOURCE: PRO, MH 12, 13061; WSRO, PHA 140; PAR 149/1/3/1; AO, Gore District Census, 1842 Nelson Twp

Kachett, Robert | 20 | *From*: Newport, Isle of Wight | 1837 | *Assistance*: Parish, House of Industry
SOURCE: IOWRO, Z/HO/44

Kemp, Ann | *Spouse*: James Kemp* | *Children*: Harry b 22 Sept 1813, bap 25 Aug 1815, bur 25 Sep 1851 Woodstock; Susannah bap 25 Aug 1815; 1 more son not found | *From*: Brighton, East Sussex | *To*: Blandford (town plot), 5-acre lot between Vincent St and Henry St | 1834 | *Assistance*: Hyam Lewis and James Collins, Earl of Chichester, parish, Brighton Emigration Committee; the family had had poor relief. | Harry and Susanah given at their baptism as son and daughter of James Kemp, late Sergeant Sussex Local Militia, under sentence of transportation. James was sentenced to 14 years' transportation in Aug 1815 at Lewes Assize for having forged Bank of England notes in his possession and was transported 16 Jan 1816 on the *Atlas* with six other Sussex convicts.
SOURCE: *Sussex Weekly Advertiser* 24, 31 Jul 1815; *Brighton Herald*, 19 Apr 1834; Brydone, *Narrative*; ESRO, PAR 255/1/2/1; PRO, ASSI 35/255/4; HO 11/2; WSRO, PHA 139; AO, Oxford Co., Woodstock, Old St Pauls Anglican Registers

Kemp, W. | *From*: Lewes, East Sussex ? | *To*: Ancaster | *Occupation Can*: "Fine shop of business" keeping on two or three men in Ancaster | Pre-1834 ? | The *Ingersoll Chronicle* for 13 Jan 1865 recorded a William Kemp, hotel keeper, who died in Ingersoll on 6 Jan 1865 formerly of Lewes, Sussex. A William Kemp, son of William and Emma Kemp of Ancaster, was b 23 Jan 1836 and bap 21 Jun 1836 (Charles Pinch, *Anglicanism in Ancaster* [Ancaster

Twp Historical Soc. c1979]).

SOURCE: *Sussex Advertiser*, 8 Sep 1834, extract of letter from Henry Harwood

Kenward, Richard | *Spouse*: Wife | *Children*: 9 children | *From*: Sussex | *Occupation Eng*: Agricultural labourer | 1837 | *Assistance*: 7 passages | Remarks on abstract of PEC emigrants "Most respectable" family.

SOURCE: WSRO, PHA 140

King, Martin | Single | *From*: Billingshurst, West Sussex | *Occupation Eng*: Agricultural labourer; no parish relief | 1836 | *Assistance*: Parish backed by Poor Law Commissioners

SOURCE: PRO, MH 12, 13060

Kingswell, James | 17, bap 23 Jan 1820 Godshill, IOW | *From*: Newport, Isle of Wight | 1837 | *Assistance*: Parish, House of Industry | Admitted to House of Industry 10 Jul 1830 aged 10; discharged 26 Apr 1837.

SOURCE: IOWRO, Z/HO/44; Z/HO/L4; Index of Baptisms, Marriages, and Burials

Kinshott, George | b 1813 | *From*: Lurgashall, West Sussex (removed from Frensham, Surrey, to Lurgashall 1817, aged 4, as a pauper) | *To*: Galt area ? | 1832

SOURCE: WSRO, Goodwood Ms 1465, f18; PAR 130/32/3/43X

Kinshott, Joseph | d 29 Jun 1832 of cholera | *Spouse*: Elizabeth Child, m 9 Jun 1826, possibly bap 20 Dec 1798 | *Children*: 3 children emigrated: Eleanor bap 5 Nov 1826, John bap 7 Sep 1828, Harriet bap 11 Sep 1830 (one child d in Jun 1832 of cholera) | *From*: Lurgashall, West Sussex | *To*: Blenheim Twp | *Occupation Eng*: Labourer | 1832 | *Assistance*: Earl of Egremont, W.H. Yaldwin, and parish

SOURCE: *No. 4 Continuation*; WSRO, Goodwood Ms 1460, f113; PAR 130/1/2/1, PAR 130/1/3/1

Knight, Robert | 25, bap 17 Jan 1813 Carisbrook | *From*: Whippingham, Isle of Wight | *Occupation Can*: Agricultural labourer | 1837 | *Assistance*: Parish, House of Industry | Admitted to House of Industry 22 Oct 1831 aged 20 and again 29 Oct 1831. Remarks on abstract of IOW emigratns: "well behaved during the voyage and subsequently."

SOURCE: IOWRO, Z/HO/44; Z/HO/L4; Index of Baptisms, Marriages, and Burials; WSRO, PHA 140

Knott, Edward | 13 | *To*: Toronto ? | *Occupation Can*: apprentice wheelwright | 1835 | apprentice to Mr Hersse; travelling with Hersse family

SOURCE: WSRO, PHA 142

Ladd, Mr | *Spouse*: Wife | *Children*: 5 children | *From*: Dorking, Surrey | *To*: Nelson Twp | Letter from W. Spencer told of their misfortunes.

SOURCE: *Continuation of Letters from Sussex Emigrants ... Written in 1836* [1837], 19–22

Laker, William | *Spouse*: Wife | *Children*: 3 children emigrated: Mary Ann bap 1825, Helen bap 1828, William bap 1832 | *From*: Wisborough Green, West Sussex | 1832 ?

SOURCE: WSRO, PHA 137

Lander (Launder), George | bap 27 Mar 1814 | *From*: Lurgashall, West Sussex | *Occupation Eng*: Agricultural labourer | 1832 | *Assistance*: Earl of Egremont, W.H. Yaldwin, and parish | Died of cholera in 1832 along with brother **Henry**.

SOURCE: *Emigration: Letters* (1833), 17–18; WSRO, PAR 130/31/6, p232; PAR 130/1/2/1; PAR 130/1/1/4

Lander (Launder), Henry | bap 15 Oct 1809 | *From*: Lurgashall, West Sussex | *Occupation Eng*: Agricultural labourer | 1832 | *Assistance*: Earl of Egremont, W.H. Yaldwin, and parish | Died of cholera in 1832, as did his brother **George**.

SOURCE: *Emigration: Letters* (1833), 17–18; WSRO, PAR 130/1/1/4, PAR 130/1/2/1, PAR 130/31/6, pp5, 232

Langley, Edward | 38 | *Spouse*: Wife | *Occupation Eng*: Farming man | 1835 | "Have place in view."
SOURCE: WSRO, PHA 142

Leggett, Charles | 20, bap 24 Apr 1814 | *From*: Walberton, West Sussex | *To*: Thornhill, York Co. | *Occupation Eng*: Agricultural labourer | 1835 | *Assistance*: Richard Prime and parish | Brother of **George** and **Ruth**; may have m Nancy Booker. A Charles Legett was on lot 25 con 10 Vaughan Twp in 1851.
SOURCE: GB, Parl. Papers, *Select Committee … Poor Law Amendment Act …* App. to 12th Report, 1837; *Letters from Sussex Emigrants*; WSRO, PAR 202/2/3; NA, RG 31, Canada Census, 1851 Vaughan Twp, agricultural schedule; Correspondent Helen Fortney

Leggett, George | 19, bap 24 Mar 1816, d 30 Aug 1894 Rainham Twp, Haldimand Co. | *Spouse*: Catherine Thompson, m 1 Dec 1842 at Vaughan Twp (Presbyterian) | *Children*: John b 9 Jun 1843 Thornhill, Jane b 15 May 1844, William b 5 Mar 1846, Samuel b 15 July 1847, Charles b 8 June 1849, William b 21 Sep 1850, Hannah b 15 Jan 1853, Jacob b Feb 1855, Elizabeth Ann b 25 May 1858, George Alburn b 29 Oct 1860 (all but John b Rainham) | *From*: Walberton, West Sussex | *To*: Vaughan Twp | *Occupation Eng*: Agricultural labourer | 1836 | *Assistance*: Richard Prime and parish | Brother of **Charles** and **Ruth**. In 1846 a George Leggett was on lot 24 con 10 Vaughan Twp.
SOURCE: GB, Parl. Papers, *Select Committee … Poor Law Amendment Act …* App. to 12th Report, 1837; WSRO, PAR 202/2/3; AO, RG 80-27-1, vol 11, Home District marriage registers, p 62; NA, RG 31, Canada Census, 1851 Vaughan Twp agricultural schedule; *Directory of Toronto & York County 1846/7*; Correspondent Helen Fortney

Leggett, Joseph | bap 7 Mar 1813 | *From*: Sutton, West Sussex | *To*: Hilton (180 miles further than York) ? | 1832 | *Assistance*: Earl of Egremont and parish
SOURCE: *Emigration: Letters* (1833), 26; WSRO, Goodwood Ms 650, f110; PAR 191/1/1/4

Leggett, Ruth | 19, bap 25 Jan 1818 | *Spouse*: George **Booker**, m 25 May 1839 at Thornhill, York Co. | *From*: Walberton, West Sussex | *To*: Thornhill | 1836 | *Assistance*: Richard Prime and parish | With Edmund Birch. Sister of **George** and **Charles**
SOURCE: GB, Parl. Papers, *Select Committee … Poor Law Amendment Act …* App. to 12th Report, 1837; *Letters from Sussex Emigrants*; WSRO, PAR 202/2/3; AO, RG 80-27-1, vol 10, Home District marriage registers, p390; Correspondent Helen Fortney

Lelliot (Elliot or Lillyott), William | 22 | *Occupation Eng*: Bricklayer | 1832 ? | *Assistance*: Mrs Goring (paid £10 down for Holden and Wm. Lelliot) | "W and M Lelliott" were masons in 19th century Thornhill (Doris M. Fitzgerald, *Thornhill, 1793– 1963* [Thornhill 1964]).
SOURCE: WSRO, PHA 137; mentioned in *No. 6 Continuation*, 47–8, letter from John Holden (originally from West Chiltington), dated Delaware, 6 Nov 1833

Lillywhite, Daniel | 27, bap 28 Aug 1808, baseborn son of Elizabeth, d 13 Dec 1853 age 47 | *Spouse*: Mary Ann Smith (née Plowman), m 10 Dec 1831 Findon | 26 | *Children*: 2 children emigrated: Elizabeth bap 30 Sep. 1832, Mary Ann bap 18 May 1834. Also Mary Ann's children by 1st marriage: George (Smith) bap 6 Jan 1828, Henry (Smith) bap 1 Nov 1829 | *From*: Findon, West Sussex | *To*: Blandford Twp? | *Occupation Eng*: Labourer | 1836 | *Assistance*: Hugh Penfold, churchwarden, and Poor Law Commissioners | A Daniel Lillywhite 46, b England, is listed in the 1851 census for Woodstock with a wife 44, b England, and a daughter Esther 14.
SOURCE: PRO, MH 12, 13128; WSRO, PAR 84/1/2/1; PAR 84/7/2; Ep IV/7/10B; NA, RG 31, Canada Census, 1851 Woodstock, p51; AO, Oxford Co., Woodstock, Old St Pauls cemetery

Lillywhite, George | 29, bap 31 Mar 1808 | *Spouse*: Sophia Floate, m 13 Sep 1828 Washington, West Sussex | 24; d 23 Sep 1882 age 70 Ingersoll | *Children*: 2 children emigrated: Ann bap 27 Sep 1829; Sarah* bap 24 Aug 1831, "killed, being run over by a horse," bur 2 Sep 1834; George bap 25 May 1833; b in Canada (1851 census): Elizabeth 15, James 9, William 7, Daniel 5, Richard 2 (d 1924, m Elizabeth Pickard 1871) | *From*: Findon, West Sussex | *To*: Blandford Twp | *Occupation Eng*: Labourer | 1836 | *Assistance*: Hugh Penfold, churchwarden, and Poor Law Commissioners
SOURCE: PRO, MH 12, 13128; WSRO, PAR 84/1/1/1, PAR 84/1/1/6, PAR 84/1/2/1, PAR 84/1/3/2, PAR 205/1/3/1; AO, Cemetery Transcriptions, Oxford Co, Ingersoll rural cemetery; NA, RG 31, Canada Census, 1851 Blandford Twp, p45; *Ingersoll Chronicle*, 7 Dec 1871; Correspondent Richard Moon

Lillywhite, John | 24 | *Spouse*: Wife | 28 | *From*: Findon, West Sussex | *Occupation Eng*: Labourer | 1836 | *Assistance*: Hugh Penfold, churchwarden, and Poor Law Commissioners
SOURCE: PRO, MH 12, 13128

Lillywhite, Reuben | bap 5 Apr 1812 Findon | *Spouse*: Frances Renment (widow), m 5 Nov 1832 | *From*: Findon, West Sussex | 1836 | *Assistance*: Hugh Penfold, churchwarden, and Poor Law Commissioners. | Brother of **George**.
SOURCE: PRO, MH 12, 13128; WSRO, PAR 84/1/1/6, PAR 84/1/3/1

Lingham, Thomas | "and family" | *From*: Upper Beeding, West Sussex (Tottington) | *Occupation Eng*: Farmer | 1833 | *Assistance*: Earl of Egremont paid £18 by draft to Messrs Stainbrook & Son 22 Exchange Buildings London "for taking out Thomas Lingham & his family to Canada" | Had been tenant of Earl of Egremont, distrained for debt Aug 1832.
SOURCE: WSRO, PHA 2691; PHA 4455; PHA 9015

Lintot, Benjamin | bap 26 Feb 1815, illegitimate son of Sarah Lintot | *From*: Walberton, West Sussex | *To*: Thornhill, York Co. ? | 1836 or before | Probably not brother of **George**.
SOURCE: *Letters from Sussex Emigrants*, 8–9; WSRO, PAR 202/2/3

Lintot, George | *Spouse*: Charlotte Turner, m 31 Jul 1832 Thornhill | *Children* b in Canada: Sarah Ann bap 23 Jul 1835; William bap 26 Jul 1837; John 3 Jun 1839; James b 27 Dec 1840, bap 28 Aug 1842; Mary Jane 10, Mariah E. 6, Margaret 4, Amelia 2 (baps not found) | *Religion*: Methodist (1851 census) | *From*: Walberton, West Sussex | *To*: Thornhill, York Co.; lot 31 con 4 Markham Twp (1851 census) | *Occupation Can*: Labourer, farmer | 1832 ? | Probably not brother of **Benjamin**. The 1851 census for Markham Twp listed George Lintot age 44, b England, his wife Charlotte age 37, b England, and 8 children.
SOURCE: Letter from John Ayling, 24 Jul 1836, *Letters from Sussex Emigrants*, 8–9; WSRO, PAR 202/2/32; NA, RG 31, Canada Census, 1851 Markham Twp, p110; ADT, Thornhill, Holy Trinity Church registers

Littleworth, James | b c1780 Hampshire, bur 27 Apr 1873 | *Spouse*: (1) Sarah Sadler, m 8 May 1819 Fittleworth | *Children*: William bap 2 Jan 1820 Fittleworth, bur 16 Feb 1820; Mary Ann bur 31 Oct 1825, age 4 Fittleworth (no bap recorded) | *From*: Fittleworth, West Sussex ? | *To*: Plympton Twp | *Occupation Eng*: Soldier; labourer | 1833 ? | *Assistance*: Applied to the Vestry for relief for emigration to North America. | According to his obituary in the *Sarnia Observer*, he had 3 wives and 30 children. One of his wives may have been a sister of James **Elliot**.
SOURCE: WSRO, PAR 86/1/2/1, PAR 86/1/3/1, PAR 86/12/1, PAR 86/31/1; NA, RG 1, L 3, Upper Canada Land Petitions, vol 292a, L18/30; RG 31, Canada Census, 1861 Plympton Twp, pp43–4; *Sarnia Observer*, 2 May 1873

Lockyer, Richard | 70 | *Spouse*: Wife | *Children*: 6 children | *To*: U.S.: "to Anondays in the States where the father and two sons of the wife reside" | *Occupation Eng*: Blacksmith | 1835
SOURCE: WSRO, PHA 142

Longhurst, George | b 1809, d c1865 Mulmer Twp, Simcoe Co | *Spouse*: Rebecca Weller, m 4 Jul 1831 Dorking, Surrey, bap 26 Feb 1809 Newdigate, Surrey, d 27 Oct 1888 Watt Twp, Muskoka District | *Children*: 1 child emigrated: Christiana bap 6 Nov 1831 Leatherhead, Surrey, d 17 Aug 1891 Watt Twp; b in Canada: Wellar b c1834; Rebeca b c1836; George b c1838; James b c1840; John b c1843; Frederick b c1845; Joseph b c1847; Moses b c1849; Albert b c1852. | *From*: Capel, Surrey | *To*: Little York (Toronto) | *Occupation Eng*: Fellmonger | *Occupation Can*: Building cottages and houses | 1832 | Eveline | *Assistance*: Mr Broadwood (piano manufacturers) | Went with Dorking party via PEC. George's parents, brothers, and sisters also emigrated. Acquired W ½ lot 5 con 1 Mulmer Twp, Simcoe Co., in 1850.
SOURCE: *Letters from Dorking*, 25–7; SRO (GMR), PSH/DOM/2/2/3; PSH/LE/4/1; NA, RG 31, Canada Census, 1851 Mulmer Twp, p5; Correspondents Donna Longhurst, Lyle Longhurst

Longhurst, Joseph | b 30 Nov 1789, bap 13 Dec 1789, d 7 Sept 1877 Fullerton Twp, Perth Co | *Spouse*: Sarah Hosmer (Osmer), b 18 Aug 1786 England, d 11 Mar 1863 | *Children*: **George**; Charles b 1811, d 22 Dec 1892 Toronto (m Martha Lepard); John bap 26 Dec 1813; James bap 7 Jul 1816 (m Flora MacDonald); Anne bap 12 Sep 1819; Frederick bap 19 Aug 1821, d 17 Oct 1899 Toronto; Jesse Isaac b 15 Jan 1824, bap 8 Apr 1827, d 11 Apr 1891 Detroit (m Mary Hoskins); Carolyn b 1827, bap 8 Apr 1827, d 4 Aug 1896 Toronto; Hester (Esther) b 1831, bap 3 Jan 1832, d at sea 1832 | *From*: Capel, Surrey | | *To*: York, Home District | 1832 | Eveline | *Assistance*: Mr Broadwood (piano manufacturer) | Went with Dorking party via PEC. Lived at Motherwell in Fullarton Twp, Perth Co, in 1850s with daughter Carolyn.
SOURCE: SRO (GMR) PSH/CAP/3/1; PSH DOM/2/2/3; Correspondents Donna Longhurst; Lyle Longhurst

Longley, Edward | *Spouse*: Wife | *Children*: Harriet* bap 17 Jul 1806; William* bap 11 Nov 1807 (was at sea in 1836); Mary* bap 22 Jul 1809; Miriam* bap 13 Oct 1812; George* bap 13 Nov 1814, d aged 5 weeks. Children apparently did not go to Canada. | *From*: Heene, West Sussex | *To*: near Guelph | *Occupation Eng*: Labourer | 1835 | *Assistance*: Parish, backed by Poor Law Commissioners | Longley's 1st wife Lucy died in 1817 at Heene aged 29; no record of 2nd marriage found but appropriate Heene records are missing.
SOURCE: *Brighton Guardian*, 11 May 1836; PRO, MH 12, 13060; WSRO, PAR 99/1/5/1; Ep IV/7/4; Ep IV/7/10B

Lowe, James | 36 | *From*: Newport, Isle of Wight | *Occupation Eng*: Labourer | 1837 | *Assistance*: Parish, House of Industry, IOW
SOURCE: IOWRO, Z/HO/44

Lower, William | *From*: Sussex | *Occupation Eng*: Jeweller | 1837 | *Assistance*: 1 passage
SOURCE: WSRO, PHA 140

Lucas, Edward (Ned) | *To*: Nelles Settlement, Niagara Dist. | 1832 | With C. Edwards; a "loose and runagate fellow": was suspected in Jul 1831 with Charles Edwards of setting fire to "the barn, part of the stable and a Hay Rick at Northlands," part of the Rev. T. Sockett's premises.
SOURCE: *Emigration: Letters* (1833), 23; WSRO, PHA 8618

Lucas, Thomas | *Spouse*: Ann Mitchell, m 22 Sep 1829 | *Children*: 2 children emigrated: William bap 1 Nov 1829, Thomas bap 15 Jan 1832 | *From*: Petworth, West Sussex | *Occupation Eng*:

Labourer for Earl of Egremont Dec 1830 | 1832 | *Assistance*: Earl of Egremont
SOURCE: *No. 4 Continuation*, 30–2; WSRO, PHA 8557; WSRO, PAR 149/1/1/2, PAR 149/1/2/1;
PAR/149/1/3/1

Lucy, James | 36 | *Spouse*: Jane | 28 | *Children*: 1 child: Emily 11 months, bap 31 Jul 1831
Dorking | *From*: Dorking, Surrey (Back Lane) | *Occupation Eng*: Labourer | 1832 | *Assistance*: Dorking Emigration Society
SOURCE: *Letters from Dorking*, 10; SRO (GMR), PSH/DOM/3/1

Lucy, John | 28 | Single | *From*: Dorking, Surrey | *Occupation Eng*: Labourer | 1832 | *Assistance*: Dorking Emigration Society
SOURCE: *Letters from Dorking*

Luff | *From*: Iping, West Sussex ? | 1832 ? | *Assistance*: Mr Smith
SOURCE: WSRO, PHA 137

Luff, Edward | *Spouse*: Wife | *Children*: 2 children emigrated: youngest d of cholera | *From*: Lurgashall, West Sussex | *To*: Hamilton ? | 1832 | *Assistance*: Parish
SOURCE: Capling, "The Capling Family"; WSRO, Goodwood Ms 1460, f113; PAR 130/31/7

Luff, John | 15 | *From*: Bury, West Sussex | *To*: Nelson Twp, Halton Co., Gore District |
Occupation Eng: Road worker | 1832 | Eveline | *Assistance*: The overseer of Bury agreed
to pay the expense of his conveyance to Canada because this lad had neither father nor
mother; £3 received from Mr Bishop to be paid to him at York. | A John Luff was
employed by the PEC to post bills advertising emigration. Luff was bound to Jacob Triller
In Nelson Twp until age 21. A John Luff age 47 died 23 May 1865 and was buried in
Toronto Necropolis cemetery.
SOURCE: *Emigration: Letters* (1833), 9–10; WSRO, PHA 137; PHA 8557; PAR 33/31/3

McCurry, M.A. | 30 | *To*: Montreal | 1835 | "joined her sister at Montreal"
SOURCE: WSRO, PHA 142

Maingy, William Anstruther | *To*: Montreal | *Occupation Eng*: engineer | 1833 (cabin passenger) | Wrote two notes from Montreal 22 Jun 1833 commending Hale's conduct, which
Sockett printed.
SOURCE: *No. 5 Continuation*

Mann, Charles | b 26 Aug 1810, bap 15 Sep 1811 | *Spouse*: Sarah Janes, m 28 Aug 1833 in
Canada | *From*: Wisborough Green, West Sussex ? | *To*: London, Adelaide / Delaware,
later Westminster Twp | *Occupation Eng*: Agricultural labourer | 1832 | England | *Assistance*: Parish and Earl of Egremont | Son of Samuel and Ann **Mann**; emigrated with his
cousin John **Downer**. Sold W ½ lot 19 con 4 SER Adelaide to Frederick **Hasted** in 1837.
SOURCE: WSRO, Letter from Ann Mann to her children in England, 2 Jan 1837; PHA 137;
PAR 210/1/1/11; AO, RG 1, C-IV, Adelaide Twp Papers; Correspondent Margaret Parsons

Mann, John | b 3 Apr 1817, bap 18 May 1817 | Episcopal Methodist (1851 census) | *From*:
Wisborough Green, West Sussex | *To*: London; Adelaide | *Occupation Eng*: Agricultural
labourer; "has been in service. No relief until now" | 1835 | *Assistance*: Parish, backed by
Poor Law Commissioners | Son of Samuel and Ann **Mann**; emigrated with brothers
Samuel Jr and **Thomas**
SOURCE: PRO, MH 12, 13060; WSRO, Letter from Ann Mann to her children in England, 2
Jan 1837; PAR 210/1/1/11; NA, RG 31, Canada Census, 1851 Adelaide, p9; Correspondent
Margaret Parsons

Mann, Mark | *b 11 Jul 1819, bap 8 Aug 1819, d 31 Oct 1904 Strathroy aged 85 years, 3 months* |
Spouse: Sophia Rapley, m 8 Mar 1841 Adelaide, b 22 Nov 1821, d 5 Apr 1903 aged 81 years |
Children b in Canada: Charles, John R., Henry, Malinda Jane, Cynthia Ann, Frances Elizabeth,

Mark Wesley, Jesse B., David Wallace, Sarah Sophia, Alice Maude Maria | From: Wisborough Green, West Sussex | Church of England 1841; Wesleyan Methodist (1851 census) | To: Adelaide | Occupation Eng: Labourer | Occupation Can: Farmer | 1836 | Assistance: Parish, backed by Poor Law Commissioners | Son of Samuel and Ann **Mann**. In Jun 1831 he had a pair of shoes (5s.) from parish.
SOURCE: WSRO, PAR 210/1/2/1; PAR 210/31/10; PRO, MH 12, 13060; NA, RG 31, Canada Census, 1851 Adelaide, p9; ADH, Adelaide, St Ann's Anglican registers, 1833-83; UCA, Wesleyan Methodist baptismal registers, Adelaide 1: 88, 96, 97; Correspondents Margaret Parsons, Jane Thompson

Mann, Noah | 33, b 13 Jan 1803, bap 13 Feb 1803 | Spouse: Elizabeth Sherwin, m 2 Jul 1826 Rudgwick by licence | 32 | Children: Noah Jr 10, bap 26 Nov 1826 Wisborough Green; Ambrose 8, b c1828; Meshec 6, bap 7 Nov 1830 (m Mary Ann **Napper**); Shadrac 4, bap 24 Jun 1832; Hannah 2, bap 28 Mar 1834; Ellen infant, bap 17 Jan 1836 | From: Wisborough Green, West Sussex | To: Adelaide ? ("North Street") | Occupation Eng: Agricultural labourer | 1836 | Assistance: Parish, backed by Poor Law Commissioners | Son of Samuel and Ann **Mann**. He and Elizabeth were removed from Rudgwick to Wisborough Green as paupers Aug 1826; received parish relief, working occasionally on parish roads.
SOURCE: PRO, MH 12, 13060; WSRO, PAR 160/1/3/1, PAR 210/1/1/9, PAR 210/1/2/1, PAR 210/1/29/1, PAR 210/32/3; Letter from Ann Mann to her children in England, 2 Jan 1837

Mann, Samuel Sr | 54, b 4 May 1782, d on arrival in Montreal 1836 | Spouse: Ann Downer, m 27 Sep 1802 Billingshurst | 53, b 25 Feb 1783 ? d 9 Nov 1845 | Children: **Noah** b 13 Jan 1803, bap 13 Feb 1803; Henry* b 29 Jun 1805, bap 18 Aug 1805; **Samuel** b 3 Jun 1807, bap 6 Sep 1807; George* b 13 Apr 1809, bap 28 May 1809 (all in Wisborough Green); **Charles** b 26 Aug 1810, bap 15 Sep 1811 Pulborough/Wisborough Green; **Thomas** b 18 Apr 1813, bap 20 Jun 1813; Hannah* b 16 Apr 1815, bap 7 May 1815, bur 9 Feb 1834 Wisborough Green; John b 3 Apr 1817, bap 18 May 1817; Mark 16, b 11 Jul 1819, bap 8 Aug 1819 (m Sophia Rapley); Eli 14, bap 17 Feb 1822; Moses 12, bap 7 Feb 1824; Edwin 9, bap 14 Jan 1827 (last 5 in Loxwood, a hamlet in parish of Wisborough Green). *did not go to Canada | From: Wisborough Green, West Sussex | To: Adelaide con 4 lot 19 "North side Road" | Occupation Eng: Labourer, generally employed on the highways on parish relief | 1836 | Assistance: Parish, backed by Poor Law Commissioners | Ann married Thomas **Holden** in 1837; she was sister of Avis Downer **Napper**.
SOURCE: PRO, MH 12, 13060; WSRO, Letter from Ann Mann to her children in England, 2 Jan 1837; PAR 21/1/1/7, PAR 210/1/1/9, PAR/210/1/1/11, PAR 210/1/2/1; AO, Middlesex Co., Adelaide Twp, 4th line cemetery, Mt Zion Old Methodist; Correspondents Margaret Parsons, I. and G. Mann, D. Mann, Blake Rapley, Jane Thompson, June Moffat, Constance Bayley

Mann, Samuel Jr | b 3 Jun 1807, bap 6 Sep 1807 | From: Wisborough Green, West Sussex | To: Adelaide ? ("North Street") | Occupation Eng: Agricultural labourer, "relieved several times" | 1835 | Assistance: Parish, backed by Poor Law Commissioners | Son of **Samuel** and **Ann**; emigrated with brothers **John** and **Thomas**
SOURCE: PRO, MH 12, 13060; WSRO, PAR 210/1/1/9; Letter from Ann Mann to her children in England, 2 Jan 1837

Mann, Thomas | b 18 Apr 1813, bap 20 Jun 1813, d 14 Sep 1882 Cass City, Michigan | Spouse: (1) Ruth **Holden**, m 1 May 1837 in Canada, bap 26 Jul 1818, d 22 Nov 1865; (2) Jane Patrick Clark | Children: 12 children b in Canada, including Eli, Harriet, George, Levi, Ruth, Emily Ann, Elmira C. | Free Will Baptist 1837; Episcopal Methodist (1851 Census) | From: Wisborough Green, West Sussex | To: Adelaide con 4 lot 19 "North side road." | Occupation Eng: Agricultural labourer; "Has been in service – no relief until now." | 1835

| *Assistance*: Parish, backed by Poor Law Commissioners | Son of **Samuel** and **Ann**; emigrated with brothers **John** and **Samuel Jr.**

SOURCE: PRO, MH 12, 13060; WSRO, Letter from Ann Mann to her children in England, 2 Jan 1837; AO, RG 80-27-1, vol 16, London District marriage register, p89; NA, RG 31, Canada Census, 1851 Adelaide, p9; UCA, Wesleyan Methodist baptismal registers, Adelaide I: 89, 90; *Strathroy Age*, 20 Jul 1882; Correspondent Margaret Parsons

Marshall, Louisa | 17, b 26 May 1815, bap 18 Jan 1818 | *From*: Haslemere, Surrey | 1832 | *Assistance*: Peter Scovell of Kings Head, Haslemere | Went with **Edsall** family.

SOURCE: WSRO, PHA 137, 28 May 1832; SRO (GMR), PSH/HME/3/1

Marshall, Thomas | 38, bap 31 Jan 1802, illeg. son of Elizabeth Marshall | *Spouse*: Rhoda Magic, m 4 Feb 1828 | 26, bap 30 Sep 1810 | *Children*: 4 children emigrated: Thomas 7, bap 5 Jul 1829; Jane 5, bap 1 Jan 1832; James 3, bap 10 Mar 1833; Charles 1, bap 8 Mar 1835 | *From*: Graffham/Woolavington, West Sussex | *Occupation Eng*: Labourer | 1836 | *Assistance*: Poor Law Commissioners

SOURCE: PRO, MH 12, 13198; WSRO, PAR 93/1/1/1, PAR 93/1/2/1/, PAR 93/1/3/1

Martin, James | 16, b 24 Aug 1819, bap 24 Oct 1819 | Church of England | *From*: Felpham, West Sussex | *To*: Guelph ? | *Occupation Eng*: Agricultural labourer; had been a pauper boy | 1835 | *Assistance*: Parish and Earl of Egremont

SOURCE: *Sussex Advertiser*, 22 Feb 1836; GB, Parl. Papers, *Select Committee ... Poor Law Amendment Act ...* App. to 12th Report, 1837; WSRO, PAR 81/1/2/1

Martin, Martin | b c1788, d 30 Mar 1872 Pilkington Twp aged 85 or 86 | *Spouse*: Fanny Hollis, m 5 Feb 1811 Felpham, bap 24 Mar 1793, d before 1851 | *Children*: Eliza* bap 14 Nov 1811, d 1 Apr 1830; Frances bap 24 Apr 1813; Mary Ann* bap 29 Mar 1814, d 3 Feb 1819; Richard bap 12 Oct 1816; Francis* bap 3 Dec 1818, d 5 Mar 1825; Louisa bap 25 Jun 1820; Jane* bap 17 Feb 1822, d 26 Feb 1822; William bap 29 Jun 1823; Marion bap 19 Jun 1825; Esther bap 3 Jan 1827 | bur Ponsonby Cemetery, Nichol Twp | *From*: Felpham, West Sussex | *To*: Guelph, Wellington Co. (later went to Gilkenson House, Elora, then Pilkington) | *Occupation Eng*: Carpenter, had been a pauper boy | *Occupation Can*: Farm labourer or carpenter, tavern keeper, farmer | 1832 | Lord Melville | *Assistance*: Parish and Earl of Egremont (£150 out of loan raised in 1832 remains to be paid off in 1835) | Fanny Hollis was probably sister of John **Hollis**.

SOURCE: *Emigration: Letters* (1833), 27–9; PRO, MH 12, 13198; *Sussex Advertiser*, 22 Feb 1836; WSRO, PHA 137; PAR 81/1/1/2, PAR 81/1/1/4, PAR 81/1/2/1; NA, RG 31, Canada Census, 1851 Pilkington Twp, p13; AO, RG 22/318, Wellington Co. Surrogate Court, file 723; information supplied by Rachel Fletcher and Marjorie Martin Dow; *Historical Atlas of Wellington County* (1906); J. Connon, *The Early History of Elora and Vicinity* (1930; repr. Waterloo: Wilfrid Laurier University Press 1974)

Martin, Thomas | bap 14 Aug 1786 | *Spouse*: Philadelphia Durrant, m 31 Oct 1808 | *Children*: Mary Ann* bap 11 Jun 1811; James* bap 9 Aug 1812 (apparently did not go); Harriett bap 18 Dec 1814; Eliza bap 24 Nov 1816; George bap 29 Jan 1819 Ardingly; Robert bap 21 Jan 1821; Eliz(abeth) bap 2 Feb 1823; Emily bap 5 Jun 1825; Martha bap 31 May 1827; Thomas bap 24 Jan 1830 | *From*: Horsted Keynes, West Sussex | *To*: America | *Occupation Eng*: Cooper | 1835 | *Assistance*: Parish, had been getting parish relief.

SOURCE: WSRO, PAR 231/1/2/1, PAR 384/1/1/3, PAR 384/1/1/4, PAR 384/1/2/1, PAR 384/12/2, PAR 384/31/1

Martin (Marten), William | *Spouse*: Jane, d 6 Feb 1835 | *Children*: 4 children emigrated: William bap 10 Nov 1816, poss d 1854; Mary bap 7 Feb 1819; Henry bap 17 Feb 1822; Sarah bap 8

Jun 1823; Charles* bap 18 May 1825, d 1832 | *From*: Brighton, East Sussex (Union St) | *To*: Blandford (town plot, lot between Barwick and 1st street) | *Occupation Eng*: Carpenter, had had poor relief | *Occupation Can*: Carpenter | 1834 | *Assistance*: Hyam Lewis and James Collins, Earl of Chichester, Parish, Brighton Emigration Committee | Brydone observed Martin and A. Muzzle finishing the roof of a frame house on 17 Jul in Blandford Twp.
SOURCE: Brydone, *Narrative*, 40–1; *Brighton Herald*, 19 Apr 1834; *Brighton Gazette*, 23 Apr 1835; ESRO, PAR 255/1/2/2/, PAR 255/1/2/3, PAR 255 1/2/4; WSRO, PHA 139; AO, RG 1, C-IVB, Township Papers, Woodstock, Martin File; OMNR, Survey Records, Plan 1834

Masters, William | 19, b 30 Mar 1818, bap 10 Apr 1818 Node Hill, Congregational Church | *From*: Newport, Isle of Wight ? | *Occupation Eng*: "no employ" | 1837 | *Assistance*: Parish, House of Industry IOW | Admitted to House of Industry 24 Apr 1837; discharged 26 Apr 1837
SOURCE: IOWRO, Z/HO/44; Z/HO/L5; Index of Baptisms, Marriages, and Burials

Meaden, William | 18, bap 2 Feb 1817 Barnham | *From*: Felpham, West Sussex | *Occupation Eng*: Agricultural labourer | 1835
SOURCE: GB, Parl. Papers, *Select Committee … Poor Law Amendment Act …* App. to 12th Report, 1837; WSRO, PAR 13/1/2/1

Mellish, Frank | 19 | *Spouse*: Eliza Savage, m 28 Nov 1839 Thornhill | *From*: Walberton, West Sussex | *To*: Thornhill, York Co. | *Occupation Eng*: Agricultural labourer | 1835 | Working for George Wells.
SOURCE: GB, Parl. Papers, *Select Committee … Poor Law Amendment Act …* App. to 12th Report, 1837; *Letters from Sussex Emigrants*, 5–6; ADT, Thornhill, Holy Trinity parish registers; NA, RG 31, Canada Census, 1851 Vaughan Twp, p25

Mercer, William Jr | 20 | Single | *From*: Dorking, Surrey | 1832 | *Assistance*: Dorking Emigration Society
SOURCE: *Letters from Dorking*, 10

Merritt, Edward | 50, possibly bap 1 Jun 1788 Shipley | *Spouse*: wife | *Children*: 5 children | *From*: Shipley, West Sussex ? | *Occupation Eng*: Farming man | 1835 | "steady, industrious, & hard working"
SOURCE: WSRO, PHA 142

Merritt (Merrit), Samuel | 35, possibly bap 15 May 1808 Washington | *Spouse*: Harriet Lulham, m 23 Nov 1834 Botolphs, bap 11 Sep 1814 | *Children*: 1 child emigrated: Thomas bap 26 Mar 1835 | *From*: Steyning, West Sussex | *Occupation Eng*: Blacksmith; "farming man" | 1835 | "For employment"; "a hard-working woman"
SOURCE: WSRO, PHA 142; PAR 26/1/1/2, PAR 26/2/1, PAR 183/1/2/1

Merritt (Meryett), James | 25, b 2 Jun 1806, bap 22 Jun 1806 | Single | *From*: Dorking, Surrey | 1832 | *Assistance*: Dorking Emigration Society
SOURCE: *Letters from Dorking*, 10; SRO (GMR), PSH/DOM/1/7

Messenger, Mark | bap 10 Nov 1793 | *Spouse*: possibly Jemima Sandford, m 26 Dec 1814 Climping "with consent of parents" | *Children*: possibly Thomas bap 18 Feb 1815, John Fleet Mitchel bap 11 Jan 1818, William bap 20 Mar 1828, Henry bap 20 May 1830 (all at Climping) | *From*: Walberton, West Sussex | *To*: Toronto (Duchess St) | *Occupation Eng*: Labourer | *Occupation Can*: Brickmaker | before 1836 | *Assistance*: Richard Prime | John Ayling stayed at his place when he arrived.
SOURCE: *Letters from Sussex Emigrants*, 26; WSRO, PAR 51/1/2/1, 51/1/3/1, PAR 202/2/3; George Walton, *City of Toronto and the Home District Commercial Directory and Register*, 1837

Miles, George | 31, bap 27 May 1804 | *Spouse*: Ann Hansfield, m 9 May 1823 "with consent of their respective fathers," bap 4 Aug 1805 | *Children*: 5 children emigrated: William* bap 12 Aug 1823, bur 21 Aug 1823; Mary bap 10 Nov 1824; Jane bap 7 Mar 1827; George bap 21 Feb 1829; Henry bap 7 Aug 1831; Ruth bap 26 May 1833 | *From*: Goring, West Sussex | *Occupation Eng*: Farming man "for employment" | 1835 | *Assistance*: Levi Bushby | A George Miles was in Brantford Twp in 1842 with 4 children b in England and 3 b in Canada. SOURCE: PRO, MH 12, 12905; Letter from W & S Jackman, *Continuation of Letters from Sussex Emigrants ... Written in 1836* [1837]; WSRO, PHA 142; PAR 92/1/1/5, PAR 92/1/2/1, PAR 92/1/3/1; AO, RG 21, Gore District Census and Assessments, 1842 Brantford Twp

Miles, Henry | b 15 Nov 1800, bap 14 Dec 1800 | *From*: Tillington, West Sussex | *Occupation Eng*: employed on Dean Farm | 1832 | Parish and Earl of Egremont SOURCE: WSRO, PHA 2415; PHA 8557; PAR 197/1/1/4, PAR 197/31/5

Milyard, James | 15, bap 19 Sep 1819, d 1899 | *From*: Walberton, West Sussex | *To*: 11 miles from Thornhill | *Occupation Eng*: Agricultural labourer | *Occupation Can*: Apprenticed to a carpenter | 1836 | *Assistance*: Richard Prime and Parish | A James Millyard of Thornhill married Rebecca Jane Wiley 6 Mar 1841 (Toronto, St James [Cathedral] marriages, 1807–1908); James, a cooper, and Rebecca had 2 children by 1851. SOURCE: GB, Parl. Papers, *Select Committee ... Poor Law Amendment Act ...* App. to 12th Report, 1837; *Letters from Sussex Emigrants*, 8–9; WSRO, PAR 202/2/3; NA, RG 31, Canada Census, 1851 Vaughan Twp, p7

Mitchell, Robert | 28, bap 3 Jan 1808 | *Spouse*: Louisa Mates, m 30 Sep 1826 Angmering, bap 31 Aug 1806 Angmering | *Children*: 4 children emigrated: Charlotte bap 21 Sep. 1828, Joseph bap 25 Jul 1830, Thomas bap 24 May 1832, Alfred bap 29 Jun 1834 | *From*: Petworth, West Sussex | *To*: Brantford | *Occupation Eng*: Bricklayer/stonemason | 1835 | *Assistance*: Earl of Egremont | Robert was probably brother of **Thomas**; Louisa was sister of Mary Ann Mates, Thomas's wife. SOURCE: WSRO, PAR 6/1/1/3, PAR 6/1/3/1, PAR 149/1/1/2, PAR 149/1/2/1; PHA 142

Mitchell, Thomas | probably bap 28 Dec 1803 | *Spouse*: Mary Ann Mates, m 9 Dec 1826 Goring | bap 5 Mar 1803 Angmering | *Children*: 1 child: Fanny, bap 13 Apr 1827 Goring | *From*: Petworth, West Sussex | *Occupation Eng*: Bricklayer | 1832 | *Assistance*: Earl of Egremont, 2½ passages | Thomas was probably brother of **Robert**; Mary Ann was sister of Louisa Mates, Robert's wife. SOURCE: *Emigration: Letters* (1833), 40; WSRO, Goodwood Ms 1465, f18; PHA 137; PAR 6/1/1/3, PAR 92/1/2/1, PAR 92/1/3/1, PAR 149/1/1/2

Mitchell, William | 74 | *To*: Brantford | *Occupation Eng*: Bricklayer | 1835 | Presumably relative (father?) of **Robert** whose family precedes William on list of emigrants. SOURCE: WSRO, PHA 142

Mitchell, William | *Spouse*: Jane (?), d 2 Oct 1855, aged 53 | *From*: Billingshurst, West Sussex | *Occupation Eng*: Tailor | 1832 ? | Ran away from his grandfather. SOURCE: WSRO, PHA 137; AO, Middlesex Co., Adelaide Twp, 4th line cemetery, Mt Zion Old Methodist

Moore, Charles | bap 23 Aug 1815 | *Spouse*: Rhoda Willett, m 29 Mar 1832 just before emigrating, bap 3 Apr 1811 Tillington, West Sussex | *Children*: Eliza Willett [Sageman] bap 11 Jul 1830 Easebourne; b in Canada: George | *From*: Tillington or Petworth, West Sussex | *To*: Blenheim, Upper Block, Waterloo | *Occupation Eng*: Agricultural labourer | 1832 | *Assistance*: Earl of Egremont, parish | Charles was a minor when he married with par-

ents' consent at Petworth. Eliza was probably child of William Sagemen.
SOURCE: *No. 3 Continuation*, 23–4; WSRO, PAR 75/1/2/1, 149/1/2/1, PAR 149/1/3/1, PAR 197/1/1/4, PAR 197/31/5

Moore, Edward | 20, bap 18 Jul 1812 | *From*: Petworth, West Sussex | *Occupation Eng*: Labourer | 1832 ? | *Assistance*: Earl of Egremont | "Wishes to go." Brother of **William**, **James**, and **Luke**. Possibly emigrated in 1835 or 1836.
SOURCE: WSRO, PHA 137; PAR 149/1/1/2

Moore, James | bap 14 Aug 1816 | *From*: Petworth, West Sussex | *To*: Sandwich, Essex Co. | 1832 | *Assistance*: Earl of Egremont | Brother of **Edward**, **William**, and **Luke**.
SOURCE: *No. 5 Continuation*, 40; Continuation *of Letters from Sussex Emigrants …Written in 1836* [1837], 9–10; WSRO, PAR 149/1/2/1

Moore, John | bap 18 Sep 1814 | *From*: Petworth, West Sussex | *To*: Sandwich, Essex Co. | *Occupation Eng*: Labourer, employed by Egremont's steward | 1836 ? | *Assistance*: Earl of Egremont | Not brother of other Moores.
SOURCE: *Continuation of Letters from Sussex Emigrants …Written in 1836* [1837], 9–10; WSRO, PHA 8557; PAR 149/1/2/1

Moore, Luke | bap 23 Dec 1820 | *From*: Petworth, West Sussex | *Occupation Eng*: Agricultural labourer | 1837 | *Assistance*: Earl of Egremont, 1 passage | Remarks on abstract of PEC emigrants: "Naughty youth." Brother of **Edward**, **William**, and **James**.
SOURCE: WSRO, PHA 140; PAR 149/1/2/1

Moore, William | bap 6 Nov 1814 | Church of England | *From*: Petworth, West Sussex | 1832 | *Assistance*: Earl of Egremont | Brother of **James**, **Luke** and **Edward**.
SOURCE: *No. 5 Continuation*, 40; *Emigration: Letters* (1833); WSRO, PHA 8557; PAR 149/1/2/1

Moorman, William | probably bap 8 Apr 1821 Carisbrooke | *From*: Carisbrooke, Isle of Wight | 1834 | *Assistance*: Parish/House of Industry | Admitted to House of Industry 5 Nov 1831 with sister Leah; discharged 16 Apr 1834 "to Canada."
SOURCE: IOWRO, Z/HO/L5; Index of Baptisms, Marriages, and Burials

Morgan, George | *From*: West Grinstead, West Sussex (area) | *To*: Toronto or Hamilton | *Occupation Can*: Apprenticed to carpenter | 1834 | According to Brydone he found work in Hamilton.
SOURCE: WSRO, PHA 139; PRO, CO 384/39, f116, Letter from Henry Heasman, 19 Oct 1834; Brydone, *Narrative*, 26

Morley, Nathan | bap 20 Mar 1781 Tillington | *Spouse*: Sarah Kinshott (Kingsett), m 21 Nov 1814, d 1832 Hamilton of cholera shortly after arrival) | *Children*: Mary bap 4 Feb 1816 (m George **Capling**); William bap 24 May 1818; George bap 2 Jul 1820, d 1908 Australia (m (1) Hannah Hall c 1845, (2) Charlotte Garrey c 1870 Nebraska); Hannah bap 5 May 1822; James bap 5 Mar 1824 (m Catharina Moss c1850); Stephen bap 29 Jan 1826; Michael bap 30 Mar 1828; Edwin bap 4 Apr 1830; Thomas bap 19 Apr or Jun 1831, d Hamilton of cholera shortly after arrival | *From*: Lurgashall, West Sussex | *To*: Huron Tract, Perth Co. ? | *Occupation Eng*: Labourer | 1832 | *Assistance*: Parish, Earl of Egremont, and W.H. Yaldwin | Family tradition holds that one baby was "given away" in Canada.
SOURCE: Capling, "The Capling Family"; WSRO, Goodwood Ms 1460, f113; PHA 8557, PAR 130/1/2/1/, PAR 130/1/3/1, PAR 197/1/1/2; Correspondents Nancy Conn, Nancy Graden

Muzzall (Muzzle), Abraham | b 6 Jan 1814, d 21 Dec 1855 Merrillville, Ind. | *Spouse*: Caroline Hayward, m 1836 Quebec | Particular Baptist | *From*: Brighton, East Sussex | *To*: Blandford Twp | *Occupation Eng*: Carpenter/builder | 1834 | Brydone saw him finishing

a roof on a frame house with W. Martin in Blandford Twp 17 Jul 1834. Of Huguenot descent.
SOURCE: Ernest L. Muzzall, *The Family of Abraham Muzzall, Huguenot Informant and Emigrant to America in 1834* (Ellensburg, Wash. 1965); Brydone, *Narrative*, 40

Muzzall, Prudence (née Boniface) | b 11 Feb 1776 | *Spouse*: (1) John Muzzall; (2) L.W. Thompson, m 1839 in Canada | *Children*: **Abraham** b 6 Jan 1814; Prudence bap 28 Dec 1815, reg 12 Apr 1834; Jane* | Salem Particular Baptist Chapel, Bond St, Brighton | *From*: Brighton, East Sussex | *To*: Blandford Twp ? | 1836 | Mother of Abraham Muzzall. Prudence and her daughter, Prudence, emigrated in 1836.
SOURCE: Ernest L. Muzzall, *The Family of Abraham Muzzall, Huguenot Informant and Emigrant to America in 1834* (Ellensburg, Wash. 1965); ESRO, Non-Conformist Registers, vol 4

Napper, Charles | *bap 6 May 1821, d 28 Mar 1907 Petrolia* | *Spouse: Amy Parker, m 27 Oct 1845 Adelaide Twp, bap 14 May 1820, d 1908* | *From: Pulborough, West Sussex* | *To: Adelaide Twp* | *Occupation Can: Confectioner in 1861* | *1832* | *Assistance: Parish* | *Son of James and Avice Napper. Charles and Amy bur 4th line cemetery, Mt Zion Old Methodist, Adelaide Twp.*
SOURCE: *AO, Middlesex Co., Adelaide Twp, 4th line cemetery, Mt Zion Old Methodist; WSRO, PAR 153/1/2/1; NA, RG 31, Canada Census, 1861 Strathroy (info. supplied by Arnold Orchard); Strathroy Age, 28 Sep 1882, 10 Jul 1885; Correspondent Jane Thompson*

Napper, James | bap 1 Jun 1788, d 12 May 1875 Petrolia | *Spouse*: Avice (Avis) Downer, m 1 Feb 1820 Wisborough Green, bap 12 Jun 1791 Wisborough Green | *Children*: 3 children emigrated: **Charles** bap 6 May 1821, d 28 Mar 1907 Petrolia; George bap 7 Dec 1823; William bap 28 May 1826, d 18 Nov 1884 Petrolia (m Susannah Jury); b in Canada: Mary Ann b 12 Sep 1834, bap 14 Jun 1835 (m Meshec **Mann**) | Wesleyan Methodist (1851 census) | *From*: Pulborough, West Sussex | *To*: York, Upper Canada; then Adelaide Twp, lot 13 con 4SER | *Occupation Eng*: Labourer | 1832 ? | *Assistance*: Mr Challen and parish; Napper was lent £47.10.0 "for to emigrate with his wife and 3 children to America." | Avis and James were parents of John **Downer**. Avis was a sister of Ann **Mann**.
SOURCE: WSRO, PHA 137; PAR 153/1/1/1, PAR 153/1/2/1, PAR 153/1/3/1, PAR 153/12/3, PAR 210/1/3/1; NA, RG 31, Canada Census, 1851 Adelaide, p13; *Strathroy Age*, 14 May 1875; Correspondent Jane Thompson

Nash, Frank | 17 | Single ? | *From*: Kirdford, West Sussex | *To*: Hamilton | *Occupation Eng*: Sawyer | 1832 | Cousin of Henry **Smart**.
SOURCE: *Emigration: Letters* (1833), 41; WSRO, Misc. Paper 1031; PHA 137

Nash, William | 21 | *Spouse*: Wife | 21 | *Occupation Eng*: Sawyer | 1832 ? | *Assistance*: Parish, 4 passages | A down payment of £8 for 4 passages is recorded opposite these two and Frank Nash. One adult or two children missing?
SOURCE: WSRO, PHA 137

Neal, Richard | bap 19 Jan 1809 | *From*: Sutton, West Sussex | *To*: Dundas, then Ancaster | *Occupation Eng*: Bricklayer | *Occupation Can*: Bricklayer and contractor | 1832 | Eveline | *Assistance*: Earl of Egremont and parish
SOURCE: *Emigration: Letters* (1833), 5–7; Woodhouse, *History of Dundas*; WSRO, Goodwood Ms 650, f110; PAR 191/1/1/4

Nesbit, William | 18 | *From*: Newport, Isle of Wight | 1837 | *Assistance*: Parish, House of Industry
SOURCE: IOWRO, Z/HO/44

Nevett, John | b 18 Jul 1806, bap 13 Oct 1806 (son of John and Ann) | *From*: Petworth, West Sussex | *To*: Westminster Twp | *Occupation Eng*: Tailor | *Occupation Can*: Tailor | 1832 ?

SOURCE: *No. 5 Continuation*, 33; *Letters from Emigrants … in 1832, 1833* and *1836*, 7; WSRO, PAR 149/1/1/1; PHA 137

Nevett, Thomas | b Mar 1816, bap 25 Jun 1830 (son of Thomas and Eliza) | *From*: Petworth, West Sussex | 1832 ?
SOURCE: *No. 5 Continuation*, 33–4; WSRO, PAR 149/1/1/2

Newman, Charles | b 23 Jul 1811, bap 21 Aug 1811 | *From*: Petworth, West Sussex | *To*: Hamilton | 1832 | *Assistance*: Earl of Egremont
SOURCE: *Emigration Letters* (1833), 37–9; *No. 2 Continuation*, 11; WSRO, PAR 149/1/1/2

Nicol, William Bulmer | 22 | *To*: Darlington, Newcastle District | *Occupation Eng*: Probably son of friends of T. Sockett | *Occupation Can*: Has commenced as a doctor. | 1835 | Nicol gave George Sockett a very bad account of Mrs Brydone's health. He practised in Bowmanville and in 1842 was appointed to staff of King's College and moved to Toronto.
SOURCE: WSRO, PHA 142; AO, MU 1717, Mary Leslie Papers, George Sockett Business Papers, Draft of part of a letter [George Sockett] to father, Eramosa, 26 Dec 1836 (sic) – Accounts in back, A. Carnie Dr to J.M. Brydone, 19 Jul 1837; Charles Godfrey, *Medicine for Ontario* (Belleville, Ont: Mika 1979), 48, 283

Norris (Noice, Noyce), Henry | b 8 Feb 1811, bap 14 Jul 1811 | *Spouse*: Charlotte Austin, m 27 Dec 1831, bap 8 Mar 1812 | *Children*: Emma bap 7 Dec 1832, Mary Ann bap 23 Jul 1835, Edward bap 1 Jun 1838 | *From*: Walberton, West Sussex | *To*: Thornhill, York Co. ? | *Occupation Can*: Shoemaker on Yonge St (1832 baptismal register) | 1832 ? | *Assistance*: Richard Prime and parish | Brother of **Thomas** and **John**.
SOURCE: WSRO, PAR 202/1/1/3, PAR 202/2/3; *Letters from Sussex Emigrants*, 9–10; John Ayling to William Ayling, Thornhill, 24 Jul 1836; ADT, Thornhill, Holy Trinity Church registers, 1831–50

Norris (Noice, Noyce), John | 18, bap 5 Jan 1817 | *From*: Walberton, West Sussex | *Occupation Eng*: Agricultural labourer | 1836 | *Assistance*: Richard Prime and parish | Located about 10 miles from George Lintot; working for $8 per month. Brother of **Thomas** and **Henry**.
SOURCE: *Letters from Sussex Emigrants*, 9–10; GB, Parl. Papers, *Select Committee … Poor Law Amendment Act …* App. to 12th Report, 1837; WSRO, PAR 202/2/3

Norris (Noice, Noyce), Thomas | 16, bap 18 Apr 1819 | *From*: Walberton, West Sussex | *Occupation Eng*: Agricultural labourer | 1836 | *Assistance*: Richard Prime and Parish | Brother of **John** and **Henry**.
SOURCE: *Letters from Sussex Emigrants*, 9–10; GB, Parl. Papers, *Select Committee … Poor Law Amendment Act …* App. to 12th Report, 1837; WSRO, PAR 202/2/3

Nott, Thomas | *Spouse*: Wife | *Children*: 7 children | *Occupation Eng*: Farmer | 1837 | *Assistance*: 7 passages | Remarks on abstract of PEC emigrants: "Most respectable" family. Possibly related to Edward **Knott**.
SOURCE: WSRO, PHA 140

Older, George | 32, possibly bap 3 Jan 1813 Billingshurst | *Spouse*: Wife, possibly Sarah Gilbert, m 7 Nov 1832 Burpham | *Children*: 2 children | *From*: Wisborough Green, West Sussex | *To*: Delaware, London District | *Occupation Eng*: Labourer, applying for poor relief | *Occupation Can*: Family were working for William Robinson | 1836 | *Assistance*: Parish, backed by Poor Law Commissioners | Brought a good character from John Drewitt, Esq.; said he was personally known to Sockett.
SOURCE: *Continuation of Letters from Sussex Emigrants … Written in 1836* [1837], 8, W. Robin-

son to Sockett, Ekfrid Park, nr Delaware, 14 Oct 1836; PRO, MH 12, 13060; WSRO, PAR 21/1/2/1, PAR 31/2/2

Older, Samuel (widower of Rudgwick) | *Spouse*: (1) Sophia Turner, m 2 Apr 1812 Slinfold; bur 21 Mar 1822 | (2) Joanna Hard, m 20 Apr 1823, b 15 Jul 1802, bap 25 Jul 1802 | *Children*: Henry bap 25 Oct 1812 Billinghurst; William bap 8 Jan 1815 Billinghurst; John* bap 16 Mar 1817 Billinghurst, bur 21 Apr 1822 Billinghurst; James bap 2 Apr 1820 Billinghurst; Mary bap 17 Aug 1823 Loxwood; George bap 13 Feb 1825 Loxwood; Samuel bap 17 Dec 1826; Caleb bap 7 Sep 1828; Harriet bap 27 Dec 1829; Sarah bap 17 Apr 1831 | *From*: Wisborough Green, West Sussex (Five Oaks) | *To*: Nelsonville, Ohio | *Occupation Eng*: Labourer | 1832 | England | *Assistance*: Parish, "employed constantly" out of the parish | Eight children were given in the Courtauld letters.
  SOURCE: *Courtauld Family Letters* I; WSRO, PAR 21/1/2/1, PAR 21/1/5/1, PAR 176/1/1/5, PAR 210/1/1/9, PAR 210/1/2/1, PAR 210/1/3/1, PAR 210//37/11(1), PAR 210/37/11(3)

Oler (Older), Thomas | bap 12 Nov 1809 | *From*: Wisborough Green, West Sussex | *To*: Nelsonville, Ohio | 1832 | England | *Assistance*: Parish and landowners
  SOURCE: *Courtauld Family Letters* I: xxi; WSRO, PAR 210/1/1/11, PAR 210/37/11(3)

Oliver, George | 22 | Single | *From*: Wisborough Green, West Sussex | *Occupation Eng*: Agricultural labourer, occasional relief | 1836 | *Assistance*: Parish, backed by Poor Law Commissioners
  SOURCE: PRO, MH 12, 13060; WSRO, PAR 210/37/11

Overdean, (Mrs) | 58 | *To*: Cobourg ? | 1835 | With her daughter and son-in-law, **C. Hammond**
  SOURCE: WSRO, PHA 142

Owen, Eliza Sophia | Congregational | *From*: Cuckfield, West Sussex (and Hurstmonceaux) | 1834 | Left for "America" Mar 1834
  SOURCE: WSRO, Nonconformist Records, NC C2/1/1

Page, Charles | *From*: Lewes, East Sussex | *To*: Montreal | *Occupation Eng*: Saddler | before 1834
  SOURCE: *Sussex Advertiser*, 8 Sep 1834

Page, Richard | 25, b 31 Mar 1806, bap 27 Apr 1806 | Single | *From*: Dorking, Surrey | 1832 | *Assistance*: Dorking Emigration Society
  SOURCE: *Letters from Dorking*, 10; SRO (GMR), PSH/DOM/1/7

Palmer, Hannah | 27, b 19 Jul 1808, bap 7 Aug 1808 | *Spouse*: Frederick **Upton**, m 15 Jul 1835 Ancaster | *From*: Petworth, West Sussex | 1835 | *Assistance*: Earl of Egremont and parish
  SOURCE: WSRO, PHA 142; PAR 149/1/1/2; Correspondent Nancy Smith

Pannell, Mary | 41 | *Children*: 4 children emigrated: Mary 16; Jane 14; William 10; Ann 4 | *From*: Tillington, West Sussex | 1836 | *Assistance*: Earl of Egremont and parish
  SOURCE: WSRO, PAR 197/12/1

Pannell, William | b 7 Oct 1805, bap 19 Jan 1806, d 17 Jun 1882 | *Spouse*: (1) Mary **Holden**, m 29 Jan 1833, bap 1815, d 29 Oct 1850; (2) Mary Marshall, m 6 May 1851 in Adelaide | *Children*: b in Canada: William 14, Alfred 11, Clara 8, James 4 (1851 census) | Wesleyan Methodist in Canada | *From*: Kirdford, West Sussex | *To*: Adelaide Twp, London District | Mr Moulton | *Occupation Eng*: Wheelwright | *Occupation Can*: Carpenter/wheelwright | 1832 | *Assistance*: Earl of Egremont and parish | Pannell and Mary Marshall both appear to have been widowed with families before their 1851 marriage.

SOURCE: *Emigration: Letters* (1833), 31–32; WSRO, Misc. Paper 1031; PHA 110; PAR 116/1/1/2; AO, Middlesex Co., Adelaide Twp, 4th line cemetery, Mt Zion Old Methodist; RG 80-27-1, vol 16, London District marriage registers, p 245; NA, RG 31, Canada Census, 1851 Adelaide, p27; *Strathroy Age*, 22 Jun 1882

Parker, James | bap 13 Aug 1797, d 29 Feb 1864 | *Spouse*: Amy Steer, m 20 May 1819 | bap 21 Dec 1800; d 25 Mar 1872 | *Children*: 3 children: Amy bap 14 May 1820 (m Charles **Napper**), George bap 21 Apr 1822 (m Sarah Ann **Hilton** 8 Nov 1848), James bap 22 Aug 1824 (m Helen Mather 27 Oct 1842) | converted to Wesleyan Methodist in 1842 | *From*: Pulborough, West Sussex | *To*: Adelaide Twp | *Occupation Eng*: Labourer, applied to parish for work Sep 1831 | 1832 | *Assistance*: Charles Challen, Pulborough, and parish | James and Amy are buried 4th line cemetery, Mt Zion Old Methodist, Adelaide Twp.

SOURCE: WSRO, Goodwood Ms 1465, f18; PHA 137; PAR 153/1/1/1, PAR 153/1/2/1, PAR 153/12/3; AO, Middlesex Co., Adelaide Twp, 4th line cemetery, Mt Zion Old Methodist; RG 1, C-I-1, Adelaide; C-IV, Township Papers, Adelaide; OLRI; RG 22/321, Middlesex Co. Surrogate Court, file 366; RG 80-27-1, vol 16, London District marriage registers, pp173, 230; *Christian Guardian*, 18 May 1864; Correspondents Jane Thompson, Blake Rapley

Parker, Maria | 22 | *To*: Cobourg | *Occupation Eng*: Maid | *Occupation Can*: Maid | 1835 | Emigrated with the family of **C. Hammond**.

SOURCE: WSRO, PHA 142

Parsons, James | *Spouse*: Anne Brooker of Ashurst, m 22 Feb 1816 | *Children*: 2 children emigrated: Charles bap 27 Feb 1820, George bap 19 Dec 1824 | *From*: West Grinstead, West Sussex | *Occupation Can*: Labourer | 1835 | *Assistance*: Parish and Mr Woodward (vicar) and possibly Sir C. Burrell and Mrs Goring

SOURCE: WSRO, PHA 142; PAR 95/1/2/1, PAR 95/1/3/1, PAR 95/12/1

Parsons, James | *From*: Hellingly, East Sussex | *Occupation Eng*: Parish labour | 1834 | *Assistance*: Parish, Earl of Chichester, Thomas Calverley

SOURCE: ESRO, PAR 375/12/5, PAR 375/31/2/6, PAR 375/31/2/7

Pay, William | 17, bap 4 Feb 1819 | *From*: Felpham, West Sussex | *Occupation Eng*: Agricultural labourer; had been a pauper boy | 1835 | *Assistance*: Parish and Earl of Egremont

SOURCE: GB, Parl. Papers, *Select Committee ... Poor Law Amendment Act ...* App. to 12th Report, 1837; WSRO, PAR 81/1/2/1

Peacock, Charles | possibly bap 3 Aug 1799 Wisborough Green | *Spouse*: (1) Amelia Cooper, m 26 Dec 1829, bap 1 Jul 1802 South Bersted; (2) Martha Hilton 8 Jun 1841 | *Children*: Frederick bap 11 Jul 1830; b in Canada: George b c1836, Isabella b 15 Jun 1844 Delaware, Henry b c1847, Alfred b c1849, Dudley b c1851 (1851 census) | *From*: Kirdford, West Sussex | *To*: Delaware | *Occupation Eng*: Shoemaker | *Occupation Can*: Shoemaker | pre 1838 | *Assistance*: Earl of Egremont and parish

SOURCE: WSRO, PAR 19/1/1/4, PAR 116/1/2/1, PAR 116/1/3/1; Letter from John Pullen, 1838; AO, Church Registers Collection, Caradoc, Ekfrid and Delaware, Anglican register 1834–51; NA, RG 31, Canada Census, 1851 Delaware, p27

Pearce | *From*: Petworth, West Sussex | 1832 ? | Belongs to Petworth, wishes to go.

SOURCE: WSRO, PHA 137

Pellett, Hugh | 37 | *Spouse*: Sarah Messenger, m 29 Jan 1824 | 36, bap 6 May 1798 | *Children*: 4 children emigrated: Mark Boniface 9, bap 7 Jan 1826; Sarah Pink 7, bap 30 Jan 1827; Jane Messenger 4, bap 8 Oct 1830; James 1, bap 17 Feb 1834 | *From*: Felpham, West Sussex | *Occupation Eng*: Farming man; had been a pauper boy | 1835 | *Assistance*: Earl of Egremont and parish | "For employment, a hard-working man"

SOURCE: GB, Parl. Papers, *Select Committee ... Poor Law Amendment Act ...* App. to 12th Report, 1837; WSRO, PHA 142; PAR 81/1/2/1, PAR 81/1/3/1

Pelling, Peter | *From*: Hellingly, East Sussex | *Occupation Can*: Labourer | 1834 | *Assistance*: Parish, Earl of Chichester, and Thomas Calverley
SOURCE: ESRO, PAR 375/12/5, PAR 375/31/2/6, PAR 375/31/2/7

Penfold, David | possibly bap 14 Feb 1815 Betchworth, Surrey | Baptist ? | *From*: Dorking, Surrey | 1832 | *Assistance*: Paid for himself, but went with Dorking group
SOURCE: *Letters from Dorking*; IGI

Penfold, James | d intestate 24 Jan 1847 | *Spouse*: Mary | *Children* b in Canada: Charlotte; William b c1847 (m Jane Dowsling) | *From*: Lodsworth, West Sussex | *To*: Galt, Dumfries Twp | 1832 | E ½ lot 6 Beasly's New Block Waterloo Twp, deeded to Jesse and James Penfold 1844. Mary may have m (2) John Lee; Charlotte and William Penfold were living with John and Mary Lee in Goderich Twp in 1861 according to the census.
SOURCE: J. Rapson to his father, Galt, 26 Oct 1832, *Emigration: Letters* (1833); AO, RG 61, Waterloo Twp Abstract Index to Deeds; RG 22/318, Wellington District Surrogate Court files; Correspondent David Rapson

Penfold, Jesse | bap 16 Apr 1781 | *Spouse*: Jane Tribe, m 2 Dec 1817, bap 10 Jun 1798 | *Children*: Matilda b 1819, bap 12 Jun 1819 (m (1) Thomas **Adsett**, (2) James Hall); Jesse bap 11 Jan 1824 (m Hannah Wismer 1842); Caroline bap 12 Aug 1827; Esther b 1832 on board ship (m Owen Roberts 25 May 1846); Harriett (m John Scully 1852) | Wesleyan Methodist (1871 census) | *From*: Lurgashall, West Sussex | *To*: Galt, Dumfries Twp | *Occupation Eng*: Carpenter, ex-soldier | 1832 | *Assistance*: Earl of Egremont, W.H. Yaldwyn, and parish; had clothes from Earl of Egremont 1831 | Jane (daughter of Henry and Charlotte **Tribe**) was carried in a chair to Durham boat at Montreal after childbirth. Petitioned for land grant for service as private for 8 years in 57th Regiment; he evidently served at Quebec City about 1814. Had land in Waterloo Twp, Woolwich Twp.
SOURCE: *No. 4 Continuation*, 25–6; WSRO, Goodwood Ms 1460, f114; Goodwood Ms 1465, f18; PHA 110; MP 3191; PAR 130/1/1/1, PAR 130/1/2/1, PAR 130/1/3/1; AO, RG 1, Ontario Land Records Index; RG 21, Gore District Census and Assessments, Waterloo Twp, 1840 Census; NA, RG 1, L3, Upper Canada Land Petitions, vol 408, P18/2; RG 31, Canada Census, 1851 Woolwich Twp agricultural schedule, 1861, 1861, 1871; *The Marriage Registers of Upper Canada/Canada West, vol.9, pt 1, Wellington District, 1840-1852*, comp. D. Walker and F. Stratford-Devai (Delhi: Norsim Publishing 1997), 40, 130; John Connon, *The Early History of Elora and Vicinity* (1930; repr. Waterloo: Wilfrid Laurier University Press 1979)

Penfold, Samuel | bap 6 May 1810 Mayfield, East Sussex, d 14 May 1875 Guelph aged 65 | *Spouse*: Mary Ann Heather, m c1845–50 Guelph, bap 20 May 1825 at Camberwell, Surrey, St Giles Presbyterian Church, d 14 Jul 1885 | *Children* b in Canada: Fannie b 1849, d 1939; Samuel, George, b 1852, d 1937 (m Epsy Lakin); Mary; Jane; Elizabeth d 26 Apr 1925 (m Harry Heather); Emily | Protestant (1861 census) | *From*: Petworth, West Sussex | *To*: Guelph | *Occupation Can*: Carpenter and builder | 1832 ? | *Assistance*: Earl of Egremont | Brother of **William**.
SOURCE: WSRO, Misc. Paper 2513; PAR 48/1/1/1; NA, RG 31, Canada Census, 1861 Guelph; AO, RG 22/318, Wellington Co. Surrogate Court, file 996; KPL, Wellington Co, Guelph, Woodlawn cemetery; Correspondent M.L. Black

Penfold, William | *Spouse*: Sarah | *Children*: Standing George bap 18 May 1820, son b on ship | *From*: Thakeham, West Sussex | *To*: Guelph | 1832 | Lord Melville | Superintendent of Lord Melville; guaranteed £100 from the fee charged parishes. Penfold Sr and family were to have a place separated off for them on the ship.

SOURCE: *Portsmouth, Portsea and Gosport Herald*, 22 Jul 1832; WSRO, Misc. Paper 2513; PHA 137; PAR 149/1/2/1; Correspondent M.L. Black

Pennicott, John | 17, bap 15 Dec 1816 Findon, West Sussex, d 19 Sep 1901, bur Innisfail, Alta | *From*: Washington, West Sussex | 1834 | *Assistance*: Blagden, vicar of Washington | Son of John Pennicott and Elizabeth Gatton. He and his son Herbert Charles Pennicott (aged 24) began homesteading near Innisfil in 1892.

SOURCE: Brydone, *Narrative*, 1; Read, "From Portsmouth ...," *Families* 28 no. 1 (Feb 1989); WSRO, PHA 139; PAR 84/1/2/1

Percival, David | *From*: Dorking, Surrey | *To*: York, Upper Canada | 1832 | *Assistance*: Dorking Emigration Society

SOURCE: *Letters from Dorking*, 21–2

Perrin (Perring), Thomas | b c1790 | *Spouse*: Charlotte | b c1798 | *Children*: 5 children emigrated: Elizabeth Sarah bap 14 Jan 1821, William Henry bap 16 Mar 1823, Ann bap 24 Apr 1825, Mary bap 25 Nov 1827 (m Henry Denman 22 Sep 1842), Jane bap 29 Jul 1832; b in Canada: Sarah Ann bap 19 Oct 1834 (m William Bassingdale 23 Sep 1853) | Wesleyan Methodist (1851 census) | *From*: Brighton, East Sussex (Crescent Cottages) | *To*: Blandford (town plot), 5-acre lot between 1st and 2nd street | *Occupation Eng*: Retired soldier (Rifle Brigade); labourer; had had poor relief | *Occupation Can*: labourer | 1834 | *Assistance*: Hyam Lewis and James Collins, Earl of Chichester, parish, Brighton Emigration Committee | Appears on Carroll 12 Jul 1834 Plan showing survey for Petworth emigrants. Deed for Warwick, E ½ lot 16 con 2SER, Sep 1834, free grant, military (AO RG 1, C13, vol 12, 95). Listed in 1851 Census, Town of Woodstock, age 64, wife, Charlotte age 62, one daughter Sarah, age 18, b in Canada, and a child, Thomas Clark Perrin, age 2; shared one-storey frame house with Matthew (?) Wilson, Scottish labourer with wife and 4 children.

SOURCE: *Brighton Herald*, 19 Apr 1834; ESRO, PAR 255/1/2/3, PAR 255/1/2/5, PAR 255/1/28; WSRO, PHA 139; OMNR, Survey Records, 1834 Plan; AO, RG 1, Ontario Land Records Index; C-IV, Township Papers, Woodstock, Perrin file; RG 80-27-1, vol 2, Brock District marriage register, pp30, 96; NA, RG 1, L3, Upper Canada Land Petitions, vol 242, H1/52; RG 31, Canada Census, 1851 Woodstock, p77

Peters, Edward | 21 | Single | *From*: Dorking, Surrey | *Occupation Eng*: Labourer | 1832 | *Assistance*: Dorking Emigration Society

SOURCE: *Letters from Dorking*, 10

Philips, James | *Spouse*: "family" | *To*: Plympton Twp. | 1833 | *Assistance*: One of Petworth party. | According to Hale, his was one of the families who embarked on the schooner for Plympton.

SOURCE: WSRO, Goodwood Ms 1469, f16

Phillips, William | bap 18 Oct 1803 | *From*: Singleton, West Sussex (Drove) | *To*: Ancaster (1832); Galt: "They are all Scotch in this part, and I do not much like it for they are very clannish." He planned on moving to Woodstock (1839). | *Occupation Eng*: Shoemaker | *Occupation Can*: Shoemaker/labourer | 1832 | Eveline | *Assistance*: Sent out by Petworth Committee in 1832; returned and permitted at "his own earnest request" to work his passage out again on the Diana in 1837. Mrs Newell. | Remarks on abstract of PEC 1837 emigrants: "Most respectable."

SOURCE: WSRO, PHA 140, 1066, 1068, letter 14 Jul 1839; PAR 174/1/1/4; *Emigration: Letters* (1833), 12–13

Phillips, William Sr | d 16 Sep 1889 age 88 years 28 days | *Spouse*: Ellen | *Children*: 1 child | *From*: Merston, West Sussex | *To*: Adelaide Twp, then Warwick Twp | 1833 | Brydone included an extract from Phillips' journal and commented that William Phillips emigrated at his own expense with his wife and child to join his son; extract described travelling up St Lawrence.

SOURCE: Brydone, *Narrative*, 20–1, 38; NA, RG 31, Canada Census, 1871 Warwick; St Paul's Anglican cemetery, Warwick

Phillips, William Jr | *Spouse*: Mary Pullen, m 13 Dec 1834 Adelaide, b 4 Sep 1827(?) Sussex, d 17 Dec 1887 age 70 | *Children* b in Canada: Alfred b 27 Jun 1836, Anne b 30 Mar 1841, Jane b 28 Feb 1843, Charles b 1 Apr 1845 (all b Warwick) | *From*: Merston, West Sussex | *To*: Adelaide Twp, then Warwick Twp | *Occupation Can*: Farmer: purchased 100 acres at $2 per acre – 1/4 to be paid in the first 3 years – the remainder within the next 3 years. | 1832

SOURCE: *Emigration: Letters* (1833), 46–7; WSRO, Goodwood Ms 1460, f35; ADH, Adelaide, St Anns Anglican registers, 1833– 83; UCA, Wesleyan Methodist baptismal registers, Warwick 1: 47, 55; AO, RG 1, Ontario Land Records Index; C-I-1 Crown Lands Petitions, Adelaide; C-IV, Township Papers, Adelaide; NA, RG 31, Canada Census, 1851 Warwick Twp agricultural schedule

Pickett, Joseph | 18 | *Spouse*: Susannah Husband, m 1841 in Canada | *Children*: 11 children b in Canada | *From*: Frensham, Surrey | *To*: Trafalgar Twp | *Occupation Eng*: Labourer | 1832 | *Assistance*: Dorking Emigration Society | Rented on lower middle road west of Trafalgar with brother-in-law Johnny Husband, eventually moved to Clarkson where he died.

SOURCE: *Letters from Dorking*, 10; Correspondent Edna Featherston

Plumbley, James | 20, bap 6 Oct 1816 Newport | *From*: Newport, Isle of Wight | 1837 | *Assistance*: Parish, House of Industry | Admitted to House of Industry 20 Dec 1823 with mother and family, "father gone to Oxford to seek employment"

SOURCE: IOWRO, Z/HO/44; Z/HO/L3; Index of Baptisms, Marriages, and Burials

Poland (Poling, Polen), George | 40 | *Spouse*: Widower, (2) Mary Grimwood, m 1 Dec 1822 West Tarring | *Children*: 6 children emigrated: including Ann bap 31 Mar 1824, Ellen bap 6 Dec 1829, Louisa bap 8 Apr 1832, Peter bap 18 Jan 1835 (West Tarring) | *From*: Heene, West Sussex (near Worthing) | *To*: Brantford? | *Occupation Eng*: Farmer's labourer, received £3.8.6 parish relief in last year; "farming man" | 1835 | *Assistance*: Parish, backed by Poor Law Commissioners | Edward Longley saw him last at Hamilton en route for Blandford (probably Brantford). "An industrious hard-working man, handy with carpenter's tools and well-behaved on voyage."

SOURCE: *Brighton Guardian*, 11 May 1836, letter of E. Longley, 28 Sep 1835 and 20 Mar 1836; PRO, MH 12, 13060; WSRO, PHA 142; PAR 99/1/2/1; EP IV/7/10B

Pratt, John | b 6 May 1818, bap 5 Jun 1818 | *From*: Petworth, West Sussex ("Barnet's Mill") | *To*: Blandford (town plot) | 1836

SOURCE: *Continuation of Letters from Sussex Emigrants ...Written in 1836* [1837], 15–16; WSRO, PAR 149/1/2/1/; Letter from James Cooper, May 1838, *Brighton Herald*, 25 Aug 1838

Puddock, (Jesse?) | *From*: Sullington, West Sussex ? | *To*: Woolwich Twp | 1832 | In 1838 a Jesse Puddock was on lot 86 Woolwich Twp; in 1837 Edmund Thomas was on lot 86.

SOURCE: Letter from George and Ann Hills, WSRO, Goodwood Ms 1460, f36; AO, RG 21, Gore District Census and Assessments, 1838 Woolwich Twp

Pullen, Richard | 36, bap 22 Feb 1801, d 22 May 1872 Delaware | *Spouse*: (1) Frances Holden, m 5 Sep 1825, bap 10 Feb 1805, d 14 May 1848; (2) Mary | *Children*: Ann bap 20 Nov 1825, d 20 May 1837 on board the Diana of "brain fever"; Sarah bap 13 May 1827;

William bap 21 Sep 1828; Hannah bap 24 Jul 1831; Henry bap 24 Mar 1832; Richard bap 14 Sep 1834 (m Elecia Brown 11 Apr 1858); Elizabeth bap 24 Jul 1836 (m Shadrac **Randall** 12 Jan 1852); at least six more children born in Canada: George, James, Mara Ann, Emily, Frances, John | *From*: Northchapel, West Sussex (Colhook Common) | *To*: Caradoc Twp, Middlesex Co., lot 18, range 2, Delaware at the Thames (village) | *Occupation Eng*: Agricultural labourer, had parish relief 1830 and 1836 | *Occupation Can*: Farm labourer | 1837 | *Assistance*: PEC and parish, 5 passages | Richard and Frances bur Christ Church, Delaware. Family history has it that three of Richard's sisters emigrated with him but evidence seems to be against it. Remarks on abstract of PEC emigrants: "Very respectable." SOURCE: *Letters from Emigrants* (1839), 5–7; PRO, MH 12, 13029; WSRO, Misc. Paper 1031; PAR 116/31/1, PAR 142/1/1/2, PAR 142/1/2/1, PAR 142/1/3/1; *Continuation of Letters from Sussex Emigrants ... Written in 1836* [1837]; *Sussex Agricultural Express*, 2 Sep 1837; NA, RG 31, Canada Census, 1851 Caradoc Twp, p 45; AO, Middlesex Co., Delaware Twp, Christ Church Anglican cemetery; RG 80-27-1, vol 16, London District marriage register, p167; RG 80-27-2, vol 36, Middlesex Co. marriage register, p13; Correspondents W.R. Thompson, Jai Williams

Pulling, George | *From*: Tillington, West Sussex | 1834 | *Assistance*: Parish
SOURCE: WSRO, PAR 197/31/5

Puttock, Sarah | bap 10 Oct 1813 | *From*: Kirdford, West Sussex | *To*: Waterloo Twp, 30 miles from Ann | *Occupation Can*: In service | 1832 | *Assistance*: Earl of Egremont and parish | She emigrated with her sister Ann and brother-in-law Edmund **Thomas**. Her father **Thomas** emigrated in 1833.
SOURCE: WSRO, Misc. Paper 1031, PAR 116/1/2/1

Puttock, Thomas | 64 | *Spouse*: Jane*, deceased | *Children*: Thomas bap 12 Nov 1797, **Ann** bap 4 Nov 1804 (m Edmund Thomas 11 Apr 1826), William bap 16 Nov 1806, **Sarah** bap 10 Oct 1813 | *From*: Kirdford, West Sussex (Strood Green) | *Occupation Eng*: Agricultural labourer | 1833 | *Assistance*: Earl of Egremont and parish | His sons Thomas and William may have gone with him. Ann and Edmund **Thomas** emigrated in 1832 with Sarah.
SOURCE: WSRO, PAR 116/1/1/6, PAR 116/1/2/1; Letter from Edward Bristow, *No. 6 Continuation*, 41–2; Letter from Ann Thomas, *Emigration: Letters* (1833)

Racher, John | bap 6 Mar 1808 | *Spouse*: (1) Edith Titmouse, m 15 Oct 1828, bap 1 Apr 1810; (2) Ann Burns, m between 1846 and 1852, b 1828 Ireland | *Children*: 2 children emigrated: Charles bap 9 Oct 1829 (m Mary Ann —); Stephen b 7 Mar 1830, bap 9 Apr 1831, d 1903 (m Margaret Shaver); b in Canada: George b 17 May 1834, d 12 Oct 1894 (m Margaret Duncan); Mary Ann b 9 Jun 1836, d 1931 (m (1) Robert Chambers, (2) John N. Westover); Charlotte b 13 Jun 1838, d 1934 (m Andrew Stocton); Francis b 1840, d 1910 (m Harriet Innis); John b 1842 (m Olive Innis); Asher b 1846, d 1909 (m Mary Brodley); Peter b 1852, d 1919 (m Cath McLeod); Rachel b 1854 (m James Mulllin); Elizabeth b 1856 (m Thomas Yerk); Sarah d 1934 (m Peter Valad); Margaret b c1859 (m Andrew Valad); Ann Jane b 1861, d 1941 (m Jacob Brindley); Edith b 1864, d 1954 (m Joel Stauffer); Jessie b 1866, d 1953 (m Charles Brindley) | *From*: Bassingbourn, Cambridgeshire | *To*: Dundas, ½ lot 32, con 6 Beverly Twp, Wentworth Co | *Occupation Eng*: Labourer | *Occupation Can*: Labourer | 1832 | *Assistance*: Vestry and Charles Beldam | Edith Racher was the sister of Mary **Shambrook** and Simeon **Titmouse**. John was said to be at Dundas in 1841.
SOURCE: *Emigration: Letters* (1833), 19–21; Cambridge County Record Office, P11/1/3, P11/1/4, P11/1/10, P11/12/5; NA, RG 31, Canada Census, 1861 Beverly Twp, 1871 Kincardine Twp; Correspondents Glenn W. Racher, Margaret Stockton; Wilson Family Papers,

Maria Wilson to her son Obediah, 21 Jun 1841; Mary Munsey (sister) to Obediah Wilson, Kneesworth, nr Royston, Cambridgeshire, 27 Mar 1876

Rackett, Robert | 20, b 1 May 1815, bap 4 Sep 1816 (at House of Industry, Newport) | *From*: Newport, Isle of Wight | *Occupation Eng*: Agricultural labourer; "out of employ" | 1837 ? | *Assistance*: Parish/House of Industry | Son of John Rackett (baker), widower, and Anne Baker (servant) of Newport. Admitted to House of Industry IOW 25 Apr 1837; discharged 26 Apr 1837. Robert was half brother of **William**. Remarks on abstract of IOW emigrants: "well behaved during the voyage and subsequently."

SOURCE: IOWRO Z/HO/L5; Z/HO/44; Index of Baptisms, Marriages, and Burials; WSRO, PHA 140

Rackett, William | 25, b 30 Mar 1809, bap 7 May 1809 | *From*: Newport, Isle of Wight | *To*: Montreal | *Occupation Eng*: Apprenticed by the House of Industry as a boy of 15 | 1834 | Son of John Rackett and Mary (d 1810). Brydone reported that he left at Montreal without permission with George Townsend, Charles Crossing, and George Walden. Half-brother to **Robert**.

SOURCE: Brydone, *Narrative*; IOWRO, Z/HO/M1; Index to Baptisms, Marriages, and Burials

Randall, Abraham Sr | d 16 Jun 1836 drowned at Montreal | *Spouse*: Sarah Edwards, m 29 Oct 1809, b c1775, d 1867 aged 92 | *Children*: **Isaac** bap 4 Jun 1809; Harriet bap 9 Jun 1811 Alfold; **Jacob** b 27 Dec 1811, bap 24 Dec 1820; Shadrack b 28 Jan 1813 [sic], bap 24 Jan 1813, bap 24 Dec 1820; **Mesheck** b 23 Feb 1814, bap 27 Feb 1814, bap 24 Dec 1820; Abednego (1) b 10 Mar 1816, bur 28 Apr 1816, (2) bap 10 Dec 1820, bur 20 Jul 1821; Abraham b 11 Apr 1817, bap 13 Apr 1817, bap 24 Dec 1820; Sarah bap 10 Dec 1820 (m John Fisher) | *From*: Dunsfold, Surrey | *To*: Plympton Twp | *Occupation Eng*: Labourer; had poor relief | 1836

SOURCE: SRO (GMR), PSH/AL/1, PSH/AL/2/2(3), PSH/AL/4, PSH/DUN/1/2, PSH/DUN/2/2, PSH/DUN/8/2, PSH/DUN/8/3; Letter from John Barnes, 1 Jan 1837, *Continuation of Letters from Sussex Emigrants* (1837), 1–5; Beers, *Biographical Record*, 420; NA, RG 31, Canada Census, 1861 Plympton Twp, p42; AO, RG 1 C-IV, Township Papers, Plympton; E. Nielsen, *The Egremont Road*

Randall, Isaac | bap 4 Jun 1809 | *Spouse*: Hannah Cooper, m 17 Oct 1830 Alfold | *From*: Dunsfold, Surrey | *To*: Plympton Twp, E ½ lot 17 con 8 until 1848; Warwick Twp 1851; St Clair, St Clair Co., Michigan, 1854 | *Occupation Eng*: Labourer | 1833 | *Assistance*: Vestry | Son of **Abraham** and **Sarah**; brother to **Mesheck** and **Jacob**. Sold Plympton Twp land to brother Abraham in 1848. In 1838 he served in militia unit under Cornet William M. Johnston of Adelaide.

SOURCE: SRO (GMR), PSH/AL/2/2(3); PSH/DUN/1/2; PSH/DUN/8/2; NA, RG 31, Canada Census, 1851 Warwick Twp agricultural schedule; E. Nielsen, *The Egremont Road*

Randall, Jacob | b 27 Dec 1811, bap 24 Dec 1820 Alfold, d 9 Jan 1887 Enniskillen Twp | *Spouse*: "family"; Louisa 37 b England (1861 census) | *Children* b in Canada: Alfred Henry, Mary Elizabeth, James, George Edward, Sarah, Martha Ann | *From*: Dunsfold, Surrey | *To*: Plympton Twp, E ½ lot 17 con 7 | *Occupation Eng*: Labourer | 1833 | *Assistance*: Vestry, £7.10.0 | Son of **Abraham** and **Sarah**; brother to **Isaac** and **Mesheck**. Estate valued at $1200 at time of death.

SOURCE: SRO (GMR), PSH/AL/3/1; PSH/DUN/8/2; WSRO, Goodwood Ms 1469, f16, Hale to Lord Egremont's Emigration Committee, 2 Jul 1833; AO, RG 1, C-IV, Township Papers, Plympton; RG 22/273, Lambton Co Surrogate Court, file 1083; NA, RG 31, Canada Census, 1861 Plympton Twp, pp30-1

Randall, Mesheck | b 23 Feb 1814, bap 27 Feb 1814 Alfold and 24 Dec 1820 Alfold, d 1834 | *From*: Dunsfold, Surrey | *To*: Plympton Twp, E ½ lot 17 con 8 | 1833 | *Assistance*:Vestry | Son of **Abraham** and **Sarah**; brother to **Isaac** and **Jacob**. Died intestate in 1834 and Isaac, who shared the lot in Plympton with him, inherited.
SOURCE: SRO (GMR), PSH/AL/3/1, PSH/DUN/8/2; AO, RG 1, C–IV, Township Papers, Plympton

Randall, Shadrack | *b 24 Jan 1813, bap 24 Dec 1820 Alfold* | *Spouse: Elizabeth Pullen, m 12 Jan 1852* | *Children: Jane* | *From: Dunsfold, Surrey* | *To: Plympton Twp, lot 16 con 8* | *Occupation Eng: Labourer* | *1836* | *He was in Johnston's militia unit raised in Adelaide in 1838. Child of Abraham and Sarah.*
SOURCE: *SRO (GMR), PSH/AL/2/2(3); E. Nielsen, The Egremont Road; AO, RG 80-27-1, vol 16, London District marriage register, p167*

Rapley, Charles (widower) | bap 12 Aug 1798 Egdean, West Sussex, d 18 Sep 1862 Adelaide, age 62 | *Spouse*: Frances Adams*, m 11 Nov 1822 Stopham, bap 24 Apr 1802, d Oct 1826 | *Children*: Sophia bap 22 Dec 1822, d 5 Apr 1903 (m Mark **Mann** 8 Mar 1841); Elizabeth bap 5 Dec 1824 (m John Payne 29 Nov 1842); Sarah* bap 29 Oct 1826, d 1827 | *From*: Wisborough Green, West Sussex | *To*: Adelaide Twp, Upper Canada; Spring Farms, lot 19 con 5 SER | *Occupation Eng*: Brickmaker | *Occupation Can*: Farmer | 1832 | Lord Melville | *Assistance*: Earl of Egremont and parish | Drummer in militia in 1837 Rebellion; buried 4th line cemetery, Mt Zion Old Methodist, Adelaide.
SOURCE: *Letters from Emigrants* (1839), 2–5; WSRO, Misc. Paper 1031; Ep 1/24/113; PAR 187/1/1/3, PAR 187/1/3/1, PAR 210/1/2/1; AO, Middlesex Co., Adelaide Twp, 4th line cemetery, Mt Zion Old Methodist; *History of the County of Middlesex*; ADH, Adelaide, St Ann's Anglican registers, 1833-83; AO, RG 80-27-1, London District marriage registers, vol 16, p160; Correspondents Margaret Parsons, Jane Thompson

Rapley, James | bap 4 Mar 1781 Fittleworth, d 18 Oct 1832 of ague contracted on voyage | *Spouse*: Mary Collins*, m 3 Jun 1805 Pulborough, bap 5 Oct 1783 Pulborough, d 1831 Wisborough Green aged 47 | *Children*: James* b 1806; Charles* bap 1807, d 1875; George* b 1808, d 1830; Mary* bap 1810; Sarah* bap 1812, d 1831 Wisborough Green; William bap 1814, d 24 Sep 1896 (m (1) Jane Hilton, 8 children; (2) Jane Page 28 Aug 1873, 2 children); Jane* bap 1815; David bap 1817, d 1915 (m Harriet Hilton); Charlotte bap 1818, d 19 Dec 1895 (m George Buttery); Anne (m Richard Biddulph); James* bap 1820; Jesse bap 1822, d 25 Nov 1878 London, Ont (m (1) Cynthia O'Dell; (2) Miranda O'Dell); Lucy bap 1824, d 12 Apr 1905 Adelaide (m John **Downer**); Thomas bap 1826, d 20 Feb 1906 Yale, Mich. (m Emily **Cooper**); children up to William bap Pulborough, thereafter bap Wisborough Green | *From*: Wisborough Green, West Sussex | *To*: Adelaide Twp | *Occupation Eng*: Labourer | 1832 | *Assistance*: Earl of Egremont and parish
SOURCE: WSRO, Misc. Paper 1031; PAR 153/1/1/1, PAR 153/1/1/3, PAR 210/1/2/1; NA, RG 1 L 3, Upper Canada Land Petitions, vol 438a, R2/46; *History of the County of Middlesex*; E. Nielsen, *The Egremont Road*; Correspondents Blake Rapley, Jane Thompson

Rapson, James | 30, b 27 Oct 1802, bur 24 Sep 1889 Ball's Cemetery Hullett Twp, Huron Co | *Spouse*: Sarah Tribe, m 30 Oct 1821 | 32, bap 17 Aug 1800, d 12 Nov 1857, bur Ball's Cemetery | *Children*: Charlotte, daughter of Sarah Tribe, b 9 Jul 1819, d 5 Mar 1852 (m Thomas Rapson); Hannah b 13 Nov 1822; Mary b 15 Aug 1824 (m Jesse Penfold); Phillip b 22 May 1826; Isaac b 24 May 1828; Rhoda b 2 Mar 1830, bap 6 Jul 1830; James b 1 Jan 1832, bap 17 Jan 1832, d 2 Jun 1832, bur Montreal; b in Canada: Jane b 1833; Sarah b 15 Aug 1834; Ruth b May 1836; Martha b 14 Aug 1838; John b 14 May 1840; Maria b 25 Mar 1842; Hester b 25 Dec 1843 | Rhoda and James were baptized at Petworth Independent and Congregational Chapel, Petworth; Church of England (1840 census); Baptist (1871 census) | *From*: Lodsworth, West Sussex | *To*: Galt, Dumfries Twp; then Waterloo Twp, Goderich Twp | *Occupation Eng*: Sawyer | 1832 | Lord Melville | *Assistance*: Earl of Egremont, W.H. Yaldwin, and parish | James was brother of Rhoda **Thair**. Sarah's parents also with them. Brydone visited them 21 Jul 1834 at their hut a few miles past Waterloo.

SOURCE: *Brighton Guardian*, 16 Oct 1833; *No. 4 Continuation*, 27–8; *Portsmouth, Portsea, and Gosport Herald and Chichester Reporter*, 22 Jul 1832; *Continuation of Letters from Sussex Emigrants …Written in 1836* [1837], 10–11; Brydone, *Narrative*, 42, map; WSRO, Goodwood Ms 1640, f114; PHA 137; MF 678, Petworth Independent Chapel Register; PAR 128/1/1/2; PAR 128/1/3/1; PAR 149/1/1/2; PAR 149/1/3/1; AO, RG 1, Ontario Land Records Index; RG 21, Gore District Census and Assessments, 1840 Waterloo Twp; OGS, *Index to the 1871 Census of Ontario, Huron County*; Correspondents James M. MacDonald, Helen Rapson Kerr, David Rapson; James and Sarah Rapson Family Bible

Rapson, William | b 26 Sep 1808 | *Spouse*: Maria Thaere (Thair), m 10 Jun 1829, bap 29 Jul 1808 | *Children*: Fanny bap 1 Aug 1830; girl (b 12 May 1833 during voyage) | *From*: Lodsworth, West Sussex | *To*: Galt or Preston; Waterloo Twp 1834 | *Occupation Eng*: Soldier in 24th Regiment of Foot over 8 years | 1833 | *Assistance*: Earl of Egremont and W.H. Yaldwin | Brother of James **Rapson**; the family returned to Lodsworth in late 1840s it seems. William and Maria were listed in the 1851 census for Lodsworth Common along with Fanny age 20 and 3 children born in Upper Canada: William 14, John 8, and Sarah 6 (PRO, HO 107/1654, f.62); George age 9 was listed on 1861 census (RG 9 626, ff38-54). Maria was a sister of George **Thair**.

SOURCE: Brighton *Herald*, 27 Jul 1833; *Letters from Emigrants* (1839), 1–2; WSRO, PAR 128/2/6; PHA 138; OGS *Families* 35, no 2 (May 1996): 105; AO, RG 1, Ontario Land Records Index; RG 21, Gore District Census and Assessments, 1834, 1837 Waterloo Twp, 1842 Dumfries Twp; NA, RG 1, L3, Upper Canada Land Petitions, vol 434 R 18/45; Correspondents Helen Rapson Kerr, David Rapson

Raynor, C. | *To*: York (area) | *Occupation Can*: Labourer: hired in a sawmill | 1832 | Raynor was presumably related to Mary Ann Rayner, wife of Henry **Goldring** and came out at same time.

SOURCE: *No. 3 Continuation*, 17–18; WSRO, Misc. Paper 1705

Read, James | 20, bap 19 Jul 1812 St Helens, Isle of Wight | *From*: West Cowes, Isle of Wight | 1833 | *Assistance*: Parish/House of Industry | Admitted to House of Industry 12 Mar 1831; discharged 25 Apr 1833.

SOURCE: IOWRO, Z/HO/15; Index of Baptisms, Marriages, and Burials

Read, James | b 14 Sep 1816, bap 22 Dec 1816 Congregational Church, Node Hill, Isle of Wight | *From*: Brighstone (Brixton), Isle of Wight | 1834 | *Assistance*: Parish/House of Industry | Son of James and Elizabeth of Newport (innkeeper). Admitted to House of Industry with father and two sisters (?) 15 Jan 1833 removed from Portsea (James 47, Elizabeth 17, and Anne 12); discharged 16 Apr 1834 "to Canada." Had also been in House of Industry in 1825.

SOURCE: IOWRO, Z/HO/13, Z/HO/15; Index of Baptisms, Marriages, and Burials

Reeves, George | 18 | *From*: Felpham, West Sussex | *Occupation Eng*: Agricultural labourer | 1835

SOURCE: GB, Parl. Papers, *Select Committee … Poor Law Amendment Act …* App. to 12th Report, 1837

Reeves, William | *From*: Littlehampton, West Sussex | 1832 ? | To have a passage to Montreal.
SOURCE: *No. 3 Continuation*, 18–20; WSRO, PHA 137

Reeves, William Dyer | 13 | *From*: Felpham, West Sussex | *Occupation Eng*: Agricultural labourer | 1835 | Travelling with James **Irish** and family. Son of Mrs Irish.
SOURCE: GB, Parl. Papers, *Select Committee … Poor Law Amendment Act …* App. to 12th Report, 1837; WSRO, PHA 142

Rice, Mary | possibly bap 17 Apr 1814 | *From*: Fittleworth, West Sussex | 1833 | *Assistance*: Earl of Egremont and parish | Illeg. daughter of Mary Rice, sister of Frances who emigrated in 1845. Went with Hannah and James **Tilley**; she was sick and and left at Montreal with the Captain as she "turned out so very bad."
SOURCE: Letter from Hannah Tilley, 29 Jul 1833, *No. 4 Continuation*; WSRO, PAR 86/1/2/1

Rich, Frank | 18 | *From*: Newport, Isle of Wight | 1834 | *Assistance*: Parish | Admitted to Newport Bridewell 27 Mar 1834; discharged 16 Apr 1834 "to Canada."
SOURCE: IOWRO, Z/HO/L5

Rich, James | 35 | *Spouse*: Sarah (Hilton ?) | 38 | *Children*: 6 children emigrated: Charles 15; Henry 11; James 9, bap 17 Aug 1828 (m Deborah Welman 5 Aug 1851); Mary Ann 5, bap 1 Jan 1832; Harriett 3, bap 12 Jan 1834; George 1 ½, bap 3 Jan 1835 | *From*: New Fishbourne, West Sussex | *To*: In Caradoc Twp, Middlesex Co., 1851-2 | *Occupation Eng*: Agricultural labourer | *Occupation Can*: Labourer | 1837 | *Assistance*: Parish, backed by Poor Law Commissioners, 5½ passages | "The family are most anxious to join some relatives in Toronto. They are incapable of supporting themselves in this country and it is considered by Persons who take an interest in them that they are proper subjects for Emigration" (PRO, MH 12, 13199). Remarks from abstract of PEC emigrants: "Most respectable" family.
SOURCE: PRO, MH 12, 13199; WSRO, PHA 140; PAR 85/1/2/1; NA, RG 31, Canada Census, 1851 Caradoc Twp, p47; *Middlesex County Marriages and Baptisms, 1848-1858*, comp. D. Walker and F. Stratford-Devai (Delhi: Norsim Publishing 1998)

Richard, Charles | 21, bap 4 Jun 1815 | *From*: Walberton, West Sussex (and Ferring) | *Occupation Eng*: Agricultural labourer | 1836 | *Assistance*: Richard Prime and parish | A Charles Richards of Caradoc m Amy Parker of Ekfrid 2 Dec 1844; Richards was granted S 1/2 lot 2 con 3 Ekfrid Twp 14 Jan 1848.
SOURCE: GB, Parl. Papers, *Select Committee … Poor Law Amendment Act …* App. to 12th Report, 1837; WSRO, PAR 202/2/3; AO, RG 1, Ontario Land Records Index; Church Records Coll., Delaware, Ekfrid, and Caradoc, Anglican register, 1834–51

Richardson, Samuel | Single | *From*: Hellingly, East Sussex | *Occupation Eng*: Labourer; had been on parish relief | 1834
SOURCE: ESRO, PAR 375/12/5, PAR 375/31/2/6

Riddill, William | boy | *From*: Scotland? | 1835 | One emigrant from Scotland is noted on Sockett's chart in 1835. Riddill was to work passage out as steward; apparently he was a protégé of Brydone and known to Sockett.
SOURCE: Letter from Sockett to Brydone in possession of Barbara Brydone; WSRO, PHA 8679

Ripley, William | possibly bap 3 Sep 1815 | *From*: Hellingly, East Sussex | 1834 | *Assistance*: Parish, Earl of Chichester, Thomas Calverley | Son of William, a hawker, and Letitia. The Ripleys seem to have been a family of hawkers with several branches of the family in Hellingly.
SOURCE: ESRO, PAR 375/12/5, PAR 375/31/2/6, PAR 375/31/2/7

Rivers | *Spouse*: Wife | *Children*: 6 children | *To*: Blandford (town plot) | *Occupation Eng*: Labourer | 1834 | Brydone asked by Hawke to take charge of family which arrived at Toronto by way of New York at the same time as Petworth group. They received a lot in Woodstock but were not sponsored by the PEC.
SOURCE: Brydone, *Narrative*, 25-6, 40

Robinson, George | *Spouse*: Wife | *From*: Angmering, West Sussex | *To*: Delaware, London District | John Holden was boarding with them in Nov 1833.
SOURCE: *No. 6 Continuation*, 47-8

Rogers, Joseph | 31 | *From*: Godshill, Isle of Wight | 1834 | *Assistance*: Parish/House of Industry | Admitted to House of Industry 21 Apr 1833; discharged 16 Apr 1834 "to Canada."
SOURCE: IOWRO, Z/HO/L5

Rose, James | 28 | Single | *From*: Dorking, Surrey | *To*: Trafalgar Twp, Gore Dist. ? | *Occupation Eng*: Labourer | 1832 | *Assistance*: Dorking Emigration Society | In 1838 he was on part of lot 34 con 3 Trafalgar Twp.
SOURCE: *Letters from Dorking*, 10, 24–5; AO, Gore District Census and Assessments, 1838 Trafalgar Twp

Rowland, James | 23, b 28 Nov 1808 baseborn, bap 18 Dec 1808 | Single | *From*: Dorking, Surrey | *Occupation Eng*: Labourer | 1832 | *Assistance*: Dorking Emigration Society
SOURCE: *Letters from Dorking*, 10; SRO (GMR), PSH/DOM/1/7

Ruddick (Ruddock), (Mrs) | 1833 | Hale noted that she was in labour on 26 Jun during trip up St Lawrence; no child recorded.
SOURCE: WSRO, PHA 138; Goodwood Ms 1469, f16

Russell, Henry | 27, bap 11 Mar 1810 Chale, Isle of Wight | *Spouse*: Harriet Holbrook, m 28 Jun 1834 Mottistone, Isle of Wight | 22, bap 13 Apr 1816 Brighston, Isle of Wight | *Children*: 1 child emigrated: William 2, bap 7 Jun 1835 | *From*: Shalfleet, Isle of Wight (previously Newbridge/Calbourne, Isle of Wight) | *Occupation Eng*: Agricultural labourer, "working on crossroads" on parish relief 1834 | 1837 | *Assistance*: Parish, House of Industry | Remarks on abstract of IOW emigrants: "Respectable."
SOURCE: IOWRO, Z/HO/44; Z/HO/L7; Index of Baptisms, Marriages, and Burials; WSRO, PHA 140

Russell, James | 17, b 28 Nov 1819, poss bap 6 Dec 1819 in House of Industry, son of Charlotte Russell | *From*: Newport, Isle of Wight | 1837 | *Assistance*: Parish, House of Industry | Apparently not brother of Henry.
SOURCE: IOWRO, Z/HO/44; Index of Baptisms, Marriages, and Burials

Sageman, William | 42, bap 21 Apr 1793 | *Spouse*: Mary Willett, m 28 Oct 1817 Easebourne, bap 21 Apr 1793, d 23 Oct 1827 | *Children*: Birtha 17, 1819; Charles 15, bap 16 Apr 1820; Mary Ann 13, bap 10 Jul 1822; Daniel 11, bap 27 Jun 1824; Emma 9, bap 9 Apr 1826 | *From*: Petworth, West Sussex (or Tillington) | *To*: Amherstburg, 20 miles from | *Occupation Eng*: Soldier, 52nd Regiment of Foot | 1836 | *Assistance*: Earl of Egremont and parish | His pension papers sent to Sockett. Mary was possibly the mother of Belinda **Willett**. In his army records, William was described as 5'7" tall, with brown hair, grey eyes, and a fresh complexion. A William Sageman, widower, d 3 Sep 1861 intestate at Sandwich West, leaving an estate valued at $100; his daughter Bertha was married to John Clark, a miller in Sandwich West. Charles and a Thomas Sedgeman [sic] lived among the Petworth cluster in 1851-2.
SOURCE: PRO, CO 385/10, 17, Pinnock to Sockett, 22 Mar 1836; WO 97/659; WSRO, PAR 75/1/3/1, PAR 149/1/2/1/, PAR 197/1/1/4, PAR 197/1/2/1; Letter from James Cooper, May

1838, *Brighton Herald*, 25 Aug 1838; AO, RG 22/311, Essex Co. Surrogate Court, file 1020;
NA, RG 31, Canada Census, 1851 Adelaide, pp9, 27

Sanders (Saunders), John | bap 19 Apr 1793 | *Spouse*: Possibly wife and children | | *From*:
Lurgashall, West Sussex | *To*: York | *Occupation Eng*: Bricklayer; pauper of Lurgashall |
1833 | *Assistance*: Earl of Egremont and parish | Petworth party
SOURCE: WSRO, Goodwood Ms 1470, f217; PHA 5557; PAR 130/1/1/4, PAR 130/1/2/1, PAR
130/1/3/1

Sandford, William | 17 | Single | *From*: Dorking, Surrey | *Occupation Eng*: Labourer | 1832
| *Assistance*: Dorking Emigration Society
SOURCE: *Letters from Dorking*

Saunders, James | 24 | *From*: Newport, Isle of Wight | 1837 | *Assistance*: Parish, House of
Industry
SOURCE: IOWRO, Z/HO/44

Saunders, William | b 6 Dec 1805, bap 19 Jan 1806 | *Spouse*: Matilda Peskett, m 23 Jan 1826
at Billingshurst | *Children*: 4 children emigrated: Susan bap 9 Jul 1826; Eliza bap 28 Mar
1830; Jane bap 15 Apr 1832 | *From*: Wisborough Green, West Sussex | *To*: Nelsonville, Ohio
| *Occupation Eng*: Bricklayer | 1832 | England | *Assistance*: Parish and landowners | 4th
child not found.
SOURCE: *Courtauld Family Letters* I: xxi; WSRO, PAR 21/1/3/1, PAR 210/1/2/1, PAR
210/37/11(3)

Saxby, Charles | 39, bap 25 Dec 1796 | *Spouse*: (1) Mary*; (2) Charlotte Carver, m 7 May
1831 Binstead, West Sussex | 29 | *Children*: 2 children emigrated: Emily 15, bap 6 May
1820 Climping, West Sussex (d of Mary); Mary Ann 1, bap 21 Feb 1834 (d of Charlotte)
| *From*: Yapton, West Sussex | *Occupation Eng*: Farming man; husbandman; "For employ-
ment" | 1835 | *Assistance*: Richard Prime and parish | Charles was described at time of
marriage to Charlotte as widower of Littlehampton.
SOURCE: GB, Parl. Papers, *Select Committee … Poor Law Amendment Act …* App. to 12th
Report, 1837; WSRO, PHA 142; PAR 22/1/3/1/, PAR 51/1/2/1, PAR 225/1/2/1

Sayres (Sayers), James | bap 17 Oct 1813, b Pulborough Poorhouse | *From*: Pulborough,
West Sussex | *To*: America | 1833 ? | *Assistance*: Given £10 to "send him to America"
25 Apr 1833 | Illegitimate son of Lucy Sayers, Humphrey Cooper cited as father in bas-
tardy bond.
SOURCE: WSRO, PAR 153/12/3

Scott. See also Scutt

Scott, George | 26, b 27 May 1805, bap 21 Jul 1805 | Single | *From*: Dorking, Surrey | *To*:
Trafalgar, Gore Dist. | *Occupation Can*: Farm labourer | 1832 | *Assistance*: Dorking Emi-
gration Society | Brother of **John**.
SOURCE: *Letters from Dorking*, 10; SRO (GMR), PSH/DOM/1/7

Scott, John | 20, b 6 Jun 1811, bap 21 Jul 1811 | Single | *From*: Dorking, Surrey | *To*: Trafal-
gar, Gore Dist. | *Occupation Can*: Farm labourer | 1832 | *Assistance*: Dorking Emigration
Society | Brother of **George**.
SOURCE: *Letters from Dorking*, 10; SRO (GMR), PSH/DOM/1/7

Scutt (Scott), John | 46 | *Spouse*: Sarah | *Children*: 6 children emigrated: including John
bap 30 Sep 1832, Ellen bap 19 Apr 1835 | *From*: Sullington, West Sussex | *To*: Upper Canada
| *Occupation Eng*: Farming man | 1835 | *Assistance*: Parish and G.J. Gibson | Was turned
out of his house "without a shilling" on 1 Apr 1835. "For employment" in Upper Canada.
SOURCE: WSRO, PHA 142; PAR 190/1/2/1, PAR 190/31/1

Shambrook (Shambrink), John | *Spouse*: Mary Titmouse, m 15 Mar 1821, bap 5 Jan 1800 | *Children*: Lydia bap 7 Jul 1822; Hannah bap 31 Oct 1824; George bap 1 Aug 1830; Sophia b 26 May 1831, bap 1 Apr 1832 | *From*: Bassingbourn, Cambridgeshire | *To*: Dundas ? | *Occupation Eng*: Labourer | 1832 | Lord Melville or Evelyn) | *Assistance*:Vestry and Charles Beldam | Mary Titmouse was a sister of Edith **Racher** and Simeon **Titmouse**.
SOURCE: *Emigration: Letters* (1833), 19–21; WSRO, PHA 137; Cambridge County Record Office, PII/1/3, PII/1/4, PII/1/10, PII/12/5

Sharp, David Clowser (Cloudesley, Clousley) | bap 16 Feb 1806, son of Sarah Clowser at Fittleworth | *Spouse*: Clara Ware, m 26 Mar 1827 Northchapel, bap 1 Mar 1807 | *Children*:Thomas bap 19 Aug 1827 Fernhurst, David bap 13 Feb 1829, Sarah bap 27 Mar 1831, Edmund bap 10 Jan 1834, George bap 27 May 1835 | *From*: Petworth, West Sussex (and Fittleworth) | *To*:Amherstburg | *Occupation Eng*: Labourer | constant poor relief | 1836 | *Assistance*: Earl of Egremont; had been on parish relief
SOURCE: *Brighton Herald*, 2 Aug 1834; *Continuation of Letters from Sussex Emigrants ...Written in 1836* [1837]; WSRO, PAR 82/1/2/1, PAR 86/1/1/5, PAR 86/31/1, PAR 142 1/1/2, PAR 142 1/3/1, PAR 149 1/1/2, PAR 149 1/2/1; Letter from James Cooper, May 1838, *Brighton Herald*, 25 Aug 1838

Sharp, Edmund Sr | bap 22 Jan 1784 | *Spouse*: Sarah Clowser, widow, formerly West, m 30 Mar 1806 Fittleworth | *Children*: David Clowser **Sharp** bap 16 Feb 1806 Fittleworth; Elizabeth b 6 Apr 1807, bap 10 Apr 1807; Mary b 17 Aug 1809; Edmund bap 16 Apr 1816, d 15 Aug 1836 | *From*: Petworth, West Sussex | *To*: Sandwich | 1833 | *Assistance*: Earl of Egremont | Described by Sockett as "a man of extremely bad character." His daughter Elizabeth was married to George **Turner**, army pensioner from Petworth. Brother to Thomas **Sharp**.
SOURCE: *Brighton Guardian*, 16 Oct 1833; *No. 5 Continuation*; WSRO, Goodwood Ms 1469, f13, Sockett to Richmond, 4 Oct 1833; PAR 86/1/1/4, PAR 86/1/1/5, PAR 149/1/1/1, PAR 149/1/1/5, PAR 149/1/2/1

Sharp, Thomas | 51, bap 3 Oct 1788 | *From*: Petworth, West Sussex | *To*: Amherstburg | *Occupation Eng*: Army pensioner, discharged as "worn out" after serving 20 years | 1836 | *Assistance*: Earl of Egremont | Brother of Edmund **Sharp** Sr. Uncle to David Cloudsley **Sharp**, Edmund Jr, and Elizabeth Turner. He emigrated in 1832 in a Petworth ship, returned to England in autumn of 1832, and went back to Canada on the Heber in 1836 with nephew David Sharp and family. His army record states he was 5'7" tall with brown hair, grey eyes, and a fair complexion. He served in both the East and West Indies.
SOURCE: PRO, MH 12, 13060; PRO, WO 97/527; WO 120/25; WSRO, PAR 149/1/1/2; Letter from James Cooper, May 1838, *Brighton Herald*, 25 Aug 1838

Sheath, Ed | *Spouse*: Wife | *Occupation Eng*: Agricultural labourer | 1837 | *Assistance*: 2 passages | This could possibly be Edward Sheath, bap 1804 in Gosport (Portsmouth) Hants, m Eliza May in 1829 at Portsea, Hants. Remarks on abstract of IOW emigrants: "Dissipated."
SOURCE: WSRO, PHA 140

Sheath, James | 45 | *Spouse*: Mary Munday, m 23 Apr 1837 Carisbrooke, just before the Diana sailed | 26 | *From*: Carisbrooke, Isle of Wight | *Occupation Eng*: Labourer; had been on parish relief | 1837 | *Assistance*: Parish, House of Industry | Mary was sister of Jane Munday, Job **Hodge**'s deceased wife.
SOURCE: IOWRO, z/HO/44; z/HO/L3; Index of Baptisms, Marriages, and Burials

Shepherd, Thomas | 18, bap 26 Jan 1818 | *From*: Petworth, West Sussex | *Occupation Eng*: Labourer | 1836 | *Assistance*: Earl of Egremont and Poor Law Commissioners
SOURCE: PRO, MH 12, 13060; WSRO, PAR 149/1/2/1

Shepherd, William | b 19 Jan 1814 | *From*: Petworth, West Sussex | *Occupation Eng*: Labourer, poacher | 1832 | William Shepherd was in process of being sued by Earl of Egremont for trespass but "not proceeded in as he afterward emigrated to Canada but returned." He must have returned very quickly as he was being prosecuted again in Mar 1833, and was in Horsham Gaol for trespass and unpaid fines in Aug 1833. Was prosecuted again in 1834/5.
SOURCE: WSRO, PHA 4454, Apr 1832; PHA 4455, Mar 1833; PHA 4457; PHA 8543

Sheppard, George | "boy" | *From*: Egdean, West Sussex | *To*: Blandford Twp | 1834 | *Assistance*: Parish and Earl of Egremont
SOURCE: WSRO, PAR 79/31/1; Brydone, *Narrative*, 42

Sherring, John | 20, b 13 Jul 1813, bap 26 Sep 1813 St James St Independent Church, Newport | *From*: Newport, Isle of Wight | 1834 | *Assistance*: Parish/House of Industry | Admitted to House of Industry 22 Feb 1834; discharged 16 Apr 1834 "to Canada."
SOURCE: IOWRO, Z/HO/L5; Index for Baptisms, Marriages, and Burials

Short, Henry | *From*: West Grinstead, West Sussex | *Occupation Eng*: Labourer, intermittently on parish relief | 1835 | *Assistance*: Parish and Mr Woodward, vicar | He had broken his leg at the beginning of 1835.
SOURCE: WSRO, PAR 95/12/1, PAR 95/38/1

Simmonds (Simmons), Charles | 31 | *From*: Carisbrooke, Isle of Wight | *Occupation Eng*: Servant | 1837 | *Assistance*: Parish, House of Industry | In Mar he was on the list for Australia. Admitted to House of Industry IOW Feb 1837; discharged 26 Apr 1837.
SOURCE: IOWRO, Z/HO/44; Z/HO/L5

Sims, William | 19, bap 23 Feb 1817, d 5 Mar 1857 | *From*: Yapton, West Sussex (and Tortington) | *To*: Blandford (Woodstock) | *Occupation Eng*: Agricultural labourer | *Occupation Can*: Carpenter | 1835 | *Assistance*: Parish and Richard Prime | A William Sims died 3 Mar 1857 in West Oxford Twp; his estate was valued at £2410 and his wife Jane was sole executor (AO, RG 22/221, Oxford Co. Surrogate Court, file 250 (old ser.)).
SOURCE: GB, Parl. Papers, *Select Committee … Poor Law Amendment Act …* App. to 12th Report, 1837; WSRO, PAR 198/1/2/1; AO, Oxford Co, Woodstock, Old St Pauls Cemetery; NA, RG 1, L3, Upper Canada Land Petitions, vol 242, H1/52, vol 534, W19/88

Slipper, Robert | 46, bap 27 Mar 1785 | *Spouse*: Harriet Bixley, m 10 Mar 1810 Guildford Holy Trinity | 44 | *Children*: 7 children emigrated: George 21; Harriet 14, bap 26 Apr 1818; Robert 13, bap 26 Apr 1818; Rose 12, bap 9 Feb 1820 (all Guildford St Mary); Jane 8, bap 19 Oct 1823 in the workhouse; Levi 6, bap 13 Oct 1826 (m Catherine Rines 27 Dec 1862); John 2, bap 11 Apr 1830 in the workhouse (m Louisa Reynolds 27 May 1860) | Methodist (1851 census) | *From*: Dorking, Surrey (South St) | *To*: eventually Huron Co. | *Occupation Eng*: Shoemaker | *Occupation Can*: Shoemaker (1851 census) | 1832 | *Assistance*: Dorking Emigration Society | They were living in Wilmot Township at time of 1851 census.
SOURCE: *Letters from Dorking*, 10; SRO (GMR), PSH/DOM/1/6, PSH/DOM/3/1, PSH/GUM/2/1, PSH/GU/HT/1/3; NA, RG 31, Canada Census, 1851 Wilmot Twp, p17; AO, RG 80-27-2, vol 1, Brant Co. marriage register, p89; vol 20, Huron Co. marriage register, p79

Smart, Henry | 29, bap 26 Sep 1802 | *Spouse*: Jane Baker, m 31 Dec 1829 at Petworth, d of cholera shortly after arrival | *Children*: Frederick bap 2 Jan 1831 Wisborough Green, d soon after arrival; infant, d at birth at Quebec | *From*: Kirdford, West Sussex | *To*: Ancaster | *Occupation Eng*: Labourer; had parish relief 1830 | 1832 | *Assistance*: Earl of Egremont, Rev. J.K. Greetham, and parish | Jane was sister of William **Baker**.

SOURCE: *Emigration: Letters* (1833), 37–41; WSRO, Misc. Paper 1031; PAR 116/31/1, PAR 149/1/3/1, PAR 210/1/2/1; Correspondent Lesley Parker

Smart, James | bap 2 Apr 1797 | *Spouse*: Ann(e) Gumbrell, m 20 Feb 1816 | *Children*: Benjamin* bap 16 May 1819, bur 2 Jan 1820; Rhoda bap 6 May 1821; another child | *From*: Wisborough Green, West Sussex | *To*: Nelsonville, Ohio | *Occupation Eng*: Labourer | 1832 | England | *Assistance*: Parish and landowners
SOURCE: *Courtauld Family Letters* I: xxi; WSRO, PAR 210/1/2/1, PAR 210 1/3/1, PAR 210/37/11(3)

Smith, Daniel | 44 | *Spouse*: Mary Kench, m 5 Feb 1821 Birdham, bap 21 Mar 1802 Birdham | *Children*: 6 children emigrated, all under 14: Daniel bap 23 Sep 1821; Mary Ann bap 28 Sep 1823; Sarah bap 25 Sep 1825; Harriet bap 27 Jan 1828; Henry bap 27 Jun 1830; Elizabeth bap 21 Jul 1833 | *From*: Linchmere, West Sussex | *Occupation Eng*: Labourer, farming man | 1835 | *Assistance*: £60 raised on rates
SOURCE: PRO, MH 12, 13028; WSRO, PHA 142; PAR 23/1/3/1, PAR 23/1/1/5, PAR 124/1/2/1

Smith, Daniel | 52 | *Spouse*: Maria Lucas, m 15 Nov 1815 Amberley | 45, bap 18 Sep 1791 Amberley | *Children*: 6 children emigrated: Mary 18, bap 18 Mar 1816; Jemima 17, bap 23 Dec 1818; Lucy 15, bap 28 Oct 1821; John 13, bap 19 Sep 1824; Daniel 9, bap 24 Jun 1827; Emma 6, bap 13 Dec 1830 | *From*: Tillington, West Sussex | *To*: Amherstburg | *Occupation Eng*: Labourer and soldier | 1836 | *Assistance*: Earl of Egremont and parish | Sockett wrote to Pinnock, the emigration agent, and the Chelsea Hospital to negotiate the paying of Smith's pension in Toronto. First three children baptized in Amberley; next three at Lodsworth. In his army record he was given as 5'5½" tall, brown hair, grey eyes, and fair complexion. Possibly died 2 Feb 1844 (note in army records). "A most impudent & insolent man; for employment. Is known to William Spencer, Wellington Square, Gore District; and to Edward Berry, Township of Louth, Niagara."
SOURCE: PRO, CO 385/10, 17 Pinnock to Sockett, 22 Mar 1836; WO 97/742; WSRO, PAR 3/1/2/1, PAR 3/1/3/1, PAR 128/2/6, PAR 197/12/1; Letter from James Cooper, May 1838, *Brighton Herald*, 25 Aug 1838

Smith, George. See Lillywhite, Daniel
Smith, Henry. See Lillywhite, Daniel
Smith, John | 33, bap 22 Jan 1804 Woolbeding | *Spouse*: Rebecca Turrell of Horsham, m 12 Nov 1822 Petworth | 32, possibly bap 3 May 1801 Horsham | *Children*: Thomas 14, bap 30 Mar 1823 Horsham; Leonard 11, bap 16 Apr 1826 Horsham; Matilda 9, bap 28 Sep 1828 Midhurst; Caroline 6, bap 1 May 1831 Woolbeding; Jane 3, bap 19 Jan 1834 Heyshott; John 1 ½ | *From*: Woolbeding, West Sussex | *To*: Dundas | *Occupation Eng*: Agricultural labourer | 1837 | *Assistance*: Parish 5 passages | Son of Jane Smith. Remarks on abstract of PEC emigrants: "Most respectable" family.
SOURCE: PRO, MH 12, 13028; WSRO, PHA 140; PHA 1068; PAR 101/2/2, PAR 106/1/1/3, PAR 106/1/2/3, PAR 106/1/3/1, PAR 138/1/3/1, PAR 149/1/3/1, PAR 216/1/1/3, PAR 216/1/2/1

Smith, John | 28 | *From*: Newport, Isle of Wight (previously Arreton, Isle of Wight) | 1837 | *Assistance*: Parish, House of Industry | Discharged from House of Industry, IOW, 26 Apr 1837.
SOURCE: IOWRO, Z/HO/44; Z/HO/L5

Smithers, Charles | *From*: Wisborough Green, West Sussex | *Occupation Eng*: Labourer, relieved in provisions during winter | 1835 | *Assistance*: Parish, backed by Poor Law Commissioners; had been in Wisborough Green Work House | Related to **Lucy, William, Edward**, and **Stephen**.
SOURCE: PRO, MH 12, 13060; WSRO, PAR 210/31/10 (1818); PAR 210/37/4, PAR 210/37/5

Smithers, Lucy | 46 (widow) | *Children*: Probably mother of **Charles, Edward, Stephen, William** | *From*: Wisborough Green, West Sussex | 1836 | *Assistance*: Parish, backed by Poor Law Commissioners; had been in Wisborough Green Poor House.
SOURCE: PRO, MH 12, 13060; WSRO, PAR 210/31/10 (1818), PAR 210/37/4, PAR 210/37/5

Smithers, Ned [Edward] | *From*: Wisborough Green, West Sussex | *To*: Nelsonville, Ohio | 1832 | England | *Assistance*: Parish; had been in Wisborough Green Poor House | Probably related to **Lucy, William, Charles,** and **Stephen**.
SOURCE: *Courtauld Family Letters*, I: xxi; WSRO, PAR 210/31/10 (1818), PAR 210/37/4, PAR 210/37/5

Smithers, Peter | bap 26 Dec 1792 | *Spouse*: Mary Pacey, m 23 May 1817, bap 7 Dec 1794 | *Children*: Sophy b 5 Mar 1818, bap 19 Apr 1818; Susannah bap 13 Jan 1822; Elisabeth bap 27 Jun 1824; Mary bap 3 Dec 1826; Ann bap 20 Sep 1829; Peter bap 22 Apr 1832 | *From*: Wisborough Green, West Sussex | *To*: Pittsburgh, Penn. | *Occupation Eng*: Labourer | 1832 | England | Mentioned in a letter from Mr Job Mitchell of London in 1831 with regard to emigration: "I believe you have some that would goe such as P. Smithers."
SOURCE: *Courtauld Family Letters*, I: xxi; WSRO, PAR 210/1/1/9, PAR 210/1/2/1, PAR 210/37/11(3)

Smithers, Stephen | *From*: Wisborough Green, West Sussex | *Occupation Eng*: "Has been in service" | 1835 | *Assistance*: Parish, backed by Poor Law Commissioners; had been in Wistborough Green Poor House | Related to **Lucy, William, Edward, Charles**.
SOURCE: PRO, MH 12, 13060; WSRO, PAR 210/31/10 (1818); PAR 210/37/4, PAR 210/37/5

Smithers, William | 23, b c1812/13 | *From*: Wisborough Green, West Sussex | *Occupation Eng*: Labourer | 1836 | *Assistance*: Parish, backed by Poor Law Commissioners; had been in Wisborough Green Poor House | Related to **Lucy, Edward, Charles, Stephen**
SOURCE: PRO, MH 12, 13060; WSRO, PAR 210/31/10(1818), PAR 210/37/4, PAR 210/37/5

Snelling, Henry | *Spouse*: Sarah | *Children*: 1 child emigrated: Henry bap 1833 | *From*: Isle of Wight ? | *To*: Blandford (town plot, lot between Barwick and 1st street) | *Occupation Can*: Labourer | 1834
SOURCE: Brydone, *Narrative*, 4, 14, 26; WSRO, PHA 139; AO, RG 1, C-IV, Township Papers; OMNR, Survey Records, 1834 Plan

Snelling, John | 32, bap 1 Jan 1802 | *Spouse*: Eleanor (Ellen) Welling, m 17 Feb 1823 | 31 | *Children*: 6 children under 12 emigrated: Eleanor bap 14 Dec 1823; Sarah, Anne, and Julia bap 13 Nov 1825; William bap 30 Sep 1827; Frances Jane bap 5 Apr 1829 | *From*: Broadwater, West Sussex | *Occupation Eng*: Shoemaker | 1834 | *Assistance*: Notice in MH 12 says "run away" and underneath "emigration account" £27.6.5d. | Did they emigrate with PEC?
SOURCE: PRO, MH 12, 12905; WSRO, Goodwood Ms 1476, f277; WSRO, PAR 29/1/2/2, PAR 29/1/2/1, PAR 29/1/3/1

Snow, George | 15, bap 27 Oct 1816 | *From*: Carisbrooke, Isle of Wight | *Occupation Eng*: Apprentice returned to House of industry by William White, 2 years unexpired | 1833 | *Assistance*: Parish, House of Industry | Admitted to House of Industry 20 Oct 1832; discharged 25 Apr 1833.
SOURCE: IOWRO, Z/HO/L5; Index of Baptisms, Marriages, and Burials

Snow, James | 17, b 31 Jul 1810, bap 26 Aug 1810 | *From*: Godshill, Isle of Wight | *Occupation Eng*: Apprentice returned to House of Industry by P. Colenutt | 1833 | *Assistance*: Parish, House of Industry | Admitted to House of Industry 12 May 1832; discharged 25 Apr 1833. No evidence that George and James are brothers.
SOURCE: IOWRO, Z/HO/L5; Index of Baptisms, Marriages, and Burials

Southerton (Sutherton), Charles | bap 20 May 1798 | *Spouse*: Esther Smart, m 10 Jun 1819 | bap 28 Jul 1793 | *Children*: Sophy bap 6 Feb 1819; Elisabeth bap 2 Sep 1821; Thomas bap 25 Jan 1824; Olive bap 29 Apr 1832 | *From*: Wisborough Green, living in Chichester, West Sussex | *To*: Sunday Creek, Ohio | *Occupation Eng*: Shoemaker, cordwainer | 1832 ? | England? | *Assistance*: Parish and landowners | Esther was not sister of James Smart.
SOURCE: WSRO, PAR 210/1/1/9, PAR 210/1/2/1, PAR 210/1/3/1, PAR 210/37/11(3)

Spencer, William | *Spouse*: Sarah Cooper, m 7 Jun 1829 | bap 14 Dec 1809, d of typhus fever shortly after arrival | *From*: Petworth, West Sussex | *To*: Nelson Twp 1833 | *Occupation Can*: Labourer; farming on shares | 1832 | *Assistance*: Earl of Egremont | Purchased a town lot in Bronte, Trafalgar Twp, by late 1836.
SOURCE: *Continuation of Letters from Sussex Emigrants ... Written in 1836* [1837], 19–22; *Emigration: Letters* (1833), 24; *No. 3 Continuation*, 18–20; WSRO, PAR 149/1/1/2, PAR 149/1/3/1

Squibb, George | 14, bap 6 Jun 1819 | *From*: Calbourne, Isle of Wight | 1834 | *Assistance*: Parish/House of Industry | Admitted to House of Industry 1 Nov 1833. Returned from London, "brot" back by his Brother (Parish Calbourne). Discharged from House of Industry 16 Apr 1834 "to Canada." Brother to **James**.
SOURCE: IOWRO, Z/HO/L5; Index to Baptisms, Marriages, and Burials

Squibb, James | 24, bap 17 Feb 1811 Brightstone, Isle of Wight | *From*: Newport, Isle of Wight | 1834 | *Assistance*: Parish/House of Industry | Admitted to Newport Bridewell 22 Feb 1834; discharged 16 Apr 1834 "to Canada." Brother to **George**.
SOURCE: IOWRO, Z/HO/L5; Index to Baptisms, Marriages, and Burials

Squibb (Squib), William | 22 | *From*: Newport, Isle of Wight ? | 1837 | *Assistance*: Parish, House of Industry
SOURCE: IOWRO, Z/HO/44

Stamford, William | poss bap 14 Jul 1788 Bassingbourn, d by 1859 | *Spouse*: Elizabeth Chapel, m 30 Jul 1822 Meldreth | *Children*: James bap 13 Aug 1822, Maryann bap 26 Feb 1826, Charles Augustine bap 13 Jan 1830 | *From*: Bassingbourn, Cambridgeshire | *Occupation Eng*: Gardener | 1832 | *Assistance*: Vestry and Charles Beldam | William may be a relation of Maria (Stamford) Wilson.
SOURCE: Cambridge County Record Office, P 11/1/4, P 11/12/5; Wilson Family Papers, Obed Wilson Correspondence, Maria Wilson to Obediah Wilson, Bassingbourn, 22 Aug 1839, 4 May 1859

Stamp, William | 38 | *Spouse*: Jane | *Children*: 5 children evidently emigrated: Edward bap 4 May 1808, William bap 1 Feb 1811, Susan bap 27 Sep 1812, Maria bap 30 Jul 1815, James bap 29 May 1818, Sarah bap 5 Jul 1820, John bap 25 Dec 1822, Henry bap 30 Aug 1829 | *From*: Ware, Hertfordshire | *To*: St Catharines | *Occupation Eng*: Farming man; "very hard working man" | 1835
SOURCE: IGI; WSRO, PAR 149/1/1/1; PHA 142; Robert T. Bell family papers

Standing, William | *To*: Nelson Twp ? | Possibly William and Sarah Standing whose son Henry was bap 19 Nov 1826 in Petworth. Mentioned by James and Hannah Tilley; also by William and Elizabeth Daniels: "they go on the same way they did when they were at home."
SOURCE: *No. 4 Continuation*, 30-2; *No. 5 Continuation*, 34-5

Stedman, John | poss bap 23 Jan 1799 Dorking | *From*: Hascomb, Surrey | (near Godalming) | *To*: Malahide, Middlesex Co. | *Occupation Can*: Farm labourer | 1832 | Eveline | "Matthew" is with him (this could be Matthew Stedman, bap 25 Jun 1820, not his brother).
SOURCE: *Emigration: Letters* (1833), 33–5, Letter from John Stedman, 7 Aug 1832; SRO (GMR), PSH/DOM/1/1/7

Stemp, Arthur | b 20 Nov 1803, bap 19 Dec 1803 at Petworth | *Spouse*: Mary Tanner, m 16 Jul 1826 at Petworth, bap 21 Jul 1805 | *Children*: Jane bap 20 Jun 1830; Hannah bap 2 Oct 1831; b in Canada: George b 11 Sep 1838 [1837?] bap 3 Jun 1838 | *From*: Kirdford, West Sussex | *To*: Dundas | *Occupation Eng*: Labourer; going to seek for haymaking Jun 1830 | 1832 | *Assistance*: Earl of Egremont, Rev. J.K. Greetham, and parish
SOURCE: WSRO, Misc. Paper 1031; PAR 116/1/2/1, PAR 116/31/1, f47, PAR 149/1/1/1; *No. 4 Continuation*; C. Pinch, *Anglicanism in Ancaster, 1790-1830* (Ancaster Historical Society 1979)

Stephenson, William | 28, b 23 Nov 1813, bap 30 Jan 1814 | *Spouse*: Hannah (possibly a sister) | 20 | *From*: Yarmouth, Isle of Wight (removed from St Clements, London, to Yarmouth IOW) | *Occupation Eng*: "out of employ" | 1833 | *Assistance*: Parish/House of Industry | Admitted to House of Industry 12 Feb 1833; discharged 25 Apr 1833
SOURCE: IOWRO, Z/HO/L5; Index to Baptisms, Marriages, and Burials

Stevens, Henry | 40, bap 15 May 1796 Midhurst | *Spouse*: Jane Lawrence (Laurence), m 5 Oct 1818 | 36, bap 4 Feb 1798 Selham | *Children*: Henry 17, bap 24 May 1818 (m Elizabeth Simmons in Canada); Elizabeth* bap 26 Dec 1819; James* bap 15 Apr 1821; Ann 14, bap 13 Apr 1823; Maria 11, bap 11 Sep 1825; Stephen 9, bap 13 May 1827; Jonathon* bap 8 Mar 1829; Timothy 4, bap 19 Jan 1834; child b c1838-40 Norwich, Canada | *From*: Easebourne, West Sussex | *Occupation Eng*: Labourer | 1836 | *Assistance*: Parish, had considerable poor relief to 1834. | A witness to Henry and Jane's marriage was Edward **Burt** (Birt); he was married to Elizabeth Lawrence and they emigrated in 1843. It would seem Mary Cooper had a child by Henry Stevens (presumably Jr) in Canada. Asterisked children are not listed in PRO, MH 12, as emigrating.
SOURCE: PRO, MH 12, 13028; WSRO, PAR 75/1/2/1, PAR 75/1/2/2, PAR 75/1/3/1, PAR 75/12/2; PAR 165/2/2, PAR 138/2/3; Letter from James Cooper, May 1838, *Brighton Herald*, 25 Aug 1838; Correspondent Shirley Blakely

Stowe | *pre* 1833 |
SOURCE: WSRO, Misc Paper 1705

Streeter, George | bap 2 Jan 1814, d 5 Jul 1898 Weidman, Mich | *Spouse*: Susan Isenhauer b New York, d 17 May 1884 Elmira, Woolwich Twp, Waterloo Co. | *Children*: b Canada: Adaline b 8 Sep 1839, d 15 Nov 1936; George W. b 8 Nov 1841; Michael b 5 Jun 1843, d 21 Dec 1927; John M. b Dec 1845; Leonard I. b 22 May 1847; Mary b 28 Jan 1850; James b 10 Sep 1853; Lavinia b 19 Jan 1858 | *From*: Shipley, West Sussex | *To*: Waterloo Twp, then Elmira | *Occupation Can*: Blacksmith apprentice | 1832 | Lord Melville | Brother of Hannah **Bristow** née Streeter.
SOURCE: Mentioned in letter from Edward Bristow, *No. 6 Continuation*, 41–2; WSRO, PAR 168/1/2/1; Correspondents Virginia Sande, Roger Miller

Sturt, John | *From*: Dorking, Surrey | 1832 | *Assistance*: Paid for himself | Was coming back to England for his family.
SOURCE: Letter from George Scott, *Letters from Dorking*

Sturt (Start), William | 38 | *Spouse*: Elizabeth Fowler, m 4 Dec 1820 South Bersted | 39, bap 7 May 1797 Birdham | *Children*: Olive 13, bap 28 Apr 1822; James 10, bap 6 Jun 1824 South Bersted; Martha 7, bap 28 May 1826; Eliza 4, bap 29 Sep 1828; Isaac bap 30 Jan 1831; George 2, bap 2 Mar 1833 | *From*: Felpham, West Sussex | *To*: St Catharines | *Occupation Eng*: Agricultural labourer; had been a pauper boy | 1835 | *Assistance*: Parish and Earl of Egremont
SOURCE: *Sussex Advertiser*, 14 Mar 1836; WSRO, PHA 142; GB, Parl. Papers, *Select Committee ... Poor Law Amendment Act ...* App. to 12th Report, 1837; WSRO, PAR 19/1/2/1, PAR 19/1/3/1, PAR 23/1/1/5, PAR 81/1/2/1

Suter, George | bap 13 Jan 1811 Walberton, West Sussex, d 21 Nov 1887 Thorah Twp, bur Stone Church Cemetery, Beaverton | *Spouse*: Mary Sayers, m in Canada, b c1811, d 14 Jul 1897 Beaverton | *Children* b in Canada: George b c1837 Woodstock, d 1 Nov 1916 Thorah; James b c1839, d 3 Feb 1917; William b c1841; Henry b c1843, d 18 Dec 1920; John b c1846; Robert b c1849, d 12 Aug 1906; Mary Theodora b 30 May 1855, d 13 Jun 1933 | Presbyterian (1871 census) | *From*: Walberton, West Sussex | *To*: Woodstock c1837; Balsam Lake (Bexley Twp) c 1847, Thorah Twp by 1850 | *Occupation Can*: Carpenter | 1835 ?
SOURCE: *Letters from Sussex Emigrants*, 6–7; WSRO, PAR 202/2/2; NA, RG 31, Canada Census, 1851 Thorah Twp, 1871 Thorah Twp; Correspondents S.R. Suter, Rachel Fletcher

Tanner, Eliza | 16, bap 1 Dec 1816 | *From*: Petworth, West Sussex | *To*: Dundas | 1832 | *Assistance*: Earl of Egremont | In service at Dundas, emigrating with her sister **Mary** and brother-in-law Arthur **Stemp**.
SOURCE: WSRO, PHA 137; PAR/149/1/2/1

Tanner, Richard | *From*: Haslemere, Surrey (or Lurgashall?) | *To*: Toronto Twp ? | 1833 | Does not appear to be near relation of Eliza or Mary Tanner. Living with James Helyer "Toronto near York Upper Canada."
SOURCE: Letter from James Helyer, *No. 6 Continuation*, 43–4

Tarrant, – | 1834 | A young man
SOURCE: WSRO, PHA 139

Taylor, John | 21, b 9 Jan 1811, bap 27 Jan 1811 | Single | *From*: Dorking, Surrey | 1832 | *Assistance*: Dorking Emigration Society
SOURCE: *Letters from Dorking*, 10; SRO (GMR), PSH/DOM/1/7

Terry, Thomas | 27 | *Spouse*: Sarah Sherman King, m 22 Feb 1830 Dorking, bap 9 Feb 1811 Wonersh, child of Sarah King | *Children*: 1 child emigrated: Thomas bap 20 Mar 1831 Dorking | *From*: Dorking, Surrey (Holmwood) | *To*: Yarmouth Twp, London District | *Occupation Eng*: Labourer | 1832 | *Assistance*: Dorking Emigration Society | By 1851 census they were living in Vittoria, Charlotteville Twp, Norfolk Co, and stayed there the rest of their lives.
SOURCE: *Letters from Dorking*, 10; SRO (GMR), PSH/DOM/2/2/3, PSH/DOM/3/1, PSH/WON/1/4; IGI for Surrey; Correspondent C. William Terry

Thair (Thaire), George | bap 9 May 1806 at Lurgashall, d by 1838 | *Spouse*: Rhoda Rapson, m 27 May 1831 | *Children*: 3 children emigrated: John b 19 Dec 1831, bap 29 Jan 1832; Tom; Fanny | Baptist Independent and Congregational Chapel, Petworth; Methodist in Canada. | *From*: Lodsworth, West Sussex | *To*: Dundas, then Galt, Dumfries Twp; Waterloo Twp (1834) | *Occupation Eng*: Brickmaker | 1833 | *Assistance*: W.H. Yaldwyn and parish | His wife, Rhoda, was a sister of James **Rapson** and his sister was married to William **Rapson**. Travelled and settled in a party with the Rapsons and John **Dearling**'s party.
SOURCE: *Brighton Guardian*, 16 Oct 1833; *No. 4 Continuation*, 29–30; *No. 5 Continuation*; WSRO, MF 678, Petworth Independent Chapel; Goodwood Ms 1469, f 16; Letter from John & Caroline Dearling, *Continuation of Letters … Written in 1836* [1837], 1–3; *Letters from Emigrants* (1839), 1–2; WSRO, PAR 130/1/1/4, PAR 130/1/2/1; AO, RG 21, Gore District Census & Assessments, Waterloo Twp

Thaire (Thayre), William | *Spouse*: Mary Ann Hampshire, m 20 Jul 1823, b 16 Apr 1803, bap 24 Jul 1803 | *Children*: Mary bap 26 Oct 1823; James bap 13 Apr 1828 | *From*: Wisborough Green, West Sussex | *To*: Nelsonville, Ohio | *Occupation Eng*: Labourer | 1832 | England | *Assistance*: Parish and landowners

SOURCE: *Courtauld Family Letters*, I: xxi; WSRO, PAR 210/1/2/1, PAR 210/1/3/1, PAR 210/37/11(3)

Thomas, Edmund | bap 21 Apr 1805 | *Spouse*: Ann Puttock, m 11 Apr 1826 | *Children*: Mary bap 31 Jul 1826, William bap 16 Dec 1827, George bap 22 Mar 1829, Edmund bap 19 Sep 1830, Peter b on ship 3 Jun; b in Canada: Elizabeth 16; Elijah 14; Jesse 12; Harriett 8; Jane 5 (1851 census) | *From*: Kirdford, West Sussex | *To*: Waterloo Twp, Gore Dist; Woolwich Twp (1834), lot 88 con D (1851) | *Occupation Eng*: Labourer | *Occupation Can*: Farm labourer | 1832 | Lord Melville | *Assistance*: Earl of Egremont, Rev. J.K. Greetham, and parish | Brother of **James** and **Thomas**. Ann's sister, Sarah **Puttock**, was with them. William, Edmund, and youngest six children listed with parents in 1851 census.
SOURCE: *Emigration: Letters* (1833), 34–5; WSRO, Misc. Paper 1031; PAR 116/1/1/6, PAR 116/1/2/1, PAR 116/1/3/1; AO, RG 21, Gore District Census and Assessments, Woolwich Twp; NA, RG 31, Canada Census, 1851 Woolwich Twp, p45; Census Index, 1871 Waterloo Co

Thomas, James | bap 22 Feb 1807 | *Spouse*: Mary Ball alias Boxall, m 29 Jul 1829 | *Children*: Henry bap 21 Feb 1830, William bap 7 Aug 1831 | *From*: Kirdford, West Sussex | *Occupation Eng*: Labourer | 1832 | *Assistance*: Earl of Egremont, Rev. J.K. Greetham, and parish | Brother of **Edmund** and **Thomas**.
SOURCE: WSRO, Misc. Paper 1031; PAR 116/1/1/6, PAR 116/1/2/1, PAR 116/1/3/1, PAR 116/31/1 f47

Thomas, Thomas | b 1795, d 24 Mar 1868 | *Spouse*: Elizabeth Durrant (Deront in Canada), m 30 Dec 1821, b 1795, d 2 May 1891 | *Children*: 2 children emigrated: Rhoda bap 28 Dec 1823 (m Thomas Randall?); David, d 15 Apr 1894 (m (1) Hannah Cope); b in Canada: George b c1833 | Episcopal Methodist (1851 census) | *From*: Kirdford, West Sussex | *To*: Adelaide Twp, London Dist. | *Occupation Eng*: Labourer; Private soldier 5th Regiment of Foot, 5 Apr 1814 – 2 Mar 1817 | 1832 | *Assistance*: Earl of Egremont, Rev J.K. Greetham, and parish | Brother of **Edmund** and **James**. Thomas mistakenly called Elijah in his wife's obituary. Army records noted Thomas as "under size," 5' 2¼", dark brown hair, brown eyes. Bur 4th line cemetery, Mt Zion Old Methodist, Adelaide Twp. Military grant E ½ lot 18 con 4 SER Adelaide.
SOURCE: *Emigration: Letters* (1833); WSRO, Misc. Paper 1031, 1399; PAR 116 1/2/1, PAR 116/1/3/1; AO, Middlesex Co., Adelaide Twp, 4th line cemetery, Mt Zion Old Methodist; RG 1, L3, Upper Canada Land Petitions, vol 504, T21/5; Ontario Land Records Index; RG 22/321, Middlesex Co. Surrogate Court, file 607; NA, RG 31, Canada Census, 1851 Adelaide Twp, p9; *Strathroy Age*, 7 May 1891, 15 Apr 1894

Thomas, William | *From*: Pulborough, West Sussex | 1833 ? | *Assistance*: "Resolved that Mr Thomas be sent to America"; no further details.
SOURCE: WSRO, PAR 153/12/3

Tickner, William | bap 20 Sep 1795 or 23 Aug 1797, d 10 Aug 1877 Lobo Twp | *Spouse*: Sarah Boxall, m 26 Nov 1816, bap 12 May 1798 | *Children*: Jane bap 1 Nov 1818, Thomas bap 5 Nov 1820, Caroline bap 19 May 1822, Ann bap 4 Apr 1824, William bap 13 Apr 1826, Eliza bap 11 May 1828, George bap 16 May 1830, James bap 1 Jan 1832 | *From*: Lurgashall, West Sussex | *To*: Adelaide; Caradoc Twp; Lobo Twp con 8 | *Occupation Eng*: Labourer; pauper | 1832 | *Assistance*: Earl of Egremont, W.H. Yaldwin, and parish | Youngest child d in crossing. William was in Carodoc by 1838 when he sold his right to E ½ lot 17 con 5SER Adelaide. According to the *Strathroy Age*, William was alive in Jan 1877: "yet quite smart," and a great hunter; his wife, Sarah "Bond" had died in 1838.

SOURCE: Capling, "The Capling Family"; WSRO, Goodwood Ms 1460, f113; PHA 8557; PAR 130/1/1/4, PAR 130/1/2/1, PAR 130/1/3/1; AO, RG 1, C-IV, Adelaide Twp Papers; RG 80-8-0-39, deaths 1877, vol C, Waterloo Co., 8055; "A Few of the Old Folks," *Strathroy Age*, 12 Jan 1877

Tilley, James | bap 2 Dec 1781 Lodsworth | *Spouse*: Hannah Chesman, m 3 Mar 1801, bap ? Dec 1782 Witley, Surrey | *Children*: Sarah* bap 27 Jul 1804 Thursley, Surrey; **Mary** bap 24 Jan 1807 Thursley; Ann* bap 22 Apr 1810 Thursley; Elizabeth* bap 28 Jun 1812 Thursley; **William** bap 24 May 1814 Thursley; Maria bap 5 Jan 1817 Thursley; Henry bap 14 May 1820; Frederick bap 1 Sep 1822; possibly George | *From*: Petworth, West Sussex | *To*: Nelson Twp (9 miles from Dundas) | *Occupation Eng*: Labourer | *Occupation Can*: Labourer; tavern keeper 1836 | 1833 | *Assistance*: Earl of Egremont | Daughter **Mary** married George **Boxall**, and emigrated in 1832; **William** also emigrated with them. Sarah, Ann, and Elizabeth were not mentioned in Hannah Tilley's letter.

SOURCE: *Brighton Guardian*, 16 Oct 1833; *No. 4 Continuation* (1833), 30–2; IGI for Surrey; WSRO, PAR 128/1/1/1, PAR 149/1/1/5, PAR 149/1/2/1

Tilley, William | bap 24 May 1814 Thursley, Surrey | *Spouse*: Eliza Helensly, m 18 Oct 1839 Burlington | *From*: Petworth, West Sussex | *To*: Nelson Twp(?); Saltfleet Twp in 1839 | *Occupation Can*: Sawing for steamboats in 1833 | 1832 | *Assistance*: Earl of Egremont | Emigrated with his sister **Mary** and her husband **George Boxall**. Child of **James** and **Hannah**. William, age 40, and Eliza, age 35, were in Saltfleet Twp with 3 children in 1851.

SOURCE: *Emigration: Letters* (1833); IGI for Surrey; NA, RG 31, Canada Census, 1851 Saltfleet Twp; ADN, St Pauls, Burlington, registers

Tilt, William | 27, b 25 Jun 1805, bap 31 Jul 1805 Dorking, d 4 Apr 1883 Blair | *Spouse*: (1) Jane Cosens, 27, d 17 Oct 1832 in childbirth, bur Turner Cemetery, Tuckersmith Twp (2) Caroline **Cosens** m 1834 in Canada, b 17 Jan 1817, d 13 May 1907 Blair | *Children*: William 5, bap 23 Apr 1827 Capel; Jane 3, bap 3 Jan 1830 Capel; John bap 7 Aug 1831 Capel; b in Canada: Ellen b 5 Apr 1852 Blair; Caroline b c1855 (m Dr John A. Oatman 5 Jun 1883); George b c1857; Elizabeth b c1859 | Presbyterian (1871 census) | *From*: Dorking, Surrey (also Capel) | *To*: German Mills, Waterloo Co | *Occupation Eng*: schoolmaster | 1832 | *Assistance*: Dorking Emigration Society | Jane was a daughter of Charles **Cosens**, who also emigrated; Caroline, another daughter, was listed as age 15 when she emigrated. William was clerk of Waterloo South Township in 1871. According to his obituary, he had 17 children.

SOURCE: *Letters from Dorking*, 10; Letter from Ann Cosens, 31 Mar 1833; SRO (GMR), PSH/CAP/3/1; PSH/DOM/1/7; KPL, Waterloo Co., Waterloo Twp, Blair Cemetery (OGS transcription); OGS, Huron Co. cemeteries, Tuckersmith Twp, Turner Cemetery; UCA, Wesleyan Methodist baptismal registers, Town of Blair 3:379; NA, RG 31, Canada Census, 1851 Waterloo Twp; 1871 Census Waterloo South Twp, 3: 16; *Dumfries Reformer*, 12 Apr 1883; *Berlin Daily Telegraph*, 13 May 1907; Correspondent Eunice M. Brake

Titmouse, Simeon | bap 13 Apr 1802 | *Spouse*: (1) Sarah Jackson, m 8 Oct 1823, bap 20 Apr 1806 | *Children*: 3 children emigrated: Charles bap 8 Jul 1824 Litlington, Ann bap 9 Nov 1828, George bap 1 May 1831 (m Izabel McKenzie 1854); b in Canada: Richard 14, William 12, Joseph 8 (m Jessie Wishart 4 Apr 1866), Elizabeth 8; Benjamin 6 (1851 census) | *From*: Bassingbourn, Cambridgeshire | *To*: Dundas, Nelson Twp | *Occupation Eng*: Farm labourer, employed by parish | 1832 | Lord Melville or Evelyn | *Assistance*: Vestry and Charles Beldam | Simeon was brother of Mary **Shambrook** and Edith **Racher**. The 1842 Flamborough census listed 3 children born England and 3 born Canada. The 1851 census of West Flamborough listed Simeon's wife as Catherine, age 38, b Ireland.

SOURCE: *Emigration: Letters* (1833), 19–21; Cambridge County RO, PII/I/3, PII/I/4, PII/I/10, PII/I2/5, PII/I2/6, P108/2; NA, RG 31, Canada Census, 1851 West Flamborough Twp, p23; Correspondent Maurice Titmouse

Townsend, Charles | *From*: Lewes, East Sussex | *To*: Montreal | 1834
SOURCE: *Sussex Advertiser*, 8 Sep 1834

Townsend, George | 20, b 18 Oct 1814, bap 27 Nov 1814 | Wesleyan Methodist | *From*: Lewes, East Sussex (St Mary's Lane) | *To*: Montreal | 1834 | Brydone reported he left at Montreal without permission.

SOURCE: Brydone, *Narrative*; ESRO, Sussex Non-conformist Registers, vol 5, RG 4/2943

Tribe, Benjamin | *bap 2 May 1813, d 22 Aug 1848 Woolwich Twp* | *Spouse: Mary Ann Lepard, m 10 Apr 1837 in Canada* | *Children: Robert Andrew b c1838/9, Sarah Jane, Catherine, Thomas b 1844?, Mary Ann b 24 Apr1848* | *From: Lurgashall, West Sussex* | *To: Galt, Dumfries Twp* | *1832* | *Assistance: Earl of Egremont, W.H. Yaldwin, and parish* | *Son of Henry and Charlotte. Described as "of Pilkington" Twp when he died. The 1851 census also lists a Peter and Henry 4 in the household.*

SOURCE: *No. 4 Continuation, 25–6; WSRO, MP 3191, "The Tribe Tribe"; PAR 130/1/2/1; AO, RG 22/318, Wellington Co Surrogate Court, file 184; NA, RG 31, Canada Census, 1851 Pilkington Twp; UCA, Wesleyan Methodist baptismal registers, 1:363*

Tribe, George | bap 26 Jun 1814 | *Spouse*: Sarah Heather, m 25 Oct 1831 | *From*: Wisborough Green, West Sussex | *To*: Nelsonville, Ohio | 1832 | England | *Assistance*: Parish and landowners

SOURCE: *Courtauld Family Letters* I: xxi; WSRO, PAR 210/1/2/1, PAR 210/37/11(3)

Tribe, Henry | bap 9 Mar 1776? d winter 1833 after 12 Feb | *Spouse*: Charlotte Tickener, m 1 Aug 1797 | *Children*: **Jane** b 1798, bap 10 Jun 1798 (m Jesse **Penfold** 1817); **Sarah** b 1800, bap 17 Aug 1800 (m James **Rapson** 1821); Charlotte b 1803, bap 9 Jan 1803 (m Joseph Evans); Henry* b 1805, bap 3 Mar 1805, bur 23 Jan 1807; Caroline* b 1808, bap 31 Jan 1808, bur 29 Feb 1808; Henry b 1808, bap 18 Dec 1808; Robert* b 1811, bap 20 Apr 1811 (m Mary Puttick); Benjamin b 1813, bap 2 May 1813, d 22 Aug 1848 (m Mary Ann Lepard 1837); Mary b 1815, bap 28 Mar 1815 (m Thomas Irvine); Richard b 1817, bap 10 Oct 1817; Ann b 1820, bap 23 Apr 1820; Jonathan b 1822, bap 9 Jun 1822, d 12 Mar 1872 (m Martha Broderick) *did not go to Canada | *From*: Lurgashall, West Sussex (Dial Green) | *To*: Galt, Dumfries; Woolwich Twp | *Occupation Eng*: Bricklayer; had been on poor relief | *Occupation Can*: Farmer and farm labourer | 1832 | *Assistance*: Earl of Egremont, W.H. Yaldwin, and parish. Richard was evidently working at York in Jul 1833 (*No. 4 Continuation*, 25–6).

SOURCE: WSRO, Goodwood Ms 1465, f18; PHA 8557, MP 3191, "The Tribe Tribe"; PAR 130/1/1/3; PAR 130/1/1/4, PAR 130/1/2/1, PAR 130/31/7; WCA, Genealogies Collection; Tribe-Penfold ms notes

Tribe, James | *From*: Chiddingfold, Surrey | 1832 | Brother of John
SOURCE: WSRO Index

Tribe, John Allen | *Spouse*: Unis Ward, m 29 Apr 1839 Malahide | *Children*: b in Canada: Elisha 12, Susana 9, Sheldon 6, Emily 2 (1851 census) | Baptist (1851 census) | *From*: Chiddingfold, Surrey | *To*: Port Talbot, close to Southwold, London Dist. | *Occupation Can*: Farm labourer | 1832 | *Assistance*: Mr Sadler | He emigrated with his brother **James** and his uncle **Thomas**.

SOURCE: *Emigration: Letters* (1833), 32–4; AO, RG 80-27-1, London District marriage register, vol 16 p113

Tribe, Thomas | b 28 Nov 1803 | *From:* Chiddingfold, Surrey | 1832 | Uncle of **James** and **John Allen**

SOURCE: Guildford Local History Centre, MF 1042/95, Chiddingfold Parish Register

Trusler (Trussler), John | b 7 Apr 1787, bap 10 Jun 1787 Chiddingfold, Surrey, d 29 or 31 Jan 1878, 90 years and 9 months Camlachie, bur Presbyterian Cemetery | *Spouse:* Jane Childs, m 6 Feb 1812 Lurgashall;, bap 13 Oct 1793 Lurgashall, d 5 Nov 1853 | *Children:* Timothy bap 12 Jun 1812 Lurgashall; Thamar bap 23 Jan 1814 Lurgashall; Absalom b 1815; Eliza[beth] bap 28 Dec 1817; Ruth bap 27 Feb 1820; Martha bap 17 Feb 1822; Eleanor bap 30 Oct 1824; Reuben bap 28 Jan 1827; Harriett bap 4 Oct 1829; Walter bap 18 Dec 1831, d 1833 Sarnia; Obediah d 1833 Sarnia; b in Canada: Arthur bap 3 Sep 1836 Plympton; Alvah b 4 Oct 1838 | *From:* Fernhurst, West Sussex | *To:* Plympton Twp | *Occupation Eng:* Labourer | 1833 | *Assistance:* W.H. Yaldwin and parish | According to Hale, Trusler's was one of the families who embarked on the schooner for Plympton. Walter and Obediah died on Henry Jones's wharf on the St Clair River while John and others were clearing land grant. Settled on land Jul 1833, purchased 50 acres crown land for £12 10s, Nov 1833; John and Timothy purchased E ½ lot 9 con 9 ser Plympton 1843. According to *Commemorative Biographical Record* of Lambton Co., John eventually owned 340 acres. Brother of **George**.

SOURCE: *Letters from Sussex Emigrants; No. 4 Continuation,* 29–30; WSRO, Goodwood Ms 1469, f16; PAR 82/1/2/1, PAR 130/1/1/3, PAR 130/1/1/4, PAR 130/1/2/1; NA, RG 31, Canada Census, 1861 Plympton Twp; Biography in Lambton Co. Library; *Sarnia Observer,* 8 Feb 1878; Correspondents Helen Stover, Jean McKenzie Brownhill, William Cairns, Janet Fisher, John D. Trussler

Trussler, George | b 7 Apr 1797, bap 9 Apr 1797, d 1 Sep 1882, bur Rosebank Cemetery, Wilmot Twp | *Spouse:* Elizabeth Gilbert, m 15 Jan 1820 Easebourne, West Sussex, b 5 Jan 1796, bap 20 Mar 1796, d 27 Oct 1867 | *Children:* John b 3 Oct 1820, bap 20 Jan 1821; James b 24 Feb 1822, bap 28 Feb 1823 Lodsworth, d 1 Jul 1833, drowned at York; Frances b 2 Mar 1825, bap 17 Apr 1825; David b 5 May 1827, bap 17 Jun 1827; William b 24 Aug 1829, bap 4 Oct 1829; Thomas b 10 Dec 1831, bap 1 Jul 1832; Harriet bap 1 Jul 1832, d on voyage in 1833; b in Canada: George Gilbert b 5 Jun 1838 Waterloo Twp, Waterloo Co, near Fischers Mills | *From:* Fernhurst, West Sussex | *To:* Plympton Twp; then German Co Tract, lots 144, 145, 146, Waterloo Twp Galt | *Occupation Eng:* Sawyer, poacher | *Occupation Can:* Farmer | 1833 | *Assistance:* W.H. Yaldwin, parish | Elizabeth Gilbert had twin daughters, Sarah and Mary, baptized 26 Jun 1819 at Easebourne Poorhouse (Mary bur 30 Jun 1819). Hale, on board ship, and Henry Jones, crown lands agent at Plympton, described Trussler as a complainer. Trussler turned down Jones's offer of work at $1.00 a day and took a house and land to become a farmer.

SOURCE: *No. 4 Continuation,* 29–30; WSRO, Goodwood Ms 1469, f16; PAR 75/1/1/5, PAR 75/1/3/1, PAR 82/1/2/1, PAR/128 1/2/1; PHA 138; AO, RG 1, A-1-6, 10531, Henry J. Jones to Peter Robinson, 10 Aug 1833; NA, RG 31, Canada Census, 1851 Waterloo Twp, p278; Correspondent Helen Stover

Tugwell (Mrs) | *Spouse:* Widow | *From:* Warnham, West Sussex | 1834 ? | *Assistance:* Parish | Did she go?

SOURCE: WSRO, PAR 203/31/7

Turner, Edward | *From:* Billingshurst, West Sussex | *Occupation Eng:* Seaman | 1832 ? | Offered an opportunity work out his passage.
SOURCE: WSRO, PHA 137

Turner, George | *Spouse:* Elizabeth Sharp, m 5 Apr 1824, bap 10 Apr 1807 | *Children:* 5 children emigrated: Thomas bap 17 Apr 1825; George bap 6 Aug 1826; Charles bap 24 May 1829; Edmund bap 24 Jul 1831; Hezekiah bap 31 Mar 1833 | *From:* Petworth, West Sussex | *To:* Plympton Twp ?; then Sandwich area | *Occupation Eng:* Army pensioner; also ragman/labourer | 1833 | *Assistance:* Earl of Egremont | Elizabeth was a daughter of Edmund **Sharp**. Turner was described by Capt Hale as "the black sheep of the party." According to Hale, his was one of the families who embarked on the schooner for Plympton. Sockett wrote that at some point before he emigrated George was condemned to be hanged for house breaking, but was reprieved and then pardoned because he intervened to prevent murder at the time of the robbery.
SOURCE: *Brighton Guardian,* 16 Oct 1833; *Continuation of Letters from Sussex Emigrants ... Written in 1836* [1837], 9–10; WSRO, Goodwood Ms 1469, f.13, Sockett to Richmond, 4 Oct 1833; Goodwood Ms. 1469, f16; PAR 149/1/2/1, PAR 149/1/3/1

Turner, Jane | 17 | *To:* Toronto ? | *Occupation Can:* Maid | 1835 | Travelled with Mr **Hersse** and family
SOURCE: WSRO, PHA 142

Tutt, [John] James | bap 10 Jun 1804 | Single | *From:* Hellingly, East Sussex | *Occupation Eng:* Labourer | 1834 | *Assistance:* Parish, Earl of Chichester, and Thomas Calverley
SOURCE: ESRO, PAR 375/12/5, PAR 375/31/2/6, PAR 375/31/2/7

Upton, Clifford | bap 13 Apr 1819 | *From:* Petworth, West Sussex | *To:* Guelph | *Occupation Can:* Apprentice carpenter | 1832 | *Assistance:* Earl of Egremont | Apprentice fee of £21 paid to William **Penfold** for Upton 6 Apr 1832. Emigrated with Penfold in the same year as his brother **William**.
SOURCE: WSRO, PHA 137; PHA 9015; PAR 149/1/2/1; *Emigration: Letters* (1833), 22–3

Upton, Egbert | bap either 11 Jan 1821 or 16 Feb 1825 | *From:* Petworth, West Sussex | *To:* Hamilton | 1834 | *Assistance:* Earl of Egremont | Probably went with **Frederick** and **Percival**, his brothers. According to Brydone the 3 Uptons found work in Hamilton.
SOURCE: Brydone, *Narrative,* 26; WSRO, PAR 149/1/2/1

Upton, Frances Taylor | 49, bap 17 Aug 1785 | *Spouse:* William Upton*, m 7 Aug 1804 at Petworth ("both minors") | *Children:* **William Taylor** b 16 Sep 1806, bap 31 Dec 1806; George b 5 May 1808, bap 15 Dec 1808; **Frederick** b 17 Jun 1809, bap 19 Jul 1809; Frances* b 9 Nov 1810, bap 21 Dec 1810; Emma* b 30 May 1812, bap 5 Aug 1812, bur 1 Aug 1834; Clara* b 1 Jul 1814, bap 25 Jul 1814, bur 12 Nov 1834; Mary Jane* bap 25 Jul 1817, bur 21 Jul 1818; **Percival** bap 25 Jul 1817; **Clifford** bap 13 Apr 1819; **Egbert** bap 11 Jan 1821 and 16 Feb 1825 | *From:* Petworth, West Sussex | *To:* Hamilton | *Occupation Eng:* William was a timber merchant | 1835 | *Assistance:* Earl of Egremont | Frances Jr emigrated to Tasmania in 1829. Frances Joined her sons in Hamilton. (William Sr had deserted her by 1831.) William and Clifford emigrated in 1832. Fred, Percival and Egbert in 1834. Other children may have gone with Frances in 1835.
SOURCE: WSRO, PHA 142; PAR 149/1/1/1, PAR 149/1/1/2, PAR 149/1/1/5, PAR 149/1/2/1; MP 1193; Correspondent Nanette Neville

Upton, Frederick | b 17 Jun 1809; bap 19 Jul 1809; d 1 Mar 1861, bur Toronto Necropolis | *Spouse:* Hannah **Palmer**, m 15 Jul 1835 Ancaster | *Children:* b in Canada: Frederick

Marshall, Walter, Teresa, Amanda, Adeline, Sidney, Edwina | Church of Engand (1851 census) | *From:* Petworth, West Sussex | *To:* Hamilton; then Toronto Twp (Port Credit?) | *Occupation Eng:* Seaman | *Occupation Can:* Harbourmaster (1851 census) | 1834 | *Assistance:* Earl of Egremont | Emigrated with brothers **Egbert** and **Percival**, following **Clifford** and **William**. Frederick acted as Brydone's steward on the *British Tar*. Brydone reported that the 3 Uptons found work in Hamilton, but that Frederick had volunteered to assist him in taking party to Blandford. Hannah accompanied Frederick's mother **Frances** in 1835. On 24 Aug 1835 Frederick petitioned for a free grant of land, citing 6 ½ years of service in the navy. The 1851 census lists Frederick 42 b Eng, harbourmaster, Hannah 43 b Eng, children b Canada: Frederick 15, Walter 13, Jessie 12, Female 10, Amanda 8, Sidney 3, Sarah 1, Adeline 5; servant Margaret Blackhall 15 b Ire.
SOURCE: Brydone, *Narrative,* 26; WSRO, PAR 149/1/1/2; P. Tripp and Laura Upton Newell, "The Upton Family"; NA, RG 5, A–1 Correspondence of Civil Secretary, vol 156, pp85567–70; RG 31, Canada Census, 1851 Toronto Twp; C. Pinch, *Anglicanism in Ancaster, 1790–1830*

Upton, Percival | bap 25 Jul 1817 | *From:* Petworth, West Sussex | *To:* Hamilton | 1834 | Emigrated with brothers **Frederick** and **Percival**, following **Clifford** and **William**.
SOURCE: Brydone, *Narrative,* 26

Upton, William Taylor | b 16 Sep 1806, bap 31 Dec 1806 | *From:* Petworth, West Sussex | *To:* Nelles Settlement, Niagara District | (Ardross Mills) | *Occupation Can:* Sawyer | 1832 | *Assistance:* Earl of Egremont | Emigrated with brother **Clifford**. Others of family followed.
SOURCE: *Emigration: Letters* (1833), 23; WSRO, PAR 149/1/1/2

Urry, Thomas | 53, bap 16 May 1781 or 1 May 1782 Calbourne, Isle of Wight | *From:* Isle of Wight | 1833 | *Assistance:* Parish/House of Industry | Admitted to House of Industry 29 Oct 1831; discharged 25 Apr 1833.
SOURCE: IOWRO, Z/HO/L5; Index of Baptisms, Marriages, and Burials

Varndell (Varndel), George | 48 | *Spouse:* Jane Stedman* (widow), m 15 Oct 1820, bur 16 Dec 1821 Petworth | *Children:* 2 children: Fanny (Francis sic) 16, bap 20 Nov 1820, daughter of Jane Stedman; George 6 | *From:* Tillington, West Sussex (and Petworth) | *To:* Woodstock | *Occupation Eng:* Soldier (?), labourer | 1836 | *Assistance:* Earl of Egremont, 2 parishes, and Poor Law Commissioners
SOURCE: PRO, CO 385/9; MH 12, 13060; WSRO, PAR 149/1/2/1, PAR 149/1/3/1, PAR 197/12/1; Letter from James Cooper, May 1838, *Brighton Herald,* 25 Aug 1838

Varndell, James | 19, bap 16 Mar 1817 | *From:* Petworth, West Sussex | *Occupation Eng:* Tailor | 1836 | *Assistance:* Earl of Egremont, parish, and Poor Law Commissioners | Illegitimate son of Massey Varndel.
SOURCE: PRO, MH 12, 13060; WSRO, PAR 197/1/2/1

Verrall, Ann | *To:* Blandford ? | 1834
SOURCE: AO, RG 1, C–IV, Township Papers, Town of Blandford

Verrall, John Henry ? | b Feb 1811 | *Spouse:* Fanny Margherita Charlotte | *Children:* Fanny bap 6 Jan 1832 | *From:* Seaford, East Sussex | *To:* Downie Twp | *Occupation Eng:* Surgeon | 1834 ?
SOURCE: Brydone, *Narrative,* 33, map; ESRO 30/167, MF XA, Parish of Seaford Register

Viney (Finey), Emily E. | 21, bap 25 Sep 1813 | *From:* Climping, West Sussex | 1835 | Travelled with 19-year-old **Frances** Viney; possibly a sister. Married William **Anscombe** in Canada.
SOURCE: WSRO, PHA 142; PAR 51/1/2/1

Viney, Francis (Frances) | 19, bap 14 Apr 1816 (female) | Church of England | *From:* Climping, West Sussex | 1835 | *Assistance:* Parish | James Viney, Francis's father, had intermittent parish relief. Possibly sister of **Emily** Viney. Married James **Birch** in Canada. SOURCE: WSRO, PHA 142; PAR 51/1/2/1, PAR 51/31/2

Vinson (Vincent), Wellington | 22, b 23 Apr 1814, bap 13 Aug 1814 | *From:* Petworth, West Sussex | *Occupation Eng:* Agricultural labourer | 1836 | *Assistance:* Earl of Egremont | "Mr Vinson being possessed of a few pounds, no allowance was made him by the Parish of Petworth, but his passage etc was given him by Lord Egremont." His brother George Vinson was entered in PHA 137 as a potential emigrant to Canada in 1832, but it is certain from writs served on him for poaching and trespass later in 1832, and further years, that he did not go. SOURCE: PRO, MH 12, 13060; WSRO, PAR 149/1/2/1

Voice (Foice), Ham | bap 1 Mar 1789 and 20 Dec 1790, d 30 Dec 1861 Blandford Twp | *Spouse:* (1) Mary Seaker, m 28 Jan 1812, d 15 Apr 1815; (2) Sarah | *Children:* Frederic bap 12 Jul 1812, Ham bap 9 Oct 1814 | *From:* Billingshurst, West Sussex | *To:* Woodstock by 1842 | *Occupation Eng:* Yeoman | 1836 | *Assistance:* Parish, backed by Poor Law Commissioners | Ham Jr died on arrival in Canada. Jul 1844 purchased park lot 3 range 1 Woodstock; sold it 1849. In 1851 on west part lot 11 con 16 East Zorra Twp. SOURCE: PRO, MH 12, 13060; WSRO, PAR 21/1/1/5, PAR 21/1/1/9, PAR 21/1/2/1, PAR 21/1/5/1; AO, RG 1, C-IV, Township Papers, Woodstock, Budd file; p72; Ontario Land Records Index; RG 22/221, Oxford Co. Surrogate Court, file 85; NA, RG 31, Canada Census, 1851 East Zorra agricultural schedule

Voice, Cornelius | b 1787, bap 23 Sep 1787 | *Spouse:* Elizabeth Smallwood, m 4 Aug 1807 Horsham, West Sussex | b 1789, bap 19 Jul 1789 Horsham | *Children:* Mary* bap 1807 (m James Elliot 1827); William bap 6 Jan 1811, Elizabeth b 9 Jun 1817, bap 28 Sep 1817 (m George **Coleman** Jr in Canada); Cornelius bap 12 Sep 1819; Martha b 10 Jun, bap 18 Nov 1821; George bap 9 Jan 1831; Joseph bap 9 Jan 1831 | Congregational | *From:* Billingshurst, West Sussex | *To:* Blandford, Town Plot, London Dist., lot between Barwick and 1st Street | *Occupation Can:* Carpenter/joiner and farmer | 1834 | *Assistance:* Earl of Egremont, parish | Children baptized at Hayes Independent Chapel, Slinfold, except George and Joseph who were bap at Billingshust Parish Church since there was no longer a registered Congregational minister in Slinfold. Letter annotation says they emigrated with 5 sons, 2 daughters and a nephew [John]. Fifth son not found. Brydone reported that Voice, 2 sons, and nephew were together making £6 per week in summer of 1834. SOURCE: *Continuation of Letters from Sussex Emigrants,* 9–11; Brydone, *Narrative;* PRO, RG4, 2365; WSRO, Goodwood Ms 1476, f307; PAR 21/1/2/1, PAR 106/1/1/3, PAR 106/1/1/5; AO, RG 1, C-IV, Township Papers, Woodstock; omnr, Survey Records, 1834 Plan

Wackford (Wakeford), James | d 21 Dec 1870 aged 77, 2 days | *Spouse:* Elizabeth Nash, m 22 Jun 1817, bap 19 Sep 1794 Selham, d 10 Jan 1871 | *Children:* Sarah bap 24 Jun 1821 Northchapel, d 1854 (m Michael **Ford**); James; Emma bap 12 Oct 1817; Thomas bap 22 Jan 1826 Lurgashall; William bap 30 Dec 1827 Lurgashall; Abraham bap 8 Nov 1829 Lurgashall; b in Canada: Martha ? (m John Douglas), Isaac 16, Fanny 14 (last 2 listed in 1851 census) | Church of England (1851 census) | *From:* Petworth, West Sussex (also Lurgashall) | *To:* Waterloo, near Galt; then Woolwich Twp and Peel Twp | *Occupation Eng:* Labourer | *Occupation Can:* Elizabeth is a hatmaker: | 1832 | *Assistance:* Earl of Egremont and Mrs Sarah Green SOURCE: *No. 3 Continuation,* 21–3; WSRO, PAR 130/1/2/1, PAR 149/1/2/1, PAR 149/1/3/1,

PAR 165/1/1/1; KPL, Waterloo Co, Waterloo Twp, Martins Mennonite Cemetery, local transcription; NA, RG 31, Canada Census, 1851 Peel Twp, p45; 1861 Peel agricultural schedule; AO, RG 1, Ontario Land Records Index; RG 22/318, Wellington Co. Surrogate Court, file 643; RG 21, Gore District Census and Assessments, 1834 Woolwich Twp; Correspondents Frances Acres, Roy Marvel

Wackford (Wakeford), William | bap 27 Oct 1793 | *Spouse:* Maria Jennings, m 29 Sep 1823 | *Children:* Maria bap 14 Nov 1834, bur 16 Nov 1834; possibly other children. | *From:* East Lavant, West Sussex | *To:* America | 1835 | *Assistance:* Parish | "In want of work & in great distress." May be relations of James and Elizabeth Wackford.

SOURCE: WSRO, PAR 120/1/1/1, PAR 120/1/3/1, PAR 120/1/2/1, PAR 120/1/5/1, PAR 120/30/1

Walden, George | 1834 | Disembarked at Montreal without permission.

SOURCE: Brydone, *Narrative*

Walden, John | bap 18 Mar 1798 | *Spouse:* Ruth Rewell (Rule), m 11 Dec 1819 Walberton, bap 12 Jun 1796 | *Children:* Elizabeth bap 3 Aug 1824, Mary bap 25 May 1828, Ann bap 25 May 1828, Charles bap 31 Jan 1831, Jane bap 29 Jun 1834 | *From:* Climping, West Sussex | *To:* St Catharines | *Occupation Eng:* Farming man and seaman | 1835 | *Assistance:* Parish | Ruth was probably a cook and confectioner. "Hard-working man for employment."

SOURCE: *Sussex Advertiser*, 14 Mar 1836; WSRO, PHA 142; PAR 51/31/2, PAR 51/1/2/1, PAR 202/1/3/1

Ware, William | 25 | Single | *From:* Boxgrove, West Sussex | *Occupation Eng:* Sawyer/Carpenter | 1832

SOURCE: WSRO, PHA 137

Warne, Charles | 21 | *From:* Carisbrooke, Isle of Wight | *Occupation Eng:* "no employ" | 1837 | Admitted into House of Industry 27 Mar 1830 aged 15 "by suspended order of removal from Chatham, Kent, with £9.12.3d expences ..." with parents(?) James and Eliz and Emma, James, Leonard, and Ellen. Admitted to House of Industry IOW 20 Apr 1837; discharged 26 Apr 1837. Brother of **Leonard**.

SOURCE: IOWRO Z/HO/44, Z/HO/L4, Z/HO/L5

Warne, Leonard | 22 | *From:* Carisbrooke, Isle of Wight | *Occupation Eng:* "no employ" | 1837 | *Assistance:* PEC, House of Industry, parish | Admitted into House of Industry 27 Mar 1830 aged 15 "by suspended order of removal from Chatham, Kent with £9.12.3d expences" ... with parents(?) James and Eliz and Emma, James, Charles and Ellen. Admitted to House of Industry 20 Apr 1837; discharged 26 Apr 1837. Brother of **Charles**.

SOURCE: IOWRO, Z/HO/44; Z/HO/L4; Z/HO/L5

Warren, William | *Spouse:* Mary | *Children:* child | *From:* Isle of Wight ? | *To:* Quebec | *Occupation Can:* Labourer | 1834 | "William Warren, his wife and child were left here [Quebec]."

SOURCE: Brydone, *Narrative*

Waters, Henry | *Occupation Eng:* Farmer | 1837 | *Assistance:* 1 passage | Remarks on abstract of PEC emigrants: "Most respectable"

SOURCE: WSRO, PHA 140

Watts, Eleanor | 22, bap 28 Apr 1813 | With sisters **Sophia** bap 20 Apr 1820, **Catherine Ludby** bap 6 Oct 1824 | *From:* Petworth, West Sussex | *Occupation Eng:* Schoolmistress (Eleanor); Sophia: mantuamaker, dressmaker | *Occupation Can:* "for a situation" | 1835 | *Assistance:* Earl of Egremont | Daughters of Jesse and Sarah Watts.

SOURCE: WSRO, PAR 149/1/2/1; PHA 142

Webb, Joseph | *Spouse:* Ann(e) Richards, m 16 Oct 1821 South Bersted, bap 12 Dec 1802 South Bersted | *Children:* Sarah bap 5 Oct 1823 South Bersted; Joseph bap 26 Sep 1824; Ann(e) bap 9 Sep 1827; William bap 11 Dec 1831; James | *From:* Felpham, West Sussex (Flansham) | *To:* St Catharines | *Occupation Eng:* Labourer; had been a pauper boy | 1832 | *Assistance:* Parish and Earl of Egremont | £150 of sum borrowed by Felpham remained to be paid off in 1835
SOURCE: PRO, MH 12, 13198; *Sussex Advertiser,* 22 Feb 1836; WSRO, PAR 19/1/1/4, PAR 19/1/2/1, PAR 19/1/3/1, PAR 81/1/2/1

Welbeloved, John | 23 | Single | *From:* Dorking, Surrey | 1832 | *Assistance:* Dorking Emigration Society
SOURCE: *Letters from Dorking,* 10

Wells, George | *From:* Goring, West Sussex (and Findon) | 1835
SOURCE: WSRO, PHA 142, p9; PAR 5/37/4, p24

Wells, William | 18 | *From:* Wisborough Green, West Sussex | *Occupation Eng:* Labourer; called for service in Sussex militia Dec 1831 | 1832 | *Assistance:* Mr Napper
SOURCE: WSRO, PHA 137, 4 Apr 1832; PAR 210/36/1

West, William | bap 30 Dec 1792 | *Spouse:* Mary | 30 | *Children:* Mary 11, b 2 Oct 1821, bap 20 Oct 1821 (m Alfred **Harwood** 3 Oct 1839); John 10, b 17 May 1823, bap 3 Aug 1823; Edward 8, b 23 Jun 1825, bap 31 Jul 1825; William 6, bap 18 Mar 1827; Hannah 5, bap 2 Aug 1829; Eleanor 3, bap 17 Jul 1831; Francis 2, bap 30 Dec 1832; b in Canada: Elizabeth Jane bap 1834 Woodstock | *From:* East Hoathly, East Sussex (parish house, Scallow Bridge) | *To:* Blandford (town plot), 5-acre lot between 2nd and 3rd streets | *Occupation Eng:* Farm labourer; constantly needing parish relief. | 1834 | *Assistance:* Parish, Mr Smith of Lewes, and possibly the Earl of Chichester | Base-born son of Sarah West, pauper. When William was 5 his mother married a Charles Warden and William is sometimes referred to as Warden. Brydone wrote that the party had to search for West at Lachine where he got drunk and quarrelsome and hid intending to leave his family and return to England. Mrs West went into labour 21 June at Vanorman's Inn.
SOURCE: Brydone, *Narrative,* 14–15; PRO, MH 12, 13160, 11 Jun 1842; ESRO, PAR 378/1/2/1, PAR 378/31/3/27, PAR 378/35/4; WSRO, Goodwood Ms 1476, f277; AO, RG 1, C-IV, Township Papers; OMNR, Survey Records, 1834 Plan of Blandford; Old St Pauls Anglican Registers, Woodstock

Wheeler, Charles | bap 20 Jan 1799 | *From:* Wisborough Green, West Sussex | *To:* Nelsonville, Ohio | 1832 | *Assistance:* Parish and landowners | He probably sailed on the England but arrived in Nelsonville, Ohio, 11 days before main party.
SOURCE: *No. 5 Continuation;* WSRO, PAR 210/1/1/9; *Courtauld Family Letters* 1: xxi

Wheeler, Mark | 20, bap 29 Sep 1816 | *From:* Chale, Isle of Wight | *Occupation Eng:* Tailor | 1837 | *Assistance:* Parish, House of Industry | Admitted to House of Industry, IOW, 6 Apr 1837; discharged 26 Apr 1837
SOURCE: IOWRO, Z/HO/44; Z/HO/L5; Index of Baptisms, Marriages, and Burials

Wheeler, Thomas | 44, bap 11 Mar 1792 | *Spouse:* Jane Saulter, m 31 Jan 1819 Northwood, Isle of Wight | 37 | *Children:* 3 children emigrated: Thomas 14, bap 15 Apr 1824; George 8, bap 31 Oct 1830; Charles 5, bap 31 Oct 1830 | *From:* Node Hill, Isle of Wight | *Occupation Eng:* Labourer | *Occupation Can:* Well digger | 1837 | *Assistance:* Parish, House of Industry, 4 passages | Remarks on abstract of IOW emigrants: "Dissipated."
SOURCE: IOWRO, Z/HO/44; Z/HO/L5; Index of Baptisms, Marriages, and Burials; WSRO, PHA 140

White, – (2) | *From:* Bignor, West Sussex ? | pre 1834 | *Assistance:* Squire Hawkins , Bignor Park | "The two Whites told me they had their expences paid by the kind interposition of Squire Hawkins … for which they seemed grateful" (Frederick Hasted).
SOURCE: *Brighton Herald,* 17 May 1834, letter from Hasted, 7 Feb 1834; WSRO, Bignor Bishop's Transcripts Ep 1/24/11

White, Edward | 25 | *Spouse:* Louisa Lotton, m 29 Oct 1832 | *From:* Lodsworth, West Sussex | *To:* Toronto | *Occupation Eng:* Farming man | 1835 | *Assistance:* Parish and landowners | Michael **Ford (Foard)**, an agricultural labourer, emigrated with them. Brother of **John** White, shoemaker.
SOURCE: *Continuation of Letters from Sussex Emigrants …Written in 1836* [1837], 15–16, WSRO, PHA 142; PAR 128/12/2

White, Harriet | *From:* Lodsworth, West Sussex (or Lurgashall) | *To:* York | 1833 | Travelled with **George** and **Rhoda Thair**.
SOURCE: *No. 4 Continuation,* 28–30

White, John | *Spouse:* Elizabeth West, m 27 Aug 1831 Fernhurst | *Children:* William bap 29 Jan 1832 Fernhurst; "young England" b at sea 8 May 1833; b in Canada: 2 more boys by Aug 1836 | *From:* Lurgashall, West Sussex, but "belongs to Boxgrove" | (and Lodsworth) | *To:* Guelph | *Occupation Eng:* Shoemaker | *Occupation Can:* Shoemaker, working for John Jorning, boot and shoemaker; Elizabeth worked at "binding of shoes" | 1833 | *Assistance:* W.H. Yaldwin and parish | Probably brother of **Edward** White.
SOURCE: WSRO, Goodwood Ms 1862, f9, Sockett to Richmond 12 Mar 1833; PHA 138; PAR 82/1/2/1, PAR 82/1/3/1; Letter from John White and his wife, 27 Oct 1833, *No. 6 Continuation;* Letter from Jas Rapson, 1836, *Continuation of Letters from Sussex Emigrants …Written in 1836* [1837]

White, John | 33 | *From:* Newport, Isle of Wight | 1837 | *Assistance:* Parish, House of Industry
SOURCE: IOWRO, Z/HO/44

Whitington, George | bap 11 Dec 1808 | *From:* Goring, West Sussex | *Occupation Eng:* son of a tailor | 1835 or 1836 | *Assistance:* parish and landlords
SOURCE: *Continuation of Letters from Sussex Emigrants …Written in 1836* [1837], 23–4; PRO, MH 12, 12905; WSRO, Emigrants Index; PAR 92/1/1/5

Whitmaish, William | 16, b 3 Mar 1823, bap 3 Jul 1823 | *From:* East Cowes, Isle of Wight | 1833 | *Assistance:* Parish/House of Industry | Admitted to House of Industry May 1832; discharged 25 Apr 1833.
SOURCE: IOWRO, Z/HO/L5; Index of Baptisms, Marriages, and Burials

Whittington, Mark | 19, b 12 Nov 1814, bap 11 Dec 1814 Gatcombe, Isle of Wight | *From:* Carisbrooke, Isle of Wight | *Occupation Eng:* "no employment" | 1834 | *Assistance:* Parish/House of Industry | Admitted to House of Industry 11 Feb 1834; discharged 16 Apr 1834, "to Canada."
SOURCE: IOWRO, Z/HO/L3; Z/HO/L5; Index of Baptisms, Marriages, and Burials

Willard, William | d 6 Dec 1861 age 75 years, 2 months, 28 days (Sheffield Cemetery, Beverly Twp) | *Spouse:* Charlotte Longhurst, m 22 Apr 1812 Ockley, Surrey, b 23 Aug 1790, bap 5 Sep 1790 Abinger, d 26 Nov 1864 | *Children:* Maria b 10 Nov 1812 (m John **Worsfold** 12 Sep 1834); William b 17 Mar 1815, bap 23 Apr 1815, d 8 Sep 1898 (m Abigail Smith 17 Jul 1839); James b 13 Feb 1817, bap 23 Mar 1817, d 7 Jul 1884 (m (1) Harriet Smith, (2) Eleanor Cornell); John b 19 Nov 1818, bap 10 Jan 1819, d 9 Dec 1900 (m Mary Davis 13 May 1845); Charlotte b 21 Nov 1821, bap 14 Jan 1821?, d 4 Feb 1901 (m John Proctor 14 Sep 1841); Henry b Feb 1823, bap 6 Apr 1823, d 13 Jun 1887 (m Amy McKay c1856);

George b Feb 1825, bap 10 Apr 1825, d 3 Apr 1845; David b 19 Jun 1827, bap 14 Oct 1827, d 10 Dec 1911 (m Mary Jane Blackburn 13 Nov 1865); Charles b 31 Jan 1830, bap 4 Aug 1830, d 3 Mar 1916 (m Sarah Moore 26 Feb 1859) (all bap Dorking) | William was received into the Congregational Church, West St., Dorking, 30 Jan 1828 | *From:* Dorking, Surrey (Milton) | *To:* Beverly Twp, near Sheffield, lot 6 con 5 | *Occupation Eng:* Carpenter | *Occupation Can:* Labourer ? | 1832 | Lord Melville | *Assistance:* Dorking Emigration Society and Dorking, Shere, and Albury parishes. The parishes were in dispute over where he had a settlement but combined to pay for his family's passage. | Charlotte worked as a domestic. William's father and his brother, Henry, were also with them.
SOURCE: *Letters from Dorking,* 15–20; SRO (GMR), PSH/DOM/3/1; United Reformed Church (West St, Dorking), List of Members, Dorking Congregational Church Book 1826; NA, RG 31, Canada Census, 1851 Beverly Twp agricultural schedule; AO, RG 80-27-2, vol 79, Wellington Co. marriage register, p165; Correspondent Rosemary Ambrose

Willett, Belinda | b 3 Mar 1815 Easebourne Poor House, bap 19 Mar 1815 | *From:* Tillington, West Sussex | 1834 | *Assistance:* Parish and Earl of Egremont | Illegitimate daughter of Mary Willett and James Jenner
SOURCE: WSRO, PAR 75/1/2/1, PAR 197/31/5

Willett, Richard | *Spouse:* Martha Skilton, m 26 Dec 1804 Galton? | Congregational Church | *From:* Dorking, Surrey | 1833 | Recorded as emigrants to Canada in Congregational Church Records, Dorking. Possibly PEC.
SOURCE: United Reformed Church (West St, Dorking), List of members in Dorking Congregational Church Book 1826

Williams, William | 41, b Whippingham, Isle of Wight | *Spouse:* Catherine Robbins, m 22 May 1820 Whippingham | 43 | *Children:* 4 children emigrated: William 16, b 3 Jul 1822, bap 28 Jul 1822; Alfred 12, b 26 May 1824, bap 1 Aug 1824; Mary Anne 10, b 8 May 1826, bap 4 Jan 1826; Thomas Henry 9, bap 24 May 1829 | *From:* Newport, Isle of Wight (Paradise Row) | *Occupation Eng:* Blacksmith/painter; "a painter by trade but is always on the Parish during the winter months" | 1837 | *Assistance:* Parish/House of Industry , 4.5 passages | Had been apprenticed to Mr Harris, coachmaker. Remarks on abstract of IOW emigrants: "Dissipated."
SOURCE: IOWRO, Z/HO/L7; Z/HO/44; Index of Baptisms, Marriages, and Burials; WHIP/REG/MAR/3; WSRO, PHA 140

Wills, William | 18 | *From:* Wisborough Green, West Sussex ? | 1832 ? | *Assistance:* Mr J. Napper
SOURCE: WSRO, PHA 137

Wilson, Charles | *From:* Poss Bignor or Sutton | *To:* Westminster Twp | 1832 or 1833
SOURCE: *No. 5 Continuation,* 37–8

Wilson, Obediah | 18, b 11 Apr 1814, bap 10 Jul 1814, d 10 Feb 1894, bur Harndon Cemetery, Whitby Twp | *Spouse:* Elizabeth (Betsey) Maria Martin, m in Canada 16 Feb 1847, b 1831, d 14 Jan 1893, bur Harndon Cemetery, Whitby Twp | *Children:* 13 b in Canada | Church of England | *From:* Bassingbourn, Cambridgeshire | *To:* Ernest Town: he was with Silvester Lambkin, Ernest Town, 13 miles from Kingston. Mariposa, Newcastle District, Upper Canada. Then moved to East Whitby Township wH lot 10 Concession 9 | *Occupation Eng:* Labourer | *Occupation Can:* Farm labourer; farmer | 1832 | *Assistance:* Mr Beldam
SOURCE: *Emigration: Letters* (1833), 21; Cambridge County Record Office, P 11/1/4; NA, RG 31, Canada Census, 1851 Whitby Twp, p85; 1871 Whitby East Twp, 3:39; AO, RG 22/264,

Ontario Co. Surrogate Court, file 268; Wilson Family Papers, Obed Wilson Correspondence; Correspondents Robert Bell, W.H. Wilson

Winham (Wonham ?), (Mr) ? | *From:* Westbourne, West Sussex | 1832 | Mrs Winham applied for relief since her husband had "gone to America." See also entry for R. Wonham.
SOURCE: WSRO, PAR 206/12/6

Wolfe, John | 16 | *From:* Newport, Isle of Wight | 1837 | *Assistance:* Parish, House of Industry
SOURCE: IOWRO, Z/HO/44

Wonham, R. | *Children:* 1 son | 1832 | Seen in 1832 by J.S. & W. Goldring in Canada. Referred to by them in letter as going back to England in 1833 to fetch his family, leaving eldest boy in college in Canada until his return.
SOURCE: *No. 3 Continuation,* 17–18; WSRO, Misc. Paper 1705

Woodford, George | *From:* Bury, West Sussex | 1833 | *Assistance:* Parish
SOURCE: WSRO, PAR 33/12/1

Woods, James | *Spouse:* Ann | *Children:* 1 child: "Little George" | *From:* Tillington, West Sussex | *To:* Blandford (Woodstock), London Dist. | 1836
SOURCE: *Continuation of Letters from Sussex Emigrants ... Written in 1836* [1837], 20

Woods, Richard | *From:* Angmering, West Sussex | 1832 | *Assistance:* Parish and Miss Susan Loud
SOURCE: WSRO, PAR 6/12/1

Woods, Thomas | 21 | *Spouse:* Ann | 36 | *From:* Petworth, West Sussex | *To:* Blandford (town plot) | *Occupation Eng:* Labourer | 1836 | *Assistance:* Earl of Egremont and parish, backed by Poor Law Commissioners
SOURCE: PRO, MH 12, 13060; Letter from James Cooper, May 1838, *Brighton Herald,* 25 Aug 1838

Woolgar, Ann | Congregational Church | *From:* Dorking, Surrey (Milton) | 1833 | Possibly PEC. Recorded as emigrating to Canada in 1833 in Congregational Church Records. Possibly related to Charlotte and William Willard, see their letter in *Letters from Dorking,* 15-20.
SOURCE: United Reformed Church (West St, Dorking), List of members in Dorking Congregational Church Book 1826

Worsfold, John | *Spouse:* Maria Willard, m 12 Sep 1834 in Canada | Congregational Church | *From:* Dorking, Surrey | *To:* Hamilton | *Occupation Can:* Painter and decorator | 1832 | *Assistance:* Dorking Emigration Society | The 1842 census for Beverly Twp lists a John Worsfold, his wife Mariah, 1 son, and 2 daughters.
SOURCE: *Letters from Dorking,* 35–8; United Reformed Church (West St, Dorking), List of members in Dorking Congregational Church Book 1826

Worsfold, William | 29 | Single | *From:* Dorking, Surrey (Dorking area) | *Occupation Eng:* Labourer | 1832 | *Assistance:* Dorking Emigration Society
SOURCE: *Letters from Dorking,* 10

Wright, William | bap 6 Feb 1814 Chertsey | *From:* Dorking, Surrey | *To:* Nelson Twp | *Occupation Eng:* Labourer | *Occupation Can:* Farm labourer | 1832 | *Assistance:* Dorking Emigration Society | Travelled with his brother who was apprenticed to a blacksmith. (His brother could be James, bap 7 Jan 1816 Dorking; David, bap 6 Apr 1817 Dorking; or George, bap 18 Jul 1819 Dorking.)
SOURCE: *Letters from Dorking,* 22–4; SRO (GMR), PSH/DOM/3/1

Young, James | *Spouse:* Jane Pigley, m 18 Nov 1821 Horsham | *Children:* Jane b 17 Jun 1823, Robert b 30 Dec 1826 (both bap 4 Apr 1832) | *From:* Petworth, West Sussex | *Occupation Eng:* Labourer | 1832 | *Assistance:* Earl of Egremont and Sockett | Sockett wrote 15 Apr 1832 to Chelsea Hospital about Young's pension money payable.
SOURCE: WSRO, PHA 137; PAR 106/1/3/2, PAR 149/1/2/1

Young, William | 21 | *From:* Newport, Isle of Wight | 1837 | *Assistance:* Parish, House of Industry
SOURCE: IOWRO, Z/HO/44

Appendix A
Sockett and Wyndham Debate Poverty and Assisted Emigration

A correspondence between Wyndham and Sockett, begun in 1838 and continued into 1840, on the relief of poverty and assisted emigration records a debate in which Sockett defended attitudes formed under Egremont and Wyndham relied on opinions prevailing in the late 1830s to justify his point of view. Although their relationship was changing to reflect Wyndham's new position as Egremont's successor, they wrote with the frankness of tutor and pupil.[1]

Sockett, at least in his own mind, was open to change in methods of administering poor relief. His emphasis was on local discretion. What he could not stomach about poor law reform as embodied in the poor law commissioners' administration was the doctrinaire certainty of their attempts to fit the same solution to every pauper. He believed that they condemned the poor for the fact of poverty, and he reacted against their cynicism about the motives of people struggling to feed their children.

The opinions Wyndham expressed in his correspondence with Sockett took shape as he travelled in Yorkshire and Ireland to visit his new estates. In Yorkshire, Wyndham saw a sturdy self-reliance in rural labourers that he believed to be lacking in the people around Petworth. He jumped quickly to the prevailing opinion that the moral fibre of labourers in the south had been undermined by "a system which makes beggars of a whole population." His views on the subject were provoked by a question from Sockett's Petworth curate about continuing Egremont's practice of making annual gifts of clothing and shoes to the deserving poor. This kind of expectation, Wyndham wrote to Sockett, "has materially tended to make the People different from those in Yorkshire & elsewhere, and not half so pleasant to live amongst."[2] He believed that people (including the farmers who pushed the unemployed onto his father's charities) had taken advantage of his father's benevolence in his later years, and he intended to make changes. His wife seems nevertheless to have taken over a number of these small charities and to have used Sockett as her emissary.

Sockett reflected on past experience in this correspondence. A question from Wyndham about roads turned his mind back to his arrival at Petworth in 1796. In those days, roads through the Weald had been impassable for wheeled vehicles. He recalled that two or three years later he had been "mired down on horseback in the regular road from Petworth to Kirdford."[3] From about 1810, many Sussex roads had been improved, provided with a hard surface and brought to a state of perfection – built by parish paupers during the years when Sockett was active in dispensing Egremont's charity. As this form of relief had been cut off under the new poor law, the condition of the roads had begun to deteriorate. Because he was well aware that there had been many abuses in parish employment, Sockett was willing to concede the need for reform to Wyndham. In this case, they were able to agree that work on the roads should be deliberately saved for the "pinching season," when labourers had most need of this source of income.

On the subject of the poor law commissioners and their reforms, their disagreement was profound. Sockett promoted assisted emigration to Wyndham, as he had to Egremont, as a remedy for a redundant population and a happy alternative to Malthusian outcomes, but the poor law commissioners had shifted the ground of the debate. The commissioners argued that England had the capacity to employ its workers once the ties that held them to their parish were cut and they had incentives to move in search of work. Sockett did not deal much with the question of the redistribution of the workforce beyond reporting what labourers had told him. He believed them when they said that they had walked as far in search of work as they could travel in a day and that they lacked the resources to go further. His attention by 1838 had shifted from unemployment to low wages as "our crying evil among the labourers."[4]

Sockett disputed the poor law commissioners' claim that they could raise wages by forcing labourers onto a free market. He tried to be objective in telling Wyndham that the new poor law might have done much good "if a few of the clauses had been softened and if its execution had not been committed to such very bad hands." His real feelings came closer to the surface in his concern that men of influence had been blinded by a "set of wild theories." He seems to have meant men of influence like Richmond, of whose pronouncements on the new poor law he wrote in 1838: "he is either very ill informed; has a very bad memory; or (which I am unwilling to think) states what he knows to be untrue in several instances."[5]

Sockett's point was that workers with a trade or a needed skill had some bargaining power, but that the majority of labourers in his district had to accept that "the farmer will not give more wages than he can get a job done for."[6] As a result, the earnings of day labourers were falling at a time when the price of grain was rising, and the poor were "sinking" into a lower standard of living under the new law. Sockett believed labourers were rendered uncompetitive by there being too many others equally able to do the same job. Under the new law, they had to work for whatever they could get in order to keep out of the workhouse. For him, this was reason enough to keep emigration flowing from West Sussex.[7]

Was it not, Wyndham asked Sockett in another letter, time to disband the Sutton Union and bring these parishes into line with the new poor law? He suggested that Sockett needed a rest and should take it by making himself less accessible to the poor and idle – he crossed out "poor idle people," knowing his clergyman.[9] At his lowest moments, Sockett characterized the people who "invaded" the rectory "from morning to night" with their endless needs as a duty attached to his calling.[9] Even as he wrote this passage in a letter to Mary Wyndham, Sockett thought better and scratched it out. Sockett recognized in Wyndham both fear born of mistrust and the disappointment of too high expectations, and he hoped that knowledge would bring Wyndham compassion. Rather than shutting himself off from their clamour, he urged Wyndham to learn more about the people he condemned. Sounding very like the tutor he had been, Sockett expressed the wish that he could induce Wyndham "to make, as occasion arises, minute enquiries into the *actual condition* of the cultivator of the soil."[10]

Wyndham wrote of assisted emigration from Sussex as no more than a favour to offer individuals who had some claim on his patronage. When he considered assisted emigration as a solution to poverty in Britain, he thought principally of Ireland. Wynhham's walks among the people on his Irish estates did not, however, have the effect on him that Sockett hoped. Wyndham was struck not by the living conditions of individual families but by the daunting scale of the problems of a redundant population in rural Ireland. He brought home the conviction that only the government could implement assisted emigration at a level that would make a difference. Sockett accepted his patron's decisions, but they did not change his thinking. His actions in continuing to seize every remaining opportunity to send emigrants from his neighbourhood a few at a time spoke for his own view of poverty as an individual and personal matter that he addressed one person and one family at a time.

APPENDIX B

Table B.1
Emigration from the British Isles, 1821–1851

Year	North American Colonies	United States	Australian Colonies New Zealand	All Other Places	Total
1821	12,995	4,958	–	384	18,297
1822	16,081	4,137	–	279	20,429
1823	11,355	5,032	–	163	16,550
1824	8,774	5,152	–	99	14,025
1825	8,741	5,551	485	114	14,891
1826	12,818	7,063	903	116	20,900
1827	12,648	14,526	715	114	28,003
1828	12,084	12,817	1,056	135	26,092
1829	13,307	15,678	2,016	197	31,198
1830	30,574	24,887	1,242	204	56,907
1831	58,067	23,418	1,561	114	83,160
1832	66,339	32,872	3,733	196	103,140
1833	28,808	29,109	4,093	517	62,527
1834	40,060	33,074	2,800	288	76,222
1835	15,573	26,720	1,860	325	44,478
1836	34,226	37,774	3,124	293	75,417
1837	29,884	36,770	5,054	326	72,034
1838	4,577	14,332	14,021	292	33,222
1839	12,658	33,536	15,786	227	62,207
1840	32,293	40,642	15,850	1,958	90,743
1841	38,164	45,017	32,625	2,786	118,592
1842	54,123	63,852	8,534	1,835	128,344
1843	23,518	28,335	3,478	1,881	57,212
1844	22,924	43,660	2,229	1,873	70,686
1845	31,803	58,538	830	2,330	93,501
1846	43,439	82,239	2,347	1,826	129,851
1847	109,680	142,154	4,949	1,487	258,270
1848	31,065	188,233	23,904	4,887	248,089
1849	41,367	219,450	32,191	6,490	299,498
1850	32,961	223,078	16,037	8,773	280,849
1851	42,605	267,357	21,532	4,472	335,966

SOURCE: Extracted from H.I. Cowan, *British Emigration to British North America: The First Hundred Years* (rev. ed. Toronto: University of Toronto Press 1961), 288.

ABBREVIATIONS

Add Ms	Additional manuscript
ADH	Anglican Diocese of Huron
ADN	Anglican Diocese of Niagara
ADT	Anglican Diocese of Toronto
AO	Archives of Ontario
ASSI	Assize record
BPP	British Parliamentary Papers
CO	Colonial Office
DCB	*Dictionary of Canadian Biography*
EP	Bishop's Transcript
ESRO	East Sussex Record Office
GB	Great Britain
GMR	Surrey Record Office, Guildford Muniment Room
HO	Home Office
IGI	International Genealogical Index
IOWRO	Isle of Wight Record Office
KPL	Kitchener Public Library
MH	Ministry of Health
MP	Miscellaneous paper
NA	National Archives of Canada
OGS	Ontario Genealogical Society
OMNR	Ontario Ministry of Natural Resources
P	Parish record (Cambridge County Record Office)
PAR	Parish record (ESRO, WSRO)
PEC	Petworth Emigration Committee
PHA	Petworth House Archives
PRO	Public Records Office, England
PSH	Parish record (Surrey Record Office)
QR	Quarter Sessions record (WSRO)
SRO	Surrey Record Office
Wilts RO	Wiltshire Record Office
WO	War Office
WSRO	West Sussex Record Office

NOTES

NOTE: Abbreviated sources are given in full in the bibliography; complete citations are given for sources that only appear in the notes.

INTRODUCTION

1 Elliott, "Regional Patterns," and Brunger, "Distribution of the English," have found that these were areas favoured by English immigrants of the 1830s.

2 Webb and Webb, *English Poor Law Policy*; Rose, *English Poor Law*. Ann Cole, *An Introduction to ... Poor Law Documents before 1834* (Birmingham: Federation of Family History Societies Publications 1993), is one of several short introductions available.

3 Brandon and Short, *South East from AD 1000*, 331.

4 William Cobbett, *Rural Rides* (London: Reeves and Turner 1908), 1, 221.

5 WSRO, Goodwood Ms 1491, p. 398, Richmond to Grey, 21 November 1830; McCann, ed., *Goodwood Estate Archives*, 3:73–113, Appendix 1. McCann describes agriculture as the "overriding" interest in the duke's correspondence.

6 T.A. Jenkins, *The Liberal Ascendancy, 1830–1886* (London: Macmillan 1994); E.A. Smith, *Lord Grey 1764–1845* (Oxford: Oxford University Press 1990), 302–6; WSRO, Goodwood Ms 689, confidential letters, E.G. Stanley to Richmond, p. 25, 2 April 1834, and p. 48, 22 December 1834. Richmond, Sir James Graham, Edward George Stanley (the colonial secretary at the time and later Earl of Derby), Frederick Robinson, and Viscount Goderich (Stanley's predecessor as colonial secretary, later Earl of Ripon) resigned to protest a perceived threat to the established church in Ireland, the same issue that had precipitated Richmond's break with the Duke of Wellington in 1830.

7 Cannadine, *Aspects of Aristocracy*, 10–11. Richmond, who inherited the Scottish estates of his maternal uncle the fifth Duke of Gordon, also fits Cannadine's picture of the noblemen who prospered in this era. An obituary in the *Gentleman's Magazine* 9 (January 1838): 88–92 claimed that Egremont's rental income alone was £81,000 annually by 1837. Wyndham, *A Family History*, vol. 2. Egremont, *Wyndham and Children First*, guessed an annual income of £100,000.

8 Egremont, *Wyndham and Children First*, 56, 197; Wynne E Baxter, *The Doomsday Book for the County of Sussex* (Lewes and London 1876). John Bateman, *The Great Landowners of Great Britain and Ireland* (London 1883), writing after some of Egremont's property had gone to others, described his grandson, the second Lord Leconfield, as the largest landowner in Sussex and eighth among the twelve largest landowners in England and Wales.

9 Butlin et al., *Turner at Petworth*; Patrick Younghusband, "'That house of art': Turner at Petworth," *Turner Studies* 2 (1983), 16–33. The May 1977 issue of *Apollo* has several articles on Petworth and its art, which include sculpture and architectural features.

10 Strachey and Fulford, eds., *Greville Memoirs*, 2:335–6, and 3:399; *The Times*, 18 November 1837, Egremont's obituary; Max Egremont, "The Third Earl of Egremont and His Friends," *Apollo* (1985), 280–7; Egremont, *Wyndham and Children First*.

11 Timothy J. McCann, *The Goodwood Estate Archives: A Catalogue*, 3:73–7. Poynter, *Society and Pauperism*, 299, and Chester Kirby, *The English Country Gentleman: A Study in Nineteenth Century Types* (1937), 122, both quote Charles Greville's description of Richmond as "prejudiced, narrow-minded, illiterate, and ignorant, good-looking, good humoured and unaffected, tedious, prolix, unassuming and a duke." Greville, who repeated versions of his assessment of the duke more than once, also admitted to his diary his envy of his aristocratic school fellow's rank and popularity. Strachey and Fulford, *Greville Memoirs*, 1:258 (1829); 2:111 (1831); 3:322–3 (1832);3:399–400 (1833).

12 J.H. Adeane, *The Girlhood of Maria Josepha Holroyd* (London 1896), 286, and project files.

13 WSRO, PHA 1679, Sockett's journal, kept between 12 September 1805 and 8 March 1807; Povey, "Rise of Thomas Sockett"; Evelyn Morchard Bishop, *Blake's Hayley* (London 1951). J.H. Adeane, *The Girlhood of Maria Josepha Holroyd* (London 1896), 286, records the year from June 1794 to June 1795, which Sockett spent as a very junior secretary to Lord Sheffield.

14 WSRO, PHA 1679, Sockett's journal, 8 March 1807; Guildford Public Library, Guildford, Surrey, East Horsley Parish Register, 15. Sockett was christened as an adult on 24 August 1806 "according to the directions of his Grace the Archbishop of Canterbury."

15 As an absentee, Sockett held Tadcaster in Yorkshire from 1808 to 1811 and North Scarle, Lincolnshire, from 1811 until his death. He was curate at Northchapel in 1810, then rector of Duncton 1815–59 and of Petworth 1816–59. Povey, "Rise of Thomas Sockett"; WSRO, PHA 2681, William Tyler's letterbook (Tadcaster); PHA 2682 (North Scarle); Northchapel parish register; Petworth parish register; clergy lists; Lincolnshire Archives, COR B 5/4/105/2 and 5/4/124/2, has correspondence from Sockett to the Bishop of Lincoln about North Scarle from 1829, 1842, 1846, 1850, and from the curate in 1852. Sockett described the rectory in 1829 as a "mere cottage" only fit for the "lowest class of farmer" to whom the glebe was rented; the parish was served by a non-resident curate who in 1846 was receiving a stipend of £90 from Sockett.

16 BPP 1837–38 (658), XX, pt 2, Select Committee on Postage, Second Report, Sockett, 23 May 1838.

17 Checkland and Checkland, eds., *The Poor Law Report*.

18 Poor Law Amendment Act, 4&5 Will. 4, c. 76. The commissioners were George Nicholls, T. Frankland Lewis, and J. Shaw-Lefevre. Their secretary was Edwin Chadwick.

19 Webb and Webb, *English Local Government*, 171–2.

20 Rose, *Relief of Poverty, 1834–1914*.

21 Dunkley, *Crisis of the Old Poor Law* and "Whigs and Paupers"; Brundage, *Making of the New Poor Law* and *England's "Prussian Minister"*; Anthony Brundage, David Eastwood, and Peter Mandler, "Debate: The Making of the New Poor Law Redivivus," *Past and Present* 127 (May 1990).

22 Dunkley, "Whigs and Paupers," 135–9.

23 Senior, *Remarks on the Opposition;* Chadwick, "Article on the Principles and Progress of the Poor Law Amendment Act"; Crowther, *Workhouse System*; Driver, *Power and Pauperism*.

24 For an exchange between Brundage and Dunkley on the "Landed Interest and the New Poor Law," see *English Historical Review* 87 (1972): 27–48; 88 (1973): 836–41; and 90 (1975):

347–51. Roberts, *Paternalism*, 127–8, mistakenly thought that none of the large landowners of Sussex opposed the new law and numbered Egremont among its supporters.

25 Henry Pilkington was assistant commissioner until September 1835 when William Toovey Hawley took over. Hawley had responsibility for West Sussex unions until he departed for Ireland in 1840.

26 Driver, *Power and Pauperism*, 42–7. The final configuration of the Petworth Poor Law Union was so awkward that the commissioners had difficulty defending it.

27 PRO, MH 32/38, Hawley to Nicholls, 22 July 1836; WSRO, Goodwood Ms 1574, f. 120, the Reverend Robert Tredcroft to Richmond, 17 June 1835; WSRO, Goodwood Ms 1627, f. 1052, Henry Pilkington (a former assistant poor law commissioner for Sussex) to Richmond, 9 August 1841. Chakrit Choomwattana, "The Opposition to the New Poor Law in Sussex, 1834–1837," chronicles opposition in Petworth in a wider context.

28 *Hansard*, 3d ser., 36 (1837), 991–7, 1034. The government blocked any possibility of opening up the Amendment Act for new debate; the committee was to "inquire into the administration of the relief of the poor under the orders and regulations issued by the Commissioners."

29 Brundage, *Making of the New Poor Law*, 163; Finer, *Life and Times*, 129–39; WSRO, Goodwood Ms 1585, f. 64, Chadwick to Richmond, 10 July 1834, and f. 72, Chadwick to Richmond, 4 September 1837. Chadwick described the committee's report as a "severe blow" that had weakened the resolve of the "firm guardians" in several unions.

30 PRO, MH 32/39, Hawley to Chadwick, 7 March 1837; BPP 1837 (131), XVII, pt 1, and (138), XVII, pt 1, first and second reports from the Select Committee on the Poor Law Amendment Act. In order to supply a rebuttal of sorts, the government majority on the committee designated Richmond's Westhamptnett as the next union for examination.

31 PRO, Prob 11/1889 1-E, The Last Will and Testament of the Right Honourable George O'Brien Wyndham, Earl of Egremont and Baron of Cockermouth. *Gentleman's Magazine*, 9 (January 1838). Henry was given the Cumberland property, including Cockermouth Castle and valuable mines and collieries; Charles and three daughters received monetary settlements.

32 McCalla, *Planting the Province*, 249, Table 1.1.

33 Elliott, "English"; B.R. Mitchell, *British Historical Statistics* (Cambridge: Cambridge University Press 1988); N.H. Carrier and J.R. Jeffery, *External Migration: A Study of the External Statistics, 1815–1950*, Studies on Medical and Population Subjects, 6 (London: HMSO 1953); Baines, *Emigration from Europe*; W.S. Shepperson, *British Emigration to North America: Projects and Opinions in the Early Victorian Period* (Oxford: Basil Blackwell 1957); Walter Nugent, *Crossings: The Great Transatlantic Migrations, 1870–1914* (Indianapolis: Bloomington University Press 1992); Cowan, *British Emigration*.

34 *Canadian Emigrant*, 2 June 1832.

35 Baines, *Emigration*, 46.

36 Bruce Wilson, *As She Began: An Illustrated Introduction to Loyalist Ontario* (Toronto and Charlottetown: Dundurn 1981), 13, 18, 120n1; Craig, *Upper Canada*, 5–9; McCalla, *Planting the Province*, 13–18.

37 Cowan, *British Emigration*; Johnston, *British Emigration Policy*; Gates, *Land Policies*.

38 Gates, *Land Policies*, 92.

39 Johnston, *British Emigration Policy*, 1.

40 Barbara C. Murison, "Poverty, Philanthropy and Emigration to British North America: Changing Attitudes in Scotland in the Early Nineteenth Century," *British Journal of Canadian Studies* 2 (December 1987): 264–5, 283.

41 Buchanan's annual reports and, from 1834, an appendix showing these numbers were printed in the British Sessional Papers. His report for 1833 exists only in manuscript: PRO, CO 384/35, f. 123v.

42 Elliott, "English."

43 BPP 1826, IV (404), First Report of the Select Committee on Emigration from the United Kingdom, and BPP 1827, V (550), Third Report; Cameron, "Wilmot Horton's Experimental Emigrations"; Horton, *Causes and Remedies.*

44 Burroughs, *Colonial Reformers and Canada.* Spring, *English Landed Estate*, points out that Wakefield began his career based in London as an agent in the sale and purchase of land and as a land steward.

45 Peter Burroughs, *Britain and Australia 1831–1855: A Study in Imperial Relations and Crown Lands Administration* (Oxford: Clarendon Press 1967), 39.

46 Alan Wilson, "Colborne, John, 1st Baron Seaton," DCB, 9:137–44; C.G.M. Smith, *The Life of John Colborne, Field Marshall Lord Seaton* (London 1903).

47 S.F. Wise, "Head, Sir Francis Bond," DCB, 10:342–5. Head, "English Charity"; Baehre, "Paupers and Poor Relief," 77; Wise, ed., *A Narrative*, xi–xxii, 192. In this last source, Head described himself as the senior of the twenty assistant commissioners.

48 Baehre, "Pauper Emigration to Upper Canada" and "Paupers and Poor Relief."

CHAPTER I

1 WSRO, Goodwood Ms 648, f. 52.

2 WSRO, Goodwood Ms 1469, f. 64.

3 *Hansard*, 2d ser., 23 (1830): 476–85.

4 Mitchell, *British Historical Statistics*, 9, 30.

5 Caird, *English Agriculture*; G.E. Mingay, ed., *Agrarian History of England and Wales*, vol. 6, *1750–1850*; F.M.L. Thompson, ed., *Cambridge Social History of Britain, 1750–1950*; Snell, *Annals of the Labouring Poor*; Brandon and Short, *The South East from AD 1000.* Chambers and Mingay, *Agricultural Revolution, 1750–1880*, justify using the term revolution in their title because the impact of change in agriculture was social as well as economic.

6 Blaug, "Myth of the Old Poor Law"; Baugh, "Cost of Poor Relief"; Digby, "Labour Market"; Boyer, *Economic History of the English Poor Law.*

7 Hobsbawm and Rudé, *Captain Swing*, devote a section to each of these regions. Hammond and Hammond, *Village Labourer*; Charlesworth, *Atlas* and *Social Protest*; Stevenson, *Popular Disturbances*, 262–71. Stevenson, 5–12, attempts definitions of "disturbances, riots, crowds, and mobs" as the terms apply to the period 1700–1832.

8 Hobsbawm and Rudé, *Captain Swing*; Thompson, *Making of the English Working Class*, and "Moral Economy" and "The Crime of Anonymity," in Hay et al., *Albion's Fatal Tree*; Hobsbawm, "The Machine Breakers," in *Labouring Men*; Rudé, *Crowd in History*; Stevenson, *Popular Disturbances*, and "Social Control and the Prevention of Riots …," in Donajgrodzki, ed., *Social Control.*

9 PRO, HO 52/10, Sussex, Egremont, 12 November 1830. Hobsbawm and Rudé, *Captain Swing*, 190, explain that the paths followed by the risings were not "the main arteries of national or even county circulation, but the complex system of smaller veins and capillaries which linked each parish to its neighbours and to its local centres."

10 *Brighton Gazette*, 25 November 1830. E.P. Thompson, *Making of the English Working Class*, 250, quotes the Duke of Wellington, Lord Lieutenant of Hampshire, calling on magis-

trates to attack and disperse the "mobs" at the head of a mounted force of their "servants and retainers, grooms, huntsmen, game-keepers."

11 E.P. Thompson, "The Patricians and the Plebs," in *Customs in Common*, describes the relationship between the "gentry" and the "labouring poor," exemplified in Egremont's realm. Roberts, "The Patriarchy of Sussex," in *Paternalism in Early Victorian England*, sets out the new directions in which this relationship was developing.

12 WSRO, PHA 8853, Fitzroy Somerset to Peel, copy, 13 November 1830, and a memo of the same date showing the stations of troops in Kent and Sussex; PRO, HO 52/10, Sussex, Egremont, 15 and 19 November 1830.

13 WSRO, Goodwood Ms 613, f. 33, Burrell to Richmond, 2 December 1830; PRO, HO 52/10, Sussex, Horsham. In Royal Commission on the Poor Laws, *Extracts*, 76, C.H. Maclean wrote of Horsham in 1831 and 1832: "the more respectable inhabitants live in continual dread of the destruction of their property."

14 *Sussex Advertiser*, 15 November 1830; Francis W. Steer, ed., *"I am, my dear Sir ..."': A Selection of Letters written mainly to and by John Hawkins* (n.p.: West Sussex County Council n.d.), 84, Richard Prime to Hawkins, 16 November 1830. Prime added a note in red ink that since writing he "had had a visit from abt 150 of the mob." Prime became one of Sockett's most reliable sponsors.

15 WSRO, Goodwood Ms 635, f. 51, Richmond to Melbourne, 31 July 1831.

16 WSRO, Goodwood Ms 1432, f. 102, Richmond to Melbourne, 23 December 1830. Hobsbawm and Rudé, *Captain Swing*, 217: one incendiary was hanged at Lewes; the second, the young Thomas Goodman, saved his life by recanting. Hobsbawm and Rudé, 262–3 and app. 2, report that across the country 19 of 252 people condemned to death were hanged and hundreds more were transported and jailed. Sussex was not one of the counties visited by a special commission. Stevenson, *Popular Disturbances*, 268.

17 *The Times*, 26 November 1830; WSRO, Goodwood Ms 635, f. 51, Richmond to Melbourne, 31 July 1831; Clive Emsley, *The English Police: A Political and Social History* (New York: St Martin's Press 1991), 30–8. Emsley does not discuss emigration, but there is a familiar ring to his impression of the reception of the Rural Constabulary Act of 1839, p. 38: "It seems that those counties which had experienced serious disturbances against the New Poor Law were those most sympathetic to adopting the act, while estimates of the potential expense were the most powerful disincentive."

18 WSRO, Goodwood Ms 1484, p. 4, Richmond to J.B. Freeland, 30 December 1830.

19 PRO, HO 52/10, Sussex, Egremont, 19 November 1830; *Hansard*, 2d ser., 1 (1830): 424. Dunkley, "Paternalism, the Magistracy and Poor Relief," 397, states that large landowners of this era typically saw themselves as protectors of the poor and their tenants and freeholders as insensitive to the plight of their labourers.

20 Brandon and Short, *The South East from AD 1000*, 236, provide a map of rural protest in the 1830s.

21 *Sussex Advertiser*, 15 and 29 November 1830. The meetings described in these articles were chaired by Lord Chichester of East Sussex, who later sent emigrants on Sockett's *British Tar* in 1834.

22 WSRO, PHA 2684, William Tyler to Rev. Dr Challen, 21 November 1830; *Portsmouth, Portsea and Gosport Herald*, 2 January 1831 (Sockett is mentioned); *Sussex Advertiser*, 22 November 1830 (Lord Surrey promised reductions on behalf of his father the [12th] Duke of Norfolk); *Brighton Herald*, 1 January 1831 (voluntary reductions by tithe holders Richard Hasler and W.S. Poyntz).

23 PRO, HO 52/10, Sussex, Egremont, 13, 19, and 26 November 1830.

24 WSRO, PHA 2690, Tyler to Coppard, 17 November 1830: Egremont's agent giving permission for a farmer to dismantle a threshing machine.

25 *The Times*, 23 November 1830, report headed Petworth, 19 November.

26 WSRO, PHA 8558, Egremont, 27 November 1830, setting a wage retroactive to 15 November; Egremont, 3 February 1831, excluded "Helpers etc" at the house from the advance. They already received a twelve-shilling wage (2s. a day for a six-day week) and were "very well off," probably because of perquisites. Thos. Sherwin to W. Tyler, n.d., wrote concerning payments to estate employees, such as shepherds and carters, who worked on Sundays, and gatekeepers, who had their cottages rent free.

27 PRO, HO 52/10, Sussex, Egremont, 19 November 1830; BPP 1837, XVII, pt 1 (138), Second Report from the Select Committee on the Poor Law Amendment Act, 337, John Stapley, 14 June 1837. Stapley described the collapse of consensus in his parish of South Bersted. South Bersted belonged to the Sutton Gilbert Union controlled by Egremont, but it was on the coast, apart from the other parishes, and probably too far away for him to assist.

28 Roberts, *Paternalism*, ch. 4, "The Patriarchy of Sussex," sets out the limits of aristocratic concern for the poor. Dyck, *William Cobbett*, 139–40, and "William Cobbett and the Rural Radical Platform," 193, states that the radical politician and writer set community standards at defiance when he set the wages of labourers on his small farm at a level to make them independent of parish aid.

29 *Brighton Herald*, 9 November 1839, Mr Acland's report on the agricultural population of Sussex. Looking back from the end of the decade, Acland stated that raises won during the Swing disturbances in Sussex had lasted "for the period of the duration of the fear which Swing-fires had excited and no longer." Snell, *Annals*, 128–30, traces a decline in wages in the south from 1834 to 1850.

30 Royal Commission on the Poor Laws, *Extracts*, reports some of the examples collected by assistant commissioners.

31 WSRO, PHA 133, Richmond to Egremont, 18 November 1830, reported the agreement reached at Aldingbourn: the farmers promised twelve shillings a week and the men said they would return to work. WSRO, Goodwood Ms 1484, p. 3: In replies to the petition of three labourers from the parish of Aldingbourn, 16 December 1830, and a similar letter to the labourers of Oving, 11 January 1831, Richmond warned that the law against combination had serious consequences and reminded them that each labourer must represent his individual case to a magistrate. Blaug, "Myth of the Old Poor Law," summarizes opinions on parish work and discontent.

32 *Brighton Herald*, various reports, February 1831.

33 Dunkley, *Crisis of the Old Poor Law*, iv, describes "worried politicians groping for some means of ensuring social stability without impeding further agricultural development or endangering the interests of landed proprietors."

34 Mandler, *Aristocratic Government in the Age of Reform*, 135 George Rudé, "English Rural and Urban Disturbances on the Eve of the First Reform Bill, 1830–1831," *Past and Present* 37 (July 1967): 87–102. In addition to the Swing disturbances of the countryside and urban agitation for reform, Rudé describes a third centre of unrest in the manufacturing districts of the Midlands and the north and west that did not reach its high point until 1834.

35 *Hansard*, 3d ser., 6 (1831): 379–89. Richmond was moving second reading of a bill permitting overseers to lease up to fifty acres for cultivation by applicants for seasonal relief.

36 *Hansard*, 3d ser., 18 (1833): 671.

37 BPP 1831 (227), VIII, Select Committee of the House of Lords on the Poor Laws and Petitions Praying for Relief from Pauperism.

38 Poynter, 299; *Hansard*, 3d ser., 18 (1832): 898–900; 19 (1833): 665–8; 20 (1833): 357–9.

39 Goodwood Ms 1461, f. 173, Sockett to Richmond, 15 November 1832; BPP 1837 (131) and (138), XVII, pt I, First and Second Reports from the Select Committee on the Poor Law Amendment Act, Petworth Union, Sockett, 15 and 20 March. The subject of Sockett's tithe came up on 15 March. He made a second appearance, apparently at his own request, to clarify what he had said about payments in money and in kind.

40 WSRO, Goodwood Ms 647, f. 88, Burrell to Richmond, 14 February 1832. Burrell described the rate in terms familiar to all who study emigration as a "safety valve to parochial disquiet."

41 In the parish of Petworth, the annual spending on the relief of able-bodied paupers had averaged £235 for the decade from 1810 to 1820 and £340 over the next ten-year-period. In the one year of 1830–31, it was £1,127. Expenditure was continuing at a rate of over £475 for the three months from 8 October 1831 to 13 January 1832.

42 WSRO, Goodwood Ms 647, f. 81 and f. 91, Sockett to Richmond, 23 February, and petition; GB, House of Commons, *Journals*, 87 (1831–32), 17 February 1832, petitions from Ifield, Rusper, Petworth, and Pulborough to allow a majority of two-thirds of ratepayers by value to adopt a plan for employing the able-bodied poor (a labour rate).

43 BPP 1837 (131), XVII, pt I, First Report from the Select Committee on the Poor Law Amendment Act, Sockett, 9 March, 21.

44 WSRO, Acc. 5927, Papers of Sir Charles Merrik Burrell, Charles Murray to C. Burrell, 11 November 1837.

45 WSRO, Goodwood Ms 1435, Egremont to Richmond, 10 February 1832; Ms 648, f. 52, Egremont to Richmond, 22 March 1832.

46 BPP 1826 (404), IV, First Report; BPP 1827 (550), V, Second and Third Report.

47 *Hansard*, 2d ser., 18 (1828): 938, 1547; 21 (1829): 1720; 23 (1830): 782.

48 BPP 1832 (334), Copy of the Report of Mr Richards.

49 Peter Burroughs, *Britain and Australia 1831–1855: A Study in Imperial Relations and Crown Lands Administration* (Oxford: Clarendon Press 1967), 39.

50 Dunkley, "Whigs and Paupers," 131, quoting Goderich from a letter to Brougham, 28 December 1830.

51 WSRO, Goodwood Ms 634, f. 93, Goderich, 5 March 1831, and f. 94, "*Paper upon the Poor Laws: Emigration etc.*" The article on Goderich in *Australian Dictionary of Biography*, 456–7, describes him as having "little liking" for Wakefield's theory of systematic colonization.

52 Durham University Library, Grey Papers, GRE/BIII/7, "Observations on Lord Howick's Emigration Bill," encl. in Horton to Howick, 20 February 1831.

53 Johnston, *British Emigration Policy*, 168, comes closest among historians to Senior's view when he says that "for the right cause the money would have been available."

54 Senior, *Remarks on Emigration*, 4–6, and *Three Lectures on the Rate of Wages*, v, xv–xix; Leon S. Levy, *Nassau W. Senior*.

55 Durham University Library, Grey Papers, GRE/BIII/7, Horton's "Observations," 20 February 1831.

56 BPP 1830–31 (178), I, Bill to facilitate Voluntary Emigration to H.M. Possessions Abroad; as amended by Committee: BPP 1830–31 (358), I.

57 *Hansard*, 3d ser., 2 (1831): 880.

58 Durham University Library, Grey Papers, GRE/B124/6J, Poulett Scrope to Howick, 10 December 1831; GRE/V/CI, Howick, Private Letter Book, 26–9, Howick to Poulett Scrope, 14 December 1831.

59 Durham University Library, Grey Papers, GRE/B121/4E, Richmond to Howick, 3 April 1831.

60 PRO, CO 384/27, 5–10, Goderich to the commissioners, 1 July 1831: Instructions. The members of the commission in addition to Richmond and Howick were Francis Baring, Henry Ellis, and R.W. Hay.

61 PRO, CO 384/27, 11–13v, commissioners to Goderich, 30 July 1831, f. 15, circular 8 July 1831, and f. 17, circular 18 July 1831; CO 384/28, 579–85v, Poulett Scrope to Ellis, 8 and 12 August 1831.

62 House of Lords, *Journals*, 70 (1838), app. 2, Select Committee on New Zealand, 191; BPP 1847 (737), VI, Report of the Lords Committee on Colonization from Ireland, T.F. Elliot, 11 June 1847. Elliot, the commissioners' secretary, built a career on this initiative in the Colonial Office and as a commissioner of the Colonial Land and Emigration Commission in the 1840s.

63 Haines, *Emigration and the Labouring Poor*; Richards, "How Did Poor People Emigrate."

64 *Hansard*, 3d ser., 3 (1831): 11; WSRO, Goodwood Ms 671, f. 8, Map: "The Parishes in Sussex with the number of Able bodied Labourers in each out of employ, 1831–32," in Michael Irish to Richmond, 18 February 1834. Irish was one of several people reporting to Richmond in 1831–32.

65 WSRO, Goodwood Ms 1489, f. 92, Richmond's letter book, Richmond to Howick, 5 January 1832.

66 WSRO, Goodwood Ms 647, f. 30, Howick to Richmond, 10 January 1832.

67 GB, House of Lords, *Journals*, 64 (1831–32), 439, and app. 2, Minutes of Evidence; Brock, *Great Reform Act*.

68 PRO, HO 52/15, Sussex 1831; 52/20, Sussex 1832; and 52/23, Sussex 1834; Mingay, *Unquiet Countryside*. The *Journal of Peasant Studies* ran a series of studies of popular protest in England in this era: Wells (1979–81), Charlesworth (1980), Archer (1982), Mills and Short (1982), Read (1984 and 1986), and Mills (1988). Roger Wells, "Resistance to the New Poor Law."

69 Lloyd C. Saunders, ed., *Lord Melbourne's Papers* (London 1889), 152, Melbourne to Wellington, 10 November 1832. Melbourne had been home secretary in 1830.

70 WSRO, Goodwood Ms 647, f. 8: "The Duke of Richmond's remedy for relieving the Labouring Poor by the appointment of a Commission to enquire into Their Condition. Submitted and agreed to by the Government, 18 January 1832." Richmond had been discussing a commission or a select committee for this purpose since 1829.

71 BPP 1834 (44), XXVII–XXXIX; Checkland and Checkland, *Poor Law Report of 1834*.

72 Crowther, *Workhouse System*, 22–3.

73 University of Durham, Grey Papers, GRE/B144[6], Report, as submitted in February 1832.

74 BPP 1831–32 (724), XXXII, Report of the Commissioners for Emigration, 15 March 1832.

75 BPP 1831–32 (724), XXXII, Report of the Commissioners for Emigration, 15 March 1832, Information, 9 February 1832, 211, 215.

76 WSRO, Goodwood 648, ff. 2, 28, 29, Elliot to Richmond, March 1832.

77 WSRO, Ms 1460, f. 98, Sockett to Richmond, 15 October 1832. Sockett wrote of submitting a recommendation to the commissioners of emigration.

78 WSRO, Goodwood Ms 1463, f. 434, Sockett to Richmond, 12 February 1833.

79 WSRO, Goodwood Ms 1473, f. 73, Sockett to Richmond, 21 January 1834, and f. 219, Sockett to Richmond, 25 February 1834. The parishes Sockett named were Kirdford, Lurgashall, Lodsworth, and Fernhurst to the northeast of Petworth and Pulborough, Billingshurst,

and Rudgwick to the east. PRO, MH 12/13198 and MH 12/13199, Westhamptnett Union, December 1835 to January 1837, give the history of borrowing and repayment by the parishes of Walberton, Felpham, and Yapton for emigration from 1832 to 1836.

80 *Emigration: A Letter to a Member of Parliament. Brighton Herald*, 22 June 1833, identifies the member of Parliament who received this pamphlet as Wolwyrch Whitmore. WSRO, Goodwood Ms 1473, f. 73, Sockett to Richmond, 21 January 1834; BPP 1837–38 (658), XX, pt 2, Select Committee on Postage, Second Report, Sockett, 23 May 1838.

81 Mackay, *History of the English Poor Law*, 120; Dunkley, "Whigs and Paupers," 136–7; Checkland and Checkland, *Poor Law Report of 1834*, 490. Senior advised separate legislation for assisted emigration such as he had proposed in 1830, but the committee ignored his advice.

82 *Poor Law Amendment Act*, 4 & 5 Will. 4, c. 76.

83 BPP 1836 (595), XXIX, pt 1 and pt 2, app. D, 571–4, "Statement of the Number of Persons who have Emigrated ... between June 1835 and July 1836." More emigrants for 1836 would be included in this number than for 1835. Report from the Secretary of the Treasury relative to the Deportation of Paupers from Great Britain, 24th Congress, 2d session (1836–37), Senate doc. 5, serial 297. Rye was the Sussex port identified as sending significant numbers since 1829. Yarmouth in Norfolk, where fourteen emigrant ships had sailed for Quebec in place of the usual four, sent the only report of a sharp increase in 1836. Elliott, "English"; Howells, "For I was tired of England, Sir."

84 Elliott, "English"; William Cattermole, *Emigration: The Advantages of Emigration to Canada* (London 1831), PRO, CO 384/28, 239–41, Cattermole, 23 April 1831; CO 384/30, 428–9v.

85 PRO, CO 384/45, Parker to Elliot, 7 November [1837].

86 PRO, CO 384/41, 245–7v, John Phillips (secretary to Lord John Russell) to the Colonial Office, 27 February 1835, conveying Russell's support of Stradbroke's plan and enclosing a copy of Stradbroke's letter to Russell.

87 PRO, MH 12/11729, Blything Union.

88 PRO, MH 12/38, Hawley, Report as to the Operation and Effects of the Poor Law Amendment Act, in the County of Sussex, 16 June 1836, 496; BPP 1836 (595), XXIX, pt 1, Second Annual Report, app. B, no. 3, Report of W.H.T. Hawley; PRO, MH 12, 13061, John Ellis [the chairman of the Petworth Union], 23 January 1837: Hawley replied to Ellis, 30 January 1837, and reported to the commissioners, 11 February 1837. Ellis rather than Sockett testified on this report for the 1837 select committee.

89 *London Standard*, 22 February 1837. Sockett to John Walter, 15 February 1837.

CHAPTER 2

1 WSRO, Goodwood Ms 1464, 513.

2 Oliver Macdonagh, *A Pattern of Government Growth 1800–1860: The Passenger Acts and Their Enforcement* (London: MacGibbon and Kee 1961). Guillet, *Great Migrations*, 25–7, discusses emigrant vessels sailing to Quebec from 1770 until steamboats took over the trade.

3 Houston and Smyth, *Irish Emigration*, 47, 54–60, 71; Elliott, *Irish Migrants*; Donald Harman Akenson, *The Irish in Ontario: A Study in Rural History* (Kingston and Montreal: McGill-Queen's University Press 1981); Fingard, "The Poor in Winter," in Cross and Kealey, *Readings in Canadian History*, 2; Way, *Common Labour.*

4 Cowan, *British Emigration*, 153. Durham University Library, Grey Papers, GRE/B144[6], Report ... February 1831. The report suggested that passages from Dublin to Quebec, expected to be thirty shillings in 1832, represented the last possible reduction in the price.

5 Jones, *Background to Emigration*; Cowan, *British Emigration*; Gillet, *Great Migration*; William Forbes Adams, *Ireland and Irish Emigration to the New World from 1815 to the Famine* (New Haven:Yale University Press 1932), 80–1, 114–18, 235. Adams estimates that children probably accounted for two-thirds of deaths during emigration.

6 WSRO, Goodwood Ms 1464, f. 511, Sockett to Richmond, 8 March 1833, and f. 512, Sockett to Charles Barclay, 8 March 1833 (copy).

7 Senior, *Remarks on Emigration*, 24.

8 Cowan, *British Emigration*; Macdonagh, *Pattern of Government Growth*; Peter Dunkley, "Emigration and the State, 1803–1842: The Nineteenth-Century Revolution in Government Reconsidered," *Historical Journal* 23, no. 2 (1980): 353–80.

9 PRO, CO 384/36, ff. 161–1v, Thomas Buckley, mayor of Portsmouth, 10 February 1834.

10 *Brighton Gazette*, 8 March 1832, Waddell's advertisement; PRO, CO 384, ff. 269–70, Custom's Office, Portsmouth, 10 February 1832, with an enclosure from Garratt and Gibbon of the same date. With provisions, Garratt and Gibbon charged £5 17s. 6d. Waddell asked £6 10s.

11 Charles Barclay, ed., *Letters from the Dorking Emigrants*, 12–13.

12 PRO, MH 12/13060, 123817, and CO 384/41, 352, "Emigrants sent out to Upper Canada by the Petworth Emigration Committee," n.d., received by the poor law commissioners 15 December 1836. The thirteen parishes were Sutton, Coates, Fittleworth, Barlavington, West Grinstead, Billingshurst, Wisborough Green, Kirdford, Lurgashall, Pulborough, Sullington, Storrington, and Felpham and Merston (combined on the list).

13 WSRO, PHA 1068, Sockett's notes on a proposed handbill and on the scheme [28 August 1838]. Sockett suggested a ship that would carry about 200 adults and 60 or 70 children; the *Waterloo* sailed with 181 emigrants.

14 Sidney Webb and Beatrice Webb, *English Local Government*, 1:364–84; GB, Royal Commission on the Poor Laws, *Extracts*.

15 WSRO, PHA 1068, Sockett's comments [28 August 1838]; BPP 1847 (737), VI, Colonization from Ireland, Brydone, 18 June 1847, 137–8: Sockett to Chichester, 12 November 1833, with later additions.

16 BPP 1834 (44), Royal Commission on the Poor Laws, app. A, C.H. Maclean, "Emigration."

17 Biographical information from project files.

18 AO, RG 1, A-1-6, 13780-81, Cattermole to R.B. Sullivan, 27 July 1836. Cattermole received £190 from the company for this tour, an amount he claimed to be less than it cost him. He claimed to have influenced the emigration decision of some 6,000 people.

19 Cameron, McDougall Maude, and Haines, *English Immigrant Voices*; Cameron, "'Til they get tidings.'"

20 WSRO, PHA 137; PHA 691. Sockett rented the house in Littlehampton for some time prior to 1838.

21 WSRO, MP 4317, Ann Mann to sons and friends, 2 January 1837.

22 *Emigration: A Letter to a Member of Parliament*, 9.

23 *Emigration: A Letter to a Member of Parliament*. Sockett's experience was mainly in parishes conforming to Gilbert's Act of 1782; he took his proportioning of the expenses from the formula for financing a parish workhouse set out in this act.

24 Barclay, ed., *Letters from the Dorking Emigrants*, 7. In the parish of Walberton in 1832, Sockett's formula was reversed, the parish paying two-thirds. In South Bersted, the parish matched the amount paid during the previous year in support of the people sent.

25 WSRO, PAR 210/37/11 (1), Samuel Older to parish authorities at Wisborough Green, a begging letter for clothing. He hoped for a single set of clothes to outfit his son for service.

WSRO, PHA 6572, Earl of Egremont's Bounty (items of clothing given to paupers selected for good behaviour). In 1832, shirts and blankets for this purpose were supplied by Messrs Colebrook and Blunden, who seem to have been employed in providing outfits for Petworth emigrants as well as clothing for the local poor.

26 WSRO, PHA 137, Petworth Emigration Committee, Minute Book, 1832. The Minute Book is a primary source for much of the account that follows. Sockett's published account of the 1832 emigration is in the introduction to *Emigration: Letters … 1832*, and his *Emigration: A Letter to a Member of Parliament* touches on the emigrations of 1833 and 1834.

27 PRO, CO 384/30, 151, Office of the Privy Council, 14 March 1832; CO 384/30, 126, Council Office, 28 March 1832, and supplement to the London *Gazette*.

28 PRO, CO 385/6, Elliot's letter book for 1832, pp. 33–6, to Moon and Carter, 31 March and 3 April; pp. 39 and 50, to Pym and Carter, 7 and 9 April; p. 66, to Sockett, 25 April; WSRO, Goodwood Ms 648, ff. 112 and 124, Elliot to Richmond, 21 and 28 April 1832. Haines, ed., "*No Trifling Matter*," 24, "Medicines supplied …," has some identifications and descriptions.

29 Other ships named in 1832 were the *Moffat*, the *Ocean*, the *Esther*, and the *England*. The committee had to get the name of the *England* changed to the *Lord Melville* in letters already prepared at the Colonial Office for the governors of the Canadas.

30 WSRO, PHA 1069, memorandum of agreement with Carter and Bonus for the *British Tar*, 1834; PHA 140, abstract memo for the *British Tar*, memoranda for the *Heber* with Carter and Bonus, 1836, and for the *Diana* with Tebbull, Stoneman and Spence, 1837. PHA 1069 contains a similar contract with Carter and Bonus and related correspondence from 1839 for the *Waterloo*.

31 WSRO, Goodwood Ms 641, "Information to Persons desirous of emigrating from the Neighbourhood to Upper Canada," 1 March 1832.

32 Goodwood Ms 648, f. 61, "Information …," updated, 19 March 1832.

33 WSRO, PHA 137, Minute Book, 1832. The *Brighton Herald*, 3 March, 7 April, and 28 April 1832, reported the formation of a committee set up to consider emigration from Brighton. It recommended Canada as the cheapest destination, but the cost seems to have been more than sponsors were willing to pay at that time. Brighton *Gazette*, 10 May 1832, reported a thinly attended vestry meeting that turned down the few people who had applied for assisted emigration.

34 *Portsmouth, Portsea, and Gosport Herald*, 8 and 15 April 1832; *Emigration: Letters* (1833). Egremont's share in Lurgashall seems to have been negotiated from three pounds ten shillings up to four pounds (two-fifths of the total); Yaldwyn's other parishes were Lodsworth, Fernhurst, and "Hampshire End" (unidentified). Sockett identified Surrey parishes that in 1832 sent emigrants through the Petworth Emigration Committee (rather than the Dorking Society) as Chiddingfold, Hascomb, Haslemere, Frensham (acting in conjunction with Linchmere, Sussex), Stoke (Guildford), Southwark (London), and Witley. Beldam may have learned of the scheme through the Prime family, who sent emigrants with the Petworth committee from Walberton in Sussex and owned land near Beldam in Cambridgeshire.

35 *Emigration: Letters* (1833), xiii.

36 PRO, CO 385/6, Elliot to Sockett, 7 March 1832; PRO, CO 385/10, 32–4, Pinnock to Buchanan, 26 March 1836. Four years after Sockett, Pinnock also arranged on behalf of the parishes dealing with him to transfer money from London through the Canada Company.

37 AO, Canada Company Papers, section 1 C, 2, 278, [John Perry] to the commissioners, 27 March 1832; p. 258, Charles Bosanquet to commissioners, 13 April 1832; p. 278, Charles Franks to commissioners, 3 May 1832, sending a similar order for emigrants on the *England* for £150; Canada Company, C-6, Letters of Credit: vols. 1–4 record these transfers in the years 1833–37.

38 Sockett to Richmond: WSRO Goodwood Ms 1447, f. 306, 1 April 1833; Ms 1465, f. 23, 12 April 1833; Ms 1465, f. 61, 20 April, f. 62, 19 April, and f. 67, 21 April 1833.

39 WSRO, Goodwood Ms 1459, f. 607, Sockett to Richmond, 15 August 1832. Accidents occurred even at this stage, and one woman was badly injured when her cart overturned on the steep hill between Petworth and Duncton.

40 *Portsmouth, Portsea and Gosport Herald*, 15 April 1832, 6 May 1832.

41 *Brighton Gazette*, 17 April 1834; *Brighton Herald*, 19 April 1834; *Brighton Guardian*, 16 and 23 April 1834.

42 *Hampshire Telegraph*, 27 April 1835.

43 WSRO, PHA 137; *Portsmouth, Portsea, and Gosport Herald*, 15 April 1832 (the pheasants belonged to Sir Charles Taylor of Holleycombe, near Liphook); *Sussex Advertiser*, 16 April 1832.

44 *Hampshire Telegraph*, 2 April 1832 (Chandler's death); Goodwood Ms 1447, f. 306, Sockett to Richmond, 1 April 1832 (asking his help in bringing the *Lord Melville* into the harbour).

45 *Portsmouth, Portsea, and Gosport Herald*, 28 April 1833.

46 Brydone, *Narrative*, 3; Haines, ed., *"No Trifling Matter,"* 8, includes a reconstructed sketch of the 'tween decks of the *British Tar*.

47 Letters from Sockett to Richmond about his son George, his army career, and his plans to sell his commission and emigrate to Upper Canada in 1833 are in WSRO, Goodwood Mss 1460, 1461, 1463, 1465, 1647, and 1648. George sailed in the autumn, and he was never associated with the Petworth emigrations in any official capacity.

48 WSRO, PHA 138 [Hale's report, 1833].

49 Cobbett, *Emigrant's Guide*, Letter v; WSRO, Goodwood Ms 1464, f. 512, Sockett to Barclay, 8 March 1833.

50 *Emigration: Letters* (1833), 72–80, and published by Phillips as a separate pamphlet; WSRO, PHA 1063, Phillips's account for printing 300 copies, 5 April 1843. Hale's strong recommendation of the Canada Company suggests that he wrote the *Instructions* before his association with Sockett. Cobbett in his *Emigrant's Guide* covered some of the same ground with reference to ships sailing to the United States.

51 WSRO, PHA 1069, "Berthing List," *Waterloo*, 1839, shows emigrants assigned space on the same ratio as on the *Lord Melville*.

52 *Emigration: Letters* (1833), 72. *Brighton Gazette*, 3 May 1832, describes "hundreds" of people visiting an emigrant ship moored at Shoreham before leaving for Montreal. The writer noted the failure of the emigrants to secure their possessions or their provisions and feared that in a gale they would be "tumbled and tossed and soiled and spoiled rarely."

53 WSRO, PHA 139, [Brydone] to the Petworth committee, report up to 2 June 1834.

54 *Emigration: Letters* (1833), 34–5.

55 *Emigration: Letters from Sussex Emigrants*, 8–9.

56 Brighton *Guardian*, 11 May 1836, Edward Longley, 28 September 1835

57 Barclay, *Letters from the Dorking Emigrants*, 8. Sockett was stung by Barclay's use of an earlier publication date than his; Barclay had used four letters from Sussex emigrants that Sockett knew he had published after January. As Barclay's version of these letters is the same as the handwritten copies that Sockett sent to Richmond, Richmond could have supplied them to Barclay and Barclay may be innocent of advancing his date.

58 WSRO, Goodwood Ms 1464, f. 512, Sockett to Charles Barclay, 18 March 1833 (copy). Sockett did not give the amount of Mitchell's quotation.

59 *Portsmouth Herald*, 7 April 1833.

60 WSRO, PHA 141, "Emigration to Upper Canada," 29 January 1836.

61 *No. 6 Continuation*, 44–5, John and Elizabeth White, 27 October 1833.

62 WSRO, PHA 8622, William Tyler to Willard and Hasting, 18 March, and 6 and 11 April 1832; PHA 137, Minute Book, 1832.

63 *Emigration: Letters* (1833), 27, Martin Martin, 24 September 1832.

64 *Emigration: Letters* (1833), 3–4, Stephen Goatcher, 6 July 1832; WSRO, Goodwood Ms 1465, f. 18, Goatcher, 17 January 1833; Barclay, ed., *Letters from the Dorking Emigrants*, 28–34, James Tewsley, 9 November [1832]. Tewsley reported that Able was visiting him in New York State but that Able's opinion was in favour of Canada.

65 Reports, 1833, from Hale to the Petworth Committee: WSRO, PHA 138, report on the crossing; PHA 140, Account of Expenses, Lower and Upper Canada; Goodwood Ms 1469, 16, 2 July 1833 (copy).

66 WSRO, Goodwood Ms 1469, f. 13, 4 October 1833.

67 Examples are the *Brighton Guardian*, 16 April 1833, and the *Montreal Gazette*, 2 January 1833 (copied from the *Courier*).

68 WSRO, Goodwood Ms 1469, f. 87, 30 October 1833, and Ms 1470, f. 94, 2 November 1833. At least one of Sockett's sponsors, Henry Seymour, had had good reports of Hale, but he reported complaints from two returned emigrants of a lack of attention from Hawke.

69 *No. 5 Continuation*.

70 WSRO, PHA 138, Hale's journal of the voyage, 1833; *No. 5 Continuation*, the two emigrants quoted are Hannah Tilley and Henry Habbin; *Portsmouth, Portsea, and Gosport Herald*, 13 October 1833; *Brighton Guardian*, 16 October 1833. The *Montreal Gazette* of 2 January 1834 reprinted Sockett's *No. 5 Continuation* from the *Courier*.

71 WSRO, Goodwood Ms 1470, 94, Sockett to Richmond, 2 November 1833. The *Hampshire Telegraph*, 7 April 1834, carried a notice of circulars advertising Hale's intention to charter and conduct an emigrant ship in May.

72 WSRO, PHA 734, Sockett to Wyndham, 2 February 1838.

73 Barbara (Brydone) Calder, private family papers, Sockett to Brydone, 24 February 1834.

74 WSRO, Goodwood Ms 1504, f. Q86, Sockett to Richmond, 12 January 1834; Ms 1505, f. R28 and 29, Sockett to Richmond, 6 March 1834, and enclosed memorandum concerning Brydone.

75 WSRO, Goodwood Ms 1474, 369, Sockett to Richmond, 1 April 1834.

76 Brydone, *Narrative*; WSRO, PHA 139, Brydone, report up to 2 June 1834.

77 Brighton *Gazette*, 8 March 1832, advertisement; PRO, MH12/13061, Sockett to Poor Law Commission, 12 April 1837.

78 BPP 1847 (737), VI, pt 1, Robert Carter (of Carter and Bonus), 16 July 1847. Carter may have advised Sockett.

79 PRO, CO 386/19, Elliot to Stephen, 14 July 1837, reporting on a case investigated by the emigration agent at Bristol.

80 *Emigration: A Letter to a Member of Parliament*, 7–8; WSRO, PHA 138, [Hale], Report, 1833. Horton's emigration committees collected similar information, especially from Buchanan, about providing Irish families with familiar foods.

81 *Hampshire Telegraph*, 2 May 1836.

82 *Brighton Patriot*, 28 November 1837.

83 WSRO, PHA 139 [Brydone], Report, 2 June 1833; Brydone, *Narrative*; PHA 1069, Scale of Provisions, Ship *Diana*, 1837, and Ship *Waterloo*, 1839. Haines, ed., *"No Trifling Matter,"* 25–9, compares shipboard fare with the diet of the Petworth Poorhouse and with cooking traditions in Sussex.

84 Barbara (Brydone) Calder, private family papers, "Narrative Journal by Naval Surgeon James Marr Brydone."

85 *Brighton Patriot*, 28 November 1837.

86 *Brighton Patriot*, 12 December 1837.

87 *Brighton Patriot*, 12 December 1837.

88 PRO, CO 385/9, pp. 64–71, Pinnock to PLC, 9 May 1835.

89 PRO, CO 384/39, 373–3v, "Emigration …," 5 March 1835.

90 BPP 1834 (44), Royal Commission, app. B.1, Answers to Rural Questions, Kirdford, Richard Hasler.

91 WSRO, PHA 1068, Sockett, 28 August 1838.

92 WSRO, Goodwood Ms 647, f. 85, Sockett to Richmond, 12 February 1832.

93 WSRO, Goodwood Ms 648, f. 49, William Holmes to Richmond, 4 March 1832, and f. 48, Holmes to Richmond, 24 February 1832. The mayor had hoped for aristocratic backing in selling parish property to raise funds to assist emigration.

94 WSRO, Goodwood Ms 1473, f. 101, Lord Suffield to Richmond, 20 January 1834, and Ms 1474, f. 381, Suffield to Richmond, 5 April 1834. Suffield sent seven single men and two families from his lands in Norfolk through the port at Yarmouth.

95 WSRO, Goodwood Ms 1469, f. 64, Sockett to Richmond, 22 October 1833.

96 BPP 1847 (737), VI, Colonization from Ireland, Brydone, 18 June 1847, 137–8: Sockett to Chichester, 12 November 1833, with later additions.

97 *Brighton Gazette*, 14 November 1833; *Brighton Herald*, 16 November 1833.

98 *Brighton Gazette*, 17 April 1834, article describing the proceedings of the Brighton committee. After 1834, emigrants from East Sussex areas around Brighton and Lewes seem to have been sent from London or Rye rather than having them travel all the way to Portsmouth.

99 *Hampshire Telegraph*, 21 April 1834.

100 IOWRO, House of Industry Minute Book, 1837.

101 PRO, MH 12/13061, Sockett, letters of 27 and 28 March and 2 and 12 April 1837.

102 PRO, MH 12/12830, Cuckfield Union, C. Strong, one of the Cuckfield guardians, to the poor law commissioners, 17 March 1837.

103 PRO, MH 12/12830, Cuckfield Union, Strong to the poor law commissioners, 21 March 1837.

104 PRO, MH 12/12830, Poor Law Commissioners, 21 March 1837. The broker was a Mr Saunders.

105 BPP 1838 (389), Emigration: Canada and Australia, No. 9, Extracts from a portion of the weekly reports of the acting chief agent for emigration …, 40, weeks ending 17 June and 1 July [1837]. PRO, MH 12/12830, has further correspondence concerning the emigrants sent on the *Auxilier* written in July and September.

106 Cameron, "Wilmot Horton's Experimental Emigrations."

CHAPTER 3

1 Gash, "Rural Unemployment"; E.P. Thompson, *Making of the English Working Class*; Snell, *Annals*; Mingay, ed., *The Agrarian History of England and Wales*, 6: *1750–1850*; F.M.L. Thompson, ed., *The Cambridge Social History of Britain, 1750–1959*, vol. 1: *Regions and Communities*.

2 Stevenson, *Popular Disturbances*, 118, 124.

3 Baugh, "The Cost of Poor Relief"; Oxley, *Poor Relief in England and Wales, 1601–1834*, 112,

believes the Speenhamland magistrates gave their name to this form of relief because Sir Frederick Eden chose to use their table for 1795 in his influential book. GB, *Hansard*, 2d ser., 20 (1829): 539, Robert Aglionby Slaney. Slaney, an advocate of rural reform, claimed that the Speenhamland allowance began as a support for children who were classed as "impotent poor" within the sense of the Tudor statute, 43 Eliz. 1, c. 1.

4 WSRO, Goodwood Ms 671, f. 8, map in Michael Irish to Richmond, 18 February 1834; Goodwood Ms 1456, f. 87, Irish to Richmond, 1 February 1832. Irish states that he and his associate, Barratt, have "completed the account for Sussex of the unemployed labourers." They were compiling papers on turnpike roads, which may be why this map, despite its handsome presentation, has blanks and appears to be incomplete.

5 Blaug, "The Poor Law Report Re-examined," 245; Baugh, "The Cost of Poor Relief in South-East England, 1790–1834."

6 Blaug, "Myth of the Old Poor Law" and "The Poor Law Report Re-examined"; Baugh, "Cost of Poor Relief in South-East England, 1790–1830"; Digby, "The Rural Poor Law," in Fraser, ed., *New Poor Law*; Boyer, *Economic History*.

7 BPP 1837 (131), XVII, pt 1, 37, Sockett, 9 March 1837; Reay, *Microhistories*, 129. Using the 1841 census and excluding newcomers, Reay estimates that over 80 per cent of labouring households in the Kent parish of Hernhill had received poor relief at some stage in the life cycle.

8 *Brighton Herald*, 9 November 1839, Acland's Report. Snell, *Annals of the Labouring Poor*, 125–31, discusses literary and statistical evidence of wage rates in England in this period. The weekly averages for Sussex he gives in table 3.1, p. 130, are 12/6 (1833), 10/7 (1837), and 10/6 (1850). He attributes the drop in wages in 1837 to the introduction of the new poor law.

9 BPP 1837 (138), XVII, pt 1, 160, Edward Butt, 20 March 1837. Butt spoke of his own parish, but he seemed to mean Petworth and Kirdford. He had resigned as relieving officer just before coming to London, and he was trying to avoid a controversy over whether he did so in protest or because the salary was reduced.

10 Anderson, "The Social Implications of Demographic Change," in F.M.L. Thompson, ed., *Cambridge Social History of Britain*, 2:14, 39, 46. Average life expectancy was around forty; a married woman might expect, on average, to bear six children in her lifetime.

11 BPP 1837(131), XVII, pt 1, 28, Sockett, 9 March 1837.

12 Snell, *Annals*, 129–30.

13 Jones, "Agricultural Labour Market in England, 1793–1873"; Mingay, ed., *Victorian Countryside*; Armstrong, *Farmworkers*; George R. Boyer and Timothy J. Hatton, "Did Joseph Arch Raise Agricultural Wages? Rural Trade Unions and the Labour Market in Late Nineteenth-Century England," *Economic History Review* 47, no. 2 (1994): 310–34.

14 Quoted in R.B. Madgwich, *Immigration into Eastern Australia 1788–1851* (1937; Sydney: Sydney University Press 1969), 91. Hay probably sought to control some of the damage Horton had done to the cause of assisted emigration by writing of absolute paupers when he had actually meant emigrants who could not pay their own passage.

15 Rose, *Relief of Poverty*, 1 (quoting *Wealth of Nations*, book v, ch. 2, par. ii).

16 James Caird, *English Agriculture in 1850–51* (London 1852), frontispiece.

17 Alun Hawkins, "In the Sweat of Thy Face: The Labourer and Work," ch. 3 in G.E. Mingay, ed., *The Vanishing Countryman* (London: Routledge 1989), 43.

18 WSRO, Goodwood Ms 657, f. 79, J. Cuming, 24 June 1833.

19 E.J.T. Collins, "The Coppice and Underwood Trades," in Mingay, ed., *Agrarian History*, 6:484–500. Collins described the middle decade of the nineteenth century as the high-water mark of the many crafts and industries that used coppice wood for their raw material.

20 WSRO, Goodwood Ms 669, f. 41, Robert Weale, Midhurst Vestry, Statement, 7 March 1834.

21 Robert C. Allen, "Labour Productivity and Farm Size," 479. Based on a survey in the South Midlands, Allen gave 145 acres as the average size of an open-field farm in the early nineteenth century.

22 WSRO, PHA 2415, Dean Farm, also Heyshott and Goffs and Garlands; PHA 2416, Frithfold Farm; PHA 2417, Heyshott Farm; PHA 2418, Heyshott Farm. These accounts span the period from November 1829 to June 1833.

23 Of these, John and Ann Sageman are probably the John and Ann Sageman who left Tillington for Upper Canada in 1844.

24 WSRO, PHA 2415, accounts for Dean Farm, Tillington.

25 Snell, *Annals of the Labouring Poor*, 263.

26 *Portsmouth Herald*, 15 April 1832.

27 *Emigration: A Letter to a Member of Parliament.*

28 *Brighton Guardian*, 5 April 1832.

29 Michael Reed, "Social and Economic Relations in a Wealden Community: Lodsworth, 1780–1860," unpublished MA thesis, University of Sussex, 1982; WSRO, MP 2027; Mills, *Lord and Peasant*, 46–8.

30 Hampshire *Telegraph*, 21 April 1834.

31 WSRO, Goodwood Ms 1474, f. 329, Sockett to Richmond, 22 March 1834.

32 *Brighton Herald*, 2 May 1835.

33 WSRO, PHA 140, Abstract of the families and single men … by the *Diana*, 1837.

34 As indicated in the introduction, there are no ship's lists for Petworth ships in official sources. WSRO, PHA 142, contains a twentieth-century copy prepared from a list for the *Burrell*, 1835, and PHA 140 has an abstract of the list for the *Diana*, 1837.

35 PRO, MH 12/13060, Emigrants sent out to Upper Canada by the Petworth Emigration Committee, received 15 December 1836. The same table is in CO 384/41, 352.

36 *Emigration: Letters* (1833), "Introduction"; *Emigration: A Letter to a Member of Parliament*. There are minor differences in the numbers attributed to some parishes in these two sources.

37 Erickson, "Emigration from the British Isles to the U.S.A. in 1831," 185–7.

38 *Portsmouth Herald*, 15 April 1832. Sockett may have kept these figures because he was considering counting these children as one-third of a passage (a standard practice in Ireland). If so, he abandoned early on any thought of a reduction in cost that would have added to crowding on his ships rather than reducing it, as he chose to do in 1833.

39 WSRO, PHA 140, Abstract of the families and single men … by the *Diana*, 1837.

40 Stapleton, "Inherited poverty," 345. Stapleton writes of a "multigenerational deepening poverty trap from which it became increasingly difficult to escape."

41 Peter Laslett, "Introduction," in Laslett and Richard Wall, *Household and Family in Past Time* (Cambridge: Cambridge University Press 1972). Thomas Sokoll, *Household and family among the poor: the case of two Essex communities in the late eighteenth and early nineteenth centuries* (Bochum: Universitätsverlag Dr N. Brockmeyer 1993), 45, defines "household" as a "residential group" distinct from "family," a "demographic unit."

42 Hobsbawm and Rudé, *Captain Swing*, 247.

43 Reay, *Last Rising*, 135–7.

44 PHA 734, 1838, Sockett's observations on a list of persons employed by Colonel Wyndham.

45 Kussmaul, *Servants in Husbandry in Early Modern England*, 126–30, summarizes the shift in the status of young men from servants to labourers as revealed in the census of 1831 and the 1834 report of the Royal Commission on the Poor Laws. On page 7, she defines a

"servant" as a worker hired for the year and resident with the farmer. A labourer was a worker hired for a shorter term and resident elsewhere.

46 Great Britain, Poor Law Commissioners, *Report on the Sanitary Condition of the Labouring Population* (London 1842). This report, the work of Edwin Chadwick, is in BPP 1842 (006), XXVI, pt 1.

47 David Davies, *The Case of the Labourers in Husbandry* (London 1795; repr Fairfield, N.J.: Kelley 1977); Pamela Horn, *A Georgian Parson and His Village: The Story of David Davies, 1742–1819* (Abingdon, Oxford: Beacon Publications 1981). Davies and Sockett were both products of middle-class poverty and both worked for their education as secretaries and tutors until their patrons provided them with livings.

48 *The Times*, 6 August 1832.

49 BPP 1837 (131), XVII, pt 1, 33, Sockett, 9 March (Sockett first suggested Pullen).

50 BPP 1837 (131), XVII, pt 1, 17 March 1837, 132–9, Sopp; 139–44, Slements; 145–7, Pullen; 147–50, Ayling.

51 D.J. Oddy, "Working Class Diets in Late Nineteenth Century Britain," *Economic History Review*, 2d ser., 23 (1970): 321. Tufnell in his 1842 report warned that comparisons between diets at different times and places should take quality into account as well as quantity. One of his examples was tea, which might be drunk without sugar, be adulterated, or be replaced by a substitute such as burnt crusts.

52 D.C. Barnett, "Allotments and the Problem of Rural Poverty, 1780–1840," in E.L. Jones and G.E. Mingay, ed., *Land, Labour and Population in the Industrial Revolution*, 172. On the evidence of a select committee of 1843, Barnett states that in the southeast a comparatively high proportion of agricultural labourers had adequate ground attached to their cottages for gardens.

53 WSRO, PHA 693, Sockett to Wyndham, 26 March 1838.

54 BPP 1837 (138), XVII, pt 1, 160, Edward Butt, 20 March 1837, and 349, John Stapley, 14 June 1837. Butt had earlier attributed his resignation to a sharp reduction in salary. Other witnesses from the Petworth Union speaking of labouring lives and the hardships caused by removing the child allowance were Sockett; James Foard, a magistrate and guardian; John Napper, chairman of the Petworth Board of Guardians; Arthur Daintry, clerk to the board; and John Luttman Ellis, the vice-chairman. Hawley was called to answer them.

55 Robert C. Allen, "Reply: Labour Productivity and Farm Size in English Agriculture before Mechanization," *Explorations in Economic History* 28 (October 1991): 478–92. Gang labour by women and children was a later phenomenon and seems to have been unknown in Sockett's district in the 1830s.

56 Hugh Cunningham, "The Employment and Unemployment of Children in England, c. 1680–1851," *Past and Present* 126 (February 1990): 115–50, see especially 133–5.

57 Snell, *Annals of the Labouring Poor*, 51–7, writes that after nearly a century of increasing sexual specialization in farm work, women field workers had been relegated to a few poorly paid jobs in spring and the possibility of a subsidiary role helping men during harvest.

58 Peter King, "Customary Rights and Women's Earnings: The Importance of Gleaning to the Rural Labouring Poor, 1750–1850," *Economic History Review* 44, no. 3 (1991): 461–76. King offers a figure of between three and eight bushels of wheat as possibly typical for poor families gleaning in eastern and central England in the 1830s. Sopp mentioned two bushels. Slement's children (his wife had just given birth) obtained one and a half.

59 Snell, *Annals of the Labouring Poor*, 322–34, discusses the age of leaving home and the occupations that took children away.

60 WSRO, PHA 693, Sockett's handwritten notes on the printed list of premiums offered in 1837 by the West Sussex Association for the encouragement of industrious and meritorious agricultural labourers.

61 WSRO, Goodwood Ms 648, f. 61, "Information."

62 WSRO, Goodwood Ms 1476, f. 307, Sockett to Richmond, 14 September 1834; PRO, CO 384/39, ff. 312–14, Sockett to Hay, 14 February 1835.

63 PRO, CO 384/39, f. 373v, "Emigration to Upper Canada."

64 Snell, *Annals of the Labouring Poor*, 251–63, on the decline of apprenticeship in England. Jeremy Webber, "Labour and the Law," in Craven, ed., *Labouring Lives*, 124, 127–30, discusses apprenticeship in Upper Canada with reference to English precedent and as a form of foster care. Joy Parr, *Labouring Children: British Immigrant Apprentices to Canada, 1869–1924* (1980; Toronto: University of Toronto Press 1994).

65 Barbara (Brydone) Calder, private family papers, Sockett to Brydone [1835]. Cowan, *British Emigration*, 221, cites Buchanan's report for the arrival of two groups of these children in 1835. PRO, CO 384/28, f. 315. The full title given this society in a pamphlet published and sent in by Gouger in 1831 was the Society for the Permanent Support of Orphan and Destitute Children by means of apprenticeship in the Colonies.

66 BPP 1834 (44), app. A, report of Captain Pringle; *Portsmouth Herald*, 26 June 1831.

67 *Portsmouth Herald*, 21 June 1834.

68 PRO, CO 384/28, ff. 636–6vff., Richard Walton White, 4 February 1831. The Isle of Wight also sent assisted emigrants to the United States and Australia and to the Canadas on ships other than those of the Petworth committee.

69 Brighton Reference Library, Sussex Pamphlets, Box 38, "Autobiography of Charles Adsett."

70 Esther Chantler Dennis to her children, c. 1896, manuscript copy given to the Petworth project by descendant Berenice Smith.

71 PRO, CO 384/36, f. 453, Richmond to ?, 26 March 1834, sent to Colborne, 31 March 1834. The list was received, but we have been unable to find it.

72 Howells, "For I was tired of England, Sir"; Haines, "Shovelling out Paupers"; Donald Harman Akenson, *The Irish Diaspora: A Primer* (Toronto: P.D. Meany; Belfast: Queen's University 1993), 35–7.

73 WSRO, Goodwood Ms 670, f. 18, Sockett to Richmond, 19 May 1834, Remarks on the Poor Law Bill.

74 BPP 1834 (44), First Report of the Royal Commission on the Poor Laws, Remedial Measures, Emigration, 22d recommendation.

75 WSRO, PHA 1068, Sockett to Wyndham, 23 August 1838.

76 BPP 1834 (44), app. A, report of C.H. Maclean.

77 *Hansard*, 3rd ser., 92 (1847): 936. In a debate about limiting the hours of factory work, Richmond was provoked by colleagues who took the annoying position that all was well with farm workers because their even longer hours of labour took place in the healthy outdoors. *Hansard*'s recorder heard him say something to the effect that half of agricultural workers died prematurely from overwork.

78 WSRO, Goodwood Ms 647, f. 88a, Burrell to Richmond, 14 February 1832.

79 WSRO, Goodwood Ms 1862, f. 9, Sockett to Richmond, 12 March 1833. This man seems to be the shoemaker John White on our list. He was working in Boxgrove, in Richmond's sphere of influence, which was why Sockett made enquiries about him through Richmond.

80 WSRO, PHA 140, Abstract of the families and single men … by the ship *Diana* in 1837, and a similar abstract for the families and single men and women from the Isle of Wight.

81 WSRO, PHA 137, Minute Book, 1832.

82 Brydone, *Narrative*, 14–15; ESRO, PAR 378/35/2/3, documents relating to William West, alias Warden.

83 WSRO, Goodwood Ms 1469, f. 16, Hale to the Petworth Emigration Committee, 2 July 1833, copy.

84 WSRO, Goodwood Ms 1496, f. 13, Sockett to Richmond, 4 October 1833. Turner was reprieved and then pardoned because he had intervened to prevent murder at the time of the robbery.

85 *Brighton Gazette*, 27 February and 17 April 1834. We have identified Grafenstein in a report that spoke only of a young man.

86 PRO, CO 384/28, f. 636, Richard Walton White, 4 February 1831.

87 Howell, "For I was tired of England, Sir" 186–9, cites poor men threatening to emigrate alone and leave the parish to support their wives and children if authorities would not send them out. He found other East Anglian paupers who had refused to depart without an additional small sum of money.

88 BPP 1837 (138), XVII, pt 1, 348, John Stapley, 14 June 1837.

89 *Portsmouth, Portsea, and Gosport Herald*, 15 April 1832.

90 *Emigration: A Letter to a Member of Parliament*, 10.

91 *Continuation of Letters from Sussex Emigrants … Written in 1836* [1837], 1–3.

92 AO, Canada Company Papers, C-6, Letters of Credit, vol. 3, no. 892, 24 April 1835; no. 1170, 21 April 1836.

93 Stapleton, "Inherited poverty and life-cycle poverty," bases his conclusions on family reconstructions within the Hampshire parish of Odiham, which sent seven emigrants with the Petworth committee in 1832.

94 BPP 1834 (44), app. A, report of C.H. Maclean, Dorking. Although he arrived in both communities after the emigrants had left, Maclean knew that the Dorking emigrants went on a Petworth ship. In his report, he repeated what he had heard in each community without attempting a rationalization.

95 McCalla, *Planting the Province*, table 57, 271, summarizes the sales records for twelve Canadian farms in the period 1798–1850.

96 BPP 1843 (510), XII, Reports of Special Assistant Poor Law Commissioners on the Employment of Women and Children in Agriculture, 171, Vaughan, Kent, Surrey, and Sussex; W.A. Armstrong, "The Flight from the Land," in G.E. Mingay, ed., *The Vanishing Countryman*, 63. Jeffreys Taylor, *The Farm; A New Account of Rural Toils and Produce* (London 1832), emphasized these points for his young readers.

97 AO, MU 1717, Mary Leslie Papers, George Sockett Family Business Papers.

98 *Historical Atlas of Canada*, vol. 2, ed. R. Louis Gentilcore (Toronto, Buffalo, London: University of Toronto Press 1993), plate 14; AO, Ontario Land Records Index.

99 WSRO, PHA 142, notes in Lord Leconfield's hand. The list is a copy.

100 BPP 1841 (1) (298), XV, 447, no. 26, Sydenham to Russell, 26 January 1841; BPP 1842 (373), XXXI, pt 1, 22–31, extracts from Hawke's correspondence and his report for 1841.

101 Columbia University, Butler Library, Hawke, X325 T63, vol. 1, 172–4, Hawke to Harrison, 2 September 1839.

102 Flatting was the painting of a flat undercoat; graining involved painting to imitate the grain of wood or marble.

103 Baehre, "Pauper Emigration," 347.

104 BPP 1834 (44), app. A, report of C.H. Maclean, Petworth.

105 David Cannadine, *Class in Britain* (New Haven and London: Yale University Press 1998), xi, describes political history as "a study of the visions of society entertained by British politicians, and of the ways in which they conceived their task to be that of imposing their vision *of* the people *on* the people." The changing view of parish relief seems a good example.
106 Richards, "How Did Poor People Emigrate?" 262.
107 Haines, *Emigration and the Labouring Poor*, 46–53.
108 Haines, *Emigration and the Labouring Poor*, 5.
109 *London Standard*, 22 February 1837, Sockett to John Walters, 15 February 1837.
110 Research notes prepared by Leigh Lawson in 1994.
111 Merriman, *Emigrant Ancestors of a Lieutenant Governor*.

CHAPTER 4

1 Canadian Settler, *Emigrant's Informant*, 124–5.
2 R.J. Morris, *Cholera 1832: The Social Response to an Epidemic* (London: Croom Helm 1976), 25. Morris believes that approximately 32,000 people died of cholera in Great Britain in 1831–32 (79).
3 Bilson, *Darkened House*; C.M. Godfrey, *The Cholera Epidemics in Upper Canada 1832–1866* (Toronto and Montreal: Seccombe House 1968).
4 Baehre, "Pauper Emigration," 346–7.
5 BPP 1831–32 (724), XXXII, 231, Buchanan's report for 1831.
6 BPP 1831–32 (724), XXXII, 224–7, Enclosure no. 6, extract of a despatch from Lord Aylmer, 12 October 1831.
7 Buchanan first gained attention as a prominent witness before Horton's emigration committees. He restated his position in *Emigration practically considered*.
8 BPP 1831–32 (724), XXXII, 228, Report, no. 1 in no. 7, extracts from the report of the resident agent, 12 December 1831.
9 WSRO, Goodwood Ms 1460, f. 98, Sockett to Richmond, 15 October 1832; PRO, CO 384/41, 35–7, selected documents from Buchanan, including a list of vessels lost in 1834, a chart of the gulf, and his recommendations.
10 Brydone, *Narrative*, 10.
11 Cowan, *British Emigration*, 295, table VI.
12 WSRO, PHA 139, Brydone to Sockett, report covering the period between entering the St Lawrence and 2 June 1834.
13 Brydone, *Narrative*, 11; WSRO, PHA 140, Brydone to Sockett, 27 February 1835.
14 *Emigration: Letters* (1833), 5–7, Neal. Nathaniel Gould, *Sketch of the Trade of British America* (London 1833), 15, described the *John Bull* as 260 h.p., consuming 512 cubic feet of wood per hour. The 180-mile trip took nineteen hours, and the steamer had taken as many as 1,800 persons. He confirmed that the *John Bull* (when less heavily laden) could tow six vessels.
15 Brighton *Guardian*, 11 May 1836. Edward Longley, 28 September 1835, claimed the trip from Quebec to Montreal stretched out to a week because Brydone refused to pay the steamboat and insisted on the *Burrell* making its own way.
16 WSRO, PHA 138, Hale, report for 1833.
17 PRO, CO 384/36, 483–6, Sockett to Richmond, 14 April 1834; Jas Bowell to ? Sockett, Monday evening (copy); Sockett to Hay, 18 April 1834.
18 PRO, CO 384/39, Sockett to Hay, 2 April 1835; WSRO, PHA 140, Brydone to Aylmer, 9 June 1835 (copy). Sockett noted elsewhere that Egremont paid this tax himself rather than passing it on in increased fares.

19 *Montreal Gazette*, 22 June 1837.

20 Brydone, *Narrative*, 20–1, quoting Phillips. Later in the journey, Phillips mentions borrowing the sail from a Durham boat for a tent.

21 PRO, CO 384/28, 223–4v, Buchanan to Hay, 16 December 1831.

22 PRO, CO 42/411, 224, Colborne to Hay, 4 May 1832; also 203, Colborne, private, 9 April 1832.

23 PRO, CO 384/30, 391, Buchanan's printed notice "For the Information of Persons intending to settle in Upper Canada," 1 September 1832. Buchanan listed nine agents for Upper Canada, four at Lachine, Cornwall, Prescott, and Bytown (Ottawa) and five positioned to take charge of sales in the various districts. Buchanan's list omitted people whose connection with Robinson's office was through charitable societies and also agents appointed temporarily to help cope with the heavy immigration of 1832.

24 PRO, CO 384/32, ff. 86–7, RHH to Howick, 20 March 1833; CO 384/35, ff. 155–7v, Buchanan to Hay, 5 September 1834. The crisis in Lower Canada over control of the civil list lent urgency to Buchanan's attempts to have his salary paid from money not controlled by the Assembly.

25 AO, RG 1, A-1-4, vol. 2, Letter Book, Emigration, 1832–33, Robinson to Cheesman Moe, 10 May 1832 (Moe was reassigned to Cornwall), and Robinson to Hawke, 30 June and ? July 1832.

26 WSRO, Goodwood Ms 1460, f. 114, James Rapson, [August] 1832.

27 WSRO, Goodwood Ms 1460, f. 98, Sockett to Richmond, 15 October 1832.

28 WSRO, Goodwood Ms 1460, f. 114, Rapson. J.M. Trout and Edward Trout, *The Railways of Canada for 1870–1* (Toronto: Monetary Times 1871), 24–6, described bateaux as flat-bottomed, made of pine board and narrowed at bow and stern. The crew was typically four men and a pilot, and sails, oars, and poles were all used. They sometimes had a makeshift upper cabin. The Durham boat was also a flat-bottomed barge, but it had a ship keel and nearly twice the capacity. In the opinion of these authors, the balance of safety was with the bateaux, which could run on shore if they got into difficulties.

29 Firth, *Town of York*, 2:240, notes that the *Sir James Kempt*, a steamer of only 200 tons, did not usually sail as far up the lake as York and intended to meet the larger *Great Britain* (500 tons) at Kingston. She was "compelled" to continue to York, arriving 18 June 1832.

30 Bilson, *Darkened House*; C.M. Godfrey, *The Cholera Epidemics in Upper Canada 1832–1866* (Toronto and Montreal: Seccombe House 1968).

31 AO, Misc. Coll 1832, MU 2106, John Chantler to his uncle Joseph Chantler and his wife, Newmarket, 27 July 1832, and to his brother, n.d.; Esther Chantler (Dennis), memoir written for her children c. 1896, manuscript donated to the project by Berenice Smith; Wendy Cameron, Mary McDougall Maude, and Brenda Merriman, "History of the Petworth Emigration Scheme: Report for Families, 1995," and Brenda Dougall Merriman, "Some Descendants of Nathaniel Chantler," *Families* 34, no. 2 (1995): 85–9.

32 Berenice Smith, family papers, mss copy, Hester Mary Chantler to her children, c. 1896.

33 Cameron, McDougall Maude, and Merriman, "History of the Petworth Emigration Scheme: Report for Families, 1995," *Families* 34, no. 2 (1995): 85–9.

34 Firth, *Town of York*, lxiii–lxv, 254–7, and Baehre, "Pauper Emigration," 355, report the work of Bishop John Strachan's Society for the Relief of Orphan, Widow, and Fatherless. This society had Colborne's patronage and may have taken up the Chantler's case.

35 WSRO, Goodwood Ms 1463, f. 434, Sockett to Richmond, 12 February 1833.

36 AO, Ms 564, Canada Company, Commissioners: Letters and Reports, 2, 314–34, letters written between 25 October 1832 and 6 April 1833.

37 Robert Legget, *Ottawa River Canals and the Defence of British North America* (Toronto: University of Toronto Press 1988), and *Rideau Waterway* (2nd ed., Toronto: University of Toronto Press 1986); Robert Passfield, "Waterways," in Ball, ed., *Building Canada*; John P. Heisler, *The Canals of Canada* (Canadian Historic Sites, Occasional Papers in History and Archaeology, no. 8, Ottawa 1973).

38 Brydone, *Narrative*, 21.

39 WSRO, PHA 138, Hale, report for 1833; *No. 5 Continuation* (1833), 35, Rhoda Thair, 13 July 1833.

40 Brydone, *Narrative*, 21. Phillips described the typical wagon of the Canadas as having "one straight board, on each side, one at the head, and one behind, just like a great chest, without a lid."

41 WSRO, PHA 138, Hale, report for 1833.

42 *No. 5 Continuation*, printed as an addition.

43 WSRO, Goodwood Ms 1470, f. 105, extract from Hale's journal (copy); PHA 138, Hale, report on 1833 emigration, n.d.; PHA 140, "Table shewing the distances ... Rideau Canal ...," annotated by Hale.

44 WSRO, PHA 140 [Additional instructions, 1834]; Brydone, *Narrative*, 23–4.

45 Brydone, *Narrative*, 13.

46 NA, Upper Canada, State Book J, 345, Tolls on the Rideau Canal, authority for a proclamation of new rates, 10 November 1835. The rates indicate the hierarchy of travel between Ottawa and Kingston. First was the steamboat with a premium for cabin passengers like Brydone. Rates for towed vessels carrying deck passengers were as follows: barge, ten shillings; Durham boat, seven shillings; large bateaux, five shillings; small bateaux, three shillings. Rates for the return journey downriver were half these amounts in each class.

47 Firth, *Town of York*, 2:240.

48 Brydone, *Narrative*, 23.

49 WSRO, Goodwood Ms 1463, f. 488, C. Rowan to Richmond, 27 February 1833.

50 *Emigration: Letters* (1833), 13–15, Stedman.

51 *Emigration: Letters* (1833), 90–1; John C. Weaver, *Hamilton: An Illustrated History* (Toronto: James Lorimer and National Museums of Canada 1982).

52 AO, Fonds 129, Canada Company, series A-6-2, vol. 2, 278–9, 29 March 1832.

53 *Emigration: Letters* (1833), 68–9, information published by the commissioners of the Canada Company in 1831, detailing their arrangements for conveying emigrants "from the Head of Lake Ontario to the Huron Territory"; Karr, *Canada Land Company*, 73, 80, maps of roads and mills and services in the Huron Tract. The services included taverns maintained along the Huron and London roads.

54 WSRO, Goodwood Ms 1460, f. 113, Capelain (Capling), 28 August 1832 (Sockett dropped this passage from the letter when he printed it in *Emigration: Letters* (1833); Robina and Kathleen MacFarlane Lizars, *In the Days of the Canada Company ... 1825–1850* (Toronto 1896), 417–18. The Lizarses described the losses among Egremont's immigrants and wrote of graves lined with bark.

55 WSRO, Goodwood Ms 1460, f. 113, Capling (Capelain), 28 August 1832; in f. 112, Sockett to Richmond, 21 October 1832.

56 *Emigration: Letters* (1833), 13–15, Stedman.

57 AO, RG 1, A-1-4, vol. 2, Letter Book: Emigration, 1832–33, entries between 20 and 27 June 1832.

58 *Emigration: Letters* (1833), 46–7, Phillips.

59 *The Times*, 14 July 1832, reported that U.S. authorities were not allowing anyone over the border. British Library, Courtauld Family Letters, vol. 1 and vol. 6, 2039–47, James Knight to George Courtauld (II), 15 December 1832; WSRO, MP 1790, Sarah (Redman) Knight, memoir of her early life and diary, 1861–67.

60 AO, RG 1, A-1-4, vol. 1, Robinson to Rowan, 29 August 1833; NA, UC State book J, 585, Hawke, Memorial, 22 March 1837 (entry for 20 July 1837); DCB, IX, 377, Anthony Bewden Hawke. Hawke was sent to England in 1859–60, where he opened the first Canadian emigration agency overseas at Liverpool. He remained in charge of the emigration office until his retirement in 1864.

61 *No. 5 Continuation* (1833), 35, Barnes.

62 *No. 4 Continuation*, 27–8, James Rapson, 9 July 1833.

63 *No. 4 Continuation*, 28–9, Rhoda Thair, 13 July 1833. Hale reported that he sent this "Petworth party" to Dundas; Rhoda mentioned only Hamilton. Apart from the Thair and William Rapson families, the group included the families of John Dearling, George Trussler, and John White.

64 WSRO, PHA 138, Hale's report.

65 *Western Mercury* (Hamilton), 11 July 1833, copied from the York *Courier*.

66 *Courier of Upper Canada*, 17 July 1833.

67 Nielsen, *Egremont Road*; AO, RG 1, A-1-6, 13220-1, J. Boyce to Robinson, 19 October 1835. Lord Mountcashel's agent described a trip when he had had to make a detour around a swampy, central section of the road in dry weather. He expressed concerns that the state of the road would impede the development of the townships of Warwick and Plympton.

68 WSRO, Goodwood Ms 1469, f. 16, Hale to Petworth committee, 2 July 1833 (copy); Goodwood Ms 1470, f. 95, Hawke to Sockett, 16 September 1833 (copy).

69 WSRO, PHA, 138, Hale, Report, 1833.

70 WSRO, PHA 140, Hale, Account of Expenses.

71 PRO, CO 42/426, 318–23v, Hawke to Rowan, Emigration Report for the Year 1834, Hawke's account of the 1834 cholera epidemic.

72 Brydone, *Narrative*, 24–9, 43.

73 PRO, CO 42/426, ff. 324–5v, Hawke, Disbursements, 1 January to 30 June 1835.

74 WSRO, PHA 142, return of emigrants with remarks [Brydone, 1835] (copy).

75 Columbia University, Butler Library, X325 T63, vol. 1, 103, Hawke to John Hatch, 4 July 1837.

76 WSRO, Goodwood Ms 1461, f. 173, Sockett to Richmond, 15 November 1832.

CHAPTER 5

1 PRO, CO 384/35, 117–18.

2 Gates, *Land Policies*, 179–85, adds the positions of Upper Canadian politicians to this picture.

3 Fowke, "Myth of the Self-sufficient Canadian Pioneer," Jones, *History of Agriculture in Ontario*, McCalla, *Planting the Province*, and Crowley, "Rural Workers," in Craven, *Labouring Lives*, all discuss the resources of skill, knowledge, and money needed by pioneer farmers.

4 Bercuson et al., *Colonies: Canada to 1867* (Toronto: McGraw-Hill Ryerson 1992), 150, place the "ultimate cost" of loyalist resettlement in all the various British North American colonies in the millions of pounds. The children of these loyalists still claimed grants at the time the Petworth immigrants were arriving.

5 McLean, *People of Glengarry*, table 6 (83) and 210.

6 Elliott, *Irish Migrants in the Canadas*, 61–7, 82–115.

7 Andrew Haydon, *Pioneer Settlement in the District of Bathurst*, vol. 1 (Toronto 1925); Robert W. Passfield, *Building the Rideau Canal* (Don Mills, Ont.: Fitzhenry and Whiteside 1982), 70; Elliott, *Irish Migrants*, 120–2; WSRO, Goodwood Mss 1947, 1986, and 2021. Richmond's father, the fourth duke, toured the military settlement named for him as governor in 1818 and died there of rabies after being bitten by a pet fox.

8 Haydon, *Pioneer Settlement*, vol. 1; Elliott, *Irish Migrants*; Jean S. McGill, *A Pioneer History of the County of Lanark* (Toronto: privately printed 1968); Robert Lamond, *A Narrative of the Rise and Progress of Emigration from the counties of Lanark and Renfrew ...* (Glasgow 1821).

9 Wendy Cameron, "Robinson, Peter," DCB, VII, 752–7; and "Wilmot Horton's Experimental Emigrations."

10 Gates, *Land Policies*, 154–5, records Lieutenant-Governor Maitland's difficulties in attracting paupers to fifty-acre lots in selected locations in the 1820s using a reduction in fees as the only incentive.

11 Robert John Wilmot Horton, *Ireland and Canada* (London 1839); Edwin C Guillet, ed., *The Valley of the Trent*, Champlain Society, Ontario Series, no. 1 (Toronto 1957); Wendy Cameron, "Peter Robinson's Settlers in Peterborough," in Robert O'Driscoll and Lorna Reynolds, eds., *The Untold Story: The Irish in Canada* (Toronto: Celtic Arts of Canada 1988), 1:343–53.

12 PRO, CO 384/26, f. 118v. This volume contains Richards's correspondence and a draft and printed version of his report.

13 BPP 1831–32 (724), XXXII, 224, Report, no. 4, extract of a despatch from Sir J. Colborne, 24 November 1831.

14 BPP 1834 (616), XLIV, 307, Goderich to Colborne, 31 October 1831.

15 BPP 1834 (616), XLIV, 309, Colborne to Goderich, 7 April 1832; PRO, CO 42/411, 213–18, Colborne to Goderich, 4 May 1832.

16 Gates, *Land Policies*; Manning, "Colonial Policy," pt 1, 209; Cowan, *British Emigration*. McCalla, *Planting the Province*, tables 9.3 and 9.6, attempts to tabulate spending on emigration in the context of total spending by the governments of Upper Canada and Great Britain.

17 BPP 1834 (616), XLIV, 308, Goderich to Colborne, 1 February 1832.

18 Wendy Cameron, "Roswell Mount," DCB, VII, 521–3.

19 *Canadian Emigrant*, 19 January and 29 September 1832; Surveyor General's Office, "Information ... (for the use of emigrants)," 30 November 1832.

20 PRO, CO 42/411, 217, extract of instructions to John Patton at Prescott, 26 April 1832, with Colborne's despatch of 4 May 1832.

21 AO, RG 1, A-1-4, vol. 2, Robinson to Mount, 27 June 1832, with enclosure, Goderich to Colborne, 26 March 1832.

22 NA, RG 1, E 15 B, vol. 77, Mount's accounts.

23 PRO, CO 42/415, 118, Mount to Robinson (copy), 14 March 1833, gives his most complete account of the settlement. See also Radcliff, ed., *Authentic Letters*; James J. Talmon, "Early Immigration to Adelaide Township in Middlesex County," London and Middlesex Historical Society, *Transactions* 13 (1929): 481; Nielsen, *Egremont Road*. Katesville no longer exists; it was located about three miles west of Strathroy on the sixth concession, in the northeast corner of the present Township of Metcalfe.

24 AO, RG 1, A-1-6, 11096, Rowan to Robinson, 4 February 1834; PRO, CO 42/418, 97, Colborne to Stanley, 5 February 1834. Because deeds had already been issued, neither Adelaide nor Warwick townships could be renamed Egremont. The Grey County township later given Egremont's name had no connection with his emigrations.

25 AO, RG 1, A-1-4, vol. 2, Robinson to Mount, 7 August 1832.

26 AO, RG 1, A-1-6, 70500-3, Mount to Rowan, 24 November 1833. Mount estimated that using immigrant labour increased the cost of opening a road by two-thirds.

27 Cameron, "Petworth Emigrants in Adelaide," 27; Columbia University, Butler Library, x325/63, vol. 1, 121–5, Hawke to Joseph, 12 September 1837. Hawke estimated that by 1837 perhaps 350 of the roughly 800 pensioners sent to Upper Canada had died; many of the 300 still on their lots were kept there only by relief provided annually by the government. These men were not capable of bringing enough land into cultivation to support their families for a full year.

28 Cameron, "Petworth Emigrants in Adelaide," 26; Radcliff, ed., *Authentic Letters*, 88–9. Thomas Radcliff's log house in Adelaide was thirty feet by twenty-five feet, two storeys high, and cost him thirty pounds currency.

29 *Emigration: Letters* (1833), 43–4.

30 *Emigration: Letters* (1833), 46–7, William Phillips, 28 July 1832.

31 *Emigration: Letters* (1833), 43–4, Mary Holden, 21 November 1832; *No. 1 Continuation*, 5–6, William Cooper, 5 February 1833, and 7–8, Edward and Catharine Boxall, 9 February 1833. *Letters from Emigrants ... in 1832, 1833, and 1837*, 9; the writer of an anonymous letter from West Flamborough, 17 January 1839 explained that she obtained very good yeast from the brewery at Dundas, but people living up-country could not get yeast and had to use a salt rising.

32 Project files. Hasted's transactions are recorded in NA, RG 1, L3, Upper Canada Land Petitions, vol. 240, H21/58, and AO, RG-1, C-IV, Township Papers, Adelaide, w½ lot 19 con 4 SER (south of Egremont Road). Hasted probably did not get his money out of his sale, which was fraught with legal difficulties.

33 *No. 2 Continuation*, 9–10, Henry Smart, 1 March 1833.

34 Cameron, "Wilmot Horton's Experimental Emigrations," 41–2, and "Peter Robinson," DCB, VII, 752–6.

35 PRO, CO 42/414, 2, Colborne, 10 January 1833; CO 42/415, 94, Colborne, 3 September 1833. By the spring of 1833, the cost of Mount's settlement alone had risen to £7,558 provincial currency.

36 AO, RG 1, A1, 71116–23, McDonell to Robinson, 10 May 1833. This series contains much detailed correspondence on the subject of Mount and his settlement. Cameron, "Petworth Emigrants in Adelaide," 28–9.

37 NA, RG 1, E15 B, vol. 17, Roswell Mount, accounts for supplies. When neither the governor nor the Crown Lands Office gave them satisfaction, William Robertson and Brothers, the firm with the largest debt, pursued payment through the courts.

38 Cameron, "Wilmot Horton's Experimental Emigrations"; DCB, VI, 521–2, Roswell Mount; NA, Upper Canada, State Book J, 446–7, 30 June 1836. Hawke and the council were still struggling with Mount's unauthorized spending on roads in the spring of 1836.

39 PRO, CO 42/414, 3, Colborne, 10 January 1833; CO 42/415, 146, Mount to Robinson, 31 August 1833.

40 PRO, CO 42/414, 2, Colborne to Goderich, 10 January 1833; CO 42/414, 144, Colborne to Stanley, 14 September 1833, and 146, Mount to Robinson, 31 August 1833; CO 42/415, 94, Colborne to Stanley, 3 September 1833, and 118, Mount to Robinson, 14 March 1833. Extracts from this correspondence were printed in the British sessional papers.

41 PRO, CO 42/411, 151, Colborne, 29 March 1832.

42 Columbia University, Butler Library, x325/T 63, vol. 8, Robinson in account current ... This account included a few items carried forward from 1831, and there may have been

further payments for the Adelaide settlement after this date. In the spring of 1833, Colborne used figures of £7,558 provincial currency for Mount's settlement and a total figure of £13,286 for the relief and settlement of immigrants in 1832.

43 NA, RG 5, A-1, 70341, Hawke to Rowan, ? March 1833.

44 Columbia University, Butler Library, X325/T63, vol. 1, 47–56, Remarks on the present system of disposing of crown lands. Hawke pointed out that the government had already relinquished claims amounting to upwards of £25,000 for advances to settlers in the Bathurst District.

45 DCB, VII, 335–9, John Galt.

46 AO, RG 1, A-1-6, 10027, Rowan to Robinson, 16 March 1833.

47 Lampton County Library (Sarnia), Henry John Jones diary, transcript, 9 May 1833. Jones reported that Mount's spending had made it impossible for the legislature to provide funds for pauper emigration in 1833. He did not give Colborne as his source, but he had just met with him.

48 WSRO, Goodwood Ms 1470, f. 95, Hawke to Sockett, 16 September 1833 (copy).

49 Lambton County Library, Jones diary, original, 20 May 1833? to 14 July 1833, and typescript, entries for 11, 14, and 18 July 1833; AO, RG 1, A-1-6, 10408, 10512, Jones, 16 July 1833; DCB, VIII, 436–9. Henry John Jones was the son of Henry Jones, who since 1829 had been trying to establish an Owenite community of settlers from Scotland at Maxwell in the Township of Sarnia.

50 AO, RG 1, A-1-6, 10512, 10531, 10814, Jones, 6 and 10 August, 6 November 1833.

51 The Montreal Gazette of 24 September 1833 copied material from the Sandwich Canadian Emigrant, the Prescott Gazette, the Toronto Courier, and the Montreal Daily Advertiser. The news probably reached Sussex in the Montreal Weekly Abstract.

52 Canadian Emigrant, Sandwich, 17 August 1833; Montreal Gazette, 12 and 24 September 1833. Material published in the Gazette on 24 September came from the Canadian Emigrant, the Prescott Gazette, the Courier, and the Montreal Daily Advertiser, and concluded with an original addition. The Gazette of 2 January 1833 copied Sockett's response in No. 5 Continuation from the Courier.

53 Canadian Emigrant, 5 and 26 October 1833.

54 AO, RG 1, A-1-6, 70500, Mount to Rowan, 24 November 1833; Columbia University, Butler Library, X325/T63, vol. 2, Hawke to Murdock, 4 November 1840. Hawke did not specify if he meant currency or sterling.

55 PRO, CO 323/170, 297, Colborne to Hay, 13 September 1833, private, with estimates prepared at the Emigrant Office, York, 13 August 1833, 305, of the outlay and proceeds, and, 306, of the cost of providing teams and implements and of contingent expenses.

56 Columbia University, Butler Library, X325/T63, vol. 1, 78–9, Hawke to Sullivan, 21 February 1837.

57 AO, RG 1, A-1-4, Robinson to Rowan, 19 June 1834.

58 PRO, CO 42/414, 293, Colborne to Hawke, 20 April 1833, private.

59 BPP 1841 (298), XV, 429–35, Sydenham to Russell, 14 January 1841, and enclosures, no. 1, Arthur to Sydenham, 26 December 1840, and no. 4, Hawke to Harrison, 17 December 1840.

60 AO, RG 1, Series CB-1, survey diary, Blandford, Peter Carroll, 24 June–12 July. Columbia University, Butler Library, X325/T63, vol. 1, 67, recording two small payments in 1836; vol. 8, account book, 1831 to 1841: most references in this connection are to 1834, but Hawke recorded a payment to Brydone in 1837; vol. 9, ledger, advances on account of emigration for 1835.

61 *Courier of Upper Canada*, 23 October 1833, from the *Hamilton Mercury*.

62 Columbia University, Butler Library, x325/T63, vol. 9, ledger, 1 January 1835. Hatch's account with Hawke was for both shanties and log houses but did not specify use.

63 Brydone, *Narrative*, 24–6; PRO, CO 384/39, 316–16v, Henry Heasman, 19 October 1834.

64 Errington, *Wives and Mothers*, 107–30; WSRO, Goodwood Ms. The anonymous author of this work on Upper Canada blamed English settlers for sending their children into service so young that they never formed any attachment to the land and never settled down as farmers.

65 *Brighton Gazette*, 23 April 1835, John Gamblen, 18 February 1835. Errington, *Wives and Mothers*, 127–9, discusses married women and domestic work but not their families' views of the various possible arrangements.

66 PRO, CO 384/39, 317–18v, William Voice, 27 October 1834, printed by J. Phillips, Petworth; *Continuation of Letters from Sussex Emigrants* (1837), 9–11, Cornelius Voice, 20 September 1835; Crowley, "Rural Labour," in Craven, ed., *Labouring Lives*, 32–6.

67 Project files; "A History of Brighton: Being the Story of a Woodstock Settlement from the Early Thirties," Oxford Museum *Bulletin*, no. 7, reprinted from the *Woodstock Daily Express*, 1900–1901. Printed by Phillips on a single sheet: James and Ann Woods, 20 August 1836; James and Sarah Lannaway, 24 September 1840.

68 AO, RG 1-100, Map Collection, C-69, Plan of the Town of Woodstock.

69 PRO, CO 42/426, 324–4v, Hawke to Rowan, 3 September 1835.

70 NA, RG 1, E15 B, vol. 88, nos. 46 and 47, Brydone, Expenses ... Toronto to Brantford, 1835; Burwell in account with Hawke, 24 June and 31 December 1835, for items of account for the erection of emigrant shanties and supplies for the emigrants. The cost of these shanties averaged out a bit below the £3 10s. he was allowed for a single shanty at Brantford in 1836.

71 *Continuation of Letters from Sussex Emigrants ... Written in 1836* [1837], 22–4.

72 Butler Library, x325 T63, Hawke papers, vol. 1, 103, Hawke to Hatch, 4 July 1837.

73 AO, RG 1, A-1-6, John Willson et al., 15 August 1835. They wrote from St Catharines.

74 *Continuation of Letters from Sussex Emigrants ... Written in 1836* [1837], 22–4; Merriman, *Emigrant Ancestors*, 1–16.

75 BPP 1841 (298), XV, 435, no. 1, Hawke, Memorandum, 9 July 1839.

76 Cameron, Haines, and McDougall Maude, *English Immigrant Voices*.

77 Brydone, *Narrative*, 32–3.

78 Crowley, "Rural Labour," in Craven, ed., *Labouring Lives*, 28–9. David Gagen, *Hopeful Travellers: Families, Land, and Social Change in Mid-Victorian Peel County, Canada West*, Ontario Historical Studies Series (Toronto: University of Toronto Press 1981), presents the different opportunities of a rural community after the land was cleared and occupied.

79 Gates, *Land Policies*, 132–41. These regulations were in force until 1835.

80 Gates, *Land Policies*, 132–3; WSRO, PHA 138, Hale's report. We have been unable to identify these families with any certainty.

81 *Continuation of Letters from Sussex Emigrants ... Written in 1836* [1837], cover sheets, W. Robinson, 14 October 1836.

82 *Continuation of Letters from Sussex Emigrants ... Written in 1836* [1837], 17–18, George and Mary Hills, 18 September 1836.

83 *Emigration: Letters* (1833), 22, Upton.

84 *Continuation of Letters from Sussex Emigrants* (1837), 1–5, 1 January 1837.

85 WSRO, PHA 1052, Brydone to Wyndham, 21 May 1839, "Canada."

86 [Canada Company], *A Statement of the Satisfactory Results which have attended Emigration* …, 3rd ed. (London 1842), 63, Dr Ayling to the commissioners, 16 December 1840.

87 Barclay, ed., *Letters from the Dorking Emigrants*, 15–22, Charlotte Willard, 26 August 1832.

88 *Continuation of Letters from Sussex Emigrants … Written in 1836* [1837], 3–7, Lydia Hilton, 10 September 1836.

89 *Continuation of Letters fom Sussex Emigrants … Written in 1836* [1837], 9–10, David (Cloudesley) Sharp, 21 August 1836.

90 *Continuation of Letters from Sussex Emigrants* (1837), 6–8, William Courtnage, 10 January 1837.

CHAPTER 6

1 WSRO, PHA 1068.

2 WSRO, PHA 730.

3 Poor Law Amendment Act, 4 & 5 William IV, c. 76, clauses 62 and 63. The act received royal assent 14 August 1834.

4 WSRO, Goodwood Ms 1504, f. 86, 12 January 1834.

5 PRO, CO 385/6, 12–13, Elliot to Sockett, 26 March 1832.

6 *Emigration: A Letter to a Member of Parliament*, 11.

7 WSRO, PHA 140, Project for the Earl of E," 1 November 1834.

8 "Robert Pilkington," DCB, VI, 582–3; AO, MU 2319 and 2320, Pilkington Estate Papers.

9 WSRO, PHA 140, "Project …," 1 November 1834.

10 Barbara (Brydone) Calder, private family papers, "Narrative Journal by Naval Surgeon James Marr Brydone, 1779–1866."

11 "John Galt," DCB, VII, 335–40. Roger Hall and Nick Whistler list several studies of Galt and the Canada Company and include a bibliography of Galt's extensive writings on North America and colonial matters.

12 Brydone, *Narrative*, map and 30–1; Gilbert A. Stetler, "David Gilkison," DCB, VIII, 327–8. David's father, William, a cousin and associate of John Galt's, returned to Canada from Scotland in 1832 and bought the land in Nichol. On his death, the land was divided between six surviving sons. David acted as resident manager until 1837 when he appointed his father-in-law as agent and moved away.

13 Fergusson, *Practical Notes Made during a Tour … in 1831* and *Agricultural State*. WSRO, PHA 137, has Sockett's notes taken from Fergusson.

14 William Dunlop, *Tiger Dunlop's Upper Canada*, New Canadian Library no. 55 (Toronto: McClelland and Stewart, 1967), reprint. Sockett included Dunlop's *Statistical Sketches* by "a backwoodsman" in his bibliography (*Statistical Sketches* first published 1832).

15 Wilson, *New Lease*, 54, describes Lord Mount Cashell's purchases in this area as stereotypical speculation. Nielsen, *Egremont Road*, 39, remarks that "the extent of [John] Elmsley's settlement efforts is difficult to ascertain," but she found little evidence that he put much into the nearly 20,000 acres he acquired in Warwick and Plympton townships.

16 Brydone, *Narrative*, 39.

17 Brydone, *Narrative*, 31–40, 9–17 July 1834; Andrew Picken, *The Canadas* (London 1832).

18 WSRO, Goodwood Ms 1570, f. 137, Sockett to Richmond, 3 February 1835, and Ms 1493, f. 20, Richmond to Sockett, 6 [7] February 1835.

19 WSRO, Goodwood Ms 1493, f. 20, Richmond to Sockett, 6 [7] February 1835.

20 WSRO, PHA 140, Sockett to Thomas Mercer Jones, 16 February 1835, and Jones to Sockett, Liverpool, 10 March 1835.

21 PRO, MH 12/13127, Sutton Union, 27 March 1835, Hasler to Pilkington.

22 PRO, MH 12/13060, Sockett, 2 April 1835. He wrote that the letter was from Tuxford.

23 WSRO, PHA 140, R.W. Hay to Sockett, 21 February 1835.

24 WSRO, Goodwood Ms 1487, p. 74, Richmond to Holland, 23 August 1834, and Ms 1491, p. 465, Richmond to Melbourne, 12 November 1834; Fletcher, "Early Years of the Westhamptnett Union," 82.

25 PRO, MH 12/1398, Westhamptnett Union, Pilkington to the Poor Law Commission, 4 December 1834 and 21 February 1835; Fletcher, "Early Years of the Westhamptnett Union," 20.

26 WSRO, Goodwood Ms 1580, f. 612, Prime to Richmond, 13 December 1834, and Ms 1573, f. 478, Prime to Richmond, 16 May 1835.

27 PRO, MH 12/13060, Sockett to Lefevre, 20 March 1835.

28 PRO, MH 12/13060, Chadwick to Sockett, 4 April 1835.

29 WSRO, PHA 140, Authority for Brydone.

30 Barbara (Brydone) Calder Papers, Brydone, Diary, 30 June to 9 September 1835. This tract is outlined on the map accompanying Brydone's *Narrative*.

31 Barbara (Brydone) Calder Papers, Brydone, Diary, 1 September 1835.

32 PRO, CO 42/427, 265–9v, Brydone to Rowan, 12 September 1835; WSRO, PHA 140, Sockett to the Colonial Secretary [Glenelg], 2 December 1835.

33 WSRO, PHA 1068, Map of the Eastern Townships of Lower Canada: a printed map with a note by Sockett identifying the red ink as marking Brydone's route in October 1835.

34 WSRO, PHA 1068, Brydone to Nathanial Gould, deputy governor of the British American Land Company, 1 February 1836 (copy).

35 WSRO, PHA 1068, Brydone to Sockett, 12 October 1838; Map of the Eastern Townships showing Brydone's route in red. Henry P. Bruyers, secretary to the company, tried in vain to encourage Brydone to reconsider and to visit at a more "genial" time of year (Bruyers to Brydone, 19 February 1836).

36 Philip Buckner, "Acheson, Archibald, 2nd Earl of Gosford," *DCB*, VII, 5–9.

37 Mackenzie presented his "Seventh Report … on Grievances" with its indictment of the Crown Lands Department in 1835, Upper Canada, House of Assembly, *Journals*, 1835, app. 21.

38 Cowan, *Land Policies*; Hodgetts, *Pioneer Public Service*.

39 PRO, CO 384/39, ff. 392–3v, Memorandum, 11 December [1835], on Colborne's despatch no. 59, 3 October 1835, and Sockett's letter, 2 December 1835.

40 PRO, CO 384/39, ff. 391–1v, draft for "Sir G. Grey's consideration," 12 December [1835]; WSRO, PHA 140, [Under-secretary] Grey to Sockett, 18 (?) December 1835.

41 BPP 1837 (131), XVII, pt 1, First Report of the Committee on the Poor Law Amendment Act, W.H.T. Hawley, 14 March 1837.

42 Columbia University, Butler Library, x325/T63, vol. 1, 30–1, Hawke to Joseph, 30 March 1836.

43 McCalla, *Planting the Province*, 191. Leo A. Johnston, *History of Guelph, 1827–1927* (Guelph: Guelph Historical Society 1977), 48, states that in this area the harvest of 1836 was almost entirely ruined by continuous rain.

44 Columbia University, Butler Library, x325/T63, vol. 1, 40–1, Hawke to Joseph, 23 May 1836.

45 Brydone, *Narrative*, 36.

46 WSRO, PHA 3491, has two maps of the area prepared in 1835 which are based on Chewett's map of Upper Canada. A third from 20 October 1836 is of the new Township of Ashfield. Winearls, *Mapping Upper Canada*, A 124, Ashfield, gives the date of instructions for the sur-

vey as 10 February 1836 and of the map as 21 July 1836. The surveyor was William Hawkins, who accompanied Brydone in 1835.

47 PRO, MH 12/38, Petworth Board of Guardians, 24 December 1835; PRO, MH 32/38, Hawley to Nicholls, 22 July 1836; Mary MacKinnon, "English Poor Law Policy and the Crusade against Outrelief," *Journal of Economic History*, XLVII, 3 (1987): 603–25. Writing of the late 1860s and early 1870s, MacKinnon states that the perceived poor quality of workhouse facilities in the early years of the new poor law made it politically impossible to enforce the rule against outdoor relief to the "deserving" poor before this time.

48 PRO, MH 12/38, Hawley, 16 June 1836, 497v, quoting Sockett.

49 *The Times*: the Petworth evidence was printed in issues of 25 and 27–30 March 1837. On 18 April 1837, *The Times* reported that the chair of the committee had forbidden daily printing of the evidence and the paper had to wait until it was reported to the House.

50 Brundage, *Making of the New Poor Law*, 163; Finer, *Life and Times*, 129–39; WSRO, Goodwood Ms 1585, f. 64, Chadwick to Richmond, 10 July 1834 and f. 72, Chadwick to Richmond, 4 September 1837. Chadwick described the committee's report as a "severe blow" that had weakened the resolve of the "firm guardians" in several unions.

51 *Hampshire Telegraph*, 10 April 1837.

52 PRO, MH 12/39, Hawley, 23 September 1837, a long report defending the law as implemented and arguing the case for strict adherence to the rules. He alludes twice to the opposition of the clergy (41 and 43) and to the "prejudices and unwarrantable interference" of a few of them. WSRO, Goodwood Ms 1589, f. 1229, Robert Raper (clerk of the Westhamptnett Union to Richmond): "I do not know a clergyman whom I could trust. They are all in their Hearts against us."

53 Spater, *William Cobbett*, vol. 2, 525; Fletcher, "Early Years" and "Chichester and the Westhamptnett Poor Law Union"; *The Times*, 14 July 1837; Thomas Rogers to the editor on the Westhamptnett Union workhouse; *Brighton Patriot*, 23 July 1837, Thomas Rogers to the editor of *The Times*. The *Brighton Guardian* continued to make jibes at Richmond's expense on the subject of the poor laws: 12 June 1839, 22 April 1840, 1 July 1840.

54 *Hansard*, 3d ser., 76 (1844): 1759; see also *Hansard*, 3d ser., 24 (1834): 273–4; 1071–2; 25 (1835): 273–4.

55 McCalla, *Planting the Province*, 187–93.

56 Columbia University, Butler Library, x325/T63, vol. 1, 97–8, Hawke to John Joseph, 7 June 1837.

57 Wise, ed., *Sir Francis Bond Head*, 89.

58 BPP 1837 (132) XLII, 19; PRO, CO 385/45, 158, Head to the poor law commissioners, 4 March 1837.

59 PRO, MH 32/39, Hawley to the Poor Law Commission, 1 May 1837; Columbia University, Butler Library, x325/T63, vol. 1, 110, Hawke, 24 July 1837.

60 WSRO, PHA 140, Brydone to Joseph, 14 September 1837.

61 Read and Stagg, *Rebellion of 1837 in Upper Canada*; Read, *Rising in Western Upper Canada*. Colin Read was kind enough to consult his files for two rebels we thought might be Petworth immigrants known to be in Brantford; neither of them fit the description of people with the same or similar names. Greer, "1837–38: Rebellion Reconsidered," *Canadian Historical Review* 76 (March 1995): 1–18, discusses the historiography of the rebellions.

62 Columbia University, Butler Library, x325/T63, vol. 1, 172–4, Hawke to S.B. Harrison, 2 September 1839.

63 *Letters from Emigrants … in 1832, 1833 and 1837*, 5–7, Richard and Frances Pullen, 31 December 1838.

64 WSRO, PHA 1068, Wyndham to Melbourne, 22 June 1838.

65 *Letters from Emigrants … in 1832, 1833, and 1837*, Charles Rapley, 14 October 1838; Richard and Francis Pullen, 31 December 1838, and *Brighton Herald*, 25 August 1838, James Cooper to his family, [2]6 May 1838.

66 Wilson family papers, [Maria Wilson], 22 August 1839.

67 *Brighton Guardian*, 1 January 1840, William Phillips, 14 July 1839. Phillips wrote to encourage people to come out with Thomas Rolph the following spring.

68 WSRO, Parham House Papers. An incomplete letter written 14 November 1837 gossiped that Egremont had pushed himself into his final illness by upsetting and exhausting himself firing servants he believed ungrateful cheats and hiring others.

69 WSRO, PHA 728, Klanert to Sockett, 11 November 1837, a brief note that "All is over."

70 H.A. Wyndham, *Family History*, vol. 2, 347, cited Greville's opinion that Henry would have been elected for the Western Division of Sussex had Egremont "lifted his finger." Henry's failure may have indicated Egremont's weakening hold on those beholden to him rather than his intention. WSRO, PHA 694–7, the hunting dispute; Egremont, *Wyndham and Children First*, 39, 43–52.

71 Spring, *English Landed Estate*, 28–31, discusses a similar exercise undertaken by the seventh Duke of Bedford on inheriting Woburn in 1839.

72 WSRO, PHA 728, for funeral arrangements, and PHA 729–35, containing the bulk of the correspondence between Sockett and Leconfield on these topics.

73 WSRO, PHA 733, Sockett to Wyndham, 19 March 1838. At the time this letter was written, Brydone had been busy for three weeks sorting "an immense mass of letters and papers" dating from the Commonwealth and the reign of Charles II that Sockett had found stored in a neglected chest.

74 PRO, MH 32/39, Hawley to Nicholls, 18 January 1838; Hawley, Quarterly Reports, 31 March and 30 June 1838.

75 WSRO, PHA 1068, Wyndham to Melbourne, 22 June 1838 (copy).

76 WSRO, PHA 1068, Sockett to Colonial Office, 5 November 1838 (tissue copy); WSRO, PHA 1068, Elliot to Sockett, private, 29 November 1838.

77 WSRO, PHA 729, Wyndham to Sockett, 7 January 183[8].

78 WSRO, PHA 734, Sockett to Wyndham, 21 February 1838.

79 WSRO, PHA 3492, Map of the District of Adelaide, South Australia (1839), and PHA 3493, Special Survey of the Hutt River (1842), showing Wyndham's two sections in Adelaide and ten sections on the Hutt River, a total of 960 acres.

80 WSRO, PHA 7917, South Australia. Sockett's instructions to Mitchell were dated 12 May 1838. Haines, *Emigration and the Labouring Poor*, 93–5.

81 William Forbes Adams, *Ireland and the Irish Emigration to the New World from 1815 to the Famine* (New Haven 1932), 165–7, 215–17; Cowan, *British Emigration*, 215.

82 WSRO, PHA 1052–4 and 1062–6, contain more extensive information on preparations for the *Waterloo* than is available for any of the ships sent through Portsmouth.

83 "Charles Rubidge," DCB x, 635–6.

84 WSRO, PHA 1052, Brydone [to Wyndham], n.d. (just before the *Waterloo* sailed).

85 WSRO, PHA 1061, has a clipping from one of the newspapers and correspondence.

86 WSRO, PHA 736, Memorandum of the expenses of the *Waterloo*. If the full 230 passages had been taken up, the cost per passage would have dropped by £4 to £8 6s.

87 WSRO, PHA 1069, Account of emigrants to Canada and Australia from Ireland, 1839–47; PHA 142, notes in Lord Leconfield's hand; Cowan, *British Emigration*, 215–16; Adams, *Ireland and the Irish Emigration*. Donald Harman Akenson, *The Irish Diaspora* (Toronto and Belfast 1993), brings together much recent work on Irish emigration to North America and the Australasian colonies.

88 WSRO, PHA 736, p. 49, Wyndham to Crowe, 11 December 1839.

89 WSRO, PHA 736, p. 132, Wyndham to Crowe, 5 April 1841.

90 WSRD, PHA 729, Brydone to Sockett, 9 September 1838.

91 Thomas Rolph, *DCB*, 8:764–5; J.K. Johnson, "Land Policy and the Upper Canadian Elite Reconsidered: The Canada Emigration Association, 1840–41," in David Keane and Colin Read, eds., *Old Ontario: Essays in Honour of J.M.S. Careless* (Toronto: Dundurn 1990), 217–33. In 1840 the provincial government appointed Rolph as emigration agent for Upper Canada.

92 Thomas Rolph, *Emigration and Colonization* (London 1844), 16; WSRO, PHA 1060, contains correspondence with Rolph, Colborne, Head, and Parry. PHA 731, Rolph to Sockett, 12 January 1841.

93 WSRO, PHA 1068, Brydone to Wyndham, 12 July 1839. Hawke seems to have been acting for principals who were selling privately. Wilson, *New Lease on Life*, 60, reports that Mount Cashell's chief agent was married to Hawke's daughter.

94 WSRO, PHA 1068, Sockett to Wyndham, 13 July 1839, and PHA 729, Tylee to Brydone, 10 July 1839; AO, MU 2319, Pilkington Estate Papers, Tylee Letterbook, nos. 1 and 3.

95 *Historical Atlas of the County of Wellington* (Toronto 1906); project files. His younger son, Henry, served for a time as his curate at Duncton before obtaining his own parish as rector of Sutton and Bignor.

96 WSRO, PHA 1071, Wyndham to Brydone, 29 November 1840.

97 Eric Richards, ed., *The Flinders History of South Australia*, vol. 1: *Social History* (Adelaide, South Australia: Wakefield Press 1986), 105–7; WSRO, PHA 7917, Emigration, Australia.

98 WSRO, PHA 1061, Thomson to Russell, 27 June 1840.

99 WSRO, PHA 731, Brydone to Sockett, 2 August 1840.

100 Cowan, *British Emigration*, 205.

101 WSRO, PHA 1061, Brydone to Smith, 29 July 1840 (copy), and Smith to Wyndham, 12 August 1840.

102 WSRO, PHA 1058; PRO, MH 12, 13062, William Parker to the Poor Law Commissioners, 3 February 1845, mentions three letters from Petworth emigrants of 1844 that we have not discovered.

103 PRO, MH 12/13063, March 1850, Vestry resolution. The ship was the *Laurel*. Sockett died at the age of eighty-one in 1859, "old age and increasing infirmities [having] for some years rendered him very feeble."

CHAPTER 7

1 BPP 1847 (737), VI.

2 Hodgetts, *Pioneer Public Service*, 16, 242.

APPENDIX A

1 This correspondence is mainly, although not entirely, in WSRO, PHA 729–36.

2 WSRO, PHA 729, Wyndham to Sockett, 12 November 1839.

3 WSRO, PHA 731, Sockett to Wyndham, 24 March 1840.

4 WSRO, PHA 732, Sockett to Wyndham, 18 June 1838; Sockett to Wyndham, 29 January 1838.

5 WSRO, PHA 693, Sockett to Wyndham, 26 March 1838.

6 WSRO, PHA 693, Sockett to Wyndham, 26 March 1838.

7 WSRO, PHA 734, Sockett to Wyndham, 8 January 1838.

8 WSRO, PHA 730, Wyndham to Sockett, 10 November 1840.

9 WSRO, PHA 728, Sockett to Mrs Wyndham, 16 March 1838.

10 WSRO, PHA 732, Sockett to Wyndham, 29 January 1838.

BIBLIOGRAPHY

ARCHIVAL SOURCES

Archives of Ontario
Toronto

RG I Ministry of Natural Resources, Office of the Surveyor General and Crown Lands
  Department, Upper Canada
  A-I-4 Commissioners' Letterbooks
  A-I-6 Letters Received, Surveyor General and Commissioner
  CB-I Survey Diaries and Field Notes
  C-I-I Crown Lands Department, Petitions and Applications
  C-IV Township Papers
RG 21 Municipal Records
  F 1679 Gore District Census and Assessment
RG 22 Court Records
  County Surrogate Courts
RG 40 Records of the Heir and Devisee Commission
RG 80 Records of the Office of the Registrar General
  80-27-1 District Marriage Registers
  80-27-2 County Marriage Registers
F 129 Canada Company Papers
  A-2 Court of Directors Records
    Minutes
  A-6 Correspondence
  A-6-2 Correspondence with the Commissioners
  C-6 Letters of Credit
F 170 Pilkington Estate Papers
  MU 2319, Letterbooks
F 675 Mary Leslie Papers
  MU 1717, George Sockett Family Business Papers
F 775 Miscellaneous Collections
  MU 2106, 17, Chantler letters, 1832
F 977 Cemetry Transcriptions (Ms 451)

British Library
London

Courtauld Family Letters

Columbia University, Butler Library, Manuscripts and Rare Books
New York City

X325T63 Toronto: Emigration Office Records [Hawke's papers]

Durham University Library, Archives and Special Collections

Grey Papers, papers of the third Earl Grey

East Sussex Record Office
Lewes

Sheffield Park Papers

National Archives of Canada
Ottawa

RG 1 Executive Council
    E 1, Minute Books (State Matters), Upper Canada, Executive Council,
      State Book J, 1831–1838
    E 15B, Upper Canada, Public Accounts, 1792–1841
    L 3, Upper Canada, Land Petitions
RG 5 A Upper Canada: Civil Secretary
    A 1, Upper Canada Sundries
RG 7 Canada: Governor General's Office
    G 16C, Civil Secretary's Letterbooks

Public Records Office
London

Colonial Office
    CO 42 Original Correspondence, Canada
    CO 323 Colonies General, Correspondence, private letters to R.W. Hay
    CO 384 Emigration, Correspondence
    CO 385 Emigration, Entry Books of Correspondence
    CO 386 Colonial Land and Emigration Commission
Home Office
    HO 41 Disturbances: Entry Book
    HO 52 Home Office, Municipal and Provincial, Counties, Correspondence
    HO 73 Poor Law Commissioners: Letters and Papers
Ministry of Health
    MH 12 Poor Law Union Papers
    MH 32 Assistant Poor Law Commissioners and Inspectors, Correspondence
    MH 33 Register of Correspondence
War Office
    WO 97 Regimental Lists: Attestation and Discharge Records
    WO 120 Regimental Registers

Parish Records and Related Material

The *International Genealogical Index* (IGI) is an invaluable starting point for research in English parish records, but individual record offices have to be consulted for a full list of parishes that have deposited their records. The parish records used most frequently included baptismal and marriage records, vestry minutes, and overseers' records. After 1813, baptismal records included the occupation of the father. After 1834, parish matters appear in correspondence between local poor law unions and the Poor Law Commission in London. The West Sussex Record Office holds the Bishop's Transcripts for East and West Sussex, copies of parish register entries that were forwarded annually to the bishop's registry at Chichester. Records in the following repositories were consulted:

> Cambridge County Record Office, Cambridge
> East Sussex Record Office, Lewes
> Isle of Wight Record Office, Newport
> Surrey Record Office, Guildford Muniment Room, Guildford
> West Sussex Record Office, Chichester
> Wiltshire Record Office, Trowbridge

West Sussex Record Office
Chichester

Petworth House Archives

> The archives at Petworth House are partially catalogued under the title *The Petworth House Archives: A Catalogue*, vol. 1, ed. Francis W. Steer and Noel H. Osborne; and vol. 2 and 3, ed. Alison McCann (West Sussex County Council 1968, 1979, and 1997). Alison McCann has a fourth volume in preparation and estimates that there is material for five more at least.

Goodwood Estate Archives

> *Catalogue of the Goodwood Estate Archives*, vols. 1 and 2, ed. Francis W. Steer and J.E. Amanda Venables, and vol. 3, ed. Timothy J. McCann. Vol. 3, 103–13, is an alphabetical list of correspondents who wrote ten or more letters to the fifth Duke of Richmond. Timothy McCann's card index of all correspondents with the fifth duke is available in the West Sussex Record Office.

Burrell Mss

MF 678, Petworth Independent or Congregational Chapel

MP 320, Emigrations to Canada

MP 1790, Sarah (Redman) Knight, Diary

West Sussex Quarter Session Rolls

Newspapers

ENGLAND

Brighton Gazette and Lewes Observer
Brighton Guardian
Brighton Herald or Sussex, Surrey, Hampshire and Kent Advertiser
Brighton Patriot and Lewes Free Press (1836: *Brighton Patriot and South of England Free Press*)
Cinque Ports Chronicle and East Sussex Observer
Hampshire Telegraph and Sussex Chronicle and General Advertiser
Hastings and Cinque Ports Iris or Sussex and Kent Advertiser
Political Register

Portsmouth, Portsea and Gosport Herald and Chichester Reporter
Standard, London
Sussex Advertiser or Lewes and Brighthelmston Journal
Sussex Agricultural Express, County and General Advertiser
The Times, London

CANADA
British American Journal, St Catharines
Canadian Emigrant and Western District Advertiser, Sandwich (Windsor)
Colonial Advocate, York (Toronto)
Courier of Upper Canada, York (Toronto)
Kingston Chronicle and Gazette
Montreal Gazette
Montreal Settler and British, Irish and Canadian Gazette
Niagara Gleaner, Niagara-on-the-Lake
Quebec Mercury
Patriot and Farmer's Monitor, Kingston
Western Mercury, Hamilton

PRINTED SOURCES

Ankli, Robert E., and Kenneth J. Duncan. "Farm Making Costs in Early Ontario." *Canadian Papers in Rural History* (D.H. Akenson, editor) 4 (1984): 33–49.
Apfel, William, and Peter Dunkley. "English Rural Society and the New Poor Law: Bedfordshire, 1834–47." *Social History* 10, no. 1 (January 1985): 37–68.
Armstrong, Alan. *Farmworkers: A Social and Economic History 1770–1980*. London: Batsford 1988.
Baehre, Rainer. "Pauper Emigration to Upper Canada in the 1830s." *Histoire sociale – Social History* 14 (November 1981): 339–68.
– "Paupers and Poor Relief in Upper Canada." Canadian Historical Association, *Historical Papers* (1981): 57–80.
Baines, Dudley. *Emigration from Europe 1815–1930*. New Studies in Economic and Social History. Cambridge: Cambridge University Press 1995.
– "European Emigration 1815–1939: Looking at the Emigration Decision Again." *Economic History Review* 47, no. 3(1994): 524–44.
Barclay, Charles, ed. See *Letters from the Dorking Emigrants*.
Baugh, D.A. "The Cost of Poor Relief in South-East England, 1790–1834." *Economic History Review* 28, no. 1 (1975): 50–68.
Bilson, Geoffrey. *A Darkened House: Cholera in Nineteenth-Century Canada*. Toronto: University of Toronto Press 1980.
Blaug, Mark. "The Myth of the Old Poor Law and the Making of the New." *Journal of Economic History* 23, no. 2 (1963): 151–81.
– "The Poor Law Report Re-examined." *Journal of Economic History* 24 (1964): 229–45.
Bouchette, Joseph. *The British Dominions in North America*. London 1831.
Boyer, George R. *An Economic History of the English Poor Law 1750–1850*. Cambridge: Cambridge University Press 1990.
Brandon, Peter, and Brian Short. *A Regional History of England: the South East from AD 1000*. London and New York: Longman 1990.

British Parliamentary Papers [BPP] 1824 (392), VI, Select Committee on Labourers' Wages.

BPP 1826 (404), IV, Select Committee on Emigration from the United Kingdom appointed to inquire into the Expediency of Encouraging Emigration.

BPP 1827 (550), V, Third Report from the Select Committee on Emigration.

BPP 1830–31 (178), I, Bill to facilitate Voluntary Emigration to H.M. Possessions Abroad; [as amended by the Committee] 1830–31 (358), I.

BPP 1831 (227), VIII, Select Committee of the House of Lords on Poor Laws and Petitions praying for Relief from Pauperism.

BPP 1831–32 (334), XXXII, Report of Mr Richards to the Colonial Secretary on Waste Lands in the Canadas and Emigration.

BPP 1831–32 (724), XXXII, Report of the Emigration Commissioners [chaired by Richmond]. [Buchanan's report for 1831]

BPP 1831–32 (730), XXXII, Acts passed by Colonies in North America for levying a Tax on Emigrants.

BPP 1833 (141), XXVI, Correspondence relating to Emigration, North America and Australian colonies. [Buchanan's report for 1832. Buchanan's report for 1833 (PRO, CO 384/35, 107–34) was not printed in the sessional papers.]

BPP 1833 (619), XXXII, Documents in Possession of the Poor Law Commissioners on the Labour Rate Bill.

BPP 1834 (44), XXVII.1–XXXIX.1, Royal Commission of Inquiry into the Administration and Practical Operation of the Poor Laws.

BPP 1834 (211), III, and subsequent amendments, Bill for Amendment and better Administration of Laws relating to the Poor in England and Wales.

BPP 1834 (616), XLIV, Correspondence with Colonial Governors on Emigration and the Disposal of Crown Lands.

BPP 1835 (87), XXXIX, Emigration, Correspondence and Returns. [Buchanan's report for 1834]

BPP 1835 (5000), XXXV.1, Poor Law Commissioners, First Annual Report.

BPP 1836 (76), XL, Emigration, Correspondence and Returns. [Buchanan's report for 1835]

BPP 1836 (595), XXIX, pt 1, Poor Law Commissioners, Second Annual Report.

BPP 1837 (131), XVII, pt 1, Select Committee on the Poor Law Amendment Act, First Report; 1837 (138), XVII, pt 1, Second Report; 1837 (350), XVII, Twelfth Report.

BPP 1837 (132), XLII, Emigration (Canada). [Buchanan's report for 1836]

BPP 1837 (546-I) (546-II), XXXI, Poor Law Commissioners, Third Annual Report.

BPP 1837–38 (147), XXVIII, Poor Law Commissioners, Fourth Annual Report.

BPP 1837–38 (388), XL, Report from the Agent-General for Emigration from the United Kingdom.

BPP 1837–38 (389), XL, Emigration, Canada and Australia. [Buchanan's report for 1837]

BPP 1837–38 (658), XX, pt II.1, Second Report from the Select Committee on Postage. Sockett's evidence.

BPP 1837–38 (719) (719-II), XIX, pt I.1, XIX, pt 2.1, Select Committee of the House of Lords on the Operation of the Poor Law Amendment Act.

BPP 1839 (536-I, 536-II), XXXIX, Emigration.

BPP 1840 (317), XXXII, Correspondence relative to Emigration to Canada.

BPP 1841, Session 1 (298), XV, Canada: Correspondence relative to Emigration to Canada.

BPP 1842 (373), XXXI.I, Emigration: Canada and Correspondence relative to Emigration.

BPP 1844 (543), X, Report from the Select Committee on Poor Relief (Gilbert Unions).

BPP 1847 (737) (737-II), VI.I, Select Committee of House of Lords on Colonization from Ireland.

BPP 1847–48 (343), XLVII, Returns from British Colonies. No. 9: "The Number of Persons, with their average Cost per Head to the Parishes, who have been aided in Emigration under the Provisions of the Poor Law Amendment Act," 1837–46.

Brundage, Anthony. *"England's Prussian Minister": Edwin Chadwick and the Politics of Government Growth, 1832–1854.* University Park, Pa.: Pennsylvania State University Press 1988.

– "The Landed Interest and the New Poor Law: A Reappraisal of the Revolution in Government." *English Historical Review* 87 (1972): 27–48; *see also* 347–51, "The Landed Interest and the New Poor Law: a Reply" [to Peter Dunkley].

– *The Making of the New Poor Law.* New Brunswick, N.J.: Rutgers University Press 1978.

Brunger, Alan G. "The Distribution of the English in Upper Canada 1851–1871." *Canadian Geographer* 30, no. 4 (1986), 337–43.

Brydone, James Marr. *Narrative of a Voyage with a Party of Emigrants, Sent out from Sussex, in 1834, by the Petworth Emigration Committee to Montreal ...* Petworth: John Phillips; London: Effingham Wilson 1834. Reprinted 1987 as *Voyage of Emigration to Toronto, Canada.*

Buchanan, Alexander Carlisle. *Emigration Practically Considered ... in a Letter to the Right Hon. R. Wilmot Horton.* London: Henry Colbourn 1828.

[–] *Information Published by His Majesty's Chief Agent ... for the Use of Emigrants.* Quebec: 1831 and thereafter.

– *Official Information for Emigrants Arriving at New York, and Who Are Desirous of Settling in the Canadas ...* Montreal 1834.

Buchanan, James. *Project for the Formation of a Depot in Upper Canada with a View to Receive the Whole Pauper Population of England.* New York 1834.

Burroughs, Peter, ed. *The Colonial Reformers and Canada 1830–1849.* Carleton Library No. 42. Toronto 1969.

– *The Canadian Crisis and British Colonial Policy, 1828–1841.* London: Edward Arnold 1972.

Butlin, Martin, Mollie Luther, and Ian Warrell. *Turner at Petworth: Painter and Patron.* London: Tate Gallery 1988.

Caird, James. *English Agriculture in 1850–51.* 1st ed. 1852; 2nd ed. with an introduction by G.E. Mingay. London: Frank Cass 1968.

Cameron, Wendy. "The Petworth Emigration Committee: Lord Egremont's Assisted Emigrations from Sussex to Upper Canada, 1832–1837." *Ontario History* 65, no. 4 (1973): 231–46.

– "'Till they get tidings from those who are gone ...' Thomas Sockett and Letters from Petworth Emigrants, 1832–37." *Ontario History* 85, no. 1 (March 1993): 1–16.

– "Wilmot Horton's Experimental Emigrations to Upper Canada." B.Litt. thesis, Oxford University, 1971.

Canada: Letters from Persons who have Emigrated to Upper Canada. See *No. 1 Continuation.*

Canadian Settler (late of Portsea, Hants). *The Emigrant's Informant, or, a Guide to Upper Canada.* London, Edinburgh, and Dublin 1834.

Cannadine, David. *Aspects of Aristocracy: Grandeur and Decline in Modern Britain.* New Haven: Yale University Press 1994.

Cattermole, William. *Emigration: The Advantages of Emigration to Canada ...* London 1831; Coles reprint, Toronto 1970.

Chadwick, Edwin. "An Article on the Principles and Progress of the Poor Law Amendment Act, and Also on the Nature of the Central Control and Improved Local Administration Introduced by That Statute, reprinted by permission from the *Edinburgh Review* with notes and additions." London: Charles Knight 1837.

[–] "The New Poor Law." *Edinburgh Review* 63 (1836): 487–537.

Chambers, J.D., and G.E. Mingay. *The Agricultural Revolution 1750–1880.* London: Batsford 1966.

Charlesworth, Andrew. *Social Protest in a Rural Society: The Spatial Diffusion of the Captain Swing Disturbances of 1830–1831.* Historical Geography Research Series 1. Liverpool: Liverpool University, Department of Geography 1978.

–, ed. *An Atlas of Rural Protest in Britain 1548–1900.* London and Canberra: Croom Helm 1983.

Checkland, S.G., and E.O.A. Checkland, eds. *The Poor Law Report of 1834.* Harmondsworth, Middlesex: Penguin Books 1974.

Choomwattana, Chakrit. "The Opposition to the New Poor Law in Sussex, 1834–1837." Unpublished PHD thesis, Cornell University, 1986.

Cobbett, William. *Rural Rides ... during the Years 1821–1832.* 2 vols. London: Reeves and Turner 1908.

– *The Emigrant's Guide; in Ten Letters, Addressed to the Tax-Payers of England ...* 1st ed. London: the author, 1829; new ed. 1830.

Cohen, Marjorie Griffin. *Women's Work, Markets, and Economic Development in Nineteenth-Century Ontario.* Toronto: University of Toronto Press 1988.

Commissioners for Emigration. *Information ... respecting the British Colonies in North America.* London 1832.

Continuation of Letters from Sussex Emigrants in Upper Canada. Petworth: John Phillips 1837.

Continuation of Letters from Sussex Emigrants in Upper Canada, Written in 1836. Petworth: John Phillips [1837].

Courtauld Family Letters, 1782–1900. 8 vols. Cambridge: Bowes and Bowes 1916. Printed for private circulation, a copy is found in the British library.

Cowan, Helen. *British Emigration to British North America: The First Hundred Years.* Rev. ed. Toronto: University of Toronto Press 1961.

Craig, Gerald M. *Upper Canada: The Formative Years 1784–1841.* Toronto: McClelland and Stewart 1963.

Craven, Paul, ed. *Labouring Lives: Work and Workers in Nineteenth-Century Ontario.* Ontario Historical Studies Series. Toronto: University of Toronto Press 1995.

Cross, Michael S., and Gregory S. Kealey. *Pre-industrial Canada 1760–1849.* Toronto: McClelland and Stewart 1982.

Crowther, M.A. *The Workhouse System 1834–1929.* London: Batsford 1981.

Cunningham, Hugh. "The Employment and Unemployment of Children in England c.1680–1851." *Past and Present* 126 (February 1990): 115–50.

Davies, David. *The Case of Labourers in Husbandry.* 1795; reprint, Fairfield, N.J.: Augustus M. Kelley 1977.

Dictionary of Canadian Biography. Edited by George Brown et al. 14 vols. to date. Toronto: University of Toronto Press, 1965–.

Digby, Anne. "The Labour Market and the Continuity of Social Policy after 1834: The Case of the Eastern Counties." *Economic History Review* 28, no. 1 (1975): 69–83.

– *Pauper Palaces.* London: Routledge and Kegan Paul 1978.

Donajgrodzki, A.P., ed. *Social Control in Nineteenth Century Britain.* London: Croom Helm 1977.

Doyle, Martin (William Hickey). *Hints on Emigration to Upper Canada; especially addressed to the middle and lower class in Great Britain and Ireland.* Dublin and London 1831. Letters from Petworth emigrants are included in the second and third editions, 1832 and 1834.

Driver, Felix. *Power and Pauperism 1834–1884.* Cambridge Studies in Historical Geography 19. Cambridge: Cambridge University Press 1993.

Dunkley, Peter. *The Crisis of the Old Poor Law in England 1795–1834: An Interpretive Essay.* New York and London: Garland Press 1982.

– "Emigration and the State 1803–1842: The Nineteenth-Century Revolution in Government Reconsidered." *Historical Journal* 23, no. 2 (1980): 353–80.

– "The Landed Interest and the New Poor Law: A Critical Note." *English Historical Review* 88 (1973): 836–84.

– "Paternalism, the Magistracy and Poor Relief in England, 1795–1834." *International Review of Social History* 24, no. 3 (1979): 371–97.

– "Whigs and Paupers: The Reform of the English Poor Laws, 1830–1834." *Journal of British Studies* 20, no. 2 (1981): 124–49.

[Dunlop, William]. *Statistical Sketches of Upper Canada.* London 1832.

Dutt, Monju. "The Agricultural Labourers' Revolt of 1830 in Kent, Surrey and Sussex." PhD thesis, University of London, 1966.

Dyck, Ian. *William Cobbett and Rural Popular Culture.* Cambridge: Cambridge University Press 1992.

Edsall, Nicholas C. *The Anti-Poor Law Movement 1834–44.* New Jersey: Manchester University Press 1971.

Egremont, Lord. *Wyndham and Children First.* London: Macmillan 1968.

Elliott, Bruce S. "English." *An Encyclopedia of Canada's Peoples,* ed. Paul Robert Magosi. Toronto: University of Toronto Press 1999.

– *Irish Migrants in the Canadas: A New Approach.* Kingston and Montreal: McGill-Queen's University Press 1988.

Emigration: A Letter to a Member of Parliament … [Wolryche Whitmore]. Petworth: John Phillips; London: Longman 1833; 2d ed. 1834. This pamphlet was written by Thomas Sockett.

Emigration: Letters from Sussex Emigrants, who sailed from Portsmouth, in April 1832 … Petworth: John Phillips; London: Longman 1833.

– "English." In Paul Robert Magocsi, ed. *Encyclopedia of Canada's Peoples.* Toronto: University of Toronto Press for the Multicultural Historical Society of Ontario 1999.

Erickson, Charlotte. *Invisible Emigrants: The Adaptation of English and Scottish Immigrants in Nineteenth-Century America.* London: London School of Economics and Political Science 1972.

– *Leaving England: Essays on British Emigration in the Nineteenth Century.* Ithaca and London: Cornell University Press 1994.

Errington, Elizabeth Jane. *Wives and Mothers, Schoolmistresses and Scullery Maids: Working Women in Upper Canada, 1790–1840.* Montreal and Kingston: McGill Queen's University Press 1995.

Fairplay, Francis. *The Canadas as they now are.* London 1833

– *A Map of the Canadas …* London 1834

Fergusson, Adam. *On the Agricultural State of Canada and part of the United States.* Cuper, Scotland 1832.

– *Practical Notes Made during a Tour of Canada, and a Portion of the United States in 1831.* 2d ed. Edinburgh 1834.

Filby, P. William. "Sailing List of Sussex Emigrants to Canada circa 1836." *Canadian Genealogist*, 4, no. 1 (1982), 9–12. This list and the copy made by Lord Leconfield in WSRO, PHA 142, have a common source. They record passengers who sailed on the *Burrell* in 1835.

Finer, S.E. *The Life and Times of Sir Edwin Chadwick*. London: Methuen 1952.

— "The Transmission of Benthamite ideas 1820–50," 11–32. In Gillian Sutherland. *Studies in the Growth of Nineteenth Century Government*. London: Routledge and Kegan Paul 1972.

Firth, Edith G., ed. *The Town of York, 1815–1834: A Further Collection of Documents of Early Toronto*. The Champlain Society for the Government of Ontario. Toronto: University of Toronto Press 1966.

Fitzpatrick, David. *Oceans of Consolation: Personal Accounts of Irish Migration to Australia*. Ithaca and London: Cornell University Press 1994.

Fletcher, Barry. "Chichester and the Westhamptnett Poor Law Union." *Sussex Archaeological Collections* 134 (1996), 185–96.

— "The Early Years of the Westhamptnett Poor Law Union 1835–38." MSc (Social Sciences), University of Southampton 1981.

Fowke, V.C. "The Myth of the Self-Sufficient Canadian Pioneer." *Transactions of the Royal Society of Canada*, ser. 3, 16 (June 1962): 23–37.

Fraser, Derek, ed. *The New Poor Law in the Nineteenth Century*. London, Macmillan 1976.

Gash, Norman. "Rural Unemployment 1815–1834." *Economic History Review* 6 (October 1835): 90–93.

Gates, Lillian F. *Land Policies of Upper Canada*. Canadian Studies in History and Government No. 9. Toronto: University of Toronto Press 1968.

Great Britain, Royal Commission on the Administration and Operation of the Poor Laws. *Extracts from the Information Received*. London [1833], 1837.

Greer, Alan. "1837–38: Rebellion Reconsidered." *Canadian Historical Review* 76, no. 1 (1995): 1–18.

Greer, Alan, and Ian Radford, eds. *Colonial Leviathan: State Formation in Mid-Nineteenth-Century Canada*. Toronto: University of Toronto Press 1992.

Guillet, Edwin C. *The Great Migration: The Atlantic Crossing by Sailing-Ship since 1770*. 2d ed. Toronto: University of Toronto Press 1963.

Haines, Robin F. *Emigration and the Labouring Poor: Australian Recruitment in Britain and Ireland, 1831–60*. London: Macmillan; New York: St Martin's Press 1997.

Haines, Sheila, ed. *'No Trifling Matter': Being an Account of a Voyage by Emigrants ... on board the "British Tar" in 1834*. Brighton: Centre for Continuing Education, University of Sussex 1990.

Hale, J.C. *Instructions to Persons intending to Emigrate*. Petworth 1833.

Hammond, J.L., and Barbara Hammond. *The Village Labourer 1760–1832: A Study in the Government of England before the Reform Bill*. London: Longmans, Green 1912.

Hart, Jenifer, "Nineteenth-Century Social Reform: A Tory Interpretation of History." *Past and Present* 31 (July 1965): 39–61.

Hay, Douglas, et al. *Albion's Fatal Tree: Crime and Society in Eighteenth-Century England*. London: Allen Lane 1975.

Head, Sir Francis Bond. "English Charity." In vol. 1, *Descriptive Essays contributed to the Quarterly Review*. 2 vols. London: John Murray 1857.

Hitchcock, Tim, Peter King, and Pamela Sharp, eds. *Chronicling Poverty: The Voices and Strategies of the English Poor, 1640–1840*. Houndsmill, Basingstoke: Macmillan 1997.

Hobsbawm, E.J. *Labouring Men: Studies in the History of Labour.* London: Weidenfeld and Nicolson 1964.

Hobsbawm, E.J., and George Rudé. *Captain Swing.* London: Lawrence and Wishart 1969.

Hodgetts, J.E. *Pioneer Public Service: An Administrative History of the United Canadas.* Toronto: University of Toronto Press 1955.

Horn, Pamela. *Labouring Life in the Victorian Countryside.* 1976; reprint, Abingdon, Oxford: Fraser Stewart Book, Wholesale Limited 1995.

Horton, Sir Robert John Wilmot. *Causes and Remedies of Pauperism in the United Kingdom.* London: Edmund Lloyd 1830.

Howells, Gary. "For I was tired of England, Sir: English pauper emigrant strategies, 1834–60." *Social History* 23, no. 2 (1998): 181–94.

Johnson, J.K., and Bruce G. Wilson, eds. *Historical Essays on Upper Canada: New Perspectives.* Ottawa: Carleton University Press 1991.

Johnston, H.J.M. *British Emigration Policy 1815–1830: Shovelling Out Paupers.* Oxford: Clarendon Press 1972.

Jones, E.L. "The Agricultural Labour Market in England, 1793–1892." *Economic History Review,* 2d ser., 17 (1964–65): 323–38.

Jones, Maldwyn A. "The Background to Emigration from Great Britain in the Nineteenth Century." In *Perspectives in American History,* ed. Donald Fleming and Bernard Bailyn, vol. 7, 1973, Harvard University, Charles Warren Centre for Studies in American History 1974.

Jones, Robert Leslie. *History of Agriculture in Ontario 1613–1880.* 1946; reprint, Toronto: University of Toronto Press 1997.

Karr, Clarence. *The Canada Land Company: The Early Years.* Research Publication No 3. Ottawa: Ontario Historical Society 1974.

Knott, John. *Popular Opposition to the 1834 Poor Law.* London and Sydney: Croom Helm 1986.

Kussmaul, Ann. *Servants in Husbandry in Early Modern England.* Cambridge: University Press 1981.

Letters from the Dorking Emigrants Who Went to Upper Canada, in the Spring of 1832. Ed. Charles Barclay. London: J. and A. Arch, Cornhill, and Dorking: Robert Best Ede 1833.

Letters from Emigrants sent out to Upper Canada by the Petworth Committee in 1832, 1833, and 1837. Petworth: John Phillips 1839.

Letters from Sussex Emigrants Gone out from the South Side of the Hills to Upper Canada. Chichester: William Hayley Mason 1837.

Levy, S. Leon. *Nassau W. Senior 1790–1864: Critical Essayist, Classical Economist and Advisor of Governments.* Newton Abbott, Devon: David and Charles 1970.

Lucas, C.P., ed. *Lord Durham's Report on the Affairs of North America.* Oxford: Clarendon Press 1912.

McCalla, Douglas. *Planting the Province: The Economic History of Upper Canada 1784–1870.* Toronto: University of Toronto Press for the Ontario Historical Series 1993.

McCann, Alison, ed. *Emigrants and Transportees from West Sussex 1675–1889.* Chichester: West Sussex County Council 1984.

Macdonagh, Oliver. "The Nineteenth-Century Revolution in Government: A Reappraisal." *Historical Journal* 1, no. 1 (1958): 52–67.

– *A Pattern of Government Growth 1800–1860: The Passenger Acts and their Enforcement.* London: MacGibbon and Kee 1961.

McDonald, Terry. "'Come to Canada While You Have a Chance.' A Cautionary Tale of English Emigrant Letters in Upper Canada." *Ontario History* 91, no. 2 (1999): 111-30.

MacGregor, John. *British America*. Edinburgh and London 1832.

McLean, Marianne. *The People of Glengarry: Highlanders in Transition, 1745–1820*. Montreal and Kingston: McGill-Queen's University Press 1991.

Mandler, Peter. *Aristocratic Government in the Age of Reform: Whigs and Liberals, 1830–1852*. Oxford: Clarendon Press 1990.

– "Tories and Paupers: Christian Political Economy and the Making of the New Poor Law." *Historical Journal* 33, no. 1 (1990): 81–103.

Manning, Helen Taft. "The Colonial Policy of the Whig Ministers 1830–37." *Canadian Historical Review* 33 (September 1952): 203–63; 33 (December 1952): 341–68.

Merriman, Brenda Dougall, *The Emigrant Ancestors of a Lieutenant-Governor of Ontario*. Toronto: Ontario Genealogical Society 1993.

Mills, Dennis R. *Land and Peasant in Nineteenth Century Britain*. London: Croom Helm 1980.

Mingay, G.E. *The Victorian Countryside*. 2 vols. London, Boston, Henley: Routledge and Kegan Paul 1981.

– ed. *The Agrarian History of England and Wales, vol. 6, 1750–1850*, gen. ed. Joan Thirsk. Cambridge, Cambridge University Press 1989.

– ed. *The Unquiet Countryside*. London: Routledge 1989.

Mudie, Robert. *The Emigrant's Pocket Companion: Containing What Emigration Is, Who Should Emigrate*. London 1832.

Murray, David R. "The Cold Hand of Charity: The Court of Quarter Session and Poor Relief in the Niagara District, 1821–1841." In W. Wesley Pue and Barry Wright eds. *Canadian Perspectives on Law and Society: Issues in Legal History*. Ottawa: Carleton University Press 1988.

Nicholls, Sir George, and Thomas Mackey. *A History of the English Poor Law*. 3 vols., 1st ed. 1854; rev. 1898; vol. 3 added by Thomas Mackey, reprinted 1967.

Nielsen, Eleanor. *The Egremont Road: Historic Route from Lobo to Lake Huron*. n.p. Lambton Historical Society 1993.

No. 1 Continuation of Letters from Sussex Emigrants in Upper Canada for 1833 [No. 1 to 6]. Petworth: John Phillips 1833. Published as six 8-page pamphlets plus covers and unnumbered pages, the letters are paginated consecutively from 1 to 48. The New York Public Library has a copy of a publication bringing all six together as *Canada: Letters from Persons Who Have Emigrated to Upper Canada, under the Management of the Petworth Emigration Committee, Written in the Year 1833*. Petworth: John Phillips, and London: Longman 1834.

Norris, Darrell A. "Migration, Pioneer Settlement, and the Life Course: The First Families of an Ontario Township." *Canadian Papers in Rural History* (D.H. Akenson, editor) 4 (1984): 130–52.

Oxley, Geoffrey W. *Poor Relief in England and Wales, 1601–1834*. Newton Abbot, England: David and Charles 1974.

Palmer, Bryan D. *Working Class Experience: Rethinking the History of Canadian Labour 1800–1991*. Toronto: McClelland and Stewart 1992.

Parr, Joy. *Labouring Children: British Immigrant Apprentices to Canada, 1869–1924*. Toronto: University of Toronto Press 1994.

Pickering, Joseph. *Enquiries of an Emigrant, Being the Narrative of an English Farmer, from the year 1824 to 1830.* 3rd ed. London 1832.

Polanyi, Karl. *The Great Transformation.* 1944; Boston: Beacon Press 1957.

Povey, Kenneth. "The Rise of Thomas Sockett." *Sussex Country Magazine* 2 (1928): 38–40.

Poynter, J.R. *Society and Pauperism: English Ideas on Poor Relief, 1795–1834.* London: Routledge and Kegan Paul; Toronto: University of Toronto Press 1969.

Radcliff, Thomas, ed. *Authentic Letters from Upper Canada.* 1833; reprint, Toronto: Macmillan 1953.

Read, Colin. *The Rising in Western Upper Canada, 1837–8: The Duncombe Revolt and After.* Toronto: University of Toronto Press 1982.

Read, Colin, and Ronald J. Stagg. *The Rebellions of 1837 in Upper Canada.* Ottawa: Champlain Society with Carleton University Press 1985.

Reay, Barry. *The Last Rising of the Agricultural Labourers: Rural Life and Protest in Nineteenth-Century England.* Oxford: Clarendon Press 1990.

– *Microhistories: Demography, Society, and Culture in Rural England 1800–1930.* Cambridge Studies in Population, Economy and Society in Past Time, No. 30. Cambridge: Cambridge University Press 1996.

Reed, Michael. "Social and Economic Conditions in a Wealden Community: Lodsworth 1780–1860." MA, University of Sussex 1982.

Richards, Eric. "How Did Poor People Emigrate from the British Isles to Australia in the Nineteenth Century?" *Journal of British Studies* 32 (July 1993): 250–79.

Roberts, David. *Paternalism in Early Victorian England.* London 1979.

– *Victorian Origins of the British Welfare State.* New Haven 1960.

Rolph, Thomas. *A Descriptive and Statistical Account of Canada.* 2d ed. London 1841.

– *Emigration and Colonization.* London 1844.

Rose, Michael E. "The Allowance System under the New Poor Law." *Economic History Review*, 2d ser., 19 (1966): 607–20.

– *The English Poor Law 1780–1930.* Newton Abbot, England: David and Charles 1971.

– *The Relief of Poverty 1834–1914*, 2d ed. Bassingstoke, Hampshire: Macmillan 1986.

Rubidge, Charles. *A Plain Statement of the Advantages Attending Emigration to Canada.* London 1838.

Russell, Peter A. *Attitudes to Social Structure and Mobility in Upper Canada 1815–1840.* Lewiston: Edwin Mellen Press 1990.

[Scope, G. Poulett, or John Fullarton]. "Condition of the Labouring Classes: Wiltshire Emigrants to Canada." *Quarterly Review* 46 (1832): 349–90.

Senior, Nassau William. *Remarks on Emigration with a Draft of a Bill.* London: R. Clay 1831.

– *Remarks on the Opposition to the Poor Law Amendment Bill by a Guardian.* London: John Murray 1841.

– *Three Lectures on the Rate of Wages ... with a Preface on the Causes and Remedies of the Present Disturbances.* 2d ed. London: John Murray 1831.

Shepperson, Wilbur S. "Agrarian Aspects of Early Victorian Emigration to North America." *Canadian Historical Review* 33 (September 1952): 254–64.

– *British Emigration to North America: Projects and Opinions in the Early Victorian Period.* Oxford: Blackwell 1957.

Short, Brian M. "The Changing Rural Society and Economy of Sussex 1750–1945." In *Sussex: Environment, Landscape and Society*, ed. Geography Editorial Committee, ch. 8. Brighton: University of Sussex 1983.

Smith, E.A. *Lord Grey 1764–1845*. 1990; Gloucestershire: Alan Sutton 1996.

Snell, K.D.M. *Annals of the Labouring Poor: Social Change and Agrarian England 1660–1900*. Cambridge Studies in Population, Economy and Society in Past Time No. 2. Cambridge: Cambridge University Press 1985.

Sockett, Thomas. Although Sockett did not use his name as author or editor on the title pages of his publications, he was responsible for the publication of letters printed by Thomas Phillips and for *Emigration: A Letter to a Member of Parliament*.

Spater, George. *William Cobbett: The Poor Man's Friend*. 2 vols. Cambridge: Cambridge University Press 1982.

Spring, David. *The English Landed Estate in the Nineteenth Century: Its Administration*. Baltimore: John Hopkins Press 1963.

Stapleton, Barry. "Inherited poverty and life-cycle poverty: Odiham, Hampshire, 1650–1850." *Social History* 18, no. 3 (October 1993): 339–55.

Stevenson, John. *Popular Disturbances in England, 1700–1832*. Rev. ed. London and New York: Longman 1992.

Strachey, Lytton, and Roger Fulford, eds. *The Greville Memoirs 1814–1860*. 8 vols. London: Macmillan 1938.

Thompson, E.P. *Customs in Common*. London: Marlin Press 1991.

– *The Making of the English Working Class*. London: Victor Gollancz 1963.

Thompson, F.M.L,. ed. *The Cambridge Social History of Britain 1750–1950*. 3 vols. Cambridge: Cambridge University Press 1990.

Wakefield, Edwin Gibbon. "Swing Unmasked, or, The Causes of Rural Incediarism." In Kenneth E. Carpenter, ed. *The Aftermath of the "Last Labourers' Revolt": Fourteen Pamphlets 1830–31*. New York: Arno Press 1972.

Way, Peter. *Common Labour: Workers and the Digging of North American Canals 1780–1860*. Cambridge: Cambridge University Press 1993.

Webb, Sydney, and Beatrice Webb. *English Poor Law Policy*. London: Longmans Green 1910.

Wells, Roger. "Resistance to the New Poor Law in the Rural South." In John Rule and Roger Wells, *Crime, Protest and Popular Politics in Southern England, 1740–1850*. London: Hambledon Press 1997.

Wilson, Catharine Anne. *A New Lease on Life: Landlords, Tenants, and Immigrants in Ireland and Canada*. Montreal and Kingston: McGill-Queen's University Press 1994.

Winearls, Joan. *Mapping Upper Canada, 1780–1867: An Annotated Bibliography of Manuscript and Printed Maps*. Toronto: University of Toronto Press 1991.

Wise, S.F., ed. *Sir Francis Bond Head: A Narrative*. Carleton Library No. 43. Toronto 1969.

Wyndham, H.A. *A Family History 1688–1837: the Wyndhams of Somerset, Sussex and Wiltshire*. Oxford: Oxford University Press 1950.

ACKNOWLEDGMENTS

From the time we began investigating the history of the Petworth emigrations and collecting material on the families and individuals involved, we have had an enthusiastic and generous response from individuals and institutions in Canada and England. We owe a great debt to all those who have helped us, from the people working in archives and record offices who have generously shared their knowledge and collections, to the descendants of emigrants who have sent us family histories, letters, photographs, and anecdotes.

The project has been underwritten by the Jackman Foundation and has been part of the Northrop Frye Centre at Victoria University in the University of Toronto. We wish to acknowledge the very generous financial assistance of the Foundation. Eva Kushner at Victoria oversaw the beginnings of the project in her dual role as president of the university and director of the Frye Centre. We are grateful to her and her successors, Roseann Runte at Victoria, and Brian Merrilees at the Centre, for a friendly and stimulating academic home for our project. We also thank the staff of the Robarts Library of the University of Toronto and in particular those on whom we made great demands for interlibrary loans and microtexts.

There are some institutions and individuals to whom we appealed time and again, and we should like to acknowledge their help. We cannot name all the individals who assisted us within public repositories but we are grateful for their knowledge and attention. In England, all the record offices in our research area were helpful – Cambridge County Record Office, East Sussex Record Office, Hampshire County Record Office, Norfolk County Record Office, Surrey County Record Office, Guildford Muniment Room, Isle of Wight Record Office, Wiltshire County Records Office, but we relied most heavily on the West Sussex Record Office and we thank archivist Richard Childs and his predecessor Patricia Gill. Special thanks are owed to Alison McCann, the archivist for the Petworth House Archives, and Tim McCann, in charge of the Goodwood Estate Archives, for sharing knowledge beyond their impressive familiarity with these wonderful collections.

Lord Egremont kindly gave us permission to consult and quote from the Petworth House Archives, and Diana Owen has been an able liaison with the National Trust. Quotations from the Goodwood manuscripts are made by courtesy of the Trustees of the Goodwood Collections and with acknowledgments to the West Sussex Record Office and the County Archives. We wish also to acknowledge the assistance of the Brighton Reference Library, the British Library Newspaper Library, Courtauld Institute of Art, Dorking and District Museum, Public Record Office,

Religious Society of Friends (Quakers) Dorking Preparative Meeting, Archives and Special Collections of the Durham University Library, Sussex Archaeological Society, Sussex University Library, Tate Gallery, United Reformed Church, West St, Dorking, and the University College Library of the University of London. Barbara Brydone Calder shared family papers left by her ancestor, James Marr Brydone.

In the United States, we thank the Rare Book and Manuscript Library in the Butler Library of Columbia University. In Canada, we relied on help from both local and national institutions, and we would like to acknowledge the assistance of the National Archives of Canada, the Archives of Ontario, the D.B. Weldon Library Regional Collection of the University of Western Ontario, the United Church Archives, the Baldwin Room at the Toronto Reference Library, Queen's University Archives, Kitchener Public Library, Hamilton Public Library, Strathroy Middlesex Museum, Stratford-Perth Archives, Special Collections at the University of Waterloo, and the Wellington County Museum and Archives. Staff and members of the Ontario Genealogical Society, both at the provincial and the branch levels, were of great assistance; in particular, we would like to mention Mary Evans of the Oxford County Branch and Claudia McArthur of the Simcoe County Branch. Sylvia Wray of East Flamborough Archives and Helen Maddock of Lambton County Library went to extra efforts to locate material for us, as did Eleanor Nielsen, Margaret Parsons, and Jane E. Thompson. Dan Walker and Gerry Tordiff helped us with research in the Huron Diocese Archives. We would also like to thank the staff of the *Dictionary of Canadian Biography* for help with many and sundry questions. Ellen Megannety deserves a special thanks for uncovering some valuable nuggets of information about some of the emigrants.

A number of our colleagues read all or part of our work, shared their own work in progress, or assisted with particular aspects of either history or genealogy. Any errors that remain are our responsibility, but we should like to acknowledge their help in making this a better book. We were most fortunate in having the advice of Professor G.S. French, who read and commented on drafts; we owe him a particular debt. We thank the readers for McGill-Queen's University Press for thoughtful comments, as well as Alison McCann and Tim McCann, who read text in addition to the help they gave us as archivists. In addition, we thank Peter Brandon, Clifford Collier, Bruce Elliott, Barry Fletcher, Brian Gilchrist, Gary Howells, Alexandra Johnston, Terry McDonald, Henri Pilon, Guy St Denis, Brian Short, Ryan Taylor, Morley Thomas, and Joan Winearls.

Many other individuals from different walks of life contributed in a variety of ways to our search for Petworth emigrants and their stories – historians, librarians, archivists, genealogists, and interested people researching their families. These contacts were made at various times and places, and we apologize to those who are not mentioned by name. Our correspondence stretched from Great Britain to Australia with stops across Canada and the United States. We wish to acknowledge the assistance of Frances Acres, Rosemary Ambrose, Roy Adsett, Phyllis Alcorn, Shelley Banks, Constance Bayley, Edna Bell, Robert T. Bell, Mary L. Black, Shirley Blakely, Elizabeth Bloomfield, Eunice M. Brake, William K. Cairns, Arthur J. Capling, Harvey Carver, Kenneth M. Cates, Roger A. Chalwin, Roy Coleman, Ken Cook, Beatrice and Harold Cosens, Ralph D. Courtnage, Ronald E. Cox, Virginia Curulla, John Dennis, Marjorie Dow, Pat Duguid, Yvette H. Dwyer, Edna Featherston, Rachel and Barry Fletcher, Helen Fortney, Elizabeth R. Gillespie, Nancy W. Graden, R.A. Golds, Doris Gray, A.J. Haines, John H., Beth, and Stuart Harwood, Alfred Haslett, Gerald W. Hilman, Elizabeth Hodges, Jean Hodges, Richard Holt, Richard H. Howick, Mavis and Tony Howlett, Patricia Pay Keefe, Agnes M. Kelcher, Helen M. Kerr, Diane Khoury, E. Jack Langstaff, Donna Longhurst, Lyle Longhurst, Sandra and David Longhurst, O.G. Luton, James M. MacDonald, Jeanette Mahler, Margaret Major, Doreen Mann, Grace and Isobel Mann, Sharon Martin, Roy Marvel, H. Roger Miller, June Moffatt, Barbara Monasch, Richard Moon, Nanette Neville, Peter A. Noice, Arnold Orchard, Lesley Parker, Betty Patterson, Janet Pennington, Glenn Racher, John W. Racher, Blake Rapley, Charlotte Rapley, David Rapson, Marjorie Robbins, Dennis Ruhl, Thomas A. Ryerson, Guy St Denis, Virginia Streeter Sande, John Sayers, Mary and Ian Short, R.J. Simmonds, John J. Skilton, Berenice A. Smith, John Ward Smith, Nancy Smith, Claire Stemp, Margaret Stockton, Clifford L. Stott, Helen Stover, S.R. Suter, Sally Swenson, C. William Terry, Wilbert and Doreen Thompson, Maurice and Vera Titmuss, Donald W. Tomlinson, Pat Tripp, Eleanor C. Tuckey, H.E. Turner, H.M. Upton, Lesley and Tony Voice, Heather Wallis, John Ward-Smith, Eileen Whitehead, Jai Williams, W.H. Wilson, and Jane Zavitz.

We would also like to thank the people at McGill-Queen's University Press. Don Akenson and Philip Cercone gave advice and encouragement at various points during the project's history. Joan McGilvray added her deft editorial touch and was always a pleasure to deal with, as were her colleagues at the press. Miriam Bloom devised an attractive design, and Judith Turnbull brought her careful attention to the copy edit of the history.

Finally, we would like to thank our families for their support, especially the late Joe Haines for research help and cheerful encouragement to both sides of the Atlantic.

Index to Part 1

Readers should also consult the alphabetical list of Petworth emigrants, 1832–1837, found in Part Two, page 201.